British Policy and the
Weimar Republic, 1918–1919

British Policy and the Weimar Republic, 1918–1919

DOUGLAS NEWTON

CLARENDON PRESS · OXFORD
1997

Oxford University Press, Great Clarendon Street, Oxford OX2 6DP

Oxford New York

Athens Auckland Bangkok Bogota Bombay
Buenos Aires Calcutta Cape Town Dar es Salaam
Delhi Florence Hong Kong Istanbul Karachi
Kuala Lumpur Madras Madrid Melbourne
Mexico City Nairobi Paris Singapore
Taipei Tokyo Toronto
and associated companies in
Berlin Ibadan

Oxford is a trade mark of Oxford University Press

Published in the United States
by Oxford University Press Inc., New York

British Library Cataloguing in Publication Data
Data available

Library of Congress Cataloging-in-Publication Data
Newton, Douglas J.
British policy and the Weimar Republic, 1918–1919 / Douglas Newton.
p. cm.
Includes bibliographical references.
1. Great Britain—Relations—Germany. 2. Great Britain—Foreign
relations—1910–1936. 3. Germany—Foreign relations—1918–1933.
4. Germany—Relations—Great Britain. I. Title
DA47.2.N49 1997 327.41043—dc21 96–52310
ISBN 0–19–820314–4

1 3 5 7 9 10 8 6 4 2

Typeset by Hope Services (Abingdon) Ltd.
Printed in Great Britain
on acid-free paper by
Biddles Ltd.,
Guildford & King's Lynn

For my Mother, with love

ACKNOWLEDGEMENTS

MY debts are many. At the top of any list of persons to whom I owe sincere thanks, I must place my friend and colleague Joy Melhuish—for making the research in the United Kingdom possible through her hospitality, for generously agreeing to undertake parts of the research which I was not able to complete (at Bowood, the University of Sussex, Richmond upon Thames, and the Kent Archives Office), for reading the entire manuscript, and for offering the benefit of her advice at every stage in the production of this book. I must offer special thanks also to my generous friend Andrew Moore, who agreed to read and comment upon every chapter of the book, notwithstanding his own pressing publication schedule at the time. For their unflagging support during my research and the writing of this book, Julie Newton and David Newton also deserve my special thanks.

I would like to thank the following family, friends, and academic colleagues for reading various chapters of this book while in draft form and for making valuable suggestions for improvement: Robert Newton, Mary Ann Anastasiadis, Ethel Mulder, John Buchner, Francis de Groen, Lucie Halberstam, Peter Munz, John Moses, Jürgen Tampke, Tania Rose, Denis Winter, Bill Gammage, and Bruce Kent. For help, support, and critical comment along the way I would like to thank Robert Lee, John O'Hara, Hilary Weatherburn, David Christian, Kerry Taylor, David Rollison, Malcolm Mackinnon, Peter McPhee, Susan Grogan, Glyn Parry, David Mackay, David Hamer, Hans Delbrück, Jill Roe, Michael Roberts, Michael Birch, Arno Mayer, John McEwen, Keith Wilson, Trevor Wilson, Paul Turnbull, Barry Smith, Margaret Lamb, Patrick Waddington, Jane Tolerton, Nicholas Boyack, Brian Croke, and the late Bill Edmonds. In particular, I must thank Cameron Hazlehurst, who gave generously of his time when the project was in its infancy, pointing me in valuable directions for source material, reading several draft chapters, and saving me from a number of errors. When I craved a little encouragement, Tom Keneally, the Australian novelist, and Bill Hayden, the Governor-General of Australia, were kind enough to read the chapter on the armistice which I sent to each of them, and to reply with an inspirational letter—I must thank them both.

Opportunities to undertake research in the United Kingdom have been essential in the production of this book. I wish to thank Professor Tim Beaglehole and the Council of the Victoria University of Wellington, New Zealand, and Professor Des Crawley of the Faculty of Arts and Social Sciences at the University of Western Sydney, Macarthur, for agreeing to release me for periods of study leave in the United Kingdom in 1990 and 1992. For assistance in putting together successful applications for research grants at the University of Western Sydney, Macarthur, I must thank Pat Bazeley, Lesley Johnson, and Warwick Wilson.

I am grateful also to those who have encouraged me in the writing of the book by providing a lectern from which to speak. In particular, I must thank Ken Stewart and the staff of the Department of Humanities at the University of Western Sydney, Macarthur, for invitations to speak at staff seminars where I introduced early versions of various chapters.

For assistance in obtaining access to archival material I must thank the staff of all the institutions at which I worked in the United Kingdom, in New Zealand, and in Australia. I owe a special debt of thanks to the following for enduring especially heavy demands on their time and expertise: Elizabeth Bennett at the Churchill Archives Centre, Helen Langley and the staff of the Modern Papers Reading Room (Room 132) at the Bodleian Library, Angela Raspin at the British Library of Political and Economic Science, Peter Liddle at the Peter Liddle Archive in Leeds, Simon Robbins at the Imperial War Museum, Jacqueline Cox at King's College Library, B. S. Benedikz at the University of Birmingham Library, Christine Woodland at the Modern Records Centre at the University of Warwick, and Lady de Bellaigue at the Royal Archives at Windsor. I must thank Wilma Bancroft and the staff of the Inter-Library Loan Section of the Library at the University of Western Sydney, Macarthur, who were superbly efficient in obtaining scarce material for me. I would like to thank also the following who generously allowed me access to archival material belonging to their families: Tania Rose (for the papers of Morgan Philips Price), William Pease and Lizzie Ormsby-Gore (Sir Henry W. Forster), Nigel Nicolson (Harold Nicolson), and the Earl of Shelburne (Lord Lansdowne). In particular, I must thank the Earl of Crawford who agreed to loan the diaries of the 27th Earl of Crawford to the National Library of Scotland for my research needs. For their sincere efforts on my behalf to gain access to the archive of General Sir Charles Fergusson, unfortunately in vain as events turned out, I must thank Adam Fergusson and Geordie Fergusson. I am especially grateful to the following who wrote to me with their personal memories of their family member's involvement in these events: Neville Masterman (Charles Masterman), John Hayes Fisher (William Hayes Fisher), Margaret Jenner and T. F. Wise (E. F. Wise).

I would like to thank the following individuals and institutions for granting me permission to examine personal papers which they own and/or to quote from personal papers over which they hold copyright: the Trustees of the Estate of the late Lord Rennel of Rodd (Lord Rennel of Rodd), the Provost and Scholars of King's College, Cambridge (unpublished writings of J. M. Keynes), Robin Farquhar-Oliver (Frederic Scott Oliver), Christine Penney, University Archivist, the University of Birmingham (Austen Chamberlain and William Harbutt Dawson), the Library of the School of Oriental and African Studies, University of London (Sir Charles Addis), the Confederation of British Industry (the Federation of British Industry Archive), the Trustees of the Broadlands Archives (Wilfrid William Ashley), Sir Edward Ford (Robert Brand), Kathleen, Viscountess Addison (Christopher Addison), Mary Bennett (H. A. L. Fisher), the Council of the Royal Historical Society (George Prothero), the Earl of Derby (Earl of Derby), New College, Oxford (Alfred Milner), Admiral Sir Ian Hogg (H. A. Gwynne), the Earl of Selborne (the Earl of Selborne), Lord Gainford (J. A. Pease), Nicholas Hammond (J. L. and L. B. Hammond), Lord Howard of Penrith (Esme Howard), Lawrence Toynbee (Arnold J. Toynbee), Mr A. Murray (Gilbert Murray), Lord Dickinson (Willoughby Dickinson), Mrs Stacey and the Trustees of the Bridgeman Family Archive (William Bridgeman), Mrs Parsons (Leonard Woolf), the National Library of Wales (Thomas Jones), Joan Simons (Alfred Emmott), Mr Peter Carnell, Library Archivist, and Mr Michael Hannon, University Librarian, the University of Sheffield (W. A. S. Hewins), the *Spectator* (J. St Loe Strachey), Churchill Archives Centre (James Headlam-Morley, Wester Wemyss), the Earl of Shelburne (the Marquess of Lansdowne), the Library of the London Borough of Richmond upon Thames (Douglas Sladen), the Guildhall Library, Corporation of London (Papers of the Association of British Chambers of Commerce and the London Chamber of Commerce), Leeds University Library (Glenesk-Bathurst and Edmund Gosse), the Robinson Library, University of Newcastle upon Tyne (Walter Runciman), the Trevelyan Family Trustees and the Robinson Library, University of Newcastle upon Tyne (C. P. Trevelyan), Wiltshire County Record Office (Walter Long), Lord Amery (Leo Amery), Lord Crawford (27th Earl of Crawford), the India Office Collection of the British Library, on behalf of the Trustees of the Kedleston Estate (George Curzon), the Earl of Halifax and the Borthwick Institute of Historical Research (Earl of Halifax), Master and Fellows of Trinity College, Cambridge (E. S. Montagu and F. W. Pethick-Lawrence), Lord Cullen of Ashborne MBE and the Northhamptonshire Record Office (Brien Cokayne), Peter Liddle (Peter Liddle's 1914–18 Personal Experience Archive), Katharine Cobbett (A. W. Allan Leeper), Trustees of the National Library of Scotland (Douglas Haig, Richard Haldane, Arthur Murray), Trustees of the National Maritime Museum (Charles Madden, Sydney Fremantle, David Beatty, Water Cowan), Nigel Nicolson (Harold Nicolson), the Trustees of the Liddell Hart Centre for Military Archives (George Aston, Alexander Godley, Frederick Maurice, Edward Spears, Hugh Montgomery-Massingberd), the *Guardian* (C. P. Scott), Mr Christopher Seton-Watson (R. W. Seton-Watson), William Pease (Henry Forster, Rachel Forster, and Mrs Harold Lubbock), the Chartered Institute of Bankers (Papers of the Institute of Bankers), Mr. Graeme Powell for the National Library of Australia (William Morris Hughes, Frederic Eggleston, John Latham, Henry Bourne Higgins, Keith Murdoch, John L. Baird, George Pearce, Ronald Munro-Ferguson, Robert Garran), William Bell (Geoffrey Dawson), the Syndics of Cambridge University Library (Charles Hardinge, Jan Smuts, Edgar Abraham), the University Archivist, Brynmor Jones Library, the University of Hull (Union of Democratic Control Archives and Mark Sykes), Norfolk Record Office (H. W. Massingham), the Trustees of Lambeth Palace Library (Randall Davidson), the Warden and Fellows of Nuffield College (Alfred Emmott and J. A. Pease), the Clerk of the Records of the House of Lords Record Office, who acts on behalf of the Beaverbrook Foundation Trustees (David Lloyd George, Andrew Bonar Law, Max Aitken, Ralph Blumenfeld, Patrick Hannon), the Clerk of the Records of the House of Lords Record Office (Herbert Samuel), Elizabeth Ogborn, on behalf of the Bank of England (the Bank of England Governor's Correspondence), Jane Bonham Carter (Herbert Henry Asquith), Christie, Viscountess Simon (John Simon), and Mrs G. B. Ingall (James Bryce). Material from the Royal Archives is reproduced by the gracious permission of Her Majesty Queen Elizabeth II.

I have attempted to contact many copyright holders beyond those listed, but unfortunately some of my letters have been returned from old addresses or have remained unanswered. If I have inadvertently infringed the copyright of any person I do apologize most sincerely.

My sincere thanks must go also to Tony Morris for his support of the original proposal for this book at Oxford University Press, and for his patience and advice during the writing of the manuscript. Finally, I would like to thank Pat Lawrence, Anna Illingworth, and Michael Belson for their invaluable assistance in preparing the manuscript for publication.

D.N.

August, 1995

CONTENTS

ABBREVIATIONS

ADM	Admiralty Papers, Public Record Office
BCU	British Commonwealth Union
BEPO	British Empire Producers' Organization
BEU	British Empire Union
BICC	British Imperial Council of Commerce
BMA	British Manufacturers' Association
BWL	British Workers' League
CAB	Cabinet Office Papers, Public Record Office
CIGS	Chief of the Imperial General Staff
DIIB	Department of Information Intelligence Branch
DMI	Director(ate) of Military Intelligence
FBI	Federation of British Industry
FO	Foreign Office Papers, Public Record Office
HMP	Headlam-Morley Papers (Churchill Archives Centre, Cambridge)
ILP	Independent Labour Party
KPD	Communist Party of Germany
NUM	National Union of Manufacturers
PID	Political Intelligence Department (of the Foreign Office)
RA	Royal Archives, Windsor
SPD	Sozialdemokratische Partei Deutschlands
UDC	Union of Democratic Control
USPD	Unabhängige Sozialdemokratische Partei Deutschlands
WO	War Office Papers, Public Record Office

Introduction

> The future peace of the world would depend more on the way in which we
> behaved after victory than upon victory itself.
>
> Lloyd George to the War Cabinet, 11 November 1918[1]

THE First World War ended not just with an armistice, but with revolution; in
fact, with a series of revolutions throughout much of central and eastern Europe.
In Germany, the revolution of November 1918 was led by various elements of
the socialist movement. The German Empire collapsed and was replaced by the
first German republic, usually known as the 'Weimar Republic' after the town
where the new National Assembly gathered in February 1919. Democratic institutions were set up and a coalition government of socialists, liberal democrats,
and Catholics took office. In May 1919, six months after the armistice, the victorious Allied and Associated Powers presented a treaty of peace to Germany.
But the Germans themselves were excluded from any genuine negotiations on its
contents. The representatives of the 'new Germany' were called upon by the victors to sign the Treaty of Versailles at the end of June 1919, whatever their reservations, under threat of invasion and full economic blockade.

The year 1994 marked the seventy-fifth anniversary of the Treaty of Versailles.
In marked contrast to the public celebrations marking the other great milestones
in European history over recent years, this one passed with no fuss, no ceremony,
no self-congratulation. In Britain, Europe, and America, the date came and went
without acknowledgement. In the popular consciousness, it seems, there remains
an abiding sense that a blunder—a momentous blunder—had somehow marred
this particular victory of the Western powers.

There are, of course, dozens of books about the blunder, written from many
points of view. This book is a study of one aspect that has been seldom examined: the British reaction to the revolution in Germany and to the advent of
German democracy at the end of the First World War. It aims to show how
important the revolution was in shaping the British government's reaction to the
defeated Germany. Indeed, it examines the hostility of the British government to
the revolution and to the new Weimar Republic, and argues that this response to
events in Germany contributed to the tragic discrediting of the new democracy
in Germany.

---

[1] Minutes of the War Cabinet, 11 Nov. 1918, CAB 23/14.

The interpretative context: the persistence of the 'German problem' and the rehabilitation of Britain's 'Great War' of 1914–1918

As the research for this book proceeded, contemporary events in Germany provided some parallels with the events of seven decades ago, superficial parallels no doubt, considering it was a 'socialist' regime in decay in Germany this time, but parallels none the less. In the autumn of 1989 a 'people's revolution' swept through the German Democratic Republic. The unrest eventually prompted the decision of the East German government to open the Berlin Wall to its citizens on 9 November 1989—as it happened, seventy-one years to the day after the proclamation of the German republic in Berlin in 1918. In a still more extraordinary rush of events, within twelve months the division of Germany was ended.

The British response to this modern German revolution was diverse. While some journalists and academics stressed the strength of democratic traditions in Germany, there was much loose talk about the uncertainties of 'the Fourth Reich'.[2] One commentator on the new European revolutions, David Selbourne, was moved to complain that the great events in Europe were eliciting only 'the most banal responses in Britain'; he lamented the British tendency to 'see in every "good German" a potential recidivist with jack-boots under his trousers'.[3] The reaction of the British government confirmed Selbourne's fears. Prime Minister Thatcher's opposition to German unification became well known. She revealed in her private exchanges the durability of language and ideas derived from the Second World War. For example, Mrs Thatcher proudly told Cabinet colleagues that on German unification she was 'not an appeaser'.[4] In July 1990, Nicholas Ridley, Secretary for Trade and Industry, resigned, following indiscreet remarks to the effect that the plan for European monetary union was 'a German racket designed to take over the whole of Europe'.[5] Then came the leaking of the so-called 'Chequers Memorandum'. This was an impressionistic record of a meeting between the Prime Minister and a group of academics held at Chequers in March 1990 to consider events in Germany. Mrs Thatcher, a firm believer in the importance of 'national character' in history, presided over a discussion of the German future in the light of the German past.[6] While the academics proved to be mildly optimistic about Germany's democratic prospects, discussion ranged

---

[2] See e.g. Conor Cruise O'Brien, 'Beware the Reich is Reviving', *The Times*, 31 Oct. 1989; Norman Stone, 'No Threat From a New Germany', *Sunday Times*, 18 Feb. 1990, and 'At the Birth of the Fourth Reich? The British Reaction', *Political Quarterly*, 61/3 (July–Sept. 1990), 278–84.

[3] David Selbourne, 'Wall of Suspicion Britain Must Raze', *The Times*, 6 Mar. 1990. See also David Selbourne, *Death of the Dark Hero: Eastern Europe 1987–1990* (London, 1990).

[4] Alan Clark, *Diaries* (London, 1994), entries for 19 and 28 Jan. 1990, 275–6.

[5] See 'Saying the Unsayable about the Germans', *Spectator*, 14 July 1990.

[6] Margaret Thatcher, *The Downing Street Years* (London, 1993), 791.

over alleged negatives in 'the German character', including 'aggressiveness, assertiveness, bullying, egotism'.[7] Looking forward in matters German has scarcely been assisted by the special brand of history-mindedness currently in favour in Britain and the West. Lavish public spectacles have been staged over recent years in order to mark historic events. Among the events specially honoured have been the seventy-fifth anniversary of the landings at Gallipoli and the fiftieth anniversary of the Battle of Britain in 1990; the seventy-fifth anniversary of Armistice Day in 1993; the fiftieth anniversary of D-Day in 1994; and the fiftieth anniversaries of victory over Nazi Germany and Japan in 1995. Naturally, the media attention generated by these public commemorations and re-enactments has had effects on popular perceptions of the two world wars. In Britain, the historian Andrew Roberts has argued that there is a 'national obsession' with the Second World War which has buttressed British belief in the nation's moral superiority. Britain's successful defiance of Nazism (and fortunate escape from the ultimate test of occupation) is believed to have given Britain a claim to 'moral cleanliness' in comparison with most other nations of Continental Europe. According to Andrew Roberts, such 'fifty-year-old myths' lie behind the deep split in the Conservative Party over the European Union.[8]

But the belief in Britain's spiritual supremacy is not sustained solely by the memories of the Second World War. For some, the aura of 'moral cleanliness' is projected back to the 'Great War'. The anniversary industry appears to have given a fillip to this tendency in its interleaving of the First World War and the Second World War anniversaries. The inclination to perceive the first war through the haze of the second, and to conflate Britain's purposes in each conflict, has certainly been encouraged. Scholars of the Great War have craved permission to crow a little over the greatness of Britain's victory in 1918. John Grigg has argued that the British commitment to the First World War was just as unselfish and noble a commitment as that which gripped the people in the so-called 'peoples' war' of 1939–45.[9] Trevor Wilson has also been forthright in his defence of the British decision to enter and prosecute the war of 1914–18 until victory. In a series of articles Wilson has proclaimed that the conflict for Britain was ultimately 'about vindicating its liberal parliamentary system against the challenge of military autocracy'.[10] Similarly, on the seventy-fifth Armistice Day in

[7] On the Ridley affair and the Chequers meeting see Charles Powell, 'What the PM Learnt About the Germans', and Timothy Garton Ash, 'The Chequers Affair', in Harold James and Marla Stone (eds.), *When the Wall Came Down: Reactions to German Unification* (New York, 1992), 233–9 and 242–6.

[8] Andrew Roberts, '1945 and All That', *Spectator*, 11 Feb. 1995.

[9] John Grigg, 'Nobility and War: The Unselfish Commitment?', *Encounter*, 74 (Mar. 1990), 21–7, an edited version of the Gallipoli lecture for 1989 entitled 'Britain's Nobler War: 1914–1918 or 1939–1945?'.

[10] Trevor Wilson, *The Myriad Faces of War: Britain and the Great War, 1914–1918* (London, 1986), 2, and see ch. 77. The same point is made in Trevor Wilson 'The Significance of the First World War in Modern History', in R. J. Q. Adams (ed.), *The Great War, 1914–18: Essays on the*

1993, Norman Stone attacked the pervasive influence in Britain of anti-war interpretations of the First World War.[11]

The British press too has recently sought to encourage the portrayal of the Great War in more favourable colours. For example, on the seventy-fifth anniversary of the armistice, an editorial in *The Times* lamented the fact that millions of Britons were still deluded by the historical and literary orthodoxy into thinking that the First World War was a futile waste of young life. According to *The Times*, 'Tragically high as the price of victory was, it was arguably worth paying'. The editorial went on to commend John Terraine and other revisionist historians for rehabilitating the British Commander, Douglas Haig, for demonstrating the dimensions of the British victory of 1918, and for reconsecrating the British cause as an essentially just and realistic one. This revisionist case, observed *The Times*, is a strong one, and it is 'strongest in its assessment of the German threat'.[12]

Thus emerges the 'sound' position towards which we are being herded. The argument goes something like this. First, historians should shrug off the sentiment and outrage of the war poets and of Bloomsbury, and begin to recognize that both world wars were absolutely necessary democratic crusades. Second, historians ought to recognize the continuity of evil in 'the German threat' as it appeared in both its Imperial and Nazi incarnations, and face up to the fact that security from such a menace was not to be purchased by any other means than war. According to this interpretation, both world wars were comparable in purpose and spirit. Horrific as the long carnage of the Great War may have been, there was no viable means of avoiding or shortening it.

The vision of the Great War as a democratic war designed to nip Nazism in the bud is indeed a seductive and consoling one. But there are problems with both elements of the vision. First, demonizing the German enemy to the point of equating the aggression and despotism of Imperial and Nazi Germany is a serious distortion of history. The invention of an irredeemably evil Germany may be, as E. M. Forster recognized in 1917, 'a menace essential to faith'.[13] But belief in the menace is not likely to be bolstered by a careful reading of recent works in modern German history. Progressive historians in Germany since the Second World War, it is true, have stressed what they call the 'continuities' in German history. The historians of the 'Fischer school' and the 'Bielefeld school' have explored the ideological links *on the Right* between Imperial and Nazi Germany;

Military, Political and Social History of the First World War (London, 1990), 24, and Robin Prior and Trevor Wilson, 'What Manner of Victory? Reflections on the Termination of the First World War', *Revue internationale d'histoire militaire*, 72 (1990), 96.

[11] Norman Stone, 'The Reason Why', *Guardian*, 11 Nov. 1993.

[12] *The Times*, editorial, 'History's Trenches. Orthodox Views of the First World War Should be Questioned', 11 Nov. 1993. For representative examples of Terraine's work see *Douglas Haig: The Educated Soldier* (London, 1963), *To Win a War: 1918 The Year of Victory* (London, 1978), *The Smoke and the Fire: Myths and Anti-Myths of War, 1861–1945* (London, 1980), and *White Heat: The New Warfare, 1914–1918* (London, 1982).

[13] E. M. Forster to Goldsworthy Lowes Dickinson, 5 May 1917, in Mary Lago and P. N. Furbank, *Selected Letters of E. M. Forster, i. 1879–1920* (London, 1983), 251.

they have postulated a destructive German *Sonderweg*, a 'special way', an illiberal path to modernity.[14] But the names of the leading German historians of these schools, Fischer, Geiss, Wehler, and Berghahn, ought not to be flourished as if their historical discoveries vindicate the caricatures peddled by British Germanophobes during both wars. In fact, these German historians do not depict the bulk of the Germans as a naturally abject people predisposed to give allegiance to dictatorship. Even the most critical amongst these historians never lose sight of the powerful internal opposition to the German *Machtstaat* (power-state) in the era of the *Kaiserreich*. Indeed, Fischer and Wehler stress the 'primacy of domestic politics' as the key to modern German history, and by this phrase they mean that aggressive foreign policy in pre-1914 Germany is best understood as a response by the beleaguered ruling élite to the growing strength of socialist and democratic opposition to the regime. It is sharp domestic division in Germany which is stressed.[15]

Moreover, in recent Anglo-American scholarship on Germany there is a growing reaction against the interpretation of Imperial Germany as unremittingly illiberal. In much new writing there is a focus on the opposition to militarism, the liberal potential of the *Kaiserreich*, the creeping parliamentarization, the power of the urban middle classes, and the favourable outlook for increasing liberal, Catholic, and socialist co-operation in pursuit of internal reforms.[16] It is

[14] See the major representative works, Fritz Fischer, *Germany's Aims in the First World War* (London, 1967); Fritz Fischer, *War of Illusions: German Policies from 1911–1914* (London, 1975); Fritz Fischer, *From Kaiserreich to Third Reich: Elements of Continuity in German History, 1871–1945* (London, 1986); Volker Berghahn, *Germany and the Approach of War in 1914* (London, 1973); Hans-Ulrich Wehler, *The German Empire 1871–1918* (Leamington Spa, 1985); and the most recent contribution to the debate, Gregor Schollgen (ed.), *Escape into War? The Foreign Policy of Imperial Germany* (Oxford, 1990).

[15] For the latest survey of socialist anti-militarism before the war see Nicholas Stargardt, *The German Idea of Militarism: Radical and Socialist Critics 1866–1914* (Cambridge, 1994).

[16] During the last twenty years a number of works have appeared which question the traditional portrait of the *Kaiserreich* as relentlessly illiberal and present the possibility of its internal reform in a more democratic direction as at least an open question. For example, see Beverly Heckart, *From Bassermann to Bebel* (New Haven, 1974), David Schoenbaum, *Zabern 1913: Consensus Politics in Imperial Germany* (London, 1982), and Stanley Suval, *Electoral Politics in Wilhelmine Germany* (Chapel Hill, NC, 1985). Some support for this view can be seen also in a number of new American works, including Joachim Remak and Jack Dukes (eds.), *Another Germany* (Boulder, Col., 1988), and Konrad H. Jarausch and Larry Eugene Jones (eds.), *In Search of a Liberal Germany: Studies in the History of German Liberalism* (New York, 1990). At a more theoretical level, the influential model of Germany as an industrialized state utterly backward in its political development and lacking a bourgeois revolution has recently come under sustained attack. A group of younger British historians, Richard Evans, David Blackbourn, and Geoff Eley, are most prominent in this movement. These historians see the 'Bielefeld school' as providing a misleading caricature of Wilhelmine Germany. In contrast, they dispute the image of a wholly deferential and manipulated bourgeoisie. See the provocative works produced by this circle, including D. Blackbourn and G. Eley, *The Peculiarities of German History* (Oxford, 1985), Richard Evans, 'The Myth of Germany's Missing Revolution', in his *Rethinking German History* (London, 1987), G. Eley, *From Unification to Nazism* (Boston, 1986), and D. Blackbourn, *Populists and Patricians* (London, 1987). This extensive debate is summarized in James Retallack, 'Wilhelmine Germany', and in Dieter Langewiesche, 'The Nature of German Liberalism', both in Gordon Martel (ed.), *Modern Germany Reconsidered 1870–1945* (New York, 1992), 33–53, and 96–116.

noteworthy that even the proponents of 'continuities' do not argue that the ambition and culture of Imperial Germany were in any way equivalent to the Nazi menace. It is Fischer himself who has stressed that 'Imperial Germany was, even in the exceptional circumstances of the First World War state of siege, a constitutional state (*Rechtstaat*) with historic roots in liberalism'. As Fischer has pleaded, 'it cannot be emphasised too often or too strongly that continuity is not to be equated with sameness'.[17]

Second, there are great problems with investing British and Empire purposes during the Great War with a modern democratic glow. We must draw a veil over a great many inconvenient facts on the British side. Britain was loyal to Tsarism and accommodated itself to Tsarist war aims for more than half the war.[18] Britain accepted constant compromises with liberal principle in pursuit of firm alliances with France, Italy, and Japan.[19] British imperial ideology was in a state of constant tension with the ideology of Wilsonianism.[20] The British 'trade warriors', whose influence was clear at the time of the Paris Economic Conference in 1916, were eager to achieve the economic subjugation of Germany.[21] British policy in Ireland in the aftermath of the Easter Rising, especially the threat of conscription in 1918, hobbled the Irish Nationalist Party and boosted the fortunes of Sinn Fein.[22] The British government's policies towards democratic Russia in 1917 were similarly disastrous. British reluctance to declare precise war aims undermined faith in the war in Russia as a progressive cause, to the enormous cost of Kerensky's democratic liberal-socialist government.[23] During 1917 the British government determinedly opposed the new Russian diplomacy of negotiating an end to the war on the basis of the formula 'no annexations and no indemnity'; the priority was to keep Russia in the war, even if this imperilled the survival of Russian democracy itself.[24] The British government's own domestic experiment in democratic reform, the Representation of the People Act of 1918, was most certainly an historic leap towards democracy, but one made most reluctantly by many in the government; the reform was hedged around with safeguards (such as the age qualification of thirty years for women) which were believed to advantage the Conservative Party.[25] To this list one might add the occasional 'excesses'

---

[17] Fischer, *From Kaiserreich to Third Reich*, 98.

[18] K. Neilson, *Strategy and Supply: The Anglo-Russian Alliance, 1914–1917* (London, 1984).

[19] David French, *British Strategy and War Aims 1914–1916* (London, 1986), and Paul Guinn, *British Strategy and Politics, 1914 to 1918* (Oxford, 1965).

[20] Edward B. Parsons, *Wilsonian Diplomacy: Allied–American Rivalries in War and Peace* (St Louis, Mo., 1978).

[21] Robert E. Bunselmeyer, *The Cost of the War: British Economic War Aims and the Origins of Reparation* (Hamden, Conn., 1975).

[22] Stephen Hartley, *The Irish Question as a Problem in British Foreign Policy, 1914–1918* (London, 1987).

[23] V. H. Rothwell, *British War Aims and Peace Diplomacy, 1914–1918* (Oxford, 1971).

[24] Robert D. Warth, *The Allies and the Russian Revolution* (Durham, NC, 1954), R. A. Wade, *The Russian Search for Peace, February–October 1917* (Stanford, Calif., 1969) and David Stevenson, *The First World War and International Politics* (Oxford, 1988).

[25] Martin Pugh, *Electoral Reform in War and Peace, 1906–18* (London, 1978).

on the part of the Lloyd George Coalition in its treatment of domestic critics: the prohibition of the overseas circulation of the Radical newspaper the *Nation* in 1917, the prosecution and imprisonment of Radical critics of British foreign policy like E. D. Morel in 1917, and the attempted exclusion of conscientious objectors from the new franchise of 1918 for a period of five years after the war.[26] As is the case in most nations at war, the democratic spirit in Britain during the First World War was an anaemic thing.

But most of all, the suggestion that Britain's war was a crusade for democratic purposes makes the behaviour of the British government in victory seem quite inexplicable. In victory, Britain did not act like a power whose first priority was to liquidate the remnants of Prusso-German authoritarianism and set up a healthy democracy in its place in Germany. As this study will demonstrate, the British government showed virtually no concern with nourishing the new German democracy in 1918–19. Policies that might have led to the consolidation of progressive politics in Germany were rarely considered. The new Weimar Republic was starved and shunned during its first crucial months of life. This had catastrophic consequences for post-war German politics.

This book, therefore, is not in the tradition of those that seek to make the human losses of the First World War more bearable by ceaselessly lauding the victorious military effort or by sanitizing the cause retrospectively. It may be comforting to believe that the British and Empire dead were part of a great sacrifice for a new democratic Europe, but it is a fairy tale. Attempts to democratize the motives of Lloyd George's 'knock-out blow' Coalition only confuse the ideological realities of the period. Neither the democratization of the British victory of 1918, nor the attempted Nazification of the German enemy, will really work. Both pander to a näive vision of the English Channel as a moat behind which the best values have held firm against lesser ones. In contrast, it is the purpose of this book to examine critically British policy towards the new Germany at a moment of opportunity in its modern history—and to suggest a British share of responsibility for a European tragedy.

The interpretative context: the historiography of peace-making and the 'aborted revolution' in Germany, 1918–1919

Clearly the subject-matter of this book brings to the fore a familiar question: why did democracy fail to 'take root' in Germany after the First World War? There are two common interpretations to be found in the literature. One stresses the 'unfinished' nature of the German revolution, the result of the mistaken moderation of the socialist and liberal leadership of the revolution. The revolutionary

---

[26] On the *Nation* episode see A. F. Havighurst, *Radical Journalist: H. W. Massingham (1860–1924)* (Cambridge, 1974), 250–5; on Morel's imprisonment see Marvin Swartz, *The Union of Democratic Control in British Politics during the First World War* (Oxford, 1971), 178–80; and on the exclusions from the Representation of the People Bill of 1918 see Pugh, *Electoral Reform in War and Peace*, 113–14 and 125–6.

government, it is often maintained, lacked revolutionary zeal and compromised too much with the old order. According to this interpretation, it is the Germans themselves who must bear most of the blame for the weakness of Weimar. A second interpretation stresses the debilitating effects of the long armistice and blockade maintained by the Allies, the imposition of the Versailles Treaty of June 1919, the abandonment of the democratic government in Germany to the vituperations of the German Right, and the pursuit of reparations during the 1920s, all of which, it is contended, discredited German democracy. According to this interpretation, the victors were chiefly at fault.

In Britain and America, the tide of historical opinion has flowed back and forth from one interpretation to the other. J. M. Keynes's brilliant attack on the peacemaking élite's bad faith and economic vandalism, *The Economic Consequences of the Peace*, seduced much educated opinion during the inter-war years.[27] Not surprisingly, this 'unpatriotic' consensus did not survive the outbreak of the Second World War. The next most influential work, Harold Butler's *The Lost Peace*, written during 1941, changed the emphasis altogether. Butler conceded the inadequacies of the Versailles settlement, but placed the chief burden of blame for Germany's weak democracy on her unfinished revolution of 1918–19. The timidities of the German socialists and liberals, Butler argued, undermined Germany's revolution from the outset. So much of the old order survived, it seemed that 'the so-called German Revolution never really happened'.[28] In the 1960s, A. J. P. Taylor refocused historical attention once again on the folly of Allied policy. In his two best-selling and intensely provocative histories, *The Origins of the Second World War*, and *The First World War: An Illustrated History*, Taylor lambasted the peacemakers as greedy, hypocritical, short-sighted, and inconsistent. 'The peace of Versailles lacked moral validity from the start', declared Taylor.[29] The Allies 'imposed peace by dictation, with hardly a pretence of negotiation'. The statesmen of Paris, concluded Taylor, had failed as spectacularly as the generals.[30] In the years since Taylor's works first appeared, a reaction against his scorn for the peacemakers of 1919 has slowly taken hold. Reviving the perspective of Butler, historians have played down the importance of the Versailles Treaty as a factor in the early debilitation of the Weimar Republic. Indeed, some scholars have gone further and have vigorously defended the treaty as a realistic attempt to contain the German threat. The treaty's critics, past and present, have been scolded as misguided idealists who merely buttressed German nationalist

---

[27] John Maynard Keynes, *The Economic Consequences of the Peace* (Cambridge, 1971; originally published in 1919).

[28] Harold Butler, *The Lost Peace: A Personal Impression* (New York, 1942), 108–9 and 111.

[29] A. J. P. Taylor, *The Origins of the Second World War* (Harmondsworth, 1964), 52. On the reaction to Taylor's views regarding the First World War as a whole, see Alex Danchev, ' "Bunking" and Debunking: The Controversies of the 1960s', in Brian Bond (ed.), *The First World War and British Military History* (Oxford, 1991).

[30] A. J. P. Taylor, *The First World War: An Illustrated History* (Harmondsworth, 1966), 263–4, 270, and 287.

illusions.[31] The chief proponents of this view, Marc Trachtenberg and Sally Marks, have combined a stout defence of French diplomacy in 1918–19 with attacks on the German politicians of Weimar for refusing to accept the verdict of Allied arms.[32]

The chief themes of West German scholarship of the revolution follow the pattern first outlined so passionately in Alfred Döblin's post-war novel *A People Betrayed*, namely, the themes of lost opportunity and betrayal.[33] According to this tradition, it was the unfinished revolution that was chiefly to blame. Most progressive West German historians minimize the importance of Allied pressure in 1918–19. As Erich Matthias wrote in 1971: 'It is possible to reproach the Allies for having pursued a policy which was in many respects unwise, and of having neglected, against their own interest, to support the democratic German Republic effectively. But they can surely not be blamed for developments inside Germany.'[34] True to this dictum, West German historians during the 1960s and 1970s focused their attention almost exclusively upon the internal political dynamics of the revolution. An introspective debate flourished about the viability of a 'third way' for Germany in 1918–19, a democratic but still socialist path, avoiding both the fatal moderation of the majority socialists (the Sozialdemokratische Partei Deutschlands or SPD) and the ardent Leninism of many of the Spartacists. According to proponents of the 'third way', a more complete revolution was a prerequisite for the building of a strong republic, but the inexperienced majority socialists lost their nerve. West German and East German scholarship has concentrated upon either the sins of the impatient Spartacists or the sins of the diffident SPD. According to either interpretation the revolution was a disappointment, at best incomplete and at worst abortive.[35]

[31] e.g. see the review of the historiography in Marc Trachtenberg, 'Versailles After Sixty Years', *Journal of Contemporary History*, 17 (1982), 487–506, Catherine Cline, 'British Historians and the Treaty of Versailles', *Albion*, 20/1 (1988), 45–58.

[32] See Sally Marks, *The Illusion of Peace: International Relations in Europe, 1918–1933* (London, 1976), and 'The Misery of Victory: France's Struggle for the Versailles Treaty', *Historical Papers* [Canada] (1986), 117–133, and '1918 and After: The Postwar Era', in Gordon Martel (ed.), *The Origins of the Second World War Reconsidered: The A. J. P. Taylor Debate after Twenty-five Years* (London, 1986), 17–48.

[33] Alfred Döblin, *A People Betrayed. November 1918: A German Revolution* (New York, 1983, first published in Munich, 1948–9).

[34] Erich Matthias, 'The Influence of the Versailles Treaty on the Internal Development of the Weimar Republic', in Anthony Nicholls and Erich Matthias (eds.), *German Democracy and the Triumph of Hitler: Essays in Recent German History* (London, 1971), 26.

[35] Typical of the work on 1918–19 is Sebastian Haffner, *Verratene Revolution: Deutschland, 1918/19* (Berne 1969). On the 'third way' controversy see Eberhard Kolb, *Die Arbeiterräte in den deutschen Innenpolitik 1918–19* (Düsseldorf, 1962), Reinhard Rürup, *Probleme der Revolution in Deutschland 1918/19* (Wiesbaden, 1968), Heinrich August Winkler, *Die Sozialdemokratie und die Revolution von 1918/19: Ein Rückblick nach sechzig Jahren* (Berlin, 1979), and Heinrich August Winkler, *Vom der Revolution zur Stabilisierung: Arbeiter und Arbeiterbewegung in der Weimarer Republik, 1918 bis 1924* (Berlin, 1984). The best summary of this historiography in English is provided by the introduction to Jürgen Tampke, *The Ruhr and Revolution: The Revolutionary Movement in the Rhenish Westphalian Industrial Region, 1912–1919* (Canberra, 1978), and Elizabeth H. Tobin, 'Revolution and Alienation: The Foundations of Weimar', in Michael N. Dobkowski and Isidor

The great exception to this almost exclusive focus upon internal political tensions is the work of Klaus Schwabe. His major work, *Woodrow Wilson, Revolutionary Germany, and Peacemaking, 1918–1919,* appeared in English in 1985. While concentrating on American foreign policy as it affected revolutionary Germany, Schwabe addressed the wider international context. In an evenhanded account, he stressed the faith the new German government placed in Wilsonianism, and the bitter recriminations which flowed from Wilson's failure to deliver a peace of reconciliation at Versailles. But Schwabe was critical also of some of Germany's diplomats, claiming that 'they were not willing to accept Germany's military defeat as a basis for the peace', and that they cultivated the political illusions of the German Right.[36] Notwithstanding Schwabe's work, most modern German historians have been unwilling to pin even a measure of the responsibility for the hobbling of Weimar democracy upon the Allied peacemakers. For example, Eberhard Kolb, the eminent historian of the Weimar Republic, asserts that the Western Allies were generally comfortable with the German revolution of 1918 and reluctant to interfere in Germany's internal politics.[37] In his major history of Weimar, he offers a mild judgement, observing only that 'it may be doubted whether the victors acted wisely in visiting the consequences of defeat on those German politicians and parties which shared Wilson's ideas concerning international understanding'.[38]

But with most German historians appearing to be content to blame Germans for Weimar's troubles, few Western scholars have felt the need to disagree. Indeed, the same themes of betrayal and lost opportunity dominate the British and American historiography of the revolution, and there is the same stress on Germany's own political mistakes.[39] Most accounts dwell upon the fatal division of the two socialist parties, the SPD and the USPD, and the overreaction of the moderate majority to the perceived threat of Bolshevism. Pressures from abroad upon the revolutionary government during the long armistice period are seldom explored, although some histories do note Allied opposition to the Workers' and Soldiers' Councils in the occupied zones and to socialist plans for the national-

Walliman (eds.), *Toward the Holocaust: The Social and Economic Collapse of the Weimar Republic* (Westport, Conn., 1983), 155–76.

[36] Klaus Schwabe, *Woodrow Wilson, Revolutionary Germany, and Peacemaking, 1918–1919. Missionary Diplomacy and the Realities of Power* (Chapel Hill, NC, 1985), 404.

[37] Eberhard Kolb, 'Internationale Rahmenbedingungen einer demokratischen Neuordnung in Deutschland 1918/19', in his *Umbrüche deutscher Geschichte 1866/71, 1918/19, 1929/33* (Munich, 1993), 261–87.

[38] Eberhard Kolb, *The Weimar Republic* (London, 1988), 33.

[39] The main works are Eric Waldman, *The Spartacist Uprising of 1919* (Milwaukee, 1958), A. Mitchell, *Revolution in Bavaria, 1918–1919: The Eisner Regime and the Soviet Republic* (Princeton, 1965); Richard A. Comfort, *Revolutionary Hamburg: Labor Politics in the Early Weimar Republic* (Stanford, Calif., 1966); A. J. Ryder, *The German Revolution of 1918: A Study of German Socialism in War and Revolt* (Cambridge, 1967); Fritz Carsten, *Revolution in Central Europe, 1918–1919* (Los Angeles, 1972); David Morgan, *The Socialist Left and the German Revolution: A History of the German Independent Social Democratic Party, 1917–1922* (Ithaca, NY, 1975); Tampke, *Ruhr and Revolution*; and Richard Breitman, *German Socialism and Weimar Democracy* (Chapel Hill, NC, 1981).

ization of industry.[40] In most accounts, the polarization of internal German politics in 1918–19 is presented as the all-important factor which led to the fragility of Weimar democracy.

In contrast, the major historians of the peacemaking in 1919 reveal an intense awareness of the counter-revolutionary preoccupations of the peacemakers. Since the appearance in the 1960s of the groundbreaking works by the German and American scholars Gerhard Schulz, J. M. Thompson, Gordon Levin, and Arno J. Mayer, the theme of Allied hostility to revolution has become well known.[41] In this tradition, recent studies of British policy by the American scholars Lloyd Gardner and Lorna Jaffe acknowledge as a factor in British policy-making the profound anxiety in government circles over the German revolution.[42]

However, most British scholarship on the peacemaking is curiously resistant to this approach. The dominant model for the analysis of British relations with Germany is that promoted by Correlli Barnett. In this model 'realists', those with no illusions about Germany, perpetually confront 'idealists', always portrayed as effete believers in both 'new Jerusalems' and a peaceful Germany. In Barnett's pages, the blame for the advent of the Second World War is laid firmly at the door of the 'idealists' even in 1919. It was the 'idealists' who allowed the decisive moment to slip by, the moment when Germany might have been properly throttled. The British had the chance to join forces with the French, to stand firm against President Wilson, and ensure that Germany was 'divided and permanently weakened in the very springs of power'. Instead, Barnett laments, the British fell into 'a confusion between realism . . . and idealism'. Thus, as Barnett contends, 'the critical weakness of the Versailles Treaty lay in its failure to deal with the problem of German national power'.[43] Significantly, he dismisses the new government in Germany out of hand, describing it as 'a flimsy republican régime of dingy, well-meaning but inexperienced working-class and middle-class politicians'.[44]

Similarly, the major histories of the British contribution to the peacemaking in Paris in 1918–19 simply ignore the new German governments thrown up by

---

[40] e.g. Ryder, *German Revolution*, 169 and 181, and Tampke, *Ruhr and Revolution*, 88.

[41] J. M. Thompson, *Russia, Bolshevism and the Versailles Peace* (Princeton, 1966); Gerhard Schulz, *Revolutions and Peace Treaties, 1917–1920* (London, 1972; published originally in Germany in 1967); N. Gordon Levin, *Woodrow Wilson and World Politics* (New York, 1968), and Arno J. Mayer, *Politics and Diplomacy of Peacemaking: Containment and Counter-revolution at Versailles, 1918–1919* (London, 1968).

[42] See Lloyd C. Gardner, *Safe For Democracy: The Anglo-American Response to Revolution, 1913–1923* (Oxford, 1984) and Lorna Jaffe, *The Decision to Disarm Germany: British Policy towards Postwar German Disarmament, 1914–1919* (London, 1985).

[43] Correlli Barnett, *The Collapse of British Power* (London, 1972), 318. The same model of idealists versus realists is promoted by Paul Kennedy, without the unqualified endorsement of the 'realist' position, in his 'Idealists and Realists: British Views of Germany, 1864–1939', *Transactions of the Royal Historical Society*, 25 (1975), 137–56, and 'The Tradition of Appeasement in British Foreign Policy, 1865–1939', *British Journal of International Studies*, 2 (1976), 195–215.

[44] Barnett, *Collapse of British Power*, 249–50. Not one of the major German political leaders of 1919 gains a place in the index of *The Collapse of British Power*.

the revolution. Neither Lowe and Dockrill's *The Mirage of Power*, nor Dockrill and Goold's *Peace Without Promise: Britain and the Peace Conferences, 1919—1923* describe the German 'enemy' of 1919 upon whom peace was imposed.[45] In the same way, Eric Goldstein's survey of British policy at the Paris Peace Conference, *Winning the Peace*, ignores the German revolution as a factor in the settlement with Germany.[46] In these accounts the revolution is a phantom; the new democratic German leadership seems not to exist. British historians, it seems, have simply not considered the question of interaction between the German revolution and British peacemaking.

Not surprisingly, there is no acknowledgement either that in exhibiting hostility to the German republicans Britain might have been in some measure responsible for the baleful political outcome in Germany in 1918–19. There is only one exception: Albert Lentin's *Lloyd George, Woodrow Wilson and the Guilt of Germany*. Lentin is forthright in his attack on British policy towards the new Germany, arguing that 'the shunning of the Germans appears in retrospect to have been a capital error of *British* psychology'. The moderate German republicans, as Lentin insists, were 'the best hope for the emergence of a liberal Germany'.[47] But Lentin's strictures have made little impact it seems. The most recent survey of the peacemaking published in Britain, Alan Sharp's *The Versailles Settlement: Peacemaking in Paris, 1919*, offers very little on this theme. Only on his last page does Sharp concede that 'the Allies did little to foster the new democratic Germany they hoped would ensure peace'.[48]

As this brief review of the existing historiography reveals, therefore, no systematic analysis has yet been made of the British response to revolutionary Germany in the protracted period of crisis between the armistice and the signing of the Versailles Treaty. This study aims to fill this important gap.

Why should there be a special focus upon Britain?

Some readers may immediately object that Britain was not alone among the Allies in making a response to the German revolution and ought not to be studied alone. Indeed, the events of the period October 1918 to June 1919 were truly international in scale; that must be conceded at the outset. Of course, it is true that Britain was but one of the 'Allied and Associated Powers'—as the victors were officially styled in deference to the Americans' refusal to be nominated as an ally of the imperialist Entente. It is true also that American, French, Italian, Belgian,

---

[45] C. J. Lowe and M. L. Dockrill, *The Mirage of Power, ii. British Foreign Policy, 1914–22* (London, 1972); M. L. Dockrill and J. D. Goold, *Peace Without Promise: Britain and the Peace Conferences, 1919—1923* (London, 1981). Ebert, Scheidemann, Erzberger, and Brockdorff-Rantzau, are not listed in the indexes.

[46] Eric Goldstein, *Winning the Peace: British Diplomatic Strategy, Peace Planning, and the Paris Peace Conference, 1916–1920* (Oxford, 1991).

[47] Albert Lentin, *Lloyd George, Woodrow Wilson and the Guilt of Germany* (Leicester, 1984), 146, italics in the original.

[48] Alan Sharp, *The Versailles Settlement: Peacemaking in Paris, 1919* (London, 1991), 196.

Australian, and other influences, were all involved in the making of policy towards defeated Germany. This study does not seek to inflate the importance of British policy over and above the many other factors operating at Versailles. Similarly, it is not the intention of the book to survey every aspect of the British contribution to the peace settlement with Germany. The objective is to examine the British reaction to the revolutionary and advanced republican politics that were so powerful a force inside Germany between the armistice and the signing of the peace, that is, at the advent of Weimar democracy.

What is offered here is obviously only a part of the much larger story of peace-making, and the much larger story of Germany's revolution. But, for a number of reasons, the British aspect of both stories seems well worth examining. The British contribution to Allied policy on Germany was by any measure a most significant one. In the first place, the decisive character of the British military effort on the Western Front in the autumn of 1918 was widely acknowledged at the time. Geoffrey Dawson, the editor of *The Times*, was not exaggerating when he wrote to a friend from Cambrai in October 1918 that 'there is no doubt at all that the present situation is mainly a *British* triumph'.[49] The sources are littered with similar statements. This sense of the decisiveness of the British military effort gave Britain great leverage in determining policy towards the defeated state. Second, the harsh decision to continue the blockade after the armistice, in order to preserve the victors' ultimate capacity to coerce the German republic in all subsequent diplomacy, was the product of British insistence. Moreover, the blockade itself was largely dependent for its operation on British naval power. Third, it was the British general election of December 1918, and more precisely the campaigning themes of the Lloyd George Coalition, which did much to inflame popular expectations of bitter retribution against Germany. Fourth, as Marc Trachtenberg and Bruce Kent have shown, it was British not French pressure that led to the expansion of the punitive 'reparations' claim at Paris beyond the level of compensations originally envisaged at the time of the armistice.[50]

Finally, according to a great many first-hand accounts of the Paris Peace Conference, Lloyd George, fresh from his electoral triumph in Britain, was widely regarded as having wielded decisive influence on a number of issues among the 'big Four' (Clemenceau, Wilson, Orlando, Lloyd George) in Paris in 1919. Of course, he did not construct the policy of the Allied and Associated Powers just as he wished. He had no constant ascendancy; but he was not easily pushed aside. In Britain, tributes to his performance at Paris were made both publicly and privately, by Liberals and Conservatives, by friends and enemies alike. Bonar Law told H. A. L. Fisher that, from the moment of the opening of

---

[49] Geoffrey Dawson to G. S. Freeman, 18 Oct. 1918, Geoffrey Dawson Papers, 67. Italics in original. For similar judgements see Bryce to A. V. Dicey, 31 Dec. 1918, Bryce Papers, 4, and Haig to Beatty, 8 Jan. 1919, Beatty Papers, 14/6.

[50] See Marc Trachtenberg, 'Reparation at the Paris Peace Conference', *Journal of Modern History*, 51 (Mar. 1979), 24–85, and Bruce Kent, *The Spoils of War: The Politics, Economics and Diplomacy of Reparations, 1918–1932* (Oxford, 1989), ch. 2.

the conference, Lloyd George was 'easily the best' among the leading speakers.[51]
After a visit to Paris in April 1919, Walter Long, a leading Conservative minis-
ter and no friend of the Prime Minister, wrote that Lloyd George was 'by far the
biggest and strongest man there and everybody knows it'.[52] When the peacemaking was over the tributes were still flowing. In June 1919 Lord Derby, the
English Ambassador in Paris, wrote to Lord Curzon 'full of admiration' for Lloyd
George's dominance at the Peace Conference, and proudly noting that 'both the
French and Americans are complaining that the peace is an English peace'.[53] Eric
Phipps, a Foreign Office diplomat in Paris, recalled in his private memoir: 'My
general impression of such meetings as I attended was that the dominating per-
sonality of the Four was Mr Lloyd George'.[54] Much of this might be dismissed
as mere boastful chatter. Indeed, it would be difficult to determine an exact balance sheet of the points won and lost in debate between the leading figures at
Versailles. Georges Clemenceau, the French Prime Minister, had the considerable advantage of the location of the conference in the French capital. President
Woodrow Wilson had the power of American economic resources behind him.
The fairest conclusion seems to be that Lloyd George, in debate, in manœuvre,
and in diplomacy, was at least the equal of any of the other major players during the period of peacemaking.

Thus, the reality of the British opportunity deserves to be stressed. British
political weight was poised somewhere between the liberal progressivism of
Wilson, on the one side, and the security-driven *revancheist* spirit of Clemenceau,
on the other. Britain was in a position to lend decisive assistance to either side,
to a negotiated peace of reconciliation and recovery, or to an imposed peace of
humiliation and impoverishment. There seems little doubt that, had Britain
declared its determination immediately after the revolution to consolidate the new
democratic forces inside Germany, as a priority of the peacemaking, this view
would have prevailed. Had Britain pursued a policy of strengthening the hands
of the new government—by declaring support for the new administration in
Berlin, by applauding the break with the imperial system and the decision for a
republic, by dispatching emergency food, by swiftly raising the economic blockade, and by insisting on a process of genuine negotiation of the peace with representatives from Berlin—then any or all of these gestures would very probably
have been supported by the United States and adopted by the powers gathered
at Paris in 1919. It was not to be. This book aims to explain why.

[51] H. Fisher to L. Fisher, 21 Jan. 1919, Fisher Papers, 205.
[52] Doreen Long to William Bull, undated but filed as early Apr. 1919, Bull Papers, 4/19.
[53] Derby to Curzon, 30 June 1919, Derby Papers, 28/2/2.
[54] Phipps, 'Light and Shade' (typescript memoir), Phipps Papers, 9/1.

The Politics and Politicians of the 'Knock-Out Blow' Coalition, 1914–1918

At present, men who wish to make the world safe for democracy are fighting shoulder to shoulder with men who thank God for the war as a means of making an end of democracy and bringing insurgent labour finally to heel.

George Bernard Shaw, 18 July 1918[1]

At the Hôtel Majestic, the headquarters of the British delegation during the Paris Peace Conference of 1919, an anonymous satirical poem entitled 'Ode on the Majestic' did the rounds of the crowded dining-room. One of the stanzas offered these insights:

> *Here's where the Foreign Office wage their war,*
> *And though the hours are, strictly, 10 to 4,*
> *Even at 5 amid the tea cups' clatter,*
> *Sit Men Who Count discussing Things That Matter.*[2]

These may have been mere recreational jottings intended to poke fun at the Foreign Office, but they serve to introduce some essentials of the world of British high politics in the period. Indeed, policy was made by an inner circle of 'Men Who Count', as they described themselves. This élite was composed not only of the politicians who took the final decisions, but also of the secretaries, diplomats, intelligence officers, and military personalities, who made up the entourage of the great men. In addition, the phrase 'Men Who Count' aptly described the men beyond the cabinet rooms who wielded considerable power, the proprietors and journalists of the mass-circulation newspapers. Naturally, the leading men were affected by all sorts of 'Things That Matter', shorthand no doubt for the myriad of pressures that were brought to bear upon them. These included not only 'the facts' mustered by experts, but also other ever-present personal and

---

[1] George Bernard Shaw to John Spargo, 18 July 1918, in Dan H. Laurence, *Bernard Shaw: Collected Letters, iii. 1911–1925* (New York, 1985), 557.

[2] 'Ode on the Majestic', handwritten copy in George Prothero Papers, Personal Correspondence 1919, PP 1/11, Wemyss Papers, 5/2, and see Basil Thomson, *Queer People* (London, 1922), pp. vii and 250–1, where the author is given as M. R. K. Burge.

domestic political considerations—in their way the most weighty of 'Things That Matter' to be discussed among political intimates over the tea cups.

To understand the making of British policy in 1918–19, therefore, it is important to take account of both elements of this general context, personalities and politics, as the governing circles perceived them. The impact of the war on British politics is, of course, essential background to the period. Fortunately a large body of scholarship exploring in detail the development of British politics during and just after the First World War is already at the disposal of readers.[3] This chapter, therefore, aims only to introduce the essential context of 1918–19, the leading figures of the so-called 'knock-out blow' Coalition, and the preoccupations of the governing élite at the moment of victory.

At the outset it is vital to appreciate that the Lloyd George Coalition was much more than a gathering of men devoted to the vision of a 'war to end all war' or a 'world made safe for democracy' as the popular slogans suggested. The 'knock-out blow' label fixed the fundamental faith of the government. Its precise meaning demands attention. The phrase derived from a sensational interview which Lloyd George had given to an American journalist in late September 1916 in which he had deprecated any intervention to achieve a negotiated peace and instead insisted that the war must be a fight 'to a finish—to a knockout blow'.[4] It is important to stress that the label was used to describe not just the government which Lloyd George led but also a great assembly of quite disparate forces supporting the notion of no peace until victory. Throughout the war, these political, economic, ideological, and journalistic forces had pressed for a military resolution of the war as the *sine qua non*. Thus, the vision of a 'knock-out blow' brought together all those who clung to the idea of a military victory as a panacea, and conversely all those who shared a horror of the alternative—not just defeat, but any adjustment downwards of British territorial and economic war aims in order that a negotiated settlement might be attempted.

Support for a 'knock-out blow' was much more than a simple 'never say die' spirit. The determination that there be no peace until victory often sprang from very different motives. Idealists and jingoes moved uneasily in the same combination. On the one side were progressive thinkers who hoped that victory would lead to a new era of peace, internationalism, and democracy. Among their ranks were journalists like C. P. Scott and C. E. Montague, writers like H. G. Wells, and progressive politicians like George Barnes and Christopher Addison. On the other side was a large assembly of nationalists, social imperialists, tariff reform-

---

[3] A useful summary is John Turner, 'British Politics and the Great War', in his *Britain and the First World War* (London, 1988), 117–38. The four indispensable works are Cameron Hazlehurst, *Politicians at War, July 1914 to May 1915: A Prologue to the Triumph of Lloyd George* (London, 1971), Kenneth O. Morgan, *Consensus and Disunity: The Lloyd George Coalition Government, 1918–1922* (Oxford, 1979), Chris Wrigley, *Lloyd George and the Challenge of Labour: The Post-War Coalition, 1918–1922* (Hemel Hempstead, 1990), John Turner, *British Politics and the Great War: Coalition and Conflict, 1915–1918* (London, 1992).

[4] John Grigg, *Lloyd George: From Peace to War, 1912–1916* (London, 1985), 424–8.

ers, and agitators from right-wing pressure groups such as the National Service League and Navy League. Their advocacy of victory sprang from a determination to extend *Imperium Britannica*, to build an exclusive economic autarky for this greater British Empire, and simultaneously to fend off the political progress of socialism and democracy at home. Their ranks included the zealots of the right-wing press, men such as Leo Maxse, H. A. Gwynne, and J. L. Garvin, the tariff reformers who dominated the Unionist Business Committee and the Federation of British Industry, men such as Dudley Docker, W. A. S. Hewins, and Halford Mackinder, the ethical imperialists of Lord Milner's Round Table movement, men such as John Buchan, Leo Amery, and F. S. Oliver, and the anti-socialists who dominated the military élite, the diplomatic élite, and the intelligence services, men like General Sir Henry Wilson, Lord Charles Hardinge, Admiral Reginald Hall, and Basil Thomson. The broad coalition included men who had been eager for war in 1914—as a chance to quash Britain's chief economic and naval rival, and as an unmatched opportunity to buttress the existing social order at home. As Basil Thomson wrote, he believed that Edwardian Britain had been drifting towards revolution 'unless there was a European war to divert the current'.[5] Such men did not regard war as an unmitigated evil. While many of these crusaders reserved the right to criticize deficiencies in the Lloyd George 'knock-out blow', all were proudly part of the great combination espousing the vision of ultimate victory through force of arms alone.

The essence of the argument presented in this chapter is that the forces gathered under the banner of the 'knock-out blow' in Britain were by 1918–19 increasingly inclined towards reaction. This domestic political orientation had clear consequences for foreign policy—the men of influence within the 'knock-out blow' government were predominantly of a political 'type' predisposed to regard the new socialist-led regime in Germany with disfavour. In completing a portrait of the political priorities of the Coalition, the following propositions are argued here. First, in spite of the Liberal background and democratic renown of Lloyd George, the Coalition government he led from December 1916 was founded primarily to fend off a negotiated peace and had no real dedication to a progressive programme. Second, as Prime Minister, Lloyd George was an essentially vulnerable leader who, even at the moment of victory, recognized the frail improvisations underpinning his premiership. Third, within the Conservative-dominated Coalition, anti-socialist passions and tariff reform expectations were in the ascendant by late 1918. Fourth, the Prime Minister's close advisers, while including some genuine idealists, were for the most part men who shared the reactionary political prejudices of the 'bitter-end' patriots, chiefly a suspicion of democracy and a disdain for all manifestations of socialism. Fifth, the leadership of the Foreign Office in the period was demoralized and steeped in Germanophobic prejudice. Sixth, even the most advanced spirits of the Foreign

[5] Thomson, *Queer People*, 265.

Office, the young men of the Political Intelligence Department, had little expertise in, or sympathy for, German socialism, anticipating instead the emergence of
a liberal Germany in defeat. Seventh, the popular right-wing pro-Coalition
newspapers were never merely compliant supporters of a Lloyd George government, but rather made plain their intention to exert pressure upon the government in favour of a profitable peace of economic aggrandizement for Britain.
Finally, during the war, new pro-business pressure groups arose which mobilized
opinion among the economically powerful classes in favour of a tough peace settlement, a peace that would deliver some measure of economic protection against
competition from any German economic revival and help deflect demands for
high taxation at home. Each of these factors helped shape the British government's response to revolutionary Germany in the aftermath of the First World
War.

The 'knock-out blow' Coalition and the priority of victory, 1916–1918

The British government that thrilled to the great victory over Germany in
November 1918 was a coalition government led by David Lloyd George. Its
political history can be swiftly summarized. The first Liberal-led Coalition government had been created in May 1915 when the Conservatives (and one Labour
Party representative) were invited into the Cabinet by the Liberal Prime Minister
of seven years, H. H. Asquith.[6] However, this government was overturned in
December 1916. Following months of mounting dissatisfaction over the alleged
inefficiencies of his leadership, Asquith was succeeded as Prime Minister by
Lloyd George, the former Secretary of State for War. Bitterly resenting his displacement, Asquith left the government but, most significantly, remained Liberal
Party leader. Lloyd George, a former Radical and hero of the left-wing 'New
Liberal' faction of the party, led a new 'patriotic' Coalition dominated by the
Conservative Party. Only a sprinkling of Liberal and Labour ministers could be
found to join this improvised second Coalition government. The new government
fiercely proclaimed its determination to prosecute the war until victory was
achieved. Surviving through the vicissitudes of two more years of struggle, it was
this Lloyd George-led Coalition which oversaw the eventual triumph of British
arms in Europe in late 1918.

For almost fifty years after the eventual fall of Lloyd George in 1922 hostile
accounts of his prime ministership held the field. Biographers and historians were
repelled by his 'slipperiness' and alleged venality, especially in the post-war government of 1919–22.[7] Scholarship since the 1960s, however, has sought to redress

---

[6] H. H. Asquith, from the 'Liberal Imperialist' wing of the party, was the dominating personality
of the Edwardian Liberal Party. He was Chancellor of the Exchequer in the Campbell-Bannerman
government of 1906–1908, and Prime Minister 1908–1916.

[7] On the record of hostile writings on the Coalition see Morgan, *Consensus and Disunity*, 1–9.

the balance. Prompted by the revisionist efforts of A. J. P. Taylor, most modern historians have presented Lloyd George in a comparatively attractive light, paying homage to his political skills and his personal vitality.[8] The television production *The Life and Times of David Lloyd George*, made by BBC TV Wales in 1980, also presented a positive image. Lloyd George was 'The People's Prime Minister', according to the book accompanying the series. Significantly, the television series gave greatest emphasis to Lloyd George's achievements as wartime Prime Minister between 1916 and 1918.[9] Similarly, in much historical writing he is often presented as a war leader, an inspirational force comparable with Churchill.[10] Evidently, Lloyd George's modern reputation still bears upon it the giant imprint of the victory of 1918.

But this popular image ought to obscure neither the realities of Lloyd George's essentially fragile political position during the First World War, nor the essentially reactionary complexion of the governments which he led. Notwithstanding the aura of victory that surrounded him in 1918, Lloyd George remained a vulnerable prime minister. A gamble underlay his premiership: he had agreed to walk away from the bulk of the senior figures of the Liberal Party in 1916 and to rely instead on the Conservatives' perceived need of him to lead the nation. To be sure, both his governments of 1916 and 1919 were coalitions in name, but the political mix within them was heavily weighted in favour of the Conservative Party. As John Turner, author of the most exhaustive study of the wartime coalition, has written, 'the Lloyd George Coalition, over the period of its wartime ministry, became a deliberately counter-revolutionary force'.[11]

To appreciate the political values of the Lloyd George Coalition, the circumstances surrounding the displacement of Asquith as premier in December 1916 must first be reviewed.[12] A crisis of leadership erupted in early December over

[8] Modern reassessments of Lloyd George include A. J. P. Taylor, 'Lloyd George: Rise and Fall', in Taylor, *Politics in Wartime* (London, 1964), 123–49; Kenneth O. Morgan, 'Lloyd George's Premiership: A Study in "Prime Ministerial Government" ', *Historical Journal*, 13/1 (1970), 130–57; A. J. P. Taylor (ed.), *Lloyd George: Twelve Essays* (London, 1971); Hazlehurst, *Politicians at War, July 1914 to May 1915*; Peter Rowland, *Lloyd George* (London, 1975); Stephen Koss, 'Asquith versus Lloyd George: The Last Phase and Beyond', in Alan Sked and Chris Cook (eds.), *Crisis and Controversy: Essays in Honour of A. J. P. Taylor* (London, 1976), 66–89; Michael Fry, *Lloyd George and Foreign Policy*, i. *The Education of a Statesman, 1890–1916*; (Montreal, 1977); David Woodward, *Lloyd George and the Generals* (East Brunswick, NJ, 1983), Grigg, *Lloyd George: From Peace to War, 1912–1916*; Martin Pugh, *Lloyd George* (London, 1988); Stephen Constantine, *Lloyd George* (London, 1992); and Wrigley, *Lloyd George*. Themes in the historiography of Lloyd George are reviewed in David Brooks, 'Lloyd George: For and Against', *Historical Journal*, 24/1 (1981), 223–30.

[9] The television series *The Life and Times of Lloyd George* was produced and directed by John Hefin and written by Elaine Morgan, with A. J. P. Taylor acting as historical adviser. See also the book accompanying the series, David Benedictus, *Lloyd George* (London, 1981).

[10] e.g. J. Ehrmann, 'Lloyd George and Churchill as War Ministers', *Transactions of the Royal Historical Society*, 11 (1961), 101–15, and Lord Beaverbrook, 'Two War Leaders: Lloyd George and Churchill', *History Today*, 23/8 (1973), 546–53.

[11] Turner, *British Politics and the Great War*, 387.

[12] There is a vast literature on the political crisis of Dec. 1916. The most judicious account is that provided in Turner, *British Politics and the Great War*, ch. 3. Other useful contributions are: P. A. Lockwood, 'Milner's Entry into the War Cabinet, December 1916', *Historical Journal*, 7/1 (1964),

Asquith's decision to resist the creation of a small War Council to be led by Lloyd George. This prompted a political showdown. Lloyd George and the leading Tories resigned. Asquith in turn resigned, miscalculating the likelihood of the Conservatives agreeing to serve under Lloyd George. The option of forming a purely Conservative government was rejected by the Conservative Party leader, Andrew Bonar Law.[13] Instead, Lloyd George was catapulted into the top job, with Conservative support. He immediately 'squared' the Labour Party 'partly by the promise of Cabinet posts and partly by promises about the nationalisation of various industries', as Labour Party leader Arthur Henderson later recalled.[14] The Labour Party Executive decided by a vote of 19 to 12 in favour of joining the new government, a less than overwhelming endorsement, but sufficient to maintain Lloyd George's claim to be leading a second 'coalition'.[15]

In essence, the new government stood for a military resolution of the war. This becomes clear when the controversies over war aims in the months leading up to the crisis are recalled. From the perspective of the 'victory at any price' hardliners who dominated the Conservative Party, the perceived 'danger' of imminent peace by negotiation formed the lurid backdrop to the whole political drama of December 1916. The new Coalition was lashed together by men convinced they were averting the menace of a 'patched-up peace'. For Lloyd George and his collaborators believed not only that Asquith was incapable of securing victory, but also that his Coalition might soon accept a German or American offer of a peace conference. Determined to resist any such outcome, Lloyd George had pushed himself forward as the leader of the 'bitter enders'. They were alerted to the 'danger' of peace by Asquith's invitation in late August to Cabinet members and the

120–34; Barry McGill, 'Asquith's Predicament, 1914–1918', *Journal of Modern History*, 39 (1967), 283–303; Cameron Hazlehurst, 'The Conspiracy Myth', in Martin Gilbert (ed.), *Lloyd George* (Englewood Cliffs, NJ, 1968), 148–57; Peter Lowe, 'The Rise to the Premiership, 1914–16', in Taylor (ed.), *Lloyd George: Twelve Essays*, 95–136; J. M. McEwen, 'The Struggle for Mastery in Britain: Lloyd George Versus Asquith, December 1916', *Journal of British Studies*, 18 (1978), 131–56; J. M. McEwen, 'The Press and the Fall of Asquith', *Historical Journal*, 21/4 (1978), 863–83; Richard Murphy, 'Walter Long, the Unionist Ministers, and the Formation of Lloyd George's Government in December 1916', *Historical Journal*, 29/3 (1986), 735–45; David French, *British Strategy and War Aims, 1914–1916* (London, 1986), ch. 12; and Michael Fry, 'Political Change in Britain, August 1914–December 1916: Lloyd George Replaces Asquith: The Issues Underlying the Drama', *Historical Journal*, 31 (Sept. 1988), 609–27.

[13] Andrew Bonar Law was a successful Glasgow-based iron merchant and businessman, leader of the Conservative Party 1911–21. In Lloyd George's wartime Coalition he was Chancellor of the Exchequer and Leader of the House of Commons.

[14] Arthur Henderson, Labour MP for Barnard Castle 1903–18, and Chairman of the Parliamentary Labour Party 1914–17. He joined Asquith's first Coalition in May 1915 and was offered a seat in the War Cabinet in Lloyd George's Coalition in Dec. 1916. Visited Russia in 1917 where he was impressed by the determination of the Russian left-wing parties to secure revision of Allied war aims if Russian support for the war was to be maintained. As a result, he supported British Labour representation at the proposed Stockholm Conference in 1917. This led to his clash with the War Cabinet and resignation in Aug. 1917. Arthur Henderson's description of the crisis of Dec. 1916 is quoted in Repington Diary, 11 Mar. 1918, in Lieut.-Col. C. à Court Repington, *The First World War 1914–1918: Personal Experiences of Lieut.-Col. C. à Court Repington* (London, 1920), ii. 242.

[15] Turner, *British Politics and the Great War*, 147.

major departments of state to submit material for a reconsideration of Britain's war aims, a move which in turn began a major Cabinet debate over the wisdom or folly of continuing the war.[16] As noted above, it was in response to this Cabinet move that Lloyd George gave his famous interview to the American press in late September, pledging himself to the policy of the 'knock-out blow'. The interview aggravated existing tensions in the Cabinet. To the surprise of many Conservatives, the first member of the Cabinet to break ranks was the Conservative Leader in the Lords, Lord Lansdowne.[17] He suggested in a memorandum of 13 November 1916 that a negotiated peace was nothing other than good sense, and he described the prospect of a 'knock-out blow' as 'to say the least of it, remote'.[18] Lansdowne's memorandum provoked panic among the 'bitter enders'. General Sir William Robertson, Chief of the Imperial General Staff (CIGS), who was due to address the Cabinet, was visited by Lloyd George; he advised the general that he should 'let himself go' so that any support for a peace conference could be 'very peremptorily stamped upon'.[19]

The 'knock-out blow' faction of the Cabinet clearly believed that, in spite of Lansdowne having initiated the movement for peace, the Asquithians were the greater danger. Sir Edward Grey, Foreign Secretary, was known to be in close touch with the American President's emissary, Colonel Edward House, and was suspected of entertaining hopes of American mediation. Grey had attacked Lloyd George very sharply for his 'knock-out blow' speech, correctly perceiving it to be an attempt to deflect American diplomacy.[20] Grey was 'not sound on the question of American mediation', as Lord Bertie, Ambassador to France, observed.[21] Asquith's reliability also was considered suspect: he had lost his son Raymond at the front in September 1916 and was observed to be shattered by the loss.[22] In fact, in late November Asquith and his closest Liberal associates declared their preference for an ongoing military struggle.[23] But both Grey and Asquith, so their critics maintained, might soon change their tune on peace.

---

[16] French, *British Strategy and War Aims*, 227.

[17] Henry Petty-Fitzmaurice, 5th Marquess of Lansdowne, Conservative elder statesman, Secretary of State for Foreign Affairs 1900–5, Minister without Portfolio in Asquith's Coalition Cabinet 1915–16.

[18] Lansdowne's memorandum of 13 Nov. 1916 is reproduced in David Lloyd George, *War Memoirs* (London, 1938), 2 vol. edn, i. 514–20.

[19] Sir William Robertson, *Soldiers and Statesmen, 1914–1918* (London, 1926), i. 280. See also David R. Woodward, 'Britain's "Brass Hats" and the Question of a Compromise Peace, 1916–1918', *Military Affairs*, 4 (Apr. 1971), 65.

[20] See Joyce Grigsby Williams, *Colonel House and Sir Edward Grey: A Study in Anglo-American Diplomacy* (Lanham, Md., 1984), ch. 5 and p. 110.

[21] Bertie to Lord Hardinge, 16 Oct. 1916, FO 800/178, Bertie Papers, quoted in David R. Woodward, 'Great Britain and President Wilson's Efforts to End World War I in 1916', *Maryland Historian*, 1 (Spring 1970), 50.

[22] Lord Riddell, *Lord Riddell's War Diary* (London, 1933), 26 Nov. 1916, 224, and Lloyd George, *War Memoirs* i. 603.

[23] French, *British Strategy and War Aims*, 234.

The inner meaning of the change of government, therefore, was plain: a Lloyd George government was virtually certain to spurn any offer of a negotiated settlement of the war. Because the Liberal Party was believed to be vulnerable on the matter of peace, the true believers in the 'knock-out blow' had combined together to ensure the dominance of the only party with an apparently unqualified commitment to ongoing war, the Conservative Party. Lloyd George provided the eye-catching emblem of a continuing Coalition. But, clearly, he was head of the government because he had promoted himself as the epitome of the Conservative war spirit. Accordingly, when the German and American governments did issue their famous 'peace notes' just a few days after the formation of Lloyd George's government, the Conservative hardliners congratulated themselves that the change of government in London had already been made. Rejection of the peace offers was considered certain. The mood of satisfaction in Northcliffe's office was typical. 'Yesterday the Germans put forth their peace proposals', Tom Clarke, the leading Northcliffe journalist, recorded in his diary; 'Apparently Lloyd George got into power in the nick of time', he added.[24]

The democratic credentials of this new government are sometimes assumed. One recent study, for example, concludes that the dynamic Lloyd George was simply 'what democracies require from time to time: the man of peace who went to war'.[25] In fact, the government of Lloyd George could scarcely be described as democratic in inspiration or temper. The realities of political alignment were clear: enthusiasm for democracy and enthusiasm for victory at any price were at opposite ends of the British political spectrum during the war. The more fervently democratic forces, the New Liberals, Radicals, and socialists, even those supporting the war, generally harboured all sorts of reservations, reservations over the foreign policy of Sir Edward Grey, over conscription, over protection, and over censorship.[26] On the other hand, the ultra-patriotic forces on the Right, constantly trumpeting their support for any measure of compulsion necessary to achieve victory, were generally the same forces that had shown most hostility to the march of Edwardian democracy.[27] In the scale of values of the new Lloyd George government democracy certainly ranked very low. The leading Conservative personalities who dominated the War Cabinet and the government, Bonar Law, Lord Milner, Austen Chamberlain, Edward Carson, Lord Crawford, Lord Curzon,[28]

[24] Tom Clarke Diary, 14 Dec. 1916, in Tom Clarke, *My Northcliffe Diary* (London, 1931), 108.

[25] R. J. Q. Adams, *Arms and the Wizard: Lloyd George and the Ministry of Munitions, 1915–1916* (London, 1978), 189.

[26] e.g. see Peter Clarke, *Liberals and Social Democrats* (Cambridge, 1978), ch. 6; Malcolm I. Thomis, 'Conscription and Consent: British Labour and the Resignation Threat of January 1916', *Australian Journal of Politics and History*, 23/2 (1977), 10–18.

[27] e.g. see Chris Wrigley, ' "In Excess Of Their Patriotism": The National Party and Threats of Subversion', in Chris Wrigley (ed.), *Warfare, Diplomacy and Politics: Essays in Honour of A. J. P. Taylor* (London, 1986), 93–119.

[28] George Nathaniel Curzon, Conservative MP 1886–98. Travelled widely in Asia, served as Viceroy and Governor-General of India 1899–1905, entered House of Lords in 1908 and created Earl Curzon of Kedleston in 1911. Lord Privy Seal in Asquith's Coalition of May 1915, and member of Lloyd George's War Cabinet 1916–19. Leader of the House of Lords 1916–24.

and Arthur Balfour,[29] had all defied the democratic programme of the pre-war Asquith government. All but Balfour and Curzon had barracked for the 'diehard' position in 1911. Yet even these two were contemptuous of democracy. Curzon, soliciting for funds among the very rich for his Anti-Suffrage League in 1910, described the idea of adult suffrage as 'socialism naked and unashamed'.[30] Such deeply entrenched hostility was not easily masked. Local Liberal Party branches during 1917–18 regarded the Lloyd George government with increasing disfavour precisely because it was believed to be indifferent to democracy.[31]

Lloyd George and the 'knock-out blow' Coalition: the underlying vulnerability of the Prime Minister

Within the new War Cabinet which Lloyd George constructed at the centre of his new government, he was in a truly exceptional position. The former scourge of the 'diehard' peers was surrounded by men who had been among his most vociferous Edwardian critics. The quality of improvisation was appreciated on both sides. It was obvious that the Conservative magnates of the government had chosen Lloyd George to lead them not because he had shown a greater determination than Asquith to defend democratic ideals. Lloyd George had been installed in office by men who could agree on the priority of victory, but not on a leader from their own ranks to whom they could entrust the task. They had rejected all Liberal leadership in the war except that of Lloyd George. They deferred, no one knew for how long, to the flamboyant Liberal man of mark. A bargain underpinned the government. Under its unwritten terms, Lloyd George was never a mere puppet of his Conservative partners, but neither was he a free agent. As Curzon had predicted in conversation with Lansdowne at the height of the crisis of December 1916, Lloyd George was framed in: 'His Government will be dictated to him by others, not shaped exclusively by himself'.[32]

The 'knock-out blow' government existed to sustain the war until victory. Lloyd George's credentials for leadership in this task were readily apparent. He had built up considerable credits with the bellicose men. His decision in favour of British intervention on the Continent in August 1914 was widely known to have been a turning-point for the waverers in the Asquith Cabinet. Then, he easily matched the ultra-patriots in the extravagant rhetoric of war. In his Queen's Hall address of September 1914, he militarized his familiar Welsh valley parables depicting the war as a chance for Britons to gaze upward and glimpse 'clad in

[29] Arthur James Balfour, a Conservative MP since 1874, and one of the most senior men in the party. Leader of the Opposition 1892–5 and 1906–11, Conservative Prime Minister 1902–5, First Lord of the Admiralty in Asquith's Coalition 1915–16, Foreign Secretary 1916–19.

[30] Curzon to Lord Astor, 11 July 1910, quoted in Derek Wilson, *The Astors: The Life and Times of the Astor Dynasty* (London, 1993), 164.

[31] George L. Bernstein, 'Yorkshire Liberalism during the First World War', *Historical Journal*, 32/1 (1989), 119.

[32] Lord Newton, *Lord Lansdowne* (London, 1929), 453, cited by McEwen, 'The Struggle for Mastery in Britain', 151.

white, the great pinnacle of Sacrifice pointing like a rugged finger to Heaven'.[33]
He rattled the cage of party loyalty, flaunting an eagerness to trim Liberal principles, even beyond the considerable trimming of the Asquithians who swallowed
both conscription and some protectionism during 1916. Above all, his support
for conscription was deeply appreciated in Conservative ranks. For example, as
early as May 1915, Lord Milner,[34] the imperial seer, and H. A. ('Taffy')
Gwynne,[35] the leading Conservative editor, agreed together that when it came to
conscription Lloyd George was 'the only man who could carry it'.[36] Even more
reassuring, Lloyd George's conversion was known not to have been a last-minute
affair. He had made plain his accommodation with the Germanophobic faith in
the aftermath of his Mansion House speech of 1911 when he had first confessed
to General Henry Wilson and to Balfour his belief in the inevitability of British
intervention in a coming war against Germany.[37] His friendly correspondence
with the leading Germanophobic journalist J. L. Garvin dated from 1910.[38] Such
men were genuinely in his debt.

From the Conservative perspective, Lloyd George's inherent value lay in the
rarity of his political combination: he was a profoundly patriotic front-rank politician of democratic renown. His leadership was useful in confounding progressive critics of the war. For instance, Lord Esher[39] wondered upon Lloyd
George's appointment if he would prove to be 'our Gambetta'.[40] Keeping the

[33] David Lloyd George, *The Great War. Speech delivered by the Rt. Hon. David Lloyd George
M. P. at the Queen's Hall, London, on September 19th, 1914* (London, 1914), 15–16. On the reception
of this address see Hazlehurst, *Politicians at War*, 178–9.

[34] Alfred Milner, Viscount Milner after 1902, leading advocate of an esoteric blend of imperialism
and social reform, as promoted in the journal *Round Table*. A founder of the Liberal Unionist
Association in 1886. Governor of the Cape Colony and High Commissioner in South Africa
1897–1901. Governor of the Transvaal and Orange River Colony 1901–5. During this period, he gathered together a number of young and idealistic civil servants in his so-called 'Kindergarten' to promote his vision of Empire. On his return to England, he was prominent in the National Service
League, and in campaigns of resistance to the policies of the Asquith Liberal government.

[35] Howell Arthur Gwynne was a senior journalist of extreme right-wing opinions. He was editor
of *Standard* 1904–11, and Lady Bathurst's *Morning Post* 1911–37. He was an unwavering advocate of
Tariff Reform.

[36] Milner to Gwynne,10 May 1915, and Gwynne to Milner, 11 May 1915, H. A. Gwynne Papers,
Imperial War Museum, HAG/21/nos. 36–7.

[37] Bentley B. Gilbert, 'Pacifist to Interventionist: David Lloyd George in 1911 and 1914. Was
Belgium an Issue?', *Historical Journal*, 28/4 (1985), 863–5.

[38] See Alfred Gollin, 'Freedom or Control in the First World War: The Great Crisis of May 1915',
Historical Reflections (Canada), 2/2 (1975), 153. James Louis Garvin, prominent advocate of Tariff
Reform and promoter of the 'German Menace' before the war, editor of *Outlook* 1905–6, editor of
the *Pall Mall Gazette* 1912–15, editor of the *Observer* 1908–42.

[39] Reginald Baliol Brett, second Viscount Esher, a confidant of King George V and of many high-
ranking military officers. Close to the Royal Family since the last years of Queen Victoria's reign.
Pursued the cause of army reform from the turn of the century onward. A prominent member of the
Committee of Imperial Defence from 1904.

[40] Lord Esher to Lord Burnham, 9 Dec. 1916, Burnham Papers, HLWL 1/no. 1 (Leon Gambetta
was the leading French Republican and Radical, an opponent of Louis Napoleon's Empire, who then
skilfully combined his radicalism and popular patriotism at the time of the Franco-Prussian War,
1870–1).

'lower orders' enthralled by the war was essentially what was expected of him in these quarters. Indeed, ultra-patriots occasionally expressed impatience with Lloyd George if he did not 'manage' the popular forces. For example, when Arthur Henderson, the Labour Party minister, supported the socialist Stockholm Conference in 1917, Gwynne noted sourly that Lloyd George should have been able to 'work the British socialists' concerning the Stockholm affair 'as he is supposed to be such a great manager of men'.[41] On balance, however, most Conservatives were more than happy with his record as a kind of lion tamer. In early 1918, Lord Crawford[42] praised Lloyd George's ability to stifle labour troubles. 'He possesses an insinuating manner and a happiness of repartee which are admirable with a popular audience', he wrote.[43] There was even a degree of Conservative dependence upon this conspicuous talent. W. E. Oliver, brother of the influential Conservative ideologue F. S. Oliver,[44] explained to his brother in December 1918 that it was only Lloyd George among the modern politicians who could protect 'the decent element at home from the Bolsheviks'.[45]

To be sure, Lloyd George grew in stature during the war. During 1918 he enjoyed a series of crucial political victories. He survived several bitter clashes with the 'brass hats'. He succeeded in his effort to secure the dismissal of Sir William Robertson as CIGS in February 1918, and then shrugged off the first real political challenge from Asquith prompted by General Maurice's allegations of dishonesty against him in May 1918.[46] However, as various commentators pointed out at the time, these victories for Lloyd George were somewhat hollow. The Conservatives exhibited no fierce loyalty to Lloyd George; rather, they simply made it plain that they would not have Asquith back as Prime Minister at any price, even if he were allied temporarily with some of the dissatisfied brass hats.[47]

Notwithstanding these assets, Lloyd George may still be described as an insecure politician in the autumn of 1918. Salvation by way of battle was in prospect, but for how long victory would lift him above challenge nobody really knew. His

---

[41] Gwynne to Esher, 17 Aug. 1917, Gwynne Papers, Imperial War Museum, HAG/8, No. 13.

[42] David Alexander Lindsay, 27th Earl of Crawford and 10th Earl of Balcarres, Conservative MP for Chorley 1895–1913 and party whip 1903–13 until proceeding to the Lords in 1913. President of the Board of Agriculture and Fisheries July–Dec. 1916, Lord Privy Seal to Jan. 1919, and then Chancellor of the Duchy of Lancaster to 1921.

[43] Lord Crawford Diary, vol. xxxi, 18 Jan. 1918 (in the care of the present Lord Crawford, examined at National Library of Scotland).

[44] Frederick Scott Oliver, a writer and successful businessman. He was a leading member of the Round Table group. His fortune derived from his directorship with the well-known stores of Debenham and Freebody. Among his close friends were other Round Tablers such as Philip Kerr and Leo Amery. Wrote *Federalism and Home Rule* (1910) and *Ordeal by Battle* (1915).

[45] W. E. Oliver to F. S. Oliver, 3 Dec. 1918, F. S. Oliver Papers, 70.

[46] Lloyd George was accused by General Sir Frederick Maurice of misleading the House of Commons over the numbers of British troops in France. See John Gooch, 'The Maurice Debate 1918', *Journal of Contemporary History*, 3/4 (1968), 211–28, and Ged Martin, 'Asquith, the Maurice Debate and the Historians', *Australian Journal of Politics and History*, 31/3 (1985), 435–44.

[47] See Turner, *British Politics and the Great War*, 300.

original elevation to the post of Prime Minister had carried with it no guarantees concerning his future. Indeed, Lloyd George's stoical acceptance of this uncertainty was remarked upon by some Conservatives as one of the Prime Minister's chief merits. For example, William Bridgeman,[48] the Conservative junior whip, wrote in early 1918 that Lloyd George was 'single-hearted about the war, and does not really think of his future position afterwards'.[49] As the political maverick who had challenged the old party labels, Lloyd George could not confidently predict his long-term political future. A safe landing upon the Liberal benches was a diminishing possibility. While a majority of Liberal MPs supported Lloyd George's government as a war government, when forced to choose at such moments as the 'Maurice debate', Lloyd George's lifeline back to the Liberal Party was dangerously frayed.[50] Freddy Guest, his 'numbers man' in the House of Commons, estimated in March 1918 that perhaps only 10 per cent of Liberal MPs supported Lloyd George personally.[51] He was detested by most of the front-rank Liberals as a self-advertising adventurer and an apostate to Liberalism.[52]

Nor was there real safety for Lloyd George in the Conservative Party. His personality had certainly made an impression upon leading Conservatives during the war. Garvin declared that Lloyd George was the only war politician 'worth a damn'.[53] 'He is a wonderful man', Sir Edward Carson[54] confessed in January 1918; 'I do not see how we could replace him.'[55] Bridgeman praised the 'glamour of his extraordinary personality'.[56] But few among the top-ranking Conservatives were permanently awestruck by these personal attributes. He was still viewed as an exotic outsider. At the top only Bonar Law presented himself as a friend. The Conservative Party leader, plainly exhausted by office and devastated by the deaths of his two sons at the front, was increasingly inclined to

[48] William Clive Bridgeman, later 1st Viscount Bridgeman, a Conservative MP for Shropshire (Oswestry) 1906–29, Parliamentary Secretary to the Ministry of Labour in Lloyd George's first government 1916–19, and Parliamentary Secretary to the Board of Trade 1919–20.

[49] William Bridgeman Diary, (no day given) Feb. 1918, Bridgeman Papers, SRO 4629/1/2/1.

[50] On the relatively small dimensions of personal loyalty to Lloyd George in the Liberal Party after Dec. 1916 see J. M. McEwen, 'Lloyd George's Liberal Supporters in December 1916: A Note', *Bulletin of the Institute of Historical Research*, 53/128 (1980), 265–72.

[51] Sanders Diary, 24 Mar. 1918, in John Ramsden (ed.), *Real Old Tory Politics: The Political Diaries of Sir Robert Sanders, Lord Bayford, 1910–1935* (London, 1984), 102.

[52] 'Memorandum by Lord Selborne, 1916', in George Boyce (ed.), *The Crisis of British Unionism* (London, 1987) 188.

[53] Garvin quoted in Alexander Whyte Diary, 14 Nov. 1917, Whyte Papers, MSS Eur D 761/1. On Garvin's friendship with Lloyd George from 1910 see Gollin, 'Freedom or Control in the First World War', 150–5.

[54] Sir Edward Henry Carson, Baron Carson, Unionist MP for Dublin University 1892–1918. Recognized as a vehement opponent of Irish Home Rule. Leader of the Ulster Unionists in the House of Commons from 1910. Attorney-General May–Nov. 1915. First Lord of the Admiralty Dec. 1916–July 1917, then entered War Cabinet as Minister without Portfolio, resigning in Jan. 1918 over Lloyd George's policy on Ireland.

[55] Carson quoted in *Lord Riddell's War Diary*, 11 Jan. 1918, 306.

[56] William Bridgeman Diary, (no day given) Feb. 1918 and 4 July 1919, Bridgeman Papers, SRO 4629/1/2/1.

defer to Lloyd George.[57] He was, he said, seduced by 'the magnificent qualities he had, especially vitality and endurance'.[58] But Bonar Law's special relationship with Lloyd George led to allegations against him of an abject servility.[59] Both Liberals and Conservatives came to regard his brand of loyalty as quite exceptional among his party colleagues.[60]

Certainly it contrasted with the simmering hostility and embarrassment felt by other powerful figures in the Conservative Party over their party's connection with Lloyd George. Austen Chamberlain,[61] Lord Curzon, Walter Long, and Lord Milner were all affronted by aspects of Lloyd George's leadership. Chamberlain had been reluctant to enter the government in December 1916, describing Lloyd George as 'quite untrustworthy'.[62] His disdain for the Prime Minister's style led him to condemn the government in the House of Commons in February 1918 for having granted government appointments to so many of the press lords. 'I cannot shout myself hoarse over the cry Great is our David or proclaim myself his prophet', he wrote. [63] Lord Curzon also had a difficult relationship with Lloyd George; the Prime Minister constantly mocked Curzon's imperial style and pretensions.[64] Another persistent and powerful critic of Lloyd George was Walter Long, the wartime Colonial Secretary and later First Lord of the Admiralty, a close ally of the Tariff Reform campaigners.[65] Lloyd George recognized Long as a disgruntled foe as early as February 1917 and privately expressed a desire to be rid of him.[66] However, Long had delivered crucial Conservative support to Lloyd George in the crisis of December 1916, so determined was Long to unseat Asquith.[67] Not surprisingly then, Long retained posts in both the Lloyd George ministries in spite of his despising the Prime Minister.

[57] C. P. Scott Political Diary, 29 Aug. 1917, C. P. Scott Papers, Box 134.

[58] William Bridgeman Diary, 4 July 1919, Bridgeman Papers, SRO 4629/1/2/1.

[59] e.g. Robert Sanders Diary, 3 Oct. 1917, in Ramsden, *Real Old Tory Politics*, 89, Selborne to Austen Chamberlain, 18 Mar. 1918, in Boyce (ed.), *The Crisis of British Unionism*, 213, and Austen Chamberlain to J. St Loe Strachey, 19 Mar. 1918, Strachey Papers, S/4/5/8.

[60] Edward Shortt, quoted in John Baird Diary, 6 Sept. 1919, Stonehaven Papers, 7. John Baird, later Viscount Stonehaven, was a Conservative MP 1910–25, and Governor-General of Australia 1925–30.

[61] Austen Chamberlain, son of Joseph Chamberlain, champion of his father's great cause, Tariff Reform. A Conservative MP 1892–1937. He was the chief rival with Walter Long for the leadership of the Conservative Party on the resignation of Arthur Balfour in 1911. Member of the War Cabinet from Apr. 1918 and Chancellor of the Exchequer 1919–21.

[62] A. Chamberlain to Hilda Chamberlain, 14 Dec. 1916, Chamberlain Papers, AC 5/1/65.

[63] A. Chamberlain to Hilda Chamberlain, 17 Mar. 1918, Chamberlain Papers, AC 15/3/10.

[64] *Lord Riddell's War Diary*, 10 Dec. 1916, 230, 13 Jan. 1918, 307, and 11 May 1918, 328, and C. P. Scott Diary, 28 Dec. 1917, C. P. Scott Papers (Rylands Library), Box 134.

[65] Walter Long was leader of the 'Country Party' in the Conservative Party. He was a Conservative MP 1880–1921. Under Lloyd George, Long served as Colonial Secretary 1916–18 and First Lord of the Admiralty in 1919. A prominent member of the Anti-Socialist Union.

[66] Frances Stevenson Diary, 17 Feb. 1917, in A. J. P. Taylor (ed.), *Lloyd George: A Diary by Frances Stevenson* (London, 1971), 145, and Hankey Diary, 16 Feb. 1917, quoted in Stephen Roskill, *Hankey: Man of Secrets*, i. *1877–1918* (London, 1970), 359.

[67] Murphy, 'Walter Long, the Unionist Ministers, and the Formation of Lloyd George's Government in December 1916', 735–45.

Mutual respect between Lord Milner and the Prime Minister also appears to have evaporated by the last months of the war. Milner was increasingly critical of Lloyd George's impulsiveness. He complained in December 1918 that following 'the Goat' (Lloyd George) was more than he could bear for 'this wild animal will go where it pleases'.[68] In sum, Lloyd George developed no genuinely close relations with any of the leading Conservatives with whom he worked during the war years, with the single exception of Bonar Law.

Even the make-shift structures of the Coalition gave to the Prime Minister's position a sense of impermanence. Lloyd George did not lead his own political party and was not likely to lead it. No real political machine of his own had been created to sustain him until a rudimentary organization was set up in the House of Commons in the middle of 1918. No constituency organization devoted to him was to be created until 1920.[69] He did not cultivate a following in the House, seldom bothering to appear there. As Peter Fraser has noted, the Commons was 'slighted and ignored' by the leaders of the Coalition government.[70] Immediate power was deemed to lie beyond the parliament—with the War Cabinet, the Imperial War Cabinet, and with the small clique of senior politicians who had given Lloyd George access to the levers of power. Here Lloyd George might presume to swagger. But such novel structures of government were not likely long to survive the war. Many observers perceived his predicament. Esme Howard of the Foreign Office detected a mood in late November 1918 that 'his time is drawing to a close and that with the end of the war his role is finished'.[71] Henry Wilson, Lloyd George's hand-picked CIGS, was equally confident that Lloyd George would not remain at the helm for long; he observed in his diary on the last day of 1918 that Lloyd George 'ought to last out a year'.[72]

There were signs of the limitations of Lloyd George's power even amidst the apparatus of war. Ultimately, Lloyd George failed to make a difference on the issue which he claimed burned brightest in his conscience, the alleged squandering of British life on the Western Front. The reason for his defeat on the issue is clear: he had bound himself to men who counted casualties by the millions in the continuing 'war of attrition' as acceptable. Curzon was typical. In March 1915 he told Colonel House that he wanted 'to make peace in Berlin no matter how long it takes to get there'.[73] Curzon advised the Cabinet in June 1915 that if 'two million (or whatever figure) more of Germans have to be killed at least a corre-

[68] Milner to F. S. Oliver, 23 Dec. 1918, Oliver Papers, 93. On the breakdown in the relationship between Lloyd George and Milner see Terence H. O'Brien, *Milner* (London, 1979), 306 and 323–4.

[69] K. O. Morgan, 'Lloyd George's Stage Army: The Coalition Liberals,1918–1922', in Taylor (ed.), *Lloyd George: Twelve Essays*, 226–7, 233.

[70] Peter Fraser, 'The Impact of the War of 1914–18 on the British Political System', in M. R. D. Foot (ed.), *War and Society: Historical Essays in Honour of J. R. Western, 1928–1971* (London, 1973), 134–5.

[71] Esme Howard Diary, 29 Nov. 1918, Howard Papers, DHW 1/4.

[72] Henry Wilson Diary, 31 Dec. 1918, Henry Wilson Papers, microfilmed diary.

[73] Colonel House Diary, 9 Mar. 1915, in Charles Seymour (ed.), *The Intimate Papers of Colonel House, i. Behind the Political Curtain, 1912–1915* (London, 1926), 393.

sponding number of allied soldiers will have to be sacrificed to effect that object'.[74] Once bound to such men, Lloyd George did not abandon his reservations about the British brass hats, but neither did the Conservatives abandon their commitment to a 'war of attrition'. Certainly, Lloyd George succeeded in creating a Supreme War Council in late 1917 as an alternative source of military advice. But Lloyd George's efforts to curb the powers of the British generals were in most instances rebuffed. Most importantly, he failed to overturn Field Marshal Sir Douglas Haig. Lloyd George might deride him as a dullard, a man who was 'more chin than head'—but the Conservative Party was loyal to Haig. The Field Marshal stayed.[75]

Finally, behind the scenes, there was a painful social gap between the Prime Minister and his Conservative allies. Condescension towards Lloyd George was habitual. Lamentably, he behaved 'in a way which showed he had never been at public school'.[76] He had no taste, according to some. Conservative visitors to Downing Street were not above observing his 'pathetic ostentation of rubbish' that passed for ornamentation.[77] Most of his Conservative colleagues claimed to detect the reek of rascality about him. Many voiced suspicions about his want of 'straightness'. Balfour observed that, after all, he was 'only a little Welsh attorney'.[78] Typically, for Clive Wigram, the King's Assistant Private Secretary, Lloyd George was 'the best man we could have to win the war but his methods are rather un-English'.[79]

Lloyd George himself could scarcely have been unaware that he was regarded as a tribune who had been admitted to the inner sanctum of power on sufferance. For all his bravado, he did occasionally confess sensitivity to his own exposed position. Edwin Montagu[80] reminded him in 1917 that he had complained early in the life of his government of his 'isolation', having no colleagues in the War Cabinet who truly thought as he thought.[81] In private, Lloyd George laughingly dismissed Conservative protestations of loyalty.[82] Well-informed Conservatives also detected Lloyd George's underlying vulnerability. Summing up all he had

---

[74] Lord Curzon, 'Registration and military service', 21 June 1915, CAB 37/130/19, cited by David French, 'The Meaning of Attrition', *English Historical Review*, 103 (Apr. 1988), 398.

[75] Lloyd George quoted in Lord Burnham memorandum, 13 July 1917, Burnham Papers, HLWL/10/no. 9. On Lloyd George's tense relations with his military leaders see Woodward, *Lloyd George and the Generals*.

[76] William Waldorf Astor, MP, quoted in John Turner, *Lloyd George's Secretariat* (Cambridge, 1980), 196.

[77] Lord Crawford Diary, vol. xxxiii, 1 Nov. 1918, Crawford Papers.

[78] Randall Davidson, Diary, 9 Dec. 1917, Davidson Papers, vol. 13.

[79] Clive Wigram to Alexander Godley, 11 May 1918, General Alexander Godley Papers, microfilmed correspondence, 3/1, Liddell Hart Centre for Military Archives.

[80] Edwin Samuel Montagu, Liberal MP for Cambridgeshire 1906–22. He made his mark chiefly in the reform of Indian affairs. Parliamentary Under-Secretary of State for India 1910–14, Financial Secretary to the Treasury 1914–16, and Minister of Munitions July–Dec. 1916. Returned to the ministry as Secretary of State for India in June 1917.

[81] Edwin Montagu to Lloyd George, 1 May 1917, Montagu Papers, Box 15, AS 4/3/4.

[82] *Lord Riddell's War Diary*, 26 May 1917, 252.

learned of the doings of the War Cabinet, F. S. Oliver wrote in March 1918 that Lloyd George was definitely the 'greatest character' among the élite, but added that he was seriously handicapped by 'the want of any devoted personal following'.[83]

The semblance of coalition: the dominance of the Conservative Party in the Lloyd George governments, 1916–1919

The political balance of the government as a whole also reveals starkly the essential vulnerability of the Prime Minister. The domination of the War Cabinet, the supreme decision-making body, by the Conservative Party was obvious from the outset. When Lloyd George formed his first War Cabinet of five members in December 1916, Sir Henry Lucy, the veteran political journalist, jotted in his diary that 'the wildest fancy' could not have imagined the cabinet's composition: 'three are not only Unionists but belong to the ultra type of the sect.'[84] The three 'ultras' were Bonar Law, Curzon, and Milner. These were balanced by Lloyd George and Arthur Henderson, the Labour Party leader. Henderson was regarded at first as 'a cipher' by his Conservative colleagues.[85] The War Cabinet appeared to reflect the ideal of national solidarity. But the new supreme body was politically lopsided. Most additions and changes to the War Cabinet over the next two and a half years only served to underline this fact. Sir Edward Carson was a member for six months from July 1917. Austen Chamberlain joined the War Cabinet in April 1918 and insisted on his reappointment in January 1919. Arthur Balfour, the former Conservative Party leader, attended the War Cabinet frequently in his capacity as Foreign Secretary.

Few voices outside the Conservative Party hierarchy gained admission to this top echelon of power. The most important new influence during the war was General Jan Smuts, the South African Defence Minister, who entered the War Cabinet in June 1917 and remained until mid-December 1918.[86] Smuts could be represented as an imported ersatz Liberal supplementing the otherwise isolated Liberalism of the Prime Minister. Smuts was certainly ecumenical in his political contacts. He included in his personal circle several Quakers. He assisted the patriotic Liberals of the League of Nations Society at its launch in May 1917.[87]

---

[83] F. S. Oliver to W. E. Oliver, 13 Mar. 1918, F. S. Oliver Papers, 77.

[84] Sir Henry Lucy, *The Diary of a Journalist: Fresh Extracts*, iii (London, 1923), 291.

[85] Austen Chamberlain to Chelmsford, 8 Dec. 1916, cited in Turner, *British Politics and the Great War*, 143.

[86] Jan Christian Smuts, born in South Africa, of Cape Dutch origin but Cambridge education, a Boer military commander during the Boer War, helped negotiate the peace in 1902. Minister of Defence in Louis Botha's government 1910–19. Conducted the successful campaign against German forces in South-West Africa in 1915. Commanded imperial forces in East Africa 1916 as a Lieutenant-General in the British army. A member of the War Cabinet 1917–18.

[87] George W. Egerton, *Great Britain and the Creation of the League of Nations: Strategy, Politics and International Organisation, 1914–1919* (London, 1979), 49. On his close friendship with the

Similarly, the trade unionist George Barnes, who replaced Henderson in the War Cabinet as the representative of the Labour Party in August 1917, was a genuinely moderate influence.[88] However, his authority was waning at the end of the war. His decision to defy the Labour Party after its abandonment of the Coalition in November 1918 left him marooned in the government, beholden to Lloyd George. He was no longer the representative of the Labour Party, but rather a speaker for the working class as the government wished it to be, patriotic and patient—not as it was. Neither Smuts nor Barnes could speak with the authority of a progressive political party behind them at the end of the war. For the crucial period of October 1918 to June 1919, the period in which British decisions regarding the German revolution were made, the War Cabinet comprised Lloyd George, Curzon, Chamberlain, Bonar Law, and Barnes. Conservative dominance of the War Cabinet, therefore, was always preserved behind the semblance of Coalition.

The weakness of progressive politics at the top of the government in 1918–19 is no mystery. The outstanding fact is that no leading Liberal agreed to join Lloyd George in December 1916. All the great Liberal names of the former Asquith-led government chose to follow the departing Prime Minister into a polite and rather ineffectual opposition. Those senior Liberal figures approached personally by Lloyd George to join him in December 1916, Herbert Samuel and Edwin Montagu, turned him down.[89] Indeed, Liberal representation in the first Lloyd George Coalition government as a whole remained paltry. In the ministries, at first only minor Liberal figures could be found, Christopher Addison at Munitions and Sir Alfred Mond as First Commissioner of Works being the most notable. Herbert Fisher, the Chancellor of Sheffield University, a man of Liberal political sympathies, was recruited as minister at the Education Board. The Labour Party, similarly, supplied only second-rank figures to command the specially created ministries of Labour and Pensions in the government. Most of the Labour Party ministers were members of the British Workers' National League. These men, in the confidence of Lord Milner, were never a formidable progressive presence in the government. Tom Jones admitted privately that the final outcome of the political manœuvring of 1916 was lamentable and astonishing: after thirty years in politics, he noted, the Prime Minister now had 'no *Liberal* backing in the Cabinet'.[90]

Quaker, Margaret Clark, granddaughter of John Bright, see Kenneth Ingham, *Jan Christian Smuts: The Conscience of a South African* (London, 1986), 51.

[88] George Nicoll Barnes, a trade unionist from the Amalgamated Society of Engineers. A Labour MP 1906–18, then a Coalition MP 1918–22. He was Minister of Pensions Dec. 1916–Aug. 1917, and then entered the War Cabinet. Resigned from the Labour Party in late 1918.

[89] Lloyd George, *War Memoirs*, i. 640.

[90] Thomas Jones to Eirene Jones, 18 Apr. 1917, in Thomas Jones, *Whitehall Diary, i. 1916/1925* (London, 1969), 31, emphasis in the original. The leading Labour ministers were John Hodge, George Roberts, Alex Wilkie, and Stephen Walsh.

Lloyd George made only one major attempt to increase Liberal representation in his wartime government, a reshuffle in the summer of 1917. Addison was shifted to a new Ministry of Reconstruction. Two former front-bench Liberals were brought into the government: Churchill was placed at Munitions, and Montagu was appointed to the India Office. Although the new Liberal ministerial appointments were balanced by the simultaneous promotion of Edward Carson to the War Cabinet, there were howls of protest from leading Conservatives.[91] For ultra-patriots like Rudyard Kipling, it was 'more disheartening to the country than any words can say'.[92] In Conservative circles, Montagu was especially reviled. His Jewish background and his sympathy for the cause of Indian reform made him unsuitable, in many Conservative eyes, to be entrusted with the supreme imperial appointment. The violence of the reaction to Lloyd George's Liberal appointments betrayed the Conservatives' beliefs about piper and tune in the 'knock-out blow' Coalition.[93] Lloyd George's capacity to carry off the reshuffle certainly testified to his tenacity. On the other hand, the furore disabled the new Liberal appointees, and both were effectively barred from a further promotion to the War Cabinet itself.[94] Conservatives regarded their enlistment as symbolic of Lloyd George's insecurity. As Bridgeman noted, it 'looked as if he were afraid of losing hold of all his old Liberal colleagues and being absorbed by us'.[95] The Prime Minister did not again seek to boost the Liberal presence in his wartime government. Similarly, following the elections of December 1918, and the crushing defeat sustained by the divided Liberal Party, Lloyd George was in no position to increase dramatically Liberal representation in his government.[96]

There were uncomfortable moments when Lloyd George was forced to confront the obvious dominance by men of a reactionary complexion in his governments. For example, C. P. Scott, owner and editor of the leading Liberal newspaper, the *Manchester Guardian*, complained to Lloyd George in September 1917 that the War Cabinet 'even now was far too Tory'. Milner and Curzon, he reminded Lloyd George, were reactionaries 'whom no one would touch before the war'. Lloyd George did not deny the substance of the claim. The leading Conservatives, he explained, had been appointed by Bonar Law following Lloyd George's debilitation by an untimely flu. Then, to mollify Scott, Lloyd George

---

[91] Arthur Murray Diary, 27 July 1917, Elibank Papers, 8815.

[92] Kipling to Gwynne, 26 July 1917, Kipling Papers, 137.

[93] On the row occasioned by these appointments see Turner, *British Politics and the Great War*, 219–23.

[94] A Unionist War Committee resolution in Feb. 1918 forbade the Prime Minister to contemplate Churchill's promotion to the War Cabinet; Repington Diary, 12 Feb. 1918, in Repington, *The First World War*, ii. 229.

[95] William Bridgeman Diary, Feb. 1918, Bridgeman Papers, SRO 4629/1/2/1.

[96] In Jan. 1919, the new Cabinet of nineteen contained eight Liberals (Lloyd George, Montagu, Churchill, Fisher, Addison, Ian Macpherson, Edward Shortt, Robert Munro). Apart from Lloyd George, these were plainly men who were regarded on both sides of the House of Commons as political mavericks or politicians of the second rank.

described Milner as 'a progressive in social questions'. Smuts, he added, 'might supply a wholesome corrective'.[97] It was not convincing. Similarly, in two of his major election speeches during the campaign of December 1918, Lloyd George was forced to answer the charge that his government included too many 'reactionary Lords'. 'I trust these men', he assured his audience, 'who for two years helped me to carry great progressive measures.'[98] He told an election meeting in Leeds that his Conservative colleagues had been politically reconstructed during the war on issues of social reform. 'Some of them were a little timid in the past, but I think the war has improved us all.'[99]

What then was the fundamental political outlook of the Lloyd George Coalition government in late 1918? Modern specialist studies are divided. Some present the governing ideology as an amalgam of 'populism', 'new imperialism', 'social imperialism', 'national efficiency', and 'resistance to socialism'. More charitable assessments describe it as a blend of genuine faith in 'reconstructionism', 'consensus', and 'national unity'.[100] The Prime Minister himself continued to make private declarations of his reformist passion. 'I am out to give the underdog a chance', he remarked to Riddell. More adventurously, he described himself to Kerr as a 'Nationalist-Socialist'. The label caught the spirit of the Prime Minister's commitment to a range of social reforms, but reforms to be pressed only so far as consensus and coalition would permit. In this way, Lloyd George hoped to prevent social conflict and 'weld together all these classes'. Seamed through the reformism, it must be conceded, there was an instinctive opportunism too. Lloyd George remarked in August 1918 that he had 'no philosophy of life beyond "Follow your nose" '.[101]

The promise—or menace—of sweeping social reforms was certainly discernible at war's end. The historic Representation of the People Bill of February 1918 gave the appearance of the beginnings of a new democratic age. Forward-looking men in the government, such as Fisher at the Board of Education and Montagu at the India Office, were eager to press on with the work of further reforms in their portfolios. Most importantly, the great 'gesture towards Labour' of 1917, the Ministry of Reconstruction established under Addison, promised epoch-making changes to Britain's economic and social life. However, by November

[97] C. P. Scott Political Diary, 28 Sept. 1917, C. P. Scott Papers, Box 134. As the war proceeded, Lloyd George occasionally made similarly unconvincing attempts in his table talk to project Milner and even Bonar Law as sincere advocates of social reform; on Bonar Law, see *Lord Riddell's War Diary*, 2 Mar. 1918, 318; and on Milner see ibid. 18 Feb. 1917, 243, and 17 June 1918, 334.

[98] Lloyd George's speech at Newcastle, 29 Nov. 1918, *The Times*, 30 Nov. 1918.

[99] Lloyd George's speech at Leeds, 6 Dec. 1918, *Daily Chronicle*, 9 Dec. 1918.

[100] For critical assessments, see especially Paul Guinn, *British Strategy and Politics, 1914–18* (Oxford, 1965), Maurice Cowling, *The Impact of Labour, 1920–1924* (Cambridge, 1971), R. J. Scally, *The Origins of the Lloyd George Coalition* (Princeton, 1976), and Wrigley, *Lloyd George and the Challenge of Labour*. For more favourable judgements see K. O. Morgan, 'Lloyd George's Stage Army', in Taylor, *Lloyd George: Twelve Essays*, 225–54, and Morgan, *Consensus and Disunity*.

[101] *Lord Riddell's War Diary*, 2 Mar. 1918, 318, Apr. 1918, 324, 23 June 1918, 334 and 13 Aug. 1918, 345.

1918, precious little of substance had yet materialized from 'the great wishing well that was reconstruction', as Paul Barton Johnson has described it. Many of the reports and recommendations which had gone forward from the Ministry of Reconstruction had been caught up in a governmental log-jam. Unfortunately, for the credibility of the government, these included Addison's schemes for public housing and a Ministry of Health.[102]

In the long run, as Ken Morgan has convincingly argued, Coalition Liberalism in the government of 1919–22 was to prove itself to be anything but a spent force.[103] From the perspective of late 1918, however, there was little reason for optimism over reform. The ranks of Labour were permeated by suspicion towards the government. The promises of 'reconstructionism' were too vague and the Ministry's actual achievements too slender to keep Labour satisfied with a place in the post-war coalition.[104] Moreover, any dispassionate analysis of Liberalism's prospects had to take account of the obvious political realities. Liberalism was the very junior partner in the coalition. It could scarcely ask for more: that the Liberal Party had been debilitated by the war was a political fact staring all in the face. The Liberal Party had buckled under the weight of the great disputes over conscription, leadership, and peace by negotiation. In addition, the danger that the Labour Party might outflank Liberalism was very real. The 'New Liberal' programme of the Edwardian period, based on social insurance and the redistribution of wealth through taxation, was unlikely to sustain a post-war working-class and middle-class alliance because of the tremendous pressure placed upon future tax receipts by war debts.[105]

Not surprisingly then, beneath the progressive rhetoric of the Lloyd George Coalition, reactionary impulses held sway. Clearly, the First World War had not reconciled the majority of Conservative MPs to a reformist programme. Meetings of the Unionist Social Reform Committee, founded in 1911, were actually suspended upon the outbreak of war and not resumed until March 1919.[106] In contrast, both the Unionist Business Committee (revived in January 1915) and the Unionist War Committee (founded in January 1916) flourished during the war. Both provided powerful platforms for the zealous tariff reformers whose influence within the Conservative Party had clearly strengthened during the

---

[102] The definitive history of the early Reconstruction Committee and the Ministry of Reconstruction that followed is Paul Barton Johnson, *Land Fit For Heroes: The Planning of British Reconstruction, 1916–1919* (Chicago, 1968). Johnson provides a review of the very limited achievements of the Ministry of Reconstruction by the eve of the armistice in ch. 11.

[103] Morgan, 'Lloyd George's Stage Army', in Taylor, *Lloyd George: Twelve Essays*.

[104] Johnson, *Land Fit For Heroes*, 232–6.

[105] The effect of the war upon the Liberal Party is a subject that has spawned a huge debate. A powerful and succinct statement of the case which I have adopted here, namely, that it was above all the First World War which had the fatal 'deliquescent effect on the Liberal Party', is put in Michael Hart, 'The Liberals, the War, and the Franchise', *English Historical Review*, 97/385 (1982), 820–32.

[106] Wood to Hewins, 27 Feb. 1919, Hewins Papers, 74, and see Jane Ridley, 'The Unionist Social Reform Committee, 1911–14: Wets before the Deluge', *Historical Journal*, 30 (1987), 391–413.

course of the war.[107] As Eric Geddes told Lloyd George in March 1919, 'if you scrape the white-wash of progress off 90% of the Coalitionists, they are hard-shelled tories still'.[108] Certainly, there were also articulate moderates voicing their belief in cautious social reform within the Conservative Party. George Lloyd and Edward Wood, two leading moderates, published their programme under the title *A Great Opportunity* in December 1918. But it scarcely set the Conservative Party aflame with a passion for social reform. Most informed Conservatives were well aware that the ruinous cost of the prolonged war had made a great programme of social reform next to impossible. Both victory in a long war *and* social reform at home could not be had. Therefore, the surviving private sources of the governing élite for the period 1918–19 show not the bright hope of reconstruction, but rather an abiding fear of social unrest. To ride out the expected post-war storm, with a minimum of concession to Labour, was the *idée fixe* of the comfortable classes. From the perspective of the Conservative Party, the great domestic battles to come were to be all about resistance—resistance to disorder, to strikes, to the Labour Party, to a levy on capital, to socialism, and to Bolshevism itself. The only great positive expectation, as demanded by the Unionist Business Committee, was for an instalment of Tariff Reform, dressed up as a patriotic precaution against any renewed penetration of the Empire by German commerce and investment.[109]

Those accustomed to power detected grave danger in the nation's democratic mood. Under the banner of 'National Unity', the forces of order prepared to secure 'society'. The war, after all, had been waged through until victory for many causes, great and small, but domestic political containment had always been one of them. As Lord Esher had written in May 1917, at a time when he believed a peace brokered by socialists was imminent: 'We shall all go down before the new forces that are coming into the war. Thrones . . . aristocrats, plutocrats and all. Peace—a thoroughly dangerous peace—is clearly in sight.'[110] Only victory could make safe the world from such a prospect.

---

[107] John Stubbs, 'The Impact of the Great War on the Conservative Party', in Gillian Peele and Chris Cook (eds.), *The Politics of Reappraisal 1918–1939* (London, 1975), 14–38.

[108] Eric Geddes to Lloyd George, 19 Mar. 1919, Lloyd George Papers, F/18/3/10, quoted in Peter K. Cline, 'Eric Geddes and the "Experiment" with Businessmen in Government, 1915–22', in Kenneth D. Brown (ed.), *Essays in Anti-Labour History: Responses to the Rise of Labour in Britain* (London, 1974), 94.

[109] On these themes see Christopher Nottingham, 'Recasting Bourgeois Britain? The British State in the Years which Followed the First World War', *International Review of Social History*, 31/3 (1986), 227–47. For a different viewpoint, stressing the long-term commitment to coalition on the part of many Conservatives in the period 1918–22, a commitment arising not only from a determination to resist Labour but also from a determination to provide stable government and economic reform, see David Close, 'Conservatives and Coalition After the First World War', *Journal of Modern History*, 45/2 (1973), 240–60.

[110] Lord Esher to Lord Derby, 31 May 1917, quoted in Keith Wilson, *A Study in the History and Politics of the Morning Post, 1905–1926* (Lewiston, NY, 1990), 146.

The 'moral warriors': social imperialism, idealism, and reaction among the Prime Minister's advisers

The small group of advisers closest to the Prime Minister must also be reviewed before embarking on a study of decision-making. The crucial question to be resolved is this: were the men advising the decision-makers in 1918–19 of a cast of mind likely to be well-disposed to a socialist-led and democratic revolution in Germany?

Two new bodies were created by Lloyd George on his assumption to power in December 1916, the Prime Minister's Secretariat and the War Cabinet Secretariat. The actual political influence exerted by the personnel of the two bodies is a contentious issue. In particular, the presence of Lord Milner in the War Cabinet (from December 1916 to April 1918), and the appointment of a prominent Milnerite in Philip Kerr,[111] as Lloyd George's principal Private Secretary in January 1917, has led historians to speculate over the influence of the Round Table movement among the Prime Minister's advisers in general.

The claim that in Lloyd George's company of advisers can be detected the overwhelming influence of Milnerite 'social imperialism' has come under sustained attack. As John Turner's exhaustive research has shown, it is a mistake to imagine that, in the group of experts assembled by Lloyd George to assist him, a conspiracy of Milnerite imperialists obtained a tremendous sway over Lloyd George. Radicals certainly alleged this at the time; it buttressed their belief in the apostasy of Lloyd George. The Milnerites sometimes claimed it too; it flattered them. In fact, both exaggerated the weight of Lord Milner and his followers.[112] Idealists and social reformers were also represented among the advisers. However, as the two secretariats evolved and new appointments were made, the limits of this moderate influence became clear. By late 1918, the political 'mood' among Lloyd George's advisers was inclined towards reaction.

In exploring this problem, the controversial Round Table group itself requires some introduction.[113] The group arose out of the so-called 'Kindergarten' of imperial civil servants established by Lord Milner during his service in South Africa between 1897 and 1905. These men, generally young and Oxford trained,

---

[111] Philip Henry Kerr, 11th Marquess of Lothian, educated New College, Oxford, with Milner's 'Kindergarten' colleagues in South Africa 1905–9, editor of *Round Table* 1910–16, Private Secretary to Lloyd George 1916–21, Liberal member of the House of Lords 1930–40, Ambassador to Washington 1939–40.

[112] John Turner, 'The Formation of Lloyd George's "Garden Suburb": "Fabian-like Milnerite Penetration"?', *Historical Journal*, 20/1 (1977), 165–84; Turner, *Lloyd George's Secretariat*; John Turner, 'Cabinets, Committees and Secretariats: The Higher Direction of the War', in Kathleen Burk (ed.), *War and the State* (London, 1982), 57–83. For the other side in this argument see Lockwood, 'Milner's Entry into the War Cabinet, December 1916', and J. Naylor, 'The Establishment of the War Cabinet Secretariat', *Historical Journal*, 14 (1971), 783–803.

[113] Scholarship on the Round Table movement in general includes Walter Nimocks, *Milner's Young Men: The 'Kindergarten' in Edwardian Imperial Affairs* (London, 1970), and J. B. Kendle, *The Round Table Movement and Imperial Union* (Toronto, 1975).

were under the personal spell of Milner. They brought to British imperialism a new idealism of great fervour. In their activities and writings they promoted a vision of imperial unity which stressed the high moral calling of Empire. The earliest devotees of this creed included Philip Kerr, Leo Amery,[114] Lionel Hichens,[115] Robert Brand,[116] Lionel Curtis,[117] and Geoffrey Robinson (Dawson).[118] In 1910, with the blessing of Lord Milner, a Round Table meeting (the 'moot') agreed to support the suggestion of Lionel Curtis that a new journal be launched, the *Round Table*. Its purpose was to promote the ideals of imperial unity.[119] Round Table groups were soon established in all the British Dominions.[120]

By 1918, the 'inner moot' of the Round Table movement comprised an impressive range of supporters from politics, business, and the press. Those prominent in political affairs included Milner, Selborne, Lord Lovat, Arthur Steel-Maitland, Chair of the Conservative Party from 1911 to 1916, and Leo Amery and Waldorf Astor, both Conservative MPs. From the world of business came the very prosperous F. S. Oliver, director of the Debenham and Freebody stores, and author of the violently anti-Liberal tome *Ordeal by Battle* (1915); Lionel Hichens, chairman of the great shipbuilding firm Cammel Laird from 1910; and Robert Brand, a successful banker. The Round Table had also cultivated a significant connection with Fleet Street. Activists among the newspaper confraternity included Edward Grigg, who had been an editor of imperial affairs at *The Times* until 1913; Amery, a former correspondent for *The Times* in South Africa; and Geoffrey Robinson, appointed editor of *The Times* in 1912 after Amery had pressed his name upon Lord Northcliffe, the legendary proprietor. Robinson was to remain editor until his dismissal in February 1919. Waldorf

---

[114] Leopold C. M. S. Amery, Fellow of All Souls, *The Times* correspondent in South Africa 1899–1900, author of *The Times History of the War in South Africa*, founder of imperialist discussion circle 'The Compatriots' 1904, Conservative MP 1911–45, Assistant Secretary to the War Cabinet 1916, Under-Secretary Colonial Office 1919–21.

[115] William Lionel Hichens, 'Nel', educated New College, Oxford, Colonial Treasurer of the Transvaal 1902–7, director of Cammell Laird & Co. 1910–40.

[116] Robert Henry Brand, later 1st Baron Brand, educated New College, Oxford, Fellow of All Souls, joined Milner's staff in South Africa 1902, Secretary of the Intercolonial Council of the Transvaal and Orange River Colony, established Imperial Munitions Board in Canada 1915, adviser to Supreme Economic Council at Paris Peace Conference 1919, banker with Lazard Brothers 1909–60.

[117] Lionel George Curtis, educated New College, Oxford, in South Africa 1899–1909, Assistant Colonial Secretary Transvaal 1903–7, published Selborne Memorandum 1907, Beit Lecturer Colonial History 1912, travelled widely in Canada, New Zealand, Australia, and India on the eve of the war, and again in India 1916–17, for the Round Table movement, attended Paris Peace Conference 1919.

[118] George Geoffrey Robinson (Dawson), served with Milner's staff in South Africa, 1901–5, editor Johannesburg *Star* 1905–10, editor of *The Times* 1912–19 and 1923–41. Robinson changed his name in 1917 to Geoffrey Dawson as a condition of a legacy.

[119] On the foundation of the journal and the demand that it be 'severely detached from the domestic issues of the day', see Nimocks, *Kindergarten*, 181.

[120] Curtis and Kerr laid the foundations of these groups during a visit to Canada in 1909, and Curtis undertook a similar trip to Australia and New Zealand during 1910. Curtis, appointed as a lecturer in Colonial History at Oxford in 1912, travelled constantly in promotion of the Round Table movement over the next five years (Kendle, *Round Table Movement*, chs. 3 and 4).

Astor was owner of the pro-Tariff Reform newspaper the *Observer*. J. L. Garvin, the powerful editor of the *Observer*, was close to several leading Round Table men, especially Oliver and Grigg. Garvin offered the movement the *Observer's* unhesitating support.[121] At the Foreign Office there were two important allies of the movement, Lord Robert Cecil,[122] the Under-Secretary to Arthur Balfour, and Eustace Percy,[123] a Political Intelligence Department officer with a special brief to cover American affairs. Academic connections with Oxford, especially New College and All Souls, were strong: the historians Reginald Coupland[124] and Alfred Zimmern[125] joined the Round Table movement in 1913 and swiftly assumed roles within the 'inner moot'. Edwyn Bevan,[126] a colleague of Zimmern from New College, also became a contributor to *Round Table*. Here was an impressive array of well-placed talent. And behind these men stood the power of great wealth.[127]

[121] In 1920 Garvin assured Brand that he had given 'standing instructions for us to have a good review of every number [of the *Round Table*]'; Brand to Garvin, 9 Sept. 1920, and Garvin to Brand, 14 Sept. 1920, Brand Papers, 42. On Garvin's association with Round Table circles see David Ayerst, *Garvin of the Observer* (London, 1985), 164.

[122] Robert Cecil, later Viscount Cecil of Chelwood, third son of former Conservative Prime Minister Lord Salisbury, Conservative MP 1906–10, then an 'independent' Conservative MP on account of his opposition to Tariff Reform 1911–23, Under-Secretary at the Foreign Office 1915–18, Assistant Secretary of State for Foreign Affairs 1918–19, Minister of Blockade 1916–18, Chair of the Supreme Economic Council at the Paris Peace Conference 1919, President of the League of Nations Union 1923–45. On Robert Cecil's connections with the Round Table see Lord Robert Cecil, *A Great Experiment: An Autobiography* (London, 1941), 250, and Nimocks, *Kindergarten*, 156.

[123] Eustace Percy, later Baron Percy of Newcastle, entered the Foreign Office in 1909, served at the British Embassy at Washington 1910–14, at the Foreign Office 1914–17 and then at the Washington Embassy 1917–18, returning to take up a position in the Political Intelligence Department in mid-1918. He was secretary to Sir Robert Cecil during the Paris Peace Conference, Conservative MP for Hastings 1921–37.

[124] Reginald Coupland, historian of the British Empire and Commonwealth, Fellow and lecturer at Trinity College, Cambridge, 1907–14, Beit Lecturer in Colonial History 1903–18, replaced Philip Kerr as editor of the *Round Table* 1917.

[125] Alfred Zimmern, lecturer in Ancient History, New College, Oxford, 1904–9, inspector with the Board of Education 1912–15, worked at the Reconstruction Committee 1915–18, Political Intelligence Department 1918–19. After the war he was Wilson Professor of International Politics at Aberystwyth 1919–21, Director of School of International Studies, Geneva, 1930–44, and Montague Burton Professor of International Relations, Oxford, 1930–44.

[126] Edwyn Robert Bevan, educated at New College, Oxford, a Hellenistic scholar, travelled widely before the war in India, wrote a sympathetic account of Indian politics in *Indian Nationalism* (1913), Political Intelligence Department of the Foreign Office 1918–19, lecturer in Hellenistic literature and history King's College, London, 1922–33, active member of the Student Christian Movement. Bevan's writings on India were especially appreciated in the Round Table; see Lionel Curtis to Reginald Coupland, 29 Sept. 1917, Round Table Papers, MSS Eng. Hist. c. 810.

[127] Contributors included Sir Abe Bailey, L. S. Jameson, and Alfred Beit, the South African mining entrepreneurs, Lord Inchcape, the P & O shipowner and prominent Liberal, Sir Thomas Royden, the deputy chairman of Cunard, Lord Leverhulme, the soap king and former Liberal politician, Lord Cowdray, the building contractor and former Liberal MP, F. C. Tiarks of the banking firm J. H. Schröder, W. W. Paine of Lloyds Bank, and F. S. Oliver of Debenhams: see pencil notes marked 'former subscribers' on a Round Table circular appealing for funds, and accompanying correspondence referring to past generous donations, dated 15 and 16 June 1920: Brand to Cowdray, to F. S. Oliver, to Eustace Percy, to W. W. Paine, to Thomas Royden, and to F. C. Tiarks (Brand Papers, 42). Financial support is also examined in Nimocks, *Kindergarten*, 143, 149–51.

What did the movement stand for? The members of the Round Table movement found common ground as enthusiasts for the moral vision of a more united and a more patriotic Empire. As Kendle has written, the members were 'unashamedly pan-anglo-saxon nationalists with a deep faith in the contribution that the commonwealth could make to humanity'.[128] There was a common style too, an almost spiritual quality in adherence to the Empire. For example, Frederic Eggleston, a young Australian Round Table man at the Paris Peace Conference in 1919, attended one 'moot' in Lionel Curtis's room at the Hôtel Majestic; afterwards he jotted in his diary that 'Curtis acts like a kind of Abbé with a special delegation from the Pope'.[129]

Hostility to socialism within the movement was axiomatic. In Round Table literature the Empire's civic virtue was often contrasted with the evils alleged to arise from the narrow politics of class. The belief that imperial pride should supplant class feeling was fundamental. Thus Milner, Amery, Steel-Maitland, and Astor decided to sponsor the British Workers' National League from early 1916 (known as the British Workers' League or BWL from March 1917) as a political experiment designed to rally the patriotic loyalties of organized labour and to counter the influence of international socialism.[130] Hichens and Selborne were active in preparing propaganda against coal nationalization for the Nationalization Committee of the Federation of British Industry in May 1919.[131] While the movement claimed to stand above party politics, the great balance of political affiliation was on the Conservative side of politics.[132]

Did the movement gain an overwhelming influence in the Prime Minister's entourage? The representation of Round Table men at the top was certainly impressive. Milner himself was Secretary of State for War in 1918 and was Secretary of State for the Colonies in the new government formed in 1919. At the centre of the government, as has been seen, Kerr became Lloyd George's Private Secretary in 1917 and remained until 1921. Astor also served on the Prime Minister's Secretariat. Amery was appointed an Assistant Secretary to the

---

[128] Kendle, *Round Table Movement*, 303.

[129] Frederic Eggleston Diary, 27 Jan. 1919, Eggleston Papers, MS 423/6/76. On the religious inspiration and moral earnestness see also Deborah Lavin, 'Lionel Curtis and the idea of Commonwealth', in D. K. Fieldhouse and John Madden (eds.), *Oxford and the Idea of Commonwealth* (London, 1985), esp. 101.

[130] See Lockwood, 'Milner's Entry into the War Cabinet', 120–34; J. O. Stubbs, 'Lord Milner and Patriotic Labour', *English Historical Review*, 87 (1972), 717–54; Roy Douglas, 'The National Democratic Party and the British Workers' League', *Historical Journal*, 15 (1972), 533–52.

[131] Minutes of the Federation of British Industry Nationalization Committee, FBI Papers, MSS 200 F/1/1/139.

[132] When the leading members opted for political careers, it was to Conservatism that a majority instinctively owed their allegiance—although Kerr was to be exceptional in becoming a Liberal peer in the 1930s. Among the senior figures, as has been seen, Milner, Selborne, Lovat, Steel-Maitland, Cecil, Astor, and Amery were prominent in the Conservative Party. Curtis tried hard to secure a candidacy for a Conservative seat in 1918. (See Arthur Steel Maitland to Col. R. A. Sanders, 17 Apr. 1918, Steel-Maitland Papers, GD 193/274.) Eustace Percy stood unsuccessfully as a Coalition Conservative in the Central Hull by-election in Mar. 1919.

War Cabinet. John Buchan was Director of the Department (later the Ministry) of Information in 1917–18. The Political Intelligence Department (PID) of the Foreign Office in 1918–19 included three prominent Round Table men, Zimmern, Bevan, and Percy.[133] Other PID men were close to key decision-makers. Percy served in 1919 at the Paris Peace Conference as an assistant to Lord Robert Cecil and then to Arthur Balfour. F. S. Oliver served as the secretary to Carson's War Cabinet Committee on Economic Offensive in 1917–18, and afterwards was invited to dine a number of times in the Prime Minister's circle.[134] Clearly, membership of the Round Table group could mean instant entrée into the company of the mighty. For example, Round Tablers from Australia, Robert Garran, John Latham, and Frederic Eggleston, all members of the Melbourne Round Table group, found themselves summoned to attend 'moots' in London in 1918 with men at the top of government.[135] This was indeed a magic circle.

But there was no outright Milnerite take-over. The Prime Minister's Secretariat, known to history as the 'Garden Suburb', was originally inspired by a gathering of Welsh Liberal supporters of the Prime Minister.[136] Of the six men who served within it from 1917 to 1919, only two were Milnerites, Astor and Kerr.[137] Thus, Round Table representation was important but not overwhelming within the Prime Minister's own secretariat. Kerr was undoubtedly the key personality.[138] He served as the Prime Minister's Private Secretary throughout the period under study here. In 1918 he was given a special responsibility for advising Lloyd George in the sphere of foreign policy. It was Milner who suggested his name to Lloyd George as a Private Secretary.[139]

---

[133] Three other PID men, James Headlam-Morley, Arnold J. Toynbee, and George Saunders, also wrote articles for *Round Table* about this time and might be judged as sympathetic to its objectives; see Minutes of an Editorial Committee meeting of the *Round Table*, 8 Apr. 1920, Robert Brand Papers, 42.

[134] Stephen Gwynn (ed.), *The Anvil of War: Letters between F. S. Oliver and his Brother*, 1914–1918 (London, 1936), 25.

[135] Frederic Eggleston, 'The Peace Conference at Paris', unpublished typed memoir, Eggleston Papers, MS 423/6/8–10.

[136] Turner, 'The Formation of Lloyd George's "Garden Suburb"'. Two men of Liberal political conviction played the key roles in setting up the new secretariat: Thomas Jones, a Welsh civil servant with a left-wing political background and Labour sympathies, and David Davies, a Welsh Liberal MP devoted to Lloyd George.

[137] The original head of the 'Garden Suburb' was Professor W. G. S. Adams, a progressive Oxford academic. Adams was Gladstone Professor of Political Theory and Institutions at Oxford. In 1914 he had co-operated with the Oxford Faculty of History in producing the patriotic pamphlet *Why We Are At War*. His closest political friend appears to have been Sir Horace Plunkett, the independently minded Irish politician, agrarian reformer, and Wilsonian idealist; see Plunkett to Charles McCarthy, 10 July 1918, Plunkett Papers, MAC/C 137. The other members were David Davies and Joseph Davies, a Liberal businessman. The Liberal MP Cecil Harmsworth, brother of Lord Northcliffe, joined the secretariat in May 1917. The politics of the members of the 'Garden Suburb' are thoroughly analysed in Turner, *Lloyd George's Secretariat*, ch. 1.

[138] The major biography is J. R. M. Butler, *Lord Lothian (Philip Kerr), 1882–1940* (London, 1960).

[139] Turner, *Lloyd George's Secretariat*, 18.

In domestic politics, it should be stressed, Kerr was by no means backward-looking. Liberal Imperialism claimed his allegiance. H. A. L. Fisher had been his tutor while Kerr was reading History at New College.[140] Fellow Round Table activists regarded him as comparatively progressive. Curtis, for example, observed in 1915 that Kerr was emerging as one of the 'real democrats' of the Round Table set.[141] Certainly, Kerr was able to promote the cause of democracy without stumbling over the word. From the first months of fighting in 1914, the *Round Table*, under Kerr's editorship, seemed to warm to the theme of the war as a great struggle between democracy and tyranny. Kerr clothed the Entente's objectives in the evangelist's language of high morality, and heaped opprobrium on 'Prussianism' as the German nation's collective sin.[142] In pursuit of Moral Redemption on Germany's part, he would insist constantly on evidence of that most singularly elusive sign of inner rejuvenation, a 'change of heart'.[143] Kerr's crusade for 'public right' was delivered in a style that may have made a special appeal to the Nonconformist in Lloyd George.[144] As an adviser to the Prime Minister on things German, however, Kerr cannot be considered to have been blessed with any special advantages. He knew no German. He had not travelled extensively on the Continent. Clearly, he knew a great deal more about the British Empire than about the enemy's internal politics.[145]

Important as Kerr may have become to Lloyd George, it must be acknowledged that he was never dependent on any single person for his views on foreign policy. But his special faith in Kerr is clear. 'Philip becomes more and more indispensable to L. G.', was Dawson's judgement in November 1917.[146] Kerr was to be entrusted with the secret negotiations for a separate peace with Austria in December 1917 and March 1918.[147] He played a major role at other crucial moments in the development of foreign policy, such as at the time of Lloyd George's famous war aims speech delivered at Caxton Hall in January 1918.[148] As Lloyd George was notoriously loath to write anything by hand himself, the man who sat at the typewriter close by the Prime Minister was in a superb position to guide the development of policy.[149]

In considering the formation of Britain's policy towards the German revolution in 1918–19, therefore, Kerr's Round Table connections must be seen as

---

[140] Butler, *Lord Lothian*, 6.   [141] Kendle, *Round Table Movement*, 187.

[142] See [Kerr], 'The War in Europe', *Round Table*, 16 (Sept. 1914); [Kerr] 'The End of the War', *Round Table*, 20 (Sept. 1915), [Kerr]; 'The War for Public Right', *Round Table*, 22 (Mar. 1916); [Kerr], 'War Aims', *Round Table*, 24 (Sept. 1916); and the discussion in Turner, *Lloyd George's Secretariat*, 146–53.

[143] Turner, *Lloyd George's Secretariat*, 157 and 166.

[144] 'The public like a high tone when a great moral issue is involved', Lloyd George remarked in 1918; quoted in *Lord Riddell's War Diary*, 29 July 1918, 341.

[145] Butler, *Lothian*, 48 and 190.

[146] Dawson to the Bishop of Pretoria, 7 Nov. 1917, quoted in John Evelyn Wrench, *Geoffrey Dawson and our Times* (London, 1955), 154.

[147] Turner, *Lloyd George's Secretariat*, 77–82.   [148] Ibid. 160–6.

[149] On Lloyd George's reluctance to write, see Frank Owen, *Tempestuous Journey: Lloyd George His Life and Times* (London, 1954), 70.

significant. Kerr moved constantly in an élite intellectual circle where imperial values were the ultimate measure of good. Among his fellow Round Tablers, while 'social reform' was espoused by some,[150] opinions remarkably hostile to left-wing labour were commonplace: F. S. Oliver, for example, advised in 1916 that the method he favoured for dealing with working-class unrest was daring organized labour 'to fly at my throat and beating him to a jelly if he does'.[151] In the Round Table's conclaves, international socialism was despised; it was the great threat to the people's will to win, and the enemy of the British Empire.

The second centre of influence closest to the decision-makers was the new War Cabinet Secretariat. Here Lieutenant-Colonel Sir Maurice Hankey, Secretary to the War Cabinet, was the key figure. His political and strategic outlook was complex. With the future of the Empire in mind, he appears to have accepted the necessity of imperialistic war aims for Britain without question.[152] But he advocated the importance of economic warfare ahead of the blood-letting of the Western Front, and his closest advisers were Admiral Fisher and Lord Esher, men who combined a fervent anti-Germanism and anti-socialism with a mild preference for reformist Liberalism.[153] His relationship with Lloyd George was especially close, founded upon 'a strong bond of intimacy and of confidence' as Hankey's biographer puts it.[154] His own personal political convictions hovered between Conservatism and right-wing Liberalism.[155] He was never more adventurous. He liked the company of the Conservative élite in command of the Foreign Office, Balfour, Eric Drummond, Balfour's Private Secretary, and Cecil. He was no Milnerite, claiming to 'hate' Milner's politics and describing the 'ultra-Imperials' of the business world brought together by Amery as 'insufferable bores'.[156] Hankey's opinions on the German enemy were closest to the ultra-patriotic outlook—he assumed the solidarity of the German nation and placed his faith in the marshalling of Allied military and economic might as the only way to subdue the enemy and end the war. His proficiency in languages included a little German, but he had never travelled in Germany, and had no expertise to offer on internal German politics.[157]

Under Hankey's command, men of Conservative politics were in the ascendant among the staff of the War Cabinet Secretariat. Among the various Assistant Secretaries, originally ten in number, the Milnerites did not dominate but Conservatives did. Indeed, at the birth of the Secretariat Hankey rebuffed a

---

[150] Steel-Maitland, Astor, Ormsby-Gore, and Amery were active members of the Unionist Social Reform Committee before 1914; see Ridley, 'The Unionist Social Reform Committee', 394–6.

[151] Oliver to Austen Chamberlain, Aug. 1916, quoted in Marlowe, *Apostle of Empire*, 303.

[152] On his ready acceptance of imperialistic war aims for Britain see Hankey Diary, 3 Aug. 1918, Roskill, *Man of Secrets*, i. 586.

[153] Avner Offer, *The First World War: An Agrarian Interpretation* (Oxford, 1989), ch. 17; James Lees-Milne, *The Enigmatic Edwardian: The Life of Reginald 2nd Viscount Esher* (London, 1986), 262; and Roskill, *Man of Secrets*, i. 109.

[154] Roskill, *Man of Secrets*, i. 394.   [155] Ibid. 339.

[156] Hankey Diary, 10 Dec. 1916 and 15 Aug.1917, in Roskill, *Man of Secrets*, i. 329 and 423.

[157] Ibid. 80.

suggestion from Milner that Steel-Maitland should be appointed as a Secretary to the War Cabinet equal in status to Hankey.[158] Two other Milnerites, however, were appointed among the Assistant Secretaries: Amery, after urgent representations from Milner, and William Ormsby-Gore, a Conservative MP and Parliamentary Secretary to Lord Milner.[159] Amery, it should be noted was no middle-of-the-road Conservative MP; he was an inveterate propagandist for tariff reform and had close connections with those who founded the ultra-patriotic right-wing National Party in August 1917.[160] Similarly, Gore was a keen Milnerite and an admirer of the National Party.[161] Gore was in a most sensitive position in the Secretariat: he undertook vital intelligence work for the War Cabinet, assisting Sir George Aston in the production of the crucial 'Appreciations of Intelligence' which accompanied the Western and General Reports circulated weekly to all members of the War Cabinet.[162] Other appointees as Assistant Secretaries to the War Cabinet during the war, Mark Sykes, Leslie Wilson, and Lawrence Burgis, were either Tory politicians or men with Conservative connections.[163]

On the other side of the political scale, but scarcely so imposing a figure as to balance it, was Tom Jones, the solitary progressive member of the War Cabinet Secretariat. He was taken on board as an Assistant Secretary in spite of warnings from J. T. Davies, one of Lloyd George's personal secretaries, that he was a 'peace monger and a syndicalist'. Lloyd George evidently overrode these objections.[164] Hankey accepted Jones, but was aware of his consorting with 'reconstructionists' and others 'rather socialist in character'.[165] Because of his good personal relations with Hankey, Jones's politics did not lead to his marginalization. Indeed, Jones was chosen to take command of the War Cabinet Secretariat

---

[158] Ibid. 343–4. [159] Milner to Henry Wilson, 4 Jan. 1918, Henry Wilson Papers, 2/88.

[160] William D. Rubinstein, 'Henry Page Croft and the National Party, 1917–22', *Journal of Contemporary History*, 9/1 (1974), 130.

[161] Gore assured Croft of his admiration for the National Party soon after its formation and promised he would come over to the National Party openly as soon as Milner did so; William Ormsby-Gore to Henry Page Croft, 7 Sept. 1917, Page Croft Papers, 1/17.

[162] The Western and General Reports are signed 'G.G.A.' or 'W.O.G'. See also Hankey to Milner, 14 Dec. 1918, Milner Additional Papers, MS Eng. Hist. C. 696/1, describing the production of the reports, and, testifying to Aston's role, see Hankey to Lord Rothermere, 15 Feb. 1919, Sir George Aston Papers, 6/8, Liddell Hart Centre for Military Archives.

[163] Mark Sykes, a Conservative MP and enthusiast for Empire, was appointed 'Political Secretary'. Leslie Wilson, a rising star among Conservative MPs, was appointed in 1918 as Parliamentary Assistant Secretary. Lawrence Burgis, also appointed in 1918, was a former private secretary and young affectionate friend to Lord Esher. Finally, there were a number of military assistant secretaries, the most important being Capt. Clement Jones, a director of the Booth Shipping Line in his civilian life. An exceptional appointment was that of G. M. Young, a Liberal historian. Young, like Amery, was suggested by Milner, but it is not clear that Young was an active member of the Round Table group. Appointed as 'Civil Secretary', Young worked officially as an Assistant Secretary serving Arthur Henderson but broke with Henderson completely over the Stockholm Conference affair. He left the secretariat soon after. On Young see Roskill, *Man of Secrets*, i. 344, 416, and 420.

[164] Hankey Diary, 12 Dec. 1916, quoted in Roskill, *Man of Secrets*, i. 339.

[165] Hankey Diary, 15 Aug. 1917, quoted in Roskill, *Man of Secrets*, i. 423, and Thomas Jones, *Whitehall Diary, i. 1916/1925* (London, 1969), 21, 24–6.

in London while Hankey was with the Prime Minister in Paris from January
1919. However, domestic policy not foreign policy, it should be noted, largely
absorbed his energy.

The key men in the War Cabinet Secretariat, therefore, during the period of
decision-making towards revolutionary Germany can be identified: Hankey, Tom
Jones, Amery, Ormsby Gore, Sykes, and Wilson. Upon the formation of the new
government in January 1919, the politicians Amery, Gore, Sykes, and Wilson
returned to political duties but their network of friendship in high places still
gave them leverage. During the first half of 1919, therefore, Hankey and Jones
were pre-eminent, Hankey at the Paris Peace Conference with Lloyd George, and
Jones in London.[166]

One other key adviser close to the Prime Minister and the War Cabinet
throughout 1918–19 must also be mentioned, the vituperative and intensely political General Sir Henry Wilson.[167] Appointed CIGS by Lloyd George after the
controversial dismissal of General Robertson in February 1918, Wilson was constantly in Lloyd George's company in London and Paris in 1918–19, attending
even the 'X' meetings of the War Cabinet (Hankey, Milner, Lloyd George).
Lloyd George appointed Wilson because he believed him to be a critic of Haig
and a supporter of 'unity of command', the concept embodied in the new
Supreme War Council created in November 1917. But Lloyd George appears
also to have liked Wilson personally. The Prime Minister's intimates noted his
fondness for Wilson's boundless confidence and for his habit of mixing serious
business with 'jokes and badinage'.[168] But it is equally clear that Henry Wilson
was a reactionary of the deepest hue: a supporter of (but not a participant in) the
'Curragh mutiny', a ferocious Germanophobe, and anti-socialist. The pages of
his diary reveal an archetypal authoritarian, Ludendorff-like in his contempt for
all politicians. These he denounced as 'frocks' (wearers of frock coats), and these
he blamed for virtually all deficiencies that appeared in Britain's war effort. His
despised enemies were all around: Bolshevism, the Labour Party, and the idealistic American President Woodrow Wilson, whom he mocked unmercifully as his
muddle-headed 'cousin'.[169] His political contacts were almost entirely with the
like-minded notables of the Right, Milner, Esher, Gwynne, Carson, and Leo
Maxse. His ADC was Viscount Duncannon, a founder of the National Party.

---

[166] Roskill, *Man of Secrets*, ii. 48; Lord Hankey, *The Supreme Control at the Paris Peace Conference,
1919* (London, 1963), 25 and 29. In Paris, the more vital location, Hankey's military secretaries and
some younger Foreign Office personnel assisted him. These included Capt. Clement Jones, and two
new men from the Supreme War Council staff, Major H. A. Caccia and Major Edgar Abraham, and
from the Foreign Office, H. C. Norman, Eric Phipps, T. A. Spring Rice, Sir Percy Loraine, and
Cecil Hurst.
[167] The best survey of Wilson's career is to be found in the introduction to Keith Jeffery (ed.),
The Military Correspondence of Field Marshal Sir Henry Wilson, 1918–1922 (London, 1985).
[168] *Riddell's War Diary*, 16 Feb. 1918, 312.
[169] The original diary is in microfilm in the Henry Wilson Papers at DS Misc. 80, but long extracts
may be found in C. E. Callwell, *Field Marshal Sir Henry Wilson: His Life and Diaries* (London, 1927),
2 vols.

During 1917 Wilson contemplated entering parliament as a member, perhaps even as the leader, of the new National Party.[170]

Lloyd George claimed in his memoirs to have been aware of General Wilson's reactionary politics, but to have ignored them as he ignored the politics of all his generals.[171] Wilson's influence upon the Prime Minister cannot be so easily dismissed. With the large resources of military intelligence at his command, Wilson was constantly advising Lloyd George from a position of apparent inside knowledge, and thus strength, on both military and political matters concerning defeated Germany in 1918–19. The leaders of the intelligence services, in turn, those who supplied the bulk of the intelligence material to Wilson and to the War Cabinet, formed a tightly knit circle of highly politicized right-wing Germanophobes. The key men included, on the military side, General Sir William Thwaites, Director of Military Intelligence 1918–20, General Sir George Cockerill, commander of the Directorate for Special Intelligence at the War Office, and Rear-Admiral Sir Reginald 'Blinker' Hall, the Director of Naval Intelligence. Domestic civilian intelligence was under the command of General Nevil Macready, former Adjutant-General to the Forces, appointed Commissioner of the Metropolitan Police in September 1918 with a brief to resist the mobilization of the police union. The Assistant Commissioner and Director of Special Branch was Sir Basil Thomson, who organized the work of political surveillance during the war and immediately afterwards. Thomson was to be appointed head of a new Directorate of Intelligence within the Home Office in February 1919. Thomson was often to allege that German socialist subversion lay behind working-class and pacifist discontent in Britain before and after the armistice. These were men for whom detestation of socialism was not just for chatter during evening cigars; it was the absorbing passion of their lives.[172]

---

[170] Keith Wilson, *A Study in the History and Politics of the Morning Post, 1905–1926* (Lewiston, NY, 1990), 140–6.

[171] Lloyd George, *War Memoirs*, ii. 2013.

[172] Reginald Hall, the Director of Naval Intelligence, was a Conservative MP from 1918, the founder of the extreme anti-socialist agency, the Economic League, in Dec. 1919, and stout defender of Basil Thomson when he was dismissed from the Directorate of Intelligence in 1924. On Hall's anti-socialism see Arthur McIvor, ' "A Crusade for Capitalism": The Economic League, 1919–39', *Journal of Contemporary History*, 23 (1988), 631–55. George Cockerill was a close friend of Sir Patrick Hannon of the right-wing British Commonwealth Union. Cockerill stood as a Conservative candidate for Reigate in Dec. 1918 and was returned unopposed. During the war, Cockerill's Directorate of Special Intelligence was the agency responsible for preparing propaganda for Germany; see typescript biography, George Cockerill Papers, 86/2/1. On Macready's appointment see Nevil Macready, *Annals of an Active Life* (London, 1924), i, ch. 12. On Basil Thomson see Rupert Allason, *The Branch: A History of the Metropolitan Police Special Branch, 1883–1983* (London, 1983), 34 and 74–7. On Basil Thomson's attempts to discredit the UDC and anti-war British socialists as traitors in the pay of Germany see Marvin Swartz, *The Union of Democratic Control and British Politics during the First World War* (Oxford, 1971), 183–7. On the intelligence community's activities see also Christopher Andrew, *Secret Service: The Making of the British Intelligence Community* (London, 1985), ch. 3 (on Hall), and ch. 7 (on Thomson), and Bernard Porter, *Plots and Paranoia: A History of Political Espionage in Britain, 1790–1988* (London, 1992), ch. 7.

What then was the political spirit dominant among the Prime Minister's advisers at the end of the war? The answer must be that the political balance among the Prime Minister's advisers by late 1918 was shifting towards reaction. The three men most likely to be leaning on Lloyd George's arm as he entered conference rooms at the end of the war were Kerr, Hankey, and Henry Wilson, respectively a Round Table man, an 'apolitical' patriot, and an extreme reactionary. All three counsellors were men who saw political danger chiefly on the Left in 1919. In essence, the Prime Minister's assistants were loyal to the philosophy of the 'knock-out blow': as Mark Sykes had asked rhetorically in the smoking-room of the House of Commons, what did 'wealth, land, or anything else matter if only we can prevent a German victory?'[173] The men who circulated with Lloyd George among the 'red chairs, gilt mirrors and bawdey [sic] tapestries' that distracted Hankey in Paris, were predominantly imperially minded 'bitter enders'.[174] Lloyd George was increasingly sharing journeys and banter with advisers for whom there were clear political lessons to be drawn from the war: an imperial Britain, with the economic might of the Dominions more closely bound to her than ever before, had triumphed over German imperialism and had shown what a more united Empire could do; the triumph had come in spite of the obstructions of unpatriotic socialists, Liberals and Radicals—the 'enemy within', the 'hidden hand'—those who had doubted that peace with victory was possible; the greatest peril to victory, the push for peace by negotiation in 1917, had been a socialist project, promoted by Russian socialists, with the connivance of German socialists, and pursued by Arthur Henderson, the Labour Party leader, his 'treachery' being a salutary warning of the unreliability of organized Labour. Thus the 'moral warriors' of the Prime Minister's secretariats shared a profound contempt for exactly the brand of socialist and anti-imperialist politics that was to burst forth in revolutionary Germany in late 1918.

An embattled élite: the Foreign Office and Diplomatic Service in 1918–1919

The place of the Foreign Office in the bureaucracy of war also deserves introduction. Three points require emphasis. First, the Foreign Office leadership in this period was self-consciously weary and seriously demoralized by the Prime Minister's tendency to undervalue its advice. Second, the breakdown in trust between Lloyd George and the leadership of the Foreign Office formed a significant obstacle to any rapid amendment of policy towards Germany following the war. Third, anti-socialist political prejudices were to be found among many men in key positions in the Foreign Office and Diplomatic Service. The problems of leadership at the Foreign Office began with Arthur Balfour.

---

[173] Alexander MacCallum Scott Diary, 18 Feb. 1919, Scott reflecting upon a wartime discussion with Sykes, Alexander MacCallum Scott Papers, MS GEN 1465.

[174] Hankey Diary, 24 July 1917, in Roskill, *Man of Secrets*, i. 416.

The Foreign Secretary turned 70 in July 1918. He encouraged an indulgent toleration towards himself through self-mockery, often making light of his age and failing memory.[175] He amused many with his affected drawing-room politeness and his patrician style of indolence. The philosopher-politician at the centre of 'the Souls', that aristocratic coterie of the beautiful and the rich, was certainly a figure of legendary charm.[176] But the charm did not distract everyone from his declining capacity to perform in office. Rumours were widespread. Leo Amery seemed to be expressing a commonplace when he wrote to Lloyd George in July 1917 to assure him that it would be no loss if Balfour left the Foreign Office.[177] In Liberal eyes he was 'fiddling while Europe is dying', a 'mountebank showman', 'a dillitante [sic] and trifler', guilty of 'indolence or rather insouciance'.[178] In February 1918 the whole House of Commons was confronted with evidence that the Foreign Secretary had not bestirred himself even to read the German and Austrian replies to Lloyd George's famous Caxton Hall address on war aims.[179] This seems to have awakened leading Conservatives to the problem. Curzon approached Hankey in March 1918 to accuse Balfour of an inefficiency that 'was losing us the war'. Remarkably, Hankey did not quarrel with Curzon's indictment but replied that 'to the best of my knowledge, the P. M. and all his colleagues shared this view'.[180] In September 1918 Milner described Balfour succinctly as 'a past number'.[181] In late 1918 Algernon Cecil, Balfour's cousin and a Foreign Office historian, confided to George Prothero[182] his belief that Balfour was '*désoriente*' in European politics.[183] In a savage indictment of his former friend and predecessor, Curzon alleged in 1924 that Balfour 'never studied his papers; he never knew the facts; at the Cabinet he had seldom read the morning's FO telegrams; he never got up a case; he never looked ahead'.[184]

The evidence indicates that Lloyd George was well acquainted with Balfour's faults. He had observed enough of Balfour during the Asquith-led Coalition to declare him unfit for his position as First Lord of the Admiralty in June

[175] e.g. Lord Crawford Diary, 4 Aug. 1918, vol. xxxii, Crawford Papers.

[176] See Angela Lambert, *Unquiet Souls: A Social History of the Illustrious, Irreverent, Intimate Group of British Aristocrats Known as 'the Souls'* (London, 1984).

[177] Leo Amery Diary, 18 July 1917, in John Barnes and David Nicholson (eds.),*The Leo Amery Diaries, i. 1896–1929* (London, 1980), 164.

[178] e.g. see Alexander Whyte Diary, 19 Mar. 1918, Whyte Papers, MSS EUR D 761/2, Asquith quoted in Randall Davidson Political Diary, 28 Apr. 1918, Davidson Papers, and Lord Bryce to J. A. Spender, 15 Dec. 1918, Spender Papers, Add. MSS 46392.13.

[179] Conservatives and Liberals conceded this in their diaries; see Lord Crawford Diary, 14 Feb. 1918, vol. xxxi, Crawford Papers, and Alexander Whyte Diary, 13 Feb. 1918, Whyte Papers, MSS EUR D 761/2.

[180] Hankey Diary, 8 Mar. 1918, quoted in Roskill, *Man of Secrets,* i. 506.

[181] Milner quoted in Lord Derby Diary, 18 Sept. 1918, Derby Papers, 28/1/1.

[182] George Prothero, historian and editor of the *Quarterly Review*, working in the Historical Section of the Foreign Office during the war, brother of Rowland Prothero, Baron Ernle, the Conservative President of the Board of Agriculture in the Coalition Government 1916–19.

[183] Algernon Cecil to Prothero, 26 Sept. 1918, Prothero Papers, PP 1/10.

[184] Curzon, 'Memorandum on some aspects of my tenure of the Foreign Office', dated Nov. 1924, quoted in Kenneth Rose, *Curzon: A Most Superior Person* (London, 1985), 380.

1916.[185] In 1918, he deliberately excluded his Foreign Secretary from several crucial foreign policy decisions; for example, in January 1918 at the time of the
Caxton Hall address on war aims, and again in Paris in late October 1918 when
the armistice was being discussed.[186] Balfour's blundering in public speeches
sometimes infuriated Lloyd George. For example, in September 1918 he complained angrily that Balfour's reference in a speech to a coming offensive on the
Salonika front 'may cost us tens of thousands of lives'.[187] Nevertheless, Balfour
remained at the helm of the Foreign Office.

Why did Lloyd George retain him? He sought to persuade his colleagues that,
in spite of Balfour's evident weariness, his analytical skills were useful.[188] Less
charitable explanations for Lloyd George's tolerance seem more likely. Lloyd
George simply regarded Balfour as tractable. On his appointment in 1916, Lloyd
George told a doubtful Geoffrey Dawson that Balfour was 'an easy man to work
with'.[189] Balfour's lethargic style may well have commended him to the Prime
Minister. When Arthur Ponsonby told Lloyd George in June 1918 that he would
get nowhere with peace until he dumped Balfour, he replied that 'he was careless and indolent but he had no power over decisions and he said he could trust
him better than many other men to stand by him when the moment [for peace-
making] came'.[190] Three months later Lloyd George told C. P. Scott the exact
opposite. He explained to the Liberal newspaper man that 'in the making of peace
Balfour would probably be the chief obstacle, not because of his jingoism but
because of his indecision'.[191] Fully conscious of his inadequacies, therefore,
Lloyd George reappointed Balfour as Foreign Secretary in January 1919, a post
he retained for the ten decisive months of peacemaking in Paris until his retire-
ment in October 1919.

At the Paris Peace Conference he provoked much adverse gossip. His deafness,
his inattention to his duties, his frequent 'colds', and his general air of distracted
superiority irritated many. Accusations that the Foreign Secretary was approaching his dotage litter the sources. Admiral Roslyn Wemyss condemned him as 'too
old'.[192] Lord Hardinge, Permanent Under-Secretary at the Foreign Office, complained that he knew little of the main business in Paris because he was reliant
on 'what happens to leak out in conversation or what Mr Balfour happens to
remember to tell me'.[193] He had his admirers, of course, who pleaded that

[185] Fry, 'Political Change in Britain', 614.
[186] Hankey Diary, 2 Jan. 1918, and 30 Oct. 1918, quoted in Roskill, *Man of Secrets*, i. 478 and 623.
[187] C. P. Scott Political Diary, 18 Sept. 1918, Box 134.
[188] *Lord Riddell's War Diary*, 1 Oct. 1916, 213, and (no day given) Aug. 1918, 348.
[189] Quoted in Wrench, *Dawson*, 144.
[190] 'Notes of an interview with Lloyd George, 27 June 1918', Ponsonby Papers, MS Eng. Hist. c.
677.
[191] C. P. Scott Political Diary, 28 Sept. 1917, Box 134.
[192] Wemyss to Mrs Wemyss, 5 Mar. 1919, Wemyss Papers, 7/11/14.
[193] Hardinge to Curzon, 11 Feb. 1919, Curzon Papers, MS EUR F 112/212.

Balfour 'knows far more than he pretends to know'.[194] He did briefly impress during February 1919 when he deputized at the Peace Conference for Lloyd George.[195] But after February, most observers agreed that the fatigue was no pretence. Edwin Montagu reported from Paris that Balfour was little more than 'an amused spectator'.[196] At press conferences he 'seemed tired and had no time to prepare'.[197] Reports of his fondness for lingering in bed until mid-morning circulated freely.[198] Even members of Balfour's family, who visited him in April 1919, learned of 'French annoyance over Nunky's [Balfour's] late lying (in bed), his insistence on tennis, his dining out, his absolute inability to make a decision, holding everything back, and the desire of the Council [of Four] that he should retire'.[199] Tennis certainly competed for his time at Paris. His family complained that he played 'too much tennis and too strenuously'. Sir William Orpen, the British delegation's official artist, was told that Balfour would only sit for his portrait 'during his lawn tennis interval'.[200]

If the Foreign Office experts were to have had any hope of winning a greater degree of influence in 1918–19 it was vital that the leadership of the Foreign Office should have included someone in the Prime Minister's special trust. In fact, a chance to place such a man, Herbert Fisher, was lost in December 1918. When Robert Cecil resigned his post as Assistant Foreign Secretary (in protest over the disestablishment of the Welsh Church), both Lloyd George and Balfour pleaded with Fisher to put himself forward as the replacement. But, after much agonizing, Fisher elected to stay on at the Education Board in order to press on with his programme of reform.[201] Instead, the Liberal Coalitionist Cecil Harmsworth, an enthusiast for economic blockade, took the post. Thus an opportunity to place a voice for moderation at the Foreign Office, one Lloyd George respected, was let slip on the very eve of the Peace Conference.

Compounding these difficulties, not one of the Foreign Office leaders below Balfour managed to establish any degree of rapport with Lloyd George. Cecil,

---

[194] Harold Nicolson quoted in Alexander Whyte Diary, 21 Jan. 1919, Whyte Papers, MSS EUR D 761/3.

[195] Lord Hankey, *The Supreme Control at the Paris Peace Conference, 1919*, 75. The Prime Minister was called away to deal with the industrial unrest in Britain.

[196] Montagu to Eric Drummond, 30 Apr. 1919, Montagu Papers, AS 6/9/18.

[197] Knatchbull-Hugessen Diary, 1 Mar. 1919, Knatchbull-Hugessen Papers, KNAT 1/3.

[198] Headlam-Morley to J. Bailey, 30 Mar. 1919, HMP, HDLM OS, Box 2.

[199] Frances Balfour to Betty Balfour, 4 Apr. 1919, Whittingehame Papers, GD 433/2/363.

[200] Lord Crawford Diary, 16 Feb. and 10 Apr. 1919, vol. xxxiv, Crawford Papers.

[201] H. A. L. Fisher Diary, 2 and 3 Dec. 1918, HMP, Acc. 800, HDLM 3 and H. Fisher to L. Fisher, 2 Dec. 1918, Fisher Papers, 205. For those advising Fisher to accept see C. P. Ilbert to Fisher, 4 Dec. 1918, Fisher Papers, 205, and Gilbert Murray to Fisher, 4 Jan. 1919, Fisher Papers, 54. For those advising Fisher to remain at education, in order to see through his education reforms, see Haldane to Edmund Gosse, 27 Dec. 1918, Gosse Papers, vol. 8; Thomas Jones Diary, 10 Apr. 1919 (on Haldane's view), Thomas Jones Papers; and L. Hichens to Fisher, 5 Jan. 1919, Fisher Papers, 63. Lloyd George claimed to have received much advice recommending the importance of Fisher in education when making the final offer of the Board of Education to Fisher; see Lloyd George to Fisher, 9 Jan. 1919, Fisher Papers, 63.

Hardinge, and Curzon, all in varying degrees detested Lloyd George. Cecil, Balfour's cousin and Assistant Secretary until November 1918, made no secret of his distrust of the Prime Minister, and Lloyd George returned the sentiment.[202] This tension certainly made Cecil's task all the more difficult when in Paris in 1919 he became a leading advocate of moderation in the peace settlement. Hardinge, the former Viceroy of India and Permanent Under-Secretary at the Foreign Office, was irritated by the Prime Minister's neglect of the Foreign Office.[203] Hardinge was regarded as a lightweight by many observers and Lloyd George certainly picked up this gossip.[204] Steel-Maitland advised him in January 1919 that Hardinge was 'hopelessly incompetent'.[205] Lloyd George was determined to squeeze Hardinge out of any real position of influence in Paris in 1919; he insisted upon Hankey taking the post of British Secretary to the Peace Conference, and fobbed off Hardinge with the post of 'Organizing Ambassador'.[206] His brooding hatred of the Prime Minister is no mystery. During Balfour's long stay in Paris to attend the Peace Conference from January to September 1919, Lord Curzon ran the Foreign Office at the London end as a virtual deputy Foreign Secretary.[207] This appointment did nothing to rescue the reputation of the Foreign Office in Lloyd George's eyes. As one official lamented in late 1919, Lord Curzon appeared not to have 'any sort of relation with the P. M.'.[208] The general accusation that the Prime Minister had only disdain for the Foreign Office and its leaders gained much currency at the time.[209] In turn, many of the staff at the Foreign Office smarted with resentment at the reign of

---

[202] On Cecil's distrust see Turner, *British Politics and the Great War*, 234, and *Lord Riddell's War Diary*, 19 Feb. 1918, 315; on Cecil mocking Lloyd George see Cecil to Walter Long, 30 Nov. 1918, Long Papers, BM Add MSS 62423 (provisional catalogue number); and on Lloyd George's opinions of Cecil see Lord Riddell Diary, 23 Feb. 1919, Riddell Papers, 62983, comments which are suppressed in the published version of the Riddell diary.

[203] Hankey Diary, 22 Nov. 1918, quoted in Roskill, *Man of Secrets*, ii. 22, and Lord Hardinge of Penshurst, *Old Diplomacy: The Reminiscences of Lord Hardinge of Penshurst* (London, 1947), 205.

[204] C. P. Scott to L. T. Hobhouse, 22 Nov. 1917, Scott Papers, Rylands Library, 132/249; Lord Crawford Diary, 9 Apr.1919, vol. xxxiv, Crawford Papers. For a similar assessment see John Baird Diary, 7 Sept. 1919, Stonehaven Papers, 7.

[205] Arthur Steel-Maitland to Lloyd George, Jan. 1919 (no day given), Curzon Papers, MSS Eur F 112/213.

[206] Hankey, *Supreme Control*, 28; Maurice Hankey to Thomas Jones, 18 Jan 1919, in Jones, *Whitehall Diary*, 73.

[207] Curzon to Lloyd George, 3 Jan. 1919, Curzon Papers, MS EUR F 112/211; Curzon to Balfour, 24 June 1919, Curzon Papers, MS EUR F 112/208.

[208] Sydney Waterlow to Keynes, 21 Dec. 1919, Keynes Papers, EC/2/1/76.

[209] e.g. see Curzon to Hardinge, 8 Nov. 1918 Curzon Papers, MS Eur F 112/212. For the historical debate on this see R. M. Warman, 'The Erosion of Foreign Office Influence in the Making of Foreign Policy, 1916–1918', *Historical Journal*, 15 (1972), 133–59; Alan J. Sharp, 'The Foreign Office in Eclipse, 1919–22', *History*, 61 (1976), 198–218; M. L. Dockrill and Zara Steiner, 'The Foreign Office at the Paris Peace Conference in 1919', *International History Review*, 2/1 (1980), 55–86; and Zara Steiner, 'The Foreign Office and the War', in F. H. Hinsley (ed.), *British Foreign Policy under Sir Edward Grey* (Cambridge, 1977), 516–31. But see also Turner, *Lloyd George's Secretariat*, ch. 4, for the argument that this has been exaggerated.

the 'amateurs', as they called the Prime Minister's own advisers.[210] These rivalries, fed by a flow of poisonous gossip, were not petty matters. Frigid relations between the Prime Minister and the Foreign Office could only hamper informed decision-making.

A final factor of significance within the Diplomatic Service requires attention too. Hostile attitudes towards German socialism among the leading men at ambassadorial level were deeply entrenched by the end of the war. This can be seen in the work of a number of key Foreign Office men in the neutral European countries who gathered intelligence on internal politics in Germany during the war. The key ambassadors or ministers in the neutral states were Sir Horace Rumbold in Switzerland, Sir Walter Townley in the Netherlands, Sir Ralph Paget in Denmark, and Esme Howard in Sweden. In the main, reports from these ambassadors were unremittingly sceptical regarding Germany's internal politics and buttressed Foreign Office opinion against any 'premature peace' with the German government.

In the collecting of intelligence on 'inner Germany', Rumbold was the most assiduous. His base in Berne proved to be a veritable 'clearing house for intelligence' and a nest of spies. He was also the most unwaveringly reactionary of the diplomats. Rumbold's reports were coloured by his own extreme chauvinism, his intense hostility to socialism, his horror at the idea of a compromise peace, and his high Tory politics.[211] Rumbold sent hundreds of telegrams and private letters to London offering his own brand of intelligence on the internal situation in Germany. None was more zealous in denouncing German socialists of the Sozialdemokratische Partei Deutschlands (SPD) and discounting rumours of democratic revolution in Germany than Rumbold. As late as August 1918, Rumbold described stories of revolutionary fervour among German youth as 'absolute nonsense'.[212] Similarly 'peace offensives' and a show of democratic pressure were depicted as the cunning tactics of socialist 'intriguers' like Scheidemann and Ebert, whose opposition to the regime was bogus, warned Rumbold.[213]

While the most extreme practitioner, Rumbold was not alone among the ambassadors in constantly belittling Germany's internal political possibilities. Typical views were also expressed by Ralph Paget in a private letter to Hardinge in June 1917. In spite of all the suffering inside Germany, wrote Paget, the people were 'absolutely united and determined' and thus 'the blockade can never bring Germany to her knees'. He noted too that the 'good deal of ferment among the

---

[210] For a typical example see conversation between Hardinge and Rennell Rodd, Rennell Rodd Private Diary, 29 July 1918, Rodd Papers, 35; or Knatchbull-Hugessen Diary, 16 Feb. 1919, Knatchbull-Hugessen Papers, KNAT 1/3.

[211] Martin Gilbert, *Sir Horace Rumbold: Portrait of a Diplomat, 1869–1941* (London, 1973), preface.

[212] Rumbold to FO, 2 Aug. 1918, FO 371/3223, file 2480.

[213] The warnings against Scheidemann and Ebert in particular are contained in Rumbold to Hardinge, 9 Sept. 1918, Hardinge Papers, vol. 39.

socialists' was 'not likely to seriously incommode the German government until after the war'. The lesson was clear: only a 'crushing military defeat' could be counted upon.[214] In Copenhagen in October 1917, Paget turned away a private visit to discuss terms for peace from Philip Scheidemann and Karl Renner, the German and Austrian socialist leaders, as 'probably merely another German intrigue', a decision immediately endorsed by Hardinge.[215] After the Bolshevik revolution, the German socialists were constantly depicted as responsible for the dissolution of the Russian war effort and as working hand in glove with the German militarists to export socialist defeatism to the Entente nations.[216] Other ambassadors were constantly submitting reports which depicted the rise of socialist movements in their countries of appointment as wholly subversive developments. The political colour of the chief internal enemy was never in doubt. It is a reminder of the social circle in which these men moved to note that Lady Georgina Buchanan, wife of Sir George Buchanan, the Ambassador to Russia, was a sister-in-law of Lady Bathurst, proprietor of the arch-Tory newspaper *Morning Post*. People from such circles were bound to see the German revolution when it came as a repugnant development and to describe it as such in their reports.

The Political Intelligence Department of the Foreign Office: the limitations of expertise

During the First World War, advice to the government on political developments abroad, including Germany, came from many sources: from military intelligence, from agents in the British legations in the neutral countries, and from the Foreign Office. The most significant group of experts working on political developments inside Germany developed from a small group of intellectuals, publicists, and academics originally set up as the Department of Information Intelligence Branch (DIIB) in the spring of 1917. According to Headlam-Morley, the leading figure among the group's experts on Germany, the new intelligence agency was originally envisaged as 'working directly under the Prime Minister'.[217] However, the group was established at the Department of Information under the leadership of Buchan, the author and Milnerite, and Count Edward Gleichen, a military intelligence officer. Here youthful scholars of great promise came to pool their expertise and write reports for the government. The *illuminati* soon included such ambitious young men and academic leaders of the future as Lewis Namier,

[214] Ralph Paget to Hardinge, 8 June 1917, Paget Papers, Add. MS 51253.
[215] Ralph Paget to Hardinge, 9, 13, and 23 Oct. 1917, Hardinge to Paget, 11 and 26 Oct. 1917, Paget Papers, Add. MS 51253.
[216] Ralph Paget to Hardinge, 15 Jan. 1918, Paget Papers, Add. MS 51253. For similar views see Derby to Balfour, 9 May 1918, Derby Papers, 28/2/1. Only Esme Howard was inclined to see in German socialism a genuine movement to oppose the power of German militarism from within; see Howard to Hardinge, July–Aug. 1917, Howard Papers, DHW, 1/21.
[217] Headlam-Morley to R. B. Howarth, 15 Oct. 1919, HMP, HDLM Acc. 688, OS Box 1.

Arnold J. Toynbee, Robert Seton-Watson, Edwyn Bevan, and Rex and Allen Leeper. As noted above, these young men had close ties with members of the Round Table group.[218] In February 1918 the branch was to evolve into a new expert intelligence agency under the command of the Foreign Office: the Political Intelligence Department of the Foreign Office (PID). The PID played a most significant role in the debate over British policy towards Germany in 1918–19 and its personnel and operations require careful examination.

The PID's evolution from the former Intelligence Branch was not an entirely happy one. The scholars became the coveted prize in a feud involving fierce interdepartmental rivalries in Lloyd George's government in early 1918. A squabble began when Lord Hardinge decided to establish a new intelligence headquarters at the Foreign Office. To staff his proposed new body his eyes lighted upon the ready-made intelligence group working for Buchan. He obtained the support of the War Cabinet, and the Department of Information itself, for his proposal simply to transplant the entire group of experts to the Foreign Office. Almost all of the staff agreed to the move.[219]

However, a smooth transfer of the staff was unexpectedly interrupted when the Department of Information was upgraded to the status of a Ministry of Information in February 1918 and placed under the command of Lord Beaverbrook. The new minister called upon the War Cabinet to reverse its decision and restore 'his' intelligence men to his new ministry. In understanding this tussle, it is important to recall that Lord Beaverbrook was one of the most unpopular men in the government. His meteoric rise to the peerage and the ministry was resented not only by Liberals but by many of his own colleagues in the Conservative Party.[220]

It is an indication of the ethos of respectability prevailing at the Intelligence Branch that the staff there were similarly affronted by the Beaverbrook appointment. They too were disturbed that, if retained in the new Ministry of Information, they would be working for a man despised as a parvenu by many in the political élite. Almost all threatened to resign unless their immediate transfer to the Foreign Office was completed.[221] Already resentful at the growing

---

[218] On the formation of the Intelligence Bureau see Erik Goldstein, *Winning the Peace: British Diplomatic Strategy, Peace Planning, and the Paris Peace Conference* (Oxford, 1991), 59, and Philip M. Taylor, 'The Foreign Office and British Propaganda during the First World War', *Historical Journal*, 23 (1980), 888.

[219] On the formation of the PID see Goldstein, *Winning the Peace*, 57–62.

[220] By this time Lord Northcliffe, owner of *The Times* and the *Daily Mail*, had led a British War Mission to the USA. His brother Lord Rothermere was Air Minister. On Conservative hostility to these connections see e.g. Austen Chamberlain to Curzon, 21 Feb. 1918, Curzon Papers, MSS Eur F 112/121. See also Lord Crawford Diary, vol. xxxi, 28 Feb. 1918, Crawford Papers, and William Bridgeman Diary, 28 Feb. and 1 Mar. 1918, Bridgeman Papers.

[221] James Headlam-Morley led the staff in a virtual 'strike' in revulsion against the idea of being transformed into 'the hacks of propaganda'; Alfred Zimmern to Graham Wallas, 3 Mar. 1918, Wallas Papers 1/61. See the diary of Alexander F. Whyte, 4 Feb. 1918, Whyte Papers, MSS Eur D 761/2, and George Saunders to William Tyrrell, 11 Mar. 1918, in George Saunders's Day Book III, HMP, HDLM Acc. 800, Box 1.

tendency of the Prime Minister and his advisers to disregard the professionals at the FO, Hardinge fought hard. Doubtless he wished to strike a blow against the Foreign Office's persistent denigration by denying one of the Prime Minister's unsavoury Fleet Street companions his victory over tradition. The War Cabinet eventually resolved the dispute in favour of the Foreign Office and the PID was set up in early March 1918.[222] The acrimony surrounding the establishment of the PID was important, for it may have diminished its influence. Certainly, it could not have assisted the PID's reputation in Lloyd George's eyes that the staff had shown such determination to serve under his enemies rather than his friends.

Who precisely then provided the intelligence assessments on Germany that flowed from the PID to the War Cabinet? First, there were those in overall charge of the new department. Hardinge appointed a director to preside over the PID and chose for this position Sir William Tyrrell, his own personal assistant. Tyrrell had much in common with Hardinge, a family friend whom he had known since his childhood.[223] In common with his superior, Tyrrell had a reputation as a convinced pre-war Germanophobe and social élitist.[224] Both had lost sons in the war. In Tyrrell's case, the death of his younger son in February 1915 induced a nervous collapse.[225] This, in addition to Tyrrell's long-standing problem with alcoholism, led to the loss of his prestigious post as Private Secretary to Sir Edward Grey in June 1915. In accepting command of the PID, therefore, Tyrrell was accepting his professional rehabilitation through his old friend Hardinge.[226]

Tyrrell's own political views in 1918–19 are more difficult to discern. He was notoriously loath to write down his own judgements.[227] Those who attempted political estimates of him at this time often reached different conclusions. Some were less than charitable. H. G. Wells condemned him as typical of the Foreign Office reactionaries.[228] Seton-Watson, leader of the pro-democratic New Europe group of publicists,[229] 'foams at the mouth at the idea of serving under Tyrrell', according to Alexander Whyte, a colleague in the New Europe group.[230] And yet,

---

[222] For more details on the tussle concerning the formation of the PID see John Buchan to Headlam-Morley, 17 Jan. 1918, Hardinge to Headlam-Morley, 21 Feb. 1918, and R. J. Campbell to Headlam-Morley, 8 Mar. 1918, HMP, HDLM Acc. 727, Box 21; and James Headlam-Morley's own account in Headlam-Morley to R. B. Howarth, 15 Oct. 1919, HMP, HDLM Acc. 688, OS Box 1.

[223] Lord Hardinge of Penshurst, *Old Diplomacy*, 228.

[224] Zara Steiner, *Britain and the Origins of the First World War* (London, 1977), 173–7.

[225] Edward T. Corp, 'Sir William Tyrrell: the *Éminence Grise* of the British Foreign Office, 1912–1915', *Historical Journal*, 25/3 (1982), 697–708, and Cynthia Gladwyn, *The Paris Embassy* (London, 1986), 204.

[226] In Oct. 1918 Hardinge secured a further promotion for him, to the post of Assistant Under-Secretary of the Foreign Office; Hardinge to Balfour, 10 Oct. 1918, Hardinge Papers, vol. 39. In promoting Tyrrell, Hardinge also overlooked Tyrrell's Catholicism, the influence of which in the Foreign Office he opposed vehemently; see Hardinge to Rennell Rodd, 3 June 1918, Rodd Papers, 19.

[227] Goldstein, *Winning the Peace*. 67.

[228] H. G. Wells, *Experiment in Autobiography*, ii (London, 1966), 704–5.

[229] On the New Europe group see Hugh and Christopher Seton-Watson, *The Making of a New Europe: R. W. Seton-Watson and the Last Years of Austria-Hungary* (London, 1981).

[230] Diary of Alexander F. Whyte, 4 Feb. 1918, Whyte Papers, MSS Eur D 761/2.

dining in May 1918 in the advanced company of Sidney and Beatrice Webb and Leonard and Virginia Woolf, Tyrrell declared in favour of the League of Nations and the abortive Stockholm Conference.[231] Similarly, in September 1918, Tyrrell impressed C. P. Scott as a 'first class Liberal, bent on a rational, non-vindictive settlement of the war'.[232] In stark contrast, the right-wing journalists Leo Maxse and H. A. Gwynne endorsed Tyrrell as trenchantly anti-German and 'sound' on indemnities.[233] Tyrrell was apparently adept at telling his listeners what they wished to hear. On balance, it seems reasonable to conclude that, in his management of the PID (which included the perusal of all its reports before printing),[234] Tyrrell would have kept in view his large debts to the Germanophobic Hardinge.

Tyrrell was fortunate to have the services of James Headlam-Morley as his Assistant Director.[235] He was a Hellenistic scholar, Professor of Ancient History at Queen's College in London, before joining the Board of Education in 1902. The real supervision of the work of the PID was undertaken by Headlam-Morley. He naturally shared and enjoyed the bookish outlook of most of the staff. From the Foreign Office perspective, Headlam-Morley's views on the war were absolutely 'sound': he believed completely in Britain's moral authority and in the necessity of a military resolution of the war.[236] Not all observers were impressed with him. Critics of the Foreign Office, men like Whyte, regarded Headlam-Morley as 'dry, a little too legalistic', and limited by 'lack of imagination'.[237]

The members of staff of the PID itself, eventually numbering sixteen, were, in every sense, academic. An Oxbridge *esprit de corps* prevailed; for social gatherings the group repaired to the Oxford and Cambridge Club. No doubt the members of the PID were flattered to be advising great men at a nerve centre of British power. Most were younger men of military age, and some had served in the army before being transferred to intelligence work. They had cause to

[231] Virginia Woolf Diary, 1 May 1918, in Anne Olivier Bell (ed.), *The Diary of Virginia Woolf, i. 1915–19* (Harmondsworth, 1979), 146. Leonard Woolf was a Radical publicist and critic of British foreign policy, and his wife Virginia Woolf was a novelist. Sydney and Beatrice Webb were prominent Fabians and political advisers to the Labour Party.

[232] C. P. Scott, Political Diary, Monday, 23 Sept. 1918, C. P. Scott Papers, Box 134.

[233] H. A. Gwynne to Lady Bathurst, 16 Mar. 1917, in Keith Wilson (ed.), *The Rasp of War: The Letters of H. A. Gwynne to the Countess Bathurst, 1914–1918* (London, 1988), 214; Maxse to W. M. Hughes, 13 Jan. 1919, Hughes Papers, MS 1538/24/12.

[234] Headlam-Morley to Tyrrell, 25 June 1918, HMP, Acc. 727, Box 16.

[235] On Headlam-Morley see the introduction to Agnes Headlam-Morley, R. Bryant, and A. Cienciala (eds.), *Sir James Headlam-Morley: A Memoir of the Paris Peace Conference* (London, 1972).

[236] In 1915 he had produced a stout defence of the actions of Sir Edward Grey during the July–Aug. 1914 crisis, *The History of Twelve Days*, which no doubt endeared him to the Foreign Office. In 1917 he produced a companion piece, *The German Chancellor and the Outbreak of War*, a book that asserted the guilt of the German leaders in having deliberately incited war in 1914. Headlam-Morley's status as a 'fight-to-the-finish' man was established by a third work, *The Issue*, published in 1917. In this collection of essays he rejected the idea of a compromise peace and asserted that Germany's people must taste defeat if the militarist spirit was to be eradicated from the national psyche.

[237] Diary of Alexander F. Whyte, 15 Apr. 1919, Whyte Papers, MSS Eur D 761/2.

appreciate their good fortune. Zimmern and Namier were also acutely conscious that their Jewish and German ancestry had not been allowed to stand in the way of their employment at the PID.[238] Unstinting service was expected, clearly enough, in recompense.

The four designated 'German experts' within the PID, as central characters in this study, require some introduction. The German section was headed by Headlam-Morley. His closest colleague, George Saunders, was a retired senior journalist.[239] Two of the PID's younger academics, Zimmern and Bevan, both originally ancient historians, completed the German think-tank. The four had much in common. All but Zimmern had worked previously at the Intelligence Branch. (Zimmern joined the PID in May 1918 after service at the Ministry of Reconstruction.)[240] Headlam-Morley and Saunders, the senior pair, had German wives. Similarly, Zimmern had German family connections.[241] Zimmern and Bevan had been classical scholars together at New College, Oxford, before the war, and, in common with Headlam-Morley, shared a devotion to ancient Greek and early Christian history. Three of the four, Headlam-Morley, Saunders, and Bevan, were devout Christians. All four German specialists had comfortable upper middle-class origins and prospects.

The political outlook of each of the four men varied, but not so much as to strain the 'patriotic' cement. Saunders was somewhat exceptional, for his politics was dominated by a relatively more strident Germanophobia. This he had cultivated and advertised in his twenty years of controversial and hostile journalism from Germany for the Conservative press. During his journalistic career he had cultivated close relations with other prominent Germanophobic publicists on the Radical Right in Britain, most notably Leo Maxse. In Maxse's opinion, Saunders was '*the* sound man on Germany'.[242] In addition, during his years as a foreign correspondent he had worked closely with Foreign Office Germanophobes like Hardinge and Tyrrell. His friendly relations with both Foreign Office men undoubtedly smoothed the way to his appointment to the PID.[243] The other three PID men had more Liberal or even Radical political inclinations. Zimmern

---

[238] In July 1918 Headlam-Morley advised Tyrrell to prepare defences for Lewis Namier and Alfred Zimmern in response to the Conservative MP Kennedy-Jones's campaign seeking the dismissal of public servants with German ancestry: Headlam-Morley to Tyrrell, 9 July 1918 HMP, HDLM Acc. 727, Box 16. On Zimmern's sensitivity on the Jewish issue, see the letter of his brother-in-law, Walter Barton, to R. Seton-Watson, 27 June 1916, R. Seton-Watson Papers, First World War, General Correspondence, Box A.

[239] George Saunders, son of the journalist D. H. Saunders (editor of the *Christian Democrat*), Berlin correspondent of the *Morning Post* 1888–97, Berlin correspondent of *The Times* 1897–1908, Paris correspondent of *The Times* 1908–14, retired Mar. 1914. See the introduction to Keith M. Wilson (ed.), *George Saunders on Germany 1919–1920: Correspondence and Memoranda* (Leeds, 1987).

[240] Goldstein, *Winning the Peace*, 77.

[241] Arnold J. Toynbee, *Acquaintances* (London, 1967), 50.

[242] Maxse to Strachey, 15 Jan. 1907, quoted in Paul Kennedy, *The Rise of Anglo-German Antagonism, 1860–1914* (London, 1980), 369.

[243] On Saunders's background and his anti-German journalism, see A. J. A. Morris, *The Scaremongers: The Advocacy of War and Rearmament, 1896–1914* (London, 1984), ch. 2.

was the most left-wing: he had even toyed with the label 'socialist' in 1915, but lamented that the name had 'fly-blown associations'.[244] He had close academic friends in Radical and Labour circles.[245] He was at this time a Milnerite enthusiast for 'Commonwealth'. But his Milnerism was tempered with a fervent internationalism which made him a genuine advocate of a League of Nations. Bevan and Headlam-Morley were less intensely political, but both had Liberal political acquaintances.[246] The Round Table movement, as has been seen, was a uniting factor for all four. Both Headlam-Morley and Saunders wrote articles for the *Round Table* at this time. Saunders certainly counted the Milnerite journalists Amery and Valentine Chirol, former colleagues at *The Times*, as friends. Zimmern and Bevan were active members. 'Zim', as his friends in the 'moot' called him, was specially valued at the Round Table, one suspects as a political oddity: he was often cited as evidence that even men of 'advanced opinions' could identify with the ideals of Milnerism.[247]

These were Britain's foremost experts advising the government on Germany's internal political development in 1918–19—a notoriously Germanophobic journalist and three well-connected ancient historians. Without intending to belittle the considerable efforts made by these four men to offer expert advice to the government, it is fair to say that there were important gaps in their expertise on Germany, most especially in the one area which came to matter a great deal during 1918–19. As Germany lurched towards political upheavals in which the socialists of the SPD were to play the decisive role, the Foreign Office's German 'brains trust' was composed of four men who had little or no personal knowledge of the German working class and its politics. While each had some experience of life in pre-war Germany, none appears to have had any direct contact with the SPD or German labour movement. Saunders had spent two decades in Germany before 1908, but his reporting on German politics had focused on the military threat and the activities of the Pan-German press, not upon the German socialists. He had moved chiefly among the privileged élites of the *Kaiserreich*. Headlam-Morley had studied in Germany in the late 1880s and early 1890s, where he met his wife, Else Sonntag, daughter of a doctor of National Liberal political affiliation. In Germany, however, Headlam-Morley moved 'almost entirely in academic circles'.[248] He had become interested in modern German

---

[244] See Zimmern's explanation to G. D. H. Cole, Zimmern to Cole, 14 Apr. 1915, Round Table Papers, MS Eng. Hist. c. 817.

[245] Zimmern even served on the Labour Party's Advisory Committee on International Questions in 1919; see Arno J. Mayer, *Politics and Diplomacy of Peacemaking: Containment and Counter-revolution at Versailles* (London, 1968), 639.

[246] Both were personal friends of Herbert Fisher. Headlam-Morley had worked with Bryce in the mid-1890s on the Royal Commission into Secondary Education. Headlam-Morley's sister-in-law, Hedwig, a musician and novelist, included in her circle of admirers such men as Graham Wallas, Sidney Webb, and Bernard Shaw (Headlam-Morley *et al.*, *James Headlam-Morley*, pp. xiii and xiv).

[247] Untitled document, a review of the *Round Table* apparently prepared for fund-raising purposes, filed in 1920 papers, Brand Papers, 42.

[248] Headlam-Morley *et al.*, *James Headlam-Morley*, p. xii.

history during the 1890s, and made a special study of Bismarckian social legislation. But he acknowledged himself the gaps in his experience. In 1917 he freely confessed to Lord Haldane that his own knowledge of Germany was 'very limited and partial'; he explained that before the war his contacts with Germans had been exclusively 'with the ordinary people of the upper middle class'.[249]

As will be seen in subsequent chapters, the working model of modern Germany upon which the PID experts made their calculations tended to marginalize the socialists. The PID experts each shared the fashionable and tendentious 'academic' diagnosis of Germany's ills. According to this theory, Germany's middle class lay at the heart of the German problem. The middle class had failed to find the nerve to mount a successful bourgeois revolution during the late eighteenth century and again in 1848. The critical weakness of German liberalism had led to the peculiar middle-class deference to the neo-feudal 'Prussian military caste'. Germany was, in contrast to Britain, a land stumbling forward without the kindly light of a successful middle-class revolution to lead it. Instead, from the unification period onward, the reactionary ideals of Bismarck, Treitschke, and Bernhardi had captured the educated German mind almost completely. Therefore, each of the PID's German experts looked forward to the infliction of a stunning defeat upon the militarist system so that educated middle-class Germans would be jolted back to their senses, would recover their morality, and revive liberalism.[250] In this model, the SPD, which in fact had gained one vote in three in the elections of 1912, giving it twice the popularity of any other political party, was either ignored or its success was patronizingly regarded as a sign of Germany's political immaturity.[251]

In fact, two of the four experts exhibited overt hostility to German socialism. In 1918 Headlam-Morley advised against Labour's claim for representation at any Peace Conference, observing that international socialism before 1914 had 'a very harmful but much overrated influence'.[252] In a private letter in March 1919, reflecting on the lamentably strong influence of Bolshevism in Britain during the immediate post-war period, as shown by the rash of strikes and mutinies, he observed that the unrest could undoubtedly be 'traced back to German influence, and especially to that of German socialism, *which I have also thought was ultimately more baneful and more dangerous than German militarism*'.[253] Saunders, similarly, found nothing to praise in German socialism. Like many other pre-war Conservative commentators, he had been inclined to blame the advanced politics

---

[249] Headlam-Morley to R. B. Haldane, 9 Jan. 1917, HMP, HDLM, Acc. 727, Box 35.

[250] This view of Germany, so popular among the academic community in wartime Britain, can be explored in Stuart Wallace, *War and the Image of Germany: British Academics 1914–1918* (Edinburgh, 1988), esp. chs. 2, 3, and 4.

[251] In the elections of Jan. 1912, the SPD had gained 34.8% of the vote and 110 deputies in the Reichstag. The next most popular party, the Catholic Centre Party, had gained 16.4% and 91 deputies. See H. W. Koch, *A Constitutional History of Germany* (London, 1984), table 4, 384–5.

[252] Headlam-Morley to Tyrrell, 2 May 1918, HMP, HDLM, Acc. 727, Box 16.

[253] Headlam-Morley to Rex Leeper, 10 Mar. 1919, HMP, HDLM, Acc. 688, OS Box 1, italics mine.

of the 'lower classes' for the foreign adventurism of the Prussian ruling class. The dangerous politics of the German workers, as he explained in 1905, 'almost compel the Emperor to engage in an exciting *Weltpolitik* in order to distract attention from internal discontent'.[254] Saunders's wartime day books and correspondence were peppered with disparaging remarks concerning German socialism.[255] The attitudes of Zimmern and Bevan to German socialism were more complex. In his writings in the *Round Table* and in his book *The War and Democracy*, as will be seen in the next chapter, Zimmern drew attention to the anti-militarism of the SPD and its record of courageous opposition to the authoritarian state. But he believed the party had collapsed ignominiously in August 1914 and expected little from it. Edwyn Bevan also wrote articles denouncing the betrayal of internationalism by the small group of social imperialists on the right wing of the SPD.[256] However, Bevan seems not to have lost sight of the progressive policies followed by the majority of German socialists, even during the war. This resulted perhaps from his specific intelligence duties at the PID which demanded a close scrutiny of the German socialist press.[257] Notwithstanding Bevan's milder line, which emerged clearly only at the war's end, it is fair to conclude that the members of the German section of the PID regarded themselves as stern critics of German socialism.

The 'newspaper warriors': the popular press, the ultra-patriotic Right, and the Lloyd George Coalitions

By the eve of victory, the British popular press was recognized as a factor of tremendous significance in the land. The great proprietors, editors, and leading journalists were figures of immense prestige. As vehicles of pro-war propaganda, the newspapers played a crucial (and not unprofitable) role in moulding public opinion. From the pro-war press a lavish stream of news and opinion flowed forth, animated by the sort of chauvinist ideals that pass for 'patriotism' in every country at war, a blend of heroic myth and sentimentalism—for sentimental it surely is to believe that the enemy forces are wholly composed of fiends capable of atrocity while one's own forces are filled with men of brave hearts and scrupulous attention to the laws of war. While the journalism of war proved to be a most effective orchestration of the war whoop, nevertheless the press was never regarded by government as a compliant servant of the state. Quite to the contrary, the apparent impulsiveness of the press inspired fear among the politicians. The government did not attempt to control the press absolutely; it relied instead

[254] Saunders to Walter, 1 Dec. 1905, quoted in Morris, *Scaremongers*, 73.

[255] Saunders to Headlam-Morley, 24 Apr. and 7 June 1919, HMP, HDLM, Acc. 688, OS Box 2.

[256] See Edwyn Bevan, 'The New Marxism', *Nineteenth Century*, 498 (Aug. 1918).

[257] Bevan's evolving views on the subject eventually led him to a much more cautious judgement upon the sins of the SPD. See his *German Social Democracy During the War* (London, 1918). In this careful study Bevan concluded that a clear majority of German socialists had loyally opposed an annexationist war from the beginning; see also Edwyn Bevan to Leo Maxse, 17 Dec. 1918, Leo Maxse Papers, vol. 475.

upon the interventions of the Press Bureau which were infrequent and left much latitude to the individual editor. The press did not repay this generous treatment with tenderness towards the government of the day. Most importantly, the 'newspaper warriors' provoked a series of domestic political crises that imperilled the lives of governments—for example, at the time of the shells scandal of May 1915 and the Maurice debate of May 1918. The tension between the press and government was visible also when the newspapers, hungry for sensation, occasionally printed military details which involved breaches of censorship; these infringements were seized upon by governments eager for some pretext to inflict minor punishment upon the most undisciplined editors and journalists.[258] In this clammy atmosphere, all political sides, and British generals not least, jostled for the ear of the powerful men of the press. Grizzled losers in this competition for editorial favours lashed out at the press barons for overreaching themselves. The newspapers were accused of unmaking the Asquith government, and then of suborning the Lloyd George government. As may be readily appreciated, the subject of the press and its political inspiration is a vast one.[259] But some consideration of the inner workings of the British press is vital to this study. The newspaper press, after all, was the sole medium supplying to the British public an image of republican Germany in 1918–19. A number of factors at work deserve emphasis: first, the growing power of the great dailies and Sunday newspapers which favoured the Conservative Party; second, the increasing dominance of ultra-patriotic opinion in the high-circulation newspapers; and third, the political influence exerted by the great proprietors and editors over the Prime Minister.

In 1918, newspapers sympathetic to the Conservative Party dominated the London market. Sales boomed during the war, sometimes doubling and trebling the 1914 estimates of circulation.[260] But Conservative dominance was never threatened. The majority of the 'big name' papers, and a majority of the mass-circulation papers, were Conservative in allegiance. Together they supplied a raucous chorus in support of a war to the finish. Without a hint of squeamishness all campaigned vigorously against all manner of 'pasty-faced pacifism' and 'defeatism'. Six morning dailies supported these Conservative politics, the mass circulation *Daily Mail*, the *Daily Express, Daily Telegraph, Morning Post,*

[258] Tania Rose, *Aspects of Political Censorship, 1914–1918* (Hull, 1995), and Deian Hopkin, 'Domestic Censorship in the First World War', *Journal of Contemporary History*, 5/4 (1970), 151–69.

[259] Essential scholarship on the press includes Alan J. Lee, *The Origins of the Popular Press in England* (London, 1976); George Boyce, James Curran, and Pauline Wingate (eds.), *Newspaper History from the Seventeenth Century to the Present Day* (London, 1978); and S. E. Koss, *The Rise and Fall of the Political Press in England* (London, 1984), 2 vols. On the ultra-patriotic organizations of the Right, see Morris, *The Scaremongers*, and Barbara S. Farr, *The Development and Impact of Right-Wing Politics in Britain, 1903–1932* (New York, 1989).

[260] John McEwen, 'The National Press during the First World War: Ownership and Circulation', *Journal of Contemporary History*, 17 (1982), 459–86. McEwen uses figures for 1914 as the only complete set of figures, while acknowledging that these figures grew significantly up to 1916 and fluctuated wildly at moments of military sensation during the war.

Standard, and, of course, the most prestigious paper in London,*The Times*. These were supplemented by three illustrated papers which were colourfully 'patriotic' if not always obviously Conservative in their politics, and also achieved mass circulation, the *Daily Mirror, Daily Sketch*, and *Daily Graphic*. Three evening papers served a Conservative readership, the *Evening News* and *Evening Standard*, both with high circulations, plus the *Globe* with its more modest circulation. In addition, four Sunday newspapers were loyal to Conservative politics, two quality papers, the *Observer*, and the *Sunday Times*, and two top-selling papers, *People* and *Weekly Dispatch*. A new pro-Conservative mass circulation paper, the *Sunday Pictorial*, was launched in 1915. In a class of its own was the hugely successful ultra-patriotic Sunday paper, *John Bull*, controlled by Horatio Bottomley.[261]

Pitted against these papers of prestige or high circulation were only two London Liberal morning papers with middle-sized circulations, the *Daily News* and the *Daily Chronicle*. As a force in its own right, the *Manchester Guardian* must be added to this list, being the Liberal newspaper read by Liberals everywhere.[262] Similarly, there were only two London evening Liberal papers, the *Star* and the *Westminster Gazette*, the latter far more influential in party circles. The only Liberal papers able to muster large circulations that rivalled the big Conservative papers were the Sunday entertainers, *News of the World, Lloyd's Weekly News*, and *Reynold's Newspaper*.[263] However, their popularity was achieved by mixing political discussion with features on celebrities, sport, crime, divorce, and the panoply of war. The only Labour paper of note, the Independent Labour Party's anti-war weekly, the *Labour Leader*, was a party paper, originating in Manchester, and serving a small party membership.[264] In sum, considering the circulation figures for the big Monday to Saturday London-based dailies, it is safe to conclude that the Conservative papers generally outsold the Liberals by a figure approaching three to one.

On the face of it, therefore, the Lloyd George Coalition governments, with Conservative representation so dominant, ought to have been able to depend upon the unhesitating support of the big Conservative papers. That happy outcome was denied the Prime Minister. The sometimes notorious relations between

[261] The circulation figures for the Conservative papers given by McEwen in 'The National Press during the First World War', generally for 1914, are *Daily Mail* (950,000), *Daily Express* (300,000), *Daily Telegraph* (190,000),*The Times* (150,000), *Morning Post* (80,000), *Standard* (80,000), *Daily Mirror* (1,000,000), *Daily Sketch* (800,000), and *Daily Graphic* (800,000), *Evening News* (600,000), *Evening Standard* (180,000), *Globe* (20,000), and *Pall Mall Gazette* (10,000), *Observer* (175,000), *Sunday Times* (35,000), *People* (550,000), *Weekly Dispatch* (500,000), *Sunday Pictorial* (2,500,000 by 1917), and *John Bull* (2,000,000 by 1918).

[262] Circulation of the *Manchester Guardian* was estimated at 30,000 in 1913 (Koss, *Political Press in Britain*, i. 412).

[263] McEwen's figures for the Liberal press are *Daily News* (550,000), *Daily Chronicle* (400,000), *Star* (500,000), *Westminster Gazette* (20,000), *News of the World* (1,500,000), *Lloyd's Weekly News* (1,250,000), and *Reynold's Newspaper* (600,000).

[264] Membership of the ILP in Mar. 1918 was estimated at about 28,000, and circulation of the *Labour Leader* was probably of similar dimensions (Fritz Carsten, *War Against War: British and German Radical Movements in the First World War* (London, 1982), 262 n. 4).

Fleet Street and Downing Street proved in fact to be a constant headache. Lloyd George himself, for all his frenetic efforts to cultivate good relations with the men of the press during the war, experienced very mixed fortunes. He was to find his leadership dangerously exposed to continuing criticism from the die-hards on the ultra-patriotic Right, and from the populist conservatism of the Northcliffe press, almost from the moment an armistice was first mooted. At the end of the war, while Lloyd George retained some friends among the proprietors and editors, by no means were the 'newspaper warriors' mere pawns at his command.

Who were the powerful men behind the newspaper banners? The broadest acres amongst the Fleet Street empires were those possessed by Associated Newspapers, the company owned by the great pioneer of the cheap newspaper revolution in Britain, Alfred Harmsworth, Lord Northcliffe.[265] The irascible 'Chief' of Printing House Square was an implacable anti-socialist, and an extreme chauvinist, but regarded himself also as a populist critic of stuffy 'old Toryism'. His rise to fame in the Edwardian period was ineluctable. His moment of greatest glory had come in 1908 when he purchased *The Times*. In addition, he owned the mass-circulation and extravagantly 'patriotic' *Daily Mail*, as well as the *Weekly Dispatch* and *Evening News*. Northcliffe's brother, Lord Rothermere, owned the mass-circulation and semi-independent *Daily Mirror* and the new *Sunday Pictorial*. Even the 1914 circulation figures show that the Harmsworth brothers together controlled 46.7 per cent of the circulation of the London dailies.[266] Their importance in the eyes of politicians is self-evident.

Lloyd George's relationship with Lord Northcliffe was especially difficult.[267] During 1915 and 1916, he had received some valuable support from Northcliffe, his papers portraying him as one of the few energetic ministers in Asquith's government. Indirectly, Lloyd George profited from the attacks of the Northcliffe press upon the inefficiencies of Asquith's leadership. Liberals loyal to the Asquithians frequently assumed that the Lloyd George premiership was a '*coup d'état* . . . performed by the newspapers': that Northcliffe had played the role of 'kingmaker' and stood as 'The Old Man of the Sea' to the government was taken for granted.[268] The truth of the relationship was more complex. The press, both Conservative and Liberal, had played a critical part in the undermining of Asquith's leadership. In fact, there was no Lloyd George–Northcliffe conspiracy.[269]

Lloyd George certainly did not believe he was under any obligation to the cantankerous newspaper king for at least two reasons. First, it was always clear to

---

[265] The definitive biography is Reginald Pound and Geoffrey Harmsworth, *Northcliffe* (London, 1959).

[266] McEwen, 'The National Press during the First World War', 471.

[267] The best summary of the relationship is J. M. McEwen, 'Northcliffe and Lloyd George at War, 1914–1918', *Historical Journal*, 24/3 (1981), 651–72.

[268] The phrases come from Bryce to C. P. Trevelyan, 18 Dec. 1916 and 22 Jan. 1918, Bryce Papers, 19; and Spencer to Fitzmaurice, 22 Dec. 1916, Fitzmaurice Papers, EFm 44.

[269] McEwen, 'The Press and the Fall of Asquith', 863–83.

him that in one critical area of controversy Northcliffe was not a reliable ally: in any clash between the military élite and the civilian government Northcliffe was generally found to be on the side of the military élite.[270] Only in the three months between December 1917 and February 1918 had the Northcliffe press failed to come to the aid of the brass hats, thus assisting Lloyd George in his efforts to displace Sir William Robertson as CIGS.[271] But this had proved to be exceptional. While Northcliffe had sacrificed Robertson, he persisted in protecting the bigger fish, Haig, from the Prime Minister's reforming zeal. A second consideration was even more fundamental: that Northcliffe was mentally unbalanced, perhaps even unhinged, was appreciated by Lloyd George from 1914. Early in the war Lloyd George and Asquith had witnessed together one of Northcliffe's especially incoherent tirades against all politicians; on his departure from their room, Asquith had turned to Lloyd George with 'an angelic smile' and decreed 'You can't hunt with Northcliffe, he turns round and bites you in the seat of your breeches'—a judgement Lloyd George heartily endorsed in retelling the story in mid-1918.[272] On the eve of the crisis of December 1916, Lloyd George told Lord Burnham that 'Northcliffe was mad with vanity'; even Rothermere agreed, according to Lloyd George, that his brother had 'entirely lost his head'. Using a simile he would employ often, Lloyd George proclaimed that 'Lord Northcliffe was like a grasshopper; he did not know where he was at the moment'.[273]

Such an imposing figure, however, could never be ignored. Soon after the beginning of his premiership, Lloyd George sought to distract the 'Chief' with a 'patriotic' duty. Northcliffe was appointed in May 1917 to lead a British mission to the United States to co-ordinate finance and supplies. He was to be away for six months. Hankey was in no doubt as to Lloyd George's motives: 'This, of course, is really a dodge to get rid of Northcliffe, of whom he is afraid.'[274] To C. P. Scott, Lloyd George readily confirmed these motives, pleading that Northcliffe was so 'jumpy' that for the public good 'it was essential to get rid of him'.[275] Then, soon after his return to Britain in November 1917, came a major embarrassment. Lloyd George apparently discussed with Northcliffe the possibility of his serving the government at some point in the future as Air Minister. In a gesture that was designed to humiliate Lloyd George, Northcliffe published a letter to the Prime Minister attacking the inefficiencies of the government and declining the alleged offer to him of the new post of Air Minister. The current Director of the Air Board, Lord Cowdray, was astonished to read in the press that his post was being hawked to Northcliffe, and he resigned immediately. The

[270] McEwen, 'Northcliffe and Lloyd George at War', 665.

[271] John M. McEwen, ' "Brass-Hats" and the British Press during the First World War', *Canadian Journal of History*, 18/1 (1983), 43–67.

[272] Rennell Rodd Private Diary, 29 July 1918, Rodd Papers, 35.

[273] 'Notes of a Conversation between Lord Burnham and Mr Lloyd George', 1 Nov. 1916, Burnham Papers, HLWL/10, nos. 5 and 6.

[274] Hankey Diary, 24 May 1917, Roskill, *Man of Secrets*, i. 391.

[275] C. P. Scott Diary, 27 June 1917, C. P. Scott Papers, Box 134.

Prime Minister and almost all the political élite were stunned by Northcliffe's grandstanding and his breach of convention. However, Lloyd George did not proceed as if there had been an irreparable rupture between himself and the press lord. Indeed, the mechanism to secure Northcliffe's elevation by the king to the rank of Viscount, which Lloyd George had set in train just before the Air Ministry affair broke, was not stopped. The honour was announced only a week later. In addition, the post of Air Minister was then offered to Lord Rothermere. There was much truth in the observation of Colonel House, President Wilson's emissary, who was in constant touch with both men at this time, that 'He [Lloyd George] evidently is afraid of him and, unfortunately Northcliffe knows it'.[276]

From the time of the Air Ministry affair, the two men traded insults when outside of each other's hearing. Lloyd George was eventually to be nicknamed the 'dishevelled conjurer' by Northcliffe.[277] The Prime Minister, in his turn, indulged constantly in ridicule of 'the grasshopper'. He was not alone. In early 1918 leading Tories, led by Carson and Chamberlain, also attacked Northcliffe's pretensions to political power. Even fellow press barons like Lord Burnham warned against Northcliffe's 'fanatical belief in a newspaper government'.[278] Asquithian Liberals, of course, had long portrayed Northcliffe as a 'curse to this country'.[279] Now, in spite of all Northcliffe's reputed services to the 'patriotic' cause, the Conservative élite also was apparently united in denunciation of the monstrous plotter from Printing House Square. The private correspondence of the leading Conservatives was liberally sprinkled with criticism of 'the octopus' of influence worked by the newspaper oligarchies, and the dangers of 'press Government'. Northcliffe, 'the power behind the throne', was depicted as waiting for the premiership itself to fall into his lap 'when the pear is ripe'.[280] It may have been consoling for Lloyd George to know that the Conservative chiefs disliked Northcliffe as much as he did. But the Prime Minister, as has been seen, was more politically vulnerable than they. Accordingly, just months after the Air Ministry affair he sought for a second time to draw Northcliffe into government work, offering him the post of Director of Propaganda in Enemy Countries in February 1918. Northcliffe accepted. It was a move that shocked many in the political élite.[281] But the explanation is clear. Lloyd George's desire to neutralize Northcliffe, if he could, apparently overrode his personal detestation of the 'Chief'.

---

[276] This incident is described in detail in Stanley Morrison, 'Personality and Diplomacy in Anglo-American Relations, 1917', in R. Pares and A. J. P. Taylor (eds), *Essays Presented to Sir Lewis Namier* (London, 1956), 461–70. [277] Wrench, *Dawson*, 161.

[278] Lord Burnham to Lord Salisbury, 10 Feb. 1918, Burnham Papers, HLWL/7, no. 2.

[279] R. B. Haldane to H. W. Massingham, 11 Aug. 1915, Massingham Papers, MC 41/98/34.

[280] e.g. Lord Crawford Diary, 17 and 24 Nov. 1917, vol. xxxi, Crawford Papers; Strachey to John Buchan, 18 Dec. 1917, Strachey Papers, S/3/2/44; Strachey to Maurice Bonham Carter, 22 Jan. 1918, St Loe Strachey Papers, S/18/5/3; Lord Esher to Burnham, 28 Jan. 1918, Burnham Papers, HLWL/1, no. 3; Walter Long to George Cave, 4 Aug. 1918, Milner to Cave, 25 July 1918, Carson to Cave, 26 July 1918, Cave Papers, BL Add MS 62497 (provisional catalogue number).

[281] A. Chamberlain to Curzon, 21 Feb. 1918, Curzon Papers, MS EUR F 112/121.

Among Northcliffe's staff at *The Times* there was little certainty of support for the Prime Minister. The chief editor, Geoffrey Dawson, was, as noted above, a distinguished Milnerite, in fact a former Private Secretary to Milner. Lloyd George expressed some confidence in 1917 that he could control Dawson through Milner.[282] During 1917–18 Lloyd George tried to get close to Dawson, dining periodically with him and his Round Table friends.[283] But no special relationship developed. While Dawson himself found Northcliffe querulous and impulsive, he remained loyal to him during the war years. Moreover, there was no doubting Dawson's own invariable high Tory political outlook and his extensive connections with the Right. Similarly, other leading journalists on *The Times*, including those in the important foreign department, were right-wing Conservative patriots. The most important journalist after Dawson was the redoubtable Henry Wickham Steed, chief foreign correspondent. Steed replaced Dawson as editor in February 1919. His first loyalty was to a new settlement in Eastern Europe, that is, to the enlargement of Allied war aims in order to include support for the national struggles of the subject peoples of the Austro-Hungarian Empire. Steed was a leader in the 'New Europe' circle of publicists, the pressure group founded by R. Seton-Watson and Bernard Pares at the School of Slavonic Studies, King's College, London. Steed was naturally an ardent enemy of all who flirted with the idea of a separate peace with Austria. Lloyd George was among the guilty.[284]

Beyond the Harmsworth press, there were other powerful Conservative voices from whom Lloyd George could expect nothing but criticism. The most staid Conservative daily, the *Morning Post*, was owned, and very much controlled, by Countess Lillias Bathurst of Cirencester.[285] Her views were those of a reactionary Conservative of the die-hard school. She campaigned ardently for conscription, fiscal reform, the expulsion of aliens, and against Home Rule for Ireland and the extension of the suffrage.[286] The National Party was the beneficiary of her lavish sponsorship in 1917–18.[287] Her doughty editor, 'Taffy' Gwynne, was slavishly loyal to his proprietor: 'We are in entire agreement about all the things that really count' he wrote to Lady Bathurst in November 1918.[288] Their views were indeed in the closest harmony. From his editorial columns came an endless flow of nationalist extremism. Rudyard Kipling, his close personal friend, was

---

[282] Lord Beaverbrook, *Men and Power, 1917–1918* (London, 1956), 172.

[283] See Wrench, *Dawson*, chs. 13 and 14.

[284] H. Wickham Steed, *Through Thirty Years* (London, 1924), 2 vols. Steed's passion for Allied commitment to the subject peoples of south and east Europe was attributed in Foreign Office gossip to the fact that Steed's live-in companion of fifteen years was one Clémence Rose, a 'southern Slav of Austria' (Rennell Rodd to Balfour, 11 Nov. 1918, Rodd Papers, 11).

[285] The best study of the views of the *Morning Post* in this period is Wilson, *A Study in the History and Politics of the Morning Post 1905–1926*, esp. chs. 4 and 5.

[286] Henry Page Croft to Lady Bathurst, 18 Oct. 1917, Glenesk-Bathurst Papers, 2980.

[287] Henry Page Croft to Lady Bathurst, 9 Mar. 1918, Glenesk-Bathurst Papers, 2979.

[288] Gwynne to Lady Bathurst, 12 Nov. 1918, and see Gwynne to Lady Bathurst, 16 July 1919, Glenesk-Bathurst Papers, 2475 and 2484.

constantly giving him tips to assist the paper in hounding 'unpatriotic' Liberals, Quakers, pacifists, and defeatists.[289] Both men gave thanks to the war for uniting the nation and deflecting the forces of reform. As an exultant Kipling told Gwynne in the first week of the war, 'I always said the Kaiser was our best friend'.[290] In a real sense the hatred of Prussianism evident in the Morning Post was a hatred fanned by family resemblance. For example, Robert Cecil was moved to write to Gwynne protesting at one editorial which had suggested that Christian sentiment was fine for women and weaklings but inappropriate for men in time of war: 'Is it that Bernhardi has his disciples in this country too?' quizzed Cecil.[291] The barb did nothing to deflect Gwynne. He continued to search for an authoritarian figure, even a military dictator, to take the nation by the throat. 'There are times when one feels that a military dictatorship is the only thing for England', wrote Gwynne in 1916.[292]

For all his extremism, Gwynne was by no means an isolated figure. Gwynne was in close touch with a host of right-wing figures within and beyond the Conservative Party. Sir Edward Carson, Lord Derby, Lord Esher, and Viscount Duncannon were all confidants. He had close friends in the military élite also, especially General Rawlinson, and was working his way into the trust of the new CIGS, Sir Henry Wilson in, 1918. 'I am always for the soldier against the politician', Gwynne assured Wilson in September 1918.[293] Gwynne and his famous military correspondent, Colonel Repington, who had defected from The Times in early 1918, cultivated the closest relationships with disgruntled members of the military élite, men such as the dismissed CIGS, Sir William Robertson, whose hatred of Lloyd George was intense.[294] The Morning Post well merited its reputation as the unforgiving critic of the Coalition politicians who had acquiesced in the leadership of Lloyd George.[295] In short, no matter how victorious in war, Lloyd George could look forward to no shift of editorial opinion in his favour here.

Lloyd George's enemies among the bawling ultra-patriots had other outlets beyond the Morning Post. Leo Maxse, owner and editor of the National Review, was a particularly well-connected Germanophobe and tariff reformer of the Edwardian 'Radical Right'. He had a wide circle of friends in the press, in pol-

---

[289] e.g. Kipling to Gwynne, 19 Feb. 1916, on Haldane; Kipling to Gwynne undated, on aliens in the Royal Society; Kipling to Gwynne, 19 July 1918, on Germans that ought be interned: Kipling Papers, Gwynne correspondence, 125, 128, and 141.

[290] Kipling to Gwynne, 7 Aug. 1914, Kipling Papers, 106.

[291] Cecil to Gwynne, 2 Jan. 1915, Gwynne Papers, 17.

[292] Gwynne to Lady Bathurst, 26 June 1916, in Wilson, Rasp of War, 182.

[293] Gwynne to Wilson, 20 Aug. 1918, Wilson to Gwynne, 23 Aug. 1918, and Gwynne to Wilson, 5 Sept. 1918, Gwynne Papers (Imperial War Museum), HAG 35, nos. 33, 34, 35.

[294] McEwen, ' "Brass-Hats" and the British Press', 62.

[295] The paper's extremism irritated many Conservatives in the government; Lord Crawford lamented that it was 'so strident', and Lord Stanhope complained that 'it never misses an opportunity for destructive criticism of the Government' (Lord Crawford Diary, 1 Mar. 1918, vol. xxxi, Crawford Papers); Stanhope to Countess Stanhope, 4 Apr. 1918, Stanhope Papers, C. 578/18.

itics, and in the military (his brother Ivor Maxse was a general). Significantly, his journalism targeted the effete Conservative 'Mandarins' as much as the 'sentimentalism' of Cobdenite Liberals and 'unpatriotic' socialists. Lloyd George had been a special enemy for some years. Maxse had worked hard in an effort to destroy the Liberal Chancellor at the time of the Marconi affair, doing his own detective work and appearing as a witness at the House of Commons Select Committee inquiring into the affair in 1913.[296] Ably supporting the *National Review* was the *Globe*, the property of the irrepressible Dudley Docker, a wealthy businessman, passionate anti-German, and, as shall be seen, an 'economic warrior'.[297] Docker appointed Maxse an editorial consultant to the *Globe* in 1917, thus giving Maxse a valuable second platform from which to proselytize. Not all the Conservative journals were as strident. The *Spectator*, as the leading free trade Tory journal, owned and edited by John St Loe Strachey, had a reputation for rather more moderate Conservative opinions. Lloyd George, however, claimed not to read the *Spectator* often because Strachey was a personal foe.[298] Indeed, the major editors on the Right were all on friendly terms. Maxse declared himself to be engaged in a common struggle as a comrade-in-arms with Lady Bathurst and Gwynne.[299] Strachey described Maxse in 1919 'as one of my oldest and indeed, dearest friends'.[300] Maxse was a lawn tennis partner with Geoffrey Dawson.[301] These firebrands of the Right could not, therefore, be written off as a mere handful of risible crackpots. Lloyd George did monitor carefully their reactions to his speeches in late 1918.[302]

Lloyd George could expect some support from the more moderate Conservative proprietors and editors. Chief among these was Harry Lawson, Lord Burnham from 1916, owner of the *Daily Telegraph*. Burnham was inclined to see merit in Lloyd George's leadership. Lloyd George in turn invited Burnham to Number 10 to share the occasional breakfast with his family. On one occasion he flattered Burnham with the remark that the *Daily Telegraph* had been 'the only sane journal throughout'.[303] Burnham's support for Lloyd George's project of a united military command (the Supreme War Council) in late 1917 was especially appreciated by Lloyd George.[304] Burnham's intense anti-socialism

---

[296] On Maxse's journalistic career before 1914 see John A. Hutcheson, *Leopold Maxse and the National Review, 1893–1914* (New York, 1989).

[297] Richard Davenport-Hines, *Dudley Docker: The Life and Times of a Trade Warrior* (Cambridge, 1984).

[298] Lord Riddell's War Diary, 1 Oct. 1916, 24 Nov. 1917, and 5 Jan. 1918, 212, 292, and 305.

[299] Leo Maxse to Lady Bathurst, 5 June 1918, Bathurst-Glenesk Papers, 3503.

[300] Strachey to Bell, 7 Feb. 1919, Strachey Papers, S/26/4/15a.

[301] G. Dawson to Maxse, 28 Oct. 1918, Maxse Papers, vol. 475; Wrench, *Dawson*, 47.

[302] e.g. see C. P. Scott Diary, 18 Sept. 1918, C. P. Scott Papers, Box 134. Lloyd George complained of the right-wing newspapers' reactions to a speech in which he had spoken of German membership of a League of Nations and warned against a peace dictated by Allied 'chauvinists'. The speech is reported in *The Times*, 13 Sept. 1918.

[303] Lord Burnham, *Peterborough Court: The Story of the Daily Telegraph* (London, 1955), 166; and 'Notes of a Conversation with Lloyd George', 13 July 1917, Burnham Papers, HLWL/10, no. 9.

[304] Lloyd George to Burnham, 15 Nov. 1917, Burnham Papers, HLWL/5, no. 2.

was also a factor in the relationship. In 1918 Burnham sought to use his influence with the Prime Minister to get action against the 'sedition and treason' which he warned were being preached openly by the Labour Party.[305]

The famous Max Aitken, Lord Beaverbrook, originally a Canadian financial entrepreneur and then a controversial Conservative MP after 1910, emerged as a major force in the press during the war. He gained control of the *Daily Express* through his investments and his close friendship with the editor R. D. Blumenfeld.[306] Beaverbrook, being an intimate of Bonar Law, was a loyal friend of the Coalition. But Beaverbrook's use to Lloyd George was limited by the fact that he was intensely disliked by the traditional élite in the Conservative Party— he was one of the 'Canadian sharks who has crossed the ocean to help eat us up' as Lord Crawford described him.[307] The editor and part-owner of the *Daily Express*, R. D. Blumenfeld, was equally significant in the formulation of the paper's position. He too was a loyal Coalitionist. His political priorities, however, may be gauged from his position on the Executive Committee of the Anti-Socialist Union of Great Britain.[308]

Support for the Coalition came in general from the remaining Tory papers of note. Waldorf Astor, owner of the *Observer*, was, as noted above, a keen Round Table man and a member of Lloyd George's Secretariat. The editor of the *Observer* was the supremely influential J. L. Garvin.[309] Doubtless Lloyd George gained great satisfaction from Garvin's support for the Coalition. He was summoned to dine at Number 10.[310] But, in spite of their apparently close friendship, Lloyd George needed no especially long memory to recall the great preoccupations of Garvin's journalism in the Edwardian period—his Germanophobic extremism at the time of the 'naval scare' of 1909, his support for conscription and tariff reform, and his trenchant opposition to the budget and Parliament Act.[311] Once again, here was support from an Edwardian reactionary that was probably good for the duration of the war, but doubtful beyond it. The same could be said of the remaining less prestigious Conservative organs. The *Standard* was owned by the Conservative MP, Davison Dalziel, who supported the Coalition. W. E. Berry, a loyal Conservative, was owner of the *Sunday Times*. Sir Edward Hulton was the owner of the big-selling Tory papers the *Evening Standard*, *Daily Sketch*, and the new *Illustrated Sunday Herald*.

In contrast, among the Liberal proprietors and editors, Lloyd George could discern few friendly faces. Only one name of great political weight in the Liberal

---

[305] Burnham to Lloyd George, 11 Feb. 1918, Burnham Papers, HLWL/5, no. 3.

[306] A. J. P. Taylor, *Beaverbrook* (Harmondsworth, 1974), 141–2.

[307] Lord Crawford Diary, 6 Aug. 1918, vol. xxxii, Crawford Papers.

[308] List of Executive Committee Members and Objects of the Anti-Socialist Union of Great Britain, 1915, copy in Wilfred Ashley Papers, BR 81/16.

[309] See A. M. Gollin, *The Observer and J. L. Garvin, 1908–1914: A Study in a Great Editorship* (London, 1960).

[310] *Riddell's War Diary*, 5 Jan. 1918, 304.

[311] See especially Morris, *The Scaremongers*, ch. 15.

Party stood out, C. P. Scott, a former Liberal MP and an essentially humane man of a Radical-leaning Liberalism. In Liberal circles, Lloyd George's salvation was the continuing if cautious support which he received from Scott at the editorial desk of the *Manchester Guardian*. Scott was constantly summoned to Lloyd George's breakfast table, and while suspicious of his opportunism and occasionally critical, he never ceased to hope in him.[312] Scott was frequently flattered with declarations that the *Manchester Guardian* was the only paper the Prime Minister cared about. Smuts confirmed this, telling Scott, 'when you attack him he squirms'.[313]

Of the other Liberal proprietors, the man who surrendered most to Lloyd George's charm was the more free-wheeling and worldly Sir George Riddell.[314] The *News of the World*, the raciest of the Coalition Liberal papers, made Riddell a wealthy man. He became a ubiquitous member of the Prime Minister's wartime entourage, renting houses for him to enjoy on his weekends and holidays, and absorbing prestige from the relationship in return. In 1918 his baronetcy arrived. No political danger for the Prime Minister could be found lurking in the pages of the *News of the World*, but little serious politics either. A third Coalition supporter was Sir Henry Dalziel, another Liberal MP, owner of the *Reynold's News*, and an early convert to Lloyd George's interest.[315] Dalziel had extended his press holdings in 1917, acquiring the formerly Conservative, small-circulation *Pall Mall Gazette*. Most spectacular of all the developments in the wartime Liberal press came in early October 1918: with the assistance of Sir Henry Dalziel, the Prime Minister himself purchased the Liberal *Daily Chronicle*. This enabled him to dump instantly the editor, Robert Donald, a former ally of the Prime Minister who had turned against him during 1918 and had committed the grievous sin of hiring General Maurice as military correspondent. After six months of trying to secure a newspaper for himself, Lloyd George at last had the unreserved support of one major Liberal paper, a significant coup now that planning for a general election was well advanced.[316]

Outside this circle of Liberal friends lay enemies and sworn enemies of the Prime Minister. The *Westminster Gazette*, the traditional Liberal Party in-house journal, was owned by a group of wealthy Liberal MPs, including Lord Cowdray and Sir Alfred Mond. Lord Cowdray, the key shareholder, had been humiliated by the Air Ministry fiasco described above. This scuppered an attempt by Lloyd George to purchase the paper in late 1917, with Cowdray vengefully spurning the Prime Minister's approach. In the aftermath of the affair, the editor of the

---

[312] The most judicious review of the relationship is the Introduction to Trevor Wilson, *The Political Diaries of C. P. Scott, 1911–1928* (London, 1970).

[313] C. P. Scott Political Diary, 22 Feb. and 5 July 1919, C. P. Scott Papers, Box 134.

[314] On the relationship, see the introduction to J. M. McEwen (ed.), *The Riddell Diaries, 1908–1923* (London, 1986), 1–18.

[315] *Lord Riddell's War Diary*, 24 Mar. 1916, 167.

[316] J. M. McEwen, 'Lloyd George's Acquisition of the *Daily Chronicle* in 1918', *Journal of British Studies*, 22/1 (1983), 127–44.

Westminster Gazette, J. A. Spender, an earnest Asquithian with much status in the Liberal Party, enjoyed an even greater freedom to turn his guns on the Prime Minister.[317] The other big Liberal daily, the *Daily News*, owned by the Cadbury family, had begun to thrive during the war, boasting a circulation of one million by 1917. Edited by the famous progressive journalist A. G. Gardiner, the *Daily News* maintained a proud Radicalism. Evangelically Wilsonian during the war, it remained fundamentally hostile to the 'knock-out blow' ideals of the Lloyd George Coalition.[318] To its left lay the Rowntree family's weekly, the *Nation*, edited by H. W. Massingham, the most unflinchingly Radical of the Liberal journalists. Massingham campaigned ceaselessly for a negotiated peace from December 1916 and, for his pains, received in March 1917 a government order suppressing the export of the *Nation* to overseas subscribers. Lloyd George defended the War Office's decision on suppression on the grounds that the *Nation*'s pages gave comfort to the enemy.[319] So hostile to Lloyd George's government were the Radical and Liberal editors by early 1918 that some even swallowed their instinctive dislike of the military élite and linked up with the clique of disgruntled brass hats, led by Robertson, in an alliance of convenience to embarrass Lloyd George.[320] No wonder that it was the dogged Radical press in particular that made Lloyd George's bile stir. Massingham he had dismissed as a 'shrieking shrew' in 1917.[321]

In sum, the Prime Minister's often unhappy and sometimes shabby relations with the press served to highlight once again the underlying realities of his political vulnerability. His feverish efforts to build press support were attempts to defy these realities. On the extremities (by no means the impotent fringes) of the big political power blocs were to be found his most implacable enemies: as a former Radical, he was hated by the Radical and the socialist press as a heresiarch; conversely, as a former Radical, he was hated also by the ultra-patriotic right-wing press as a dangerous usurper of the national leadership. As he had broken the rules, rumours of his propensity for treachery were constantly carried in the political wind into the heartland of both Liberal and Conservative Parties from the volatile extremes. Towards the centre lay safety, but not much. The moderate and serious Liberal papers, especially those party papers identifying with the fallen leader Asquith, distrusted Lloyd George in varying degrees. Only the *Manchester Guardian* was friendly, but it was clear that Scott expected Lloyd

---

[317] This episode is examined in Trevor Wilson, *The Downfall of the Liberal Party, 1914–1935* (London, 1966), 113–17.

[318] Circulation of a million is claimed in George Cadbury to Gardiner, 17 Apr. 1917 and 20 Apr. 1918, A. G. Gardiner Papers, 1/8. On Gardiner's Wilsonianism and entrenched opposition to Lloyd George see S. Koss, *Fleet Street Radical: A. G. Gardiner and the 'Daily News'* (London, 1973), chs. 8 and 9.

[319] See Alfred F. Havighurst, *Radical Journalist: H. W. Massingham, 1860–1924* (Cambridge, 1974), ch. 9. On the suppression of the *Nation*, see the debate in *Parliamentary Debates*, 5th ser., vol. xcii, 1598–1613 (17 Apr. 1917).

[320] McEwen, ' "Brass-Hats" and the British Press', 60.

[321] *Riddell's War Diary*, 24 Nov. 1917, 292.

George to deliver a peace of reconciliation and progressive reforms at home. The more moderate Conservative papers supported the Prime Minister too, but did so because he was the leader of a Coalition outfitted for war. Tory opinion-makers in the Conservative 'middle ground', men like Beaverbrook, Blumenfeld, Burnham, Astor, and Garvin, were the most useful contacts for Lloyd George, but their support set limits upon him too. For it was surely unlikely that these men would back him for long if he failed to deliver the 'dictated peace' which the Coalition Conservative press always insisted upon. Worst of all from Lloyd George's viewpoint, the most powerful Conservative press baron, Lord Northcliffe, had refused to be seduced into his circle. He had proved utterly unreliable to the Prime Minister and had embarrassed him in Conservative ranks.

It is scarcely surprising, therefore, that Lloyd George took such pains to flatter and shower with titles the 'newspaper warriors' of his day.[322] It was the behaviour of a Prime Minister aware of the danger of his becoming an expendable political captive some time after victory. Again, these 'Things That Matter' were to prey on the mind of the Prime Minister throughout the peacemaking.

The 'economic warriors': pressures on the Lloyd George government for a victory of economic aggrandizement

Domestic pressures upon Lloyd George from the 'economic warriors' also increased during his wartime premiership, and intensified especially in anticipation of victory during 1918. Such pressures were not new. From the first months of the war, government and some businessmen alike had asserted the need for British industry and commerce to move ruthlessly and imaginatively to 'capture' all former German markets. By 1916, as the blockade against Germany grew steadily more effective, arguments were raised in favour of a harsh and indefinite 'economic war' even beyond the cessation of military action, a war designed to crush German economic potential and to assist British firms to supplant their German rivals wherever possible.[323] An important instalment of protection had been granted in 1915 when the McKenna Duties were introduced on luxury imports at a rate of 33 per cent. New Empire-oriented business lobby groups, many linked to the old Tariff Reform League, pleaded with the government to go further, and to seize the opportunity presented by the flood-tide of Empire patriotism to create an exclusive imperial trade bloc, that is, a bloc which would exclude all German enterprise after the war. In the midst of anti-German press hysteria, the 'merchant state' was mobilizing. Powerful advocates of tariff reform,

---

[322] In the Honours List for Apr. 1919, Rothermere and Burnham were made Viscounts, and Davison Dalziel and Sir Edward Hulton were made Baronets; *The Times*, 29 Apr. 1919. Although promised a peerage, Hulton had to wait until 1921 following complaints from the Palace over the number of honours flowing to journalists and proprietors of the press; see Beaverbrook, *Men and Power, 1917–1918* (London, 1956), 245.

[323] John McDermott, 'Total War and the Merchant State: Aspects of British Economic Warfare against Germany, 1914–16', *Canadian Journal of History*, 21 (Apr. 1986), 61–76.

Halford Mackinder and W. A. S. Hewins most notably, were active among the Conservative MPs.[324] Hewins, Under-Secretary to Walter Long at the Colonial Office, President of the Tariff Commission, and an influential presence in the Unionist Business Committee, was especially important in promoting the protectionist cause. As Kipling had advised Gwynne in early 1916, the best hope for winning the protectionist programme was to promote hatred of Germany, for this hatred was 'the golden bridge' over which many former free traders might come over to tariff reform.[325]

Kipling's 'golden bridge' was soon thronged by business pressure groups. Anti-German hysteria had affected business circles as much as any other during the war. The British Manufacturers' Association (BMA), National Union of Manufacturers (NUM), British Empire Producers' Organization (BEPO), and British Imperial Council of Commerce (BICC) all pressed for tariff barriers to protect the Empire. Agitation for protection under the guise of anti-Germanism made much headway in the Conservative press and in the business community generally during the war years.[326] At the annual conferences of various business associations, resolutions expressing horror at any resumption of trade with Germany after the war, and pleading for protection, were passed easily. There was to be protection against 'dumping', protection for 'key industries', and protection against 'German economic penetration', the malevolence of which was taken for granted.[327]

The most powerful business pressure group, the Federation of British Industry (FBI), was founded in July 1916. Dudley Docker was the vital organizing spirit and first President of the new body. Formally, the FBI was neutral on the tariff issue itself, Docker having decided to play down this divisive point, at least to begin with, in order to gain the support of as many employer organizations as possible. The tactic worked, with some 400 employer groups enrolling in the FBI by mid-1917.[328] The FBI leadership was not shy for very long, however, in recommending economic protection, at the very least against Germany: from the

---

[324] See Brian W. Blouet, 'The Political Career of Sir Halford Mackinder', *Political Geography Quarterly*, 6/4 (1987), 355–67, and W. A. S. Hewins, *Apologia of an Imperialist: Forty Years of Empire Policy* (London, 1929), 2 vols.

[325] Kipling to Gwynne, 26 Feb. 1916, Kipling Papers.

[326] On the growth of support within the business lobby for tariff reform under the patriotic colours of anti-Germanism see Peter Cline, 'Winding Down the War Economy: British Plans for Peacetime Recovery, 1916–19', in Burk (ed.), *War and the State*, 157–181; A. J. Marrison, 'Businessmen, Industries and Tariff Reform in Great Britain, 1903–1930', *Business History*, 25/2 (1983), esp. 164–5; Forrest Capie, 'The Pressure for Tariff Protection in Britain, 1917–31', *Journal of European Economic History*, 9/2 (1980), esp. 432–3; Robert E. Bunselmeyer, *The Cost of the War, 1914–1919: British Economic War Aims and the Origins of Reparations* (Hamden, Conn., 1975), ch. 2.

[327] e.g. British Imperial Council of Commerce, *Report of Proceedings of the First Annual Meeting of the British Imperial Council of Commerce, 2 June 1915*, British Imperial Council of Commerce Papers,18283/1.

[328] On the foundation of the FBI see John Turner, 'The Politics of "Organised Business" in the First World War', in his *Businessmen and Politics* (London, 1984), and Davenport-Hines, *Dudley Docker*, ch. 6.

beginning of 1917 the FBI addressed urgent pleas to the Prime Minister on the matter of the future threats posed to British industry from German industrial competition. They pressed upon him the need for advanced planning in order to create an imperial trade bloc that could counter the anticipated German economic domination of Central Europe in the post-war years.[329] Lloyd George could not simply ignore these new employer groups.[330] Indeed, he had a genuine respect for the viewpoint of business and included several 'men of push and go' from the business community in his government, including Eric Geddes, Viscount Rhondda, and Lord Weir. As John Turner observes, in Lloyd George's governments, the 'over-riding concern was to make businessmen feel themselves to be part of government'.[331]

Among the prominent 'economic warriors', a new figure of importance had emerged during 1916, the Welsh-born Australian Prime Minister, William Morris Hughes.[332] The pugnacious Billy Hughes visited Britain in March 1916. He was invited to attend the Cabinet, and was soon mixing with those energetic patriots dissatisfied with Asquith's leadership. He expressed admiration for Lloyd George, at first. But Hughes's own fixations with the campaign for retention of the former German colonies and for protection against German economic villainy in the future led him to seek more like-minded company.[333] He was soon in close contact with leading Conservatives, especially Walter Long, the Colonial Secretary, and Hewins. Lord Milner was another government figure interested in Hughes. On Milner's suggestion, Hughes appeared as the chief speaker at a major public meeting to promote Milner's new British Workers' National League in May 1916.[334] The Northcliffe press exulted over the presence in England of a blunt-speaking workingman's leader, a 'fight to the finish' man who was striving to put some vigour into the Empire's war effort. Northcliffe himself assisted Hughes in arrangements for a publicity tour of England and Wales.[335]

The promotion of Hughes soon paid handsome dividends to the 'economic warriors'. As a result of machinations set in train by Hewins and Northcliffe,

[329] Vincent Caillard to Nugent, 13 Jan. 1917, Federation of British Industry Archive, MSS 200/F/3/DI/2/2.

[330] e.g. in Feb. 1917, in a simple gesture, Lloyd George allowed his name to go forward as an Honorary Vice-President of the British Imperial Council of Commerce; British Imperial Council of Commerce, Executive Council Committee Minutes, 22 Feb. 1917, British Imperial Council of Commerce Papers,18283/1.

[331] John Turner, ' "Experts" and Interests: David Lloyd George and the Dilemmas of the Expanding State, 1906–19', in Roy MacLeod (ed.), *Government and Expertise: Specialists, Administrators and Professionals, 1860–1919* (Cambridge, 1988), 214.

[332] The definitive biography is L. F. Fitzhardinge, *William Morris Hughes: A Political Biography.* i. *That Fiery Particle* (Sydney, 1964), and ii. *The Little Digger* (1979). This can be supplemented by W. J. Hudson, *Billy Hughes in Paris: The Birth of Australian Diplomacy* (Sydney, 1978), and Peter Spartalis, *The Diplomatic Battles of Billy Hughes* (Sydney, 1983).

[333] W. R. Louis, 'Australia and the German Colonies in the Pacific, 1914–1919', *Journal of Modern History*, 38/4 (1966), 407–21.

[334] Stubbs, 'Lord Milner and Patriotic Labour', 730.

[335] Malcolm Shepherd, Secretary to the Prime Minister's Department, typescript memoirs, Australian Archives, A 1632/1.

Asquith came under great pressure to demonstrate his confidence in Hughes. At length, Asquith meekly appointed him as a British representative to the Allied Economic Conference held in Paris in June 1916.[336] In the privacy of family correspondence Raymond Asquith denounced this as akin to appointing Charlie Chaplin.[337] But Hughes soon proved his seriousness. The French-inspired economic summit provided a big stage upon which Hughes could strut. In his speech to the conference he called for sweeping bans on post-war German commerce. The other members of the British delegation, Bonar Law, Lord Crewe, and George Foster, eventually agreed to strengthen the original British proposals.[338] The final resolutions of the conference, the Paris Resolutions as they were called, were necessarily written in imprecise terms, but in tone they owed much to Hughes. It was clear that the Entente nations were contemplating a post-war trade bloc and a prohibition on all trade with Germany for an indefinite period in order that the Entente nations might look first to their own economic recovery. The commitments enshrined in the Paris Resolutions were much cherished by the 'economic warriors', and Hughes was revered as a hero.

These pressures upon the British government, however, did not lead to any major shift in economic policy sufficient to satisfy the protectionist lobby. But there were gestures. In July 1916 Asquith created the Committee on Industry and Trade after the War, under the leadership of Lord Balfour of Burleigh, a Unionist Free Trader, to consider a response to the Paris Resolutions. By early 1917 it became clear that the tariff reformers in the committee, led by Hewins and Lord Faringdon, were guiding the majority of the committee towards post-war protection, and an interim report in February came down in favour of imperial preference. Concessions from the new Lloyd George government followed during 1917. A Department of Overseas Trade, with the tariff reformer Arthur Steel-Maitland at the helm, and a British Trade Corporation, were established with the intention of boosting British trade after the war. In addition, an Economic Offensive Committee under Carson was set up by the War Cabinet in August 1917 in order to tighten the screws on Germany. However, the government appeared to be reluctant to be tied down in advance to the details of any general measure of post-war protection. Economic experts in the various government departments advising the War Cabinet still favoured the free trade position. Thus, in April 1917, the Milner Committee, set up by the War Cabinet to review economic war aims, cast doubt on the wisdom of the Paris Resolutions, preferring the moderate advice of the Board of Trade. The government, it

---

[336] On the Paris Economic Conference and 'anti-German economics', see Marc Trachtenberg, ' "A new Economic Order": Etienne Clémentel and French Economic Diplomacy during the First World War', *French Historical Studies*, 10/2 (1977), 315–41, and Bunselmeyer, *The Cost of the War*, chs. 2 and 3.

[337] Raymond to Katherine Asquith, 7 Apr. 1916, in John Jollife (ed.), *Raymond Asquith: Life and Letters* (London, 1987), 255.

[338] Spartalis, *Diplomatic Battles of Billy Hughes*, 28–34, and Fitzhardinge, *William Morris Hughes*, i. 121–37.

seemed, was willing to make threats of an economic 'war after the war' against Germany. But government speakers often qualified these threats by noting that economic war would only be pursued in the unlikely event of an eventual compromise peace with an *un*beaten Germany.[339] Nevertheless, a series of broad commitments to the ideal of imperial preference were made at the Imperial War Cabinet in April 1917. Admittedly, the key resolutions concerning the 'safeguarding [of] Imperial resources' were vague, but they promoted the vision of an increasingly self-sufficient Empire. At the very least, the government had made a commitment to restrict the supply of raw materials to Germany 'for a period after the war'. Ardent campaigners for tariff reform like Hewins were elated: a first instalment of a great anti-German economic programme had been specified at last as official Imperial policy.[340]

But this was by no means total victory. Political agitation in favour of the full programme of the 'economic warriors' continued. New pro-imperial pressure groups continued to press for the achievement of virtual imperial autarky in the post-war era. Most notable amongst these was the British Commonwealth Union (BCU) founded in December 1916. The BCU was a gathering of tariff reform enthusiasts backed by many of the same businessmen who had launched the FBI.[341] Leading lights included Vincent Caillard, of Vickers Ltd., Richard Vassar-Smith, of Lloyd's Bank, Patrick Hannon, the first secretary of the BCU, and Sir William Bull, a leading London Conservative MP. Unlike the FBI, the new BCU openly preached the full tariff reform programme and a total anti-German economic boycott and campaigned steadily to win the more reluctant members of the FBI over to this position. However, while harmonious relations were established with the FBI, the powerful Lancashire textile manufacturers in the FBI prevented a formal adhesion to tariff reform on the part of the FBI during the war. Similarly, the British Empire Union (BEU), founded in 1915, promoted a concoction of extreme anti-Germanism and anti-socialism for true 'British race-patriots'. The BEU was also extremely well connected. Numbered among its Vice-Presidents were twenty-five peers. Lord and Lady Bathurst, Leo Maxse, Ellis Powell, editor of the *Financial News*, Lord Beresford, the naval agitator, Carson, Derby, and William Joynson-Hicks, a prominent Conservative MP, were all linked to the BEU. Billy Hughes was a Patron. The full 'economic warrior' position was eventually accepted by the BEU in July 1918, when its economic programme was announced demanding a total post-war boycott of German trade and investment for six years after peace. Never again, warned the BEU,

---

[339] On the pressures upon government over protection, the appointment of the Balfour of Burleigh Committee, and the continuing ambivalence of government policy on protection see Turner, *British Politics and the Great War*, 336–53, and V. H. Rothwell, *British War Aims and Peace Diplomacy, 1914–1919* (Oxford, 1971), 268–81.

[340] Hewins, *Apologia of an Imperialist*, ii. 141–3.

[341] John Turner, 'The British Commonwealth Union and the General Election of 1918', *English Historical Review*, 93 (July 1978), 528–59.

should the nefarious figure of the German commercial agent be free to stalk over the lands of the British Empire.[342] The National Party, founded in August 1917 by the rebel Conservative MP Brigadier General Henry Page Croft, gave the 'economic warrior' group a vociferous presence inside the parliament. Launched in response to the 'labour unrest' of the Leeds Convention in June, the new party preached tariff reform, economic boycott, conscription for Ireland, the generals' right to wage war without interference from politicians, and the inculcation of a racially conscious patriotism among the British people in order to counter working-class unrest. Anti-Semitism, anti-socialism, and hostility towards aliens underpinned the rhetoric— a similar bundle of ideas to that promoted by the Fatherland Party, formed in Germany in the same month.[343] Not surprisingly, the National Party had close connections with all the 'economic warrior' pressure groups, the BCU, BEU, BWL, the Unionist Business Committee, and the Tariff Reform League. Although only seven MPs and seventeen members of the Lords actually joined the new party, its presence as a breakaway pressure group on the fringes of the Unionist Party served as a warning to the government of the restlessness on the Right. The new party was small, but its opinions attracted much sympathy on the Unionist back bench and, as has been seen, it had some support among personnel at GHQ and in the War Cabinet Secretariat. The party was known to be regarded approvingly by close colleagues of Lord Milner, including F. S. Oliver, and it was treated sympathetically in the press by Leo Maxse, Colvin, Gwynne, and Geoffrey Dawson. As Chris Wrigley has written, the new party was 'significant as a ginger group when taken in conjunction with the more belligerent Unionist backbenchers'.[344]

The agitation in favour of protection continued during 1918, and again it was Billy Hughes who pushed himself forward as a publicity agent for the cause following his return to Britain from Australia in June. Hughes was immediately consorting with the pressure groups organized by the 'economic warriors'. During the summer and autumn of 1918, Hughes spoke at a number of public receptions, always pursuing his protectionist theme, before such sympathetic audiences as the BEU, the BEPO, and the London Chamber of Commerce.[345] His rapport with the men of the Right was remarkable. Indeed, in late 1918 he seemed to go out of his way to curry favour with some of Lloyd George's most unforgiving critics, invit-

[342] Panikos Panayi, 'The British Empire Union in the First World War', *Immigrants and Minorities*, 8 (Mar. 1989), 113–28.

[343] Hans Gatzke, *Germany's Drive to the West: A Study of Germany's Western War Aims during the First World War* (Baltimore, 1966), 206–14.

[344] On the founding of the National Party see Wrigley, ' "In Excess Of Their Patriotism": The National Party and Threats of Subversion', 94, and Rubinstein, 'Henry Page Croft and the National Party, 1917–22'.

[345] Fitzhardinge, *The Little Digger*, 329–30. He could speak with some conviction on trade matters, no doubt, as much of his time in London was occupied as a travelling trade commissioner, seeking British buyers for every conceivable Australian product; see for example the files of telegrams on trade matters, Hughes to Watt, Australian Archives, CP 290/3.

ing people like General Frederick Maurice and Leo Maxse to accompany him on tours of the Australian positions at the front line in France in the autumn of 1918.[346] Hughes's various doings usually made a splash in the press. To ensure triumphal publicity in the English press, Hughes relied upon the efforts of Keith Murdoch, the famous correspondent of the *Melbourne Herald* who enjoyed good relations with Northcliffe and worked as a virtual press officer for Hughes.[347] For example, a special lunch in honour of Hughes was given by Northcliffe at Printing House Square in August. Amery and Long were also very friendly with Hughes, both encouraging him to badger the government, especially on the issue of the Empire retaining the seized German colonies.[348] As a former Labour agitator turned 'patriot', Hughes appealed to the anti-socialists in these circles in particular; he was living proof of the power of patriotism to quell class consciousness.[349] Hughes was soon confirmed as *the* leading 'economic warrior' and his message was noticed in high places: Lord Stamfordham wrote to Ronald Munro-Ferguson, the Australian Governor General, that Hughes was 'perfectly right to insist upon the indispensability of our ending the commercial penetration of Germany which before the war had almost strangled our own position as traders in the Empire'.[350]

As will be seen, only slowly during 1918 did the government move further to appease this noisy lobby. The government reaffirmed British commitment to the Paris Resolutions and held out to the expectant 'economic warriors' the prospect of some protection from resurgent German economic enterprise. The Conservative Party itself continued to keep militant organizations like the BCU, officially at least, at a distance. For example, no seats would be offered to the BCU in the 'coupon election' of December 1918. But, by no means were the 'economic warriors' shut out of Westminster as a result. Some eighteen candidates with BCU connections were elected in December 1918 under various Coalition colours.[351] Even more impressive, in January 1919 the larger FBI rejoiced in the allegiance of forty-two MPs in the new House of Commons.[352] In February 1919, the FBI Executive Council at last decided to establish formal relations with the BCU, 'with whom many members are connected'.[353] In the House of Commons as a whole, the coupon election of 1918 produced a higher proportion of MPs classified as businessmen than ever before—including some 40.8 per cent of the parliamentary Conservative Party.[354]

[346] Hughes to Maurice, Sept. 1918, F. B. Maurice Papers, 3/5/84; Hughes to Maxse, 9 Sept. 1918, Leo Maxse Papers, vol. 475.
[347] See the file of telegrams, Northcliffe to Murdoch, many undated, in Murdoch Papers, NLA MS 2823, Folder 41.
[348] Fitzhardinge, *The Little Digger*, 330–1.
[349] Walter Long to Sir George Younger, 12 Sept. 1918, Long Papers, WRO 746/599.
[350] Stamfordham to Munro-Ferguson, 18 Aug. 1918, Novar Papers, NLA, MS 696/477.
[351] Turner, 'British Commonwealth Union', 543.
[352] FBI Bulletin, 2 Jan. 1919, FBI Papers, MSS 200/F/4/24/2.
[353] FBI Bulletin, 27 Feb. 1919, FBI Papers, MSS 200/F/4/24/2.
[354] The figure compares with 24.8% in 1914; John Turner, 'The Politics of Business', in his *Businessmen and Politics*, 15.

These new economic lobbyists, therefore, must be considered a most significant pressure group acting upon the government in the period of peace-making. Surveying the political future in November 1917, Lloyd George had remarked, 'I shall have to rely upon the business classes to a great extent'.[355] The moment appeared to have arrived. With their press and business connections, and highly placed right-wing Tory friends, the leading 'economic warriors' were formidable arm-twisters. They could not be brushed off as misguided hotheads and economic innocents. Even the egregious Hughes most certainly 'counted' in Lloyd George's eyes as a representative of these men. Here was an 'economic warrior' and an accomplished headline-maker at the table of the Imperial War Cabinet itself. He was 'built like a canary', as Lord Crawford observed, but 'when out for plunder he is invincible'.[356]

Other countervailing forces, undeniably, were at work. In most belligerent nations, the scarifying experience of the long war had eventually enlarged the company of democrats, radicals, and class-conscious socialists. In Britain too, a certain radicalisation of outlook seeped into the consciousness of the mass of ordinary people. Throughout much of Europe, old habits of deference and servility were seen to be dissolving. As Bernard Waites has shown, England too was 'a class society at war' more like than unlike her enemies: her workers also experienced a new sensitivity to deprivations, and a new impatience with the inequalities of class. In Waites's words, much contemporary evidence indicates that English workers 'sloughed off some of the servile manner which had often been part of everyday exchanges with professional men or officials enjoying considerable social command'. In a thousand ways, a new egalitarianism chipped away at the presumptions of 'station in life'.[357]

The 'knock-out blow' government, however, was most certainly not constituted in celebration of this egalitarian temper. Even the Representation of the People Bill, the so-called 'Fourth Reform Act' of February 1918, was as much the product of Conservative hopes in domestic containment as it was the product of a progressive faith in democracy. The men of the British parliamentary oligarchy did not wish to surrender political power to the common people. That the Bill was a concession for a political purpose is obvious. As Lord Crawford confessed in his diary in late 1917, 'I look upon the Bill as the strongest if not the sole bulwark between this country and revolution'. The enfranchisement of women over 30 consoled Crawford. 'I think on the whole it is a good thing', he wrote, 'that women are to be enfranchised, for the larger the new electorate the more likely we are to emerge from the dangerous years of reconstruction with

---

[355] *Riddell's War Diary*, 24 Nov. 1917, 293.

[356] Lord Crawford Diary, 26 Dec. 1918, vol. xxxiv, Crawford Papers.

[357] Bernard Waites, *A Class Society at War: England 1914–1918* (Leamington Spa, 1987), 27, 241, and ch. 7.

credit and prudence. Nothing but the widest suffrage can ensure a constitutional treatment of these problems.'[358]

The grounding faith of the 'knock-out blow' Coalition was not democracy at home but triumph at the front. As has been seen, through the political bargains embodied in the Lloyd George Coalition, belief in peace through victory and victory alone had been applied as the ultimate political test. After Asquith's departure, those with humane, financial, or political doubts about the need for an extended war were tossed aside. Henderson's departure from the War Cabinet in 1917 rammed home the lesson.

At the war's end it was widely appreciated in Conservative ranks that the leadership of the Coalition government by a former Welsh Radical and plausible democrat had sustained national solidarity. Lloyd George was widely regarded as having played a vital role in preventing a national disintegration along class lines, as was to be the immediate fate of the imperialist nations facing defeat. He was owed some loyalty. 'He can be Prime Minister for life if he likes', said Bonar Law after the Coalition electoral victory in December 1918.[359] But it was the hyperbole of the moment. Lloyd George was borne aloft on the up-draughts of war. He was still a political refugee from the great Liberal Party. As the moment of victory approached, government was largely in the hands of men from Conservative political backgrounds who were determined to shutter the traditional élite from the expected rough weather. The mass-circulation newspapers were awash with anti-socialism and jingoism. The campaign of the 'economic warriors' was simmering. Lloyd George had constructed a Coalition of 'bitterenders', a majority of whom were inclined to reaction. His freedom of action in the making of policy towards revolutionary Germany was to be limited by their expectations and his vulnerability.

---

[358] Lord Crawford Diary, 11 Dec. 1917 and 10 Jan. 1918, vol. xxxi, Crawford Papers.
[359] Beaverbrook, *Men and Power*, 325.

2

The Democratization of Germany as a British War Aim, 1914–1918

I wish people would not say England is fighting for democracy. We are not fighting for democracy. We are fighting to beat the Germans.

The views of a woman in 'Society', reported by Arthur Acland to A. G. Gardiner[1]

AT some moments during the First World War, it appeared that the British government was most definitely in favour of a German revolution to topple 'Prussian militarism' and inaugurate democratic rule. In April 1917, for example, Lloyd George told an astonished deputation of right-wing Tories that 'there might be a revolution in Germany which would end the war, the Germans would in that case become our friends, and we should want to make an arrangement with them'.[2] Similarly, in January 1918, Lloyd George told a trade union gathering that Britain would happily recognize 'any government set up by the German people, whatever it is'.[3] In the event, the British government's reaction to the advent of democracy in Germany was far from that predicted by Lloyd George. The Germans were scarcely embraced as 'friends' as a result of the revolution of November 1918. The new German republic was not welcomed but shunned and starved.

To understand the hostile British reaction to the revolution and the foundation of the Weimar Republic, one must first understand the ebb and flow of British opinion on the highly controversial subject of German democratization. For the likelihood of some democratically inspired internal revolt against the Kaiser's government was a subject of intense debate in Britain during the four years of war. Politicians, newspaper editors, and academic commentators quarrelled publicly over Germany's capacity to purge herself of authoritarian and militarist government. In this fiercely contested area, characteristic attitudes were struck and political investments were made which could not be abandoned easily when the armistice eventually came.

Of course, an extensive historical literature exists on the development of

---

[1] Arthur Acland to A. G. Gardiner, no date, but filed 1914–18, A. G. Gardiner Papers, 1/1.

[2] W. A. S. Hewins's Diary, 3 Apr. 1917, describing an interview on 2 Apr. 1917, Hewins Papers, 196/26.

[3] *The Times*, 19 Jan. 1918, 7.

Britain's general war aims during the First World War.[4] But the more narrow issue of German democratization as a British war aim has not been systematically explored. Therefore, this chapter surveys the evolution of British attitudes to this question. It aims to demonstrate how diverse were the positions adopted by politicians and other opinion-makers. The argument in outline is as follows. First, British Liberals speculated upon German democratization as the most likely end to the tragedy of the war, and perhaps even a short cut to peace. Hopes rested on the pressures of war awakening the German people to their mis-government. Second, for the majority of Conservatives, especially those who dominated the Lloyd George Coalition after December 1916, this Liberal faith in 'inner Germany' was a typical piece of self-delusion. Conservatives maintained that there was no real hope of German democratization during the struggle. It was a false hope, the shirker's hope. Third, to the Left of the major 'patriotic' political groupings, British Radicals and socialists proclaimed that German democracy was a slumbering but potentially dynamic force which could easily be awakened if the Entente sincerely disavowed its own aggressive and punitive war aims. Fourth, for the intelligence experts who advised the government, the truth lay somewhere between the mild optimism of the Liberals and the hope of the Radicals. On the one hand, these advisers argued that German democratization was likely in the future, but only after military defeat; on the other hand, they suggested, the democratic movement could probably be encouraged by more honesty and clarity in the expression of progressive war aims on Britain's part.

In this sense, the debate over German democratization spilled over into the passionate debates over war aims and a negotiated peace. As the war persisted, and political power passed to the Conservative-dominated 'knock-out blow' Coalition, those political forces most resistant to the revision of war aims were increasingly dominant in London. Thus the government was most reluctant to recognize any contribution from the progressive political forces inside Germany to the dethronement of militarism. By 1918, German democratization was regarded quite cynically as a mere propaganda ploy.

The Asquith governments, 1914–1916: German democratization as a Liberal hope

In an emotional speech early in the war, Prime Minister Asquith gave to the British nation certain imperishable phrases that served, at one and the same time,

---

[4] See V. H. Rothwell, *British War Aims and Peace Diplomacy, 1914–19* (Oxford, 1971); W. B. Fest, 'British War Aims and German Peace Feelers during the First World War (December 1916–November 1918)', *Historical Journal*, 15/2 (1972), 285–308; John Gooch, 'Soldiers, Strategy and War Aims in Britain, 1914–1918', in Barry Hunt and Adrian Preston (eds.), *War Aims and Strategic Policy in the Great War* (London, 1977), 21–40; John S. Galbraith, 'British War Aims in World War I: A Commentary on "Statesmanship" ', *Journal of Imperial and Commonwealth History*, 13/1 (1984), 25–45; David French, *British Strategy and War Aims 1914–1916* (London, 1986); A. D. Harvey, 'Britain's Aims in the First World War', *Contemporary Review*, 255 (Aug. 1989), 92–100; David Stevenson, *The First World War and International Politics* (Oxford, 1988).

to evoke a generous patriotism and to obscure detailed war aims. Speaking at the Lord Mayor's Banquet at the Guildhall on 9 November 1914, Asquith declared that:

We shall never sheath the sword, which we have not lightly drawn, until Belgium recovers in full measure all, and more than all, she has sacrificed; until France is adequately secured against the menace of aggression; until the rights of the smaller nationalities are placed upon an unassailable foundation, and *until the military domination of Prussia is wholly and finally destroyed.*[5]

From Asquith's final phrases, reproduced on countless occasions during the war, came the most popular and succinct statement of Britain's chief war aim: the nation was at war in order to 'destroy Prussian militarism'. The idealistic democrat and the instinctive jingo could both enrol under this banner. And yet, while the words 'wholly and finally destroyed' had a reassuring sense of thoroughness about them, it was not entirely clear whether Britain aimed at German *democratization* or not. Just where was Prussian militarism to be destroyed? In the field? Or in Berlin?

During the first two years of the war it became clear that the belief in German democratization was essentially a Liberal idea. Liberal politicians and commentators professed to see that the defeat of the Kaiser's military forces was not simply a military objective. It was a prerequisite for the political and even the spiritual rebirth of Germany as a democracy. This faith in German democracy rested ultimately on the distinction between the German people and their leaders. Liberals accepted the idea that the German people could not possibly be wholly corrupted by militarism. There were, after all, large numbers of moderate and democratic Germans. Thus, Liberals depicted an essentially misled German people, misgoverned by élitist and aristocratic blackguards. The war was aimed at these reactionary 'Prussian militarists', not the hoodwinked masses. Liberals predicted that, if the sufferings of war were prolonged, even a revolution to overthrow Kaiserism in Germany and bring about a negotiated peace was possible.

Within the Liberal Cabinet it was common to speak of 'the war party' and 'the peace party' in Berlin. The real enemy was 'the military caste' and the 'Prussian Junkers', phrases which implied that the commitment of the German people to the war was still an open question. Both Asquith and Sir Edward Grey, his Foreign Secretary, employed these phrases freely.[6] Early in the war, Lloyd

---

[5] e.g. see Asquith himself quoting the speech, *Parl. Debs.*, 5th ser., vol . lxx, 602 (1 Mar. 1915). Italics added.

[6] e.g. see M. G. Eckstein Frankl, 'Sir Edward Grey and Imperial Germany in 1914', *Journal of Contemporary History*, 6/3 (1971), 128–9; Lorna Jaffe, *The Decision to Disarm Germany: British Policy towards Postwar German Disarmament, 1914–1919* (London, 1985), 9–10. Asquith persisted in analysing the rise and fall in the stocks of 'the war at any price lot' and 'the peace lot' in Berlin; see Asquith to Venetia Stanley, 17 Feb. 1915, *Letters to Venetia Stanley*, ed. Michael and Eleanor Brock (Oxford, 1985), 434. Significantly, the 'peace lot' he identified as the influential men of business, men like Albert Ballin, not the German socialists.

George also insisted upon maintaining the distinction between the German people and their government. A week into the war he explained to his wife Margaret that his catch-cry was 'Beat the German Junker but no war on the German people'.[7] In his famous Queen's Hall speech of September 1914, he proclaimed impeccably Liberal opinions: 'I will not say a single word in disparagement of the German people. . . . We are not fighting the German people. The German people are under the heel of this military caste, and it will be a day of rejoicing for the German peasant, artisan and trader when the military caste is broken.'[8]

Similarly, Liberal writers speculated about the potential 'good Germans' seizing hold of the reins of power in a democratized Germany from the first weeks of the war. Arnold Bennett, for example, wrote in September 1914 of his hopes that a British victory might 'finish up Germany's activities in the war department for at least fifty years, and bring about a German revolution against the military caste'. No price was too great, he wrote, 'to secure the overthrow of a handful of men at Berlin'.[9] A. G. Gardiner, idealistic editor of the Liberal *Daily News*, drew the same distinction at the beginning of the war: 'This is not a war of peoples but of despots and diplomatists. . . . We have no quarrel with the German people', he wrote. According to Gardiner, those suffering at the hands of German militarism must not seek to avenge themselves on the German people but only on the evil men directing the state.[10] The *Contemporary Review*, edited by the Liberal historian G. P. Gooch, assiduously pursued these same themes.[11] For example, in December 1914 William Harbutt Dawson, a frequent contributor, attacked the prevailing wisdom that Germany was hopelessly illiberal. Reviewing the election results of 1912, Dawson stressed the 'glaring paradox' between the Kaiser's reactionary government and the pro-democratic parties, the German Social Democratic Party and the Progressive People's Party, that had done so well at the polls. According to Dawson, a sweeping constitutional change that would inaugurate the rule of German democracy was the true solution to the German problem.[12] As the war proceeded, the *Contemporary Review* was much encouraged by the progress of the democratic forces inside Germany. Disillusionment with the war among ordinary Germans and the pressures building for thoroughgoing democratization were repeatedly analysed.[13]

[7] Lloyd George to Margaret Lloyd George, 11 Aug. 1914, in Kenneth O. Morgan (ed.), *Lloyd George Family Letters, 1885–1936* (Cardiff and Oxford, 1973), 169.

[8] *The Great War. Speech delivered by the Rt. Hon. David Lloyd George M. P. at the Queen's Hall, London, on September 19th, 1914* (London, 1914), 11 and 13.

[9] Arnold Bennett to George H. Doran, 10 Sept. 1914, in James Hepburn (ed.), *The Letters of Arnold Bennett, ii. Letters 1889–1915* (Oxford, 1966), 351.

[10] Gardiner articles in *Daily News* and *Everyman*, Aug. 1914, quoted in Stephen Koss, *Fleet Street Radical* (London, 1975), 155–6.

[11] See Frank Eyck, *G. P. Gooch: A Study in History and Politics* (London, 1982), ch. 9.

[12] William H. Dawson, 'The German Constitutional Movement and the War', *Contemporary Review*, 106 (Dec. 1914). See also similar views in G. P. Gooch, 'German Theories of the State', *Contemporary Review*, 107 (June 1915).

[13] Hugh F. Spender, 'German Opinion', *Contemporary Review*, 110 (Oct. 1916).

But did the Asquith government aim at German democracy? There was no public commitment from Asquith beyond the original elastic slogan 'the destruction of Prussian militarism'.[14] In fact, both Asquith and Grey positively discouraged discussion of war aims in the Cabinet and parliament (much as did German Chancellor Bethmann Hollweg).[15] In British diplomacy, however, the importance of Germany's evolution into a democracy in the aftermath of her defeat could be stressed when convenient. In late 1914, for example, Sir Edward Grey appeared to embrace German democratization as a British war aim. In a private letter to Colonel Edward House, President Wilson's special confidant, Grey explained that Britain aimed to inflict such a defeat upon Germany that she would become 'a democratic state emancipated from the rule of the Prussian military party'.[16] The context was significant. Grey's commitment to German democratization was made while seeking to pour cold water on an American offer of mediation in the war. This was to inaugurate a pattern: the great goal of German democratization could always be adduced as an objective of the war whenever it was necessary to set a high price before peace negotiations could be considered.

How sincere leading Liberals may have been in nominating German democratization as a priority among Britain's real war aims remains doubtful. Britain's own Edwardian political system, even after the passage of the Parliament Act of 1911, was still nearer to a parliamentary oligarchy than to a fully representative democracy. For all the influence of New Liberalism, the Asquith government had failed to reform the British suffrage on a truly democratic basis before the war. During 1915 and 1916, the Liberals were most reluctant to face an election under a reformed 'soldiers' vote' (which was thought to be a reform of the suffrage favourable to the Conservatives). The government did not announce that a comprehensive measure of electoral reform was in contemplation until June 1916. The Speaker's Conference on suffrage reform did not finally report until early 1917, and the famous 'Fourth Reform Act' was not passed finally until February 1918.[17] In the same period, much criticism was levelled at the German government on account of its foot-dragging over the reform of the notoriously undemocratic three-class suffrage in Prussia.[18] Britain's own progress towards

---

[14] Lorna Jaffe, *The Decision to Disarm Germany* (London, 1985), 11.

[15] Rothwell, *British War Aims*, 19; Gooch, 'Soldiers, Strategy and War Aims', 26.

[16] Grey to Cecil Spring-Rice, 22 Dec. 1914, quoted by David French, *British Strategy and War Aims, 1914–1916* (London, 1986), 61.

[17] The Asquith-led Coalition turned down a proposal to place all servicemen on the register in 1915. On the reluctance of some Liberals to enfranchise servicemen see Martin Pugh, *Electoral Reform in War and Peace, 1906–18* (London, 1978), ch. 5.

[18] In contrast to the manhood suffrage operating in *Reichstag* elections, the three-class suffrage in Prussia, dating from the Election Law of 30 May 1849, divided electors into one of three classes according to taxation. It ensured that working-class voters could never control the Prussian government. As the Prussian government's representatives dominated the federal upper house, the Bundesrat, the three-class suffrage in Prussia was regarded by many observers as the great bulwark against popular government in Germany. On the Prussian constitution and attempts to reform it see H. W. Koch, *A Constitutional History of Germany* (London, 1984), 79–83, and 232–4.

democracy was scarcely achieved at a blistering gallop under the stimulus of war.

Whether sincerely committed or not to German democracy, Liberal politicians soon found it impolitic to speak publicly about so-called 'good Germans' and their potential for a democratic revolution. During the first half of 1915, increasingly hysterical anti-German attitudes took hold in Britain. The denunciation of all things German reached fever pitch, provoked especially by the sinking of the *Lusitania* on 7 May, and was further inflamed by the release of Lord Bryce's highly imaginative report on German atrocities in Belgium several days later.[19] Whipped along by articles in the ultra-patriotic press condemning the presence of enemy aliens in Britain, ruffians began serious rioting against 'German' property in many towns and cities throughout the country. The pressure to conform to a chauvinist outlook, which had already overtaken most writers and academics, swept the politicians along too.[20] The sensational political response came on 19 May 1915. Asquith stunned his Liberal colleagues by secretly stitching up a deal with the Conservative leaders and the Labour Party in order to reconstruct his government as a 'patriotic' coalition.[21] Lord Haldane was a notable omission from the new Cabinet: Haldane had been hounded for months by the ultra-patriots as 'Member for Germany' on account of his long acquaintance with German philosophy.[22] In the new Asquith Coalition, the surviving Liberals had good reason to be wary of any display of expertise or even familiarity with things German.

In private, Liberals, and even dissident Unionists, continued to weigh the chances of Germany's internal conversion to democracy. For instance, Lord Cromer,[23] a Unionist free trader, adopted the position early in the war that the German people would probably overwhelm the Hohenzollern monarchy themselves if Germany was seriously defeated in war.[24] Once 'chastened by the reality of defeat', predicted Cromer, 'all that is really good and solid in the German character would eventually reassert itself'.[25] Most Liberals now adopted this

[19] Trevor Wilson, 'Lord Bryce's Investigation into Alleged German Atrocities in Belgium, 1914–15', *Journal of Contemporary History*, 14 (1979), 369–83.

[20] See Katherine Andrews, 'The Necessity to Conform: British Jingoism in the First World War', *Dalhousie Review*, 53/2 (1973), 227–45; Stuart Wallace, *War and the Image of Germany: British Academics 1914–1918* (Edinburgh, 1988); and Panikos Panayi, 'Anti-German Riots in London during the First World War', *German History*, 7/2 (1989), 184–203.

[21] See Peter Fraser, 'British Policy and the Crisis of Liberalism in May 1915', *Journal of Modern History*, 54/1 (1982), 1–26.

[22] On the hounding of Haldane see Asquith, *Letters to Venetia Stanley*, 322–3.

[23] Evelyn Baring, 1st Earl of Cromer, Consul-General of Egypt from the 1883 to 1907, then prominent free trade Unionist in the House of Lords, proponent of ethical imperialism, author of *Ancient and Modern Imperialism* (1910), cousin of Sir Edward Grey.

[24] Lord Cromer to Dr Herbert Warren, 22 Sept. 1914, quoted in Marquess of Zetland, *Lord Cromer* (London, 1933), 343.

[25] Lord Cromer to Dawson, 29 June 1915, W. H. Dawson Papers, WHD 276. Similarly, see Haldane to Dawson, 19 Nov. 1915, W. H. Dawson Papers, WHD 283. Cromer had long shown an awareness that the political contest inside Germany was essentially between a reactionary militarist élite and the SPD; see his essay 'The Home Policy of Germany', in Earl of Cromer, *Political and Literary Essays: Second Series* (London, 1914), 157–72.

understanding of the old formula, 'the destruction of Prussian militarism': the Germans would have to be cudgelled into democracy. 'Mr Britling', the central character in H. G. Wells's novel *Mr Britling Sees it Through*, the best-seller of late 1916, epitomized the evolution of 'patriotic' Liberal opinion on the issue. In the novel, Mr Britling, a patriot of Radical inclination, painfully sheds his illusions that the German people were to be always distinguished from their government. Impressed by the apparent solidarity of the German home front, Mr Britling almost succumbs to the view that 'instead of there being a liberal and reluctant Germany at the back of imperialism and Junkerdom, there was apparently one solid and enthusiastic people'.[26] While managing to resist this position in the end, Mr Britling certainly accepts that militarism had a much tighter hold on the great mass of the German people than he had first imagined. Only a big Allied victory could be relied upon to weaken its grip.

Liberals may have wavered on the matter of German democratization, but the assertion of democratic objectives remained an important theme in Britain's diplomacy. This served to enlist American sympathy, and to distract attention from the Entente's alliance with Tsarism. Special ongoing efforts were made to persuade the United States that Britain's war aims included this democratic dimension. In conversations with the Americans, the leading Liberal political personalities would immediately resume the language of Liberalism, presenting the war as a crusade aimed against the 'military caste', the 'war party', and 'military dictatorship'. Walter Page, the American Ambassador, and Colonel House (who visited Britain in February 1916), were constantly assured that Britain felt no enmity towards the German people who were 'misguided and misled'.[27] For his part, House encouraged the British Liberal leadership to maintain the distinction between the German government and people.[28] This theme also dominated the quasi-diplomatic work undertaken by Sir Horace Plunkett, the moderate Irish politician who was Chairman of the Irish Convention in 1917.[29] Plunkett had many long-standing American connections and enjoyed a particularly cordial relationship with Colonel House.[30] In his frequent correspondence with House, Plunkett sought to present the progressive face of Britain's war aims, with much emphasis upon the need to democratize Germany in order to ensure peace in the future. Indeed, Plunkett used this argument unashamedly in pleading the case for American intervention in the war. America's entry, he explained

[26] H. G. Wells, *Mr Britling Sees It Through* (London, 1916), 273.

[27] W. H. Page Diary, 11 Dec. 1916, in Burton J. Hendrick (ed.), *The Life and Letters of Walter H. Page* (London, 1930), ii. 418. See also Page to House, 23 May 1916, ibid., ii. 157.

[28] House Diary, 15 Feb. 1916, in Charles Seymour (ed.), *The Intimate Papers of Colonel House* (London, 1926), ii. 189.

[29] Sir Horace Plunkett, proponent of agricultural co-operation, cattle rancher in Wyoming 1879–89, Unionist MP for South County Dublin 1892–1900, Vice-President of Department of Agriculture and Technical Instruction for Ireland 1899–1907, founded Plunkett Foundation to promote agricultural co-operation 1919.

[30] House to Plunkett, 7 Apr. 1917, Horace Plunkett Papers, HOU 85. 'Matters arise almost daily about which I would like your counsel', wrote House.

in January 1916, 'would facilitate the liberation of the democratic forces in Germany'.[31] Britain too hankered after German democratization; as Plunkett assured House, 'the best thought here favours such a military defeat of Germany as will enable her people to deal with their own government'.[32] But which people? If there were good democratic Germans awaiting liberation, Liberals were often coy about identifying them. Whether the German socialists of the SPD should be counted amongst them was problematic. In spite of their professed internationalism, the majority of the German socialists were known to be supporting the war, while insisting on its defensive nature. Some Liberal writers were quick to condemn the SPD. The collapse of German socialism into the militarist mire had been total, argued Austin Harrison of the *English Review*: 'Nobody, except an English Liberal, ever expected anything else', he wrote bitterly.[33] Most Liberal and Radical commentators, however, were more charitable than Harrison, presenting the German socialists as errant younger brothers, still worthy because their hearts were in the right place. Most were conscious of the German socialists' genuine fear of the Tsarist threat, the bitter internal debates in the party over the decision to support the war credits, and the continuing refusal of the majority of socialists to embrace a Pan-German position.[34] German democratization, Liberals argued, was still most likely to come from socialist pressure. Most Liberal analysts, therefore, refused to quake at the socialist tag, and ridiculed the idea that the SPD's leading men had all become toadies of the militarist state.[35] Maynard Keynes, at this time a leading Treasury official and an occasional guest at the card-table of Prime Minister Asquith, went further, openly defending the SPD: he published his own positive assessment of the internationalist record of the German socialists in the *Economic Journal* in September 1915. He applauded the revisionist socialist Eduard Bernstein in particular for his 'obviously undiminished love of internationalism and international amity'.[36]

---

[31] Plunkett's handwritten comments pinned to a memorandum entitled 'Irresponsible reflections on the part which the Pacific Nations might play in discouraging future wars', by Arthur Balfour, dated Jan. 1916, with notes explaining that Plunkett had put this argument in favour of US intervention to members of the US Cabinet, Horace Plunkett Papers, BALF/A 19.

[32] Plunkett to House, 29 Mar. 1916, Horace Plunkett Papers, HOU 53.

[33] Austin Harrison, 'The Collapse of German Socialism', in his *The Kaiser's War* (London,1914), 201, reproduced from the *English Review*.

[34] For modern scholarship on the German socialists' internal debates over the matter of war see Carl E. Schorske, *German Social Democracy 1905–1917: The Development of the Great Schism* (New York, 1955); David M. Morgan, *The Socialist Left and the German Revolution: A History of the German Independent Social Democratic Party, 1917–1922* (London, 1975); and F. Carsten, *War Against War: British and German Radical Movements in the First World War* (London, 1982).

[35] G. P. Gooch, review of W. H. Dawson, *What is Wrong with Germany?* (London, 1915), *Contemporary Review*, 107 (Mar. 1915).

[36] J. Maynard Keynes, 'The Economics of War in Germany', *Economic Journal* (Sept. 1915), reproduced in *The Collected Writings of John Maynard Keynes*, xi (Cambridge, 1983), esp. 338–40.

The Conservative position: German democratization as an irrelevancy

Such generous analyses of the enemy's progressive political potential carried little weight on the Conservative side of British politics. Here, hopeful speculation about Germany's future political development was scrupulously avoided. Reports of unrest against Kaiserdom from within Germany were generally treated with great suspicion. In particular, the alleged distinction between the German people and its government was sternly rebutted as a dangerous chimera. Instead, Conservatives stressed the solidity of the German nation, and asserted the complicity of the German people as a whole in the war. German socialist internationalism, in particular, was gleefully exposed as a pathetic illusion. For example, just a fortnight into the war, Lord Milner pleaded with H. A. Gwynne of the *Morning Post* to use his paper to puncture the dangerous fantasy that the war was likely to be short because the Germans were divided. He urged him to guard especially against 'the idea that the Germans, as a nation, are dejected, disunited, and in the face of a severe reverse will go to pieces, [and] that Socialism will become formidable'.[37] This disdain for the Liberals' optimism about inner Germany made much headway in the Conservative Party during the first months of the war. In November 1914, Bonar Law boasted of his party's realism in a speech in the House of Commons: 'I never was one of those who cherished the delusion that this was a war of the rulers of Germany alone', he proclaimed; it was 'a war of the German nation'.[38]

Indeed, Conservatives began to see the very different estimate of German political potential made by Conservative and Liberal politicians as marking a crucial divide in the outlook of the two parties. Conservatives were suspicious even of the Liberal phrase 'Prussian militarism', fearing that it implied a belief in the German evil being confined to some effete aristocratic class that might easily be separated from the German people. For example, shortly after the formation of the Coalition in May 1915, Leo Amery complained to Lord Milner that 'this harping on Prussian militarism' must be rooted out because it tended to drag Conservatives into 'a false little England position'.[39] Increasingly after May 1915, Conservatives were critical of the Liberal tendency to detect democratic dissent inside Germany. The idea that there might be some hostility to the war, perhaps even a potential for a seizure of power from the German Left, was regarded as symptomatic of a contemptible Liberal desire for some short cut to victory.

For many Conservatives, then, hope in German democratization was simply the child of fear. There was no ground for hope. In any case, from the viewpoint of the 'economic warriors' on the right of the Conservative Party, German democracy simply made no difference. It was an irrelevancy, because both an

---

[37] Milner to Gwynne, 21 Aug. 1914, Gwynne Papers, Imperial War Museum, HAG 21/24.
[38] *Parl. Debs.*, 5th ser., vol. lxviii, 15 (11 Nov. 1914).
[39] Amery to Milner, 25 May 1915, cited in Jaffe, *Decision to Disarm Germany*, 15.

autocratic Germany and a democratic Germany represented an economic threat to the British Empire. Asquith and Grey, however, had given the idea of 'Prussian militarism' and the 'war party' such currency during the first two years of war that the issue could not be ignored. The response of the Right was vehement opposition to the idea that the triumph of German democracy might be a reason for ending the war short of victory, or for treating Germany generously after the war. The Conservative and ultra-patriotic press sought to maintain a ground swell of opinion against admitting the possibility of German democratization. The whole German people had been corrupted by Kaiserism, it was stubbornly maintained.[40] Sidney Whitman warned in December 1914 that it was not just the 'Prussian Military Party' with whom Britain was at war but rather 'the vitiated instincts of a whole people'.[41] Where Conservative writers did acknowledge social democratic influence in Germany, this only added to the indictment against the enemy. For example, in the popular 'patriotic' work of 1915, *The Soul of Germany*, Thomas Smith argued that the popularity of the Jewish-led and anti-family German social democrats was further evidence of the moral corruption of working-class Germans. Thus, Smith declared, 'England must be from the very nature of things an unrelenting enemy to the doctrine of the German Social Democrats who have declared war upon the institutions of home and family'.[42] The idea that resurgent German socialism might resist militarism from within was ridiculed. Lady Bathurst, the proprietress of the *Morning Post*, gave a succinct statement of the Conservative view in early 1917: 'I am not one of those who dissociate the German people from the so-called military caste. Every nation has the government it deserves.'[43]

There were some exceptions. The *Round Table* acknowledged some rebellious potential on the part of the German people even in the first months of the war. In the context of a war for liberty, it was explained, defeat for Germany would discredit Prussia's 'satanic gospel' and shatter its hold over the German people who, 'freed from the spell which has long entranced them, will begin to move once more along the path towards self-government and freedom'.[44] But the

---

[40] See e.g. F. G. Stone, ' The "Guiltless German People" ', *Nineteenth Century* (Oct. 1914).

[41] Sidney Whitman, 'The Blight of Prussian Autocracy', *Fortnightly Review*, 96 (1 Dec. 1914). Whitman was a Conservative journalist with the *Standard*, author of *Imperial Germany* (1888), *Germany's Iron Chancellor* (1897), and other works on Bismarckian Germany.

[42] Thomas Smith, *The Soul of Germany* (London, 1915), 2, 24, and 74–85.

[43] Lady Bathurst, quoted from *The Gentlewoman* magazine, 3 Feb. 1917, in Keith Wilson (ed.), *The Rasp of War: The Letters of H. A. Gwynne to The Countess Bathurst, 1914–1918* (London, 1988), 6.

[44] [Kerr], 'After Four Months of War', *Round Table*, 17 (Dec. 1914). The democratic emphasis in *Round Table* no doubt reflected the influence of Kerr and various progressive personalities in Zimmern's circle. In Dec. 1914, Robert Seton-Watson, Zimmern, and several like-minded academics produced the first full-length study of the war as an ideological struggle for the protection and perfection of democracy; see R. W. Seton Watson, J. Dover Wilson, Alfred Zimmern, and Arthur Greenwood, *The War and Democracy* (London, 1915). On the group of academics who produced this book and their roots in the Round Table movement see Hugh and Christopher Seton-Watson, *The Making of a New Europe: R. W. Seton-Watson and the Last Years of Austria-Hungary* (London, 1981), 105–6.

German socialists were not to be relied upon to lead the domestic battle; they
'had little understanding of the practical difficulties and problems of government'
and were 'often revolutionary and extreme'. The socialists would not provide salvation. Democracy would arise in Germany through the action of the German
people only when stung by defeat, only 'once the German autocracy has met its
Sedan'.[45] Thus the *Round Table* endorsed the priority of victory. After two years
of battle, even the more bluntly Germanophobic Conservative writers were willing to consider the prospect of a division opening between government and
people inside Germany. None the less, it was always emphatically asserted that
the Germans were incapable of finding their way into the democratic light without a constant fire at their tails. Democratization from within Germany, it was
made clear, was never to be regarded as an alternative to the most energetic prosecution of the war from Britain's side. J. Ellis Barker, for example, argued in
December 1916 that defeat and starvation combined might produce a spontaneous rising in Germany. But, because the Germans were a 'nation of lackeys',
only the sting of defeat would ensure this outcome. Significantly, it would be a
rising led by the German 'intelligent middle class' rather than by the German
socialists. For, explained Barker, the SPD leaders 'are not socialists at all'; in fact,
he claimed, anti-patriots and anti-militarists were quite 'unknown' in Germany.[46]
In this way, the characteristic Conservative tendency to underestimate the internal German opposition to Kaiserism became entrenched.

   Lloyd George's opinions on internal German political developments before
becoming Prime Minister in December 1916 warrant special attention also. As
has been seen, his initial war speeches revealed him as a conventional Liberal in
approach, perhaps an even more energetic flagellator of 'the military caste' than
his Liberal colleagues. Lloyd George, of course, was on the move: his growing
distaste for the Radical wing of the Liberal Party, his personal alienation from
leading ministers such as Asquith and Reginald McKenna, his conversion to the
cause of conscription, and his gradual political alignment with 'his Tory friends',
are all well-known developments.[47] His opinions on Germany appear to have
evolved to match the requirements of his political journey. He soon inclined to
the view that faith in German democratization was a balm clutched at by those
Liberal self-deceivers without the stomach for the rigours of war. Among friends

---

[45] [Kerr], 'The Schism of Europe', *Round Table*, 18 (Mar. 1915). Zimmern's article on Germany
in his book *The War and Democracy* was similar; see Zimmern's article 'Germany' in Seton Watson,
et al., *The War and Democracy*, esp. 67–8 and 117–18.

[46] 'Politicus' (J. Ellis Barker), 'Will the German People Revolt?', *Fortnightly Review*, 600 (1 Dec.
1916). J. Ellis Barker, educated in Cologne, founder of the New Health Society (homeopathy) and
the journal *Heal Thyself*, active pamphleteer in the campaigns for Tariff Reform and National Service
before the war, author of *British Socialism, Modern Germany*, and *Foundations of Germany*.

[47] See Hobhouse's typical remarks; Hobhouse Diary, 23 May 1915, in Edward David, *Inside
Asquith's Cabinet: From the Diaries of Charles Hobhouse* (London, 1977), 247. On political alignments
in this period see Michael G. Fry, 'Political Change in Britain, August 1914–December 1916: Lloyd
George Replaces Asquith: The Issues Underlying the Drama', *Historical Journal*, 31/3 (1988),
609–27.

he paraded his scepticism. 'Some of my colleagues reassure themselves by saying the Germans are becoming exhausted. What evidence is there of that?', Lloyd George groused in October 1915. Again, when dining in February 1916 with Colonel House, Wilson's emissary recently returned from Germany, Lloyd George seized upon the Colonel's remark that he had observed 'no marked indication of privation or strain' inside Germany. By April 1916, Asquith's belief in German exhaustion had become an item on Lloyd George's litany of the Prime Minister's inadequacies.[48]

In making his choice to stand with the energetic patriots in the 'knock-out blow' Coalition in December 1916, Lloyd George was siding with the political forces dominated by 'realists', as they saw themselves, on the German issue. These were the men who had long boasted of being above the pathetic illusion that the Germans might undergo some inner conversion before they were well and truly thrashed. Lloyd George's readiness to embrace this faith emerged in a private interview with Lord Burnham, owner of the *Daily Telegraph*, on 1 December 1916, only a week before becoming Prime Minister. Lloyd George exhibited irreproachable opinions on the German question. He explained his conviction that German discipline would undoubtedly hold her forces and her people together, in spite of the mounting evidence of hunger and shortages in Germany. He pointed to the fact that, for all the suffering glimpsed in the many 'hysterical and heart-broken' letters of German soldiers that had been intercepted by British intelligence in France, the leading Entente military men at the front still reported that the German troops fought magnificently. A military victory over such a disciplined enemy was the only way forward, he concluded.[49] In short, by late 1916, Lloyd George regarded faith in German exhaustion and democratization as a self-deception. It was, in Conservative eyes, a distinguishing mark of the despised Asquithian 'Old Gang'.

The Lloyd George Coalition government of 1917: German democratization as an unwelcome distraction

The formation of the 'knock-out blow' Lloyd George Coalition on 7 December 1916 encouraged many British patriots to believe that the war would now be prosecuted with renewed energy. With victory again promoted as the first and greatest war aim, supporters of the new government must also have hoped that they had heard the last of any short cut to peace, including peace via democratization. The German Peace Note of 12 December and the American Peace Note of 18 December were seen, therefore, by the new government as most unwelcome interventions. The timing of these initiatives was appalling from the British perspective. The leaders of the 'fight-to-the-finish' Coalition had barely warmed

---

[48] Lord Riddell, *Lord Riddell's War Diary* (London, 1933). See entries for Oct. 1915, 124; 16 Oct. 1915, 126; 12 Feb. 1916, 155; 13 Apr. 1916, 171.

[49] Lord Burnham, 'Notes on a Conversation with Lloyd George, 1 Dec. 1916', Lord Burnham Papers, HLWL/10, no. 6.

their seats in the new War Cabinet. The new British leaders, therefore, laboured to ensure that both approaches were turned aside.[50] As Robert Cecil succinctly expressed it in the War Cabinet on 15 December, he assumed 'that the policy of this country is to avoid being forced into peace negotiations at the present time'.[51]

The intensifying determination on the Right in Britain not to recognize *any* exponents of restraint inside Germany underpinned the new government's approach. It must be said, however, that this determination led to serious mis-judgements of the political situation in the enemy camp. For the vision of a united people, even of a united leadership around the Kaiser, was—and is still—very much open to debate. The ebb and flow in the contest for power in Berlin, and even for the consciences of the leading politicians, created a situation where genuine doubts existed concerning who ultimately ruled in Germany. Evidence can be found pointing to either German political caricature: on the one hand, that of a proud military dictatorship in supreme authority, manipulating a con-temptible Reichstag of willing puppets, sham socialists, and counterfeit moder-ates; on the other hand, that of an impatient and principled centre-left Reichstag majority, only ever cautiously in support of a defensive war, and constantly threatening a nest of desperate generals and aristocrats.[52] Where the truth lies between these two caricatures is still contested. What is certain is that an intense struggle was taking place at the top in Germany. By 1917 Germany was, as Hans Gatzke has neatly characterized her, a 'house divided'.[53] Extreme advocates of victory at any price were locked in a fierce domestic struggle with the more mod-erate forces, of intermittent sincerity and political courage. These forces were gathered in the Centre Party, the Progressive People's Party, and the rancorous

---

[50] See Sterling Kernek, 'The British Government's Reactions to President Wilson's "Peace" Note of Dec. 1916', *Historical Journal*, 13/4 (1970), 721–66, and Fest, 'British War Aims and German Peace Feelers, 285–308.

[51] Cecil quoted in Fest, 'British War Aims and German Peace Feelers', 290.

[52] The balance of power between the militarists and moderates in the wartime German govern-ment, and in the Reichstag, is still a hotly debated issue among historians. The best recent summary of the debate is Martin Kitchen, 'Civil–Military Relations in Germany during the First World War', in R. J. Q. Adams (ed.), *The Great War, 1914–18: Essays on the Military, Political and Social History of the First World War* (London, 1990), 39–68. Some relevant works in English are listed here. The argument that the 'military dictatorship' of Hindenburg and Ludendorff was always dominant is put with great force by Fritz Fischer, *Germany's Aims in the First World War* (London, 1967), and can be followed also in G. D. Feldman, *Army, Industry and Labour in Germany, 1914–1918* (Princeton, 1966), Martin Kitchen, *The Silent Dictatorship: The Politics of the German High Command under Hindenburg and Ludendorff, 1916–1918* (London, 1967), and Hans-Ulrich Wehler, *The German Empire 1870–1918* (Leamington Spa, 1985). For moderate and revisionist interpretations, which stress that German internal politics was in a state of flux, that the opposition was still a potent force, and that Bethmann Hollweg was a sincere, if moderate, reformer, see Gerhard Ritter, *The Sword and the Scepter: The Problem of Militarism in Germany* (4 vols., Coral Gables, Fl., 1969), Konrad H. Jarausch, *The Enigmatic Chancellor: Bethmann Hollweg and the Hubris of Imperial Germany* (New Haven, 1973), and Fritz Stern, 'Bethmann Hollweg and the War: The Limits of Responsibility', in Leonard Krieger and Fritz Stern (eds.), *The Responsibility of Power: Historical Essays in Honour of Hajo Holborn* (London, 1968), 252–85.

[53] Hans Gatzke, *Germany's Drive to the West: A Study of Germany's Western War Aims during the First World War* (Baltimore, 1966), ch. III.

SPD. Nor was this inner struggle entirely hidden from outside observers. The dismissal in March 1916 of Admiral von Tirpitz, the extreme Pan-German and advocate of unlimited submarine warfare, had come as the first spectacular public exposure of the struggle taking place within the German ruling élite.[54]

Exactly where the controversial German Chancellor, Bethmann Hollweg, stood in this struggle, he effectively hid from his contemporaries by means of resolute obfuscation. His political outlook is still passionately debated by historians.[55] The exact meaning of the German Peace Note of December 1916, the Chancellor's initiative, therefore, is also subject to controversy. While the note comforted the German Right with brave assurances of the nation's determination to fight on if necessary, the essence of the message was clear: an offer 'to enter even now into peace negotiations', without any specified preconditions.[56] On balance, it seems reasonable to surmise that this note was not the product of a supremely confident militarist clique. Certainly the bellicose tone of the note, and the preparations behind the scenes for an annexationist agenda to be put forward at a peace conference, revealed the government's determination to retain for Germany some semblance of territorial victory in order to impress the German electorate. But the note was not a sinister stratagem to achieve a victor's peace. The German Conservatives, the National Liberals, and the bulk of the nationalist press, it should be recalled, all opposed the issuing of the note as a sign of weakness and prayed for its rejection by the Entente. Of course, the timing reflected the German government's confidence that, in the aftermath of the fall of Bucharest (6 December), Germany would be negotiating from a position of strength, at least in the east. But a variety of motives coexisted within the German political élite. The voices of restraint inside Germany and Austria were genuinely seeking escape from the war before the fragile domestic truce shattered completely. These moderate advisers had prevailed in the German government, if ever so briefly, even to the point of risking the negotiating table, and the inevitable flood-tide of domestic pressure which would demand that the negotiators not rise from their labours until a compromise had been struck.[57]

---

[54] For insights into this antagonism see, for example, the war letters of Tirpitz included in Grand Admiral von Tirpitz, *My Memoirs* (London, 1919), i, Appendix I.

[55] Wayne C. Thompson, *In the Eye of the Storm: Kurt Riezler and the Crises of Modern Germany* (Iowa City, Ia., 1980), and Konrad H. Jarausch, 'Revising German History: Bethmann Hollweg Revisited', *Central European History*, 21 (Sept. 1988), 224–43, which makes use of the diaries of Theodor Wolff. This portrait may be contrasted with the hostile treatment of Bethmann Hollweg in Fischer, *Germany's Aims in the First World War*. For a modern survey of the deep divisions in the wartime German Conservative camp, and the Conservatives' developing hostility toward Bethmann Hollweg whom they regarded as a dangerous moderate, much too soft on socialists and trade unionists, see James N. Retallack, *Notables of the Right: The Conservative Party and Political Mobilisation in Germany, 1876–1918* (Boston, 1988), ch. 15.

[56] The German Foreign Office Note of 12 Dec. 1916, 'Chargé Grew to the Secretary of State, 12 Dec. 1916', in James Brown Scott, *Diplomatic Correspondence between the United States and Germany, August 1, 1914–April 6, 1917* (New York, 1918), 274–5.

[57] On the German political background to the issuing of the Peace Note, and especially the Conservative and National Liberal criticism of the Chancellor's initiative, see Gatzke, *Drive to the*

None of this did Lloyd George's government dare recognize openly. It was vital for the British 'patriotic' Right to see, or profess to see, only German solidarity and an absolutely dominant Supreme Command behind the German initiative. The outcome was never in doubt; the Entente rejected the German Peace Note on 29 December 1916. The excuse given out was the Germans' failure to list their terms in advance. Supposedly, this was proof of German perfidy, although Balfour himself in the months ahead was constantly to fend off demands for more precise British war aims.[58] The determination of the new Lloyd George government to avoid any oral exchange of views with the Germans is easily explained: as Lloyd George was advised, once face-to-face negotiations were commenced, the war weariness of the people would ensure they could never be broken off.[59] As William Bridgeman told his wife privately early in 1918, 'when once we are in [negotiations], I doubt if we can ever proceed with fighting'.[60] Shunning negotiations, the government turned in a more avowedly imperial direction. The British rejection of the German Peace Note coincided with an announcement that there was to be a 'War Conference of the Empire' early in 1917, an initiative that was to lead to the establishment of the Imperial War Cabinet. This encouraged the 'economic warriors' considerably. As Hewins noted in his diary, the announcement of a more self-consciously 'imperial' direction of the war from London was 'the best reply to the Central Powers which could be given'.[61] Few in these circles lamented the lost opportunity for peace. But, in casting the German Peace Note aside so brusquely, the Entente in fact helped to consolidate the domestic position of the German annexationists.[62]

Because of American economic power and the Entente's increasing reliance

West, 139–51. See also the competing priorities evident in the preparation of war aims at this time in Fischer, *Germany's Aims in the First World War*, ch. 10, Kitchen, *The Silent Dictatorship*, ch. 5, Ritter, *Sword and the Scepter*, iii, ch. 8, and the elegant summary of the fluidity of German war aims and the 'shambles at the top' of the government in Stevenson, *First World War*, 103–6.

[58] e.g. in the House of Commons on 30 July 1917, Balfour defended his policy of refusing to enlarge upon the 'broad principles' for which Britain was fighting. Balfour argued: 'Of course, how we are going to apply those broad principles depends upon endless circumstances of great complexity—circumstances that turn upon what goes on in Allied countries and in enemy countries. It may depend on the fortunes of war; upon the changing circumstances of the military and naval conditions in the world. How can we go into details and anticipate now the work that will have to be done by the final Peace Congress? I do not believe it is possible.' He concluded his speech with the observation that 'the immediate duty before us is not to discuss in detail what kind of terms of peace we would like when the war comes to an end, but to continue the war with all the strenuous vigour which we can command'. See 'Reply of Foreign Minister Balfour in debate in the House of Commons on British Peace Terms', in James Brown Scott (ed.), *Official Statements of War Aims and Peace Proposals, December 1916 to November 1918* (Washington, 1921), 122–8.

[59] Guy Locock to Hankey, 16 Dec. 1916, Lloyd George Papers, F/60/2/2, cited by Rothwell, *British War Aims and Peace Diplomacy*, 61, and Eric Drummond, Memorandum, 14 Dec. 1916, FO 800/197, cited by David R. Woodward, 'Great Britain and President Wilson's Efforts to End World War I in 1916', *The Maryland Historian*, 1 (Spring 1970), 53.

[60] Bridgeman to Mrs Bridgeman, 7 Jan. 1918, Bridgeman Papers, 4629/1/1918/7.

[61] Hewins Diary, 27 Dec. 1916, in W. A. S. Hewins, *The Apologia of an Imperialist: Forty Years of Empire Policy* (London, 1929), ii. 101.

[62] Stevenson, *First World War*, 105; Gatzke, *Drive to the West*, 151.

upon it, Wilson's Peace Note of December 1916 was seen as even more threatening to Britain than the German 'peace offensive'. There was already considerable resentment of the President's pontifical pronouncements upon the war.[63] The President was widely distrusted in the Foreign Office as a sanctimonious idealist.[64] Most importantly, Wilson's insistence upon distinguishing the German people from their government was suspect in Conservative circles. The governing American idea, that promises of leniency for German democracy might lure the German people into a revolt, was believed to entail grave risks to Britain's imperial and economic fruits of victory. There was the question of the protectionist Paris Resolutions produced by the Paris Economic Conference of June 1916. Might these be negotiated away under pressure from Wilson, an evangelical free trader? Similarly, perhaps the former German colonies, now mostly in the hands of the Dominions' armed forces, might be subject to bargaining with a democratic Germany.[65] For example, in late December 1916, Lord Esher warned H. A. Gwynne that President Wilson's 'wishy washy' tactics of appealing to the moderate forces inside Germany were going down well with the British Radicals and Asquithians, 'our weak-kneed "psychologists" ' as he described them. 'Nothing but a good and bloody victory will avail', Esher predicted, 'to keep these devils in check, who wish to deprive us of the right to punish a burglar and murderer.' Gwynne rushed to reassure Esher that he too deplored the fatal strategy of promising leniency to 'the kind of beast we are fighting'.[66] Naturally, in such circles Wilson's diplomatic effort to end the war in December 1916, complicated by his 'Peace Without Victory' speech in January 1917, gave great offence. Faith in German democratization was effectively linked in Conservative minds with the nefarious diplomacy of Wilson.

Not surprisingly, the joint reply of the Entente to President Wilson of 10 January 1917 carefully skirted the thin ice of German democratization. The Entente no longer listed among its aims 'the *destruction* of Prussian militarism', as in the Asquithian phrase, with the implicit notion of a democratized Germany. Rather, the emphasis was placed upon securing the evacuation and restoration of invaded territories. The Entente expressed its wish 'to liberate Europe from the brutal covetousness of Prussian militarism'.[67] In Balfour's private commentary on

---

[63] Joyce G. Williams, *Colonel House and Sir Edward Grey* (Lanham, Md., 1984), 107–8.

[64] For a typical comment see Ralph Paget, Ambassador to Denmark, to Lord Hardinge, Permanent Under-Secretary at the Foreign Office, 25 Jan. 1917, Paget Papers, provisional catalogue number Add. Mss 51253.

[65] For a typically frank statement of the gap between British and American aims, the British determination to hang on to the colonies, and the need to keep such aims secret see General Robertson's conversation with Repington in Repington Diary, 4 Dec. 1916, in C. Repington, *The First World War* (London, 1920) ii. 147. On the struggle within the government over the fate of the former German colonies and the intensifying resolve not to allow any colonies to be returned see William R. Louis, *Great Britain and Germany's Lost Colonies, 1914–1919* (Oxford, 1967), ch. 3.

[66] Esher to Gwynne, 24 Dec. 1916, and Gwynne to Esher, 27 Dec. 1916, Gwynne Papers, Imperial War Museum HAG/8, nos. 6 and 7.

[67] 'Entente Reply to President Wilson, 10 January 1917', Scott, *Official Statements*, 37.

the note which was dispatched to Wilson, he appeared to retreat from any direct commitment to democracy in Germany. No longer were the Entente powers eagerly anticipating some revolt from within Germany leading to democratization in order to guarantee a durable peace; rather they hoped only that 'the aggressive aims and unscrupulous methods of the Central Powers should fall into disrepute among their own peoples'—a much vaguer commitment.[68] Balfour was quite consistent in this. In various speeches in the House of Commons in 1917 and 1918, he repeatedly portrayed faith in German democratization as a dangerous illusion, because it implied that German militarism was 'merely the doctrine of a few ambitious soldiers'.[69]

Ironically, however, within the first three months of 1917, the pressures on Lloyd George to state a British position on the issue of democratization increased markedly beyond anything Asquith had experienced. A series of epoch-making events had to be accommodated. The March Revolution transformed Russia into a republic, committed to democracy and the full range of civil liberties, with a Provisional Government of Liberal patriots watched over by a Soviet of socialists. The rousing of democratic Russia, of course, had a powerful effect upon all belligerents. Similarly, the dramatic entry of the United States into the war in April 1917 set the air trembling with political possibilities. President Woodrow Wilson proclaimed that his nation's purpose in entering the struggle was clear: 'The world must be made safe for democracy.'[70] America would fight on the side of the Entente not as an 'Ally' but rather as an 'Associated Power'. These events naturally stimulated expectations that the Entente and American causes should be harmonized around the themes promoted by Wilson, the march of democracy.

The irony of the situation for the British War Cabinet was of uncomfortable intensity. Called upon to form a ministry dedicated to the 'knock-out blow' and to sweep aside the equivocators of the Asquithian 'Old Gang', Lloyd George had formed a War Cabinet including such imperial prophets as Lord Milner and Lord Curzon. The reality that the war was unashamedly a grand struggle for the moral superiority of British imperialism over German imperialism was to be advertised to the world.[71] The emblem of the revitalized imperial crusade was to be the Imperial War Cabinet, first summoned to meet early in 1917. But suddenly, under American and Russian pressure, imperialism itself threatened to become an embarrassment. Democracy was the new watchword. However, many

---

[68] 'British Supplement to Entente Reply to President Wilson, 13 January 1917', in Scott, *Official Statements*, 48, and David Lloyd George, *War Memoirs* (London, 1938), i. 662–3.

[69] e.g. 'Reply of Foreign Minister Balfour in Debate in the House of Commons on British Peace Terms, 30 July 1917', 'Foreign Minister Balfour in Debate in the House of Commons on War Aims, 6 November 1917', and 'Reply of Foreign Minister Balfour to Chancellor von Hertling, 27 February 1918', in Scott, *Official Statements*, esp. 127, 175, 183, 293.

[70] 'Address of the President of the United States, delivered at a Joint Session of the Two Houses of Congress, April 2, 1917', in Scott, *Diplomatic Correspondence*, 324.

[71] e.g. *Round Table* always underlined the fact that high-principled British imperialism stood for freedom and 'Commonwealth', in contrast to German imperialism which allegedly stood for invariable exploitation and subjection; see 'The War in Europe', *Round Table*, 16 (Sept. 1914).

of the most prominent Conservatives in the War Cabinet and wider ministry could scarcely claim reputations as enthusiastic democrats. Bonar Law, Chamberlain, Milner, Curzon, Balfour, and Carson seemed to have been miscast as directors of a democratic war. Dying in a ditch for democracy's sake was a difficult theme for men who had, after all, been cheerleaders of the reactionary Lords in the pre-war struggle against the wickedness of democratic Edwardian New Liberalism.

Even in the midst of war, democracy remained a divisive issue at home. In fact, as the bargaining between the parties at the Speaker's Conference on franchise reform in 1916–17 revealed, the Conservative Party's representatives were instinctively hostile to the principle of adult suffrage. As Steel-Maitland explained, the Conservatives' motivation at the Speaker's Conference was not to unveil a brave new democracy, but to find a compromise package containing only such concessions as might 'meet such popular feeling as exists'.[72] The local Conservative associations were overwhelmingly against democratic reforms. A petition circulated by Carson in early March 1917 showed over 100 Conservative MPs opposed to any action on electoral reform. In the event, the case for democratic reform recommended by the Speaker's report was carried only with great difficulty at a specially enlarged War Cabinet meeting in late March 1917.[73] In the new War Cabinet, wrote Tom Jones in April 1917, 'the "atmosphere" is one to develop hesitancy and shirking issues of a democratic character'.[74]

The Conservative leaders' ambivalence towards democracy was generally increased, not diminished, by the war. 'We cannot conceal from ourselves the fact that in a life and death struggle such as this [war], intelligently directed autocracy has an immense advantage over democracy', wrote Lord Selborne in 1915.[75] A supercilious tone towards democratic propaganda pervaded the private correspondence of the Round Table leadership. 'The root mischief is that while we talk of democracy and government by the people there is no such thing', Milner wrote to Curtis in 1915. British party politics was probably 'in no way better—I think in many respects it is worse—than the despotism of the Kaiser. We are putting all our money on *Democracy*. Well, Democracy is going to fail and the British Empire with it, unless we can emancipate ourselves to some extent from

---

[72] Quoted in Pugh, *Electoral Reform*, 79.

[73] See David H. Close, 'The Collapse of Resistance to Democracy: Conservatives, Adult Suffrage, and Second Chamber Reform, 1911–28', *Historical Journal*, 20/4 (1977), 893–918, and Pugh, *Electoral Reform*, chs. 6 and 7, esp. 96. For a review of the workings of the new Reform Act, stressing that Labour was not to be the sole beneficiary of the electoral changes (which may help explain the eventual decision of the Conservative leadership to support the reform), see Duncan Tanner, 'The Parliamentary Electoral System, the "Fourth" Reform Act and the Rise of Labour in England and Wales', *Bulletin of the Institute of Historical Research*, 56/134 (1983), 205–19.

[74] Tom Jones to Eirene Jones, 18 Apr. 1917, in Thomas Jones, *Whitehall Diary*, ed. Keith Middlemass (London, 1966), i. 31.

[75] Selborne to Bobby, 6 Aug. 1915, in George Boyce (ed.), *The Crisis of British Unionism: The Domestic Political Papers of the Second Earl of Selborne* (London, 1987), 142.

machine-made caucus ridden politics'.[76] As F. S. Oliver wrote of Milner, with a degree of understatement, 'I don't think he has any warm enthusiasm for democratic institutions'.[77] Similarly, Balfour told his intimates in Paris in 1919 that all his difficulties were increased 'through having to deal with Parliamentary Governments'.[78] Lloyd George's military appointments did nothing to break down this tone. Henry Wilson, Lloyd George's choice for the post of Chief of the Imperial General Staff, was fond of telling his fellow generals that democracy 'is an autocracy of blackguards'.[79]

The Prime Minister himself, of course, found it much easier to take up the democratic theme without flinching. As has been seen, it was Lloyd George's blend of extravagant patriotism and democratic theatricality that had commended him to leading Conservatives in December 1916. He was expected to be an advocate for both imperialism and democracy. He would add democratic fizz to the old King and Empire brew. As Philip Kerr had advised Milner on 11 December 1916, Lloyd George's 'faculty for democratic oratory' was now to be exploited in making a 'patriotic' appeal for a renewed dedication to the war on the part of the whole Empire.[80] In the first days of the Lloyd George government, an amalgam of Labour Party intellectuals, Liberals, and two Round Tablers also pressed upon Lloyd George the importance of projecting a democratic war spirit, with 'unmistakable evidence that he was as much the democrat as ever'.[81] The Prime Minister complied. Indeed, at the inaugural meeting of the Imperial War Cabinet on 20 March 1917, just after the collapse of the Tsarist regime, Lloyd George presented a statement proclaiming the 'democratization of Europe' as one of the great objectives of the war, second only to the driving out of German troops from the occupied lands. Lloyd George even recorded his conviction that democracy would guarantee future peace, observing that 'if Germany had had a democracy like France, like ourselves, or like Italy, we should not have had this trouble'.[82] This unexpectedly democratic atmosphere, however, was clearly unnerving for some in the War Cabinet. As Lord Curzon wrote, the Russian Revolution had created unfortunate pressures to indulge in a contemptible 'wild worship of so-called democracy'.[83]

[76] Milner to Curtis, 27 Nov. 1915, quoted in Wilson, *A Study in the History and Politics of the Morning Post, 1905–1926* (Lewiston, NY, 1990), 119; see also A. M. Gollin, *Proconsul in Politics* (London, 1964), 314.

[77] F. S. Oliver to W. E. Oliver, 16 Jan. 1919, F. S. Oliver Papers, 65.

[78] Betty Balfour to the family, 28 Feb. 1919, Whittingehame Correspondence, GD 433/2/270.

[79] Rawlinson Diary, 29 Jan. 1919, Rawlinson Papers, 1/11.

[80] Kerr to Milner, 11 Dec. 1916, quoted in John Turner, *Lloyd George's Secretariat* (Cambridge, 1980), 125.

[81] See the Memorandum drawn up in early December 1916 by Tom Jones, R. H. Tawney, Zimmern, J. J. Mallon, and Lionel Hichens, and the conversation with Jones, David Davies, Addison, and Lloyd George in Thomas Jones to Eirene Jones, 7 Dec. 1916, *Whitehall Diary*, 3–5 and 9.

[82] 'Prime Minister's Statement to the Imperial War Cabinet, on the Military and Naval Position (20th Mar., 1917)', reproduced as Appendix A, David Lloyd George, *War Memoirs*, i. 1050. See also Rothwell, *British War Aims and Peace Diplomacy*, 71, for similar comments to C. P. Scott on the eve of the meeting.

[83] Curzon to Robert Cecil, 1 June 1917, quoted in Rothwell, *British War Aims and Peace Diplomacy*, 100.

But pressures to trumpet forth democratic purposes did not only arise on the Allied side. Democratic expectations were rising in Germany too. On 14 March 1917, just before the outbreak of the March Revolution in Russia, Bethmann Hollweg announced his support for reform of the Prussian three-class suffrage. Then came the Kaiser's 'Easter promise' of 7 April, a solemn undertaking that the notorious Prussian suffrage, the keystone of the old order, would be scrapped after the war. This above all testified to the growing power of the democratic movement inside Germany. Similarly, the formation of the breakaway Independent Social Democratic Party of Germany (the Unabhängige Sozial-demokratische Partei Deutschlands or USPD) in early April, and the unprece-dented strike wave against reduced bread rations which began in Berlin on 15 April, revealed the inspirational power of the March Revolution in Russia.[84] The likelihood of these new developments inducing a German domestic collapse remained a most controversial point among the British political and military élite. In private, the Prime Minister remained generally doubtful. Asked point-blank by Lord Riddell on 1 April 1917, the very eve of the German internal troubles, whether or not he expected a revolution in Germany, Lloyd George replied 'I don't'. But he did appreciate that a domestic political struggle was in process, and told Riddell that in his opinion Bethmann-Hollweg was seeking 'a constitu-tional government'. He even confided to Riddell that with such a government 'it would be easier to make favourable terms'.[85] In the days that followed the 'Easter Promise', however, Lloyd George appeared to retreat back to the time-honoured tactic of playing down the seriousness of any evidence of new currents at work inside Germany. In a major speech on 12 April, Lloyd George reacted cautiously and succinctly to the signs of unrest in Germany. 'Prussia is no democracy. The Kaiser promises that she will be a democracy after the war. I think he is right', Lloyd George declared.[86]

Those nearest to the Prime Minister buttressed his scepticism. His close advis-ers, as we have seen, were naturally of the dominant school of thought that min-imized the German potential for reform. The opinions of Professor W. G. S. Adams, head of the 'Garden Suburb', were typical. Adams cautioned Sir Horace Plunkett in 1916 not to underestimate in his letters to his various contacts in the United States how deeply in Germany 'this Kaiser-cult' had 'entered into the thought of the nation'. It was a perversion which could not be broken until Germany was 'humbled and delivered from th[is] state of mind', wrote Adams.[87] Sir Maurice Hankey, Secretary to the War Cabinet, had similar views. In a Cabinet paper reviewing progress in the war, dated 18 April 1917, just after the

[84] See Carsten, *War Against War*, chs. 5 and 7, and on the USPD see Morgan, *The Socialist Left and the German Revolution*, and Robert Wheeler, 'Revolutionary Socialist Internationalism: Rank-and-file Reaction in the USPD', *International Review of Social History*, 22 (1977), 334–7.

[85] *Lord Riddell's War Diary*, 1 Apr. 1917, 247.

[86] Quoted in J. Ellis Barker, 'Will Germany Follow Russia's Example?', *Nineteenth Century*, 485 (May 1917), 1097.

[87] Adams to Plunkett, 11 Apr. 1916, Horace Plunkett Papers, ADA 25.

news of the serious German strike wave, Hankey observed, somewhat incongru-
ously, that in Germany 'the habit of obedience is so ingrained that the mass of
the people will accept almost any privations which their rulers inflict on them'.[88]
The recent events seemed not to count.

This seemingly invincible faith must have been tested by the extraordinarily
detailed monthly reports on social distress and unrest inside Germany assembled
for the Foreign Office from November 1914 onward by the intelligence official
W. G. Max Müller. His graphic reports on food shortages and plummeting
morale, based on the censored German newspaper press, letters from dead and
captured German troops, and private intelligence, grew steadily more grim during the first half of 1917. While Müller continued to insist loyally that military
defeat was still required before Germany would break, whatever the privations
imposed by the economic blockade, his reports vividly surveyed the hardships
being endured by the German people, the increasingly open discontent, and the
fragility of the political situation.[89]

Evidently, the Prime Minister was encouraged sufficiently by such reports of
intensifying political anxiety in Germany from April 1917 to try at least one inex-
pensive experiment. He chose his moment well—late June, a time when the food
situation in Germany (on the eve of the next harvest) was reported to be at its
most critical.[90] In a speech in Glasgow on 29 June, Lloyd George indulged in
some ostentatious fluttering of the democratic flag. In his address he declared that
the democracies of the world had been the most reluctant nations to enter the
war and reiterated his belief that, had all the nations of Europe been constitutional democracies in 1914, there would have been no war. Anticipating the victory and the peace that lay ahead, he then explained that the best guarantee of
German good faith, to which he looked forward in any peace negotiations, was

---

[88] Untitled Memorandum by Hankey, dated 18 Apr. 1917, CAB 63/20.

[89] Max Müller was the former British Consul-General in Budapest. His reports on the economic
situation in Germany and Austria-Hungary, many of which approach twenty pages in length, are
reproduced in Kenneth Bourne and D. Cameron Watt (gen. ed.), *British Documents on Foreign Affairs:
Reports and Papers from the Foreign Office Confidential Print, Part II, From the First to the Second World
War, Series H, The First World War,* ed. David Stevenson, vols. ix–xii (University Publications of
America, 1989). Modern scholarship addresses some of the same issues, confirming the images of
mounting distress inside Germany. On the lack of preparation of the German state for a long war in
1914 and the consequent economic mismanagement during the war see Robert B. Armeson, *Total
Warfare and Compulsory Labour: A Study of the Military Industrial Complex in Germany during World
War I* (The Hague, 1964). The suffering of ordinary Germans as standards of living declined is
detailed in the work of Jürgen Kocha, *Klassengesellschaft im Krieg. Deutsche Sozialgeschichte 1914–1918*
(Göttingen, 1973), published in English with the less confronting title *Facing Total War: German
Society 1914–1918* (Leamington Spa, 1984), and Avner Offer, *The First World War: An Agrarian
Interpretation* (Oxford, 1989), chs. 1 to 5.

[90] See Max Müller's report 'The Economic Situation in Germany during May 1917', dated 23
June 1917, in which he suggested 'Between now and the middle of August the German people will
pass through some critical weeks, but they will be encouraged to hold out by the promise of better
times to come after the harvest' (*British Documents on Foreign Affairs: Reports and Papers from the
Foreign Office Confidential Print, Part II, From the First to the Second World War, Series H, The First
World War,* xi, Doc. 11, 154).

'the democratization of the German Government'. Lloyd George announced: 'It is right that we should say we could enter into negotiations with a free Government in Germany with a different attitude of mind, a different temper, a different spirit, with less suspicion, with more confidence than we could with a Government whom we knew to be dominated by the aggressive and arrogant spirit of Prussian militarism.' He would encourage his military partners, he explained, to draw this same distinction in their general attitude to peace negotiations with Germany.[91] The tone was in line with Wilson's many assurances that the United States had 'no quarrel with the German people'.[92] Here was a strong hint of a more lenient peace for a democratic Germany—but a hint that committed Lloyd George to nothing precise.

On the face of it, the tactic was productive. Hankey reported that Lloyd George was naturally 'very delighted', and keen to take the credit too, when within a fortnight of his speech a major political crisis in Germany erupted.[93] The course of the crisis deserves a short survey. On 12 July an Imperial decree appeared renewing the promise of democratic elections for the Prussian lower house. On 13 July, Chancellor Bethmann Hollweg, undermined both by the Reichstag reformers on the Left and the Supreme Command on the Right, resigned. On 19 July the famous Peace Resolution, disavowing aggressive war and annexations, passed through the Reichstag by a vote of 212 to 126, with the SPD, the Centre Party, and the Progressive People's Party supporting the resolution. Its significance has long been debated. The new Chancellor, George Michaelis, was to boast later to the Crown Prince that he had robbed the resolution of significance by means of the famous qualification in his speech, accepting the principles of the Peace Resolution 'as I understand them'.[94] But certainly the military élite took the Peace Resolution very seriously indeed. The decision to found a new popular nationalist party, the Fatherland Party, hardly reflected confidence in the home front on the Right. Nor was the political situation quickly stabilized. While the initial appointment of Chancellor Michaelis to replace Bethmann Hollweg was a clear victory for the reactionary élite, he was to last only three months.[95] His replacement by the Catholic Bavarian aristocrat Count Hertling in October 1917, with the Progressive politician von Payer also replacing Karl Helfferich as Deputy Chancellor, advertised the increasing power of the Reichstag.[96]

---

[91] *Spectator*, 7 July 1917, 4.

[92] e.g. 'Address of the President of the United States, delivered at a Joint Session of the Two Houses of Congress, April 2, 1917', in Scott, *Diplomatic Correspondence*, 322.

[93] Hankey Diary, 15 July 1917, quoted in Stephen Roskill, *Hankey: Man of Secrets, i. 1877–1918* (London, 1970), 414.

[94] Fritz Fischer, *Germany's Aims in the First World War* (London, 1967), 404.

[95] The idea that Michaelis was simply the tool of the High Command is now questioned in revisionist writing; see L. L. Farrar, 'Opening to the West: German Efforts to Conclude a Separate Peace with England, July 1917–March 1918', *Canadian Journal of History*, 10/1 (1975), 74–5.

[96] On the internal crisis in Germany during 1917, works in English include Arno J. Mayer, *Political Origins of the New Diplomacy, 1917–1918* (New Haven, 1959), ch. 2, Klaus Epstein, *Matthias*

Lloyd George may have been chuffed by these events, but it is clear that many in his government were not so sanguine. The crisis in Germany reflected a broad democratic movement towards which leading Conservative personalities, as has been seen, were deeply ambivalent. Of course, Lloyd George's Glasgow speech had not by itself prompted this major political upheaval in Germany, but certainly it had made some impact, as British intelligence assured the Prime Minister.[97] Those associated with the Peace Resolution in the Reichstag certainly looked to Lloyd George as a potential moderate. Matthias Erzberger, rising star in the Catholic Centre Party and key figure in the formation of the new Centre–Left alliance in the Reichstag, proclaimed chirpily that he and Lloyd George could 'probably agree in a few hours upon a basis of peace and reconciliation'.[98] This was not a prospect over which a 'knock-out blow' government could rejoice. From the perspective of the Conservative oligarchy, there was a dangerous side to the new German mood: the Peace Resolution gave prominence to the notorious 'Petrograd formula' for a negotiated peace, 'no annexations and no indemnities'. Russian pressure for just such a 'democratic peace' was, of course, being stoutly resisted by Britain at this time. For example, the proposals of the Russian Foreign Minister Tereshchenko for an inter-Allied Conference to reconsider war aims were simply ignored.[99]

Moreover, pressures for more 'democratic' war aims soon prompted a major political crisis for Lloyd George's government. On his return to Britain in late July after six weeks in Russia, Arthur Henderson warned of the imminent demise of Russian democracy and the dissolution of Russia's war effort if the Entente's leaders persisted in their refusal to revise war aims. His advice was turned aside. Then, in early August, the War Cabinet dug its heels in deeper. In response to the Labour Party's decision to support the socialist Stockholm Conference on a compromise peace, a decision supported by Henderson, the War Cabinet decided finally against allowing any British representation at Stockholm. Lloyd George, Curzon, Milner, Carson, and Bonar Law then agreed to expel the defiant Henderson from the War Cabinet. As the War Cabinet saw the situation, the survival of Russian democracy was not a priority.[100]

Not surprisingly, therefore, the appearance of a new assertively democratic mood in the British and American leaders' speeches did not by any means win

Erzberger and the Dilemma of German Democracy (Princeton, 1959), ch. 8, Fischer, *Germany's Aims in the First World War*, ch. 14, and Gatzke, *Drive to the West*, ch. 3, and H. W. Koch, *A Constitutional History of Germany in the Nineteenth and Twentieth Centuries* (London, 1984), 211–30.

[97] 'We may say confidently that the speech was one of the influences which helped to bring about the serious crisis at Berlin at the end of last week' (Department of Information Intelligence Bureau Memorandum, 'Comments on the German, Austrian and Hungarian Press on the Prime Minister's Speech', dated 14 July 1917, probably by R. W. Seton-Watson, R. W. Seton-Watson Papers, Box 9, item V1/8).

[98] Quoted in Epstein, *Matthias Erzberger*, 215.   [99] Stevenson, *First World War*, 155.

[100] See J. M. Winter, 'Arthur Henderson, the Russian Revolution, and the Reconstruction of the Labour Party', *Historical Journal*, 15/4 (1972), 753–73, and David Kirby, 'International Socialism and the Question of Peace: The Stockholm Conference of 1917', *Historical Journal*, 25/3 (1982), 713.

general approval in Conservative circles during 1917. Hewins summed up the prevailing Conservative outlook in his diary: 'The whole of Germany is behind the Kaiser and the discipline of the people will hold through the War. Hopes entertained here of a democratic revolution are therefore likely to be disappointed.'[101] The Conservative press was divided on the issue. John St Loe Strachey, editor of the *Spectator*, was exceptional on the Conservative side; he set great store by the supposed propaganda benefits which the trumpeting of democracy might bring through the erosion of German morale from within. 'No Peace with the Hohenzollerns' he hailed as an immensely profitable propaganda theme.[102] Other Conservatives were filled with foreboding. It was appreciated that Wilson's 'democratic' weapon might carry with it all sorts of unforeseen incendiary effects that could change the political landscape on the Allied side as much as the German. And this line of propaganda might increase pressure on Britain to revise war aims in order that Britain might appear more credibly democratic. In response to Lloyd George's Glasgow speech, a flow of articles reasserting the conviction that the vast majority of Germans were guilty of 'militarism' appeared in the Conservative journals. In the leading essay in *Nineteenth Century* for August 1917, the retired Brigadier General F. G. Stone,[103] a prominent Conservative, hurled thunderbolts at Lloyd George, President Wilson, and even those few idealists in his own party who failed to recognize 'the complicity of the German people in the plans of their Ruling Class'.[104] Similarly, Dr E. J. Dillon of the *Daily Telegraph*, reasserted his conviction that the war was necessarily aimed at the German people as a whole, who had shown unfaltering loyalty to their militarist masters. 'The German people, being politically and militarily one and indivisible, the hope that State will rise against State or class against class is a delusion.'[105] The ultra-patriots too savaged the idea that the Allies had no quarrel with the German people, the old Liberal and Wilsonian distinction now implicit in Lloyd George's speech. Leo Maxse in the *National Review* argued that Lloyd George's offer from Glasgow was 'founded on a fallacy' regarding German

---

[101] Hewins Diary,17 July 1917, in Hewins, *Apologia of an Imperialist*, ii. 152.

[102] e.g. John St Loe Strachey, editor of the *Spectator*, consistently praised both Lloyd George and Wilson for distinguishing the misled German people from their rotten government and endorsed the war as a war for liberation; see *Spectator* editorials, 'Freedom's Cause' (7 Apr. 1917), 'Peace with the People' (9 June 1917), 'The Rescue of the German People' (7 July 1917), and 'The Crisis in Germany' (21 July 1917). See also Strachey's note to Sir Robert Cecil describing his own editorial as an endorsement of the 'No Peace with the Hohenzollerns' slogan, in Strachey to Cecil, 8 June 1917, St Loe Strachey Papers, S/4/4/26.

[103] Brigadier General F. G. Stone, retired in 1914, chairman of the St George's Conservative Association and a member of the Council of National Union of Conservative and Unionist Associations.

[104] e.g. see F. G. Stone, 'At War with the German People', *Nineteenth Century*, 486 (Aug. 1917). Stone attacked those on the Conservative side, such as J. Ellis Barker, who maintained that the German people might rise in revolt against militarism. As early as Sept. 1914, for example, J. Ellis Barker, had forecast that a defeat for the Kaiser's army would 'make absolute government impossible in Germany'; see J. Ellis Barker, 'The Ultimate Ruin of Germany', *Nineteenth Century* (Sept. 1914), and 'Will Germany Follow Russia's Example?', *Nineteenth Century*, 483 (May 1917).

[105] E. J. Dillon, 'The Allies' Task', *Fortnightly Review*, 606 (1 June 1917).

psychology. 'There is no reliable evidence of any political movement in the fatherland causing anxiety to the Emperor and his advisers', asserted Maxse, in spectacular defiance of all the facts.[106] Significantly, Lloyd George did not build upon his 'offer from Glasgow', if it may be called that. His subsequent speeches on the democratic theme were much more cautious. Democracy was identified as the sacred cause of the Allies, but Germany was portrayed as incapable of achieving that goal. For example, in a major speech on 21 July to mark Belgian Independence Day, Lloyd George resorted to the Conservative view that Germany's inner political arrangements were 'entirely the business of the German people themselves'. No hope was held out for democratization. He explained that 'Democracy is in itself a guarantee of peace, and if you cannot get it in Germany, well, then, we must secure other guarantees as a substitute'. He rejected the 'sham democracy of Germany' and 'a sham peace for Europe'.[107]

Distrust of the new democratic tactic was apparently the overwhelming reaction among the political élite and the government's advisers. Max Müller, for example, played down the significance of the Peace Resolution in his first intelligence report after Bethmann Hollweg's fall. He deprecated exaggerated hopes held for German democracy in some quarters in Britain. The lessons of the crisis were simple: the Michaelis appointment showed that the 'military party' were 'the only persons who count in Germany'.[108] The War Cabinet followed this lead. A 'Committee on War Policy', comprising Lloyd George, Curzon, Milner, Smuts, and Hankey, which reported in August 1917, just four weeks after the Peace Resolution crisis, was sceptical about German internal developments. The Committee noted the reports of declining morale and of political crisis in Germany but, citing the similar reports that had been received in 1915 and 1916, disparaged the idea of 'relying too much on this factor'. The paramount importance of inflicting defeat on Kaiserism by force of arms was still insisted upon.[109]

In any case, President Wilson then proceeded to drive the democratic bandwagon down paths so adventurous that Lloyd George's government dared not follow. In Wilson's unilateral reply to the Papal Peace Note on 27 August 1917 he denounced the Hohenzollern dynasty, 'the ruthless master of the German people', as unworthy of trust. He appeared to *demand* the democratization of Germany before any peace could be contemplated.[110] The American position was

---

[106] 'The Statesman's Illusion', *National Review*, 411 (May 1917), 282–3. When Lloyd George renewed the tentative hints of mild treatment for a democratic Germany given in his Glasgow speech in the House of Commons in Dec. 1917, the *National Review* was again intensely critical; see *National Review*, 421 (Mar. 1918).   [107] *Reynold's Newspaper*, 22 July 1917.

[108] 'The Economic Situation in Germany during June 1917, being the Thirty-fifth Month of the War', dated 23 July 1917, in Bourne and Watt, *British Documents on Foreign Affairs: Foreign Office Confidential Print, Part II, Series H, The First World War*, xi. 199.

[109] Report of the Cabinet Committee on War Policy, 10 Aug. 1917, CAB 63/22.

[110] 'Reply of President Wilson to the Peace Appeal of the Pope, 27 August 1917', James Brown Scott (ed.), *Official Statements of War Aims and Peace Proposals, December 1916 to November 1918* (Washington, 1921), 133.

widely interpreted as virtually a clarion call to ordinary Germans to revolt against their authoritarian government. This disturbed a great many British commentators, Radical and Conservative. The Union of Democratic Control, advocate of a negotiated peace, confessed that it was 'most disappointing' to find the President playing with the idea of the rejection of all peace approaches before a German revolution had turned out the Hohenzollerns from Berlin.[111] Even a 'patriotic' Liberal like C. P. Scott had his qualms. For example, when William Wiseman, British confidential agent in Washington, came to question Scott in August about the President's reply to the Pope, he found the veteran Liberal editor most anxious that the President did not commit himself to a 'No Peace with the Hohenzollerns' stance. Such a demand, Scott explained, 'went beyond any terms yet proposed'.[112]

Wilson's new departure only deepened mistrust of such ultra-democratic tactics in the Conservative camp in Britain. Some were stunned that the President should play with fire. 'Wilson invites the Germans to have revolution as a preliminary to peace', Hewins entered in his diary in disgust. He condemned this as unwise and unlikely: 'The Russian revolution does not encourage imitation.'[113] Some well-informed observers were honest enough to express simple embarrassment at the patent insincerity of Britain joining in a similar democratic propaganda. For example, Algernon Cecil, a cousin of Lord Robert, working at this time in the Historical Section of Naval Intelligence, complained in a private note to his fellow historian George Prothero that Wilson and Lloyd George were simply 'catching at this notion' of German democratization in order to supplement the force of arms. Cecil confessed to disillusionment at the 'confused tangle of promises and half-promises' which Britain had made, and embarrassment at her 'imperial projects which consort ill with democratic ideas'.[114] Most Conservatives, however, simply saw democratic revolution as impossible in Germany in any case. The shibboleths about the grip of militarism on the German mind and the impossibility of separating the people from the Kaiser's militarists were most commonly invoked. Sir Arthur Nicolson, the diplomatic veteran, for example, scorned Wilson's note as an attempt to dictate democracy to Germany. He advised Lord Stamfordham, the king's Private Secretary, that it was 'an error to attempt to dissociate the Hohenzollern dynasty from the German nation—and to endeavour to create a spirit of revolt among the Germans against their sovereign house'. Attempts to instruct them in democratic ways would 'only stiffen the Germans and arouse their patriotic pride'.[115] These opinions Nicolson no doubt repeated at a lunch in the presence of the king at Windsor a week later,

[111] Editorial, *U. D. C.*, Sept. 1917, quoted in Marvin Swartz, *The Union of Democratic Control in British Politics during the First World War* (Oxford, 1971), 138.

[112] C. P. Scott Political Diary, 24 Aug. 1917, Scott Papers, Box 134.

[113] Hewins Diary, 31 Aug. 1917, Hewins, *Apologia of an Imperialist*, 164.

[114] Algernon Cecil to George Prothero, 3 Sept. 1917, Prothero Papers, 'War Letters', bundle v, packet 2.

[115] Sir Arthur Nicolson to Stamfordham, 31 Aug. 1917, RA GV Q1085/25.

attended also by General Smuts of the War Cabinet. Certainly Smuts readily adopted the same views. To Riddell in late September Smuts described the latest Wilsonian declaration as 'unfortunate', explaining that it underestimated the resilience of Prussianism and failed to take account of the fact that the Germans' ideas of liberty 'are quite different from ours'.[116] Bonar Law told C. P. Scott that such tactics were useless because 'you can't impose freedom on a country'.[117]

The influential Round Table intellectuals also maintained a fierce scepticism about Germany's capacity to produce a decisive internal challenge to its own military government during 1917. At a 'moot' held in January 1917, for example, Alfred Zimmern presented a paper arguing that, in spite of the suffering in Germany, Prussian militarism was not yet crushed or even chastened.[118] At its most extreme, this school of thought appears to have decreed in advance that even a German revolution itself would be a hollow sham. For example, in January 1917, Eustace Percy wrote to Brand giving his view that Germany's despicable character traits were so deeply ingrained that 'any revolution will be a fraud'. The change that was required in Germany, explained Percy, was not a revolutionary change—it was a change that must be accomplished slowly, over a generation following her defeat in war, so that the very roots of 'Prussianism' could be attacked.[119] Brand agreed with this assessment, adding that revolution was in any case as far away as ever. Brand did acknowledge that in the long term German socialism was 'a very serious force to be reckoned with'. However, only if the Germans were decisively defeated, Brand agreed, were any constitutional changes likely.[120]

The resilience of this view among advisers to the government can be seen in the writings of the German experts at the Department of Information Intelligence Branch. Headlam-Morley's position was typical, and a candid expression of it can be seen in a rare exchange of private correspondence with Theodore Rothstein, the British socialist, an employee of the War Trade Intelligence Department at this time. The two men had quarrelled in June 1917, Rothstein insisting that Britain was doing too little to encourage the socialist and democratic forces inside Germany. Headlam-Morley replied to Rothstein that the 'democratic revolutionary movement' left him without confidence; the ferocity of the split in German socialism was the outstanding domestic development. Defeat was the only medicine. 'I still see little hope of a real change in Germany except as the result of a

[116] *Lord Riddell's War Diary*, 26 Sept.1917, 277–8.

[117] C. P. Scott Political Diary, 29 Aug. 1917, Scott Papers, Box 134.

[118] Zimmern's 'Memorandum for Circulation at the Moot, 2 Jan. 1917', Round Table Papers, MS Eng. Hist. c. 817.

[119] Percy to R. H. Brand, 24 Jan. 1917, Brand Papers, 8.

[120] Brand to Sir Joseph Flavelle, 30 Jan. 1917, Brand Papers, 8. For similar views see [Coupland], 'A War of Liberation', *Round Table*, 27 (June 1917). See also the articles by the American Round Tabler, George Louis Beer, 'The United States and the Future Peace', *Round Table*, 26 (Mar. 1917), 'America's Entrance into the War', *Round Table*, 27 (June 1917), and [Zimmern], 'The Internal Problem in Germany', *Round Table*, 28 (Sept. 1917).

definite defeat which cannot be denied, a defeat of such a nature that it will definitely and permanently destroy the influence of the militarists.'[121]

When the Peace Resolution crisis itself unfolded in Germany the men of the Intelligence Branch did not radically revise their views. Headlam-Morley was only temporarily heartened. He welcomed the resolution as a sign that the German nation was 'beginning to recover its sanity'. By late 1917, however, Headlam-Morley was describing the Peace Resolution as the 'high-water mark' of the reform movement. The Reichstag, he lamented, had failed to attract men who were 'real leaders'.[122] Saunders agreed with him that the parties behind the Peace Resolution had shown no cohesion since the July crisis and that the process of reform had now come 'almost to a standstill'.[123] The growth of German socialism, certainly, was not identified by these intelligence advisers as the hope on the horizon. Both men consistently minimized the chances of a dramatic breakthrough on the German domestic front.[124] Zimmern added his voice. At a meeting of Labour Party intellectuals and sympathizers, including Tom Jones, in January 1918, Zimmern insisted that the militarists around Ludendorff were still 'on top in Germany' and that 'at any sign of revolution they would turn machine guns on their own people ruthlessly'.[125]

Very similar attitudes pervaded the assessments submitted to the War Cabinet by military intelligence. Lieutenant-General Sir George Macdonogh, Director of Military Intelligence, told the War Cabinet in August 1917, just after the Peace Resolution crisis, that 'no revolution can be expected in Germany'.[126] By October, however, he was willing to concede that Germany was 'vulnerable politically'. But Macdonogh insisted that the best way to weaken Germany was to remain unbending on war aims, to keep up the military effort, and to refuse to deal with the present German leaders.[127]

By the end of 1917, therefore, the government's own specialist Germany-watchers, both civilian and military, remained enemies of a negotiated peace and advocates of a war to the finish. In so doing they insisted that democracy must come to Germany at the point of a bayonet.

---

[121] Headlam-Morley to Theodore Rothstein, 25 June 1917, HMP, HDLM, Acc. 727, Box 36.

[122] Headlam-Morley, 'The Internal Crisis in Germany', *New Europe*, 8 Nov. 1917.

[123] George Saunders, 'Reform in Germany and Prussia', *New Europe*, 6 and 13 Dec. 1917.

[124] Headlam-Morley, Political Intelligence Department Memorandum entitled 'German moderates and a *Verstaendigungspartei*', undated, but filed as Mar. or Apr. 1918, reflecting on the disappointing lack of internal opposition to the war in Germany since the Peace Resolution of July 1917, HMP, HDLM, Acc. 727, Box 2.

[125] Tom Jones Diary, 3 Jan. 1918, *Whitehall Diary*, 42.

[126] Lt.-Gen. G. Macdonogh, *Cabinet Committee on War Policy, The Man Power and Internal Conditions of the Central Powers. Note by the Director of Military Intelligence*, 31 Aug. 1917, quoted in M. E. Occleshaw, 'The "Stab in the Back"—Myth or Reality?', *Journal of the Royal United Services Institute for Defence Studies*, 130/3 (1985), 49.

[127] Lt.-Gen. G. Macdonogh, *The Effect of Military Operations On the Political Situation in Germany*, 13 Oct. 1917, quoted ibid.

The British Radical position: German democratization through a negotiated peace

There were other assessments on offer—but from sources unfriendly to the government. From the first week of the war, the Union of Democratic Control (UDC) and the Independent Labour Party (ILP) had mustered the dissenting Radical and socialist voices.[128] Here, and most prominently among the score of UDC and ILP critics of the war in the House of Commons, the hope of peace by negotiation with Germany became a guiding light. In pursuit of such a peace, the Radicals and the handful of anti-war Labour MPs fashioned a typically more optimistic interpretation of political developments inside Germany. The strikes in Germany in April 1917 and the passage of the Peace Resolution in July in particular were welcomed by the British Radicals as positive indications of the emerging power of the popular demand for democratic reform and a negotiated peace inside Germany. Such momentous developments, they argued, required an imaginative British response. During the summer and autumn of 1917, the Radical journals debated the likelihood of more far-reaching democratic reforms inside Germany. They attacked the British government for its failure to buttress moderate opinion in Germany by reformulating British war aims unambiguously in the Wilsonian spirit.[129] In particular, the Radicals called on the government to keep open the possibility of the return of the German colonies to a democratic Germany and to dump the 'war after the war' threats contained in the Paris Resolutions.[130] For example, H. N. Brailsford, the Radical journalist, warned that to proclaim indefinite economic war against Germany was to unite the German people 'as one man' against Britain. 'This is not to crush Prussian militarism, but to destroy German liberalism', Brailsford fumed.[131]

The most revealing debate on this subject took place in the House of Commons on 26 July 1917, just two weeks after the passage of the Peace Resolution through the Reichstag. The Radical speakers, led by Charles Trevelyan, a Radical MP, and Ramsay MacDonald, the former Labour Party leader, submitted a resolution acknowledging the Reichstag Peace Resolution and calling on the Lloyd George government and the Allies to restate their war aims in the light of the Reichstag's historic disavowal of annexations and indemni-

---

[128] The authoritative history of the Union of Democratic Control is Swartz, *The Union of Democratic Control in British Politics during the First World War*. Also useful are Keith Robbins, *The Abolition of War: The 'Peace Movement' in Britain, 1914–1919* (Cardiff, 1976), A. J. A. Morris, *C. P. Trevelyan, 1870–1958: Portrait of a Radical* (London 1979), Carsten, *War Against War*, and Raymond A. Jones, *Arthur Ponsonby: The Politics of Life* (London, 1989).

[129] e.g. W. H. Dawson, 'Germany after the War', *Contemporary Review*, 111 (Mar. 1917); W. H. Dawson, 'The New Orientation in Germany', *Contemporary Review*, 112 (Dec. 1917).

[130] e.g. W. H. Dawson, 'The Future of the German Colonies II: The Case for Conditional Return', *Contemporary Review*, 112 (Sept. 1917). The Union of Democratic Control had added a condemnation of plans for economic war after the war to its programme on the eve of the Paris Economic Conference, that is, in May 1916 (Swartz, *Union of Democratic Control*, 78).

[131] H. N. Brailsford, 'The Reichstag and Economic Peace', *Fortnightly Review*, 609 (1 Sept. 1917).

ties.[132] The silence of the government on the July crisis in Germany, and the virtual suppression of the Reichstag's resolution in the British press, they condemned.[133] The Radicals were careful not to exaggerate their optimism about events in Germany. But, while openly admitting the very limited constitutional authority of the Reichstag, they argued that a resounding vote in favour of democratic peace by a body elected by universal male suffrage was of tremendous importance. The Peace Resolution, the Radicals claimed, was a powerful expression of the emerging opinion of the great mass of the German people; it pointed to the probability of a fruitful outcome if face-to-face negotiations to end the war could only be commenced. German domestic opinion would work against a bellicose stance on the part of the German government in any negotiations. The Radicals also spoke in respectful terms of the democratic movement in Germany and predicted the inevitable ejection of the militarist élite. The discrediting of Kaiserism was bound to come, they argued, whether the war ended in compromise or clear defeat for Germany. As Trevelyan reasoned, 'a deadlock, which necessarily for all countries in the War means a non-annexation peace, is the death knell to German militarism'.[134]

The Radicals' linking of a faith in internal German politics with a demand for the revision of British war aims was another crucial feature of the debate. The Peace Resolution, the Radicals asserted, indicated the genuine belief held in Germany that she was fighting a war of defence against predatory enemies. This in turn signalled the need to revise war aims if the genuine fears of Entente aggrandizement and economic boycott, held in good faith by so many in Germany, were to be dispelled. Common sense dictated that it was essential not to 'damp down people who pass such a resolution', as R. D. Denman argued, but rather 'in every way to encourage every atom of sanity we see in that nation'.[135] The Radicals urged the government to dump the notion of a post-war economic boycott and to renounce plans to retain the German colonies. Nor was this required, they argued, simply to encourage German democracy to press for a negotiated peace. Russian democracy was at risk. The Radicals insisted that the deteriorating Russian situation made the revision of Entente war aims imperative in order to accommodate peace negotiations and thus save the democratic fruits of the Russian revolution. 'Abandon all these ideas of Colonies and conquests and economic war', urged the Radical H. B. Lees-Smith. If the government refused, he warned, 'it pronounces Mr Kerenski's doom'.[136]

The government's response to the debate showed its continuing refusal to place any faith in the internal developments inside Germany. Bonar Law jeered at the Radicals as 'living in a world of unreality'. He sought to diminish the

---

[132] *Parl. Debs.*, 5th ser., vol. xxvi, 1479 (26 July 1917).

[133] Trevelyan noted that many in the House of Commons itself had been unaware of the passage of the Reichstag's resolution, so carefully had this been 'hidden from the British public', a claim that was not challenged by government speakers (ibid. 1497).

[134] Ibid. 1503.   [135] Ibid. 1538.   [136] Ibid. 1518.

significance of the July crisis in Berlin and described the Reichstag as 'a body which does not exercise the smallest power'. Bonar Law coldly renewed the government's commitment to a war of attrition, for the war was now a matter of 'staying power'. The revision of war aims was not required. The only necessity was to avoid giving the Germans the impression that 'we are faltering in our task'.[137] Most significantly, Asquith lined up behind Bonar Law. The Liberal leader made a great effort to distance himself from his Radical and ILP critics. He sneered at their assumed 'superior moral standpoint'. He too sought to belittle the Reichstag as a body of 'a practically negligible quantity'. Its Peace Resolution he described as an 'array of more or less ambiguous generalities'.[138] Not surprisingly, the Trevelyan-MacDonald resolution was lost 148 votes to 19.[139]

The Radicals' faith in German democratization in the wake of a negotiated peace also created tension with the American President. In pursuing the revision of war aims, most Radicals believed they were in harmony with the Wilsonian position. Several Radical leaders were in friendly correspondence with Colonel House during the war, and they were confident that moderation of the Entente's war aims, in order to appeal to the democratic opposition in Germany, was also the American President's preferred tactic.[140] However, only a month after the Peace Resolution debate in the House of Commons, the Radicals' relationship with American diplomacy came under strain. The President's truculent reply to the Papal Peace Note of August 1917, as noted above, declaring that he would only make peace with the German people, perplexed Radicals as well as Conservatives.[141]

Many on the Left foresaw that the new Wilsonian position, in appearing to *insist* on sweeping democratic reforms inside Germany *before* the Allies would consent to treat with her, might sink all hopes of a negotiated end to the slaughter. Some critics argued that the President's democratic catch-cries could well be cynically commandeered by 'patriotic' agitators on the Right as 'fight-to-the-finish' slogans. In fact, Wilson's note was soon interpreted by the Conservative British press in exactly this manner, as in harmony with the Northcliffe slogan 'No Peace with the Hohenzollerns'—for democracy's sake. This, the Radicals feared, was an insincere attempt to democratize jingoism.

This reinforced Radical suspicion that the democratization theme was already being widely misused by pro-war pressure groups. Under the banner of the democratization of Europe, a long-running campaign was already in progress for an Allied commitment to the break-up of the Austro-Hungarian Empire in order

---

[137] *Parl. Debs.*, 5th ser., vol. xxvi, 1522–7.   [138] Ibid. 1505.   [139] Ibid. 1588.

[140] e.g. Noel Edward Noel-Buxton in a letter to House described his Radical colleagues as in sympathy with Wilson's method by which 'he seeks to fortify democratic forces in Germany', Noel-Buxton to House, 12 Nov. 1917, copy in Massingham Papers, MC 41/93/7. On relations between America and the Liberals in Britain see L. W. Martin, *Peace Without Victory: Woodrow Wilson and the British Liberals* (New Haven, 1958).

[141] Swartz, *Union of Democratic Control*, 138.

to achieve nationhood for the 'subject races', the Czechs and Yugoslavs in particular.[142] The British reply of 10 January 1917 to President Wilson's Peace Note had hinted at British insistence upon the liquidation of the Austro-Hungarian Empire and Ottoman Empires in order to achieve liberation for the subject peoples. (There was silence on colonies and post-war economic arrangements.)[143] The Radicals, of course, refused to believe that this commitment to democracy in Europe followed from any greater enthusiasm for democratization in the Lloyd George Cabinet compared to the late Asquith Cabinet. The fear that the Entente was using the slogans of democratization, quite selectively, to promote an indefinite war against the empires of Central Europe, undermined Radical faith in these same democratic slogans.[144]

From the middle of 1917, therefore, British Radicals made it clear that, while they supported German democratization, they were not enthusiasts for this goal *as a war aim*, that is, as a reason for pursuing the war to a military resolution. They were increasingly disappointed by Wilson's apparent insistence upon it.[145] In the *Nation* H. W. Massingham pleaded that the world was not made safe by democracy alone but by disarmament and an end to 'secret diplomacy'. To subordinate the search for peace to the achievement of democracy in Germany by force of arms, he warned, would prolong the war and imperil democracy in Russia. The Allies must not use the excuse that the war was being prolonged for democracy's sake: democracy in Germany would come in any case, he predicted, as 'the probable upshot of the first German general election after the war'.[146] Quite genuinely, judging from their private and family communications, the Radicals believed that the progressive forces seeking democratic reform inside Germany were pressing at the gates of power.[147] The British government, they

---

[142] The campaign was centred upon the *New Europe* group of publicists; see W. R. Calcott, 'The Last War Aim: British Opinion and the Decision for Czechoslovak Independence, 1914–1919', *Historical Journal*, 27/4 (1984), 979–89, and Hugh Seton-Watson and Christopher Seton-Watson, *The Making of a New Europe* (London, 1981).

[143] The note listed as an Entente objective 'the reorganisation of Europe, guaranteed by a stable regime and founded . . . upon respect of nationalities', 'the liberation of Italians, of Slavs, of Roumanians and of Czecho-Slovaks from foreign domination', and 'the enfranchisement of populations subject to the bloody tyranny of the Turks'; see 'Entente Reply to President Wilson, 10 January 1917', in Scott, *Official Statements*, 37.

[144] See H. Hanak 'The Union of Democratic Control during the First World War', *Bulletin of the Institute of Historical Research* (Nov. 1963), 173–4. Some Radical writers had opposed the 'No Peace with the Hohenzollerns' slogan from the beginning; see e.g. Headlam-Morley to W. H. Dawson, 20 Apr. 1917, W. H. Dawson Papers, WHD/326.

[145] H. N. Brailsford to A. G. Gardiner, 29 Aug. [1917], Gardiner Papers, 1/4.

[146] 'Will Germany become Democratic', *Nation*, 1 Sept. 1917. See also W. Runciman, 'No Peace with Napoleon and the Consequences', *Contemporary Review*, 112 (Dec. 1917). This argument, that Germany would rapidly reform herself under socialist pressure following a negotiated peace, a view supported by the opinions of neutral diplomatic observers, also circulated freely in the correspondence of many Liberals and Radicals at this time; for example, see Alfred Emmott to Robert Cecil, 28 Dec. 1917, Emmott Papers, 6; and Noel Buxton to Gilbert Murray, 22 Feb.1918, Gilbert Murray Papers, 36.

[147] e.g. see Charles Trevelyan to M. K. Trevelyan, 10, 21, 24, and 30 July, 1917, Trevelyan Papers, CPT EXIII [2].

believed, was seriously underestimating the German Left, and missing opportunities to fortify it. The Allies' best tactic was to present their armed struggle as a genuinely democratic cause, by shedding imperialist war aims, in order to 'hasten the cleavage between the masses of the German people and the Junkers', as Trevelyan expressed it.[148] This the 'knock-out blow' Coalition firmly refused to consider.

The British Radicals' faith in German democratization, therefore, should be distinguished from the positions of both Wilson and Lloyd George. According to the Radicals it was not the business of the Allies to *impose* democracy by force of arms in Germany. Democracy, they believed, would follow as the consequence of a negotiated end to the war. A spectacular defeat of German militarism was not required to give it life. A socialist and democratic challenge was inevitable in the post-war settling of accounts, even after a compromise peace (as every German and Austrian Conservative feared—and some were even willing to admit privately).[149] A peace dictated by the victorious Entente powers, with democracy emerging only in the midst of defeat, under the shadow of the invader's rifles, might serve to discredit German democracy. A. G. Gardiner and Colonel House had warned in 1915 that 'A humiliated Germany will not make for a democratic Germany'. Peace by means of an honourable compromise, a peace 'which would leave no wound to rankle', would be even more destructive of the Prussian militarist clique than a crushing defeat, argued Gardiner, for the German people would be free to demand a reckoning with their warmongers.[150] In this same spirit, W. H. Dawson argued, prophetically, in the *Contemporary Review* in May 1918:

There are British statesmen who, while convinced that German militarism must be destroyed, still cling to the idea that this end will only be attained as soon as the German armies are beaten in the field. No delusion could be more complete or more dangerous. Never will German militarism be uprooted by feats of arms alone, however decisive these may be. Far from that, it is even conceivable that defeat on the battlefield, if followed by such a peace as our own mail-fisted retaliationists clamour for, might have the effect of reinvigorating the military dictatorship and of inducing the German nation to accept it willingly, where in the past it has been accepted under protest, in the hope of retrieving defeat and rehabilitating the national reputation.[151]

---

[148] *Parl. Debs.*, 5th ser., vol. xxvi, 1501 (26 July 1917).

[149] e.g. Count Czernin, Austrian Foreign Minister, wrote in the summer of 1917 to Count Tisza, the Hungarian Prime Minister, in defence of his decision to support socialist representation at the Stockholm Conference: 'we shall be forced to have Socialist policy after the war whether it is welcome or not, and I consider it extremely important to prepare the Social Democrats for it. Socialist policy is the valve we are bound to open in order to let off the superfluous steam, otherwise the boiler will burst' (Czernin to Tisza, undated (mid–1917), in Count Ottokar Czernin, *In the World War* (London, 1919), 168–9).

[150] A. G. Gardiner, reporting the views of Colonel House, in *Daily News*, 24 July 1915, quoted in Koss, *Fleet Street Radical*, 211.

[151] W. H. Dawson, 'The Allies and the Supreme Issue', *Contemporary Review*, 113 (May 1918).

Of course, this interpretation contrasted sharply with the analyses upheld both by the government and its intelligence advisers. Weighing the worth of these arguments, certainly it must be conceded that the Radicals' claim that robust German democratization would follow a compromise peace was hypothetical. Critics deprecated it as a 'psychological' argument. But equally 'psychological' were the analyses preferred by the government. After all, the popular idea that a compromise peace would inevitably 'entrench Prussianism' was also a matter of speculation. The idea that democratization could only be achieved at the point of a sword was also based on various 'psychological' imponderables: that only a catastrophic military defeat in the field could sufficiently discredit the 'Prussian military caste', that only such a disastrous defeat endured by the old order would give German democracy a chance to grow, and thus only a military decision could create the circumstances for a 'lasting peace'. All these competing analyses were based equally on guesswork. All were unprovable. The analyses of inner Germany preferred by the British government were, of course, self-serving in the political sense, for the refusal to see any dependable new currents in Germany assisted the government in rebuffing demands for the revision of the Entente's war aims.

The Lansdowne letter and the Caxton Hall speech of January 1918: defining the limits of British hope in German democratization

However, as the fourth winter of the war approached, even the Lloyd George Coalition's commitment to 'seeing it through' faced a stern test. Two dramatic developments intervened. First, the cause of the Entente suffered a massive political blow in Russia: in early November 1917 a political coup swept the Provisional Government from office in Petrograd and Lenin's Bolshevik-led socialist government assumed power with the support of the All-Russian Congress of Soviets. Negotiations for an armistice on the eastern front followed and the Bolsheviks spoke enthusiastically of the prospect of a general peace. Second, a senior Conservative figure attacked the continuation of the war: none other than Lord Lansdowne, former Conservative leader in the House of Lords, Foreign Secretary, and the original architect of the Entente Cordiale. A letter from Lansdowne was published in the *Daily Telegraph* on 29 November 1917 (Dawson having refused to publish it in *The Times*). Lansdowne pleaded for moderation in Britain's war aims in order to smooth the way for a compromise settlement with Germany. The letter was widely interpreted as a plea for the government to seek a negotiated peace in place of its faith in the fiction of a 'knock-out blow'. The eminence of the writer ensured that a crisis followed.[152]

---

[152] On the Lansdowne letter and the resulting response, see Harold Kurtz, 'The Lansdowne Letter', *History Today*, 18 (1968), 84–92, Robbins, *The Abolition of War*, ch. 7, and Lord Newton, *Lord Lansdowne* (London, 1929), ch. 20.

The Lansdowne letter, it should be stressed, went beyond a simple plea for the costs of continuing the war to be honestly weighed. Implicitly, Lansdowne asked also (as he had argued in 1916) whether more moderate German leaders open to reasonable peace negotiations might not come to the surface in Germany if Britain moderated her war aims. For Lansdowne urged both a reformulation of Britain's war aims and a moral offensive against the German government. In this sense, the Lansdowne letter was a major contribution to the debate over German democratization. This added to the ferocity of the controversy which followed; for Lansdowne appeared to endorse the Radicals' long-standing complaint that the government had seriously underestimated the potential for reform inside Germany. As Lansdowne explained to an outraged Gwynne, who had written angrily to accuse him of inspiring Germany to fight on, he believed on the contrary that his views had 'given a fillip to the Peace Party in that country [Germany]: a party which to my mind deserves all the encouragement we can give it'.[153]

The Radicals were naturally the first to rejoice over Lansdowne's views, and they did so both privately and publicly.[154] Two of the key Asquithian figures, Grey and Haldane, were also cautiously supportive of Lansdowne's position. But they would not incur the 'patriotic' wrath by proclaiming their support publicly.[155] Grey complained that peace was made more difficult by the 'desire of the German people (it amounts to that) *not* to be masters in their own house and *not* to know anything except what their Gov[ernmen]t tells them'.[156] Haldane heaped praise on Lansdowne for his courage in writing the famous letter but explained to him that the timing was not propitious: 'This moment is not a difficult one, I think, for the German leaders', he confessed ruefully.[157] Asquith himself persisted in his refusal to sully himself with 'pacifism', as it was wrongly labelled, and would not give a clear lead to the Liberal Party in any campaign for a negotiated peace.[158] Scepticism about German inner politics still prevailed, even among those well-disposed to Lansdowne's position. Baron Eversley, the Liberal elder statesman, wrote to Lord Fitzmaurice, Lansdowne's brother, arguing that 'the only people who can put down militarism and autocracy in Germany are the Germans themselves.' But he was not confident: 'In view of their stupendous victory over Russia how can we expect the Germans to repudiate their army, their Emperor, their autocracy?'[159]

---

[153] Lansdowne to Gwynne, 24 Mar. 1918, Gwynne Papers, Imperial War Museum, HAG 14/no. 2.

[154] See Arthur Ponsonby to Lansdowne, 5 Dec. 1917, Lansdowne MSS [5] 85 [10], *Nation*, 8 Dec. 1917, and Robbins, *The Abolition of War*, 150–1.

[155] A. F. Whyte Diary, 3 Dec. 1917, Whyte Papers, MSS EUR D 761/1.

[156] Grey to Runciman, 15 Dec. 1917, quoted in Keith Robbins, *Sir Edward Grey: A Biography of Lord Grey of Fallodon* (London, 1971), 347.

[157] Haldane to Lansdowne, 29 Nov. 1917, Lansdowne MSS [5] 85 [10].

[158] On Asquith's response to the Lansdowne letter see John Turner, *British Politics and the Great War* (London, 1992), 251–6, and on the Liberal Party's response see Edward David, 'The Liberal Party Divided, 1916–1918', *Historical Journal*, 13/3 (1970), esp. 513–14.

[159] Baron Eversley to Fitzmaurice 19 Dec. 1917, Fitzmaurice Papers, Special Correspondence, Box 3, C–E.

The 'patriotic' press sought to minimize the impact of the letter. This was achieved by smearing Lansdowne as a faint-hearted and elderly aristocrat (at 72 he was in fact just three years older than Arthur Balfour). As an effete reactionary peer, it was said, Lansdowne had never had his heart in the struggle to make the world safe for democracy. Some in the government followed the newspapers' lead and dismissed Lansdowne as a 'nerve-wracked wobbler' still smarting with resentment over his exclusion from office in 1916.[160] The military élite, on the other hand, was divided. Robertson and Haig signalled that they were in favour of an early peace, but, in effect, only if the civilian government accepted the blame for failing to mobilize the resources which might have enabled the generals to win the war—which the civilians naturally refused to accept.[161] Moving among the soldiers in France, Sir John Simon found more straightforward support for Lansdowne: he detected a marked reluctance to fight for expansionist French war aims and reported that the soldiers in France were 'not nearly such fire-eaters as some of those who speak in their name'.[162] Support for Lansdowne among some officers was enduring. As late as August 1918, George Pitt-Rivers wrote from the front to assure Henry Forster, Financial Secretary to the War Office, that 'practically all fighting and thinking soldiers out here agree on this point [Lansdowne's letter], in spite of the fact that the bloodthirsty fellows at Westminster say it's treason!'.[163]

The issue of German democratization was very clearly tied up with this debate. For example, the Lansdowne letter led to a bitter quarrel at the editor's desk of the *New Europe* magazine. Alexander Whyte, editor of the magazine at this time, argued that the press had passed over the most important aspect of the Lansdowne letter, namely, its plea to the Allies to use the moral force of the democratic message to convert Germany to peace. He prepared an editorial urging the Allies to 'use the undoubted political power of their democratic ideals as an effective reinforcement of their military measures'. He attacked the Lloyd George government for having failed to stamp upon the 'wild talk by British politicians and newspapers' which had 'assisted the German Jingos in their campaign against German Liberalism'. Whyte was immediately denounced by Steed, who realized that any revision of war aims to appeal to German moderates might imperil the fragile Allied commitments to new states in eastern Europe.[164] In this way, the debate on German democratization often led to wrangles over how much 'ballast'—imperial, economic, or 'New Europe'—Britain should jettison from her war aims in order to reinvigorate the moderate Germans.

---

[160] e.g. see Lord Crawford Diary, 1 Dec. 1917, vol. xxxi, Crawford Papers.

[161] David R. Woodward, 'Britain's "Brass-Hats" and the Question of a Compromise Peace, 1916–1918', *Military Affairs*, 4 (1971), 63–8.

[162] John Simon to Herbert Samuel, 28 Dec.1917, Samuel Papers, A/155/V/6, and see also Esher to Lord Burnham, Burnham Papers, HLWL/1, no. 2.

[163] George Pitt-Rivers writing from the HQ of the 61st Infantry Brigade to the wife of Harry Forster, Mrs Forster,13 Aug. 1918, Lord Forster Papers. Similar evidence is presented in Turner, *British Politics and the Great War*, 266–7.

[164] Whyte Diary, 3 Dec. 1917, Whyte Papers, MSS EUR D 761/1.

Those who wanted no ballast tossed out still talked the loudest. During December, the consensus emerged that Lansdowne's suggested tactic of appealing to the reformist forces inside Germany was unlikely to work at this point of the war. The Bolshevik Revolution, in virtually ensuring Russia's exit from the war, was said, not inaccurately, to have bolstered the political stocks of the Prussian élite. The flame of democracy in Germany, it was argued, would flicker only flimsily now. If there had been a moment when internal revolt was possible, it was now judged to have been in the summer of 1917—although virtually no one in the government confessed to missing the boat.[165] Lloyd George himself still clung to the sceptical view. In his first parliamentary response to Lansdowne, he chose to use the evident lack of progress in German democratization as part of his government's argument for persistently rejecting the option of negotiation. He drew attention to his generous 'offer from Glasgow' in July, even adding the comment that the requirement for German democratization 'goes to the very root of things'. There had been 'no response' from the German moderates, he complained—ignoring altogether the Peace Resolution crisis. Therefore, he asserted, the evident resilience of the militarist clique was one more reason why 'victory alone' could be relied upon to dislodge them. 'Victory is an essential condition', he explained, for only an Allied triumph would suffice to get a popular government in Germany, and only a popular government could provide an 'enduring peace'. When the time came to make peace and establish a League of Nations, Lloyd George insisted, 'the people of Germany must be there'.[166] Just as the Radicals feared, here was the theme of German democratization transformed into a shield to deflect any demand for an end to the slaughter.

The pressures upon the Prime Minister for some redefinition of Britain's war aims, however, eventually proved overwhelming. The upshot was Lloyd George's famous speech to the trade union delegates at the Caxton Hall on 5 January 1918. The Prime Minister's various domestic, diplomatic, and military motivations in choosing this moment to redefine British war aims have been surveyed by several other historians.[167] It is clear that the Bolshevik appeal at the Russo-German peace talks at Brest-Litovsk for a general peace on the basis of the slogan 'no annexations and no indemnities', an appeal which threatened to undermine the loyalty of the British working class and perhaps the army, was a challenge which could not be left unanswered.[168] After nine months of unbending resistance to

---

[165] Only Smuts was willing to make this admission. He told C. P. Scott in Mar. 1918, 'The psychological moment for negotiating with Germany, if we wished to negotiate—was last July and August' (C. P. Scott, Political Diary, 20 Mar. 1918, Scott Papers, Box 134).

[166] *Parl. Debs.*, 5th. ser., vol. xxvii, 2221–4 (20 Dec. 1917).

[167] Mayer, *Political Origins of the New Diplomacy*, ch. 8; Rothwell, *British War Aims and Peace Diplomacy*, 145–53; David Woodward, 'The Origins and Intent of David Lloyd George's January 5 War Aims Speech', *The Historian*, 34 (Nov. 1971), 22–39; Turner, *Lloyd George's Secretariat*, 161–6; Turner, *British Politics and the Great War*, 268–71.

[168] At a War Cabinet meeting on 19 Oct. 1918 this exchange took place: Haig 'reminded the Prime Minister that in late 1917 the Army had been asking what they had been fighting for (the PM interpolated that this was one of the reasons why he had made his war aims speech)' (Minutes of the War

Russian pressure for some revision of Entente war aims, only now, with Russia lost, was it conceded that some effort to achieve the appearance of a progressive revision of war aims was necessary after all.

There were elaborate preparations for the speech. The phrasing of the main points was the result of characteristically frantic consultations over various drafts written by Smuts, Cecil, and Kerr.[169] Precautions were taken to secure the widest political support. As Lloyd George himself advertised at the beginning of the speech, he had consulted with Grey, Asquith, and 'the Labour leaders' in the lead-up to delivery. Another source of input is not so well known. In preparing his draft for the Prime Minister, Kerr also invited Headlam-Morley and his colleagues at the Intelligence Branch to submit a speech for consideration.[170]

The Intelligence Branch submitted a draft speech to Kerr that could only be read as an attempt to administer a tonic to the German democratic movement. The draft speech showed that Headlam-Morley and Saunders did not wish to miss the opportunity to offer the 'reasonable' Germans generous handfuls of hope. The spirit of the document was that of a warm invitation to embrace democracy, with promises spelled out offering a lenient peace to follow, including the safeguarding of German commerce and German membership of a 'League of States'. Among the sentences the intelligence men wished to place in the mouth of Lloyd George was a denial that the Allies sought 'the permanent exclusion of Germany from commercial intercourse'. Similarly, according to the draft speech, Lloyd George was to assure the Germans that Britain watched 'with interest and sympathy' the struggle for democracy in Germany. He was to proclaim that he knew 'on indubitable evidence that our objects would be welcomed by large numbers of the German nation'. The recommended wording of a final appeal to the German people was bold:

And to the peoples of Germany and of Austria-Hungary we would say: our cause is your cause. You are fighting against, not for, your own interests; our enemies are your enemies. Those who have destroyed the peace of the world are the same men who wish to deprive you of your liberty at home. Before the war you made a general protest against the spirit of Zabern against which we are fighting. Your true interest is the same as ours and your Government must be forced to agree to the law of the common good.[171]

The final version of the Caxton Hall speech, as eventually delivered by Lloyd George on 5 January, was tepid compared with this draft speech. The contrast

Cabinet) (X Minutes), 19 Oct. 1918, CAB 23/17). Tom Jones also stresses these motives in his account, Diary, 1 Jan. 1918 (Jones, *Whitehall Diary*, 42).

[169] See e.g. Cecil's complaints about the rush: R. Cecil to Curzon, 8 (5?) Jan. 1918, Curzon Papers, MS EUR: F 112/121.The letter would appear to be incorrectly dated.

[170] Kerr to Headlam-Morley, 7 Jan. 1918, thanking him for the memorandum he sent in on 1 Jan. 'which was very useful when Lloyd George's statement was being prepared', HMP, HDLM, Acc. 727, Box 35.

[171] Memorandum entitled 'Draft of Proposed Proclamation for New Year's Day 1918', by Headlam-Morley, undated, but suggested amendments by Saunders dated 27 Dec. 1917, HMP, HDLM, Acc. 727, Box 35.

between the two testified to the government's continuing reluctance to place any real hope in German democratization. Certainly, Lloyd George did seek to exploit the emotional capital in the words 'democracy' and 'self-determination'. He did hint at the old Asquithian distinction between the German people and their leaders, although without insisting on the innocence of the one and the guilt of the other. He proclaimed simply, 'We are not fighting a war of aggression against the German people'. But the crucial paragraph on the democratization issue was brief and unremarkable. It read:

Nor did we enter this war merely to alter or destroy the Imperial constitution of Germany, much as we consider that military autocratic constitution a dangerous anachronism in the twentieth century. Our point of view is that the adoption of a really democratic constitution by Germany would be the most convincing evidence that in her the old spirit of military domination had indeed died in this war, and would make it much easier for us to conclude a broad democratic peace with her. But, after all, that is a question for the German people to decide.[172]

Here was an assurance that German democracy would be well regarded, but precious little was offered to the Germans by way of an inducement to transform their political order.[173] The proponents of democracy in Germany had only the 'broad democratic peace' to rely upon.

The one major gesture towards the moderation of war aims was the disavowal of any insistence upon the liquidation of the Austro-Hungarian Empire (as Steed had feared). This was designed to keep alive hopes of luring the Austrians towards a separate peace. However, almost all the difficult questions concerning Germany were avoided or shrouded in a fog of phrases. Most importantly, the issues connected with post-war trade and access to raw materials were simply dodged. The speech was silent on the Paris Resolutions. Lloyd George simply offered the ominous remarks that post-war economic conditions would be 'in the highest degree difficult' and that it was 'inevitable that those countries which have control of the raw materials will desire to help themselves and their friends first'. Similarly, for Germans who looked to the proposed League of Nations as offering some economic protection for Germany there was nothing in the speech. At the tail-end of his address Lloyd George praised the idea of 'some international organisation' to banish war and ensure disarmament, but there was no suggestion of it safeguarding free trade. Nor was it proposed that Germany would be a member.[174] Similarly, the most difficult territorial questions of all, the fate

---

[172] Lloyd George's Caxton Hall Speech is reproduced in Lloyd George, *War Memoirs*, 1510–17.

[173] Commentators from various perspectives interpreted this invitation as distinctly lukewarm. Maxse attacked 'the invitation to Germany to democratise herself', which he noted 'was renewed but in a less confident tone' (*National Review*, 420 (Feb. 1918)). Similarly, see the views of Rennell Rodd, British Ambassador in Italy, in Rodd to Hardinge, 7 Jan. 1918, Rodd Papers, 19.

[174] Critics of the Lloyd George government pointed this out. The General Council of the Union of Democratic Control passed a resolution regretting that at the Caxton Hall 'Mr Lloyd George has made no clear repudiation of the commercial war implied in the resolutions of the Paris Economic Conference' (General Council of the UDC Minute Book, 20 Feb. 1918, Union of Democratic Control Papers, DDC 1/1).

of the former German colonies and of Alsace-Lorraine, which were linked to German foreboding about post-war economic opportunities, were fudged by Lloyd George. The former German colonies, it was announced, were 'held at the disposal of a Conference' and were subject to the great principle of 'self-determination'. This, Lloyd George made plain, was hardly likely to favour the former colonial masters. For Alsace-Lorraine there was to be a 'reconsideration of the great wrong of 1871', a piece of diplo-babble which sidestepped the issue of a plebiscite. At one point only in the speech did Lloyd George resort to unvarnished words. He specifically disavowed 'a war indemnity' and indeed any 'attempt to shift the cost of warlike operations from one belligerent to another'— a promise that would later haunt him.

What did the speech add up to? The tone of the speech was clearly dictated by the immediate domestic background. Barely a week before Lloyd George appeared at the Caxton Hall, the Labour Party and TUC had adopted a memorandum on war aims proclaiming that 'the fundamental purpose of the British Labour Movement in supporting the continuance of the struggle is that the world may henceforth be made safe for democracy'.[175] Lloyd George's attempt to impersonate Wilson in the Caxton Hall, therefore, was meant to reassure British Labour and rally domestic support for the war. And yet, Lloyd George must have known that a speech strewn with assurances of democratic purposes would be far from popular in the ruling circles. Just three days before Caxton Hall, for example, Douglas Haig had told the king that, while 'a few unambiguous sentences' were required so that the British soldiers would understand the objectives of the war, his brother officers had no interest in the democratic outcome of the war. 'Few of us feel that the "democratising of Germany" is worth the loss of a single Englishman! I also pointed out that the removal of the Hohenzollerns from Germany is likely to result in anarchy just as was the case in Russia', wrote Haig in his diary.[176] Nevertheless, from Lloyd George's perspective, the assertion of democratic objectives for the war was an irresistible domestic political requirement.

Indeed, the domestic purposes of the speech in the end prevailed over the international. Viewed from Berlin, the speech was not likely to do much damage on the German home front. Lloyd George claimed at a lunch immediately after delivering the speech that he was 'appealing to the German people and detaching the Austrians'.[177] But there was little expen ded in the appeal to the German people. Indeed, the elements of vagueness within the speech appear to have made most appeal to the Prime Minister. For example, in the afterglow of his oration Lloyd George was reputedly very proud of the ambiguity of the word

[175] Labour Party and the TUC, *Memorandum on War Aims as presented to the Special Conference of the Labour Movement at the Central Hall, Westminster, London, Friday 28 Dec. 1917.*
[176] Haig Diary, 2 Jan. 1918, in Robert Blake (ed.), *The Private Papers of Douglas Haig, 1914–1919* (London, 1952), 277.
[177] *Riddell's War Diary*, 5 Jan. 1918, 304.

'reconsideration' as it applied to Alsace-Lorraine.[178] But the speech was hardly a great address designed to rally the like-minded forces of progress in Germany. Fear of defeat would still outweigh fear of war. And Lloyd George knew it. In a postcard to his family three days after Caxton Hall, the Prime Minister revealed his intentions with candour: 'The speech is still the sensation. It has rallied the Allies but it does not mean peace. Never thought it would.'[179]

Nevertheless, Lloyd George's speech was malleable enough to earn him some support from all the major political groups in Britain. The belief in the moderation of the speech was assisted in part by the intervention of President Wilson. In his Fourteen Points speech, delivered just three days after Caxton Hall, Wilson included generous references to Lloyd George's address, thus felicitously enrolling him under the progressive banner. Among leading Liberals and Labour figures there was 'relief' at first at Lloyd George's decision to redefine war aims.[180] And yet, it is noteworthy that some cynics in the ruling circle were privately bemused. 'He talked much rubbish' Henry Wilson snorted in his diary.[181] As William Bridgeman explained to his wife, Lloyd George had said 'nothing very novel', but it had impressed the Labour men and that was the important thing.[182] On the fringes of politics there were murmurs of discontent. Some of the Radicals, on reflection, realized that the speech had been more in the nature of a 'non-declaration' of war aims, as Lord Courtney dubbed it.[183] On the Right, the irreconcilable ultra-patriots of the new National Party were outraged that any moderation in war aims had been suggested.[184]

But most revealing was the reaction of those experts paid to monitor German opinion, Headlam-Morley's men of the Intelligence Branch. They were crest-

---

[178] C. P. Scott Political Diary, 8 Jan. 1918, Scott Papers, Box 134. A. F. Whyte, however, claimed that Liberal gossip attributed the word to Asquith (Whyte Diary, 6 Jan. 1918, Whyte Papers, MSS EUR D 761/2). The phrase, in dodging the critical issue of a plebiscite in Alsace-Lorraine, helped head off French pressure for a deal involving the German return of Alsace-Lorraine in exchange for the return of the German colonies. Lloyd George was aware of this perspective. For example, when discussing Hertling's reply to the Caxton Hall in mid-Jan. 1918, Riddell remarked that 'it all boils down to Alsace-Lorraine and the German colonies' and Lloyd George agreed; see *Riddell's War Diary*, 27 Jan. 1918, 309. French pressure on the German colonies issue was well known. For example, see the journalist Robert Dell's opinion from Paris that 'Everybody here thinks that the German colonies should be returned' (Dell to Massingham, 1 Jan. 1918, Massingham Papers, MC 41/98/91).

[179] Lloyd George to Margaret Lloyd George, 8 Jan. 1918, in Kenneth O. Morgan (ed.), *Lloyd George Family Letters: 1885–1936* (Cardiff, 1973), 185.

[180] Tom Jones Diary, 9 Jan. 1918, describing a dinner with R. H. Tawney, A. Greenwood, A. Zimmern, and A. G. Gardiner.

[181] Henry Wilson Diary, 6 Jan. 1918, DS MISC 80, Henry Wilson Papers.

[182] Bridgeman to Mrs Bridgeman, 5 and 7 Jan. 1918, Bridgeman Papers, 4629/1/1918/5–7.

[183] For critical comments see C. P. Scott Political Diary, 8 Jan. 1918, Scott Papers, Box 134, and Lord Courtney to C. P. Scott, 7 Feb. 1918, Scott Papers, 335/12. The Radicals mocked the ambiguity of the word 'reconsideration' in particular; see Walter Runciman to A. G. Gardiner, Massingham Papers, MC 41/98/27.

[184] See *National Review*, 420 (Feb. 1918). Maxse deplored the specific disavowal of a war indemnity. Henry Page Croft wrote to Lady Bathurst, owner of the *Morning Post*, that Lloyd George 'has given all and kept nothing to bargain with' (Croft to Lady Bathurst, 11 Jan. 1918, Bathurst-Glenesk Papers, 2978).

fallen. Headlam-Morley wrote politely to Kerr that the Caxton Hall speech was 'admirable' so far as it went. But he could not hide his disappointment. He pleaded with Kerr to do all he could to stress the economic factor in future pronouncements. The Germans must be convinced, Headlam-Morley wrote, that while the Allied economic blockade would be applied 'ruthlessly' during the war, 'when it is over, if terms of peace otherwise satisfactory are attained, then they need not fear their permanent exclusion from world commerce'. The German government ceaselessly pounded their people with the message that they must fight on or face 'economic ruin' from a post-war economic boycott. The Allies must seek to banish this fear, Headlam-Morley advised.[185] In particular, the promise of German membership of a League of Nations must be held out to the Germans, for this was perceived in Germany as a guarantee against economic boycott. The best way to erode the will to win in Germany, he advised, was to make the Germans less afraid of defeat than war. Clear, solemn promises, proclaimed to the world, could do it.[186] Pledges such as these, of course, were precisely those studiously avoided by the Prime Minister.

German democratization as propaganda

At the beginning of 1918, therefore, it was clear that the British government had decided to spend little more than ambiguous phrases in an effort to arouse the forces of democratization and peace inside Germany. The chief consideration underlying this was transparent: the government's determination not to dilute war aims. This neatly reinforced its determination to see only the most slender prospect of German internal democratization acting as a viable force for ending the war. And yet, events early in the new year must have jolted this analysis. The Russo-German peace talks at Brest-Litovsk produced a violent response inside Germany. A great wave of strikes in favour of democratization and a negotiated peace 'without annexation and indemnities' engulfed the major cities in the last week of January 1918. The strikers' objectives were highly political, and this time even the SPD leaders gave some support to the strike.[187]

There was a response in Britain. The strikes set the seal on a new plan to boost British propaganda inside Germany. But the government's choices for directors of the operation were not without controversy. Two of the Prime Minister's plutocratic allies in Fleet Street were enlisted, Lord Beaverbrook and Lord Northcliffe. In mid-February, the Department of Information was upgraded to the status of a ministry and placed under the command of Beaverbrook. At the same time, Northcliffe took control of a separate department, the Department of Propaganda in Enemy Countries, which was to be located at the famous Crewe

---

[185] Headlam-Morley to Kerr, 9 and 15 Jan. 1918, HMP, HDLM Acc. 727, Box 35.

[186] Typed Memorandum, 'Certain suggestions as to the Propaganda value of the Idea of a League of Nations', undated, but filed 1918 HMP, HDLM Acc. 727, Box 2.

[187] On the strike wave in Germany see Stephen Bailey, 'The Berlin Strike of January 1918', *Central European History*, 13/2 (1980), 158–74.

House in London.[188] As the Radicals were to point out, these were not credible Wilsonian figures; Denman told the House of Commons in May that 'Lord Northcliffe is to the German what Count Reventlow is to us'.[189]

The appointments underscored the government's real intentions. Skill, not sincerity, was required. The propaganda that was to be disseminated was not to compromise Britain's vital interests. The incitement of faith in democracy and 'the League of Nations' inside Germany were to be the main ingredients. In fact, the British government had done very little to encourage support for the League of Nations idea even in Britain since first lauding the concept in the reply of the Entente to Wilson's Peace Note in January 1917. Only now did things begin to move. Balfour's appointment of the Phillimore Committee to enquire into the proposed League of Nations in January 1918 constituted a show of British support for the concept which could be exploited for propaganda purposes.[190] Some highly placed individuals were keen to encourage genuine adventures in a new propaganda of this type. For example, in March 1918 Esme Howard, British Ambassador in neutral Sweden, wrote to both Gilbert Murray, the well-known advocate of the League of Nations, and to Philip Kerr, to alert both men to the potential of such a propaganda campaign behind the lines of the Central Powers. 'There is no doubt that the German nation as a whole wants peace more than anything else', Howard explained to Kerr. If Britain proposed a progressive peace, with the League of Nations as the centrepiece, Howard predicted, 'I believe that it would not be long before the working men in Germany would produce such a ferment there that the German government would have to accept such terms.'[191] Zimmern and Percy at the PID also argued that the League of Nations would make excellent propaganda in Germany. The government itself, however, remained lukewarm. Throughout the remainder of the war, the War Cabinet refused to commit itself absolutely to the concept of a League of Nations, and it was left to several leading ministers, most notably Balfour, Barnes, and Cecil, to declare their personal sympathy.[192]

---

[188] See the account of the appointments in Reginald Pound and Geoffrey Harmsworth, *Northcliffe* (London, 1959), ch. 22, and the analysis in Philip M. Taylor, 'The Foreign Office and British Propaganda during the First World War', *Historical Journal*, 23 (1980), 875–98. The entries in *Lord Riddell's War Diary*, for 13 Jan. and 27 Jan. 1918 (308–9) show that the idea to appoint Northcliffe to a foreign propaganda post was being discussed in Lloyd George's inner circle only a week after the Caxton Hall speech.

[189] *Parl. Debs.*, 5th ser., vol. 106, 596.

[190] George W. Egerton, *Great Britain and the Creation of the League of Nations: Strategy, Politics and International Organisation, 1914–1919* (London, 1979), 44–5, 65, 72–4.

[191] Howard to Gilbert Murray, 25 Mar. 1918, Gilbert Murray Papers, 36; Howard to Kerr, 28 Mar. 1918, and Kerr to Howard, 22 Apr. 1918, Kerr Papers, GD 40/17/210. It was typical that, in his reply, Kerr noted the dangers of 'insidious pacifism' in this proposal which might undermine the war effort in Britain as much as in Germany.

[192] On Robert Cecil's struggle to get the War Cabinet to make a serious and public commitment to the League of Nations project, and the PID's support for this as a propaganda theme, see Peter Yearwood, ' "On the Right and Safe Lines": The Lloyd George Government and the Origins of the League of Nations', *Historical Journal*, 32 (Mar. 1989), 131–55, and Egerton, *Great Britain and the League of Nations*, 74–80.

On such rickety bases, from about the spring of 1918, the British undertook a revitalized propaganda campaign directed at Germany and Austria-Hungary. Two agencies were involved. Lord Northcliffe's Department of Enemy Propaganda at Crewe House naturally enjoyed the greater notoriety, but in fact it was not the first in the field. When Crewe House began to produce new German propaganda in August 1918, it was in fact supplementing the material already produced in the War Office by General Macdonogh's military intelligence network. From as early as 1915, the Directorate of Military Intelligence had been trying to foment political discontent inside Germany by directing cash and propaganda to left-wing German socialists. In the autumn of 1917, the Military Intelligence unit known as MI7(*b*) 'Press, Publicity and Propaganda', was directed by Macdonogh to begin work on a major propaganda offensive behind the German lines. Millions of leaflets were prepared for distribution, designed to incite discontent against the German government among both soldiers and civilians. The undemocratic nature of Germany's government was described in these leaflets as the chief impediment to an early peace. That these were deliberately 'inflammatory' leaflets, intended to foment civil unrest, even revolution, was willingly conceded by Macdonogh's staff. The MI7(*b*) leaflets were dropped first by plane in late 1917. The campaign was suspended from February to May 1918 when two Royal Flying Corps pilots were shot down over Germany, tried by court martial, and sentenced to ten years imprisonment for inciting treason. But, in June 1918, the distribution of leaflets over German lines was resumed using paper balloons. The number of leaflets dropped was very large, increasing from about one million in June 1918 to over five million in October 1918. These were supplemented by the first leaflets produced by Crewe House which were dropped in September 1918.[193] Thus was Britain's democratic propaganda cannonade directed at German morale.

Paradoxically, this blossoming of the British propaganda effort did not mean that the British government had changed its mind about the chances of something big resulting from the forces favouring German democratization. The government leaders hoped that the German opposition would make a difference, but they did not expect it to make *the* difference. An exchange in the War Cabinet in early February was revealing in this respect. In discussion of the effect of Bolshevism on the internal situation in Germany, Lloyd George announced that 'Russia is our most powerful ally now in Germany'. He was immediately contradicted by Milner: 'I don't see it. It is marvellous how miserably feeble the effect of socialism in Germany is'.[194] In spite of the decisions in February 1918 to boost propaganda, it appears that the German strike wave of January did not transform

[193] See Michael Occleshaw, *Armour Against Fate: British Military Intelligence in the First World War* (London, 1989), ch. 9, where examples of the leaflets are given, also Occleshaw, 'Stab in the Back', 52, and Michael Sanders and Philip M. Taylor, *British Propaganda during the First World War, 1914–18* (London, 1982), 210.

[194] Jones Diary, 8 Feb. 1918, in Jones, *Whitehall Diary*, 50.

thinking at the top of the British government. The reasons for this are obvious enough. The unrest was short-lived and soon overshadowed by other events. By the middle of March the annexationist Treaty of Brest-Litovsk was accepted by the Reichstag. On the Reichstag benches fear of Bolshevism in the eastern territories swayed a large majority to accept the annexationist aspects of the treaty: the SPD abstained and only the USPD opposed the treaty at the crucial vote. The Reichstag's revolt against Pan-Germanism seemed to have come to naught—for the moment. Then, most importantly, military events on the Western Front took centre-stage as Ludendorff let loose the last great German offensive on 21 March 1918. Hope of a German internal collapse naturally dwindled in the British ruling circle.

Fear of Russian Bolshevism had an effect too. After the socialist-led January strikes in Germany, so obviously linked to the events at Brest-Litovsk, signs of domestic unrest in Germany could now be attributed to the influence of Bolshevism not just German social democracy. Naturally, there were few advisers around the Prime Minister who were willing to identify the 'Bolshevistic' German socialists as exponents of moderation to whom should be directed promises of a lenient peace. The forces of German liberalism seemed to have been eclipsed by a 'Bolshevized' German socialism. The British revulsion of Bolshevism in all its forms, therefore, helped chill the zeal of many erstwhile advocates of German democratization during 1918. For example, Randall Davidson, Archbishop of Canterbury and a supporter of the Lansdowne letter, was careful to tell Asquith in February that, of course, 'peace due to revolutions in the different countries is uncertain, and certainly not what I would advocate'.[195] Indeed, the reluctance of some leading figures to contemplate inner change in Germany lest it incite revolution was now plain. As early as February 1918, George Buchanan, the former British Ambassador in Petrograd, was impressing fellow guests at dinner parties with 'his fear of a revolution in Germany, which he thinks would spread like wildfire in this country'.[196] Enthusiasm for Wilsonianism diminished in some Liberal quarters for the same reason. Even Lord Bryce complained that the 'catch-penny talk about democracy' promoted by Wilsonian slogans was making people much too tolerant of 'the criminal lunacy of the Bolsheviks'.[197]

Not only faith in German democratization, but faith in democracy itself was at a discount among some enthusiastic 'patriots'. Notwithstanding the passage of the Reform Bill in February 1918, there was much anxiety about where democracy might lead. For example, Harold Williams of the *Daily Chronicle*, a man close to the intelligence set and recently returned from Russia, complained to Whyte in April 1918 that his New Europe group had much too simple a faith in democracy. 'You have not seen a society break up, you have not seen democracy

---

[195] Davidson Political Diary, 9 Feb. 1918, Randall Davidson Papers, vol. 13.
[196] Lord Crawford Diary, 5 Feb. 1918, vol. xxxi, Crawford Papers.
[197] Bryce to G. O. Trevelyan, 11 June 1918, Bryce Papers, 19.

shipwrecked through its own successes, you have not seen socialism monstrously parodied. You have not been in hell', wrote Williams.[198] Sometimes the most passionate 'patriots' were also the least committed to democratic war aims. The Australian Prime Minister, Billy Hughes, and his press assistant Keith Murdoch, found their faith in democracy severely shaken by the rejection of conscription for a second time by the Australian electorate in December 1917. *'War weariness in a people who have escaped all the consequences of this awful war'*, wrote Hughes in bewilderment to Murdoch.[199] Some in this circle drew the obvious conclusion that democracy itself was expendable in the struggle to defeat German imperialism. 'I admit that democracy must be cast aside by all patriotic men if the labouring classes become selfish and indolent under the authority it gives them', wrote Murdoch in May 1918.[200]

During this period of military danger Lloyd George himself appeared not to entertain any hope of salvation through an internal German democratic revolt. In April he told Lord Burnham that reports of hardship and starvation in Germany were 'exaggerated'. Privation was real 'but it had probably been much the same for some time. It was not sufficient to stop the war'.[201] The Foreign Office pressed such sceptical opinions on the War Cabinet. For example, in early March 1918 Harold Nicolson prepared an assessment of German politics for circulation to the Cabinet. According to Nicolson, the victory in the east had transformed the domestic situation of the Kaiser's regime. There was now 'considerable confidence' in Germany, wrote Nicolson, for 'public opinion is in the mass pan-German and annexationist'. Revolution or widespread disruption was 'so improbable as to be outside the range of practical conjecture'. The contempt of the Foreign Office for the fortunes of German socialism may be gauged from the fact that not once in ten printed pages did Nicolson's report even mention the SPD, the USPD, or any German socialist leader by name.[202] Lloyd George appears to have accepted this analysis. He told Ponsonby, the leading Radical MP, in June 1918 that the war must be resolved by a military victory in order to change Germany. Ponsonby replied with an attack on the British political leaders and diplomats who 'had never attempted to strengthen the moderate party in Germany'. Lloyd George stressed, however, that the current military crisis ruled out any fresh appeal along these lines to the German Left. As Ponsonby recorded, 'he only kept on repeating this was not the time'.[203] With the Allied line

[198] Williams to A. F. Whyte, 28 Apr. 1918, Seton-Watson Papers, Filing Cabinet Correspondence, Whyte File.

[199] Hughes to Murdoch, 31 Jan. 1918, Murdoch Papers, MS 2823/33.

[200] Murdoch to H. E. Elliott, 9 May 1918, Murdoch Papers, MS 2823/34.

[201] 'Notes of a conversation', 2 Apr. 1918, Burnham Papers, HLWL/10, no. 12.

[202] Confidential Memorandum, printed for the War Cabinet, 'Consideration of Future political and Diplomatic Developments', 10 Mar. 1918, by Harold G. Nicolson, Nicolson Papers, Box marked 'Paris Peace Conference 1919'.

[203] Notes of an interview with Lloyd George in his room at the House of Commons, 27 June 1918, Ponsonby Papers, MS Eng. Hist. c. 667.

crumpling, Lloyd George's anxiety about the timing of any appeal to the German domestic opposition cannot be doubted.

But this was not simply a response to military events. Domestic pressures upon Lloyd George from the 'economic warriors' also increased at this time. From the middle of 1918, as the situation in France stabilized and then the German line began to sag, the government was urged to prepare plans for an economic victory. The National Union of Manufacturers and the British Imperial Council of Commerce mounted a sustained propaganda campaign against a levy on capital at home and for economic protection. When the long-awaited report of Lord Balfour of Burleigh's Committee on Commercial and Industrial Policy was delivered to the government in June 1918, the business lobby lauded it as a cogent plea from a former free-trader for a post-war economic boycott of Germany in harmony with the Paris Resolutions of 1916.[204] This long-running campaign was not without effect at the top of the government. In May 1918, Bonar Law had reaffirmed government support for the Paris Resolutions. The Prime Minister himself, much to the chagrin of President Wilson, appeared to endorse the notion of a post-war economic boycott of Germany in July 1918.[205] The pressure for protection at home was a constant pressure also against the government making any commitment to a 'free-trade peace' for a democratic Germany.

The progressive propaganda of the Lloyd George government during 1918, therefore, concealed paradoxes in substance and timing. In the aftermath of the Caxton Hall address there was no real shift in the ideology of the government. Lloyd George's speech was, in essence, an effort to wrap up British objectives in democratic verbiage rather than to revise war aims. As to timing, the British propaganda crusade was embarked upon in the midst of a military crisis, when the government had little faith in the movement for German democratization. The campaign appeared to be a desperate effort to throw grit in the gears of the German military machine, rather than a genuine effort to strengthen German democrats with solemn commitments of a progressive peace for a new democratic Germany.

But not all those involved in this enterprise were content that democratic propaganda directed at Germany should be a mere ruse of war. The Political Intelligence Department (PID), which was established at the Foreign Office in February 1918, at the same time as the drive for a new propaganda began, was uneasy with the direction of events. As has been seen, the attitudes of the four personalities at the German section, Headlam-Morley, Saunders, Bevan, and Zimmern were generally in conformity with the views of the 'knock-out blow'

---

[204] On post-war economic boycott and indemnity see British Imperial Council of Commerce, *Report of Proceedings at the Fourth Annual Meeting, 5 June 1918*, and British Imperial Council of Commerce, *Fifth Annual Report, 1918*, Executive Resolutions, British Imperial Council of Commerce Papers, 18,282/2; and National Union of Manufacturers, *Conference at Central Hall, Westminster, 23 July 1918*, Hewins Papers, 71, and report of the conference in *Evening Standard*, 23 July 1918.

[205] Rothwell, *British War Aims*, 279–80; Edward B. Parsons, *Wilsonian Diplomacy: Allied–American Rivalries in Peace and War* (St Louis, Mo., 1978), 145, 149.

school. They were generally not optimistic about Germany's capacity for internal conversion. However, as the advice tendered to Kerr at the time of the Caxton Hall speech shows, the leaders of the PID did retain some residual hope that, if genuine efforts were made to appeal to advanced opinion inside Germany, the war might at least be shortened. While not doubting the need for military resolution, the PID men believed that honest propaganda offering the League of Nations as a guarantee of a peace of justice would strengthen Liberal Germany.[206]

Headlam-Morley was the most closely involved in propaganda work. He agreed in May of 1918 to join a committee advising Northcliffe's new Department of Enemy Propaganda on effective themes to be incorporated in propaganda destined for consumption in Germany. The new Department of Enemy Propaganda met at Crewe House during May and June 1918. Here, on a committee considering 'Great Propaganda', as it was called, Headlam-Morley worked closely with H. G. Wells, the leading Fabian. Wells had been among the first to insist that the war was a great moral crusade for progressive purposes, and he had given to the Allied cause the serviceable phrase 'the war to end all wars' in his pamphlet of that title in 1914. His intentions had not changed. In late 1917 he had written to President Wilson pleading for the President to press forward the idea of a League of Nations as the centre-piece of a 'Just Peace'. As Wells expressed it, 'Germany as much as any country fights on and is helpless in the hands of her military caste, *because there is no confidence in Germany in the possibility of a Just Peace*'.[207] It was the Allies' task to plant and nurture that confidence, and they were not doing so. As Wells told Colonel Repington in May 1918, 'we have done nothing to bring the German proletariat over to us, and so have fought with only one hand'.[208]

However, in the new committee both men came rapidly to the view that it was impossible to compose effective and honest 'Great Propaganda' projecting Britain's progressive intentions unless the British government clarified progressive war aims. A plan was prepared to put pressure on the Lloyd George government to proclaim a further statement of war aims, in clear and unadorned language. It was argued that only such a statement, genuinely embracing idealistic, democratic, and moderate war aims, in harmony with the League of Nations vision, could make credible the planned appeals to the moderate political forces in Germany.[209] In May 1918, Wells prepared a draft memorandum along these lines that was typically bold. He called for a new Caxton Hall address that made precise promises to Germany on economic access and the League of Nations. It concluded that, if the war was to be won by and for high democratic ideals, then

[206] e.g. see Memorandum by A. Zimmern and E. Percy, 17 July 1918, FO 371/3474.

[207] H. G. Wells to Bainbridge Colby, Nov. 1917, reproduced in H. G. Wells, *Experiment in Autobiography* (London, 1966), ii. 709.

[208] Repington Diary, 2 May 1918, in Repington, *First World War*, ii. 293.

[209] See Minutes of the Committee on Propaganda in Enemy Countries, 14, 27, and 31 May and 25 June 1918, HMP, HDLM Acc. 727, Box 16.

'a Revolution in Germany becomes the primary war aim of the Allies'.[210] This last rallying cry was too much for Headlam-Morley. Asked to comment on Wells's draft, he pronounced himself in favour of the argument as a whole, but sounded a note of caution:

I am a little anxious about the specific mention of a *Revolution* in Germany. . . . [It] would certainly have a bad effect in Germany itself; it would suggest that we are looking forward to and counting on a revolution similar to that which has taken place in Russia and that the ulterior object is so to breakdown the cohesion of government as to destroy Germany and all she has won in the last 40 or fifty years. I should therefore prefer to say something like: there must be fundamental change in Germany. . . . If it can be achieved by peaceful and constitutional methods, all the better.[211]

Wells accepted the recommended softening of the phrases in his draft. The vital paragraph in the memorandum now declared that 'the changing of Germany becomes a primary war aim, the primary war aim, for the Allies'. The memorandum explained that 'the word revolution is perhaps to be deprecated'. For the great change to come 'we look, therefore, not so much to the German peasant and labourer as to the ordinary, fairly well-educated, mediocre German'.[212]

The efforts of Headlam-Morley and Wells to ensure that the propaganda was underpinned by real commitments on Britain's part ended in failure. At a meeting of the governing committee of the Department of Enemy Propaganda on 31 May 1918 (which Northcliffe himself missed on account of illness), Wells and Headlam-Morley prevailed at first. It was decided to send a letter to Balfour, enclosing the Wells memorandum, and urging a new public declaration from the government on war aims. 'Hitherto, Allied policy and Allied war aims have been defined too loosely to be comprehensible to the Germans', observed the polite introduction to the memorandum. 'Successful propaganda in Germany presupposes the clear definition of the kind of world settlement which the Allies are determined to secure and the place of Germany in it', it was argued.[213] Balfour replied in two sentences. He declared that 'on a cursory reading' he was in 'general agreement with the line of thought', but added the essential caveat: 'I notice that you make no specific mention of a very difficult question—the German colonies.'[214] As Northcliffe was still unwell, the committee prepared in his name an emollient reply to Balfour on behalf of the Department. The committee

[210] H. G. Wells, 'Memorandum on War Aims, prepared by a select committee of the Enemy Countries Propaganda for guidance in the Department of Great Propaganda', with an undated covering letter from Wells to Headlam-Morley, HMP, HDLM, Acc. 727, Box 16.

[211] Headlam-Morley to Wells, 22 May 1918, HMP, HDLM, Acc. 727, Box 16.

[212] Amendments to the Wells memorandum, HMP, HDLM, Acc. 727, Box 16. Exactly the same view, the encouragement of German demoralization on the part of the German people, but 'not necessarily to a spirit of revolt', was put by Zimmern and Percy of the PID in a memorandum dated 17 July 1918 (FO 371/3474).

[213] Department of Enemy Propaganda, minutes of meetings, 31 May and 11 June 1918, HMP, HDLM, Acc. 727, Box 16.

[214] Balfour to Northcliffe, 11 June 1918, HMP, HDLM, Acc. 727, Box 16.

reaffirmed that it recognized that Britain was not in the same 'moral situation' as Germany and that the fate of the colonies would be decided by the 'Fighting League of Free Nations'.[215] The memorandum went nowhere. At a meeting of the Department on 25 June, Wells announced that 'the German sub-committee was still embarrassed in its action, as they had been unable to obtain any official statement of policy. There were still scores of foreign policies being followed in this country by different people with conflicting and possibly disastrous results.'[216] Balfour's displeasure at these activities of the Department of Enemy Propaganda was plain: he complained to Lloyd George in July that Crewe House was straying well beyond the field of propaganda and even attempting to influence foreign policy itself.[217] The gap between the two approaches was clear. The government wished to use democratic slogans merely to demoralize inner Germany. Wells and Headlam-Morley, on the other hand, were pleading for a scrupulously honest propaganda which might regenerate inner Germany. 'We were in fact decoys', Wells complained.[218] He protested against Northcliffe's 'two-faced' position and resigned from his propaganda duties in July 1918.[219]

Headlam-Morley stayed. He did compose a note to Tyrrell complaining that the German propaganda committee was seriously handicapped by the imprecision of the Allies' war aims and urging a binding restatement of the Allies' progressive principles as a matter of 'extreme urgency'. Propaganda was impossible and dishonest, he wrote, unless the Allies made a 'formal adoption' of the League of Nations and were absolutely open about 'the use which they would make of victory'.[220] In spite of his reservations, he got down to work for Northcliffe's committee, now under the command of Hamilton Fyfe, a Northcliffe journalist. The guidelines to the propaganda which survive in Headlam-Morley's files show that, during the months that followed, the German propaganda committee acted *as if* Britain was steadfastly maintaining the distinction between German government and people, *as if* Britain was prepared to offer a peace of reconciliation to a democratic Germany. The 'Maxims' for the guidance of the committee included the following:

Never blame your propagandee. Blame his government, blame his leaders. Never blame 'the German' or 'Germany'. For the purpose of Propaganda in Germany at any rate, the German is a brave, honest, orderly, clean, able, good-hearted man, gentle-natured and cultured *but scandalously misled*; he was, in Switzerland, the first republican in Europe; he

[215] Northcliffe to Balfour, 13 June 1918, HMP, HDLM, Acc. 727, Box 16.

[216] Department of Enemy Propaganda, minutes of meetings, 25 June 1918, HMP, HDLM, Acc. 727, Box 16.

[217] Balfour to Lloyd George, 31 July 1918, cited in Taylor, 'The Foreign Office and British Propaganda', 892.

[218] Wells, *Experiment in Autobiography*, ii. 704; Henry Wickham Steed, *Through Thirty Years* (London, 1924), ii. 224.

[219] Norman and Jean MacKenzie, *H. G. Wells* (New York, 1973), 317, and Sanders and Taylor, *British Propaganda*, 237.

[220] Headlam-Morley to Tyrrell, 10 June 1918, and another draft of a letter, undated, both marked 'Not sent', HMP, HDLM, Acc. 727, Box 16.

flourishes in the republics of America; Tacitus witnesses to his virtuous and democratic past.[221]

As Headlam-Morley put it to a friend, his committee's task was to persuade the Germans that 'once they have accepted defeat and if they will accept the political principles of the Allies, a reasonable future will be kept open to them'.[222] While her propagandists sat down to write leaflets attesting to Britain's careful distinction between the 'scandalously misled' German people and their government, the British government was determined to make no such distinction at the end of the struggle. In fact, there was almost no chance of the Lloyd George Coalition mustering the political will to meet the expectations within Germany which such a propaganda would raise.

In conclusion, by the autumn of 1918, the battle lines dividing British political opinion on the subject of German democratization were firmly entrenched. Even in the fourth year of war, the government's position excited critics on both the Left and the Right. From the Radical perspective, no clear or sincere promise of a lenient peace to a democratic Germany had been made by the Lloyd George government. Thus, the Radicals maintained, even in the midst of the Ludendorff offensive, the chance to galvanize the forces of moderation in Germany was never exploited.[223] On the other hand, even the government's stammering commitments to a 'broad democratic peace' were attacked by the ultra-patriots and 'economic warriors'. In associating Britain with Wilsonianism, both Lloyd George and General Smuts were said to have imperilled plans for retention of the German colonies and for economic strangulation of the German industrial competitor.[224] Throughout 1918, the ultra-patriots continued to condemn all distinctions between the German people and government, and to ridicule all suggestion of revolution. As Rudyard Kipling explained to Gwynne in February 1918, the importance of the exit of Russia from the war was that it would bring home even to the 'abject fools' in the Lloyd George government 'the remoteness of any German revolution'.[225]

Lloyd George and his ministers seldom ventured beyond the safety of the Caxton Hall speech. This scarcely invited Germany to strike out boldly for a democratic future. While Wilson produced points, particulars, and principles

---

[221] 'Maxims', listed in 'Revised Draft Organisation—Directorate of Propaganda (German)', undated, italics added, HMP, HDLM, Acc. 727, Box 16.

[222] Headlam-Morley to Selby, 16 Aug. 1918, HMP, HDLM, Acc. 727, Box 2.

[223] See Ponsonby's notes for a speech at the Cannibal Club, Holborn Restaurant, 14 Mar. 1918, Ponsonby Papers, MS Eng. Hist. c. 667. For example, see also Balfour to Gilbert Murray, 29 Mar. 1918, and Murray to Balfour, 29 Mar. 1918, Gilbert Murray Papers, 36, and L. P. Jacks to Murray, 22 Sept. 1918, Gilbert Murray Papers, 37.

[224] 'Episodes of the Month', *National Review*, 424 (June 1918). The War Cabinet as a whole was denounced as 'much too amiable where Germany is concerned' because, in Maxse's opinion, it continued to hope for some internal democratization; see 'Episodes of the Month' in *National Review*, 425 and 426 (July and Aug. 1918).

[225] Kipling to Gwynne, 26 Feb. 1918, Kipling Papers, 139.

assuring a democratic Germany of a peace of reconciliation in a world of free trade, the Lloyd George government continued to dodge all precise commitments. The governing political assumptions in the 'knock-out blow' Coalition limited Lloyd George's capacity to follow Wilson in attempting to coax German democracy into a grab for power. Among the leading men, there simply was no real commitment to democratization. As F. S. Oliver confessed in a private letter in March 1918, 'I don't care a damn about democracy; but I do care a great deal about beating the Hun'.[226]

---

[226] F. S. Oliver to W. E. Oliver, 13 Mar. 1918, F. S. Oliver Papers, 77.

3

Towards a Democratic Germany and a Conditional Armistice, October–November 1918

. . . from the point of view of the British Empire, we could not finish the war at a better moment. On all hands, it is admitted that the turn of the tide which has taken place since July has been due to the efforts and surpassing heroism of the British Army. We are entitled to take a front place at the council table which will settle peace and the future of mankind. But we cannot go on at this rate. In 1919 we shall be liable, on account of national exhaustion, to give place to the Americans on whom will depend the success of the final campaign.

General Rawlinson to Lord Stamfordham, 22 October 1918[1]

THE armistice of 11 November 1918 still possesses the power to move the emotions. Commemorated in Britain and in the former Dominions of the Empire each Armistice Day, the event has long been at the centre of the cult of the fallen soldier. An event laden with such an emotional burden has naturally attracted its share of historical controversy. There are arguments over the merits or deficiencies of the original decision for armistice in 1918. Contemporary critics of progressive or Wilsonian diplomacy can still be found attacking the armistice as a monumental error. The armistice, it is suggested, was a premature suspension of hostilities that denied to Allied arms, and to British arms in particular, an imminent 'knock-out blow'. Had the war proceeded to an occupation of Berlin, it is argued, then the dictation of peace to a humbled nation would have concluded the war decisively. In this argument, the dichotomy between idealism and realism is often invoked; idealists are charged with having undermined the realists in London and Paris who wished to fight on in order to complete the conversion of Germany. The unfortunate interruption to the final advance, it is said, enabled reactionary Germans to represent their cause as unbeaten. Thus, the exorcizing of German militarism was left unfinished, the German people were denied enlightenment, and the German problem was unresolved.

[1] Rawlinson to Stamfordham, 22 Oct. 1918, RA GV Q2522/2/148.

None of this is new. Opposition to the idea of any armistice was voiced on the Right in Britain from the moment of the first rumour of the German request. Those right-wing politicians, journalists, and 'economic warriors' who were used to repelling all German 'peace offensives' during the war naturally denounced the German request for armistice in October 1918 as yet another 'peace trap'. When the armistice was concluded, regret over the missed opportunity to drive on to Berlin was common in these same circles. For example, Lord Ampthill, a National Party supporter, told Lady Bathurst in June 1919 that his one disappointment was the Allies' failure to dictate terms in an occupied Berlin, a humiliation which would have 'made the people realize that they were beaten which does not seem to have been impressed on them yet'.[2] By the mid-1920s, when the Versailles peace had failed to satisfy the 'hard men', when republican Germany had refused to play the role of contrite international pariah, and when her nationalist extremists were again active, the 'premature' armistice was signalled out for blame. For example, Wickham Steed wrote in his memoirs that his regrets over the armistice of 1918 were now 'justified'. What had been required, argued Steed, was a still more stark and unambiguous Allied military victory: 'Many of the difficulties that afterwards arose between the Allies and Germany would not have arisen had the German people been given ocular proof of their defeat. The belief that the downfall of Germany was due solely to mutinies in the army, fostered by enemy intrigues, would not have been implanted so firmly in German minds.'[3] Similarly J. L. Garvin wrote that the Allies' mistake was 'not to have crossed the Rhine in full massiveness in 1919'.[4]

The same argument for more war in 1918 can be found in contemporary histories. John Terraine, in his admirable defence of the British military achievement of 1918, *To Win a War*, has argued that it was the British politicians after the armistice who betrayed the soldiers. The politicians were guilty of 'disparaging the soldiers' capacity to win a war' and of allowing 'the sinews that should have upheld the victory to wither away'. A wider occupation of Germany was required, argues Terraine: 'It was not enough for the Allies to occupy Cologne, Coblenz and Mainz; when the German Army returned to Berlin in 1918 it did so with oak-leaves on its helmets and under triumphal arches. This accolade should have been reserved for the Allies themselves, and indeed, so it was—but not until 1945.'[5] More recently, Sally Marks has argued that the victorious powers had a choice in 1918, either to accept armistice or to fight on to Berlin; the victors' decision for armistice in 1918 was 'their greatest single mistake' for it fostered 'German self-delusion'.[6] The idea that democratic blessings would have been won for Germany from a continuation of the war has seduced even

[2] Lord Ampthill to Lady Bathurst, 1 June 1919, Bathurst Papers, 3808.
[3] W. H. Steed, *Through Thirty Years* (London, 1924), ii. 251.
[4] Quoted in Martin Gilbert, *The Roots of Appeasement* (London, 1966), 141.
[5] John Terraine, *To Win A War—1918. The Year of Victory* (London, 1978), 14.
[6] Sally Marks, '1918 and After: The Postwar Era', in Gordon Martel, *The Origins of the Second World War Reconsidered: The A. J. P. Taylor Debate after Twenty-five Years* (Boston, 1986), 23–4.

Golo Mann who laments in his memoir that the Allies did not proceed with war in 1919 as they did in 1944. 'Then the Germans would have known that their defeat was a genuine one, and the legend of the stab in the back of the fighting army, of the victory out of which they were cheated, would have had no chance to get started.'[7] According to this school of thought, therefore, the armistice of 1918 was the child of Wilsonian weakness; it robbed the Entente of an overwhelming victory and even prepared the ground for the 'stab in the back' legend. The sources do not provide support for such an interpretation of the events of October–November 1918. No Wilsonian armistice was forced on Britain, and British leaders did not express any desire to fight on into Germany for democracy's sake. This chapter examines the various factors at work in the eventual British decision for armistice. In essence, the chapter develops the argument that the armistice proposals accepted by the Associated Powers on 4 November made for an armistice which was neither Wilsonian nor 'premature'; and certainly it was not forced upon a reluctant Britain. After initial resentment over Wilson's apparent willingness to entertain the German request for armistice, the British government itself embraced the idea of an armistice as a military and political necessity in late October. Those who initially resisted the projected armistice in Britain did not do so from any concern for the completion of Germany's conversion to democracy.

What was the British attitude to armistice in 1918? The British government was quite determined from the outset that there should be no armistice in place of victory. The aim was clear and consistently pursued: victory, if not through fighting, then through armistice. The British achieved their objective. After a diplomatic struggle, a military victory beyond any argument, a complete victory as desired by the British government, was written in to the armistice terms. The need for an armistice was, after much inner struggle, eventually accepted by the British government. It is the purpose of this chapter to explain the British retreat from the position of obdurate opposition to any armistice, the position adopted in the first week of October. The analysis here seeks to emphasize the importance of three factors: domestic political preoccupations, entrenched hostility to Wilsonianism, and waning confidence in British military capability. These factors above all guided the British political élite during the making of the armistice. British acceptance of the armistice came about only when domestic political containment was judged to be secure. An armistice was embraced only when the prospect of a Wilsonian armistice had been successfully subverted. Finally, the armistice was accepted not from confidence in overwhelming British military strength, but rather from fear of an imminent exposure of military weakness.

---

[7] Golo Mann, *Reminiscences and Reflections: Growing up in Germany* (London, 1990), 102.

The German background: the beginnings of Germany's democratic transformation and the request for an armistice

On 25 September 1918, military intelligence advised the British War Cabinet that the German government was about to announce a major new domestic initiative, nothing less than 'the projected pseudo-democratization of Germany'.[8] Only a few days later, on 30 September 1918, a German Imperial decree was published announcing major changes in the government: Chancellor Hertling was stepping down from the chancellorship and a fresh government was to be formed. The bombshell within the message was the Kaiser's declaration of his wish that 'the German people shall cooperate more effectively than heretofore in the determination of our country's fate'.[9] Some form of democratization of the government was imminent. On 1 October the experiment began. The chancellorship was offered to a man of liberal and humane reputation, Prince Max, heir to the Grand Duke of Baden. The Prince immediately came to Berlin and set about the formation of a new progressive coalition government with the support of a clear majority in the Reichstag. By 5 October, he had formed the new government comprising leading figures from the Catholic Centre Party, the Progressives, and, most importantly, the SPD. Parliamentary government had arrived.

Was this merely a case of pseudo-democratization? It was no secret that the experiment of a new government had been determined from above. Prince Max undoubtedly wished to save the dynasty. Of course, such a government was not instantly democratic. The momentum of political events, however, soon drove both the Chancellor and his government down more progressive paths than originally intended by the makers of the revolution from above. In the negotiations to form a government, the Reichstag leaders had insisted that the Conservatives and National Liberals be excluded from any share of office. The socialists demanded concessions; to ensure their support, they were promised a government responsible to the Reichstag and the liquidation of the Prussian three-class suffrage.[10] Among the new Secretaries of State were Matthias Erzberger of the Centre Party, the principal figure behind the passage of the Peace Resolution of 1917, and Philip Scheidemann, the Majority Socialist, who had emerged as a prominent critic of annexationism following the suppression of the anti-war strikes in Berlin in January 1918. Their presence in the government signalled to all German observers that this government was an altogether new departure. The political pendulum in Germany was poised to swing decisively to the left.

More and more of Germany's political leaders were setting their course under the influence and perhaps the spell of Wilsonianism. Only a few days before

---

[8] Western and General Report, no. 87, 25 Sept. 1918, CAB 24/149.

[9] Prince Max of Baden, *The Memoirs of Prince Max of Baden* (London, 1928), i. 366.

[10] On the formation of the new government see *Memoirs of Prince Max of Baden*, ii. 12–14 and 28–30; on the deal with the SPD see Philip Scheidemann, *Memoirs of a Social Democrat* (London, 1930), ii. 158.

Prince Max's appointment, another major address by President Wilson had fanned German hopes that a peace of justice and reconciliation would be available for a democratically regenerated Germany. In his famous Five Particulars speech in New York on 27 September, Wilson promised impartial justice to friend and foe alike, and the special protection of the League of Nations for all. Most importantly, he denounced economic combinations and any idea of 'economic boycott' within the League. The speech had a decisive impact in Berlin. The argument was accepted that Germany must accommodate to President Wilson's desire for a more democratic government before applying for peace. The appointment of Prince Max as Chancellor, charged with the formation of a popular government, signalled the victory of the Wilsonian influence at court.[11]

Prince Max's momentous speech to the Reichstag on 5 October showed how complete was their victory. Max announced that his government would pursue both internal democratization and a peace based upon Wilson's programme. The most dramatic news was that a diplomatic note to Wilson seeking an armistice had already been dispatched via Switzerland. It arrived in Washington on 6 October. The simple note comprised just three sentences. First, it requested the American President 'to take steps for the restoration of peace', and 'to notify all belligerents of this request'. Second, without any specified reservations, the note tied Germany to the Wilsonian programme: 'The German Government accepts, as a basis for the peace negotiations, the programme laid down by the President of the United States in his message to Congress of January 8, 1918, and in his subsequent pronouncements, particularly in his address of September 27, 1918.' Finally, in order to avoid further bloodshed, as the note asserted, Germany requested Wilson's assistance in achieving 'the immediate conclusion of a general armistice on land, on water, and in the air'.[12] The meaning of the note was scarcely debatable. The wording of the second sentence made plain the faith in Wilsonian ideals underpinning the request. The Fourteen Points, the Four Principles, and the Five Particulars were all accepted.

In so doing Germany submitted to certain costs and looked forward to certain protections. Under any reading of the Fourteen Points, Germany would almost certainly lose Alsace-Lorraine; in addition, Germany undertook the heavy obliga-

---

[11] On Wilson's speech and the impact of Wilsonianism in Germany during Sept. 1918 see Klaus Schwabe, *Woodrow Wilson, Revolutionary Germany, and Peacemaking, 1918–1919* (Chapel Hill, NC, 1985), 30–9, and Edward B. Parsons, *Wilsonian Diplomacy: Allied–American Rivalries in War and Peace* (St Louis, Mi., 1978), 155.

[12] The text of the American translation is used here as given in Schwabe, *Woodrow Wilson*, 30. The text of the English translation of the German note, as given in several official publications, is in fact defective. It includes the German commitment to the Fourteen Points speech of 8 Jan. 1918, but omits the important allusions to Wilson's other speeches; see the document reproduced from the Foreign Office Confidential Print, 'German Government to the President of the United States', in *British Documents on Foreign Affairs: Reports and Papers From the Foreign Office Confidential Print, Part II, From the First to the Second World War. Series H, The First World War*, ed. David Stevenson (University Publications of America, 1989), iv. 60, and again in Harold Temperley (ed.), *A History of the Peace Conference of Paris* (London, 1920), i. 448–9. The full version of the original German note reappears in David Lloyd George, *War Memoirs* (London, 1938), ii. 1953.

tion that Belgium and Northern France would be 'restored'. But the protections for Germany under Wilson's programme were very plain. The President had made solemn commitments to fairness, free trade, self-determination, and the League of Nations. The President had given an assurance on 11 February 1918 that there would be 'no annexations, no contributions, no punitive damages'.[13] The specific reference in the German note to the speech of 27 September was significant too. It demonstrated how fervent was the hope that Germany would not be shut out of world trade.

Domestic political pressures in Britain on the eve of the armistice: peace with victory as a shield against social discontent

How then did the British government react to these epoch-making developments? To understand decision-making at the top in Britain, the domestic political priorities of the Coalition politicians must be appreciated. As the war entered its closing weeks, two related domestic preoccupations stood out: first, mounting fear of widespread post-war unrest; and second, intensifying pressure from the constituency of the Conservative-dominated Coalition in favour of securing for Britain and the Empire the maximum economic and territorial objectives of the war. Both require some elaboration.

The post-war let-down was dreaded among governing élites in all the belligerent nations. In Britain, political figures from both Liberal and Conservative Parties were much perturbed by the premonition that the end of the war would unleash a dangerous domestic radicalism. Conservative writers explored this theme as early as 1916, urging the political élite to prepare for the troubles ahead.[14] The war, it was feared, had greatly heightened expectations of social reform, elevated the bargaining power of industrial and political Labour, and generally eroded deference. In October 1916, for example, the Federation of British Industry (FBI) produced a confidential report, 'Notes on Post-War Industrial Problems', which drew attention to the danger posed by 'the special considerations which have been given to Labour during the war'. A dangerous spirit of expectancy, fired by 'cases of generosity and friendliness towards Labour', as the FBI warned, was spreading through industry and might be easily exploited by organized labour after the restoration of peace.[15] Anxiety over war debt, and fear of a resort to confiscatory taxation in the aftermath of the war, was also especially intense. These fears of post-war domestic unrest no doubt encouraged many leading personalities to express instant opposition to anything that smacked of a 'peace without victory'. Only a great historic victory, only a

---

[13] President Wilson's key speeches of 1918 are reproduced in Appendix III of Temperley (ed.), *A History of the Peace Conference of Paris*, i. 431–48.

[14] e.g. Arthur Shadwell, 'The Trials to Come', *Nineteenth Century*, 471 (May 1916), esp. 946–9.

[15] Sir Vincent Caillard, 'Notes re Post-War Industrial Problems', marked 'confidential', dated 25 Oct. 1916, FBI Archives, MSS 200/F/3/D1/2/2.

great 'Waterloo', it was widely believed, would arm the governing élite with the 'patriotic' prestige required to keep the rough men with burry voices in line.

Sir Edward Grey had been one of the first to glimpse these aspects of a post-war future: he told the Austrian Ambassador in his last talk with him during the July–August 1914 crisis that the imminent war was 'the greatest step towards socialism that could possibly have been made . . . We should have Labour Governments in every country after this'.[16] As the war unfolded, many figures in the traditional governing élite, both Liberal and Conservative, expressed similar fears. A handful of examples shall suffice here to illustrate the mood. As early as the summer of 1916 Earl Spencer confessed to Lord Fitzmaurice of his 'horrible anxiety' about the future of Britain when peace came.[17] In June 1917, Lloyd George, Riddell, Kerr, and Smuts agreed in discussion that after the war 'drastic changes in the social fabric would be proposed'.[18] In December, Lord Buckmaster told Lloyd George that 'The next government will be a Labour Government, I don't mean that there will be a Labour Ministry but Labour will be strong enough to dictate policy and they will insist that wealth shall pay'.[19] Fears that the aristocracy was faced with ruinous taxation were already widespread. Earl Stanhope feared 'all sorts of -isms after the war which, as in Russia, [are] certain to fall on land first'.[20] Charles Bathurst, the future Viscount Bledisloe, told Lord Crawford in July 1918 that 'fresh land legislation coming upon the top of our present scale of taxation will squeeze the country gentlemen out of existence'. 'I fear he is right', Crawford recorded in his diary.[21] 'To avoid a revolutionary upheaval after the war, we must lay our plans now', Gwynne wrote to Asquith in May 1918.[22]

Therefore, the spectre of a 'premature peace' was bound to raise fears of exposure of the government to domestic unrest. More precisely, the armistice request of early October threw into doubt the plan at the core of the British government's strategy for domestic political containment, the plan for a general election. For several months before the news of the armistice request broke, and certainly throughout the next six weeks, Downing Street was often preoccupied with preparations for a general election. An appreciation of the fact that Lloyd George and his close companions were absorbed in preparations for a general election throughout October, at exactly the same time as they considered the diplomacy

[16] Grey quoted by the Austrian Ambassador, cited in K. Zilliacus, 'Economic and Social Causes of the War', in Dwight E. Lee (ed.), *The Outbreak of the First World War: Causes and Responsibilities* (Lexington, Mass., 1975), 32. Confirmed in 'Conversation of Grey with Professor Gilbert Murray, January 10, 1918', in G. M. Trevelyan, *Grey of Fallodon* (London, 1937), 302.
[17] 6th Earl Spencer to Lord Fitzmaurice, 1 Aug. 1916 and 19 Oct. 1916, Fitzmaurice Papers, EFm 44.
[18] Lord Riddell, *War Diary, 1914–1918* (London, 1933), 4 June 1917, 254.
[19] C. P. Scott Political Diary, 28 Dec. 1917, C. P. Scott Papers, Box 134.
[20] James Earl Stanhope to 6th Countess Stanhope, 6 Mar. 1918, Stanhope Papers, C 578/18.
[21] Lord Crawford Diary, vol. xxxii, 10 July 1918, Crawford Papers.
[22] H. A. Gwynne to Asquith, 8 May 1918, Gwynne Papers (Bodleian Library), 14.

of the armistice, is vital to understanding the evolution of opinion on the armistice.

Lloyd George had talked constantly of the need for a fresh election for more than a year. He floated ideas for various political combinations among his trusted friends.[23] By late July, Riddell described him as 'full of it, and palpitating with energetic enthusiasm'.[24] The government had been promised that a new register, with the soldiers included, would be ready by 1 October 1918. Election planning for a 'win the war' campaign increased in intensity after July with an election date in November favoured by Lloyd George.[25] This was to be a general election like no other, in fact a 'great Election Stunt' as Lord Milner cynically referred to it.[26] Complex negotiations with the Conservatives, and with Asquith and other Liberals, proceeded throughout September and into October.[27] While the Conservatives had grave doubts about the utility of an election, many accepted that they had little choice but to persist with Lloyd George as Prime Minister. As Milner described the situation in private to Lord Derby, Lloyd George was 'the only possible anti-Bolshevik leader and whether we like it or not we shall have to support him'.[28] Similarly, Geoffrey Dawson, editor of *The Times*, accepted the need for an election by late September, and for the same reason, that is to assist in domestic containment. He informed Lloyd George that the case for the election had 'been greatly strengthened by recent Labour troubles' which, in his view, were due to 'sheer Bolshevism'. Only a fresh parliament would have the necessary constitutional authority to deal with the post-war trouble-makers, advised Dawson.[29] It was quite openly admitted, therefore, that the primary purpose of a snap election was to paralyse the Left and to prolong the Conservative-dominated wartime coalition. Only in a 'khaki election' would the patriots be able to lump the disloyal Radicals, Asquithian Liberals, and the new rising force of Labour together as discredited and unpatriotic, and hence unfit to lead Britain at the moment of victory. The 'win the war' election strategy which Lloyd George had been planning for months was undermined entirely by the armistice request.

The second element of the domestic context that shaped the British response to the armistice request was the intensifying domestic pressure for the 'spoils of

---

[23] e.g. C. P. Scott Political Diary, 21 Oct. 1917, C. P. Scott Papers, Box 134; *Riddell's War Diary*, 24 Nov. 1917, 27 Jan., 17 June, 23 June 1918.

[24] *Riddell's War Diary*, 29 July 1918, 342.

[25] *Riddell's War Diary*, Aug. (no day given)1918, 349, Christopher Addison Diary, 20–2 Aug. 1918, Addison Papers, Box 99, File 55.9. For details of the increasing pace of election planning from July 1918 see Roy Douglas, 'The Background to the "Coupon" Election Arrangements', *English Historical Review*, 339 (1971), 318–36, and Barry McGill, 'Lloyd George's Timing of the 1918 Election', *Journal of British Studies*, 14/1 (1974), 109–24.

[26] Milner to F. S. Oliver, 3 Aug. 1918, Oliver Papers, 93.

[27] Arthur Murray gives the details of one rejected approach to Asquith as late as Sept. 1918 (Arthur Murray Diary, 25 Sept. 1918, Elibank Papers, 8815).

[28] Derby Diary, 18 Sept. 1918, Derby Papers, 28/1/1.

[29] Dawson to Lloyd George, 26 Sept. 1918, Dawson Papers, 67.

war'. On the British Right, President Wilson had long been identified as a dangerous idealist likely to obstruct British plans for the full realization of her economic and territorial war aims. From the moment of the armistice request, directed to President Wilson alone, Germany linked both her democratization and her armistice diplomacy to Wilson. This virtually guaranteed a hostile reaction on the British Right. In addition, it posed a grave problem for the British political élite. For, in spite of the lip service Lloyd George and several of his ministers had paid to Wilsonian idealism, in private they had long scoffed at the 'holier-than-thou' President Wilson, identifying the programme outlined in his various speeches as a most serious threat to British plans for a profitable peace settlement. The government, therefore, was most receptive to anti-Wilsonian pressures coming from the 'economic warriors' and the ultra-patriotic Right.

For many months there had been a rising tide of anxiety in business circles about the economic content of the inevitable peace settlement with Germany. The government, it was insisted, must seize the economic opportunities presented by the moment of victory over Germany. With victory in sight, a variety of these right-wing economic interest groups and political forces increased pressure upon the government, urging it to plan for a peace of aggrandizement for Britain. An effort was made to goad the government into some action beyond the vague phrases which had so far characterized official British economic statements during the war, especially on the matter of indemnity.[30] Lloyd George, as has been seen, had specifically ruled out any indemnity designed to transfer war costs in his Caxton Hall speech. In the last months of the war, therefore, three demands were pressed upon the government by economic and nationalist pressure groups: a punitive indemnity, the protection of British industry, and the retention of the former German colonies.

First and most insistent was the demand that the government commit itself to the exaction of an indemnity from Germany, an indemnity large enough to assist in the recapitalization of British industry, and to deflect demands for post-war taxation of wealth. The danger of confiscatory post-war taxation had prompted much anxiety among people of wealth in Britain throughout the war. Conservative writers warned of 'the millstone of enormous debt' and urged the justice of indemnities to relieve Britain's debt burden.[31] Prominent men in the City, even Robert Brand, a relatively liberal banker, had long been in favour of some kind of an indemnity.[32] Other influential men close to the top in both political parties, such as Vaughan Nash, Asquith's former Private Secretary, and

---

[30] For a review of the moderation and restraint shown by Treasury and Board of Trade officials see Bruce Kent, *The Spoils of War: The Politics, Economics and Diplomacy of Reparations, 1918–1932* (Oxford, 1989), 28–31.

[31] e.g. H. J. Jennings, 'The World's War Bill', *Fortnightly Review*, 606 (1 June 1917), and 'Politicus' (J. Ellis Barker), 'No Annexations and No Indemnities?', *Fortnightly Review*, 607 (2 July 1917).

[32] Brand to P. B. Blackett (Treasury), 17 July 1916, Brand Papers, 5B.

Leo Amery, now serving the War Cabinet, promoted the necessity of an indemnity.[33]

During October 1918, a number of prominent political figures inside the Conservative Party sought to focus popular and educated attention on the indemnity issue. In early October, for example, Sir William Bull, Chairman of the London Conservatives and a prominent member of the Anti-Socialist Union, agreed to present material to *The London Magazine* for an illustrated article designed to highlight 'the importance of compelling the Germans to pay for or replace every building, ship, cargo, and work of art which they have wantonly destroyed'.[34] Sir Gilbert Parker, Conservative MP and another Anti-Socialist Union member, was also active from the first week of October promoting a project for a huge 'society committee' whose task it would be to disseminate propaganda in favour of the personal punishment of guilty Germans. As Parker expressed it, his policy was 'a big indemnity, town for town, ship for ship, and grind the brutes to the last step of endurance'.[35] It is noteworthy also that fear of post-war taxation of wealth, so sustaining to the indemnity demand, was not confined to the Conservative benches. On 12 October Grey and Herbert Fisher talked gravely of the problems of 'the taxation of capital as a means of liquidating the debt'. Fisher recorded afterwards that 'Grey thinks the great danger will be that the working class will desire to get all the necessary revenue out of direct taxation'.[36]

From outside the political élite also, direct pressure upon the government concerning the issues of indemnity and taxation increased once the armistice request was known. The Navy League, for example, petitioned Balfour not to entertain any peace proposal until Germany accepted 'ton for ton', that is, compensation for Allied shipping losses from the German merchant fleet, a plea which Balfour circulated to the War Cabinet.[37] The Dominion leaders, unlikely to gain anything from simple 'restoration', also began to appeal for an indemnity. For example, on 21 October, Lord Edward Morris, the former Prime Minister of Newfoundland, addressing the nationalist Entente People's Alliance, called on the government to 'exact in this case the pound of flesh' so that the Empire would be spared the 'millstone' of war debt. Other speakers at the function asked bluntly that 'the debt of this country in the matter of the war should be borne by Germany'.[38] The business lobby was active during October also. At the end of the month the FBI had its second Annual General Meeting and among resolutions passed was one urging the government, in framing its taxation policy, to be mindful of the

[33] Amery to Brand, 3 Feb. 1917, Brand Papers, 8.

[34] E. Middleton to Bull, 4 Oct. 1918, Sir William Bull Papers, 4/18.

[35] Dr E. Maclaren to Gilbert Parker, 1 Oct. 1918 and Gilbert Parker to Beaverbrook, 5 Oct. 1918, Beaverbrook Papers, BBK/E/3/46.

[36] H. A. L. Fisher to Mrs Fisher, 12 Oct. 1918, HMP, HDLM Acc. 800/3.

[37] V. Tritton (Chairman of the Navy League) to Balfour, 17 Oct. 1918, CAB 24/68.

[38] *Evening Standard*, 22 Oct. 1918. On pressures from New Zealand, Canada, and Australia see Kent, *Spoils of War*, 30 and 34–5.

vital need to ensure a flow of capital to industry in the post-war setting. Various FBI speakers pointed to the extraordinary war debts run up by Britain. The President of the FBI, Sir Richard Vassar-Smith, cautioned the government that manufacturers viewed 'with the greatest apprehension the depletion of their resources by taxation' after the war.[39] There were direct political pressures too. The National Party released its new programme in late October; it included demands for the retention of German colonies, the surrender of the German merchant marine, and, most succinctly, 'Germany to pay the costs of the war'. General Page Croft, National Party leader and former Conservative MP, thoughtfully sent Bonar Law a copy.[40]

The problems of war financing were in fact constantly in the news during October 1918, because a new campaign for war bonds had only just been launched. As an imaginative advertisement for the 'Feed the Guns' campaign, Trafalgar Square itself had been turned into a replica of no man's land, complete with thousands of sandbags, stacks of timber, field guns, and shattered trees.[41] In launching the campaign Bonar Law continued to avoid any absolute commitment to indemnity. But he was certainly aware of the huge problem of debt and not above pointing the way to a victorious peace for the men of the City as the solution. For example, speaking in late September at the Guildhall, Bonar Law acknowledged the 'immense burden of debt' facing Britain whenever the war ended. However, the Chancellor explained, the effect of this war debt upon Britain would depend 'more than anything else upon the way in which this war ends (Hear! Hear!)'.[42]

Second, the government was subjected to renewed arm-twisting on the issue of protection. As has been seen, the need for some protection in the short term against German competition after the war had won wide support among the business pressure groups. Demands that British industry be given a head start in post-war trade by keeping Germany economically debilitated for as long as possible were often voiced by the business organizations. For example, throughout the war the FBI's publications gave great prominence to German plans for industrial reconstruction and urged Britain to prepare for a resumption of economic competition with Germany.[43] In particular, the business lobbies sought to bind the government to the Paris Resolutions of 1916 and to the report of Lord Balfour of Burleigh's Committee on Commercial and Industrial Policy after the War, both of which sought to throttle German competition in the post-war setting. During October, the Tariff Reformers mounted an exhibition on Britain's

[39] Federation of British Industry, Report and Resolutions of the Second Annual General Meeting, 30–1 Oct. 1918, Hewins Papers, 71.
[40] Page Croft to Bonar Law, 31 Oct. 1918, Bonar Law Papers, 84/2/15.
[41] *Evening Standard*, 1 Oct. 1918.   [42] *Evening Standard*, 30 Sept. 1918.
[43] e.g. in the *Federation of British Industry Circular* (a fortnightly) there were fifty-four articles on German industry, trade, cartelization, and economic war aims during 1918. The *FBI Bulletin* also focused upon the German trade rival periodically; see e.g. the issues of 4 July 1918 and 7 Nov. 1918, Federation of British Industry Archive, MSS 200 F/4/24/2.

'Key Industries'—the industries that must be protected as vital to the economy—at the Central Hall in Westminster.[44] On 3 October the National Union of Manufacturers sent a deputation to Walter Long to convey the 'very strong feeling of discontent' among manufacturers regarding the government's lack of any definitive position on the vexed issue of post-war economic arrangements.[45] The Association of British Chambers of Commerce followed this up in mid-October with a letter to the Prime Minister urging his government to commit itself to protectionism, industry support, and measures to ensure British exploitation of the Empire's raw materials, as recommended by Lord Balfour of Burleigh's committee. At least a twelve month ban on all goods of enemy origin entering Britain after the peace was recommended. Before the war, warned the letter to Lloyd George, 'the Germans deliberately dumped goods into this country with the object of ruining British trade'. [46] Hughes was again to be found making public speeches urging that Germany be denied access to the Empire's raw materials after the war.[47]

That the government favoured some measure of protection, however, was taken for granted in many quarters. Robert Brand, generally not a supporter of the 'economic warriors',[48] advised that it would be in Britain's interest to frustrate Germany's efforts to restock raw materials at the war's end for 'everyday that her exports are delayed in making their appearance in foreign markets is a day gained by her neutral and enemy competitors'.[49] In September 1918, John Buchan, the government's propaganda bureaucrat, proposed that Britain mount an Allied trade exhibition in Brussels 'as soon as possible after the declaration of peace' to promote the products of Allied industry to a grateful European population.[50] Similarly, General Edward Spears, head of the British Military Mission in Paris, advised Henry Wilson in mid-October 1918 that one way of 'paralysing German trade for a long time to come' would be to demand the repatriation of American troops in German ships from German harbours. As Spears suggested, 'the bottling up of German harbours for a couple of years would give our trade a long and much needed start'.[51] Prominent Conservatives associated with the

[44] Advertised in the *Globe* during Oct. 1918.

[45] Long to Bonar Law, 3 Oct. 1918, and Long to Lloyd George, 3 Oct. 1918, Bonar Law Papers, BL 84/2/4. The impatience of the manufacturers was clear: Long had been assured that the manufacturers were seeking an informal and private gathering, but George Terrell, MP, leader of the protectionist National Union of Manufacturers, leaked the interview to the press. Much to Lloyd George's annoyance, the deputation's dissatisfaction gained some press coverage.

[46] Association of British Chambers of Commerce, Executive Council Minutes, 15 Oct. 1918, Association of British Chambers of Commerce Papers, 14,476, vol. 9, minute book.

[47] e.g. Hughes's speech to Australian merchants at the Baltic Exchange, *Globe*, 9 Oct. 1918.

[48] See Brand to Geoffrey Dawson, 17 July 1916, Brand Papers, 5B, attacking the British Empire Producer's Association and Dudley Docker's views on political economy.

[49] Brand, paper entitled 'The Bearing of American Intervention upon German Post-War Economic Plans', dated 6 Mar. 1917, Brand Papers, 8.

[50] Buchan to Addison, 23 Sept. 1918, Addison Papers, 69, file 304.

[51] E. Spears to Henry Wilson, 23 Oct. 1918, Spears Papers, 1/20, Liddell Hart Centre for Military Archives.

Unionist Business Committee willingly conveyed these concerns of the business lobbies to the heart of the government. Walter Long, the Colonial Secretary, Arthur Steel-Maitland, in command of the new Department of Overseas Trade, and Lord Derby, the British Ambassador in Paris and a business tycoon in his own right, all manœuvred during October to advance the cause of industry assistance.[52] Thus, the expectation of an ongoing trade war with Germany beyond the armistice was very strong. The British government's eventual insistence on the continuation of the economic blockade of Germany during the armistice period must be seen in this context.

Third, the government came under sustained pressure not to surrender the captured German colonies in any armistice bargaining initiated by Wilson. As Lord Derby observed in his diary on 13 October, there would be 'endless difficulty' over the Fourteen Points because they directly threatened the 'German colonies we have conquered'.[53] Those leading political figures most adamant concerning the right of Britain to retain her conquests, Long, Curzon, Milner, and Balfour, were soon agitating on this issue. On the orders of Long and Curzon, teams of public servants and academics were drafted to organize the collection of as much information as possible on the failings of the former German colonial masters, and on the merits of British administration everywhere, in order better to justify the British claims in the weeks and months ahead.[54] Milner's Round Table movement mobilized on this issue also. On 15 October Kerr wrote to Curtis, to explain a counter-strategy: a *Round Table* moot had decided to launch a great campaign against the American view that imperialism was itself immoral. 'America still has a childlike faith in the virtues of democracy and laissez-faire', he lamented.[55] Kerr's companions on the *Round Table* needed little prompting. The editor, Reginald Coupland was already encouraging contributors to defend Britain's inevitable additions to her empire as a result of the war, and to encourage the United States to do more in the way of taking up the imperial burden.[56] Curtis immediately began collecting material reflecting well on the 'free institutions of the British Commonwealth' for Lord Reading to use in re-educating the Americans concerning the benevolence and humanity of the British Empire.[57] The business pressure groups stepped into the fray also. For example, on 10 October the London Chamber of Commerce declared 'in the strongest terms' their resolute support for the position that 'in the interests of civilisation, none of the former German possessions beyond the seas should be restored to Germany'.[58]

[52] e.g. see Derby to Balfour, 17 Oct. 1918, and, alluding to Steel-Maitland's role, Balfour to Derby, 21 Oct. 1918, Derby Papers, 28/2/1.

[53] Derby Diary, 13 Oct. 1918, Balfour Papers 49744.

[54] e.g. see Long to Curzon, 22 and 30 Oct. 1918, Curzon Papers, MS EUR F 112/122.

[55] Kerr to Curtis, 15 Oct. 1918, Round Table Papers, MSS Eng. Hist. c. 810.

[56] A. J. Glazebrook to R. Coupland, 4 Oct. 1918, and Coupland to Glazebrook, 16 Oct. 1918, Round Table Papers, MS Eng. Hist. c. 819.

[57] Curtis to Amery, 23 Oct. 1918, Round Table Papers, MS Eng. Hist. c. 803.

[58] London Chamber of Commerce, Minutes of the Council, 10 Oct. 1918, London Chamber of Commerce Papers, 16459, vol. 8, Council Minutes.

The threat to colonial conquest made Wilson a despised figure among the governing élite. According to F. S. Oliver, Wilson's armistice negotiation with Germany showed him to be 'a lower form of worm even than we thought him to be'.[59] Lord Esher was particularly jittery that President Wilson might seek to deprive Britain of her colonial spoils in bargaining with Germany over democratization. At the end of October, Esher wrote to Lord Stamfordham:

I wonder what you think of Wilson's alternative. Abolish the Kaiser and you get an easy armistice and peace. Keep him and you get neither!

Later on he may say to us keep the German colonies and Syria and you will be boycotted by the USA. Hand them over to an International authority, and you shall have my good wishes!

This mentality is disturbing![60]

Balfour in particular did his best to shore up the resolve of the War Cabinet on the colonial question. Speaking at the Savoy Hotel on 23 October, at a function to honour the Australian and New Zealand politicians and military leaders then in London, Balfour declared that 'under no circumstances was it consistent with the safety, security and unity of the British Empire that the German colonies should be returned to Germany'. The British Empire's wish to retain the colonies was, said Balfour, 'in the interests of the whole civilised world'.[61]

These mounting pressures upon the government to secure the 'spoils of war' could not be taken lightly: they reflected currents of opinion within the constituency of the 'knock-out blow' Coalition. In addition, the exposure of Lloyd George on these issues was increased by a further domestic political complication. At exactly the moment when the saga of armistice began, Lloyd George fell out with one of his most important, if unreliable, allies from the years of war: Lord Northcliffe. The newspaper magnate, whose support for Lloyd George had been so important in 1916 and 1917, finally overstepped the mark on 2 October. Fully persuaded of his own indispensability, Northcliffe demanded a say in the formation of the next coalition government before he agreed to support it, a proposal that Lloyd George abruptly dismissed.[62] This split between the Prime Minister and Northcliffe made Lloyd George suddenly vulnerable to the power of the popular 'patriotic' dailies. To be caught up in a German peace overture was fraught with danger for Lloyd George on the domestic front.

All these domestic complications helped shape the British response to the German armistice request. The British government was determined to deflect an early peace and to keep free of any entangling commitments to a Wilsonian

---

[59] F. S. Oliver to W. E. Oliver, 24 Oct. 1918, Oliver Papers, 65.

[60] Esher to Stamfordham, 26 Oct. 1918, George V Papers, RA GV Q724/109.

[61] *Evening Standard*, 23 Oct. 1918.

[62] *Riddell's War Diary*, 3 Oct. 1918, 366, and see entries for 12 Aug., 345, and Aug. (no day given), 348. Since August at least relations had been very strained; see Bonar Law to Walter Long, 20 Aug. 1918, Long Papers, WRO 947/567. See also the very full coverage of the reasons for the split in J. M. McEwen, 'Northcliffe and Lloyd George at War, 1914–1918', *Historical Journal*, 24/3 (1981), 651–72 and in Reginald Pound and Geoffrey Harmsworth, *Northcliffe* (London, 1959), 673–683.

programme. It followed that the Lloyd George government was bound to resist the German armistice request and to pour scorn on the simultaneous democratization of Germany. For the first three weeks of October at least, this was exactly the response of the Lloyd George government.

Resistance to armistice: the British effort to deflect the Wilsonian challenge and to discredit German democratization, 5–13 October 1918

How then did the British élite judge the arrival of Prince Max of Baden in the Chancellery on the Wilhelmstrasse? The prince, heir to the Grand Ducal throne of Baden, was related by marriage to the English Royal Family: he had married Princess Marie Louise of Great Britain and Ireland, a daughter of the Duke of Cumberland, in 1900. At home, the prince had a Liberal and humanitarian reputation arising principally from his work with the Red Cross in caring for Allied prisoners of war held in Germany. His interventions on behalf of especially well-connected and high-ranking British prisoners had earned him praise among the handful of people who had knowledge of this in Britain, a handful which included George V and Lord Stamfordham.[63] Soon after Max was appointed Chancellor, Margaret, the Crown Princess of Sweden (a daughter of the Duke of Connaught), wrote enthusiastically to the Duchess of Argyll at Kensington Palace in praise of Prince Max. The prince was well known to the young princess as she had acted as a go-between for several titled Englishmen seeking Prince Max's assistance for their relatives inside Germany during the war. The Crown Princess wrote that she was certain that Max's historic speech to the Reichstag was 'honestly meant' and that he did 'not approve of militarism or Junkers or anything of that sort'.[64] King George himself may not have heard any discussion favourable to Prince Max. During the first two weeks of October he was at Sandringham shooting.[65] Certainly, neither the king nor Lord Stamfordham appear to have undertaken any efforts to spread good opinions of the new Chancellor. The reasons for this continuing silence on Prince Max can only be speculated upon, but one consideration suggests itself. George V was still occasionally troubled by rumours that he had privately promised British neutrality to Prince Heinrich, the Kaiser's

---

[63] Positive assessments of Prince Max in the Royal Archives, arising from his Red Cross work, include Margaret ('Daisy'), Crown Princess of Sweden to 'Aunt Louise' (Princess Louise, Duchess of Argyll, the king's aunt), 15 Nov. 1916, RA Add. A17/1267, and 'Daisy' to Lady Egerton, 3 July 1917 and 27 Feb. 1918, RA Add. C22/199 and 207; Arthur Stanley to Stamfordham, 16 May 1916, RA GV Q918/14; and Lt.-Col. W. Wyndham, Military Attaché to Berne Legation, to Stamfordham, 1 June 1916, RA GV Q890/26.

[64] 'Daisy', Crown Princess of Sweden to Lady Egerton (her main English contact on these POW matters), 7 Oct. 1918, RA Add. C22/213. Princess Louise, Duchess of Argyll, did go to see Basil Thomson, the intelligence chief, to tell him 'a good deal about the Kaiser and the probable revolution in England etc.'; see Basil Thomson Diary, 5 Nov. 1918, in Thomson, *The Scene Changes* (New York, 1937), 414.

[65] Godfrey-Fausset Diary, 5–12 Oct. 1918, Godfrey-Fausset Papers, 1/70.

brother, during his visit to Britain on the eve of the war in 1914. Now, on the eve of peace, he was presumably reluctant to draw to anyone's attention the special considerations he might owe to another German prince.[66] Beyond Buckingham Palace, Prince Max was virtually unknown. Among the Foreign Office staff, Herbert Dering, Envoy Extraordinary in Bangkok at this time, put together a confidential estimate of him. Dering conceded that Prince Max was 'the nearest approach to a gentleman that one might expect to find in Germany nowadays'. However, he undercut this by portraying him as a man of lightweight intellect, almost certainly a cipher of the Kaiser.[67] Similarly, Admiral 'Rosy' Wemyss, the First Sea Lord, had met Prince Max before the war and confirmed that he was 'humane and gentleman like', but 'quite incapable of satisfactorily filling the post of Chancellor'.[68] These were, at best, ambivalent assessments.

From the point of view of Britain's political leadership, however, Prince Max's character was beside the point. The armistice request was the crucial matter, and news of it reached Lloyd George in a manner most likely to irritate him. Lloyd George travelled to Paris on 4 October for top-level discussions with the French and Italians. It was at Versailles on the afternoon of 5 October that Clemenceau suddenly produced an intercept from French intelligence showing that the Germans had approached Wilson for an armistice. This news was bound to fuel resentment against the President in the Entente camp. During the preceding week, the British and the French had been annoyed by American attempts to intervene in the armistice negotiations with Turkey and Bulgaria.[69] Another typically disagreeable incident had occurred on the very eve of the armistice news: in a speech to the Senate in advocacy of women's suffrage, Wilson had pointed out that women's suffrage was now supported even by 'old governments like that of Great Britain, which did not profess to be democratic'. The alert British Embassy in Washington protested to Colonel House immediately, and requested London to protest as well, observing that 'there will be no harm in "rubbing it in" a little'.[70] On the eve of the armistice, relations between the Associated Powers were anything but fraternal.

The realization that Wilson was considering a response to the German armistice request, without even consulting his European partners, stung all the Entente leaders. After all, the German note had invited him to 'acquaint all belligerent states with this request'. In addition, William Wiseman, Britain's special

---

[66] On the king's anxiety on this issue, see Lord Burnham's 'Notes of a Conversation between Burnham and the King', dated 21 Aug. 1917, Burnham Papers, HLWL/10/no. 10, and Harold Nicolson, *King George V: His Life and Reign* (London, 1952), 245–6. The king's only response to Max's appointment in Oct. 1918 in his diary was the unimpeachably patriotic note that the professions of peaceful intent coming from Berlin contrasted with the damage still being done by Germany's retreating armies in France and Belgium (entry for 7 Oct. 1918, RA George V Diary).

[67] Dering to Eric Drummond, undated, FO 800/201.

[68] Wemyss to David Beatty, 8 Oct. 1918, Wemyss Papers, 11.

[69] War Cabinet minutes, 482 A, 3 Oct. 1918, CAB 23/14.

[70] Wiseman to Reading, 3 and 4 Oct. 1918, Elibank Papers, 8807.

confidential agent in Washington, made special representations to House urging consultations.[71] After much fulminating against the President, Clemenceau, Lloyd George, and Orlando decided to use their fortuitous gathering in Paris as an opportunity to draw up draft terms of armistice so that the Entente would have a position prepared in advance of Wilson.[72] The next day, the military and naval chiefs at Versailles were drawn into the process and instructed to respond to an initial draft of armistice terms prepared by the politicians.[73] The outpouring of vitriol against Wilson worried some observers. For example, so angry did Lloyd George and Clemenceau seem to Robert Cecil upon his arrival at the talks on 7 October, that he cabled Balfour immediately with the suggestion that Wilson or House must come to Europe as soon as possible to heal the breach. 'Lloyd George and Clemenceau vie with one another in scoffing at the President', reported Cecil.[74] Hankey, too, noted that Lloyd George was 'very contemptuous of President Wilson'.[75] Rather lame American explanations of Wilson's unilateral action began to flow in to Paris and London almost immediately in an effort to smooth over the furore, but these failed to mollify the British.[76]

Over the next four consecutive afternoons, from 6 to 9 October, the Entente leaders pored over the political and military requirements for the mooted armistice, the very idea of which was repugnant to them. The debates were most revealing of British aims and perspectives. From these discussions, four points need emphasis: first, the British believed that the war weariness of the Allies would render any armistice the absolute end of the war; second, the British pushed for the maintenance of the blockade beyond any armistice; third, the British depicted the issue of German democratization as irrelevant to the issue of an armistice; and fourth, the British stoked the fires of Entente hostility towards Wilson. In sum, the Entente's initial effort to subvert the Wilsonian armistice was driven by the British leaders.

First, the British argued from the outset that an armistice, in the sense of a temporary cease-fire, was not really possible. Bonar Law and Lloyd George quickly scotched Clemenceau's initial suggestion that the Entente could support a very short armistice in order that 'the Allies should not open themselves to the reproach of exposing thousands of men to be killed simply because they would not accede to reasonable conditions'. Bonar Law and Lloyd George both argued

---

[71] Wiseman to Reading, 7 Oct. 1918, telegram marked 'very urgent', Elibank Papers 8807.

[72] Minutes of an International Conference at the Quai d'Orsay, Paris, 6 Oct. 1918, CAB 28/5.

[73] Minutes of an International Conference at the Quai d'Orsay, Paris, 7 Oct. 1918, CAB 28/5.

[74] Derby to Balfour, message from Cecil, 7 Oct. 1918, Balfour Papers, 49738.

[75] Hankey Diary, 6 Oct. 1918, Hankey Papers, 1/5.

[76] According to Wiseman, House had advised Wilson to consult his partners, but Wilson 'feared that consultation would mean considerable delay which would be bad for morale of our troops and peoples generally. Moreover note was in his opinion too vague too justify reference to the Allies' (Wiseman to Reading, 9 Oct. 1918, Balfour Papers, 49741). Balfour passed on this explanation to Derby, adding the qualification 'How far this is the full explanation I do not know, but it is the one given to us, and is doubtless true as far as it goes' (Balfour to Derby, 21 Oct. 1918, Derby Papers, 28/2/1).

strongly that once the Allied armies agreed to even a short armistice, the outpouring of relief that would follow would make it impossible to resume the struggle.[77] Similarly, it was Lloyd George who introduced the related argument in favour of a 'tough' armistice, namely, that armistice terms must approximate as far as possible to the peace terms really desired by the Entente. Underlying these discussions was an acute awareness of the war weariness of the Allied peoples and armies. The armistice had to be delayed in order that this perceived weakness should not be exposed.

Second, from the beginning of these discussions, Lloyd George pushed for the maintenance of the economic blockade after any armistice. This was accepted from the first day of these discussions. In his memoirs Lloyd George explained that this 'harsh' decision was required because 'we were anxious that the period of the Armistice should not be used to re-equip Germany for a renewal of the war'.[78] This was half the story; there was a grimmer purpose. The blockade also had the additional advantage of placating the protectionist economic lobby in Britain. Significantly, Cecil, Britain's minister for blockade, expressed doubts about the plan, asking whether the blockade could really be maintained throughout a long period of negotiation in view of the 'great want of food' already prevailing in Germany and Austria. His humane reservations were pushed aside.[79]

Third, it is striking that from the beginning there was virtually no discussion of German democratization. In fact, Lloyd George was the most dismissive of this aspect of the question, remarking on 6 October that Prince Max's speech of the previous day 'really meant nothing at all'.[80] By the time of the final discussions of 9 October, Lloyd George had revised his view somewhat. He announced that he had reread Prince Max's speech the previous evening and interpreted it simply as evidence that Germany was in a 'thoroughly bad way'. It was the squeal of 'a defeated Empire'. He conceded that 'the Peace Party had come to the top', but advised the conference to recall that 'we had seen that before in 1917'. The promises of democratization in the speech Lloyd George ignored altogether. When the the text of Wilson's reply to the Germans became available on 9 October, the President's abiding concern for democratization was immediately evident from his question asking if the new government of Prince Max spoke for the German people or the old authorities. To this Lloyd George responded with derision. This aspect of the note, he said, he 'did not pretend to understand'. Cecil had doubts of another kind, noting that Wilson's question appeared to set the condition that the President would not make peace with the Hohenzollern. 'We should be very careful not to commit ourselves to this', Cecil recommended.[81] The British position appeared to be that the question of internal German political reform was simply irrelevant.

[77] Minutes of an International Conference at the Quai d'Orsay, Paris, 7 Oct. 1918, CAB 28/5.
[78] Lloyd George, *War Memoirs*, ii. 1955.
[79] Minutes of an International Conference at the Quai d'Orsay, Paris, 7 Oct. 1918, CAB 28/5.
[80] Minutes of an International Conference at the Quai d'Orsay, Paris, 6 Oct. 1918, CAB 28/5.
[81] Minutes of an International Conference at the Quai d'Orsay, Paris, 9 Oct. 1918, CAB 28/5.

Fourth, the British were determined to challenge Wilson's assumption of the right to deal diplomatically with the Germans. This issue dominated the last day of discussions, 9 October, by which time Wilson's first reply to the German note was known in Paris. In essence, Wilson's note was noncommittal, asking for proof of German commitment to Wilson's programme and seeking guarantees that the Germans would withdraw from all occupied territories. In addition, Wilson sought an assurance that the new government in Berlin spoke for the German people and not the old militarist élite. In conformity with Wilson's Point One on open diplomacy, his reply to the Germans was released to the world's press. The Entente leaders were perplexed. Clemenceau, however, initially welcomed the Wilson note as 'an excellent document' and counselled against intervening in the German–American correspondence. The British representatives dissented. Lloyd George worked hard to discredit Wilson and to avert a 'premature armistice'. He explained that he 'was afraid of the document'. The Wilson note, he argued, threatened to tie Britain and France to the odious Fourteen Points. Nor was the evacuation of occupied territory, which Wilson insisted upon in his note, a sufficient condition of any armistice. If one took account of German desperation, reasoned Lloyd George, the Allies could get much more than the territorial withdrawals Wilson was seeking. He still railed at Wilson for communicating with the Germans without consulting his fighting partners, pronouncing it as 'a very grave matter'. It was at Lloyd George's insistence, therefore, that it was decided to send a long telegram to Wilson cautioning him against any rush towards armistice. The telegram urged him to turn the matter over to the military experts who alone should be entrusted with the task of fixing certain military conditions. A second telegram advised Wilson to send a representative to Europe as soon as possible to improve Entente–American communication.[82]

The British leaders had not closed their minds, however, to an *eventual* armistice. This became clear from their reaction to the excessive armistice terms drawn up by the military and naval chiefs at their request. Spurred on, no doubt, by their political leaders' indignation directed at Wilson and his 'premature armistice', the Entente generals and admirals responded with a wish-list of extreme demands. Two drafts of military terms, one drawn up by Foch and one drawn up by all the Military Representatives at Versailles, were submitted to the civilians. Foch's list of armistice terms included the occupation of three bridge-heads over the Rhine, the surrender of vast amounts of war material, and, most significantly, the occupation of the Rhineland as a 'possession of security for the reparations to be exacted'.[83] The Entente statesmen were taken aback. 'This amounted virtually to an unconditional capitulation' observed Bonar Law. There was some concern over the reaction of the public if such tough terms leaked out. While the political leaders had made no secret of their desire to sabotage any premature armistice, they did not wish to advertise exaggerated military objectives

---

[82] Minutes of an International Conference at the Quai d'Orsay, Paris, 9 Oct. 1918, CAB 28/5.
[83] Foch's initial draft is reproduced in Lloyd George, *War Memoirs*, ii. 1955.

as the reason for rejecting the German offer. As Lloyd George explained, the generals' documents constituted ' "No" with a swagger' whereas the political requirement was a simple 'No'. In any case, it was agreed that there was no point discussing the hypothetical terms dreamt up by the military experts until Wilson's next move was clear.[84] When Wilson's note was known, the military terms were officially shelved as merely conjectural. Nevertheless, the foundations of tough military-driven armistice terms had now been laid in Paris and Lloyd George had played a key role in this.

When Lloyd George returned to London on 10 October he was still denouncing Wilson. He assailed those in his circle with warnings about the perils of a precipitate armistice, the menace of the Fourteen Points, and the harm done by Wilson's wanting 'to pose as the great arbiter of the war'.[85] His Cabinet colleagues and advisers agreed. Austen Chamberlain's attitude was typical. On 4 October he informed his sister Ida that German democratization was 'sure to be a sham at any rate at first', and praised the press in Britain and America for fulminating against the idea of an armistice.[86] News of the armistice request summoned the horror of 'an inconclusive peace', as Lord Crawford described it, a peace achieved by the machinations of pacifists, socialists, and interfering American idealists.[87] Leo Amery too detected that one of the objects of the armistice request was to incite 'our pacifists'.[88] Churchill had been telling his various political confidants succinctly that 'Wilson has lost us the victory'.[89] In a speech at Glasgow he mocked the Prince Max government as a government of manœuvre and camouflage.[90] Kerr wrote to Balfour observing that the great danger behind the new Chancellor's peace offer was that it might 'range America more definitely on the side of the premature peacemakers'.[91] Similarly, Beaverbrook was speaking for many of his colleagues when he reminded a Canadian friend that the Entente powers could not possibly be considered to be bound by the Fourteen Points, for 'No declaration to that effect had ever been made by the Allies in categorical terms'.[92]

The response from the Foreign Office was instantly hostile too, as exemplified in Balfour's reaction. A cold had prevented his attendance at the Paris discussions and so he was at the Foreign Office when news of the armistice request first broke.[93] Balfour was immediately alert to the grave danger of a rush towards

---

[84] Minutes of an International Conference at the Quai d'Orsay, Paris, 8 Oct. 1918, CAB 28/5.

[85] *Riddell's War Diary*, 10 Oct. 1918, 366–7.

[86] Chamberlain to Ida Chamberlain, 4 Oct. 1918, Birmingham University, Chamberlain Papers, AC 5/1/106.

[87] Lord Crawford Diary, vol. xxxiii, 6 Oct. 1918, Crawford Papers.

[88] Leo Amery Diary, 6 Oct. 1918, Amery Papers.

[89] Alexander MacCallum Scott Diary, 12 Oct. 1918, Alexander MacCallum Scott Papers, MS Gen. 1465.

[90] *Daily Mail*, 8 Oct. 1918.

[91] Kerr to Balfour, undated but from context must be 7 or 8 Oct. 1918, FO 800/201.

[92] Beaverbrook to Victor Mitchell, 11 Oct. 1918, Lord Beaverbrook Papers, BBK E/3/46.

[93] Balfour to Derby, 10 Oct. 1918, Derby Papers, 28/2/1.

peace, and even to the grave danger, so it seemed, that democracy might indeed be dawning in Germany. The young diplomat Hugh Knatchbull–Hugessen recorded in his diary a fascinating exchange with the Foreign Secretary on these matters on the afternoon of 7 October:

I met Mr Balfour just after luncheon and asked him for his views [regarding Prince Max's government]. I said that even if the democratic move in Germany were a sham they had taken a step and could not go back. He agreed but said he thought it was a sham. 'Of course', he added, 'I think they want it to succeed, but I hope it won't . . . However', he said, 'that all rests with Wilson. *I* shall have nothing to do with it'.[94]

The British popular press, meanwhile, had been raising a hue and cry against the peril of an 'inconclusive peace' with the enemy. There was almost unanimous condemnation of the 'trickery' of the armistice request. The themes of the 'patriotic' newspapers were familiar ones: the democratization proclaimed by Prince Max's government was a hoax, the socialists within the government were compliant tools of the military party, and the armistice request was a mere dodge in order to obtain a breathing space for the German army. The German 'experts' of the Northcliffe *Daily Mail*, Frederick Wile, the former Berlin correspondent, and Charles Tower, the Hague correspondent, were particularly vehement in denouncing the new government. Wile condemned the 'pretended parliamentary character of the new government' and assured his readers that, behind the Prince Max government, the Kaiser and the militarists were 'left in unchecked control'. The new 'socialist' ministers (the adjective always appearing in quotation marks when the *Daily Mail* referred to the German SPD), wrote Wile, 'will be clay in the hands of Germany's military caste'. The new ministers were all 'peace decoys'. Erzberger was ridiculed as 'a political windbag and limelight chaser'. Scheidemann was 'the tamest socialist of all, the unspeakable Scheidemann'. Prince Max himself, it was asserted, was 'about as far remote from concession to the "democratic spirit" as an appointment imaginable'. The *Daily Mail* editorial of 7 October drew the lesson: 'A request for an armistice means not peace but trickery.'[95] Other Coalition newspapers pursued similar arguments. The Beaverbrook *Daily Express* conceded that the new government was a 'half-hearted democratic government', but warned that Prince Max's intentions were to 'save not Germany but the Hohenzollerns and the Junkers'. The *Express* took comfort from the stiff attitudes of the Allied press towards the armistice request and concluded that there was 'complete agreement among the Allies that there can be no haggling over terms and that an armistice is out of the question'.[96] The Hulton *Evening Standard* noted that Prince Max was a relative by marriage to the Kaiser

[94] Knatchbull-Hugessen Diary, 7 Oct. 1918, Knatchbull-Hugessen Papers, 1/3.
[95] F. W. Wile, 'Germany Day by Day', *Daily Mail*, 3 and 4 Oct. 1918; C. Tower, 'Junkers Still in Control: Germans' Own Admission', and editorial, *Daily Mail*, 7 Oct. 1918.
[96] *Daily Express*, editorials 'Hard Road to Peace', 'Mixed Metaphor Max', 'Germany Under Pressure', 3, 4, and 7 Oct. 1918, and article 'German Appeal for an Armistice', 8 Oct. 1918.

and condemned the 'farcical nature of parliamentarisation'.[97] Dudley Docker's ultra-patriotic *Globe* perceived only 'autocracy camouflaged as democracy'.[98] Prince Max's appointment was a transparent ruse to give 'a democratic veneer to the old firm', announced the *News of the World*.[99] *Reynold's Newspaper* commented that it was 'too early yet to say' whether democracy was coming in Germany, but warned that the German oligarchy was undoubtedly hoping to retain real power 'while giving only the semblance of that power to the people'.[100]

The Liberal papers were generally more moderate but still suspicious of developments inside Germany. C. P. Scott in the *Manchester Guardian* was the most moderate commentator. He was careful to note that Max claimed to be the head of a representative government, but acknowledged that 'in truth nothing in the [German] constitution has been altered'. Nevertheless, Scott argued, the Allies did not have to wait for 'a complete transformation' before commencing negotiation with the new German government, for 'when the people are disillusioned they will take their own regeneration in hand'.[101] But the mood of the majority of newspapers was scarcely favourable to this type of moderation. Scott caught the prevailing atmosphere in a private note to L. T. Hobhouse: 'Things are very much as I expected. Success at once inflames our people as it did the Germans and Americans. People want two things: victory and retribution. It's quite natural. I want them myself. But I fancy there will be time enough for both before we can get our full terms.'[102]

Those determined to ridicule the reforms in Germany as a 'shamocracy', found two developments of great assistance to their cause. First came the celebrated Hohenlohe letter affair. On 8 October the *Daily Mail* printed a damaging private letter which Prince Max had written back in January 1918 to his cousin Prince Alexander von Hohenlohe, a maverick among German aristocrats who had connections with the German pacifist exiles in Switzerland. In the letter Prince Max had sought to distinguish his own more 'patriotic' but still moderate political position from his cousin's pacifism. He condemned both Pan-Germanism and the Reichstag Peace Resolution of 1917, he expressed doubts about the worth of a full-blown parliamentary system for Germany, and he defended Germany's right to compensations after the war.[103] The letter had found its way into the Northcliffe press via the efforts of Horace Rumbold at the Berne legation and his friend, F. Sefton Delmer, the Berne correspondent for the *Daily Mail*, both of

---

[97] *Evening Standard*, editorials 'What Germany Should be Told' and 'Max and Mummery', 3 and 5 Oct. 1918.
[98] *Globe*, 2 Oct. 1918.   [99] *News of the World*, 6 Oct. 1918.
[100] *Reynold's Newspaper*, editorial, 'The Hope of Democracy', 6 Oct. 1918.
[101] *Manchester Guardian*, editorial, 'Approaches to Peace', 7 Oct. 1918.
[102] C. P. Scott to L. T. Hobhouse, 8 Oct. 1918, Scott Papers, 132/273.
[103] The letter is reproduced in *Memoirs of Prince Max of Baden*, i. 198–200, and the political crisis this caused is explained ibid., ii. 77–83.

whom had cultivated connections with the German pacifist exiles in Switzerland, including Hohenlohe.[104]

The 'patriotic' British press seized upon the letter as proof of German duplicity. The new Chancellor was ridiculed as a mere cat's-paw of the Kaiser who had now been exposed to the world as secretly contemptuous of democracy and a peace of reconciliation. The lesson was obvious: there could be no question of negotiating an armistice with such a man. The *Globe* praised the American press which was now insisting on 'no truck with Prince Max', and concluded that 'the suggested democratization of Germany is a palpable sham'. The *Daily Mail* was quick to draw attention to the Prince's willingness to support 'compensation' for Germany at any peace conference. Under headlines 'THE REAL MAX' and 'GLUTTON FOR INDEMNITIES', the *Daily Mail* condemned the new government as a fraud. Max 'reveals himself to the whole world as an impudent hypocrite' proclaimed the *Daily Mail*.[105] The *Evening Standard* drew the conclusion that, as the new Chancellor had 'sneered at democracy and parliamentarisation' only months previously, clearly the Prince Max government was merely a façade behind which the Junkers were still in command. 'We must not mistake a change of attitude for a change of heart', warned the *Evening Standard*.[106] Some of the Liberal papers too hardened against Prince Max in the aftermath of the affair. In the Asquithian *Star* Prince Max was condemned as a mere 'scene-shifter'.[107]

Even more damaging for Prince Max's government were two submarine 'outrages' which occurred on 10 October. A Japanese ship the *Hirano Maru* and the Irish Mail boat *Leinster* were torpedoed in the Irish Sea and sank in heavy seas with large losses of life. The *Leinster* sinking was the more serious of the two. Some three hundred and fifty troops as well as civilians were killed. The military casualties were hidden from the public at the time, the press focusing upon the fact that the ship was a passenger ship.[108] Thus, the sinking of the *Leinster* was a disastrous propaganda setback for the new German government. The Germans' use of the submarine weapon had long been a leading theme in

[104] F. Sefton Delmer was an Australian-born former university teacher in Germany who had been imprisoned in Ruhleben prison camp in 1914–15. See his son's memoir, Sefton Delmer, *Trail Sinister* (London, 1961), i. 55. Either Dr Mühlon, an emissary for the pacifist exiles, or Rumbold himself, gave a copy of the Hohenlohe letter to Delmer. The Foreign Office was much perturbed over how such an important document got into the hands of the press: see Rumbold to Tyrrell, 7 Oct. 1918, and Rumbold to Cecil, 7 Oct. 1918, Bodleian Library, Horace Rumbold Papers, 25; Rumbold to Balfour, 8 Oct. 1918, FO 800/201; A. W. G. Randall to Gaselee, 14 Oct. 1918, HMP, HDLM Acc. 727, Box 36, and Headlam-Morley to Gaselee, 22 Oct. 1918, HMP, HDLM Acc. 727, Box 16.

[105] *Daily Mail*, 8 Oct. 1918.

[106] *Evening Standard*, editorial, 'Prussia's White Flag', 7 Oct. 1918.

[107] *Star*, editorial, 'The Scene Shifter', 23 Oct. 1918.

[108] The War Cabinet of 11 Oct. 1918 was told that 50 officers and 300 other ranks perished (War Cabinet 484, 11 Oct. 1918, CAB 23/7). Even in his memoirs Lloyd George did not acknowledge that these were military casualties (David Lloyd George, *War Memoirs*, ii. 1962). The number of military casualties was confirmed by George Bernard Shaw who was in Ireland at the time staying with the transport officer who had to identify and count the bodies; see Shaw to C. P. Scott, 18 Nov. 1918, C. P. Scott Papers, 335/55.

American and Entente propaganda, symbolic of German 'barbarism' and 'frightfulness'. These fresh submarine attacks so close to the British coast made it still more difficult for the new Prince Max government to project itself as quite different to the militarist governments of the past. The response to the tragedy in Britain was especially strong. Various British ministers cited the *Leinster* sinking as evidence that the old Germany was still unreconstructed. Arthur Balfour reacted with unusual passion, seizing upon the disaster to emphasize the point that all the German people shared complicity in such crimes. At an English Speaking Union luncheon on 11 October he proclaimed that the 'Huns' had changed their constitution but had not changed their hearts. He went on to supply a frequently quoted indictment:

Brutes they were when they began the war, and, as far as I can judge, brutes they remain at the present moment . . . I wish I could think that these atrocious crimes were crimes of a small dominant military caste. I agree that the direction of national policy may be in the hands of a small class, but it is incredible that crimes perpetrated like this, known to all mankind from one end of the civilised world to the other, should go on being repeated month after month, after four years of warfare, if it did not mean that it is all the population which commits them.[109]

If decorum prevented the use of the word 'godsend', this tragedy was at the very least a happy accident for those who wished to avert a sudden armistice. 'The disaster of the *Leinster* has come at a useful moment', wrote General Rawlinson to Henry Wilson, 'for it finds him [the German government] asking for an armistice with one hand and murdering innocent civilians with the other.'[110] 'One marvels at the clumsiness of the Germans. That they should have chosen this moment when protesting their peaceful ideals and their democratization, to perpetrate such an outrage, will harden opinion against them', Lord Crawford observed in his diary.[111]

The hardening of opinion began immediately. The British 'patriotic' press fixed upon the tragedy of the *Leinster* to strengthen the campaign already under way against the armistice. Two arguments in particular began to dominate in the press coverage of the armistice issue from this point. First, the press insisted that such atrocities as the sinking of the *Leinster* only served to underline the guilt of the whole German people. This in turn pointed to the need for a decisive military decision enabling the imposition of a tough peace, including economic punishment for the whole German nation. Thus, the notion of the complicity of 'the whole German people' was used to foster a ground swell of opinion in favour of such long-standing objectives of the 'economic warriors' as large indemnities, the

---

[109] *Daily Mail*, 12 Oct. 1918. Balfour's remarks were almost certainly influenced by the experiences of several relatives who had been caught up in the tragedy. His niece Ruth Balfour lost a close friend. See Ruth Balfour to Lady Betty Balfour, 11 Oct. 1918, Whittingehame Papers, GD 433/2/362.

[110] Rawlinson to Wilson, 13 Oct. 1918, Wilson Papers, HHW 13.

[111] Lord Crawford Diary, vol. xxxiii, 11 Oct. 1918, Crawford Papers.

deprivation of colonies, and the protection of British industry. Second, the press insisted that the *Leinster* incident had revealed how hollow was the German claim to have entered upon a new democratic path under Prince Max. According to the press, any so-called democratic reforms inside Germany were obviously quite inadequate if such atrocities could continue. A pretence of democracy on Germany's part was no reason to make peace. In supporting the continuation of the military struggle, therefore, the press redoubled its efforts to expose the reforms announced by Prince Max as bogus. The test of democratic good faith in Berlin was set so high that every reform short of revolution itself was condemned. With spectacular irony, the organs of the press most vehement in denouncing revolutionaries in Russia and Britain appeared to argue that only revolution in Germany could be regarded as convincing evidence of a repudiation by the German people of their militarist government. Indeed, it is not an exaggeration to say that the British popular press did its best to incite a revolution in Germany. Throughout October 1918, the jingoistic British editors taunted the German people, citing their failure to revolt as a proof of the guilty race's inability to undergo a genuine 'change of heart'. In the pages of the jingo papers incitements to revolution and indictments of the whole German people as irredeemably guilty were run throughout October.[112] The *Daily Mail* was the most strident, condemning Prince Max and the armistice as trickery, and calling for a more radical outcome in Germany: 'The German people have not set their house in order. They have not cut off a King's head, as the English did in 1649 and as the French did in 1793.'[113]

This was the bellicose atmosphere being whipped up in the pages of the 'patriotic' press as the British and Empire politicians began to consider the armistice issue in the second week of October. The issue naturally dominated all others when the Imperial War Cabinet met on 11 October to hear Lloyd George's report on his armistice discussions in Paris. The meeting opened with a sombre announcement of the *Leinster* casualties. The Prime Minister then spoke of his deep suspicion of the Fourteen Points and his fear of an early armistice. Then, summarizing the days of complex discussions in Paris, Lloyd George chose to emphasize the governing premiss behind his own response to the armistice proposition, namely, that 'if an armistice were once granted there would probably never be any resumption of hostilities'. This was why, he explained, an effort had been made to set such tough armistice terms in Paris, terms approximating 'as closely as possible' to the final peace terms which Britain desired.

---

[112] e.g. see *Globe*, editorial, 'To Whom', 9 Oct. 1918; *Globe*, editorials, 'The Hypocrites' and 'Let Justice be done', 11 and 12 Oct. 1918, and article, 'Mr Hyndman on Foe Peoples' Guilt', 15 Oct. 1918; *Spectator*, 'German Shipping—the Crime and the Penalty', 12 Oct. 1918; *Spectator*, 'President Wilson's Vindication', 19 Oct. 1918; and *Evening Standard*, editorials 'What Germany Should Be Told', 'Voice of the Allies', 'The President's Probe', and 'League of Nations and Germany', 3, 8, 9, and 11 Oct. 1918.

[113] *Daily Mail*, editorial, 'The German Trick and How to Read It', 14 Oct. 1918.

Lloyd George's account of his stout opposition to Wilsonianism in Paris did not insulate him from attack from his right-wing critics on the Imperial War Cabinet. Immediately he finished speaking, William Morris Hughes, voice of the ultra-patriots and 'economic warriors', was cross-examining the Prime Minister.[114] Hughes reminded all that the Germans' Brest-Litovsk Treaty had included economic clauses seeking commercial advantages for Germany in Eastern Europe. The Western armistice, when it came, should include similar measures which would safeguard the Empire's economic interests after the war, argued Hughes. In response, Lloyd George sought shelter in Clause 17 of the terms drawn up in Paris. Here it was specified that the economic blockade was to be prolonged as part of any armistice. 'This power would provide a lever for the enforcement of conditions such as Mr Hughes spoke of without the renewal of hostilities', Lloyd George assured the Cabinet.[115]

The exchange was most significant. Lloyd George was seeking to placate his right-wing critics by suggesting that a prolonged blockade would give them all the power over German economic life they needed. This was an ominous commitment. Certainly, it was all the encouragement Hughes needed: a few days later in Paris, Derby reported that Hughes was on his way to see Pichon, the French Foreign Minister, to work for tough armistice terms. According to Derby, Hughes intended to put the view that 'when it comes to peace Germany must be so handicapped by the withholding of raw material from her as to prevent her getting a start in the markets of the world'.[116] That Lloyd George felt threatened by the 'economic warriors' was obvious. In Hankey's opinion, the Prime Minister deliberately sought to evade an Imperial War Cabinet discussion concerning the armistice over the next week in order to avoid another encounter with Hughes.[117]

Almost immediately after the Cabinet, however, General Smuts offered a fresh insight which would make much headway among the decision-makers over the next ten days. Lunching alone with Hankey, Smuts suggested that he was 'very keen that we should make peace this year when the victory is due mainly to British arms, and not next year when it may be due mainly to American'.[118] He was, of course, still loyally opposed to a 'premature armistice'. But Smuts was the first to suggest that an armistice in 1918 would suit Britain best. Perhaps an armistice was a chance for the British to steal a march on the Americans and seize the victory now. Hankey passed on Smuts's suggestion to Lloyd George the next day.[119]

This view, however, was still a dissenting one. The Prime Minister remained wedded to the view that any armistice brokered by Wilson must be avoided at all

---

[114] On Hughes's political alliances in Britain see L. F. Fitzhardinge, *William Morris Hughes: A Political Biography, ii. The Little Digger, 1914–1952* (Sydney, 1979), chs. 4, 5, and 14.

[115] Minutes of the Imperial War Cabinet, 11 Oct. 1918, CAB/42.

[116] Derby to Balfour, 13 Oct. 1918, Derby Papers, 28/2/1.

[117] Hankey Diary, 17 Oct. 1918, Hankey Papers, 1/5.

[118] Hankey Diary, 11 Oct. 1918, Hankey Papers, 1/5.

[119] Stephen Roskill, *Hankey: Man of Secrets* (London, 1970–2), i. 612.

costs. This emerged clearly from a series of conferences among the Prime Minister's key advisers whom he summoned to join him on the weekend of 12–13 October at Danny Park, a huge Elizabethan country house near Hurstpierpoint in Sussex leased by Lord Riddell as a retreat for Lloyd George.[120] Relaxing with Riddell and Lord Reading on the Saturday, Lloyd George gave full vent to his anger at President Wilson's intervention, so much so that Reading quipped that if ever the two were to meet 'only feathers would be left to tell the tale'. In the evening the text of the German reply to Wilson's first note was phoned through from Downing Street. An astute document, it reaffirmed German acceptance of the Fourteen Points and pointedly announced the German assumption that the other Allies were similarly bound. The German note accepted the need for immediate withdrawals and insisted that the new German government spoke for the German people. Lloyd George flew into a rage announcing that an armistice on the basis of the Wilson programme was imminent.[121]

The next morning, Sunday, 13 October, Lloyd George, Reading, and Riddell climbed Wolstonbury Hill behind Danny Park for the view of Brighton and the Channel beyond. According to Riddell, Lloyd George was still 'declaiming all the time against Wilson's action in replying without consultation with the Allies, and also in regard to the terms of the [German] note'. So agitated was Lloyd George that he immediately summoned his trusted colleagues and advisers for a series of conferences that very afternoon. Balfour, Bonar Law, Churchill, Milner, Henry Wilson, and later Wemyss and Hankey, joined the Danny Park house party for lunch and afternoon conferences over cigars. It is clear from the surviving diary entries of some of the participants that this sudden meeting was insisted upon by the Prime Minister in an atmosphere of mounting panic. There were 'extraordinary scenes' as Balfour recalled later.[122] Lloyd George made plain his dread of two perceived dangers: the possibility of an imminent armistice, based upon the Fourteen Points, being presented as a *fait accompli*; and the peril of a sudden collapse of fighting morale among civilians and troops once news of the latest German reply was widely known. After a long conference, Kerr, Hankey, and Balfour were sent to separate rooms in the grand house to compose drafts of a long letter to President Wilson. The drafts were soon prepared, Balfour's contribution becoming the basis of a cable to Wilson protesting against any armistice, and insisting that the Fourteen Points could not possibly supply the basis of an armistice. The cable was sent the same evening. In addition, it was decided that the press must be guided in their treatment of the armistice issue. In Henry

---

[120] On the Danny Park conferences, see Balfour's memoir of the occasion quoted in Lord Riddell's Diary, 16 Mar. 1919, British Museum, Riddell Papers, 62983, and 'Notes on Conference at Danny, 13 Oct. 1918', Reading Papers, 121, Hankey Diary, 13 Oct. 1918, Hankey Papers, 1/5, Henry Wilson Diary, 13 Oct. 1918, Henry Wilson Papers, DS MISC/80, and *Riddell's War Diary*, 12 and 13 Oct. 1918, 368–72.

[121] *Riddell's War Diary*, 12 Oct. 1918, 370.

[122] Balfour's memoir of the occasion quoted in Lord Riddell's Diary, 16 Mar. 1919, British Museum, Riddell Papers, 62983.

Wilson's words, it was agreed that the press must assure the public 'that the war is *not* over, that the 14 Points are *not* an armistice, and that an armistice is *not* a peace'. Summarizing the feeling of the afternoon summit, Wilson jotted in his diary: 'Everyone angry and contemptuous of Wilson. A vain ignorant weak ASS.'[123] The Danny Park conferences were without doubt the high point of British determination to avoid the armistice.

In attempting to derail an early armistice, the British were not without influence in Washington itself. Hopes rested on Sir Eric Geddes, the First Lord of the Admiralty who had arrived in Washington for naval talks at the start of October. In a luncheon in his honour at the White House on 7 October, Wilson had revealed the arrival of the German armistice request.[124] Geddes did his best in interviews with the American press over the next few days to oppose the notion of armistice, urging that the fighting must continue until Germany had been given 'a whipping'.[125] Geddes's presence in Washington provided a special opportunity to influence Wilson which London was not slow to exploit. An interview with the President was arranged for 13 October. On the preceding day a Foreign Office wire to Geddes was dispatched conveying Lloyd George's advice. The Prime Minister urged him to impress upon Wilson the need for a tough armistice with military safeguards beyond territorial evacuations. British opposition to the 'Freedom of the Seas' among the Fourteen Points was to be reaffirmed. Above all, Geddes was instructed to press upon Wilson the importance of avoiding a 'sham or humbugging peace'. In sketching his case, Lloyd George encouraged Geddes to review the overwhelming predominance of British and Empire military contributions during 1918.[126]

Geddes's interview with Wilson went very well. Geddes immediately sent home a report announcing that Wilson appeared to be 'hardening towards caution'. The *Leinster* incident in particular had done its work. When Wilson drew attention to possible mitigating circumstances, suggesting that the submarine might have been long out of touch with Germany, Geddes saw his opportunity and assured him that Germany was able to instruct its submarines daily.[127] Wilson for his part sought to soften Entente tempers. He assured Geddes that he did not wish to undermine the fighting spirit of the Allies. Without any apology for acting unilaterally so far, he explained that he was also conscious of the need for closer communication and was sending House to Europe shortly. On the armistice issue, he insisted that he did not wish to allow Germany an advantageous armistice. However, he impressed upon Geddes that he was 'outstandingly fearful' that the military and naval chiefs might urge an armistice 'so

---

[123] Henry Wilson Diary, 13 Oct. 1918, Henry Wilson Papers, DS MISC/80.

[124] Colville Barclay to Balfour, 7 Oct. 1918, Balfour Papers, 49748.

[125] See newspaper clippings from *Public Ledger, Philadelphia*, 10 Oct. 1918, in ADM 116/1809.

[126] Lloyd George to Eric Geddes, 12 Oct. 1918, ADM 116/1809.

[127] In his memoirs, Prince Max claimed that the submarines close to the United States had been cautioned, but by an oversight those operating against Britain had not (*Memoirs of Prince Max of Baden*, ii. 84–5).

humiliating that the German people could not accept it'.[128] On balance, Geddes's report was reassuring. At the very least, here was evidence that British pressure on the Americans was having an effect. Britain was successfully retarding any rush towards armistice and helping to discredit the new German government in American eyes.

The Political Intelligence Department and the peril of a German revolution

Meanwhile, what advice had been tendered to the political leadership from the British intelligence experts? At first, there was no enthusiasm for Prince Max at the PID. In common with countless others caught up in the bureaucracy of war in London, most of the staff of the PID reacted with deep scepticism to the putative victory of the democratic cause in Berlin. In fact, a sceptical reaction had been prepared even in advance of the change of government in Berlin. For example, the influential intelligence officer Arthur Murray, brother of the Liberal politician Alexander Murray, was working in the PID at that time, and he reacted to the Kaiser's initial announcement of the need for a new popular government with cynicism. On 1 October he wrote to a colleague at the British Embassy in Washington cautioning him against German democratization 'for shop window purposes'. Only 'a complete upheaval' of the German constitution could create a responsible government. It was Murray who suggested to Tyrrell on this same day that the PID produce a memorandum on the issue of German democratization in order to appraise the 'true value' of any suggested constitutional amendments by a new government. He added that the PID should also 'assist the press' in order to guide public opinion in the matter.[129]

At first the staff of the PID regarded the appointment of Prince Max as inadequate. Headlam-Morley and Saunders received their instructions from Tyrrell and produced two memoranda, both dated 3 October. But the tone was not wholly negative. The PID was willing to look ahead. The first, 'Memorandum on the Situation in Germany and Peace Overtures', opened by conceding that 'The fall of Hertling is undoubtedly the commencement of far-reaching changes in Germany'. The reform of the Prussian three-class suffrage and the creation of a government responsible to the Reichstag were probably imminent, the memorandum pointed out. If such changes did come to fruition, 'Germany will at once enter the ranks of those states which have full parliamentary government', it was admitted.[130] The bulk of the memorandum, however, addressed the diplomatic problems created for Britain by the appointment of a new German 'Liberal

[128] Geddes to Lloyd George, 13 Oct. 1918, ADM 116/1809.
[129] Arthur Murray to Charles Lyell, Military Attaché, British Embassy Washington, 1 Oct. 1918, Elibank Papers, 8807.
[130] Memorandum on the Situation in Germany and Peace Overtures, 3 Oct. 1918, PID reference number 'Germany/016', stamped as printed on 7 Oct. 1918, FO 371, 3224, file no. 2480.

Government' professing democratic objectives. The PID warned that Britain might come under pressure to honour the broad hints that had occasionally been given (by Lloyd George at Glasgow, for example) that a democratic Germany would find peace easier to obtain.[131] With great candour, the memorandum observed that if Prince Max or anyone else succeeded in establishing a liberal democracy in Germany 'we may find ourselves suddenly confronted by a curious and rather embarrassing problem'. A democratic Germany might prove to be 'very stiff about Alsace-Lorraine and the Colonies'. In order to evade this discomforting prospect, the PID had some remarkably cynical advice for the government: spokesmen should distance themselves from past statements making the time-honoured distinction between the misled German people and their government and all calls for the democratization of Germany should cease. Democratization in Germany, in fact, could land Britain in 'a very awkward and very delicate position'. As the PID memorandum explained, the British government had to avoid 'playing into the hands of international socialism or international labour'.[132]

Some surviving private sources give an intriguing glimpse behind these formal memoranda and into the informal debates taking place within the PID during the first ten days of October. The staff were not united. For example, Knatchbull-Hugessen attended a Balliol College dinner on 7 October with Eustace Percy, Arthur Salter, and Zimmern. He found Zimmern 'very enthusiastic on the situation'. As Knatchbull-Hugessen recorded in his diary:

He [Zimmern] regards the new German Government as a decisive indication that the military and internal situation in Germany has become so desperate that they have decided to get peace as quickly as possible. He regards Prince Max's speech as unconditional surrender and thinks (in which I agree) that he could not have said more in that direction.[133]

With opinions such as Zimmern's being aired in the PID office, Arthur Murray was alarmed. On 8 October he confided to William Wiseman his distress that some in the PID office thought that Prince Max's arrival in office had signalled that 'the tiger has changed or is about to change its spots'. For Murray, this only served to highlight the danger that people might imagine peace was near on account of the 'outward appearances' of German democratization.[134] Clearly, the presentation of any intelligence advice suggesting that a political reformation was

---

[131] Originally proposed by Lloyd George in a speech in Glasgow in June 1917 and most recently renewed in the House of Commons by the Prime Minister, see *Parl. Debs.*, 5th ser., vol. C, 2222 (20 Dec. 1917).

[132] Memorandum on the Situation in Germany and Peace Overtures, 3 Oct. 1918, PID reference number 'Germany/016', stamped as circulated on 7 Oct. 1918, FO 371, 3224, file no. 2480. See also Memorandum on Prince Maximilian of Baden, 3 Oct. 1918, PID reference number 'Germany 0/17', stamped as circulated 14 Oct. 1918, FO 371/3224. The PID suggested that the Prussian military élite might be making 'only a courtly show of acquiescence' to reform. The notorious Hohenlohe letter was cited also, showing that the prince was at best a reluctant and recent convert to democracy.

[133] Knatchbull-Hugessen Diary, 7 Oct. 1918, Knatchbull-Hugessen Papers, 1/3.

[134] Murray to Wiseman, 8 Oct. 1918, Elibank Papers, 8807.

indeed under way in Germany was so much at odds with entrenched prejudice and expectations that it would take much courage.

However, as early as the second week of October the initial tone of hostility towards Prince Max within the PID was beginning to fade. Reports of imminent military collapse and the rapid growth of the revolutionary spirit had awakened the PID's horror at the prospect of a German revolution. As more telegrams came in from the British legations in the neutral countries, opinion in the PID swung over to Zimmern's position. Prince Max, derided by almost all scarcely a week before, now appeared as the lesser evil. Headlam-Morley's notes to his superiors at the Foreign Office were suddenly filled with foreboding. He warned that the danger of revolution in Germany was real and that it was not in the interests of the Allies to promote a revolutionary solution to the German crisis. On 12 October he sent a personal letter to Sir William Tyrrell pleading the urgency and seriousness of the crisis developing inside Germany and its consequences for the Allies. He loyally accepted that 'the most important thing is the attainment of a decisive military victory'; but the Allies, he argued, must take account of the 'danger of a social collapse in Germany itself'. Revolution would not remain penned up in Germany but would soon threaten Switzerland, Italy, and perhaps France, he warned. Even in Britain it might have 'a serious echo'. 'The problem, therefore', Headlam-Morley reasoned, 'is how to bring it about that Germany shall suffer a military defeat but be helped to avoid this social revolution'.[135] Undoubtedly this missive had some impact upon his superiors. On 14 October, for example, Tyrrell dined with Haldane and explained the burden of all his latest intelligence to the Liberal statesman. 'Tyrrell dreads revolution in Germany' jotted down Haldane in summary of their conversation.[136]

The desire to contain revolution now controlled the view the PID took of the armistice negotiations and of Prince Max. While many in the Foreign Office and Diplomatic Service joined with the military élite and the 'patriotic' British press in a chorus demanding a tough armistice and unyielding hostility to Max's 'pretended' democratic government, the PID through Headlam-Morley gave significantly different advice.[137] Headlam-Morley's impatience with the complacent jeering at Prince Max was very evident. Prince Max's government, he argued, was doing all that any reasonable government would do. Military cata-

---

[135] Headlam-Morley to Tyrrell, 12 Oct. 1918, HMP, Acc. 727, Box 16.

[136] Haldane to Elizabeth Haldane, 14 Oct. 1918, Haldane Papers, 6013.

[137] Among those Diplomatic Service officials insisting that the democratization in Germany was pretended, Horace Rumbold, at the Berne Legation, was the most prominent. Among his FO telegrams see especially Rumbold to FO, late Sept. 1918, FO 371/3223, file 2480, Rumbold to FO, 9 Oct. 1918, FO 371/3224, file 2480. In his personal correspondence he was also unrelentingly hostile to the Prince Max government and the armistice request; see Rumbold to his mother, 10 Oct. 1918, and Rumbold to Ronald Campbell, 14 Oct. 1918, Rumbold Papers, 25, and Rumbold to Hardinge, 14 Oct. 1918, Hardinge Papers, vol. 39. Rumbold was by no means alone among Diplomatic Service staff in believing that the Hohenlohe letter had unmasked Prince Max as a 'Pan-German'. Rennell Rodd, the British Ambassador in Rome, was of the same view; see Rodd Private Diary, 14 Oct. 1918, Rodd Papers, 35.

strophe was impending. The government was driven by a fear of revolution at home because 'they know that any revolution would be to some considerable extent influenced by the anarchical doctrines coming from Russia'. The government was moderate because it quite properly sought to avoid revolution. 'It is not necessary to attribute to the German Government any special degree of dishonesty', he wrote. Prince Max and his reformist ministers simply wished 'to get out of an extremely serious situation with the least amount of loss, and the largest amount of credit'.[138] The new German government's predicament demanded Britain's understanding, pleaded Headlam-Morley.

Second thoughts: towards British recognition of the need for an armistice, 14–23 October 1918

As has been seen, an understanding of the predicament of Prince Max's government had scarcely occupied the minds of Britain's political leaders for a moment during the first fortnight of October. Through to the Danny Park conferences of 13 October one priority had been virtually absolute: heading off the threat of a Wilsonian armistice. Over the next ten days, a change of opinion slowly evolved in Lloyd George's circle. At least six factors were influential: first, an election immediately after a spectacular armistice began to be seen as the best means of delivering maximum domestic political profit to the ruling Coalition and of averting the danger of post-war social unrest; second, it was realized that the dangerously divisive policy of imminent conscription in Ireland for the 1919 campaigns could only be abandoned credibly if the excuse of an armistice intervened; third, the British succeeded in persuading Wilson to leave the details on an armistice to the military authorities in France, thus averting the danger, as they saw it, of an armistice brokered by Wilson; fourth, it was gradually accepted that Britain was only temporarily superior in military terms relative to her alliance partners during 1918 and was in a position to extract maximum diplomatic profit in competition with the United States from an early peace; fifth, fear of a German revolution if the war persisted registered on some minds; and finally, as they became aware of the weariness of Allied troops, the British military leaders slowly came round to the idea of an armistice confirming British military superiority before increasing weariness debilitated the advance. The decisive factors were primarily domestic and political in character. Military and diplomatic considerations confirmed but did not dictate policy. Each of these factors deserves some analysis and explanation in turn.

First, the direct impact of the armistice request on the election plans of the Lloyd George government needs to be considered. As has been seen, in the first days of October, the prospect of the Germans suing for peace disrupted the

---

[138] Memorandum on the Situation created by the German Request for an Armistice and Negotiations, undated but from the context and title early Oct. 1918, HMP, HDLM Acc. 727, Box 2.

Coalition's plans for a 'win the war' election. It was assumed the election would be postponed.[139] Only Lloyd George, it was rumoured, was still keen for an election, the argument being that 'it might be advisable to have the election on the new register on war issues rather than on after war issues'.[140] This argument, which amounted to an insistence that the government must seek a mandate in the flood tide of gratefulness for victory, proved compelling. By 11 October Balfour had withdrawn his reservations, announcing that he looked forward to an election in which the Coalition's watchwords would be 'Victory, Peace and National Reconstruction'.[141] Of course, the resolution of the complex negotiations between the leading Conservatives and Lloyd George on the maintenance of the Coalition was a prerequisite to the decision.[142] But there is no doubt that the progress of the armistice negotiations helped change minds too. As it became clear that no sudden armistice, imperilling the fruits of victory, was to emerge, the idea of an election to be held immediately after a victorious armistice must have gained in appeal. For example, Arthur Steel-Maitland advised Bonar Law on 17 October that 'present developments with reference to the war change the balance as to the desirability of a General Election'.[143] In arguing for the snap post-armistice election, Lloyd George made no secret of his determination to use the opportunity following a dazzling victory to crush the Radicals and socialists. He stressed this side of the election adventure to the king himself at an interview on 14 October:

> The King asked Lloyd George: 'Are you sure that if you had an election you would come in triumphant?' He replied 'Yes certainly. There is not the remotest doubt. Men like Ponsonby and Snowden would not have the ghost of a chance of re-election. Ramsay MacDonald might, but the other pacifists would be nowhere'.[144]

The need for an armistice, therefore, was never likely to be judged according to military requirements alone. An election was being planned. After a breakfast with Lloyd George on 17 October, William Bridgeman was convinced that the Prime Minister intended to have an election 'at the earliest possible moment'.[145] The decisions on the armistice and the coming election were made by the same

---

[139] 'The decision as to an election cannot be long delayed, though of course there can be no question of it as long as the offensive is going on, nor would the question arise if by any chance the Germans were to sue for peace' (Bonar Law to Balfour, 5 Oct. 1918, Bonar Law Papers, BL 95/1).

[140] H. W. Studd (at the Supreme War Council, Versailles) to James Stanhope, 10 Oct. 1918, Stanhope Papers, C. 655 Correspondence.

[141] Balfour to Bonar Law, 11 Oct. 1918, Bonar Law Papers, BL 95/1.

[142] The most complete analysis of these negotiations is John Turner, *British Politics and the Great War: Coalition and Conflict, 1915–1918* (London, 1992), ch. 9.

[143] Arthur Steel Maitland to Bonar Law, 17 Oct. 1918, Bonar Law Papers, BL 95/1. On 10 Oct. George Younger had reported to Bonar Law that 'more than half' the Executive of the Conservative Party were opposed to an election; by 25 Oct. Arthur Boscawen reported that now perhaps only 10% of the party opposed the idea of an early election; see George Younger to Bonar Law, 10 Oct. 1918, and Arthur Boscawen to Bonar Law, 25 Oct. 1918, Bonar Law Papers, BL 95/1.

[144] Stamfordham informed Archbishop Davidson of the conversation (Randall Davidson Diary, 20 Oct. 1918, Davidson Papers, 13).

[145] William Bridgeman Diary, 17 Oct. 1918, Bridgeman Papers.

people in the same rooms over the same days. In making judgements regarding the armistice, British politicians must have taken full account of these pressing domestic concerns.

An election in the immediate aftermath of victory was expected to rebound on domestic unrest. General anxiety over domestic unrest in the aftermath of peace has already been noted. In the autumn of 1918 this anxiety was profoundly felt because of a spate of labour troubles. For example, a police strike in September shocked the government and led to suggestions that German money lay behind trade union unrest. During the police strike Lord Derby cautioned Lloyd George to be on guard against this 'dangerous state of affairs' on the home front. Henry Wilson too felt that this particular strike testified to 'the uneasy spirit in the country'.[146] Alarm over the mood of labour merged with a fear of an imminent outburst of social unrest during the inevitable period of demobilization to come. Again, dozens of leading figures expressed their dread of the demobilization problems that lay around the corner during October, but nobody with more vehemence than Christopher Addison, the Minister of Reconstruction. He was to warn Lloyd George at the end of the month that unless reconstruction and demobilization were properly planned 'nothing can save this country from chaos and disaster'.[147] Lord Esher told Hankey that he should stay in harness at the Cabinet Secretariat after the war in case, as Hankey recorded it, 'some Bolshevik should become Prime Minister, as he [Esher] argued may very well happen'.[148] Esher had serious intentions in spreading this advice. As he outlined his underlying conviction to Derby, 'if history repeats itself we should expect the troubles of 1816–20 upon a vastly magnified scale'.[149] Similarly, Esher told Stamfordham that 'Unless tact and sympathy are pronounced features of the demobilisation of the vast horde of men and women now employed under government, Bolschevism [sic] is inevitable!'.[150] Lord Crawford spoke for many: 'I notice a wave of anxiety as to our own future', he wrote in his diary on 5 November.[151] This domestic anxiety explains much about the cold-blooded determination of the British government to achieve an awe-inspiring victory—if not by a continued war, then by a crushing armistice. Victory was a domestic political panacea.

Second, the armistice request also coincided with another focus of anxiety in the War Cabinet, the long-standing dispute over the alleged necessity to impose conscription in Ireland in time for the 1919 campaign. The background may be swiftly summarized. Thrown off balance by the massive German offensive of

---

[146] On anxiety during the police strike see Walter Long to Bonar Law, 1 Sept. 1918, Walter Long Papers, 746/682, George Buchanan to Lady Bathurst, 9 Sept. 1918, Bathurst Papers, 2848, Walter Long to George Cave, 13 Sept. 1918, George Cave Papers, Add. MS 62497, provisional catalogue number, Derby to Lloyd George, 13 Sept. 1918, Derby Papers, 28/2/7, and Henry Wilson to Haig, 2 Sept. 1918, Henry Wilson Papers, HHW 7.

[147] Addison to Lloyd George, 29 Oct. 1918, Addison Papers, Box 99, File 55.9, diary file.

[148] Hankey Diary, 15 Oct. 1918, Hankey Papers, 1/5.

[149] Esher to Derby, 25 Oct. 1918, Esher Papers, 4/10.

[150] Esher to Stamfordham, 26 Oct. 1918, RA GV Q724/109.

[151] Lord Crawford Diary, vol. xxxiii, 5. Nov. 1918, Crawford Papers.

March 1918, the British War Cabinet had hastily decided in favour of Irish conscription. The Military Service Bill of April included provision for conscription
being extended to Ireland. However, Lloyd George had promised that conscription would only be introduced simultaneously with 'a measure of self-government
in Ireland'. Home Rule, ill-defined, had thus been linked to conscription.
Meanwhile, voluntary recruiting was persisted with temporarily. The forces for
and against conscription in Ireland lined up over the summer of 1918. The Prime
Minister stood resolutely for imposing conscription. The military leadership,
especially Sir Henry Wilson and Field Marshal Sir John French, now Lord
Lieutenant of Ireland, was determined that no peace be entertained until the
Empire had invested all available manpower. The king also stood firm for conscription. Among the cooler heads on the other side advising at least a further
delay in a decision were Sir Horace Plunkett, head of the Irish Convention,
Edward Shortt, Chief Secretary for Ireland, and the Liberal politicians Herbert
Fisher and Lord Haldane. Fisher understood the essential political problem very
well. As he explained to Lloyd George on 11 October, grave difficulties arose precisely because the government had announced its determination to enforce conscription 'so emphatically' that it was bound to 'suffer loss of credit, both in
Ireland and outside Ireland' if it now cancelled the decision.[152] During the first
two weeks of October the problem threatened to boil over. It was rumoured that
Sir John French would resign if the government did not adhere to the date of
1 November 1918 for a final decision.[153]

Finally, on 16 October, Lloyd George veered away from the materializing
calamity in Ireland. Following a series of tense interviews with Shortt, Lord
Islington, and Haldane, he agreed that a final decision on conscription for Ireland
must be delayed still further.[154] What had intervened? It must be recalled that

---

[152] Fisher to Lloyd George, 11 Oct. 1918, Lloyd George Papers, LG F/16/7/29. On the back-
ground to this problem, see Alan J. Ward, 'Lloyd George and the 1918 Irish Conscription Crisis',
Historical Journal, 17/1 (1974), 107–29, John McEwen, 'The Liberal Party and the Irish Question
during the First World War', *Journal of British Studies*, 12/1 (1972), 109–31, and John O. Stubbs,
'The Unionists and Ireland, 1914–1918', *Historical Journal*, 33/4 (1990), 867–93. For examples of
Lloyd George's resolution on the issue, Lord Crawford Diary, vol. xxxi, 18 Dec. 1917, Crawford
Papers; William Bridgeman Diary, 25 Apr. 1918, Bridgeman Papers; Sir John French Diary, 14 June
1918, French Papers, PP/MCR/C 32. Lloyd George was not so determined in private conversation;
for example 'Notes of a Conversation. Lloyd George and Lord Burnham, 2 Apr. 1918', Burnham
Papers HLWL/10 no. 12. On the military's position see Henry Wilson to Milner, 4 Jan 1918, Wilson
Papers, HHW 11. On the king's position see Stamfordham to French, 15 Sept. 1918, French Papers
75/46/11. On the moderates see Plunkett to Col. House, 26 Apr. 1918, Plunkett Papers, HOU 91;
Plunkett to W. G. S. Adams, 13 Aug. 1918, Plunkett Papers, ADA 69.

[153] Plunkett to W. G. S. Adams, 24 Sept. 1918, Plunkett Papers, ADA 69; French to Lloyd
George, 12 Oct. 1918, French Papers, 75/46/11; Henry Wilson Diary, 10–13 Oct. 1918, Henry
Wilson Papers, DS MISC/80.

[154] W. B. Yeats to Haldane, 12 Oct. 1918, and Islington to Haldane 16 Oct. 1918, Haldane Papers,
5914; Haldane to Elizabeth Haldane, 18 Oct. 1918, Haldane Papers, 6013; Wilson Diary, 16 Oct.
1918, Wilson Papers; French Diary, 16 Oct. 1918, French Papers, PP/MCR/C 32. On 26 Oct. Lloyd
George told C. P. Scott that he would not withdraw the actual threat of conscription. 'If there were
peace there would be no conscription, but otherwise there would because we should need the men',
Lloyd George explained (C. P. Scott Political Diary, 26 Oct. 1918, Scott Papers, Box 134).

on 15 October the text of President Wilson's second reply to the Germans was known in London. The note was harsh in tone and indicated there would be no headlong rush towards armistice, and certainly that it would not be an armistice granted by the President and presented to his partners as a *fait accompli*. But, with the newspapers filled with speculation on armistice, the prospect of an eventual armistice did offer an escape from the difficulties in Ireland. Those closest to the Irish conscription tangle were certainly aware of this side of the armistice question. For example, in the privacy of his diary as early as 6 October, the seemingly intractable Sir John French had reported Curzon's and Bonar Law's arguments that a 'new factor' had to be considered on the Irish conscription issue, namely, 'all that is happening in other different theatres of war'. That French had the armistice in mind is clear. French admitted that there was 'a good deal to be said for the "new factor" in the argument and the next two to three weeks will throw considerable light upon it'. Here was a perfect escape hatch through which the Prime Minister and his colleagues could crawl away from the Irish conscription crisis.[155]

A third factor may be dated from the receipt of the text of President Wilson's second note on 15 October. From that point it became clear that Britain had succeeded in deflecting Wilsonian control over the armistice. The American President still commanded the diplomatic exchanges with Germany, but he had caved in to British pressure on the issue of military control of the actual terms of an armistice. On the previous day Lloyd George had told the king over lunch that he thought the Germans would be ready for peace 'very soon'. The terms of Wilson's note must now have boosted Lloyd George's confidence that he was making a difference in the negotiations. The note itself, insisting upon stringent military conditions, criticizing the Germans over recent atrocities, and demanding more proof of democratic good faith, pleased many in the British camp simply because of its 'tough' tone. Although the note was sent once again without any direct consultation with Lloyd George or Clemenceau, it was clear that the strong British cables after the Versailles discussions and again after the Danny Park conference had made some impact. The argument against a hasty armistice made without reference to the military experts appeared to have been heeded. The President was now lecturing the Germans. On the morning of 15 October Hankey found Lloyd George, Reading, Milner, and Sir Henry Wilson on the terrace of 10 Downing Street discussing the President's second note. All were still full of contempt for the President, suggesting that he had now lurched from 'excessive leniency to austere strictness'. But the essential satisfaction of the top men can be gauged from the fact that the War Cabinet, reassured also by a

155 French Diary, 6 Oct. 1918, French Papers, PP/MCR/C 32. Lloyd George was still trading on his being the last civilian War Cabinet member to abandon a determination to impose Irish conscription months later (Lloyd George to Curzon, 8 July 1919, Curzon Papers, MS EUR F 112/211). Henry Wilson quarrelled with Lloyd George over his tactical retreat on the Irish conscription issue as late as 22 Oct.; see Henry Wilson Diary, 22 Oct. 1918, Wilson Papers, DS MISC/80.

reading of Geddes's report from Washington, decided against any action in response to the second Wilson note.[156] Tempers appeared to have cooled. The armistice in prospect would be controlled by Foch; the threat of a Wilsonian armistice was receding.

Fourth, the idea that Britain was only temporarily superior in military terms relative to her alliance partners during 1918 began to win adherents. An armistice before the end of the year, rather than in 1919, an armistice which would give Britain the decisive voice at a Peace Conference over and above the United States, was seen to provide a means of shielding Britain's costly victory from the peril of Wilsonianism. This in turn matched the government's determination to avert the damaging domestic political consequences of a less than dazzling Wilsonian peace, a peace with only minimum gains for Britain. The theory that Britain must use her temporary military preponderance relative to the United States as a diplomatic tool in 1918, promoted as we have seen by Smuts, was calculated to appeal to the prevailing anti-Wilsonian temperament of many of the key people.

Reinforcing this argument, less sanguine assessments of the military situation as a whole were coming in to play as a factor in the British reaction to the armistice proposal. This was especially evident at a breakfast at Downing Street on 16 October. Lloyd George for the first time was willing to acknowledge that perhaps the Allied armies were not as dominant as had first been thought. The German armies were being defeated, but, the Prime Minister reported, 'they are by no means broken'. Therefore, the German armistice request was probably as much inspired by fears concerning the internal state of the country as the military situation, he explained. Herbert Fisher, fresh from a reading of Max Müller's latest survey of the internal condition in Germany, was inclined to agree; he was convinced that with the home front cracking up Germany '*must* have peace'. Lloyd George agreed that the Germans were indeed greatly debilitated by their internal situation. But he acknowledged that the Allied armies were tiring rapidly too. 'We [the British armies] are doing all the fighting now', he observed.[157] At discussions at breakfast on the following day, the day of the opening of the new session of Parliament, Lloyd George held forth once again upon the disappointments of the Allied military effort. He confirmed the 'sinister rumours which are spreading over London' that the Americans were 'hopelessly jammed'. He confessed his own conviction that the prospects for a great victory, achieved by military might on the ground, were rapidly fading.[158] This consciousness of

[156] On Lloyd George's confidence see King George V Diary, 14 Oct. 1918, RA GV Diary. On widespread support for Wilson's tough stand see H. Fisher to L. Fisher, 15 Oct. 1918, Fisher Papers, 205, and Knatchbull-Hugessen Diary, 15 Oct. 1918, Knatchbull-Hugessen Papers 1/3. On the leadership's reaction, see Hankey Diary, 15 Oct. 1918, Hankey Papers, 1/5.

[157] Addison Diary, 16 Oct. 1918, Addison Papers, Box 99, File 55.9; H. Fisher to L. Fisher, 16 Oct. 1918, and another letter undated but in an envelope also dated 16 Oct. 1918, Fisher Papers, 205.

[158] Lord Crawford Diary, vol xxxiii, 17 Oct. 1918, Crawford Papers. William Bridgeman noted Lloyd George's words that the Americans were in a 'great muddle', and that, as a result, the chances of a 'great Sedan' had faded (Bridgeman Diary, 17 Oct. 1918, Bridgeman Papers).

dwindling Allied military capacity was the abiding impression left upon Lord Crawford who attended the breakfast. He noted dismally in his diary that 'there is little confidence that under present conditions we shall achieve a Sedan'. Recalling Britain's own difficulties with fuel and food shortages in the coming winter, Crawford asked rhetorically whether the winter might not be as dangerous for Britain as for Germany. He added the most revealing observation that 'In some ways we want an early victory more than the Germans want an early peace'.[159]

In this context, Smut's theory that an armistice before the end of 1918 was actually to Britain's advantage was bound to look more and more attractive. The idea that the fresh American army would inevitably become the dominant army on the Western Front, if the war continued into 1919, was already commonly accepted among British officers. Smuts appears to have worked assiduously to bring these arguments to the politicians' attention. For example, on 14 October he outlined his theory to Addison and he became a convert instantly. Addison noted in his diary Smuts's argument that 'with our superhuman efforts this year in the field, our armies and the French are greatly exhausted, whilst the Americans are rapidly growing, and that we might be in danger next year if things went on until then'.[160]

This analysis, however, required support from the generals. Not until mid-October was this military opinion detectable. At first, of course, the leading British generals had thrown up their hands in horror at the thought of an armistice. The emotional desire to fight on German soil was very strong. With their troops advancing at speed, most of the officers in positions of high command were exhilarated and the initial talk of an armistice was very unwelcome. Most of the leading generals professed eagerness to fight on into Germany even if this meant fighting on through the winter and into 1919 if necessary. There was also much support for the idea of seeking 'guarantees' beyond the mere evacuation of invaded territories. The sinking of the *Leinster* inflamed the desire to impose a decisive defeat on German soil. Encouraged by the politicians, the generals too were insistent on 'getting full value for our victories', as Rawlinson put it. Most shared the politicians' dread of German trickery, fear of the 'breathing space' that might be afforded the enemy by an armistice, and the abandonment of the spoils of war when they were at last within military reach.[161]

[159] Lord Crawford Diary, vol. xxxiii, 17 Oct. 1918, Crawford Papers.
[160] H. W. Studd (British Section, Supreme War Council, Versailles) to Earl Stanhope, 1 Sept. 1918, Stanhope Papers, C. 655 Correspondence; Addison Diary, 14 Oct. 1919, Addison Papers, Box 99, File 55.9.
[161] Rawlinson Diary, 13 Oct. 1918, General Sir Henry Rawlinson Papers, RWLN 1/11, Cambridge; H. W. Studd to Stanhope, 10 Oct. 1918, Stanhope Papers, C. 655 Correspondence; Godley to Mrs Godley, 12 Oct. 1919, Godley Papers 6/2; Rawlinson to Sir Henry Wilson, 13 Oct. 1918, Wilson Papers, HHW 13; Wilson to Rawlinson, 13 Oct. 1918, Wilson Papers, HHW 13; Duff Cooper to Diana Manners, undated, and same to same, 18 Oct. 1918, Duff Cooper Papers, DUFC 1/3/7.

Similarly, the British naval élite was initially hostile to any idea of armistice. The disappointment that there might be no Trafalgar was painful. On 8 October Admiral Wemyss comforted Beatty, his impatient Admiral of the Grand Fleet, with assurances that the Entente politicians were determined not to be 'bamboozled into a bad armistice'. The highest ranking naval officers in the Admiralty appear to have been consumed with fear that the war might end before the craved showdown with the German High Seas Fleet. Jealous of the army's share in the glory of battle in 1918, the admirals were violently opposed to a 'premature armistice'. Beatty's views were extreme: 'It is terrible to think that it is possible after all these weary months of waiting we shall not have an opportunity of striking a blow', he wrote to his wife in late September 1918.[162]

However, by mid October, the highest ranking British army officers were having second thoughts. A number of fresh considerations suggesting that an armistice might after all be a useful stratagem began to make an impact. The weakness of the French military effort, and the dreadful inefficiencies hampering the progress of the inexperienced American army, began to cast doubt on the inexorable advance of Britain's partners. The American problems, in particular, became widely known. The realization that the American effort had stalled, of course, served to underline the merit of Smut's proposition about Britain being the 'top dog' in 1918. The corrosive effect upon the morale of the Allied troops produced by the widespread expectation of armistice was also observed. There were special fears about the Italian Front, while even the British trenches were not immune from hopes for deliverance through armistice. So concerned was Haig over the draining of the energy of his forces that he thought it advisable to warn his own troops on 12 October that an armistice could not be counted upon and that they must go on with their efforts.[163]

Fear of a German revolution was a fifth—and a very controversial—factor. In mid-October, as a result of military intelligence, the possibility of an uprising in

---

[162] Wemyss to Beatty, 8 Oct. 1918, Wemyss Papers, 11; Beatty to Lady Beatty, 22 Sept. 1918, Beatty Papers, BTY 17/52; Wemyss's manuscript entitled 'Admiralty II', in the hand of Wemyss's wife, Victoria Wester Wemyss, Wemyss Papers, 11. For other examples of the officers' eagerness for action and of their deep disappointment at the prospect of an armistice depriving the Grand Fleet of action see Admiral Roger Keyes to Beatty, 16 June 1918, Beatty Papers BTY 13/24/4; Admiral Plunkett E. E. Drax to Admiral Cowan, 11 Sept. 1918, Admiral Cowan Papers, COW 13/3/84; Wemyss to Beatty, 2 Oct. 1918, and Beatty to Wemyss, 4 Oct. 1918, Wemyss Papers, 11.

[163] General Spears reported Clemenceau's convictions on the the weakness of the American army to Henry Wilson and to Milner as early as 3 Oct. 1918 (Spears to Milner, relaying message from Henry Wilson, 3 Oct. 1918, Spears Papers, 1/11). Lord Crawford noted that Lord Derby in Paris had definite information on American military weakness (Lord Crawford Diary, vol. xxxiii, 15 Oct. and 17 Oct.). On the weakness of the Italian front after the news of the armistice request see Lord Cavan to Henry Wilson,13 Oct. 1918, Henry Wilson Papers, HHW 28/B, and for Lloyd George's awareness of this see William Bridgeman Diary, 17 Oct. 1918, Bridgeman Papers. Samuel Hoare, Chief of Field and Special Intelligence with the British Military Mission in Rome, described the destructive impact of the armistice news on the Italian army, and the dangers of a socialist-led revulsion against the war, in great detail; see Hoare's 'Weekly Notes', dated 21 Oct. 1916, Templewood Papers, III/6. On the news of the armistice debilitating British morale see Derby to Balfour, 12 Oct. 1918, Derby Papers, 28/2/1.

Germany began to be taken seriously among the British military élite. The prospect of revolution, raising the possibility that there might be no enemy officer corps with which to deal in any armistice negotiations, alarmed the officers around Haig at British headquarters. When Geoffrey Dawson, editor of *The Times*, visited the headquarters of the British army in France in mid-October he discovered the leading British officers in this conservative temper, full of apprehension that Wilsonian demands for inner transformation might drive Germany into a revolution against the government. 'The soldiers' view is that you must have a government and not a revolution on which to impose terms', Dawson reported to a Fleet Street colleague. Reflecting the intensifying fear for the safety of the spoils of war, Dawson added the significant observation that he opposed Wilson's pressure for democratic change for another reason too: 'I feel strongly that Wilson's concentration on it [internal change] is dangerous because the Germans might concede it in return for more practical advantage.'[164] Out of such discussions at Headquarters, a more favourable view of armistice began to emerge and various generals ceased their posturing against 'premature armistice'.

The idea that President Wilson's words were an encouragement to revolution in Germany was common at the time. For example, Knatchbull-Hugessen wrote in his diary: '[The President's reply] will result, I should say, either in a military dictatorship or a revolution in Germany.' Others in the War Cabinet and its secretariat certainly foresaw this risk. The disaster of a revolution in Germany had been raised by Hankey and Henry Wilson when the War Cabinet considered President Wilson's second note with its insistence upon a decisive demonstration of the triumph of democracy in Germany. 'The end of it is an encouragement to Bolshevism', Hankey had lamented. Henry Wilson likewise fumed in his diary that the President's demands were 'mad because we shall have no one to treat with [in Germany] except Bolsheviks'. Soon after, Balfour received fresh warnings from French Foreign Minister Pichon that Germany was 'as full of Bolshevism as Russia itself was before the revolution'. Lloyd George also received two communications and supporting German press cuttings from Alfred Mond, his First Commissioner of Works, insisting that the new government of Prince Max was the most genuinely democratic Germany had ever possessed. As part of his case, Mond documented the German conservatives' intense hostility to Max's government. Therefore, argued Mond, the new German government ought not be dismissed out of hand as a sham; it was worth defending against the danger of both revolution or counter-revolution. But, in spite of these suggestions, neither Balfour nor Lloyd George chose to pursue the issue in public.[165]

[164] Dawson to G. S. Freeman, 18 October 1918, Freeman File, *The Times* Archive.
[165] Knatchbull-Hugessen Diary, 15 Oct. 1918, Knatchbull-Hugessen Papers, KNAT 1/3; Thomas Jones Diary, 15 Oct. 1918, Thomas Jones Papers; Henry Wilson Diary, 17 Oct. 1918, Henry Wilson Papers, DS MISC/80; Derby to Balfour, 17 Oct. 1918, Balfour Papers 49744; Sir Alfred Mond to Lloyd George, 12 Oct. and 16 Oct. 1918, Lloyd George Papers, F/36/6/34 and 36.

In mid-October, a major controversy erupted in the British press which put the issue of the danger of a revolution in Germany momentarily at the centre of attention. The controversy was provoked by Lord Milner. He alone among the members of the War Cabinet, it appears, considered seriously the warnings of revolution in Germany now dominating the PID's memoranda. These prompted Milner to attempt a bold intervention; he decided to argue publicly the case for a more moderate treatment of the new government in Berlin lest Germany be driven towards Bolshevism. Apparently acting on his own initiative, Milner made use of a scheduled interview he had promised to Arthur Mann, the editor of the *Evening Standard*. On 17 October a report of the interview appeared with an explanatory article and an editorial by Mann. 'Victory not Vengeance' was Milner's essential message, as Mann interpreted it for his readers. But from the detail of the interview it was clear that Milner was preoccupied by the dangers of Bolshevism in Germany. Milner argued that the risk was there if a moderate German government was denied an armistice, a policy which Milner believed Wilson was mistakenly pursuing. Prince Max's government was indeed a government of 'new men'. Accordingly, Milner suggested 'we should not be in too great a hurry to denounce it as a sham'. Most controversially, Milner also suggested that it was 'a serious mistake to imagine that the German people are in love with militarism'. The German people 'may be relied upon to put Kaiserism in its place'. Milner argued that Britain had an interest in preserving a stable government in Germany. 'As reparation has to be obtained, we do not wish to see Bolshevism and chaos rampant there'.[166] He had no doubts that militarily Germany was already broken, a view he confided to friends as well as proclaiming in his interview.[167]

The organs of the Northcliffe and the ultra-patriotic press were instantly blazing away at the unfortunate Milner. 'A tremendous racket in the press about my interview', Milner recorded succinctly in his diary.[168] The *Daily Mail* in particular thundered against his intervention, ridiculed the idea that Bolshevism was a threat in Germany, and depicted Milner as a reactionary who was attempting to 'make the world safe for monarchy'. For almost a month, the Northcliffe papers continued to snipe at Milner unmercifully.[169] The *Globe*'s reaction was typical of the ultra-patriotic papers: it strongly rebutted the claim that the German people as a whole were not militarist, insisting that the German government and people

[166] *Evening Standard*, 17 Oct. 1918. Milner had evidently held these views for some time. In late 1915 he had written privately of his opposition to the notion of crushing Germany militarily and of his faith in the power of the German people to 'make an end of Junkerdom' themselves in the aftermath of the war: see Milner to Hugh Glazebrook, 8 Dec. 1915, quoted in John Marlowe, *Milner: Apostle of Empire* (London, 1976), 239.

[167] H. Fisher to L. Fisher, 13 Oct. 1918, Fisher Papers, 205; Milner to Thornton, 31 Oct. 1918, Milner Papers, 46. See also Milner's views as reported by Fisher in Anne Olivier Bell (ed.), *The Diary of Virginia Woolf, i. 1915–19* (London, 1979), 15 Oct. 1918, 203.

[168] Milner Diary, 23 Oct. 1918, Milner Papers, vol. 89.

[169] *Daily Mail* 23 Oct.1918, and see also editorials 'Lord Milner's Blunder', *Daily Mail*, 4 Nov., and 'Milner's Mischief', *Daily Mail*, 6 Nov. 1918.

had 'worked as a unit' in making war. No democratic transformation was under way, according to the *Globe*. As for the risk of Bolshevism in Germany, this was 'a piece of unconscious German propaganda'.[170] The *National Review* also attacked Milner as 'Lord Feebleguts'.[171] The old stories about Milner being a Müllner did the rounds with the gossip merchants.[172] Some Liberal papers did offer support for Milner's view, but this no doubt was a mixed blessing for a man who had suddenly lost caste among the ultra-patriots.[173] The vehemence of the ultra-patriotic reaction ought to have been no surprise. Milner was pilloried because he endangered the justification for a harsh peace which the British Right were determined to see imposed upon the defeated enemy.

The Milner interview affair also sharpened existing tensions between Northcliffe and the government. The unfortunate Milner represented the archetypal reactionary Tory 'Junker' in Northcliffe's imagination, the sort of man who invited Bolshevism in Britain because of his inability to act as a credible post-war reformer. For the next month the Northcliffe papers pursued Milner. The brawl even spilled over into public 'scenes'. Before a dinner with Lord Derby at the Paris Embassy on 1 November, Northcliffe himself came striding over to collar Balfour, directing 'violent abuse' at him before the other astonished guests on account of Milner's interview and his presumed role in the armistice negotiations.[174] The frantic newspaper denunciation of Milner must have highlighted for Lloyd George the potential for troubles ahead if he dared to depart from the patriotically correct line. The lesson was clear enough. A politician might agonize in private about the danger of a revolution sweeping away moderate government in Berlin, but not in public. No one high in the government, it should be noted, leapt to Milner's defence. Bonar Law dashed for cover in the Commons, twice explaining that Milner's remarks were 'made on his own responsibility'.[175]

Faltering military confidence provided the sixth factor which helped convert the leading minds to the need for an armistice. The decisive counsel came from Haig. Addressing the War Cabinet on 19 October, Haig presented very moderate terms for an armistice. He limited his essential claims to the German evacuation of Belgian and French territory, and a German cession of Alsace-Lorraine to an Allied occupation force. Haig thus departed from the views maintained by Foch and Henry Wilson that the victorious powers should demand the occupation of the Rhineland and bridgeheads across the Rhine. Underpinning Haig's

[170] *Globe*, 'Milner and Morgenthau', 18 Oct., 'The Milner Interview', 5 Nov., and 'Milner's Mischief', 6 Nov. 1918.

[171] Leo Maxse, 'Can Downing Street Save Germany', *National Review*, 429 (Nov. 1918).

[172] For examples of the Müllner rumour see Arthur R. Roper to Douglas Sladen, 7 Nov. 1918, Sladen Papers, SLA 38.

[173] e.g. *Star*, editorial, 'Victory or Vengeance?', 18 Oct. 1918, and Frederick Maurice's article 'Victory First', *Star*, 19 Oct. 1918.

[174] Pound and Harmsworth, *Northcliffe*, 679–80 and 694; Amery Diary, 21 Oct. and 11 Nov. 1918, Amery Papers; Derby Diary, 1 Nov. 1918, Derby Papers, 28/1/1.

[175] *Parl. Debs.*, 5th ser., vol. 110, 772 (23 Oct. 1918), and 1114 (28 Oct. 1918).

modest claims was his portrait of a tired British army that would not be pushed much further unless the purposes were clear. He reminded Lloyd George that the questioning within the army as to the ultimate purposes of the war had been going on for at least a year. Lloyd George agreed that this had been one of the reasons behind the Caxton Hall speech of January 1918. Haig explained that now, in the context of widespread armistice talk, if very stiff terms were addressed to Germany and she refused, the effect on the morale of the British army would be 'bad'.[176]

Military assessments dominated discussion. Indeed, it is noteworthy that Haig, who had impressed Dawson only days before with his serious fear of Germany being driven into Bolshevism, did not once refer to the politics of this issue. Nor did Milner. Nevertheless, that Haig was supporting the Milner position was obvious, and Lord Milner was especially gratified. In his diary he wrote: 'Haig was the while very reasonable and counselling moderation.' Lloyd George emerged as sympathetic to Haig's standpoint. He was struck by the alarming vision of a British army approaching exhaustion. In the twilight following the meeting Lloyd George played golf with Kerr and Riddell. Lloyd George explained to Riddell that Haig had looked 'worn' at the Cabinet and was 'anxious for peace'. Then the Prime Minister asked searchingly, 'If the Commander in Chief is tired out, what must the Army be?'[177]

Doubts concerning British military power grew stronger in the days that followed. On 21 October Haig again addressed the War Cabinet. He presented a memorandum summarizing his estimate of the relative strengths of the opposing armies. It was a compellingly lucid document. 'The French Army seems greatly worn out,' Haig noted. The Americans were 'disorganized, ill-equipped and ill-trained'. If the Allied armies were capable of a serious offensive this year he would support it, but 'they are not', Haig observed definitively. Underscoring this pessimism, Haig delivered an unequivocal judgement that 'the Allies had not the strength to finish the war this year'. The Germans were neither so badly mauled nor so disorganized as to justify the view that they would accept any terms, reasoned the Field Marshal.[178] The impact of this upon Lloyd George is clear. Over the days that followed, he did his bit to ensure that Haig's new pessimistic insights percolated through the ranks of his Conservative allies: at a breakfast on 24 October, Sir Robert Sanders found the Prime Minister 'not nearly so full of buck' as he recounted Haig's sombre assessment.[179]

Lloyd George's acceptance of the need for an armistice emerged also in the simultaneous discussion of proposed naval terms for armistice at the War Cabinet

---

[176] Minutes of the War Cabinet, X meeting, 19 Oct. 1918, CAB 23/17.

[177] *Riddell's War Diary*, 19 Oct. 1918, 374; Milner Diary, 19 Oct. 1918, Milner Papers, 89.

[178] Haig Memorandum, dated 19 Oct. 1918, filed as Appendix II to Minutes of the War Cabinet, 21 Oct. 1918, CAB 23/14.

[179] Lord Bayford Diary, 27 Oct. 1918, reflecting on conversations of 24 Oct., in John Ramsden (ed.), *Real Old Tory Politics: The Political Diaries of Sir Robert Sanders, Lord Bayford 1910–1935* (London, 1984), 110.

meetings of 19 and 21 October. As he had done in Paris, Lloyd George upbraided the Admiralty for bringing forward extreme demands for the surrender of most of the German High Seas Fleet and all submarines. In the Prime Minister's opinion, the extreme terms presented by Admirals Wemyss and Beatty reflected the navy's preference for no armistice at all rather than an armistice that fell short of all the officers hoped to gain by way of a final conflict in the North Sea. Although opposing the admirals for their recalcitrance, on one other aspect of the naval terms, Lloyd George himself remained adamant. It was Lloyd George himself who first suggested and insisted that a continuation of the economic blockade of Germany must be built into the armistice terms as this would supply the most effective 'gauge' over the enemy in the months following the armistice.[180] In addition, it should be noted that, as he had done in Paris, Lloyd George drew the link between the blockade and reparations. He continued to advocate that a continuing economic blockade of Germany as part of an armistice would provide the key instrument of coercion in order to ensure the payment of reparations.[181]

In the middle of the afternoon of 21 October, these discussions were interrupted by the arrival of the text of the latest German reply to President Wilson, which was read to the meeting. The German government's eagerness for an armistice was now readily apparent. The announcement of a suspension of U-boat warfare against passenger ships and the German government's insistence upon the genuine character of the democratization of Germany was especially remarked upon. A change came over the meeting. Haig immediately came under some pressure to stiffen his terms to the level of 'unconditional surrender' as the demands in the naval terms were now described. For the first time, various speakers now foresaw and spoke openly of the possibility that Britain might be in a position to exploit the fear of internal disorder in Germany.[182]

The democratization issue being pushed forward by President Wilson was also debated. There was evident disquiet over President Wilson's decision to screw up pressures for internal democratization for Germany. Most of those around the War Cabinet table still refused to contemplate political outcomes in Germany from any point of view other than that of British military advantage. No one supported the President's stand on the issue. It was agreed that Wilson's demands for more thoroughgoing constitutional reform in Germany were 'not of a very practical character'. The Cabinet eventually decreed that demands for German democratization 'would not in themselves justify the prolongation of hostilities and the sacrifice of life involved therein'.

The continuing references to the Fourteen Points in the President's notes to Germany, and in the latest German reply, also caused a good deal of agitation in the War Cabinet. Here a consensus quickly emerged that Britain was *not* bound by the Fourteen Points. At length it was decided to send another cable to Wilson seeking a further toughening in his position on the military terms of an armistice

[180] Minutes of the War Cabinet, X meeting, 19 Oct. 1918, CAB 23/17.
[181] Minutes of the War Cabinet, 21 Oct. 1918, CAB 23/14.   [182] Ibid.

but suggesting little in detail. Naval terms must be included in any armistice, and German territory including Alsace-Lorraine must be occupied too, pleaded the British cable. The cable maintained perfect silence, however, on the issue of German democratization. Britain thus presented a face of complete indifference to the issue at the centre of Wilson's exchanges with Prince Max, the issue building to a crisis inside Germany over the abdication of the Kaiser.[183] Clearly personal animosity towards President Wilson was still a potent factor shaping the British response to Wilsonian diplomacy. The next day, 22 October, Lloyd George led the War Cabinet in a fresh airing of grievances against the American President for claiming that his diplomacy with Germany was far in advance of the Entente's 'old-fashioned, secret and revengeful diplomacy'.[184] In addition, British hostility to the Fourteen Points programme was now attracting political attention. Under questioning in the House of Commons at this time, government speakers still refused to make any endorsement of the Fourteen Points. Cecil, Balfour, and Bonar Law all dodged questions from the Radical Joseph King on 17, 21, and 23 October, insisting that it was 'inadvisable' to speak of such matters while negotiations were in progress.[185]

However, this continuing tension should not be permitted to obscure the great change that had come over the top decision-makers of the War Cabinet. It was now possible to speak warmly in anticipation of the armistice. For example, at a small gathering of his chief advisers on 23 October, Lloyd George expressed his fears that 'under the influence of the bellicose attitude of the American public' Wilson might actually write such a belligerent reply to the Germans that the prospect of armistice might disappear altogether. Those who had pleaded for a hardening in Wilson's attitude in early October were now concerned that he may have become too adamant.[186] Thus, under the influence of the various factors here outlined, outright opposition to the concept of an armistice had disappeared.

The British decision for an armistice, 24–26 October 1918

British discussions reached a climactic point upon the appearance of Wilson's third note on 24 October. In this portentous document the President agreed to submit the details of an armistice to his partners on the strength of German acceptance of the Fourteen Points, but pressed once again for the Germans to take action against 'the military masters and monarchical autocrats of Germany' if they wished to avoid 'surrender'.[187] This provoked three final days of discussions in the British War Cabinet on the merits of an armistice.

A consciousness of the gap between the American and British outlook still pervaded the arguments. In particular, the continuing reluctance of the British to

[183] Minutes of the War Cabinet, 21 Oct. 1918, CAB 23/14.
[184] Minutes of the War Cabinet, 22 Oct. 1918, CAB 23/14.
[185] *Parl. Debs.*, 5th ser., vol. 110, 255, 417, 768.
[186] Minutes of a War Cabinet 'Conversation', 23 Oct. 1918, CAB 23/17.
[187] Temperley, *Peace Conference of Paris*, i. 455–6.

follow Wilson in pressuring Germany upon the democratic issue was very plain. At the first meeting of the War Cabinet after the publication of the Wilson note on 24 October, Sir Henry Wilson asked if the new note meant that easier armistice terms might be offered to a constitutional regime compared with the old autocratic Germany. Lloyd George responded that no such distinction was to be drawn. Balfour assured the War Cabinet that, in any case, no substantial internal reforms had yet taken place in Germany.[188] This, of course, was in flat contradiction to the advice being given to him from his Political Intelligence Department. At the same meeting of the War Cabinet, Lloyd George revealed also more details on the faltering performance of the American army, remarking that this 'had completely upset Marshal Foch's great strategical plan for the present year'.[189] Awareness of the military difficulties of Britain's partners on the Western Front, therefore, formed a continuing backdrop to the War Cabinet's final decision upon the utility of an armistice.

Before armistice could be accepted, however, the Fourteen Points issue had to be faced. Acting on advice from Hewins, Balfour raised the matter at the War Cabinet.[190] He expressed grave disquiet over the possibility that Britain might be ensnared in the Americans' Fourteen Points through the process of the armistice. Britain's rights to retain colonies, to build an imperial trade bloc, and to impose a substantial indemnity, were all at risk. Unless Britain protested, Balfour warned, the Germans would have an 'unanswerable' argument that nothing beyond the Fourteen Points could be added to the peace settlement.[191] In response, it was agreed at first to send another cable to Wilson alerting him to British reservations on the Fourteen Points, especially British opposition to the Freedom of the Seas. The Cabinet's determination to evade the Fourteen Points dominated the discussion. However, a communication from Washington provided a way out; the British were invited to attend a major conference in Paris with Colonel House to hammer out a position on the armistice beginning on 29 October. At length, therefore, Lloyd George persuaded the Cabinet against the proposed cable to Wilson. Instead it was resolved to entrust to the Prime Minister the task of negotiating personally with Colonel House over Britain's position on the Freedom of the Seas and the Fourteen Points at the impending conference at Paris. As Lloyd George argued, with some candour, this would be more profitable than an indignant cable because 'in a speech you could use all sorts of diplomatic and friendly phrases, and so render it innocuous, without losing the force of what you wished to say'.[192]

---

[188] Minutes of the War Cabinet, 24 Oct. 1918, CAB 23/7.
[189] Minutes of a War Cabinet 'Conversation', 24 Oct. 1918, CAB 23/17.
[190] Hewins to Balfour, 25 Oct. 1918, and accompanying notes, dated 6 Nov. 1918, Hewins Papers, 71. See also Balfour's assurance given to Hewins that, at the subsequent gatherings at Versailles to discuss the armistice terms, Hewins' Points were crucial to the British argument against being bound to the Fourteen Points (Hewins Diary, 31 Oct. and 6 Nov. 1918, Hewins Papers).
[191] Minutes of the War Cabinet, 25 and 26 Oct. 1918, CAB 23/14.
[192] Minutes of the War Cabinet, 26 Oct. 1918, CAB 23/14.

The invitation to Paris also prompted Lloyd George to call at last for a final decision from his War Cabinet colleagues on the armistice question. Did Britain want an armistice at all? Did Britain want an armistice on the basis of 'a good peace now', as he put it, or should she seek to 'impose such drastic terms for an armistice now that the enemy could not accept, our intention being utterly to crush him next year with the idea of obtaining better security for peace for the future'? On 26 October the decisive debate took place. Lloyd George, astutely defending himself perhaps from the charge of leading a Conservative Cabinet down the path to peace, began by playing the role of super-patriotic advocate. In launching the debate, he announced that there was a school of thought, 'which at times made considerable appeal to him', that Britain should fight on until Germany was 'smashed'. Peace should be dictated on German soil and the enemy taught that war could not be made with impunity, as Lloyd George explained the argument. 'At the first moment when we were in a position to put the lash on Germany's back she said "I give up", the question arose whether we ought not to continue lashing her as she had lashed France', he contended. Remarkably, no one followed the lead Lloyd George had set. One by one each of the leading decision-makers declared himself in favour of 'a good peace now'. All seemed confident that Britain could obtain all she required to register an unequivocal victory by way of armistice, even without carrying the war on to German soil. Fighting on would be to gratify a desire for pure vengeance, remarked Chamberlain, and vengeance was too expensive. Balfour believed that the terms being contemplated for armistice gave Britain and her partners all they required, and that Allied occupation of German territory was hardly necessary to confirm the scale of the German defeat. Bonar Law agreed. Geddes argued similarly that the armistice terms would reduce Germany to 'a second class power' without the necessity of war on German soil.

Nobody at the War Cabinet table, it should be noted, argued that the war should be ended to avoid revolution in Germany. Similarly, nobody argued that the war should be pressed on into Germany in order to ensure her conversion from militarism to democracy. Rather, Britain's power to dictate peace terms which would realize her territorial, economic, and military objectives was the fundamental consideration. Smuts himself argued that if the war went on into 1919 only America could profit. 'As Europe went down, so America would rise', he predicted. Peace in 1918, on the other hand, would be dictated by Britain. Lord Reading, speaking as the recently returned ambassador at Washington, added his weight to Smuts's argument. He agreed that it was in Britain's best interest relative to the United States to conclude the war in 1918, observing that 'by continuing the war it might become more difficult for us to hold our own'. The critical decision was then taken: the War Cabinet passed a resolution that, in the negotiations at Paris in the days ahead, Lloyd George and Balfour should 'base their attitude on the question of an armistice on the assumption that the British Government desires a good peace if that is now obtainable'. The die was cast.

Britain was no longer seeking to delay and derail an armistice. Lloyd George had roped his colleagues in behind him in pursuit of an early end to the fighting.[193] What did these decisions amount to? In establishing its guidelines for Lloyd George and Balfour, the War Cabinet had set a high 'reserve price' for an armistice, without actually nominating an exact figure. Lloyd George's satisfaction was very real. He had wrung from the War Cabinet a sufficiently vague formula that preserved his freedom of action for negotiation in Paris on the precise terms. It is important to stress that the decision had not been forced on Britain by American pressure when the British military were still keen to fight on to Berlin. The British government's own estimates of its political requirements, and of its military capabilities, had persuaded it that an armistice over the next few days was best for Britain. The confessions of Haig, first delivered to the War Cabinet on 19 October, had created a realization that Britain's own military preponderance was fragile. The weakness of the American effort, and anxiety about the French army, highlighted the case for Britain embracing the armistice now as her opportunity. Military opinion had shifted noticeably behind Haig on this point since early October.[194] The state of the German army was still a matter for debate. At one point in the discussions at the War Cabinet on 26 October General Harington had suggested that the German army was 'in such a state that they might accept very harsh terms for an armistice'. However, he also confirmed Haig's view that not much more could be expected from Britain's military partners. General Harington had remarked that the French army was 'leaning against the enemy' and that the Americans were 'tripping over their own feet', two phrases that Lloyd George himself commended to his intimates afterwards as having proved to be important in swaying the War Cabinet.[195] However, at the time, it was Smuts's 'top dog' argument that left the greatest impression upon members of the War Cabinet. For example, Chamberlain explained his decision in favour of armistice, in a letter to his sister Ida written on the evening of the War Cabinet, in these terms:

If we fight on Germany is ruined, but at what cost to ourselves? Our armies must dwindle, the French are no longer fighting; a year hence we shall have lost how many thousands more men? American power will be dominant. Today *we* are top dog. *Our* fleets, *our* Armies have brought Germany to her knees and today (more than at any later time) the peace may be our peace.[196]

Buckingham Palace too proved most receptive to this view. A few days later Lord Stamfordham visited Archbishop Davidson to relay the latest news and Davidson recorded the burden of his remarks in his diary:

[193] Minutes of the War Cabinet, 25 and 26 Oct. 1918, CAB 23/14.

[194] e.g. General Sackville West wrote to Henry Wilson from Paris on 21 Oct. asking him to 'Come over soon and keep an eye on these Frenchmen who now do everything except fight' (Sackville West to Wilson, 21 Oct. 1918, Henry Wilson Papers, 12).

[195] Minutes of the War Cabinet, 26 Oct. 1918, CAB 23/14, and see *Riddell's War Diary*, 27 Oct. 1918, 376.

[196] A. Chamberlain to Ida Chamberlain, 26 Oct. 1918, Chamberlain Papers, AC 5/1/110.

Some people, notably Smuts, are very anxious that the settlement of peace should be expedited with the utmost speed . . . because Smuts, with whom Stamfordham fully agrees, is most anxious that the peace should be made at a time when the victory has been won by us rather than by the Americans. If the Germans fight for some months, and the French vigour of attack wanes, as some fear, and the American forces increase, it may be called in the end an American victory, and America will claim the right to dictate the terms. This would be harmful.[197]

Ironically, the armistice, previously reviled as a Wilsonian conspiracy, was now accepted as a weapon against Wilsonian influence.

The Versailles Council and the making of the armistice terms, 28 October to 4 November 1918

Before turning to the making of the actual armistice terms, it is vital to be aware also of the state of planning for a general election which continued throughout October and reached a crisis on the very eve of the Prime Minister's departure to Paris. A blunder had been discovered in the preparation of the registers. Lloyd George informed his colleagues that there were serious difficulties in organization for the soldiers' votes, and that 'if there were an election tomorrow half our soldiers would be unable to vote'. But Lloyd George's enthusiasm for an election as soon as possible after victory seemed undiminished by the discovery that many of those British soldiers who survived the final battles might not be granted a valid vote. As Bridgeman noted, 'he passed that over rather lightly, though not without a show of irritation'. For the expediency of the election had now seduced the Prime Minister. He also fully appreciated which arguments would weigh most heavily in the minds of his Conservative supporters. It was a ghost story which he used in selling the election at a breakfast on 17 October: he explained that 'if we put it off till some time after peace the inevitable discontent that would arise during the period of settling down might lead to a regular Bolshevic [*sic*] Government'. This conversation obviously impressed Robert Sanders who recalled early in 1919 that from this point he had done his best to promote Lloyd George's argument that an election must be held before Christmas 'in order that we might get a majority large enough to stand the racket'. With his intentions firming, Lloyd George's only acknowledgement of the disaster of the registers was that those 'responsible' for the disfranchisement of the soldiers (excusing, of course, those like himself who wished to rush forward to a khaki election), were to pay dearly for the embarrassment that might be caused. On 18 October, 'in a characteristic explosion' as Milner complained, Lloyd George attacked Milner and the War Office for their alleged inefficiencies with regard to the voting registers, inefficiencies which he acknowledged would disfranchise 'thousands of soldiers'. It was on the next day, 19 October, that Lloyd George apparently made his fateful decision to come to terms with Bonar Law and confirm an electoral

---

[197] Davidson Diary, 3 Nov. 1918, Davidson Papers, 13, describing a meeting on 2 Nov.

deal for a continuing coalition—as has been seen, the same day Haig's sober reflections on the military position and Britain's need for an armistice sooner than later had begun to swing opinion in the War Cabinet in favour of armistice. A week of political deal-making followed, with a final review of election arrangements on 27 October, the eve of Lloyd George's departure to Paris.[198] The crucial point to note, therefore, is that pressing election matters were being discussed among the British political élite at exactly the same time that decisions regarding the armistice were reaching a climax. So crowded was the Prime Minister's schedule that the electoral deal-making continued on his trip to Paris: he took with him from London the vital draft 'letter' to Bonar Law, a letter embodying a declaration of Coalition policy for the coming election. In addition, the scandal of the electoral registers followed Lloyd George to Paris. For, in a fury at this last minute hitch to his election planning, Lloyd George had turned on Hayes Fisher, President of the Local Government Board, whom he now blamed for the bungle over the soldiers' franchise. Before crossing the Channel on 28 October, Lloyd George had dispatched an angry letter to the unfortunate Fisher asking for his resignation within twenty-four hours. In his letter Lloyd George again freely acknowledged that in the imminent election 'large numbers of soldiers and sailors would be disfranchised'. Bonar Law prevented the letter from being sent and phoned Lloyd George in Paris on Fisher's behalf. Bonar Law could not guarantee, he explained, Unionist support in the Commons if Fisher chose to defend himself there. This, of course, would have meant public exposure of the soldiers' vote scandal and this in turn might have brought the hastily improvised election into total disrepute. Not surprisingly, therefore, Lloyd George generously announced a stay of execution until he could meet with Bonar Law in Paris in two days time. A 'fairly heated conversation', as Bonar Law described it, took place in Paris with Lloyd George during a break in the armistice conversations with House. As a compromise, Fisher was forced out of the Local Government Board, but the whole thing was dressed up as a reshuffle, with Fisher 'consoled', as Sir Robert Sanders put it, with the Chancellorship of the Duchy of Lancaster and elevation to the title of Lord Downham.[199] Bonar Law's presence in Paris, of course, was not simply to save Hayes Fisher. According to Hankey, it was at a private dinner on 2 November, in the middle of the armistice meetings in Paris, that Lloyd George, Bonar Law, Balfour, and Milner finally 'fixed up the general election and the Coalition programme'.[200]

[198] Lord Crawford Diary, vol. xxxiii, 17 Oct. 1918, Crawford Papers; William Bridgeman Diary, 17 Oct. 1918; Lord Bayford Diary, 20 Oct. 1918, reflecting on conversations of 17 Oct. and 8 May 1919, in Ramsden, *Real Old Tory Politics*, 110 and 125; Milner to Herbert Fisher, 18 Oct. 1918, Bodleian Library, Milner Adds., MS Eng. Hist. c. 696/1; McGill, 'Lloyd George's Timing of the 1918 Election', 120.

[199] Lloyd George to Hayes Fisher, 28 Oct. 1918, Bonar Law to Lloyd George, 28 Oct. 1918, Bonar Law to Hayes Fisher, 29 Oct. 1918, Bonar Law to Long, 29 Oct. 1918, Bonar Law to Curzon, 31 Oct. 1918, Bonar Law Papers, 84/7/97–103, and Lord Bayford Diary, 3 and 10 Nov. 1918, in Ramsden, *Real Old Tory Politics*, 111–12.

[200] Hankey Diary, 2 Nov. 1918, Hankey Papers, 1/5.

The crucial point to note, therefore, is that the looming khaki election was preying on Lloyd George's mind even in Paris when the vital meetings over the armistice terms were proceeding. This is no surprise: Lloyd George had a war—and an election—to win.

With these domestic political distractions lurking constantly in the background, the priorities of Lloyd George and Balfour, the key British negotiators at Paris from 28 October to 4 November, can be readily grasped. First, it was their overall objective to secure a discernible military triumph within the armistice. Second, they had to ensure that the terms of the armistice were still realistic enough to lure the Germans to lay down their arms—for Britain needed an end to the fighting too. As has been seen, Haig and Smuts had persuaded the War Cabinet that Britain's fortunate military superiority in late 1918 was a wasting asset. In selling the armistice to the Germans, the packaging of the Fourteen Points could prove a useful lure. Third, it was a priority to avoid any such entanglement in the sticky Fourteen Points as might jeopardize British territorial or economic objectives. If these priorities could be met, then a solid basis would be laid for a snap election. The heroes of the moment would easily ride out the challenge of Labour and of disaffected Liberalism in an election to be called immediately after the awesome victory within the armistice was unveiled.

But first the difficulty of Colonel House and his master's Fourteen Points had to be faced. At a dinner with Balfour, Derby, and Reading at the Paris Embassy on 28 October, Lloyd George debated the hovering threat of the Fourteen Points. As coached by Hewins, Balfour voiced his dread of being held in bondage to the American diplomatic effort. In the light of Wilson's domination of the armistice correspondence with Germany, Balfour argued, Britain would be bound hand and foot to the President's Fourteen Points if she now accepted an armistice. Reading agreed with Balfour that if Britain signed such an armistice 'we *ipso facto* accept the whole of Wilson's articles of faith'.[201] Lloyd George would have none of this. He insisted that, having been ignored in the armistice correspondence so far, Britain was not committed in advance to any of the Fourteen Points. The strategy was straightforward: Lloyd George was determined to have an armistice but to evade, or if necessary to dilute, the Fourteen Points in obtaining it.

Further insights into Lloyd George's thinking on the eve of the discussions with House are afforded by C. P. Scott's record of a conversation with Lloyd George over breakfast on 26 October. To the Liberal editor Lloyd George expressed his confidence that peace was imminent as 'Germany is *absolutely done* and has not a kick left in her'. He anticipated that the only trouble might come from 'our stupid Admirals' and their impossibly high terms.[202] With regard to the Fourteen Points, he appeared ready to accept them as a 'basis'. However, Lloyd George added that he had already prepared two crucial 'variants' or 'reser-

---

[201] Derby Diary, 28 Oct. 1918, Derby Papers, 28/1/1.
[202] C. P. Scott to L. T. Hobhouse, 28 Oct. 1918, C. P. Scott Papers, Box 132/275.

vations' to the Fourteen Points which he intended to push in discussion with House. In his diary Scott recorded Lloyd George's explanation:

As the military terms were not to maintain any balance of force, but completely to disarm Germany, it was necessary that she should know the extent of the political demands upon her—the Fourteen Points of the Wilson Programme were the basis, but we had certain reservations to make (1) as to Freedom of the Seas (2) as to a claim for damages in respect of all merchant vessels sunk contrary to right and to the laws of war.[203]

It is worth stressing that the more important of the two anticipated reservations, in terms of its direct impact upon Germany, was the second, that concerning the British 'claim for damages'. At this point, Scott was in no doubt that this reservation, as Lloyd George had expressed it to him, was a limited claim for reparation. In two letters to L. T. Hobhouse written over the next two days outlining the conversation with the Prime Minister, Scott described the claim as 'an indemnity for all merchant ships illegally sunk' and as 'compensation for sea losses'.[204] At its birth, therefore, this reservation, so controversial in the years ahead, was undoubtedly originally designed as a device for registering a limited claim to marine compensation—not an indemnity.

The long-awaited discussions between the British, French, and Italian leaders and Colonel House began on 29 October in the room of M. Pichon, the French Foreign Minister, at the Quai d'Orsay in Paris. The discussions naturally turned upon the famous pronouncements from Washington which Wilson and the Germans had succeeded in pushing to the fore. These talks have been described in detail in a number of other studies and so only those issues of concern to this analysis of the process of British policy-making towards Germany need to be noted here.[205] Two vital points stand out.

First, at the beginning of the discussions the British imposed their will on the procedure to be adopted. At the insistence of Lloyd George and Balfour, it was agreed that the armistice terms to be assembled in Paris were not to be revealed to the public. Even more important, the leaders agreed that the terms were not to be sent to Wilson for approval and then on to Germany; rather, they were to go to Wilson *and then to Foch* who would reveal them to the Germans and negotiate with them.[206] This procedure ensured that the most intractable of the military advisers would have the last word in negotiating the terms, a crucial step in limiting the Wilsonian influence.

Second, Lloyd George succeeded in maintaining over seven days of discussion his two prepared objections to the Fourteen Points, and no others. At the very

[203] C. P. Scott Political Diary, 26 Oct. 1918, C. P. Scott Papers, Box 134.

[204] C. P. Scott to L. T. Hobhouse, 28 and 31 Oct. 1918, C. P. Scott Papers, Box 132/ 275–6.

[205] See esp. W. B. Fowler, *British American Relations, 1917–1918: The Role of Sir William Wiseman* (Princeton, 1969), 223–7; Inga Floto, *Colonel House in Paris: A Study of American Policy at the Paris Peace Conference 1919* (Aarhus, 1973); Edward B. Parsons, *Wilsonian Diplomacy: Allied American Rivalries in War and Peace* (St Louis, Mo., 1978), 153–8; and Schwabe, *Woodrow Wilson, Revolutionary Germany, and Peacemaking*, 81–92.

[206] Minutes of a Conversation in M. Pichon's Room, 29 Oct. 1918, CAB 28/5.

first meeting of the leaders with House, Lloyd George cut to the essence of the debate: he asked if the German government was 'counting on peace being concluded on the basis of the Fourteen Points'. He was assured by House that 'this was undoubtedly the case'. A tense discussion followed, with French, Italian, and British representatives all criticizing the Fourteen Points. Clemenceau 'looked unutterable things' when Wilson's wishes were explained by House, but it was Lloyd George who came to dominate the conversation.[207] He announced his two prepared reservations. He dwelt upon Point Two, the Freedom of the Seas, in particular, which he declared was totally unacceptable to Britain. He then outlined his dissatisfaction also on the matter of 'indemnities':

There was no word in President Wilson's speech about indemnities, by which he meant reparation for the wanton destruction of property in Belgium and France, and the sinking of ships. The British Government insisted on reparation to the wives and children of every sailor who had been illegally killed or drowned at sea.[208]

Once again, it is important to note that in this opening reference to demands for compensation for Britain, as in every other reference in the discussions that followed, Lloyd George indicated that Britain's claim for reparation was a limited one. Compensation for merchant shipping losses was indicated as the end in view. Although the word 'indemnities' was used, there was never a suggestion that this involved a claim for war costs as a whole.[209]

The first day's debate with House climaxed in House's celebrated threat to make a separate peace with Germany if America's partners in the struggle refused to accept the Fourteen Points. Lloyd George smoothed over the rupture. True to his brief from the War Cabinet in London, Lloyd George did not wish to imperil the possibility of armistice itself. In any case, having gained Foch's control of the ultimate negotiations with Germany, Britain and France had won some protection from Wilsonian idealism already. It was agreed, therefore, that Britain, France, and Italy should simply list their reservations to the Fourteen Points for ongoing negotiation. In the discussion that followed, Lloyd George's words betrayed his contempt for the Wilsonian programme. He remarked hopefully at one point that 'apart from Clause II, the others of the Fourteen Points appeared to him sufficiently elastic to enable us to put our own interpretation upon them'. Even the eventual outcome was hinted at in this first meeting. In a remark of naked realism, Lloyd George observed that 'If Germany would accept the terms of an armistice proposed by Foch, the Allies could interpret President Wilson's Fourteen Points as they wished'.[210] This prefigured the nub of the compromise

[207] Hankey Diary, 29 Oct. 1918, Hankey Papers, 1/5.

[208] Minutes of a Conversation in M. Pichon's Room, 29 Oct. 1918, CAB 28/5.

[209] For example, at the Supreme War Council Lloyd George again described the second of his reservations as a claim for 'reparation for the sinking of ships at sea' (Minutes of the Supreme War Council, 2 Nov. 1918, CAB 28/5).

[210] Hankey Diary, 29 Oct. 1918, Hankey Papers, 1/5; Minutes of a Conversation in M. Pichon's Room, 29 Oct. 1918, CAB 28/5.

that would be struck: the Entente would dictate harsh armistice terms, and they would concede the appearance of a commitment to the Fourteen Points. The following morning, 30 October, Lloyd George, Clemenceau, and House knocked up 'in twenty minutes' a draft telegram for Wilson summarizing Britain's two essential reservations to the Fourteen Points. When formal discussion resumed that afternoon, Lloyd George's telegram was accepted, and the French and Italian representatives eventually acquiesced in this as the sole statement of Allied equivocations on the Fourteen Points.[211] Most importantly for House, in this telegram he gained the appearance of a victory. For, on the face of it, the Allies appeared to have caved in to the Fourteen Points. The note began with a reference to the correspondence between Germany and President Wilson and then announced the vital concession, namely, that the Allied governments 'declare their willingness to make peace with the Government of Germany on the terms of peace laid down in the President's address to Congress of the 8th January 1918, and the principles of settlement enunciated in his subsequent addresses'. Then followed the wording of the British equivocations, which Lloyd George proudly proclaimed was his own:

They [the Allied Governments] must point out, however, that Clause 2, relating to what is usually described as the Freedom of the Seas, is open to various interpretations, some of which they could not accept.

They must therefore reserve to themselves complete freedom on this subject when they enter the Peace Conference.

Further, in the conditions of peace laid down in his Address to Congress of the 8th January, 1918, the President declared that the invaded territories must be restored as well as evacuated and freed, and the Allied Governments feel that no doubt ought to be allowed to exist as to what this provision implies. By it they understand that compensation will be made by Germany for all damage done to the civilian population of the Allies by the aggression of Germany by land, by sea, and from the air.[212]

This original compromise proved enduring. Acrimonious discussions on British objections to the Freedom of the Seas were to continue spasmodically until 4 November. But even the disarming gloss on the Fourteen Points, hastily written by House's advisers, Walter Lippmann and Frank Cobb (which was not communicated to the Germans), failed to tempt the British to abandon their reservations.[213] Lloyd George successfully clung to his formula on Freedom of the Seas, which amounted to a demand that the Americans and British should

---

[211] Hankey Diary, 30 Oct. 1918, Hankey Papers, 1/5; Minutes of a Conversation in M. Pichon's Room, 30 Oct. 1918, CAB 28/5.

[212] Lloyd George, *War Memoirs*, ii; 1979–1980; Minutes of a Conversation in M. Pichon's Room, 30 Oct. 1918, CAB 28/5.

[213] See Ronald Steel, *Walter Lippmann and the American Century* (Boston, 1980), 149–50. The failure to submit this honestly to the Germans was deeply troubling for those involved even long afterwards; see Charles Seymour to Harold Nicolson, 18 April 1934, Sissinghurst, Nicolson Papers. However, the Germans did obtain a copy via an intelligence intercept; see Schwabe, *Woodrow Wilson, Revolutionary Germany, and Peacemaking, 1918–1919*, 110.

agree to differ. He offered only the sop of a secret promise to discuss the issue again at the Peace Conference to soften the blow for House.[214] His stand on the second reservation proved to be less offensive to the Americans, and the reason is clear. Certainly, Lloyd George was widening the concept of simple 'restoration' of damaged territory originally envisaged by Wilson. But he was not opening the door wide to war costs. Indeed, he ruled this out specifically. In discussions on 3 November he turned aside a Belgian suggestion that the wording of the second reservation be widened still further to include 'all damage caused by the war'. The Belgians argued that it should be made clear that all public and private property must be restored. Lloyd George argued strongly against any alteration in the wording. He explained that the inclusion of the Belgian phrase 'would be to tell Germany that she had to pay such a huge indemnity that it would probably be better for her to go on fighting'.[215] On the matter of reparation, therefore, Lloyd George continued to play the role of the moderate who eschewed any notion of all damages or war costs being transferred to Germany.

Lloyd George's resolute defence of his two reservations can be readily understood in the light of the pressures exerted upon him by his colleagues in London during this week. At a meeting of the War Cabinet in London on 1 November, an anxious discussion took place. Members of the Cabinet, possibly prompted by Long, were now fretful that the Prime Minister might be forced to accept the Fourteen Points in his Paris discussions. The two reservations he was known to be pursuing were not sufficient for some ministers.[216] More qualifications were suggested. Wilson's Point Three, promising an end to economic barriers, endangered the protectionist Paris Resolutions and all the plans for post-war Imperial Preference and an economic boycott of Germany, so dear to the influential 'economic warriors'. Point Five, promising an 'impartial adjustment of colonial claims', placed the captured German colonies at risk. Long reminded the Cabinet that Balfour had more than once promised that the colonies would not be returned. The Dominions would be outraged and there would be 'serious trouble' if the colonies were to be bargained away in pursuit of an armistice at meetings where the Dominions were not even represented, he warned. Long must have pricked a conscience or two in pleading earnestly that 'it was not honest for us to go to the Peace Conference with apparently an open mind in respect of the disposal of these captured territories but really intending to retain them.' In response, Smuts argued against entreating the Prime Minister to make a formal third or fourth qualification to the Fourteen Points, pointing out that sowing dissension among the Allies was the German game. However, the mood of alarm in the War Cabinet was such that Smuts's arguments were pushed aside. It was

---

[214] Fowler, *British American Relations, 1917–1918*, 226.

[215] Minutes of a Conversation at Colonel House's Residence, Paris, 3 Nov. 1918, CAB 28/5.

[216] Hankey kept the War Cabinet Secretariat in London informed of the Paris discussions throughout the week; see Hankey Diary, 5 Nov. 1918, Hankey Papers, 1/5.

agreed to send an urgent telegram to Lloyd George asking him to place on record and make perfectly clear Britain's reservations on these additional points, even if it was too late to include them in a formal memorandum.[217] Even in Paris, therefore, Lloyd George was made aware of the unflagging demands of his political colleagues for a peace free of Wilsonian restraint.

At the same time as Lloyd George and Balfour were sidestepping the ensnarements of the Fourteen Points, simultaneous discussions were proceeding among the generals and admirals on the military and naval terms of the armistice. The Foch documents from early October, which were drawn up as we have seen in the white heat of resentment over Wilson's original and unilateral consideration of the German armistice request, had been still further strengthened by the generals at a gathering at Senlis on 25 October. The terms still reflected the generals' reluctance to consider any armistice short of a total military triumph. Opinion among the generals had hardened behind the Foch plans for extensive occupation of the Rhineland, with the American General Pershing lining up defiantly behind Foch rather than Haig. The civilians were now wary of setting such a high price for armistice. Lloyd George and his political colleagues were agreed in seeking an armistice that would deprive Germany of all means of continuing war beyond her borders, and even severely compromise her capacity to defend her own territory. For example, Milner wrote on 31 October: 'We are all agreed that they [the armistice terms] must be such as to completely paralyse the enemy and prevent his even dreaming of a renewal of the fight.' But Lloyd George still believed that Haig's more moderate terms delivered all that was required and stood a greater chance of acceptance by the Germans.[218]

On this military front, Lloyd George in particular sought to moderate the ambitions of the men in uniform lest there be no armistice. At a conference of the leaders at Colonel House's residence on 1 November he argued at length in favour of Haig's more moderate military terms and against Foch's insistence upon bridgeheads over the Rhine. However, with Clemenceau and Foch pointing to the collapse of Germany's allies, Austria-Hungary and Turkey, and the critical situation now facing Berlin, the weight of opinion swung behind the stiffer terms insisted upon by Foch. What had seemed unreasonable in mid-October now seemed realizable. In pleading his case, Foch also made reference to indemnities, an argument that could not have left Lloyd George unmoved. Under Haig's terms, the Marshal asked, 'what ga[u]ges and securities should we have to secure the indemnities we require?'. His decisive argument, according to Hankey, was that the soldiers would not fight again if called upon to do so unless they were across the Rhine. As has been seen, Haig too had stressed that the troops would not fight again once armistice was declared. At this, even House, abandoning his President's preference, announced that he was willing 'to leave

---

[217] Minutes of War Cabinet 495A, 1 Nov. 1918, CAB 23/14.
[218] Bullitt Lowry, 'Pershing and the Armistice', *Journal of American History* 55 (1968–9), 281–91; Milner to Hugh Thornton, 31 Oct. 1918, Milner Papers, 19.

the matter in Foch's hands'. Faced with this united front, and similarly encouraged by the armistice developments involving Turkey and Austria-Hungary, Lloyd George too fell in behind the Foch terms. The military terms, involving the paralysis of the German military effort, were ready.[219]

The naval terms were another story. Here Lloyd George argued strongly that the appetite of the admirals was endangering any real possibility of an armistice with the Germans. He hoped that his resolute stand against Freedom of the Seas would buy him some goodwill with the British admirals, especially Lord Wemyss. But Wemyss was under extreme pressure from his admirals, especially from his rival for the top naval job, the disgruntled Admiral Beatty, to achieve a spectacular naval triumph by way of armistice. The mood in the naval élite as a whole was poisonous. The demand for wholesale surrender of the German fleet and all submarines reflected a burning desire for some share in the glory. 'We have won a passive victory and are entitled to its fruits just as much as if an action had been fought', as one document circulating among the top naval officers put it. In their private letters the admirals openly confessed their desire that impossibly high armistice terms might drive the Germans into risking a final sea battle. Wemyss resolutely resisted Lloyd George's private suggestions that the terms be revised.[220]

At a Supreme War Council on 1 November, therefore, Lloyd George insisted that the politicians force the admirals to moderate their terms. In particular, he suggested, the internment of German battleships in neutral ports 'would appear much less hard to the Germans' as against the large number of ships which the admirals wished to see simply surrendered to the Allies. Among the civilians

---

[219] Hankey Diary, 1 Nov. 1918, Hankey Papers, 1/5; Minutes of a Conversation at Colonel House's Residence, Paris, 1 Nov. 1918, CAB 28/5. According to Klaus Schwabe, House's support of Foch occurred as a result of a technical problem in the decoding of a telegram from Wilson to House in which Wilson's exhortation to House to support the Haig formula was garbled and House misled; see Schwabe, *Woodrow Wilson, Revolutionary Germany, and Peacemaking*, 88. At the meeting on the following day, Lloyd George explained that his change of mind followed from the Turkish armistice and the imminent Austrian armistice which added to the desperate nature of the German position; see Minutes of a Conversation at the Ministry of War, Paris, 2 Nov. 1918, CAB 28/5.

[220] Wemyss's 'Notes on Paris Conversations', entry for Tuesday, 29 Oct. 1918, Wemyss Papers, WMYS 7/11/4, and also Wemyss Diary, 30 Oct. to 1 Nov. 1918, WMYS 5/7; untitled document arguing the case for the surrender of all German submarines, Admiral Fremantle Papers, FRE 317, and 'Remarks on Armistice Terms' by the C.O.S., Beatty Papers, BTY 7/11/5; 'The Case for the Surrender of the High Seas Fleet', dated 13 Oct. 1918, prepared by Admiral Fremantle for the Admiralty Board, Fremantle Papers, FRE 318, Hankey to Beatty, 25 Oct. 1918, Beatty Papers, BTY 14/7/2, and Rodman to Beatty, 31 Oct. 1918, Beatty Papers, BTY 16/13/1; Admiral Charles Madden to Admiral Dreyer, 18 Oct. 1918, Dreyer Papers, DRYR 4/3; Wemyss to Beatty, 26 Oct. 1918, Wemyss Papers, WMYS 11; Wemyss Diary, 1 Nov. 1918, Wemyss Papers, WMYS 5/7. On the quarrel between Beatty and Wemyss, on account of Wemyss's alleged deliberate exclusion of Beatty from discussion of armistice terms see the acrimonious exchange of letters, Wemyss to Beatty, 16 and 18 Oct. 1918, and Beatty to Wemyss, 17 and 19 Oct. 1918, Wemyss Papers, WMYS 11. See also Fremantle to Beatty, 27 Oct. 1918, Beatty Papers, BTY 13/12/2. On Beatty's pressure to stand firm in Paris for tough terms see Wemyss to Beatty, 3 Nov. 1918, and Beatty to Wemyss, 5 Nov. 1918, Wemyss Papers, WMYS 11. On Beatty's rivalry with Wemyss for the post of First Sea Lord see Wemyss's manuscript entitled 'Admiralty II', Wemyss Papers, WMYS 11.

Lloyd George prevailed. But for three days of discussion, the Allied Naval Council stuck to their figures of German ships they wished to have surrendered (10 battleships, 6 battle cruisers, 8 light cruisers) and refused to contemplate the lesser scheme of internment if any possibility of the return of the ships to Germany was contemplated. Eventually the Supreme War Council ended the debate by simply insisting on internment and asking the naval officers for their support. The admirals sulkily caved in to the civilian leaders, but only after they had been assured that the proposed internment was a subterfuge. Thus, on 4 November, the Allied Naval Council announced its acquiescence to internment, but 'on the understanding that this is an armistice term only, and that these ships will not, under any circumstances, be returned to Germany on the conclusion of the armistice, or at any time'. A transparent duplicity had won the day. The naval terms were ready.[221]

It is important to note that during the week of discussion in Paris much had happened within Germany to worsen the internal crisis and dissolve military discipline. The French were careful to acquaint the political leaders from Britain and America with the latest French intelligence on this score. The purpose, of course, was to add weight to the case for very tough military terms, Germany's inability to resist them being pressed as the decisive argument in their favour. For example, at the commencement of the Prime Minister's gathering with House on 1 November, Clemenceau read a report he had just received from Switzerland on the internal situation in Germany 'showing the situation to be extremely bad'. Similarly, in the Allied Naval Council on the same day, Admiral le Bon argued that in the light of the serious internal disorders in Germany 'victory on our own terms was absolutely assured, and there was no reason whatever for timidity in fixing the terms of Armistice'. Therefore, the idea that the Allies might exploit the threat or even the reality of revolution in Germany in the final determination of armistice terms with Germany was already circulating among the decision-makers in Paris from 1 November.[222]

With the military and naval terms settled, and the British established as immovable on the two reservations concerning the Fourteen Points, the Versailles Council was wound up on 4 November. House agreed to send the correspondence on to Wilson showing that the Allies were willing to negotiate peace on the basis of the Fourteen Points—just in time, as the critical British negotiators noted cynically, for Wilson to seek profit from this announcement before the voting for the mid-term Congressional elections of 5 November.[223] The Lloyd George

[221] Minutes of a Conversation at Colonel House's Residence, Paris, 1 Nov. 1918, CAB 28/5; Minutes of the Allied Naval Council, Monday, 4 Nov. 1918, in Allied Naval Council, *Report of the Sixth Meetings held in Paris and Versailles from 28 Oct. to 4 Nov. 1918* (dated 11 Nov. 1918), copy in the Beatty Papers, BTY 7/11/9; Minutes of the Supreme War Council, 4 Nov. 1918, CAB 28/5.
[222] Minutes of a Conversation at Colonel House's Residence, Paris, 1 Nov. 1918, CAB 28/5; Minutes of the Allied Naval Council, Friday, 1 Nov. 1918, in Allied Naval Council, *Report of the Six Meetings held in Paris and Versailles from 28 Oct. to 4 Nov. 1918.*
[223] Leo Amery Diary, 4 Nov. 1918, Amery Papers.

statement regarding the British reservations had to be accepted by the reluctant Americans. Accordingly, on 5 November, Wilson sent his famous note to Berlin above the signature of Robert Lansing, his Secretary of State, hence the 'Lansing Note', informing the Prince Max government of the key outcome of the Versailles Council. The Lansing Note informed the Germans that all the Associated Powers were ready to make peace on the basis of a qualified acceptance of the Wilson programme. In order to clarify the extent of the qualification, the complete text of the telegram composed by Lloyd George giving the two British reservations to the Fourteen Points, word for word, was incorporated in the text of the Lansing Note. With this established, the Lansing Note informed the Germans that Marshal Foch was willing to receive German delegates and to communicate the terms of an armistice to them. An armistice was possible. Most importantly, the Lansing Note, agreed to by all the Associated Powers as an accurate summary of the diplomatic position of the victors, offered to the Germans a conditional basis to the armistice. All sides, so it seemed, were to accept an armistice because a peace on the basis of the Wilsonian programme was to follow. Britain too was solemnly and publicly committed to this conditional character of the armistice.

For the British, however, the Wilsonian conditions underpinning the diplomacy of the armistice were quite overshadowed in importance by the spectacular military victory that would be delivered by its terms. Lloyd George was exultant. The outcome of the Versailles Council was certainly a success from his point of view. Assuredly, the terms were stiffer than he would have liked. He told Lord Derby on 31 October that he believed that the terms were 'more severe than they need to be to secure immunity from the recrudescence of war'. But their acceptance by the Germans, now further debilitated by reports of a naval mutiny in Kiel, was judged by most observers to be more likely than not. Most importantly, the armistice in prospect was to be an armistice with victory. As a buoyant Balfour explained to Derby, the disarmed Germans would be in no position to resist any Allied demands after submitting to such an armistice: Germany 'would practically therefore have to accept any terms that we chose to dictate to her'.[224] Lloyd George had succeeded too in escaping any unequivocal commitment to the Fourteen Points. Under the terms of the provisos built into the Lansing Note, he had repelled the Freedom of the Seas and inserted a claim to compensation for 'damage done to the civilian population'. He had driven a hard bargain with Wilsonianism.

Lloyd George returned to London on 4 November. On the domestic front, he had good reason to hope that the coming victory would impress all his critics. His resistance to Wilson might buy him the respect of most of his Conservative colleagues, and perhaps even some immunity from the 'economic warriors' of the Right. Hankey was full of praise, telling even the Prime Minister's enemies of

---

[224] Derby Diary, 31 Oct. 1918, Derby Papers, 28/1/1.

his sterling performance. He wrote to Curzon that Versailles had witnessed 'an extraordinarily effective and indeed crushing piece of dialectics on the part of the Prime Minister'.[225] Victory was imminent. An electoral *coup de main* would be irresistible.

[225] Hankey to Curzon, 5 Nov. 1918, Curzon Papers, MS EUR F 112/121.

4

Revolution, Armistice, and 'Surrender' November 1918

Our real danger now is not the Boches but Bolshevism. Wires came in during the Cabinet to say Kaiser and Crown Prince had escaped to Holland, and German towns were in the hands of revolutionaries . . . We are not blowing bugles. An exciting day. It is certain that Bolshevism will sweep over Germany.

General Sir Henry Wilson, 10 November 1918[1]

WHEN the armistice terms were fixed at Versailles on 4 November, it was clear that the leaders of the Entente and the United States were prepared to offer an armistice to the existing government of Prince Max—whatever its alleged lack of democratic credentials. In the Lansing Note of 5 November, Wilson's final message to the Germans prior to the armistice, no fresh demands for democratization were made.[2] Neither a popular revolution nor the abdication of the Kaiser was definitely required after all. News that the Entente had accepted the Wilsonian programme and that armistice talks would soon begin was seized upon as a lifeline by the government in Berlin. Prince Max proudly announced the departure of the Armistice Commission from Berlin on the evening of 6 November. In a message to the German people, he promised that peace was only days away and called for order and patience.

By this date, however, even the promise of imminent armistice seemed insufficient to stabilize the internal political situation in Germany. It was not that the domestic reform programme promised by Prince Max's government was stalled. Quite to the contrary, Germany's transformation towards a parliamentary monarchy under the so-called 'October Constitution' was achieved in quick time. On 22 October the Chancellor introduced to the Reichstag a package of constitutional amendments which was to transform the Reich, on paper at least, into something approaching a modern liberal democratic state. In his speech Prince

---

[1] Henry Wilson Diary, 10 Nov. 1918, Henry Wilson Papers, DS MISC/80.

[2] 'President Wilson's Note of November 5th, 1918, in Reply to the Fourth German Note of October 27th', in Harold Temperley (ed.), *A History of the Peace Conference of Paris* (London, 1920), i. 457–8.

Max announced the key reform: the Chancellor was to be made responsible to the Reichstag. Over the next two days the Reichstag endorsed a package of sweeping reforms. The Kaiser lost most of his independent powers. The military agencies were subjected to the civilian authorities. The Prussian three-class suffrage, in many eyes the bulwark of the old order, was abolished. The principle of equal suffrage was proclaimed, not only in Prussia but in many of the other states also.[3] The durability and sincerity of this October Constitution is still open to debate, but it is noteworthy that the reforms were passed through the Reichstag against the 'helpless protests' of the German Conservative Party; the defenders of the old order certainly believed that genuine reform was taking place.[4]

Nevertheless, these breathtaking reforms failed to shore up support for the existing government. Undoubtedly, intensifying pressures on the government, perceived to be coming from abroad, were chiefly responsible for this. The response of the Western powers to the inner renewal of Germany had been distinctly lukewarm. President Wilson's enigmatic diplomatic notes of 14 and 23 October were interpreted widely in the German press as a demand for more thorough democratization, and even for the abdication of the Kaiser.[5] Significant gestures followed. Liebknecht, the leading anti-war socialist, was released from prison on 23 October. The Kaiser dismissed Ludendorff on 26 October for defying the authority of the new government and advocating preparation for another winter of war. On 28 October the Kaiser signed into law the changes of the October Constitution. However, at about this time Prince Max received intelligence from confidential American sources in both Berne and Copenhagen assuring him that the deposition of the Kaiser himself was exactly the ultimate prize sought by President Wilson before he would grant a 'Wilsonian' peace to Germany.[6] A political and personal crisis threatened to engulf Prince Max for the Kaiser was intransigent on the issue of abdication. Indeed, on 31 October he abandoned Berlin and returned to Spa to be with his generals, 'sheltering behind the broad backs of the soldiers'.[7] Consequently, during the first week of November, German national political attention focused upon the Kaiser and demands for him to relinquish the throne in the interests of the nation erupted in the press.

---

[3] The reforms of the October Constitution are summarized in Eberhard Kolb, *The Weimar Republic* (London, 1988), 6, H. W. Koch, *A Constitutional History of Germany* (London, 1984), 245–6, and Gerhard Schulz, *Revolutions and Peace Treaties, 1917–1920* (London, 1967), 105–9.

[4] James N. Retallack, *Notables of the Right* (London, 1988), 221.

[5] Klaus Schwabe, *Woodrow Wilson, Revolutionary Germany, and Peacemaking, 1918–1919* (Chapel Hill, NC, 1985), 105.

[6] See Klaus Schwabe, 'U.S. Secret War Diplomacy, Intelligence, and the Coming of the German Revolution in 1918: The Role of Vice Consul James McNally', *Diplomatic History*, 16 (Spring 1992), 175–200, and Schwabe, *Woodrow Wilson, Revolutionary Germany, and Peacemaking*, 103.

[7] Theodor Wolff, *Through Two Decades* (London, 1936), 124.

Premonitions of revolution: the PID renews its advice to avoid revolution in Germany

The experts on Germany at the PID in London were enormously encouraged by these internal developments, but also increasingly fearful that the leaders of the governments in Paris and London were blind to their significance, and to the very real danger of revolution. As has been seen, up until the final acceptance of the armistice proposals at the Versailles Council on 4 November, British ministers apparently thought little about the risk of revolution in Germany. Fending off a Wilsonian armistice, and then political deal-making for the snap post-armistice election, were the constant preoccupations. Only Milner had raised the issue of a German revolution and he had been slapped back down by the Northcliffe press. There was widespread disbelief that Germany could really be so close to revolution. Thus, in the last week of October, Headlam-Morley redoubled his efforts to persuade his Foreign Office superiors to take seriously the political tremors shaking Germany. The moderate government in Berlin deserved support, he argued, for 'it is in our interest to make easy the task of any organized government established on Liberal or democratic principles'.[8] Previous PID memoranda had stressed that the changes introduced and promised by Prince Max were insufficient.[9] Now the PID revised this judgement. Prussian militarism was described now as 'irretrievably defeated'. The greatest peril was that the war would end as in 1871 with a bloody commune, only this time the fighting was likely 'in every great city in Central Europe'.[10] In a new memorandum dated 1 November the PID stressed the overwhelming significance of the changes of the October Constitution, and pointed to the mounting pressure on William II to abdicate.[11] Headlam-Morley even went into the public arena to draw attention to the danger. In an article in *New Europe* appearing on 24 October, he proclaimed that the changes in Germany were 'deliberate, sincere and final'. They were prompted in part, he wrote, by a justifiable fear of a 'serious Socialist revolution in Germany'.[12]

[8] Typed untitled memorandum (undated, but from reference to the constitutional changes of 'last week' must be dated late Oct. 1918), in file endorsed 'Preparations for the Peace Conference', HMP, HDLM, Acc. 727, Box 11.

[9] 'Provisional Note on the German Reply to President Wilson as regards Constitutional Changes in Germany', dated 21 Oct. 1918, PID reference number Germany /018, FO 371/3224. This report stressed that the survival of the Bundesrat was still a major obstacle in Germany's evolution towards genuinely parliamentary government.

[10] Typed memorandum entitled 'The Old and the New' (undated, but from references to the imminent armistice must be late Oct. 1918), HMP, HDLM Acc. 727, Box 2.

[11] 'Memorandum on Internal Changes in Germany', 1 Nov. 1918, PID reference Germany /019, FO 371/3224.

[12] J. W. Headlam-Morley, 'Germany and Revolution', *New Europe*, 9/106 (24 Oct. 1918). The article made quite an impression on George Glasgow, the editor of the *New Europe*, who wrote to Headlam-Morley to tell him that the article was 'one of the best we have had the good fortune to publish' and pleading with him for more; Glasgow to Headlam-Morley, undated and a second letter dated 13 Nov. 1918, HMP, HDLM Acc. 727, Box 36.

The PID also offered advice on the making of the armistice. The armistice should be militarily tough, Headlam-Morley argued, but, to consolidate the political changes in Germany and preserve a stable government, the Allies should promise an immediate end to the economic blockade and immediate access to raw material to allow economic recovery as soon as Germany accepted a militarily paralysing armistice. This would buttress a 'Liberal Government in Germany', as Headlam-Morley now described it.[13] He advised that the Allies must not seek to evade the Fourteen Points. They must be genuinely embraced by Britain, as they were 'the whole ground' on which the armistice request was based, he reasoned. Without faith in the Wilsonian programme, he warned, Germany would lapse back into a hopeless recrudescence of the warlike spirit. This would be followed inevitably by a disastrous revolution.[14] In the last days leading up to the German revolution, two more memoranda on internal German politics were prepared within the PID. The memoranda depicted the widespread and genuine revulsion against Kaiserism and war in Germany, the burgeoning revolutionary movement, and yet the clear preference of the majority socialists for an orderly evolution if possible towards a parliamentary republic and a new democracy. The contemptuous tone towards the German socialists, which had long characterized PID reports, was replaced with a new respect.[15]

Headlam-Morley's colleagues and contacts supported him in warning against a German revolution. Bevan and Namier went to see Basil Thomson to warn the influential intelligence chief that Britain must make peace with the moderate government in Berlin or risk having no authority with whom to negotiate.[16] Zimmern gave a public lecture at King's College in late October warning that Bolshevism and anarchy were the new enemies 'now that Prussianism was on its last legs'.[17] 'Europe is in a dangerous ferment. It is touch and go whether we can avert widespread revolution. The chauvinists are playing with fire', Zimmern wrote to a friend on 5 November.[18] Bevan resorted to the press, writing a front-page feature article for the *Westminster Gazette* which drew attention to the great change coming over educated opinion in Germany under the new government.[19] Similarly, in the *Westminster Gazette*, George Saunders reviewed the slow but

---

[13] Typed untitled memorandum (undated, but from reference to the 'two previous memoranda on Germany', 016 and 018, must be dated shortly after 21 Oct. 1918, the date of the PID memoranda bearing the PID reference Germany /018), in file endorsed 'Preparations for the Peace Conference', HMP, HDLM, Acc. 727, Box 11.

[14] Untitled memorandum, but, judging from Prince Max's speeches quoted within, written shortly after 22 Oct. 1918, HMP, HDLM Acc. 727, Box 2.

[15] 'Memorandum on the Predicament of the Emperor William', 6 Nov. 1918 (PID reference Germany /020) and 'Internal Conditions in Germany', 8 Nov. 1918 (PID reference Germany /021), both in FO 371/3224.

[16] Basil Thomson Diary, 18 Oct. 1918, in B. Thomson, *The Scene Changes* (New York, 1937), 412.

[17] *The Times*, 31 Oct. 1918.

[18] Zimmern to Henry Bourne Higgins, 5 Nov. 1918, Henry Bourne Higgins Papers, MS 1057, series 1, item 337.

[19] Edwyn Bevan, 'The Beginning of Travail', *Westminster Gazette*, 6 Nov. 1918.

irresistible progress in the reform of the Prussian suffrage. A final bill democratizing the suffrage would emerge within a fortnight, he predicted.[20] The relative isolation of the PID in offering this brand of moderate advice is clear. The majority of the diplomatic élite, for example, were still inclined to the view that Prince Max and revolutionary Germans were all camouflage. Esme Howard was typical; noting the opinion of some in London by 14 October that Germany was on the verge of revolution, he remarked in his diary 'I cannot yet believe this'.[21] Until the last week of October, intelligence from the British legations in the neutral European countries remained suspicious of reports of dangerous unrest in Germany. Sir Horace Rumbold's weekly dispatches from the British legation in Berne remained contemptuous of 'sham democratisation' and stories of imminent revolution in Germany. On 7 October he wrote to Tyrrell assuring him that Prince Max's government was a 'mere change of facade'.[22] A week later he informed Hardinge privately of his conviction that 'the Boche would be most dangerous as we approached the end, for he will apply all his cunning to escape from the punishment he has so richly merited'.[23] Similarly, in mid-October Sir Reginald Wingate, British High Commissioner in Egypt, shared his private fears with Hardinge in this regard: 'I dread the effect on pacifists and others of these lying peace offensives. Our enemies deserve all the punishment it is possible to inflict upon them—and I hope there will be no half measures in this respect.'[24] Hardinge clearly accepted these sceptical assessments. On 27 October he wrote:

As for Germany, I do not believe that the governing classes are yet in a sufficiently repentant frame of mind to accept the very harsh terms that will be offered for an armistice, though they will not be in the least too hard, and I believe these manoeuvres have been simply 'camouflage' in order to gain time.[25]

Not surprisingly, then, the advice from the PID appears to have made little or no impact on the Foreign Office or the government. The PID in essence was arguing for an outcome that would leave a liberal-democratic Germany secure from revolution. The recommended strategy, that Britain sincerely embrace the Fourteen Points and promise rapid assistance for a regenerated democratic Germany, was politically unacceptable. It amounted to a plea that the British government revise plans for a peace profitable to the British Empire. What the government had refused to revise in the darkest days of the war they were not likely to revise at the moment of victory. It was easier to deny that the internal reforms in Germany amounted to anything at all. For example, in the House of Commons as late as 30 October, Robert Cecil was throwing cold water on the

[20] George Saunders, 'The German States and Democracy', *Westminster Gazette*, 7 Nov. 1918.
[21] Esme Howard Diary, 14 Oct. 1918, Howard Papers, DHW 1/4.
[22] Rumbold to Tyrrell, 7 Oct. 1918, Rumbold Papers, vol. 25.
[23] Rumbold to Hardinge, 14 Oct. 1918, Hardinge Papers, vol. 39.
[24] Sir Reginald Wingate (Cairo) to Hardinge, 21 Oct. 1918, Hardinge Papers, vol. 39.
[25] Hardinge to Sir Reginald Wingate (Cairo), 27 Oct. 1918, Hardinge Papers, vol. 39.

October Constitution. He replied to a question on the constitutional changes in Germany by observing that he could not explain the complex effects of the changes in a short reply for the House, but he assured his questioner that the German cabinet ministers' status was certainly not in any way comparable to those of ministers in the western democracies.[26]

The British 'patriotic' press, the incitement of revolution in Germany, and the reassertion of the guilt of the German people

This scepticism was reinforced by the ceaseless mockery of Prince Max's government in the popular press. Throughout October the Coalition and ultra-patriotic press assailed the 'shamocracy' in Germany. The German socialists, in particular, were attacked. Readers of *Nineteenth Century* were assured that the SPD had condoned 'almost everything' done by the warmongering German government.[27] The *Daily Mail* argued that even the socialists' opposition to Kaiserism was bogus. The British people, declared the *Daily Mail*, must not be fooled because 'some hairy "socialist" probably hired for the occasion shouts Down with the Kaiser'.[28] When Edwyn Bevan's book *German Social Democracy During the War* appeared in mid-October, the Conservative press picked through it for passages to show that the SPD was a tame-cat party which had always been under the thumb of the German government, much to Bevan's annoyance.[29]

In its determination to discredit Prince Max and his internal reforms, the right-wing 'patriotic' press even enlisted President Wilson as an ally. Wilson's strictures against 'arbitrary power' and the 'military masters and monarchical autocrats' in Germany brought forth lavish praise of the President as a straight-talking 'fight-to-the-finish' man: 'FOR A FREE PEOPLE—PEACE; FOR THE MILITARY AUTOCRACY—SURRENDER', boomed the *Daily Mail* in summary of Wilson's note of 23 October.[30] According to the 'patriotic' press, the President's 'cold and piti-less phrases' meant that he had seen through the deceitful Prince Max government. Wilson was demanding something more substantial in Berlin than the mere 'canvas scenery of democracy', announced the *Evening Standard*.[31] Wilson was not the kind of idealist to be hoodwinked by the crafty Prince Max and his 'democratic fiction', as *The Times* phrased it.[32] 'Democracy or Surrender', *The Times* editorial of 26 October agreed, was the choice facing the German people.

---

[26] *Parl. Debs.*, 5th ser., vol. 110, 1448 (30 Oct. 1918).

[27] A. Shadwell, 'Götterdämmerung', *Nineteenth Century*, 501 (Nov. 1918), an article clearly written before news of the German revolution.

[28] *Daily Mail*, editorial, 'Our Softies and the German Lie Factory', 30 Oct. 1918.

[29] *Spectator*, 19 Oct. 1918, *Westminster Gazette*, 5 Nov. 1918, and *Globe*, article, 'The Change of Heart', 6 Nov. 1918, and Edwyn Bevan to Leo Maxse, 17 Dec. 1918, Maxse Papers, vol. 475.

[30] *Daily Mail*, editorial, 'Surrender!', 25 Oct. 1918.

[31] *Evening Standard*, editorials, 'The Criminals Must Not Escape', 12 Oct., and 'The Only Terms',14 Oct. 1918.

[32] *The Times*, 'New German Note—The Democratic Fiction', 24 Oct. 1918.

Thus, Wilson's efforts to coax Germany further down the democratic road were interpreted hopefully as a blunt refusal to be lured into an early peace by the sly Hohenzollern. The 'patriotic' press portrayed Wilson as simply loyal to the old 'knock-out blow' slogan, 'No Peace With the Hohenzollern'. Indeed, this was his 'Fifteenth Point' announced the *Spectator*.[33] The Coalition press appeared to face the prospect of revolution in Germany with equanimity. Indeed, the German people were dared by some newspapers to prove their democratic mettle by staging an uprising, while others simply taunted the German people as too spineless to contemplate such a thing. *The Times* itself refrained from incitement towards actual revolution, but did argue that Wilson was giving the German people a 'plain choice' between surrender or democracy.[34] Garvin in the *Observer* was more adventurous; nothing was more essential, he wrote, than that a tough armistice should rouse the German people 'with execration and repentance to sweep away the authors of the war'.[35] The more popular papers openly interpreted Wilson's diplomacy as an encouragement of the German people to attempt a seizure of power. The *Daily Mail* airily dismissed the capacity of the German people to respond: 'We don't imagine that the surrender of the autocracy will come by return of post, or that the German people which has grovelled in the foulness of a slavery into which it would willingly thrust all the other peoples, will in a single day rise to the stature of a free people.'[36] Hulton's *Evening Standard* suggested that an invitation to revolution was the only possible interpretation of Wilson's diplomatic notes: 'It must be now clear to the German people that they must overthrow completely the Kaiser and the Hohenzollern family or prepare for war to the knife.'[37] When news of the Kiel mutiny reached London on 6 November, most editors were still contemplating a German revolution without flinching. Northcliffe's *Evening News* announced that it was 'willing to take the risk' of a Bolshevik outbreak in Germany and urged the merciless pursuit of the retreating German armies.[38] The *Globe* outshone all others in its confidence even at the prospect of a Bolshevik revolution: 'Let the Germans go Bolshevist if they will. It is nothing to us except in so far as the extent to which they cut one another's throats is a matter of benefit to the rest of mankind.'[39]

For the 'patriotic' press, it is important to note, the likelihood of a German revolution was in any case not the important point. Neither democratization nor revolution could absolve the German people of their guilt. The German people would have to pay for having supported the war and lost. Thus, in the weeks and

[33] *Spectator*, editorial, 'President Wilson's Answer', 12 Oct. 1918, and 'News of the Week', 19 Oct. 1918. See also *Daily Mail*, editorial, 'The President's Reply: Unconditional Surrender', 16 Oct. 1918.
[34] *The Times*, editorial, 'President Wilson's Last Word', 26 Oct. 1918.
[35] *Observer*, editorial, 'Britain's Part in the Terms', 13 Oct. 1918.
[36] *Daily Mail*, editorial, 'Surrender!', 25 Oct. 1918.
[37] *Evening Standard*, 'A Londoner's Diary', 15 Oct. 1918.
[38] *Evening News*, editorial, 'Red Flag and White', 7 Nov. 1918.
[39] *Globe*, editorial, 'Let Them Bolsh', 6 Nov. 1918.

days preceding the German revolution, the Liberal and Wilsonian distinction between the German government and the people was as passionately repudiated as at any time during the war. As has been seen, Balfour had encouraged the press to pursue this line with his 'Brutes they were, brutes they remain' speech following the *Leinster* tragedy. *The Times*, for example, endorsed Balfour's analysis, noting that, quite correctly, the Foreign Secretary 'refuses to acquit the German people of complicity in these crimes'.[40] Journals like the *National Review* needed little encouragement to beat the same drum. Leo Maxse argued as always that the German government and people were 'one and indistinguishable'.[41] Similarly, Edward Gleichen, the former Intelligence Branch official, produced a diatribe in the *National Review* arguing that the Germans were utterly incapable of any genuine repentance. 'Not one German in a million will ever admit that any crimes have been committed', he assured readers.[42] In the editorials of the *Globe*, the Germans appeared, as they had appeared throughout the war, as the 'Guilty Race'. 'We cannot—more's the pity—wipe out the German race, but we can make them pay and pay heavily for their fun' declared the *Globe* on 18 October. The *Globe*'s case left no German soul guiltless:

> It is not true that the German people do not share the guilt of their government. They do. There is no country in which the government and the people are more entirely at one, and it is utterly false to regard the average German as a kindly and good-hearted fellow who has been misled by wicked rulers and by them betrayed into excess . . . The people have been wholeheartedly behind their government . . . The German people as a whole never for a moment believed the fiction that they were being forced into a war for their own defence.[43]

The *Globe* was by no means alone in this pursuit of the very broadest indictment. Dozens of similar articles appeared during October and early November in the Coalition press. *Reynold's Newspaper*, while noting that the German people were 'sorely tried and oft deluded', agreed that a 'Peace of Justice' demanded that they make good their damage to Belgium, France, and Britain 'to the uttermost farthing'.[44] Patriotic MPs were quoted in support of an indemnity. Hay Morgan, a Conservative MP, explained that Britain ought to have 'a commission sitting in Germany taking toll of her products and manufactures for fifty or sixty years'.[45] One of the most extreme examples of this type of reasoning came from the pen of Harold Wyatt, a leading spirit in Lord Beresford's Imperial Maritime League. The German people, he declared, 'with its whole brutal heart and its whole bestial soul', had supported the Prussian warmongers from the very first moment of

[40] *The Times*, editorial, 'Deeds, not Words', 12 Oct. 1918.

[41] *National Review*, editorial, 'Why the Peace Plea?', 429 (Nov. 1918), written in Oct.

[42] Gleichen, 'The "Repentance" of Germany', ibid.

[43] *Globe*, editorial, 'The Guilty Race', 18 Oct. 1918.

[44] *Reynold's Newspaper*, editorial, 'A Peace of Justice', 27 Oct. 1918.

[45] G. Hay Morgan, 'Germany and a League of Nations', and see Oswald Stoll, 'Indemnities: How They Should be Paid', both in *Reynold's Newspaper*, 27 Oct. 1918.

bloodshed. The whole people shared complicity in each and every atrocity committed by German armed forces for, he argued, the German people had 'yelled with delight' and 'roared with joy' over every reported infamy. The people had never protested: 'Murder, rape, arson, torture, have been clasped to its foul bosom from the beginning of the huge world-outrage even up to now.' The conclusion was clear. Whatever was in Mr Wilson's points, Germany must be punished with a demand for a huge indemnity: 'The righteous punishment of Germany is that she should be made to pay—pay for the whole cost of the war.'[46]

The moderate Liberal and the Radical press had little to say on the guilt issue but did argue against inciting revolution in Germany. Scott in the *Manchester Guardian* supported the President in probing for more democratic guarantees from Germany, but only up to a point. He acknowledged the progress that had been made in Berlin. 'No doubt the present German Government is a Liberalised Government and its head is a Liberal as Liberalism in Germany is understood', he wrote cautiously on 14 October.[47] From 22 October, Scott began to speak out on the danger of a revolution in Germany. He expressed the hope that the democratic changes in Germany were sufficient and that 'President Wilson may feel he has achieved enough to go on with'.[48] Scott defended Milner's controversial position and argued that the Allies must be aware of the possibility of encouraging 'subversive changes' in Germany.[49] Similarly, the *Nation* campaigned against a revolution in Germany in the last weeks of the war. 'Peace Without Revolution' was the great objective, argued Massingham. Revolution was in no one's interest. 'Bankruptcy is at least as infectious as Revolution, and Europe stands on the threshold of both', Massingham argued.[50]

The Liberal press found no echo in the government. The Lloyd George Coalition did nothing to oppose either the incitement to revolution or the doctrine of national guilt. The last Coalition minister to insist on the old distinction between the German government and its people was George Barnes. At a crowded public meeting sponsored by the League of Nations Society at the Central Hall on 10 October, Barnes ventured the opinion that the British government's declarations of war aims did not contain 'any threat to the German people'. 'There ought to be!' called out a voice immediately. But Barnes persisted, declaring that Britain was at war, not with the German people, but rather 'at war with the system which had oppressed and debased the German people'. Some press criticism of Barnes followed immediately.[51] No minister came to his assistance.

[46] H. F. Wyatt, 'Payment by the German People', *Nineteenth Century*, 501 (Nov. 1918). The article was clearly written before news of the German revolution.

[47] *Manchester Guardian*, editorial, 'Surrender', 14 Oct. 1918.

[48] *Manchester Guardian*, editorial, 'The German Reply', 22 Oct. 1918.

[49] *Manchester Guardian*, editorial, 'Discussions of Peace', 24 Oct. 1918, and editorial, 'The President's Final Reply', 25 Oct. 1918.

[50] *Nation*, editorial, 'Peace Without Revolution', 2 Nov. 1918.

[51] *The Times*, 11 Oct. 1918. For criticism of Barnes see Lord Denbigh's letter to *The Times*, 14 Oct. 1918.

The scent of imminent danger: last-minute British trepidation at the prospect of revolution in Germany

Only in the last days of October did the danger of revolution in Germany begin to impress members of the British government. A distinct change in the intelligence submitted to the War Cabinet, from both civilian and military sources, was discernible. No longer was the PID alone in warning of a revolution overtaking the moderate government of Prince Max. Foreign Office telegrams from Lord Acton at Berne, which were read to the War Cabinet by Robert Cecil on 29 October, stressed the gathering unrest inside Germany: the campaign for the Kaiser's abdication was in full swing, and it was noted that the government and military were determined to save reliable troops 'to keep order in their own country'. There was undoubtedly 'panic in Berlin' observed Cecil. Military Intelligence confirmed that the recent dismissal of Ludendorff was quite genuine.[52] News of the fall of Ludendorff appears to have awakened many to the gravity of the internal crisis. Major-General William Thwaites, the Director of Military Intelligence, told the War Cabinet on 31 October that the choice of General Groener as Ludendorff's replacement was most significant, for Groener was a transport specialist presumably chosen to deal with the practical difficulties of withdrawal and demobilization.[53] The weekly Naval Intelligence summary confirmed on 31 October that the new government had honoured its undertakings on submarine warfare. However, dangers lurked on the German Left. The 'collapse of German militarism' had given the forces of Bolshevism inside Germany 'a new lease of life', warned Naval Intelligence.[54]

Similarly, the Foreign Office telegrams arriving in London sounded a new note. Intelligence summaries from Lieutenant-Colonel Wade, military attaché at Copenhagen, stressed the depth of the changes inside Germany: 'As regards the genuineness of the reforms introduced, it seems fair to conclude that a return to the old regime has now become impossible, as the Junker system of Government was admittedly bankrupt.'[55] Even the Foreign Office telegrams from the Berne legation began to take seriously the changes inside Germany, this striking shift in analysis no doubt a result of Horace Rumbold's departure to London for three weeks' leave in mid-October.[56] Now under Lord Acton's direction, summaries of intelligence from Berne presented Prince Max's government as engaged in a genuine struggle to defeat reaction. Acton declared that 'Ludendorff's fall is the symbolical rejection by the new regenerated and democratized Germany of the old

---

[52] Minutes of the War Cabinet, 492, 29 Oct. 1918, CAB 23/8.
[53] Minutes of the War Cabinet, 494, 31 Oct. 1918, CAB 23/8.
[54] Admiralty Intelligence, 29–31 Oct. 1918, Drax Papers, DRAX 5/4.
[55] Lt.-Col. Wade (Copenhagen), 'Notes on Political Information from Intelligence and Press Sources', 31 Oct. 1918, FO 371, 3224.
[56] Martin Gilbert, *Sir Horace Rumbold* (London, 1973), 176. Rumbold visited the king on 26 Oct. 1918; see George V Diary, 26 Oct. 1918, George V Papers.

Germany and all its works'.[57] He reported on the mounting pressure on the Kaiser to abdicate, with frequent disturbances on the streets in Berlin.[58] Acton depicted the fall of Ludendorff as the expiration of the Pan-Germans' last hopes for a coup against the new government. One of Acton's informants described the new mood in Germany: 'The spell is broken, everyone is delighted at the birth of a new Germany, and no one minds that its coming has been brought about by military defeats.'[59]

In the face of multiplying reports in this vein, the mood of the British political élite changed too. At a dinner on the evening of 30 October Archbishop Davidson found Smuts 'keenly anxious' about revolution in Austria and contemplating 'a European gendarmerie' to smother it.[60] Other ministers shared Smuts's sense of trepidation. For example, Curzon, Churchill, F. E. Smith, and Lord Crawford dined together at Downing Street on 1 November. Crawford preserved in his diary the ministers' shared presentiment that 'scenes as bloody as the incidence of open war itself' might follow armistice. 'We do not want Austria or Germany to relapse into Bolshevism', wrote Crawford. He detected too 'undercurrents of nervousness' about revolutionary outbreaks not only in Berlin, but in London, Glasgow, Sheffield, South Wales, and Barrow.[61] But, if a revolution was to come, the political élite agreed with the 'patriotic' editors that it was not to be taken as evidence of moral regeneration on Germany's part. On the contrary, it was further proof of German perfidy. Austen Chamberlain, for example, wrote on 2 November that the German people were turning on the Kaiser 'rather basely'. A revolution would only serve to underline the fact that the Germans lacked moral 'grit', in that 'when they find the game is lost they collapse morally as a people'.[62]

The military élite was equally despondent. Anxiety over revolution even led some to flirt with the possibility of the Entente exerting pressure behind the scenes to save the Hohenzollern dynasty. For example, one of the most agitated among the officers was Admiral Roslyn Wemyss, the First Sea Lord, who was visiting Paris for meetings of the Supreme War Council in late October. On 30 October Wemyss lunched with Madame de Castellane, the wife of a prominent Anglophile French Deputy, Boni de Castellane. She told the admiral that the abdication of the German Emperor would be 'a disaster' and would only encourage Bolshevism in Germany. They lamented together that amidst the sufferings of war 'Socialism has had a great shove forward'. So impressed was Wemyss by the argument for 'moderation' that he volunteered to help. He suggested that Madame de Castellane should journey to Switzerland and interview Prince Alexander Hohenlohe. Wemyss went immediately to interview Arthur Balfour at

[57] Acton to Balfour, 31 Oct. 1918, FO 371/3224.
[58] Acton to Balfour, 1 Nov. 1918, FO 371/3224.
[59] Acton to Balfour, 4 Nov. 1918, FO 371/3224.
[60] Davidson Diary, 3 Nov. 1918, Davidson Papers, 13.
[61] Crawford Diary, 1 Nov. 1918, vol. xxxiii, Crawford Papers.
[62] A. Chamberlain to Hilda, 2 Nov. 1918, Chamberlain Papers, AC 5/1/111.

the embassy in Paris and suggested this approach to Germany via Switzerland. However, as Wemyss reported in his diary, Balfour was reluctant: 'He is afraid of opening out, fears the communication. Of course it is too late really. However, I have done all I can.'[63]

Similarly, the generals continued to debate the mooted armistice and speculated on the danger of revolution in Germany. For some brass-hats, fear of revolution was balanced by their desire to exploit the impotence of the German authorities if and when they were faced with revolution. At the top, Haig continued to promote his case for a moderate armistice on the basis of the proven weariness of the French army. At Cambrai on 31 October, for example, Haig told an assembly of British generals of his opposition to the French plans for demanding bridgeheads over the Rhine. Withdrawal behind the German frontier should suffice, he argued.[64] During the first days of November he collected and forwarded to Henry Wilson the latest military intelligence showing that 'the French troops made no pretence of fighting'.[65] Haig's long-standing argument against driving Germany to revolution also gained some acceptance among the leading brass hats. Some now expressed similar fears over the disruptive consequences of a popular uprising in the defeated empires. General Rawlinson, for example, recorded in his diary on 2 November his opinion that 'Bolshevism is spreading'. Austria was in chaos, he wrote, and 'it will spread to Germany and we shall have no central authority to make terms with—still I would not make the terms easy on this account'. Indeed, Rawlinson consoled himself with the knowledge that the Germans now had no alternative but to accept bitter armistice terms.[66] He told Lord Stamfordham on 5 November that German morale was plummeting, for German prisoners now greeted new arrivals with cheers, and captured German officers openly professed that the government 'will accept any terms'.[67] Other generals such as Birdwood confessed that they still had 'very imperfect information' on inner Germany and, therefore, could not tell whether the suggested armistice terms were too harsh.[68] H. W. Studd at the Supreme War Council on 3 November admitted that 'the Boche' would probably reject the harsh armistice being planned 'unless he is really in a worse way than I think internally'.[69] The possibility of the disablement of the enemy via revolution remained a factor, therefore, in the weighing of the armistice.

Among the political élite also, the prospect of revolution was unwelcome; but, at the same time, there was an awareness that the fires of revolution at the back

[63] Wemyss Diary, 30 Oct. 1918, Wemyss Papers, 5/7.

[64] Rawlinson Diary, 31 Oct. 1918, Rawlinson Papers, 1/11.

[65] F. S. H. Cavendish to Haig, 1 Nov. 1918, enclosed within Haig to Wilson, 4 Nov. 1918, Henry Wilson Papers, HHW 7.

[66] Rawlinson Diary, 2 Nov. 1918, Rawlinson Papers, 1/11.

[67] Rawlinson to Stamfordham, 5 Nov. 1918, George V Papers, RA GEO V Q 2522/2/149.

[68] General Birdwood to Sir James Allen (New Zealand Defence Minister), Allen Papers, Miscellaneous Papers, Box 9.

[69] Studd to Stanhope, 3 Nov. 1918, Stanhope Papers, C. 655 Correspondence.

of the German authorities might force them to sign the very harshest armistice. A race between revolution and armistice was observed. On 1 November Herbert Fisher, for example, explained in a private note to his wife that Germany would be under great pressure to sign an armistice now 'rather than run the risk of a revolution'.[70] Austen Chamberlain made the same point to his sister Hilda: 'With the homeland seething with discontent, disloyalty and suffering, I think we have them at our mercy and that they must accept our terms.'[71]

Revolution as the deliverer of victory

Meanwhile in Germany, revolution itself was made inevitable by the controversial actions of the German Admiralty. Plans were made in mid-October for a last great raid involving the capital ships of the High Seas Fleet. Prince Max was briefed in the most general terms. The plan may have been intended originally as a limited strike along the Belgian coast to relieve the retreating German army. However, reactionaries within the Admiralty hoped to provoke a major battle with the British fleet which might restore the honour of the German navy, sabotage the armistice negotiations, and destabilize the democratic reforms of Prince Max's government.[72] In any case, when the fleet gathered in the Jade estuary at midnight on 29 October, mutinous sailors doused their ships' boilers. The raid was cancelled, and thus a possible political counter-revolution within Germany was forestalled. On 3 November, attempts to punish the mutineers prompted a major rally in Kiel on their behalf and then a violent attempt to release the condemned men. A full-scale revolt triumphed in Kiel the next day and a Workers' and Sailors' Council was established. The government's dispatch of Gustav Noske and Konrad Haussmann to negotiate with the Kiel mutineers stabilized the situation in Kiel temporarily, but revolutionary Workers', Sailors', and Soldiers' Councils were formed in other northern port cities in the days that followed.[73]

News of the mutiny compounded the sense of trepidation and expectation felt among the British leadership. Horror at 'Bolshevism' was intense, but balanced by the realization that the enemy would now find the armistice irresistible. This was the burden of diplomatic intelligence as early as 5 November. Acton's telegram from Berne of that date reported that the Germans 'are anxious to accept any terms, however severe, owing to their fear of Bolshevist disorders in [the] interior and their consequent desire to recall troops for the maintenance of order at home'.[74] British Naval Intelligence was naturally enthralled by the

---

[70] H. Fisher to L. Fisher, 1 Nov. 1918, Fisher Papers, 205.

[71] A. Chamberlain to Hilda, 2 Nov. 1918, Chamberlain Papers, AC 5/1/111.

[72] Leonidas E. Hill, 'Signal zur Konterrevolution? Der Plan zum Vorstoß der deutschen Hochseeflotte am 30. Oktober 1918', *Vierteljahrshefte für Zeitgeschichte*, 36 (Jan. 1988), 113–29.

[73] The naval mutiny is described in detail in F. L. Carsten, *War Against War* (London, 1982), ch. 12.

[74] Acton to Balfour, 5 Nov. 1918, FO 371/ 3224.

reports from the naval towns. On 7 November Naval Intelligence reported the rioting in Kiel and drew the conclusion that the 'internal condition' of Germany was now the decisive factor and also argued that in its aftermath the proposed armistice would undoubtedly be accepted.[75] The British generals grasped the same lesson. When General Rawlinson first learned of the draft armistice terms on 3 November he had described them as 'tantamount to unconditional surrender', and noted in his diary that the Germans could never accept such terms without much 'further fighting'. On 7 November he was informed of the uprising at Kiel where, as he expressed it, 'half the Boch [*sic*] fleet have hoisted the red flag of Bolshevism'. He immediately revised his opinion of the likelihood of the German's acceptance of an armistice: 'In view of the mutiny in the fleet at Kiel I do not see how they can possibly do otherwise than accept the armistice terms.'[76] Even Haig found the reasons for his previous caution about over-ambitious armistice conditions slipping away. In his diary on 8 November he too noted that in the context of the widening naval revolt in north Germany, it was true that the Germans would accept 'any terms for an armistice which we demand'.[77]

For various reasons, the British naval élite was not so enthusiastic. Admiral Wemyss was in Paris making preparations to accompany Foch as chief British representative in the party that would shortly meet the German armistice plenipotentiaries. News of the Kiel mutiny depressed him, for he believed it may have snuffed out the still flickering hope among the naval top brass for a grand battle with the German High Seas Fleet. Wemyss sent Beatty the first detailed reports on the Kiel mutiny on 5 November. He explained that the naval confrontation for which they both hankered was now less likely than ever. The revolutionary Sailors' Councils, Wemyss explained, may prevent any fleet movements through the Kiel Canal. Minesweepers had halted, so German excursions into the North Sea were unlikely. The armistice terms, including internment of the fleet in neutral ports, were likely to be accepted now. With great candour, Wemyss confessed that he had been counting on a German refusal 'until a few hours ago'. In making his stand for absolute naval demands over the preceding week, he admitted, he had been deliberately intending to make an armistice impossible:

In a way I was pleased with these terms as I believed that directly the Germans heard them they would refuse and would come out and fight, in which case we should have got all we wanted; but if the fleet is disintegrated as we believe it may be the whole situation is altered and God knows what may happen.[78]

[75] Admiralty Intelligence, 5–7 Nov. 1918, Drax Papers, DRAX 5/4.
[76] Rawlinson Diary, 3, 7 and 8 Nov. 1918, Rawlinson Papers, 1/11.
[77] Haig Diary, 8 Nov. 1918, Haig Papers, 152.
[78] Wemyss to Beatty, 5 Nov. 1918, Wemyss Papers 11, and also Wemyss to Beatty, 5 Nov. 1918, with handwritten additions, Beatty Papers, BTY/13/40/17.

News of the revolution only further antagonized the bitterly divided naval officers. Beatty was not about to abandon his vendetta against Wemyss, attacking his acceptance of the draft armistice terms and objecting in particular to the failure to list a demand for the surrender of Heligoland.[79] In London Admiral Fremantle was deputizing for Wemyss and attending meetings of the War Cabinet. He tried at first to keep alive some hope for battle.[80] By 8 November, however, he reported to Beatty that the mutinies had blossomed into the 'Kiel revolution' and that there was not now 'the smallest chance of their coming out to fight'.[81] None the less, Fremantle had some consolations to offer. The unfortunate revolution might yet be exploited. He advised Beatty on 9 November that his proposed demand for Heligoland could still be reinserted into the armistice demands under the convenient cover of an insurance against the threatened chaos of revolution. As Fremantle explained, Heligoland ought never have been left out of the original list of armistice terms, but, in any case, 'the circumstances have now changed, owing to the utterly unexpected revolution at Kiel'.[82]

Lloyd George and the 'economic warriors' on the eve of the armistice

At the nucleus of power throughout these climactic days, Lloyd George continued to juggle the issues associated with impending armistice, the general election, and his own political future. Domestic issues still preoccupied the Prime Minister. On the evening of 5 November, the day after his return from the Versailles discussions, Lloyd George saw the king.[83] He presented his case for a general election and gained the king's assent. The great political gamble was set in train.

When the leaders of the government sat down to contemplate the coming armistice, fear of revolution in Germany at first prevailed. There was astonishment at the news of the Kiel mutiny. When Lloyd George gathered several of his ministers at Downing Street on the morning of 6 November he read to them a proclamation calling for calm issued by the German government on the preceding evening. The document showed very clearly, in Lloyd George's opinion, that the government was intensely afraid of revolution. Herbert Fisher summarized Lloyd George's reaction in his diary: 'Nothing much to be gained from one point of view by abolition of the Kaiser. A Bolshevist revolution would be dreadful in Germany and is not to be wished for, but the German Social Democrat is a steady moderate person.'[84] None the less, Lloyd George was not blind to the

[79] Beatty to Wemyss, 7 Nov. 1918, Wemyss Papers 11.
[80] Fremantle to Beatty, 6 Nov. 1918, Beatty Papers, BTY 13/12/4, and Fremantle to Wemyss, 7 Nov. 1918, Fremantle Papers, FRE/ 311.
[81] Fremantle to Beatty, 8 Nov. 1918, Beatty Papers, 13/12/5.
[82] Fremantle to Beatty, 9 Nov. 1918, Beatty Papers, 13/12/6.
[83] Sir Bryan Godfrey-Fausset Dairy, 5 Nov. 1918, Godfrey-Fausset Papers, 1/70.
[84] H. A. L. Fisher Diary, 6 Nov. 1918, in HMP, HDLM, Acc. 800/3.

value of an incipient revolution. At breakfast with the Conservative ministers on 7 November, he was more hopeful. He expressed the view that the Germans would undoubtedly accept the armistice terms now 'in view of our menace through Austria, and the internal conditions of Germany and the revolt of the fleet'.[85] Advocates of the very toughest armistice terms were rapidly coming to the same conclusion. F. S. Oliver told his brother that 'the essence of the whole matter is that the German inside has gone wrong. I don't believe there are any terms which we could offer them which their public opinion would allow them to refuse.' As Oliver summarized the situation, 'the German people have bolted'.[86]

However, the imminent imposition of a profitable armistice did not save Lloyd George from another bruising encounter with the 'economic warriors' led by Hughes. As soon as news of the Versailles discussions broke, Hughes was complaining to his contacts in the press that he ought to have been invited to Versailles, as the Prime Minister of a belligerent power, for this most crucial of meetings on the cessation of the war. Northcliffe asked Geoffrey Dawson to 'pacify Hughes', but he did not succeed.[87] Immediately upon Lloyd George's return to London Hughes was determined to interrogate him. In the Imperial War Cabinet on 5 November Hughes attacked the armistice terms worked out at Versailles and urged that Britain at once enter a caveat 'that the 14 points were not our terms of peace'. Hughes insisted that he had no desire to be bound to 'the chariot wheel of the 14 points'. Lloyd George replied that 'the Peace Terms were not limited by the 14 points, but by all Wilson's speeches since January 1918'; these, he argued, gave to Britain all she wanted 'with the exception of the points regarding freedom of the seas and indemnities, and notice of our position in regard to these matters had been duly given'. Thus did Lloyd George seek to fend off this first attack on the Versailles Council by advertising his stand against freedom of the seas and for 'indemnities'.[88] Hughes was momentarily reassured. However, the terms of the Lansing Note appeared soon after in the British press. Even *The Times* acknowledged that an indemnity had been relinquished under the second of Britain's reservations to the Fourteen Points: 'Apparently the "point", as thus read, excludes the imposition of any penal indemnity for the costs of war—an unusual concession to the defeated enemies.'[89] Hughes perceived that the promises conveyed to the Germans within the Lansing Note did indeed commit all the Entente powers to the bulk of Wilson's idealistic package. He was infuriated. Hughes launched another slashing attack on the Prime Minister in the Imperial War Cabinet. The loyal Dominions had been taken for granted; they had not been consulted over the armistice terms, he complained

[85] Bridgeman Diary, 7 Nov. 1918, Bridgeman Papers, SRO 4629/1/2/1.
[86] F. S. Oliver to W. E. Oliver, 7 Nov. 1918, Oliver Papers, 65.
[87] Dawson Diary 1918, 31 Oct. 1918 and 1 Nov. 1918, Dawson Papers, 24.
[88] Minutes of the Imperial War Cabinet, 5 Nov. 1918, CAB 23/42.
[89] *The Times*, editorial, 'Two Momentous Events', 7 Nov. 1918.

bitterly, in spite of all British promises. The peace terms had been 'definitely settled' at Paris between House and Lloyd George. Britain would be 'bound by 14
points' at the Peace Conference 'and could neither add nor take away from them'.
Lloyd George's two reservations, he insisted, were utterly insufficient. In particular, Hughes noted, 'the words inserted in the second qualification to provide for
reparation did not cover the ground'. Wilson's dangerous free trade commitment,
Point Three, with its references to the removal of economic barriers, had not
been challenged. Now Britain would find it impossible to limit Germany's economic recovery. Hughes's intemperate speech made it clear that he was alive to
the difficulty of obtaining the two precious objectives for which the 'economic
warriors' had long been campaigning—indemnity and economic protection.[90]
Lloyd George's reply at this point was most significant. He admitted that an
indemnity was ruled out as a result of his agreements with House, but held out
the hope of a large claim to compensation, for shipping losses, under the elastic
title of 'reparations':

No sort of reparation had been ruled out by the recent decisions at Versailles. A war
indemnity had been ruled out because, beyond full reparation, Germany would have no
means of paying further. There was nothing to prevent either France, Belgium or Great
Britain asking for full reparation for all damage done, e.g. in our own case reparation for
every ship sunk by the enemy, either in cash or kind. The total reparation which might
be claimed would amount to something between a thousand and two thousand million
pounds.[91]

The Prime Minister also sought to distract the Imperial War Cabinet by seizing upon the vulnerability of Germany. In the light of reports on the Kiel revolution, he shifted his ground at last on the harsh naval terms to be imposed on
Germany. Lloyd George gave the Imperial War Cabinet the latest details of the
'serious internal situation in Germany'. These, he explained, prompted him to
suggest an 'alteration in the instructions' to be given to Admiral Wemyss in Paris.
Lloyd George moved that the Imperial War Cabinet give the British naval delegates in Paris full power to alter the terms as they saw fit considering the unfolding situation in Germany. For example, Lloyd George urged, the delegates
should now be permitted to demand internment of the German naval ships in
neutral *or* in Allied ports. This was a most important alteration, as Lloyd George
remarked, for this 'practically amounted to a demand for complete surrender'.
The Imperial War Cabinet fell in with this suggestion, agreeing to give the naval
delegates in Paris full latitude 'in view of the altered circumstances which had
that morning been communicated to them', that is, in the wake of the Kiel
mutiny.[92]
    Hughes was not pacified. Neither Lloyd George's explanations of his formal
reservations on the Fourteen Points, nor his last-minute display of eagerness to

exploit the Kiel mutiny, cooled the Australian Prime Minister's temper. Hughes took his complaints to the public platform. On 7 November Hughes lunched at the Australasian Club in the City and in his speech complained bitterly of British neglect of the Dominions. He alleged that Lloyd George had caved in to the Wilsonian ideals at Versailles. 'I object to the Peace Terms because they do not provide for indemnities', explained Hughes. The Wilsonian prospect of equal treatment for Germany in tariffs also infuriated Hughes, and he swore that 'nothing but superior force will compel us to do it'.[93] Hughes was, as usual, 'undiplomatic and made too much of [the] personal aspect', as Latham recorded.[94] At a dinner at Australia House the next day Hughes 'returned to the charge', railing against the British Prime Minister's presumption in binding the Empire as a whole to Wilson's programme without any gesture of consultation.[95] Hughes's allies in the 'economic warrior' press rushed to support him and to reassert the claim to an indemnity now imperilled by the Lansing Note.[96] So serious were Hughes's allegations that an official British Government response was issued to the press on 9 November. This rather lame note avoided the major issue of the Dominions' exclusion from the Versailles discussions: it simply insisted that the Dominions had been given every opportunity to contribute to British decision-making in general, and denied that the exact peace terms had been decided in advance at Versailles.[97] This scarcely answered Hughes's allegations. He continued to press forward his claim that Lloyd George had curtailed the Empire's freedom of action in making the peace. A number of other speeches followed, all equally pointed, all hostile to Lloyd George and Wilson, and widely reported in the London papers. The sham of the Imperial War Cabinet, and the hollowness of the imperial relationship, Hughes argued, had been exposed by the British decision to end the war and agree to the broad principles that would govern the peace without reference to the Dominions.[98]

This very public falling out had important consequences. Hughes resolved to seek separate representation for the Dominions at the coming Peace Conference. Only separate representation would safeguard the fruits of victory, and protect the interests of Australia, as Hughes saw them, from the threat of Wilsonianism.[99] Even the mild-mannered Andrew Fisher, Australian High Commissioner in London, came to the same conclusion; in view of Dominion exclusion from the recent Versailles armistice discussions, he declared, it would

---

[93] *Daily Express*, 8 Nov. 1918.

[94] John Latham Diary, 7 Nov. 1918, Latham Papers, MS 1009/20/909A.

[95] Robert Garran Diary, 8 Nov. 1918, Garran Papers, Series 5, Box 3.

[96] e.g. editorial 'Are We To Lose the Peace', *Globe*, 7 Nov. 1918, editorial, 'Dominion Rights', and article, 'Bravo Hughes', *Globe*, 8 Nov. 1918.

[97] *The Times*, 9 Nov. 1918.

[98] e.g. Hughes's speech at the British Empire Club, Garran Diary, 14 Nov. 1918, Garran Papers, Series 5, Box 3.

[99] See L. F. Fitzhardinge, 'Hughes, Borden and Dominion Representation at the Paris Peace Conference', *Canadian Historical Review*, 49/2 (June 1968), 160–9.

be 'too fantastic to have only British Isles men at the Peace Conference'.[100] In addition, Hughes evinced more determination than ever to hunt the indemnity which he claimed Lloyd George had imperilled at the Versailles Council on 4 November. In the weeks that followed Hughes asked his chief Australian advisers in London, Garran, Latham, and Eggleston, to prepare briefing papers on the right of the Entente powers to seek an indemnity from Germany notwithstanding the unfortunate Lansing Note.[101]

Lloyd George, for his part, acted as something of a hostage to Hughes's tantrums. In spite of his exceptional style, Hughes could not be brushed off by Lloyd George as an Australian bumpkin. Hughes had powerful connections which he was able to exploit in his cause. For example, as soon as the crisis broke, the Round Table influence of his advisers was mobilized. As a devoted Round Table movement member, Latham was indeed quite deeply embarrassed by the British treatment of Australia. He wrote a passionate letter of protest to Kerr on 9 November explaining his 'most grave apprehension as to the future of the Empire'.[102] This produced a summons to the Australians to attend a special 'moot' at Curtis's home in London in mid-November. There Garran and Latham confronted a powerful group of London Round Tablers. Latham delivered a heartfelt address scolding the British government over 'the breach of faith in not consulting the Dominions'.[103] While expressing regret over Hughes's tone, Latham condemned the British government for making binding commitments to the outlines of peace at the Versailles Council without inviting a single Dominion representative: 'a golden opportunity has been lost', Latham proclaimed.[104] A 'vigorous discussion' among the Round Tablers followed. Latham summarized its thrust in his diary: 'They don't like Hughes but most agree B. G. [British Government] had bungled.'[105]

The danger for Lloyd George did not begin and end with Hughes. It was obvious that Hughes had his supporters among prominent members of the government itself. Within a week of Hughes's outburst, his friend Walter Long was using the affair as an opportunity to undermine the British commitment to

---

[100] A. Fisher to M. Fisher, 7 Nov. 1918, Andrew Fisher Papers, MS 2919/1/482.

[101] Garran complied with the request; see Garran's memoranda 'The Terms of Peace', Australian Archives, CP 351/1/1, bundle 1/16. Eggleston too prepared a report in favour of the principle of indemnity; see 'Memorandum on the Economic Effects of Indemnity', undated, Eggleston Papers, MS 423/6/342–360. Latham, on the other hand, argued against the defiance of the Lansing Note; see 'Preliminary Notes on the Fourteen Points', Nov. 1918, Australian Archives, A 981/6.

[102] Latham to Kerr, 9 Nov. 1918, Latham Papers, MS 1009/19/23.

[103] Garran Diary, 21 Nov. 1918, Garran Papers, Series 5, Box 3, Diary 1918.

[104] Coupland to Latham, 11 Nov. 1918; Latham to Coupland, 13 Nov. 1918; Coupland to Latham, 14 Nov. 1918; and 'Moot Agenda: the Agreement on Terms of Peace Without Consultation with the Dominion Governments', 21 Nov. 1918, Latham Papers, MS 1009/19/24–27; and Latham, 'The Agreement on Terms of Peace without consulting the Dominions. Notes for statement to London Round Table Group, 21 Nov. 1918', in Latham Papers, MS 1009/19/43. See Kerr's late response to the original protest, Kerr to Latham, 13 Dec. 1918, Latham Papers, MS 1009/19/47. See also Eggleston, 'The Peace Conference at Paris', Eggleston Papers, MS 423/6/14.

[105] Latham Diary, 21 Nov. 1918, Latham Papers, MS 1009/ 20/909A.

Wilsonianism. Long advised the Australian Governor-General that Hughes had no need to worry about aspects of the coming peace as they affected Australian interests, especially the issue of the former German colonies. Long asserted that his own recent statements, and those of Balfour, promising that the German colonies would never be returned, were statements made with the support of the whole War Cabinet. The policies dear to Hughes—and dear to Long—would be upheld, it was implied, whatever forms of words Lloyd George may have signed at Versailles.[106]

From this point onward Lloyd George had every political incentive to deny that he had ever caved in to the Wilsonian programme in his discussions with Colonel House. Political safety lay in denying the plain meaning of the Lansing Note. The solemn undertaking to make peace on the basis of the American President's pledges of 1918, the basis of the agreement to a conditional armistice as reported to the Germans in the Lansing Note of 5 November, had been exposed by Hughes and his allies in the press for what it was: a binding agreement—and a political incubus. The agreement had been made by a Prime Minister genuinely eager to have an armistice and still believing it would be achieved only by hard bargaining with an enemy still deploying considerable military power. It was an agreement made by a Prime Minister who believed he needed a quick armistice, and for whom there were still doubts over the rapidity with which victory could be obtained by military strength alone. Only days later, Germany was debilitated by revolution and her military forces in chaos. The temptation for Lloyd George and the government as a whole to wheedle free of the politically dangerous Wilsonian commitments was overpowering. The eruption of revolution in Germany was to provide the opportunity.

Revolution and the opportunities of armistice: Britain and the armistice negotiations in the Forest of Compiègne

Meanwhile, the events leading to the making of an actual armistice had begun. The members of the commission had been appointed in haste by Prince Max. The party comprised Matthias Erzberger, the well-known Catholic Centre Party deputy, Count Alfred von Oberndorff, a diplomat, and Major-General von Winterfeldt and Captain Vanselow, two military advisers. At 7 a.m. on Friday, 8 November, the train bearing the German negotiators arrived at a small siding originally built for heavy artillery near the station of Rethondes in the Forest of Compiègne. About one hundred and fifty yards away on a parallel track lay the special train of Marshal Foch. Here was the isolated site chosen by Foch, secure from all press photographers and reporters. In marked contrast to Wilson's correspondence with the Germans during October, which had been carried out in the full glare of the world's press, the final fixing of the armistice conditions was to be achieved here in the utmost secrecy. The Wilsonian example was shunned.

---

[106] Long to Munro-Ferguson, 15 Nov. 1918 (cable), Novar Papers, MS 696/5131.

The chief British representatives were Admiral Roslyn Wemyss, the First Sea Lord, and his deputy Admiral George Hope, plus their two naval assistants, Captain Bagot and Captain Marriott. In his diary, Wemyss reflected upon the 'curious' scene chosen for the talks: 'in the middle of the Forest, raining and leaves falling, and yet there is nothing sad—at any rate for us.'[107] The British party was accommodated in its own wagon-lit with telephone connections to Paris and London, an important point as the talks unfolded.[108] Wemyss's personal situation at this point is worth recalling. As has been seen, he was still embroiled in a quarrel with David Beatty who accused Wemyss of weakness over the armistice provisions. This undoubtedly placed Wemyss under considerable pressure to achieve a triumph at Compiègne during the final bargaining with the Germans.

The story of the four days of tense discussions in the Forest of Compiègne leading to the signing of the armistice has been told many times.[109] The politics of the British contribution, and especially the impact made by the German revolution on the negotiations, is the special interest here. Three points require emphasis. First, the British and French military leaders at Compiègne resisted any suggestion that the armistice negotiations were underpinned politically by Wilson's exchanges with the Germans, or that the changed political character of the German government was in any way relevant. Second, the news of the revolution in Berlin on 9 November was initially most unwelcome to the Entente negotiators. Thrown off guard momentarily, they believed the revolution imperilled the credentials of the German commissioners and thus the viability of the negotiations. Third, the news of the widening revolution and military disintegration encouraged the Entente negotiators to stand firm on the toughest armistice terms. The British negotiators sought to exploit the evident helplessness of the Germans and enlarged upon the naval conditions of armistice.

The gap in political expectations between the Germans and the Entente's military leaders is clear from the surviving sources. The German Armistice Commission was led by a civilian in the expectation that, as the representative of the new democratic order in Germany, he would be met by other civilian negotiators, including Americans. In fact, Erzberger was surprised to be confronted by French and British military representatives only, with no civilians present.[110] In contrast, on the Entente side, there was an eager anticipation that the humiliating armistice would be delivered to the hated 'Prussian militarists' of the

---

[107] Wemyss Diary, 8 Nov. 1918, Wemyss Papers, WMYS 5/7.

[108] Admiral George Hope, 'The Signing of the Armistice—11 November 1918', Hope Papers, and Wemyss Diary, 8 Nov. 1918, Wemyss Papers, WMYS 5/7, and Wemyss Appointments Book, 7 Nov. 1918, Wemyss Papers, WMYS 12/5.

[109] The classic account is Harry Rudin, *Armistice 1918* (New Haven, 1944). The most detailed first-hand account is in Ferdinand Foch, *Memoirs of Marshal Foch* (London, 1931). More recent accounts include Gordon Brook-Shepherd, *November 1918: The Last Act of the Great War* (London, 1981), and Stanley Weintraub, *A Stillness Heard Round the World: The End of the Great War: November 1918* (London, 1986). The intensively researched novel by Thomas Keneally, *Gossip From the Forest* (London, 1975), also deserves mention.

[110] Weintraub, *Stillness Heard Round the World*, 52.

German Supreme Command. Thus, there was resentment directed at the civilian leadership of the German delegation. 'The Boches [*sic*] evidently wish to make it principally a civilian affair and the French and we are very angry with them for only sending military and naval officers of a rather subordinate rank', wrote Hope.[111] The British representatives' reactions to the German delegates themselves were remarkably hostile. Marriott reported that the German delegates were 'a real blackguard typical Hun type of the worst sort, mostly crawling'.[112] Wemyss found them 'horrid to look at'.[113] Erzberger was correctly described by Admiral Hope as 'the Catholic Liberal Deputy'.[114] Erzberger's politics, however, were evidently not widely understood among the British military leadership in France; Haig, for example, scribbled in his diary that the German delegation at Compiègne was being led by Erzberger 'the socialist'.[115]

Foch received the German delegates in his train at 9 a.m. Wemyss attended the first encounter. His task was to examine the Germans' credentials. He noted that they were signed by Prince Max, and, to Wemyss's disappointment, that the Chancellor reserved the right to signal his approval before the plenipotentiaries made any final commitment to armistice.[116] Next a telling, if rather theatrical, exchange took place. The Germans were asked their mission and announced they had come to hear Foch's 'proposals' for armistice. In a carefully rehearsed gesture, Foch refused to divulge any such 'proposals'. Oberndorff began to read from President Wilson's last note, the Lansing Note, but was cut off, Foch announcing that he did not wish to hear the note. The Germans were asked to restate their purpose, that is, to ask directly for an armistice, whereupon the 'terms' would be read to them—the point being, of course, that 'terms' were non-negotiable.[117] At the very outset, the clash of interpretations was evident: the Germans insisted upon brandishing the Lansing Note, viewing this document as the essential exchange underpinning the entire peace process, while the Entente military leaders had only disdain for Wilson's interventions. For their part, the British negotiators were evidently most appreciative of Foch's gesture, for they proudly told the story again and again over the days that followed.[118]

The main business of the conference began. The long list of armistice conditions, as hammered out at Versailles over the previous week, was read to the German party and then orally translated. Both Foch and Marriott later alleged

[111] Hope, 'Signing of the Armistice', Hope Papers.
[112] Godfrey-Fausset Diary, 14 Nov. 1918, Godfrey-Fausset Papers, 1/70.
[113] Wemyss to Lady Wemyss, 'Saturday Morning', Wemyss Papers, WMYS 7/11/4.
[114] Hope, 'Signing of the Armistice', Hope Papers.
[115] Haig Diary, 8 Nov. 1918, Haig Papers, 152.
[116] Wemyss Diary, 8 Nov. 1918, Wemyss Papers, WMYS 5/7.
[117] These details based on extracts from the memoirs of Captain Marriott, broadcast as 'Armistice 1918', BBC Radio, 1985, Hope, 'Signing of the Armistice', Hope Papers, Esme Howard Dairy, 12 Nov. 1918, Howard Papers, DHW 1/4, and Sassoon to Esher, 18 Nov. 1918, Esher Papers, ESHR 4/10.
[118] e.g. it was the first story Wemyss told to Esme Howard on his return to Paris; see Esme Howard Dairy, 12 Nov. 1918, Howard Papers, DHW 1/4.

that tears rolled down German cheeks as the terms were read.[119] The Germans were told that they had seventy-two hours, that is until 11 a.m. on Monday morning, to agree to the terms. No paper copy of the terms in German translation had been prepared for them. A request for more time to consider the terms was refused. Then Winterfeldt suggested an immediate interim cease-fire 'in order to save life', but this also was turned aside. Finally, Foch insisted on the armistice terms being relayed to the German government in code. However, as the Germans had brought no ciphers, it was agreed that a German courier should be returned through the German lines to Spa with a copy of the terms.[120] At noon Captain Marriott saw the courier leave, 'terribly cut up about the terms, with a bottle of beer in each pocket, crying his eyes out'.[121] Thus began the 'new diplomacy'.

The British representatives soon realized that the German negotiators facing them had little bargaining strength. The Germans appeared not to resist the drastic naval and military terms. These, as Wemyss noted, 'did not seem to affect them so much as the civil and financial [terms]'.[122] In the discussions, the fact that German military power was almost spent was openly admitted. In arguing for more time to be allowed for German withdrawal, the Germans openly attested to the confusion in the German army, and to the exhaustion of reserves. From the very first interview the Germans focused their efforts upon mitigating those elements of the armistice terms which they pleaded could only worsen the food crisis and increase the threat of 'Bolshevism' in Germany. Such measures as the continuation of the economic blockade and the surrender of large numbers of railway wagons and trucks absorbed their attention. When Hope and Marriott interviewed Vanselow in the afternoon of the first day to review the naval terms, he dwelt at length on the risk of starvation in Germany. Hope recorded that 'he positively cringed to us and was like a whipped dog'.[123] This stress on the food crisis was matched by anecdotal evidence. For instance, the French staff serving in the German coaches reported the Germans' open expressions of amazement at the butter served with their meals.[124] Wemyss's and Hope's own observations confirmed the sagging spirit of the Germans. Wemyss noted that all the German delegates looked 'very much distressed'.[125] 'It is remarkable', wrote Hope, 'that

[119] As related in Clemenceau to Lloyd George, 9 Nov. 1918, reproduced in David Lloyd George, *War Memoirs* (London, 1938), ii. 1983, and Marriott's descriptions given to Godfrey-Fausset, in Godfrey-Fausset Dairy,14 Nov. 1918, Godfrey-Fausset Papers, 1/70.

[120] Wemyss Diary, 8 Nov. 1918, Wemyss Papers, WMYS 5/7.

[121] Marriott, 'Armistice 1918', BBC Radio, 1985.

[122] Wemyss Diary, 8 Nov. 1918, Wemyss Papers, WMYS 5/7. Foch also noted that the Germans made 'no protest . . . concerning the surrender of arms'; see Ferdinand Foch, *Memoirs of Marshal Foch* (London, 1931), 554.

[123] Hope, 'Signing of the Armistice', Hope Papers.

[124] The story was repeated in British circles within hours; see e.g. Margaret Lloyd George's relating the story to Frank Balfour, Frank Balfour to Betty Balfour, 9 Nov. 1918, Whittingehame Papers, GD 433/2/362, and General Godley to Lady Godley, 9 Nov. 1918, Godley Papers, 6/2.

[125] Wemyss Diary, 8 Nov. 1918, Wemyss Papers, WMYS 5/7.

there is not a sign of the usual German arrogance and insolence from any party.'[126] In the light of all this surprising information, the depth of the internal crisis in Germany began to dawn on Wemyss and his companions. Later in the day, the arrival of the daily newspapers provided more details of the German predicament, Wemyss noting that 'the whole story of the naval mutiny is out'.[127] The great difficulties experienced by the first German courier in crossing back through the German lines appeared to confirm the delegates' reports of great confusion in the German army.[128] The British and French officers were now fully alive to the fact that the unravelling of German military discipline was working in the Entente's favour. Hope noted that the Germans must have been prepared for the tough terms they were now studying 'as they must know the present military position and the state of mutiny in their fleet'.[129] In a long private interview with Foch that evening, Wemyss learned from the latest military intelligence of the spontaneous surrenders by large numbers of German soldiers during the day. Even if Erzberger refused to sign, Foch enthused, he would be able to destroy the German army in three weeks.[130] Wemyss summarized his impressions of the first day's discussions in a letter to Lady Wemyss on the morning of Saturday, 9 November: 'I fancy—indeed I am now sure that matters are much worse, and have been for some time, in Germany than we ever suspected. I think they must have peace, and will surely sign the armistice.'[131]

But the idea that the nation as a whole was on the edge of revolution was still not appreciated. Wemyss took offence at Captain Vanselow's suggestion that the prolongation of the economic blockade would drive Germany to revolution: 'He is afraid of the blockade and seems actually to think that we shall keep it up for the purpose of starving their country during the Armistice. Such is their mentality, so I suppose that that is what they would have done had the cases been reversed', wrote Wemyss—with dreadful irony as events turned out.[132] Similarly, Wemyss rejected Vanselow's insistence that the German army itself had been infected with Bolshevism. Wemyss observed in his diary that 'to speak of the decline of morale as Bolshevism is ridiculous'.[133]

Naturally, there was genuine shock among the Entente officers when, on late Saturday afternoon, the news of revolution in Berlin arrived in Compiègne by wireless.[134] At first details were sketchy. Wemyss recorded the reports of the

[126] Hope, 'Signing of the Armistice', Hope Papers.
[127] Wemyss Diary, 8 Nov. 1918, Wemyss Papers, WMYS 5/7.
[128] Wemyss Diary, 10 Nov. 1918, Wemyss Papers, WMYS 5/7. A second courier was eventually dispatched to Spa via aeroplane.
[129] Hope, 'Signing of the Armistice', Hope Papers.
[130] Wemyss Appointments Book, 8 Nov. 1918, Wemyss Papers, WMYS 12/5, and Wemyss Diary, 8 Nov. 1918, Wemyss Papers, WMYS 5/7.
[131] Wemyss to Lady Wemyss, 'Saturday Morning', Wemyss Papers, WMYS 7/11/4.
[132] Wemyss Diary, 8 Nov. 1918, Wemyss Papers, WMYS 5/7.
[133] Wemyss Diary, 8 Nov. 1918, Wemyss Papers, WMYS 5/7.
[134] Marriott, 'Armistice 1918', BBC Radio, 1985, and Wemyss Diary, 10 Nov. 1918, Wemyss Papers, WMYS 5/7.

abdication of the Kaiser, the appointment of Ebert as Chancellor in place of Prince Max, the formation of a 'Socialist Democratic Government', and the proclamation of a republic in Bavaria. The mood of confidence among the Entente military leaders evaporated. The revolution had arrived, it seemed, as a thief in the night to steal victory from under the noses of the Entente negotiators. 'All seems to be confusion', Wemyss noted in his diary. 'It would appear that the plenipotentiaries have no longer any powers and one would think that Erzberger at any rate has no longer any standing.'[135] Hope was equally crestfallen. 'Now that there is a new government in power it is impossible to find out who we are really dealing with', he wrote.[136] The Germans themselves were to learn of the upheavals in Berlin and the proclamation of a republic only from the French newspapers delivered to their railway car on Sunday morning.[137]

The threat of revolution in Germany had been welcome to the Entente negotiators as a bargaining tool—revolution itself now provoked them to recoil in fear. The British were nervous that the revolution had destroyed the chances of an orderly internment of the German High Seas Fleet. Wemyss's first response was to warn the Prime Minister regarding the German internal situation. In the evening of 9 November he telegraphed to Lloyd George to tell him of the Germans' repeated insistence that the maintenance of the blockade would mean 'the starving of the country' and a fillip to Bolshevism. Wemyss proposed to tell the Germans, he explained, 'that we should consider the revictualling of the country'.[138] The German negotiators were equally amazed at the news from Berlin. They could do little but assure the Entente military leaders that any new government in Berlin would be equally eager to conclude an armistice.[139] The depth of British anxiety over the outbreak of the revolution can scarcely be doubted. As Wemyss was to explain to Esme Howard in Paris a few days later, the intervention of the revolution was 'the great difficulty' of the armistice negotiations.[140]

Meanwhile in London, 9 November was, as usual, a day of traditional celebration: the Lord Mayor's Show. An intercepted wireless report of the Kaiser's abdication and the appointment of the Social Democrat Ebert as Chancellor was received at Naval Intelligence in London at 4.15 p.m.[141] For Lloyd George the abdication of the Kaiser was the really fortuitous event. The Prime Minister was

---

[135] Wemyss Diary, 10 Nov. 1918, Wemyss Papers, WMYS 5/7.

[136] Hope, entry marked 'Sunday', in 'Signing of the Armistice', Hope Papers.

[137] Naval Intelligence, 10–12 Dec. 1918, Drax Papers, DRAX 5/4.

[138] Wemyss Diary, 10 Nov. 1918, Wemyss Papers, WMYS 5/7, and Wemyss to Lloyd George, 10 Nov. 1918, Lloyd George Papers, F/47/4/6.

[139] Naval Intelligence, 10–12 Dec. 1918, giving a detailed narrative of the armistice negotiations, Drax Papers, DRAX 5/4.

[140] Esme Howard Dairy, 12 Nov. 1918, Howard Papers, DHW 1/4.

[141] Intercepted Wireless Reports, 9 Nov. 1918, Fremantle Papers, FRE 318. This was confirmed when news of the revolution in Berlin was received at the Foreign Office in the late afternoon via Walter Townley at the Hague; see cable from W. Townley to Foreign Office, 9 Nov. 1918, marked as received 5.05 p.m., FO 371/ 3224.

scheduled to speak at the Lord Mayor's Banquet at the Guildhall in the evening. He was now presented with a matchless opportunity to announce the greatest news of the war to a glittering assembly of dignitaries in the heart of the City. At the Guildhall he was 'enthusiastically received' by the bankers, judges, ambassadors, brass-hats, politicians, and city fathers.[142] Indeed, the welcome was 'without parallel in my experience', as Randall Davidson observed. 'Well, the little beggar deserves it all', Arthur Balfour shouted into the Archbishop's ear as the applause reached its crescendo.[143]

A most remarkable speech followed. Many in the audience heard the story of William II's reported abdication for the first time from the Prime Minister's lips. Germany was described as 'headless and helpless', much to the amusement of the guests. Events, therefore, had vindicated at last the Coalition's founding faith, and the Prime Minister gave vent to his own sense of deep satisfaction. 'I was one of the believers in the knock-out blow', he proudly reminded the audience. Most significantly, Lloyd George immediately repudiated the old distinction between rulers and people in Germany, and this earned him a special roar of approval. While spurning anything 'vindictive', Lloyd George argued that 'we cannot forget the reckless wantonness with which the rulers of Germany, with the full assent of her people—(loud cheers)—committed this atrocious crime against humanity. They cheered their rulers for the deed; they'd have cheered them today had they won. We must bear that in mind when we seek security.' It is noteworthy too that, even at this moment of triumph, Lloyd George drew into his victory address a direct reference to his recent quarrel with Hughes, a sign of his deep embarrassment over the affair. The Dominions had helped formulate Britain's war aims, Lloyd George maintained, at a series of conferences during the war. The Versailles Council had not imperilled the Empire's war aims, he assured his listeners: 'And at Versailles my colleagues and I agreed to nothing which would preclude us from pressing at the Peace Conference, as we intend to, all the conditions which the Dominions, India and ourselves determined upon at those conferences.'[144] Thus, the British commitments of the Lansing Note were played down by Lloyd George on the very day of the German revolution.

It is important to note also that the German revolution itself was barely mentioned by Lloyd George or any of the speakers at the Guildhall on 9 November. The dimensions of Victory, the perdition that had overtaken the Hohenzollern autocrat, and the requirement for 'divine Justice' absorbed the Prime Minister's attention. Ebert's appointment was ignored. The fact that a new socialist government had been announced in Berlin was not mentioned. The Kiel mutiny did win some attention. In a warm-up speech before the Prime Minister's arrival, Eric Geddes had revealed details of the German Admiralty's projected last raid

---

[142] Brien Cokayne Diary, 9 Nov. 1918, Cokayne Papers, c. 1350.

[143] Randall Davidson Memorandum, 17 Nov. 1918, Davidson Papers, 13.

[144] Best accounts of the Guildhall speeches are in *Observer*, 10 Nov. 1918, and *Daily Express*, 11 Nov. 1918.

and its disablement by mutiny. But this too was interpreted as a British triumph; for it was the fear of British sea power, as Geddes explained, that had provoked the sailors of the High Seas Fleet to mutiny. No speaker welcomed the revolution itself.

It could not be ignored by the next day. Throughout Sunday, 10 November, as at Compiègne, the leading figures in London waited anxiously to determine whether the revolution had derailed the armistice negotiations. The king was informed that the German revolution had very probably invalidated the armistice talks.[145] In the evening Lloyd George revealed to the War Cabinet that two telegrams from Clemenceau had been received during the day, one casting doubt on the validity of the German plenipotentiaries' credentials, and a second telegram suggesting that the revolutionaries' control of the German High Seas Fleet might make its handing over impossible. At this point Geddes revealed that Naval Intelligence had just intercepted a radio message from Berlin reporting that the German government had resigned and that 'a new socialist government was being formed'. This was accurate enough. In Berlin, a compromise plan for a new government had been worked out between the SPD and USPD. At a large meeting of the Workers' and Soldiers' Councils of Berlin on the evening of 10 November it was confirmed that the new government was to be an all-socialist Council of People's Deputies. This body was led jointly by Ebert and Haase, and watched over by the Executive Council of the Berlin Workers' and Soldiers' Councils. The existing Reichstag was dissolved.[146] Here was confirmation that a real revolution had indeed taken place, not simply a transfer of the office of Chancellor to Ebert.

The initial response of the British War Cabinet to this news was most revealing. Socialist leadership of the enemy state was obviously a distasteful development. Lloyd George remarked sombrely that 'it would seem that events were taking a similar course in Germany to that which had taken place in Russia'. The members of the War Cabinet then agreed that Britain should press for the armistice notwithstanding the revolution. Milner remarked that the German army 'was no longer a danger to us', and thus, he argued, the armistice should still be signed as soon as possible. Henry Wilson argued that the case for going beyond the Rhine was now very questionable for it was important to avoid 'getting involved in Bolshevik outbreaks in Germany'. Churchill's hostility to the revolution was the most intemperate. He suggested that Britain must not give up her military objectives 'because we were dealing with a rabble'. With the revolution in mind, he advised, Britain must not 'attempt to destroy the only police force available for maintaining order' in Germany. Lloyd George agreed on the

---

[145] Balfour to Stamfordham, 10 Nov. 1918, FO 800/201.
[146] 'Deliberations on the Approval of the Armistice Negotiations, November 10, Noon', in Charles B. Burdick and Ralph H. Lutz (eds.), *The Political Institutions of the German Revolution, 1918–1919* (New York, 1966), 41, and for a survey of the events of 9–10 Nov. in Berlin see A. J. Ryder, *The German Revolution of 1918: A Study of German Socialism in War and Revolt* (Cambridge, 1967), 150–5.

dangers to which all were now exposed, observing that Bolshevism in Germany might soon infect British troops. Germany was now 'a cholera area' he said. 'It would be most undesirable to march British miners into Westphalia if Westphalia was controlled by a Bolshevist organisation.' At length it was decided that Lord Curzon, at that time staying with Lord Derby in Paris, should liaise with Clemenceau on the precarious situation arising from the German revolution.[147] Thus, within hours of the first news of the German revolution, the struggle against socialism had supplanted the struggle against 'Prussian militarism' in the minds of the British political élite.

The private sources too show that gloom pervaded at this time. 'We had a grave talk about the position of the armistice negotiations in view of the revolution in Germany. The prospect in that country appears very black', wrote Milner in his diary.[148] Austen Chamberlain was appalled at the revolution. 'When the German falls, he falls *flat*, so the Bosch [*sic*] is finished', wrote Chamberlain. At the same time, in Chamberlain's case, as in many others, news of the revolution filled him with a pleasurable sense of just deserts:

And the humour and poetic justice of it all. Not only by the sword shall they fall since they drew the sword, but by Bolshevism since they deliberately subsidised and propagated Bolshevism in Russia, in Switzerland and elsewhere to destroy the unity of their enemies. And now from Russia and Switzerland bolshevism flows back into Germany and German thrones rock and German society trembles while Entente Governments are still secure and the Entente peoples unaffected. We may not escape the contagion, but it is fitting that the poisoner should be the first victim of his own drugs.[149]

In the Forest of Compiègne, meanwhile, late in the evening of 10 November, an open dispatch arrived from the new socialist government in Berlin authorizing the existing delegates of the Armistice Commission to sign the armistice. Thus, the doubts surrounding Erzberger's status were at last cleared. Soon after, Supreme Command at Spa sent its reluctant agreement to the terms also. Thus, at 2 a.m. on the morning of Monday, 11 November, the top-level negotiations resumed in Foch's saloon.[150] There was little real bargaining. The terms were substantially those decided upon a week previously at Versailles: German withdrawal behind the Rhine, a surrender of great volumes of war material and transport equipment, the immediate release of prisoners of war without reciprocity, and the internment of the bulk of German naval forces. The Germans achieved some minor moderation in the volumes of military equipment, rolling stock, and trucks to be surrendered, and in the timing of the army's withdrawals from Belgium and the Rhineland. But no substantial changes in the terms were made. Most importantly, notwithstanding a whole hour of debate and passionate protests from the Germans, Foch and Wemyss insisted that the economic

[147] Minutes of the War Cabinet, 10 Nov. 1918, CAB 23/14.
[148] Milner Diary, 10 Nov. 1918, Milner Papers, 89.
[149] Austen Chamberlain to Ida, 9 Nov. 1918, Chamberlain Papers, AC 5/1/112.
[150] Naval Intelligence, 10–12 Dec. 1918, Drax Papers, DRAX 5/4.

blockade would remain in place. As Wemyss had anticipated in his telegram to Lloyd George, the only concession offered was the addition of a statement that the Entente and America would 'contemplate the provisioning of Germany during the armistice'.[151]

It was in the finalization of the naval terms that Wemyss made his main contributions for Britain. Whereas the military terms were revised in minor details downwards, the naval terms were made still tougher. Armed with the War Cabinet's permission of 6 November to vary the terms as he saw fit, Wemyss had already made the most significant alteration to Article XXIII so that the demand was now for German surface warships to be interned not simply in neutral ports but 'in neutral ports, *or failing them, in Allied ports*'. Fully alive to the powerlessness of the Germans, Wemyss saw his opportunity to inflate still further the British naval triumph. His chief concern, clearly, was that the German revolution might yet disrupt the planned internment of the German naval fleet. While the revolution was a genuine concern, it also afforded the pretext for inserting at last the contentious claim to the occupation of Heligoland. A special additional demand explained that, 'in view of fresh events', the Allies and Americans asserted the right to occupy Heligoland in order to ensure the delivery of the German ships to be interned. Wemyss sent a telegram of explanation to Lloyd George announcing that the new demand had been written in to the armistice as a precaution in case the delivery of the German fleet was hampered by 'the mutinous state of the fleet'.[152] A second alteration affected the numbers of German submarines to be surrendered in Allied ports under Article XXII. As the Germans insisted that the German navy did not possess the 160 submarines demanded in the original document, Wemyss rewrote the item as a demand for the internment of 'all' submarines. Both these changes, Wemyss acknowledged, afforded him much pleasure. They represented a symbolic victory over Lloyd George, and at the same time a chance to recover status in the eyes of Beatty. Wemyss had written to Beatty from Compiègne on the previous day explaining that whatever gaps Beatty discerned in the draft naval terms, these weaknesses were all the fault of Lloyd George. It was the Prime Minister who had led the charge to 'cut down the naval terms' during the Versailles discussions, Wemyss quite correctly insisted. The demand for internment in Allied ports, the demand for 'all' submarines, and the demand for Heligoland had been stoutly resisted by Lloyd George at Versailles.[153] Now Wemyss had achieved them all. Thus, Wemyss confided to his diary, it was both 'a pleasure and a satisfaction' to redraft these naval terms of armistice according to his original design.[154] Clearly it was

---

[151] Article XXVI of the Armistice; see Temperley, *History of the Peace Conference of Paris*, i. 459–76.

[152] Wemyss to Lloyd George, 11 Nov. 1918, Lloyd George Papers, F/47/4/7.

[153] Wemyss to Beatty, 10 Nov. 1918, Wemyss Papers, 11.

[154] Wemyss Diary, 10 Nov. 1918, Wemyss Papers, 5/7. Not surprisingly, relations between Wemyss and Lloyd George remained tense in the days that followed. On his return to London, Wemyss wrote to Beatty of his astonishment that the Prime Minister had not bothered to summon

the German naval mutiny and the revolution which provided the opportunity, and the pretext, for the enlargement of the British naval terms. The discussions in Foch's coach concluded soon after 5 a.m. The historic armistice document, disarming Germany more or less completely, maintaining her economic isolation, and granting an Allied army the right of occupation of the Rhineland, was made ready for signature. The bloodshed was to cease at 11 a.m. Under these conditions, no German resumption of the war was remotely possible. The victory was complete. To the last, the food issue was of paramount concern to the Germans. After signing, the Germans asked the British delegates to interview a German food expert and a transport officer 'to discuss the details of revictualling Germany'. When neither of the German experts had arrived by 9 a.m., Vanselow himself returned to the Marshal's train to enter a request that Germany be supplied with 30,000 tons of edible fats a month. As Naval Intelligence reported, Vanselow 'was informed that his remarks would be noted'.[155]

The atmosphere in which the talks were conducted deserves special emphasis. At the conclusion of a disastrous war, neither side expected affability from the other. Indeed, there were many indications of barely suppressed hostility all around. The French claimed to have served the Germans 1870 vintage champagne.[156] Wemyss was proud of the fact that all the officers had refused handshakes with the Germans upon the signing of the armistice.[157] Every indication of German discomfort was reported gloatingly by the Entente delegates.[158] But, what was more significant than these gestures of hostility was the German delegates' sense that their government had been misled in its expectations of the armistice as a first instalment of a Wilsonian peace. The German delegates clearly expected nothing less than the assertion of Allied military dominance so that the German army's capacity to resume aggressive war was destroyed; this had been demanded in Wilson's notes, and the German negotiators had not resisted these military provisions at Compiègne. But, making a judgement on the basis of Wilson's notes, the Germans also expected nothing *more* than measures to guarantee Allied military supremacy. Thus, the maintenance of the economic blockade, in particular, was regarded as an unnecessary and inhumane coercion of the disintegrating nation. Erzberger knew full well the burden of hunger and influenza inside Germany; he had buried his own teenage son, an officer cadet at Karlsruhe, a victim of the influenza, in mid-October.[159] Thus, his horror at the

him to hear first hand of the events at Compiègne. The Royal Navy, he complained, was being studiously 'ignored' while Foch was being 'exalted'; Wemyss to Beatty, 14 Nov. 1918, Wemyss Papers, 11.

[155] Naval Intelligence, 10–12 Dec. 1918, Drax Papers, DRAX 5/4.

[156] Grant, 'Notes on the Interview between Marshal Foch and the German delegates', Cowans Papers, 69/17/1A.

[157] Wemyss proudly reported his refusal to shake hands to Howard; see Esme Howard Dairy, 12 Nov. 1918, Howard Papers, DHW 1/4.

[158] Philip Sassoon to Esher, 18 Nov. 1918, Esher Papers, 4/10.

[159] Klaus Epstein, *Matthias Erzberger and the Dilemma of German Democracy* (New York, 1971), 269.

Entente military leaders' refusal to end the blockade, and his disappointment that Wilsonian principles were apparently ruled out of court at these negotiations, secret and thoroughly militarized as they were. Thus, on 10 November he had advised Berlin that immediate contact should be made with President Wilson himself to urge the commencement of the actual peace negotiations. 'Only by an immediate conclusion of a preliminary peace can the disastrous effect of the execution of the armistice terms be mitigated.'[160] For the Germans, the blockade overshadowed everything else. After signing the armistice document, the German delegates insisted on appending a personal statement: 'In view of the discussions which brought about the Armistice, we might have expected terms which, while assuring our adversary complete and entire military security, would have terminated the sufferings of non-combatants, of women and children.'[161] The protest underlined the great political burden which the armistice had just loaded on to the shoulders of the new regime: Germany's new government had failed to gain an end to the 'starvation blockade'.

The impact of the revolution on the course of these negotiations is worth careful analysis, as the issue raises the thorny problem of the so-called 'stab-in-the-back'. The political upheavals in Berlin did clearly weaken the Germans' capacity to bargain. The authority of the plenipotentiaries at Compiègne was under question. The hostility of the Entente to the political upheavals in Berlin on 9 November was also obvious. It is true that the Entente military leaders did not exploit the sudden vulnerability of Germany to the extent of making a radical revision of the whole armistice document. As noted above, the only significant toughening of the terms affected the naval conditions. The major military and economic terms were regarded as already quite sufficient to deliver the stunning military blow desired by Foch. As has been shown, these were terms designed originally to fend off the danger of armistice so that the military conquest of Germany might continue, Foch's obvious preference. Indeed, it was the improbability that Germany would accept these armistice conditions that had been their chief merit from Foch's viewpoint. He had admitted to Lloyd George himself on the eve of the armistice talks that in his view the terms were still so drastic they were unlikely to be accepted.[162] Foch was by no means alone in this judgement. When first unveiled to Milner, he described the proposed armistice terms in his diary as 'in my opinion absurd'.[163] The revolution in Germany, therefore, simply encouraged Foch in the belief that he need only stick to his original terms and they would be accepted. These 'absurd' terms were now, as a result of a combination of circumstances, the terms accepted by Germany.

[160] *Preliminary History of the Armistice: Official Documents Published by the German National Chancellery by Order of the Minister of State*, translated by the Carnegie Endowment for International Peace (New York, 1924), 148.
[161] Quoted in Foch, *Memoirs of Marshal Foch*, 570.
[162] Lloyd George had reported to the War Cabinet on 5 Nov. that this was Foch's verdict; War Cabinet Minutes, 497, 5 Nov. 1918, CAB 23/8.
[163] Milner Diary, 4 Nov. 1918, Milner Papers, 89.

Clearly, the German revolution had not defeated Germany—that notorious 'stab-in-the-back' claim was always politically motivated nonsense. It is not possible here to go into the huge debate on the reasons for the German collapse nor the disputes over the relative weight that ought to be given to military and domestic factors.[164] Nevertheless, in the light of the analysis given above, it would certainly be a mistake to minimize the significance of German inner politics or the revolution itself on the final outcome. Germany's powers of resistance and her power to bargain had collapsed, quite suddenly and unexpectedly, in the immediate aftermath of the Kiel mutiny. Many well-informed British observers were impressed at the time over the suddenness of the collapse of the German military effort, more sudden, they insisted, than could possibly be accounted for by the pressure of the Allied military effort alone. Lloyd George himself told a meeting of trade unionists on 13 November: 'Of victory I never had any doubt, but frankly I never expected it so soon; the collapse came more quickly than I had anticipated, and I think that is really true of a good many men who knew more about it than I did.'[165] Some military figures simply stressed the speed of the German disintegration. 'One is quite bewildered by the suddenness of it all', General Godley explained to his wife on armistice day.[166] Similarly, General Rawlinson confessed his amazement at the rapidity of the German dissolution, noting in his diary entry for armistice day that he never expected such a complete victory within just three months of the first great British successes of 8 August.[167] Other political figures went further to reflect on the contrast between the rapidity of the collapse and British military estimates of German military resilience given only days before. Chamberlain expressed his amazement on 9 November that scarcely a week had passed since the British military leadership had assured the politicians that no German capitulation could be expected from 'the purely military situation'.[168] Similarly, as Randall Davidson dictated for his diary on 17 November, only a fortnight previously 'almost everybody believed that we should be vehemently at war for at least six months or more to come'.[169] Of course, not all drew the distasteful conclusion that Germany's socialists and liberals must have contributed something to the disarming of the militarist élite through their campaign for democratization and peace. Simple demoralization was a more palatable explanation. For example, Bonar Law observed in the

---

[164] The essential documents may be found in R. H. Lutz, *The Causes of the German Collapse in 1918* (Stanford, Calif., 1934), and the latest discussion on this vast subject is Wilhelm Ribhegge, *Frieden für Europa. Die Politik der Deutschen Reichstagsmehrheit 1917–1918* (Essen, 1988), Avner Offer, *The First World War: An Agrarian Interpretation* (Oxford, 1989), and Anne Roerkohl, *Hungerblockade und Heimatfront. Die kommunale Lebensmittelversorgung in Westfalen während des Ersten Weltkrieges* (Stuttgart, 1991).

[165] Lloyd George quoted in *Daily Express*, 15 Nov. 1918.

[166] General Godley to Lady Godley, 14 Nov. 1918, Godley Papers, 6/2.

[167] General Rawlinson Diary, 11 Nov. 1918, Rawlinson Papers, 1/11, and Rawlinson to Henry Wilson, 11 Nov. 1918, Henry Wilson Papers, HHW 13.

[168] Austen Chamberlain to Ida, 9 Nov. 1918, Chamberlain Papers, AC 5/1/112.

[169] Randall Davidson Diary, 17 Nov. 1918, Davidson Papers, 13.

House of Commons on 12 November that the outcome of events probably indicated that the collapse of Germany 'was not caused entirely—I doubt if it was caused mainly—by the military position. It was caused by the result of the block-ade, which has sapped the whole foundations of Germany, both military and civil alike.'[170] Even Horace Rumbold, who had always belittled the importance of German inner politics and denied German privation, made frank admissions of his misjudgements in private letters. On armistice day he wrote two letters, to his friends Eric Drummond and Lord Newton, confessing to both that the only viable explanation for the events in Germany was that observers such as himself had underestimated how bleak were conditions in Germany. 'We mistrusted every report which came from Germany', explained Rumbold. 'It was a case of crying wolf and at last the wolf has come'. He admitted too that the débâcle in Germany had gone 'faster than anybody could have imagined'. Perhaps in defence of his judgements, he protested that 'Nobody could have expected the revolution to start in Bavaria'.[171] To his mother Rumbold declared flatly that 'events in Germany are perfectly extraordinary'.[172]

For those who had long ago written off German socialism and liberalism as forces for change, a characteristic attitude within the 'knock-out blow' school of thought, the turn of events inside Germany did indeed defy explanation. The truth, however, was that German political forces had been deeply divided since at least the passage of the Peace Resolution. The power of the German author-itarian Right had been seriously undermined by the growth of liberal and social-ist opinion which was increasingly inclined to trust the democratic promises emanating from the West, especially from Wilson. Some British observers did come to acknowledge privately the inner contribution to the demise of German militarism in the months that followed. For example, J. A. Salter, the Secretary to the Allied Maritime Transport Council, explained this to J. M. Keynes in late 1919: 'By the way', he wrote, 'I'm not convinced that we had really beaten the Germans to an "unconditional surrender" position in Oct. Nov. 1918. There is, and was at the time, substantial military opinion to the effect that we couldn't have done it [un]til 1919 without the political effects of the 14 points notes then passing.'[173]

The most savage irony was obvious: the German revolution, intended by its proponents to hurry forward political change and sweep away the last obstacles to a peace of reconciliation, as promised by Wilson, had made the opposite, a peace of violence, all the more likely. For, after the revolution was unleashed, Germany's only protection was the good faith of the victors. This was a slender thread. The opportunity to exploit Germany's helplessness was too great. In the wake of the revolution, with Germany disarmed and hopelessly vulnerable, the

---

[170] Parl. Debs., 5th ser., vol. 110, 2578 (12 Nov. 1918).
[171] Rumbold to Drummond and Rumbold to Lord Newton, 11 Nov. 1918, Rumbold Papers, 25.
[172] Rumbold to his mother, 13 Nov. 1918, Rumbold Papers, 25.
[173] J. A. Salter to J. M. Keynes, 16 Dec. 1919, Keynes Papers, EC/2/1/39.

temptation to rewrite recent history was very great: thus, the conditional armistice was to be quickly transformed into an abject 'surrender'. Some perceptive observers recognized this immediately. For example, Christopher Thomson, an officer at the Supreme War Council at Versailles in late 1918, noted that as soon as news of the revolution reached Versailles the words 'armistice' and 'surrender' were already being 'misused'. The politicians, wrote Thomson, were manufacturing an unconditional surrender 'if for no other reason than that they can dictate any terms they choose and Germany will have to accept them. After the revolution in Berlin the German High Command is, for a time at least, utterly helpless.'[174]

Thomson's prophecies were fulfilled within days. What had begun life as a conditional cease-fire engineered at the Versailles Council on 4 November by Colonel House, and predicated on pledges all round to proceed to a Wilsonian peace, was now presented by Coalition politicians and the right-wing press as an unconditional capitulation by Germany to military might. The 'internment' of the German Fleet was transformed into 'surrender'; German acceptance of 'reparation' for 'damage done to the civilian population' was transformed into an acceptance of an unlimited 'indemnity'; and the Entente's commitments to the Wilsonian programme in the 'pre-armistice agreement' were to be deliberately ignored. As F. S. Oliver explained privately to his brother on 14 November, 'the Armistice is not an armistice at all, but a surrender, so that your objections, which were also mine when the first news came of the proposal, fall to the ground'.[175]

Recoiling from revolution: the British response to the first wave of the German revolution, November 1918

On the morning of the first Armistice Day in London, the War Cabinet again considered the latest news on the revolution and the condition of Germany. Wemyss had reported in a telegram that 'there is no doubt that conditions in Germany are far worse than were thought'. Lloyd George seemed genuinely shaken by the reports on the food crisis inside Germany. He asked that Cecil, Sir Joseph Maclay, the shipping expert, and Sir John Beale, the food expert, consult together and report to the War Cabinet on the measures required to relieve the hunger in the enemy states as soon as possible. Sir Eric Geddes suggested that, in this situation, perhaps the blockade itself might be reduced or even removed. Lloyd George evidently recovered his composure when faced with this. He responded with the curious observation that 'the blockade was really

---

[174] Christopher Thomson Diary, 9 Nov. 1918, Thomson of Cardington Papers, 74/39/1. Christopher Thomson, later Lord Thomson of Cardington, long-serving military officer in Bucharest and Palestine during the war, resigned from the army and joined the Labour Party in 1919 and became Air Minister in the first Labour government in 1924.

[175] F. S. Oliver to W. E. Oliver, 14 Nov. 1918, Oliver Papers, 65.

"rationing" and must be kept up'. It was agreed not to release the blockade.[176] Thus, the most contentious armistice item was locked in place.

Following this rather grim Cabinet meeting the leading politicians confronted spontaneous demonstrations of relief and gratitude among the people of London. Around 11.30 a.m. a large crowd gathered in Downing Street. Responding to 'frantic cheering' and chants of 'Speech! Speech!', Lloyd George appeared at a first-floor window of Number 10, 'his face wreathed in smiles'. 'You are well entitled to rejoice', he told the sea of 'singing crowds, flags, handkerchiefs and hats'.[177] He spoke, as MacCallum Scott noted, with 'the art of a man who knows how to play with crowds and touch the emotions of men like the strings of a harp'.[178] The nagging fear that with peace would come a flood of domestic troubles did not seem to bother the victors. Lloyd George himself still professed confidence about the domestic mood. He told Riddell: 'Old Clemenceau said a great thing to me about social upheavals. "Victory" said he "is a great safeguard. Defeat stirs up internal strife".'[179] The king too was delighted by this thought. Discussing the possibility of revolution with a grave Lord Crawford on 8 November, George V had declared 'Why should our people have a revolution— we are the victors, we are the Top Dog'.[180]

At first there was little in the reaction of the crowds to concern the leading politicians. The national anthem was sung at the Bank of England at 11 a.m. and at the Stock Exchange at noon.[181] But, by midday, vast crowds singing and surging in front of Buckingham Palace began to chant for King George and to create scenes that 'beggar description', as Godfrey-Fausset, the king's equerry, noted in his diary: 'The streets were full of mad people.' A great outpouring of relief engulfed the population of London. The king, the queen, and Princess Mary entered a coach to be paraded through the rain-drenched streets and were thrilled by their reception. The king reported with pride that 'in Trafalgar Square the crowd actually lifted the carriage off the ground'.[182]

With better weather, the celebrations picked up in tempo during the next two days. 'The streets surged with processions, whirling rings, groups and clusters of dancers, single dancers, bunches of dancers, cavalcades of dancers.'[183] By the evening of 12 November the mood of boisterous revelry began to concern the authorities and rioting was feared. Mingling with the crowds, Godfrey-Fausset

---

[176] Minutes of the War Cabinet, 11 Nov. 1918, CAB 23/14, and Milner Diary, 11 Nov. 1918, Milner Papers, 89.

[177] *Evening News*, 11 Nov. 1918; *The Times*, 12 Nov. 1918.

[178] Alexander MacCallum Scott Diary, 11 Nov. 1918, Alexander MacCallum Scott Papers, MS Gen. 1465.

[179] Lord Riddell, *War Diary, 1914–1918* (London, 1933), 10 Nov. 1918, 380.

[180] Lord Crawford Diary, 8 Nov. 1918, vol. xxxiii, Crawford Papers.

[181] Sir Bryan Cokayne Diary, 11 Nov. 1918, Cokayne Papers, C. 1350.

[182] Godfrey-Fausset Dairy, 11 and 13 Nov. 1918, Godfrey-Fausset Papers, 1/70, and *Evening News*, 11 Nov. 1918.

[183] Alexander MacCallum Scott Diary, 12 Nov. 1918, Alexander MacCallum Scott Papers, MS Gen. 1465.

and MacCallum Scott watched Australian soldiers lead a group who dragged some captured German field-guns on display in the Mall to Regent Street and Trafalgar Square, there to start bonfires around the wooden wheels. A huge bonfire on the lower plinth of Nelson's column was soon stoked with anything obtainable, the wooden hoardings bearing advertisements for the war loan, a watchman's box, wheelbarrows, and even signboards from passing buses. The heat from the fire cracked off large pieces of granite from the monument—'quite unforgivable' as Godfrey-Fausset observed.[184] For the next two days and nights the revelries continued. By 14 November, Lord Crawford noted that 'the rowdies are beginning to get the upper hand'.[185] The press urged the authorities to prepare orderly celebrations, and denounced lawlessness and rioting.[186]

Such scenes of merry-making verging on rebelliousness were observed in a great many locations in Britain so that the indiscipline of the post-armistice days became legendary. That such excesses caused a degree of panic in high places is clear. In a response typical of the Tory leaders, Curzon confessed later to Herbert Fisher that he was 'very much depressed about the relaxation of moral standard in the country since the armistice'.[187] Other prominent political figures were similarly fearful of the revolutionary turn of events in the days immediately following the armistice. General Smuts wrote to Gilbert Murray on 12 November that 'the immediate future is very fateful'.[188] Milner wrote to Lloyd George on 13 November beseeching just half an hour of his time to discuss the future of the army and especially the need to prevent too rapid a demobilization. 'With the disturbed state of Europe', wrote Milner, 'and the revolutionary tendency, greater or less, in all countries, it is as dangerous to have no army as to have too big a one.'[189]

Some insight into the Prime Minister's own initial reaction to the revolution in Germany can be gained from his address to a meeting of 'patriotic' trade unionists and employers at the Caxton Hall in London on 13 November. For Lloyd George, the chief danger in Germany appeared to be incipient Bolshevism. A resumption of the war was virtually impossible, he told his audience, but it would be folly to discount the idea altogether. Amidst the 'great confusion' in Germany, anything might happen. However, he observed, he did not think personally that Germany would go Bolshevik, for 'Germany is not Russia, but has a more disciplined and better educated population'. Still, Lloyd George conceded, there was some risk that Britain might be confronted in Germany with chaos. The Foreign Secretary, he explained, took the view that there was indeed some risk of this development. In Germany, as Lloyd George summed up the

[184] Godfrey-Fausset Dairy, 13 Nov. 1918, Godfrey-Fausset Papers 1/70.
[185] Lord Crawford Diary, 14 Nov. 1918, vol. xxxiii, Crawford Papers.
[186] e.g. *Daily Express*, editorial, 'Steady On!', 14 Nov. 1918.
[187] Curzon to Fisher, no date, but probably Dec. 1918, Fisher Papers, 205.
[188] Smuts to Gilbert Murray, 12 Nov. 1918, Murray Papers, 38.
[189] Milner to Lloyd George, 13 Nov. 1918, Milner Additional Papers, MS Eng. Hist. c. 696/2.

situation, 'nothing has been quite settled there, and they are proceeding on the same lines as in Russia'.[190]

In the same way, the private sources of the naval and military élite were strewn with expressions of hostility to the German revolution and fear that the British people were in a similarly restless state. In the case of the navy, the conclusion of the armistice certainly did not prompt any festivities among the top officers. Commiserations were exchanged over the lost opportunity for a great sea battle.[191] In addition, the revolution was seen as a danger even to the internment of the German fleet. Notwithstanding the signatures obtained by Wemyss at Compiègne, the admirals were still haunted by the fear that neither the revolutionary government in Berlin nor the revolutionary sailors of the German High Seas Fleet could be relied upon to deliver the promised ships.[192] In France, fear that the mutinous revolution might spill over into the British army's lines was an immediate concern. Thus, the official orders transmitting news of the armistice to the British troops specified that, when hostilities ceased, 'All military precautions will be preserved and no communication with the enemy permitted'.[193] General Rawlinson, in common with many brass-hats, dreaded future instability in Germany. He noted with relief in his diary the day after armistice that the German revolution was 'bloodless', so far, and expressed the hope that the politicians in Berlin might establish a stable government in spite of the 'unfavourable conditions in the shape of the penalties inflicted by the armistice'.[194] General Godley wrote to his wife on 14 November that 'I can't help thinking that we may be fighting Bolshevists in Germany before we are finished'.[195] The same sense of disappointment was felt at Haig's Headquarters in France. In a letter to Lord Esher, Sir Philip Sassoon, the Conservative M.P. who was Haig's Private Secretary, captured perfectly the mixture of pride and political anxiety, if not dejection, among the brass-hats just a week after the revolutionary end to the war:

How does this Götterdämerung of the Central Powers appeal to you [?]. In the midst of one's rejoicing one has a few nervous twinges and even the bonfires in Trafalgar Square have a note of Bolshevism when one ponders over the speeches and decisions of the Labour Conference. The people are singing God Save the King in front of Buckingham Palace—but when the peace fires have subsided they may be piping a different tune. Don't think me a croaker when the sky seems all gold—but I know you share my apprehensions

---

[190] *The Times*, 15 Nov. 1918.

[191] Jellicoe to Beatty, 11 Nov. 1918, Jellicoe Papers, 49008. This was a widespread feeling. For example, see the views of Captain Geoffrey Harper, that the navy had 'nothing to show for our four and a quarter years of waiting'; Harper Diaries, 9 Nov. 1918, Harper Papers, HRPR 1/11.

[192] On the armistice Admiral Madden noted in his diary that the armistice had been signed, but added that 'it is doubtful whether there is sufficient authority in Germany to enforce it' (Admiral Madden Diary, 11 Nov. 1918, Madden Papers, MAD 16).

[193] Lt.-Colonel R. Ledingham, 'Scottish Soldier: English Politician', typescript memoir, Imperial War Museum.

[194] Rawlinson Diary, 12 Nov. 1918, Rawlinson Papers, 1/11.

[195] Godley to Lady Godley, 14 Nov. 1918, Godley Papers, 6/2.

. . . D[ouglas] H[aig] is happy—& well he may be. I am submerged with telegrams. We have had 200 in 2 days & my brain is empty and used up. I feel none of the exhilaration I *should* feel—why is that? I want a good long talk with you. I think I shall lose my seat to a Labour Candidate who has been working like a beaver & promising them everything. Well, *tant pis* [so much the worse].[196]

The British press and the legend of the 'counterfeit revolution'

In the pages of the 'patriotic' press, hostility to the German revolution was immediate and emphatic. From the outset, two interpretations of the revolution were offered to the British public. First, the German revolution was interpreted as a dangerous red revolution with many parallels to the Russian experience, a revolution that rendered Germany an untrustworthy state riddled with incipient Bolshevism. Second, and in stark contrast, the revolution was interpreted as a contemptible sham intended to mask the persistence of Prussian militarism and deceive the victors. Obviously these interpretations of the revolution as Bolshevist terror or unconvincing fraud were logically contradictory, but readers were invited to draw the same conclusion from both models: if the revolution was genuine, then the revolutionary government was not to be trusted on account of its dangerous socialist ideology; if the revolution was counterfeit, then the bogus government was not to be trusted because it was secretly controlled by Prussian militarism.

The more serious Conservative papers initially preferred the interpretation apparently adopted by the Prime Minister, namely that Germany was in a state of incipient Bolshevism. At first *The Times* reacted cautiously to the revolution, expressing the hope that a 'firm and free government' would soon be established, but warning too that this was no time to forgo the 'precautions and guarantees' which the Allies must exact. 'We remember that all Germany gave her full assent to the war', maintained *The Times*, 'and it is failure alone which now leads her to abjure it'. Justice demanded 'a stern reckoning for guilt so deliberate, so obdurate and so great'.[197] On 12 November *The Times* noted that the socialist moderates were having a difficult time persuading the Minority of the 'impossibility or unwisdom of a purely socialist *régime*'.[198] The next day the news from Germany was 'far from reassuring'. *The Times* expressed grave disquiet that the revolution had set up an all-socialist government 'from whose ranks all the *bourgeois* are shut out', and that the Workers' and Soldiers' Councils were claiming political authority over the government. *The Times* feared for the German establishment, even coming to the defence of German officials of the old order. For example, the fact that former ministers such as Dr Solf, the Foreign Minister, had been reduced to the status of mere clerks 'under the surveillance of Social

---

[196] Philip Sassoon to Lord Esher, 18 Nov. 1918, Esher Papers, 4/10.
[197] *The Times*, editorial, 'The Downfall', 11 Nov. 1918.
[198] *The Times*, editorial, 'Germany in Defeat', 12 Nov. 1918.

Democrats' was a cause for grave concern. *The Times* noted that 'this adoption of Russian precedents is ominous', and urged the German Majority Socialists to contain looming chaos.[199] A week after the revolution *The Times* endorsed the Prime Minister's position that things in Germany were much too unsettled for any optimism; the socialist government in Berlin was in essence an unreliable revolutionary force without legitimacy:

All we know for them at present is a Berlin Socialist Committee . . . Before the Allies can prudently deal with such a body it must produce convincing evidence that its claim to speak for the German people is well founded. At present all we know is that they appear to have substituted themselves for the Emperor-King of their own mere motion and without any mandate, save what they may have obtained from the street. It would be against all common sense and against all traditions of sound democracy to accept a position seized in this fashion as a clear and legitimate commission to speak and act in the name of the entire German people.[200]

The more popular Northcliffe papers and Coalition dailies were still more damning, preferring the interpretation of the revolution as counterfeit. Of course, having predicted that no revolution was possible from such an utterly docile people as the German, the theory of a sham revolution was a way out of embarrassment. The newspapers had not got it wrong, so they argued—in fact, there was no German revolution, just the same elaborate camouflage as in the case of Prince Max. In pursuit of this theme, 'patriotic' editors and foreign correspondents peddled a series of highly improbable interpretations: the revolution was largely bloodless and unresisted because it was a huge ruse organized by the Prussian militarists; the reported hunger in Germany was all a myth, a gigantic propaganda trick intended to soften the hearts of the victorious Allies and so lessen the penalties so richly deserved by the German people as a whole; the risk of real Bolshevism in Germany was non-existent, for Bolshevism also was stage-managed by the old élites; and finally, the German people and government were utterly unrepentant and there was no 'change of heart'. The intention behind all this, of course, was very plain: to deflect the notion that the German revolution should make any difference in the peace negotiations.

The Northcliffe press promoted its major theme of the sham German revolution from the first hours of the new regime, in fact even before any but the most elementary facts were available. The *Evening News*, for example, explained on 9 November itself that there were 'three Germanys' contesting for power, the Germany of the Kaiser, the Germany of Prince Max, and the Germany of Liebknecht. But, argued the leader, even the victory of Liebknecht's Germany would not redeem the nation. A revolution was 'a mere change of clothes at the last moment'. The *Evening News* fumed at the very idea that the German revolu-

---

[199] *The Times*, editorial, 'Ordered Liberty', 13 Nov. 1918.
[200] *The Times*, editorial, 'What is the German Government?', 15 Nov. 1918.

tion changed anything. 'That will not do. *Germany is responsible and Germany has got to make good the damage.*'[201]

Other papers, similarly, rushed to shore up faith in the guilt of the new as much as the old Germany. Concern for the indemnity, based on the guilt of the whole people, it should be noted, was never far away in this interpretation. The *Daily Mail* was at pains to demolish the standing of the new government in Germany and ridiculed the so-called German revolution from the outset, declaring it to be 'a change of administration [which] does not remove the necessity for reparation and restitution, as some members of the German Socialist Party seem to assume'.[202] The *Mail*'s two experts on Germany, Charles Tower and Frederick Wile, presented readers with gross caricatures of the new socialist rulers in Berlin. Ebert and Scheidemann, were described as having supported the war 'through thick and thin'. While atrocities multiplied, these socialist moderates 'lifted no finger to stop it'. They served 'as decoy ducks to deceive simple people like Mr Arthur Henderson who believed in German social democracy'. [203] Wile, the former Berlin correspondent, introduced Ebert as 'GERMANY'S NEW DICTATOR'. He had supported the war 'unreservedly', cheering himself hoarse 'in my own hearing' on 4 August 1914, recalled Wile. 'Fritz Ebert incarnates the spirit in which the German people accepted the war', he concluded. Tower warned at the outset that the socialist conversion of Germany could be a 'huge bluff'.[204]

These same themes were promoted in the pages of all the major Conservative 'patriotic' papers during the week following the armistice. To begin with the voice of the ultra-patriotic Right, the *Globe* naturally treated the revolution as a matter of indifference. Docker and Maxse held firm to their familiar line that the socialists and the German people had 'displayed precisely the same lust of blood as the Junkers themselves', and hence the revolution did not lessen the guilt of the nation. 'Let them Bolsh if they will; but whether they do or not, they must and can be made to pay', asserted the *Globe*.[205] In greeting the end of the war, the *Evening Standard* spied danger in the reaction of the British Left to the German revolution. 'We must set our faces like flint against our own Bolshevists', argued the editorial on Armistice Day, 'who will argue that the revolutionary fires will purge the German people of all complicity in the great crime.'[206] The *Daily Express* similarly defended the claim to reparation and argued that 'the German people were the accomplices of the Kaiser. It is bare justice that they should pay'.[207] *The Spectator*, previously a defender of the German people, now reversed its position: 'The German people are very much mistaken if they think, by

[201] *Evening News*, editorial, 'The Three Germanys—But Remember They Are All Huns', 9 Nov. 1918, emphasis in the original.

[202] *Daily Mail*, 11 Nov. 1918.   [203] *Daily Mail*, 11 Nov. 1918.

[204] *Daily Mail*, 12 Nov. 1918.

[205] *Globe*, editorials, 'Too Late' and 'Take Care', 12 and 13 Nov. 1918.

[206] *Evening Standard*, editorial, 'The End of the War', 11 Nov. 1918.

[207] *Daily Express*, editorial, 'Nemesis', 12 Nov. 1918.

changing their form of government, to escape the consequences of defeat in a war which they heartily approved so long as they were winning victories.'[208]

The Coalition Liberal papers were generally more moderate in their treatment of the revolution, at least initially. There was little outright denigration of the revolution as a fraud. Nevertheless, in the popular dailies, the Northcliffe theme of an essentially unrepentant Germany was sometimes repeated. For instance, in its first editorial on the German revolution, the *News of the World* proclaimed 'no belief in the repentance of the German people. They are not sorry for their inhumanities. Germany is sick and sorry. But she is only sorry she has lost.'[209] Lloyd George's new acquisition, the *Daily Chronicle*, was a little more optimistic. The paper's special correspondent in Amsterdam, George Renwick, wrote enthusiastically of the German revolution, and was even willing to acknowledge that Ebert was 'one of the finest characters in the ranks of German socialism'. The new editor, E. A. Perris, declared the advent of German democracy 'supremely important'. However, Perris instantly added the rider that 'restitution and reparation will have to be exacted much the same from Germany, whether democratised or not'.[210]

Positive estimates of the revolution were rare, and chiefly to be found in the Radical, pro-Asquith, and Labour papers. For example, Massingham in the *Nation* rejoiced over the transformation of Europe and Germany—it was a spectacular 'conversion of the world' from the abominable militarist dogmas of the past. Massingham praised the SPD for having struggled so hard to avoid the turmoil of a revolution, and then for stepping into an alliance with the USPD in order to control disorder when revolution became unavoidable. For Massingham, events in Germany were immensely promising. All that remained was for the Allies to buttress the new order. Massingham pleaded with the victors to 'treat Germany decently', and to consolidate the changes inside Germany with an offer of 'food, raw materials and free markets'.[211]

'Windows into Germany': British military intelligence and the German revolution

While the 'counterfeit revolution' thesis dominated the Coalition press, a very different picture was built up by military intelligence in the weeks that followed the November revolution. A vast array of 'facts' on the 'new Germany' was assembled by British army and naval personnel. From the moment of the armistice, 'windows into Germany' were opened. Intelligence was collected from

---

[208] *Spectator*, 'News of the Week', 16 Nov. 1918, and see also Lord Walsingham's letter to the editor, 'The Guilt of the German People', 9 Nov. 1918.

[209] *News of the World*, editorial, 'The Hour of Fate', 10 Nov. 1918.

[210] *Daily Chronicle*, editorial, 'Germany Confronted With Our Terms', 9 Nov. 1918, and Renwick's reports, 12 Nov. 1918.

[211] 'The New German Danger', editorial, *Nation*, 16 Nov. 1918, and 'The Conversion of the World', *Nation*, 23 Nov. 1918.

those who came face to face with the revolution: from the members of the Armistice Commission in Spa in Belgium, from prisoners of war returning from Germany, and from other intelligence officers on the ground in Germany as the British army advanced into the Rhineland. A picture of Germany was assembled which contrasted sharply with the journalists' land of fake revolutionaries and unrepentant militarists.

Among the first to observe the revolution were the dozen army officers comprising the British delegation of the Armistice Commission. Under the command of Lieutenant-General Sir Richard Haking, the British mission arrived in Spa on 15 November 1918 to monitor German compliance with the armistice terms.[212] There, in company with the French, Belgian, and American missions, consultations proceeded with General Winterfeldt, now leading the German delegation. Haking sent back comprehensive daily reports to the War Office giving his impressions of German morale and internal conditions. As he put it himself, 'I have been adopting the role of a military and political intelligence department'.[213] Haking was indeed in a supremely important 'observation post', even though based in Belgium; for, as a result of the Entente and American decision to isolate Germany diplomatically, during the next eight months the Armistice Commission in Spa was to provide the chief point of formal contact between the new government in Germany and the victorious powers.

Apart from personal observation, however, Haking's sources of information were limited. Most information was that volunteered by the officers of the old German army with whom the Allied missions dealt. These officers were obviously hostile to the revolution. The view of inner Germany afforded by the Armistice Commission, therefore, was a blinkered one; but, it should be stressed, this limitation was imposed by the victors themselves. Haking and his fellow Allied generals made it clear from the outset that they wished only to speak to officers from the old German army. Members of the Soldiers' Councils who approached the Armistice Commission were turned away. 'Of course we had no dealings with these men; they were treated warily by my orders', Haking reported on 18 November.[214] The Soldiers' Council at Spa closed up shop and dispersed with other retiring troops on that day.[215] Ten days later, sailors from the Soldiers' Council at Aix-la-Chapelle arrived in Spa and again sought representation in the formal conferences of the Armistice Commission. But these men were threatened with arrest and disappeared.[216] The refusal to deal with the Soldiers' Councils of course gave to the German officers an unambiguous message to be relayed to Berlin: the victorious Allies regarded the revolution as repugnant.

[212] Armistice Commission Report, 15 Nov. 1918, WO 144/1.
[213] Armistice Commission Report, 26 Nov. 1918, WO 144/1.
[214] Armistice Commission Report, 18 Nov. 1918, WO 144/3.
[215] In the Armistice Commission Report for 25 Nov. 1918, WO 144/3, there is a reference to the Soldiers' Council leaving Spa 'a week ago'.
[216] Report of Consul Busing, in Armistice Commission Report, 28 Nov. 1918, WO 144/3.

Haking's reports also provided insights into the impact of the revolution and the drastic armistice conditions inside Germany. At first Haking depicted a disarming and dissolving Germany which, he swiftly concluded, was no longer a credible military threat to the Entente and American forces. Haking's testimony does not provide evidence in confirmation of the theory that a 'premature' armistice left German militarism unscathed. Haking observed units retreating through the town of Spa from 16 November and reported that 'a great many soldiers and a great many vehicles carry red badges or a red revolutionary flag'. The men were orderly, but Haking noted that 'the Officers have no real control over them' and were evidently 'afraid of their men'. The fear of the German High Command that the retreat of the army might become a 'disorganized rout' was quite genuine, according to Haking. [217] Most importantly, within three days of arriving in Spa, Haking reported to the War Office that 'from what I have seen there is no possibility of war being continued by the Germans at the close of armistice'; indeed, the idea that the war might be resumed by the Germans was 'quite impossible'.[218] The Germans had all their cards on the table and admitted 'complete collapse', wrote Haking.[219] Time and again German officers assured Haking that Germany's capacity and desire to make war had vanished, and he endorsed this judgement as a self-evident truth. 'To sum up all this argument, I should say that the German Commissioners here do not for a moment think they can continue the war, or recommence it with any chance of success', concluded Haking by 25 November.[220]

But the changing political atmosphere prompted by the Allies' animosity towards the revolution was also detected by Haking. He was soon aware of the disillusionment of the revolutionary Left. In his only interview with delegates from the Soldiers' Council in Spa before its dispersal, Haking was told by two disgruntled soldiers that 'the governments of the Allies had always said that they were prepared to deal fairly with the German nation if they threw over the Military regime, but that now, after this had been done, there was no moderation in the terms imposed on Germany: this would rankle for ever in the minds of the German nation'.[221] The German officers at Spa were not slow to learn the political preferences of their conquerors and this clearly revived their confidence. In private interviews, German officers openly disparaged the new government in Berlin and worked to encourage Allied pressure upon the socialist elements within it. 'There is no properly constituted government in Germany. The extreme socialists have put themselves in power', one officer reported to Haking on 20 November. The outrageous elimination of middle-class representation in the government and the domination of 'the labour class' was emphasized. The

[217] Armistice Commission Report, 16 Nov. 1918, WO 144/3.
[218] Armistice Commission Report, 18 Nov. 1918, WO 144/3.
[219] Armistice Commission Report, 19 Nov. 1918, WO 144/3.
[220] Armistice Commission Report, 25 Nov. 1918, WO 144/3.
[221] Armistice Commission Report, 17 Nov. 1918, WO 144/3.

German officers constantly stressed the danger of Bolshevism in Germany because the Soldiers' Councils had 'immense power in Germany'.[222] General Winterfeldt himself invited Haking to send officers into Germany to learn for himself the disastrous socialist indiscipline and the terrible food situation.[223] However, Haking did not favour the idea, speculating that the German propaganda about Bolshevism and the food crisis was probably just an attempt to divide the victors and obtain easier terms.[224] However, Haking revised this view after a journey to Cologne following British occupation in early December, conceding in his official report that food supplies there were 'difficult if not impossible to obtain' and that children and the sick were experiencing 'very great hardship'.[225]

The Royal Navy was the next British service to come face to face with the reality of the German revolution. As specified under the terms of the armistice, a large number of German naval ships were due to be interned in mid-November. The British government immediately anticipated a problem if delegates from the socialist Sailors' Councils on the ships of the German High Seas Fleet sought to play some role in the great internment of the ships. On 14 November Eric Geddes, First Lord of the Admiralty, told Admiral Beatty that he was most concerned at reports that four rebel sailors, known to be attached to the staff of the German Admiral Meurer, might seek to attend negotiations over the internment due to begin on Beatty's flagship, the *Queen Elizabeth*, the next day.[226] Beatty resolved not to meet with the Sailors' Councils. 'Impertinence' was Beatty's reaction to a formal message from Meurer 'saying he has Bolshies on his staff'.[227] Admiral Meurer and his party, including men from the Sailors' Council, were brought alongside the *Queen Elizabeth* in the Firth of Forth by the British destroyer *Oak* on the afternoon of 15 November. Beatty immediately 'made a signal that he would *not* receive the representatives of the so-called "Workers' and Soldiers' Delegates"'.[228] As Beatty's report of the incident to the War Cabinet explained, Meurer and his officers 'appeared to be pleased with this decision'.[229]

This proved to be no isolated gesture on Beatty's part. British antagonism to the revolution was on display throughout the German fleet's internment on 21 November—or 'surrender' as the naval officers incorrectly labelled the

---

[222] 'Information volunteered by von Haniel', in Armistice Commission Report, 20 Nov. 1918, WO 144/3.

[223] 'Notes volunteered by officer of German Naval Mission SPA, 25 Nov. 1918' [Lt.-Commander Kiep], in Armistice Commission Report, 25 Nov. 1918, WO 144/3.

[224] Armistice Commission Report, 26 Nov. 1918, WO 144/3.

[225] 'Notes on Visit to Cologne, 9 Dec. 1918', in Armistice Commission Report, WO 144/1.

[226] Geddes to Beatty, 14 Nov. 1918, ADM 116/1809.

[227] On the presence of delegates of the Sailors' Council, see Commander-in-Chief of German Fleet to Beatty, 14 Nov. 1918, in Capt. Geoffrey Harper Diary, 14 Nov. 1918, Harper Papers, HRPR 1/11, and for Beatty's reaction see Harper Diary, 15 Nov. 1918, Harper Papers, HRPR 2/5.

[228] Beatty to Flag Commander, *Oak*, 15 Nov. 1918, Andrew Cunninghame Graham of Gartmore Papers, ANCG 1/1, and Harper Diary, 15 Nov. 1918, Harper Papers, HRPR 2/5.

[229] E. Geddes, 'Compliance with the Naval Conditions of Armistice', 16 Nov. 1918, CAB 24/70.

internment.[230] The rebellious German sailors were to be carefully isolated as a potential danger to the morale of the British. Elaborate orders were drawn up for the reception of the German fleet which included strict guidelines to prevent any fraternization. These orders specified that only 'reliable men' were to be employed in search parties on the German ships, that all papers or pamphlets handed to such search parties were to be immediately surrendered to officers, and that officers in command of boats proceeding alongside German ships were to ensure that no communication between the sailors took place. Men were warned that they were to be 'not even distantly friendly'. The German officers, on the other hand, were to be accorded all the normal naval courtesies, such as piping the side and saluting.[231] Even here, the political preferences of the British were advertised.

On the day of the internment, the German ships steamed to the Firth of Forth to be met by the British Grand Fleet. Admiral Beatty and many of his staff were filled with bitterness towards the Germans whose revolutionary cowardice, as they saw it, had denied the Royal Navy its share in the glory of victory. Beatty sought to wring all the publicity he could out of the handing-over ceremonies, ensuring a large number of journalists were on board the British ships to cover the triumphal events, and even inviting the king to join him on the bridge of the *Queen Elizabeth* for the day, an invitation the king turned down.[232] Beatty told his brother officers at the end of the day that 'he wished he could have wired [to the Admiralty] he'd sunk the lot'.[233] But the sources also show that many other British officers confessed to a stirring of fellow feeling towards their disgraced German counterparts. Lieutenant-Commander Alastair Denniston, Beatty's interpreter at his conferences with Admiral Meurer, recorded that he 'did feel sorry for the Senior Officers there' who were 'keen and efficient men' facing the ruin of their careers.[234] At the conferences between Meurer and Beatty, the revolutionary mood of the German sailors was regarded on both sides as the major problem bedevilling a satisfactory internment of the German ships. Admiral Madden, for example, who joined Beatty at these conferences, noted that in his opinion the Germans 'are honestly trying to carry out the terms of Armistice, but the officers have practically no authority'.[235]

[230] See 'Official Designation for Surrender of High Sea Fleet', DCNS minute, 27 Jan. 1919, Fremantle Papers, FRE/313.

[231] 'Confidential order: Fraternisation with German Officers and Men, from Admiral Sir Charles Madden to H.M. Ships concerned, 19 Nov. 1918', in Pridham, unpublished memoir, Pridham Papers.

[232] Davidson memoir, 17 Nov. 1918, Davidson Papers, 13. The king turned down the invitation explaining that he did not intend 'to crow over the fallen enemy'.

[233] Alastair Denniston, 'Account of Surrender of the German Fleet', Denniston Papers, DENN 6/3. Denniston was moved to write that 'some rich man ought to endow a society for the prevention of public and political speeches by Admirals of the British Navy'.

[234] Alastair Denniston, 'Account of Surrender of the German Fleet', Denniston Papers, DENN 6/3.

[235] Charles Madden to Jellicoe, 29 Nov. 1918, Jellicoe Papers, 49009. See also Madden to Dreyer, 16 Nov. 1918, Dreyer Papers, DRYR 4/3.

During the internment, the revolutionary sailors were regarded as pariahs. Beatty deliberately incited this as a shield against revolutionary infection. In visits to various British ships, he delivered impromptu speeches to his own sailors attacking the revolution in the German navy which had led to this 'pitiable sight', this 'horrible sight', the surrender of those hated ships which, he declared, he had 'ached, as all ached' to sweep from the oceans in battle. He urged his sailors to feel nothing but 'extreme contempt' for the German sailor, who was 'not a man at all, nothing but a murdering rascal'.[236] Beatty's officers needed little encouragement: 'They are such skunks they are almost not worthy of our contempt', wrote Captain Geoffrey Harper. Almost inevitably, incidents between British officers and the revolutionary sailors took place during inspections of the German ships. When Harper was searching the German battleship *Seydlitz* he was particularly affronted by the 'Bolshie delegates' who accompanied his search party. He joyfully recorded that his Lieutenants had refused the delegates entry to the German ward room, telling them 'that they were not fit persons to gather up the crumbs that fell from an Officer's table (German or English)'. One Sailors' Council delegate who hesitated was 'bodily projected several yards'.[237] Vice-Admiral Arthur Pridham who inspected the *Kaiser*, recorded in his diary his horror at the state of the ship, 'appalling, dirty, smelly', and he remarked on the sad fate of the remaining handful of officers.[238] Denniston accompanied the *Seydlitz* on the journey north to Scapa. He too identified with the 'dignified' officers who had to endure the presence of the Sailors' Council delegate who 'mooched' aimlessly on the bridge.[239] On the arrival of the German fleet at Scapa Flow, the bulk of the German crews were immediately returned to Germany and the remainder were penned up in their ships and not permitted to land.[240]

Beatty's detestation of the revolution that had aborted a major naval battle and climaxed in the peaceful 'surrender' of the fleet was shared by the naval officers, the British political élite, and, of course, the British right-wing press. The delivery of the fleet without bloodshed was 'a sad spectacle', 'a degradation of the Naval Traditions of this world', wrote Admiral Chatfield in a typical reaction.[241] There was support for Beatty's decision to order the German ships at Scapa not to fly the German ensign, a decision clearly in excess of his powers under the armistice and designed to underline the British claim that the ships were surrendered rather than simply interned. 'They are nothing—they belong to nobody—we could not let an ensign that the world used to respect be worn by

[236] See Beatty's speech on board HMS *Revenge* and speech on board HMS *Lion*, dated 23 Nov. 1918, Pridham Diary, Pridham Papers, PRID 4.

[237] Harper Diary, 21 and 22 Nov. 1918, Harper Papers, HRPR 2/5.

[238] Pridham Diary, 21 Nov. 1918, Pridham Papers, PRID 4.

[239] Alastair Denniston, 'Account of Surrender of the German Fleet', Denniston Papers, DENN 6/3.

[240] Pridham Diary, 6 Dec. 1918, Pridham Papers, PRID 4, signals preserved in Cunninghame Graham of Gartmore Papers, ANCG 1/1, and DCNS minute, 20 Feb. 1919, Fremantle Papers, FRE/314.

[241] Chatfield to Dreyer, 23 Nov. 1918, Dreyer Papers, DREY 4/2.

such miseries', wrote Captain Harper in his diary.[242] Lord Crawford was typical of the political élite in offering an unremittingly negative interpretation of the events of the historic day on the Firth of Forth. He confessed to feeling devastated at 'so vile and fetid an humiliation'; it 'would seem to augur ill for the prospects of strong and orderly government', observed Crawford.[243] Throughout the political élite there was sheer incomprehension at the political forces in Germany which had produced a socialist government willing to hand over dozens of battleships, destroyers and submarines as a mark of its commitment to the armistice. 'Incredible how they could have been given up so tamely', Godfrey-Fausset commented in his diary.[244] The press enthused over the 'surrender'. Beatty was praised for snubbing the 'German soviets'.[245] The *Pall Mall Gazette* gloated over the discomfort of the *Vorwärts* which was said to be stunned at the realization that Beatty had refused to meet the men of the Sailors' Councils 'because they are not representatives of any recognized Government'.[246] Thus, one of the most spectacular gestures of the good faith of Germany's new revolutionary government, the peaceful internment of the bulk of the German High Seas Fleet, was presented to the British public as evidence only of the despicable cowardice of the German 'Red Flaggers'.

Away from the public gaze, meanwhile, Admiralty Intelligence was circulating reports on the revolution and the new men in Berlin that were to say the least even-handed. A relatively positive portrait of Germany's new government emerged. The first biographical sketch of Ebert, offered in a report of 14 November, conceded that 'though he supported the government in the war, he has consistently condemned any war of conquest and has opposed all annexations'. The report noted that both Ebert and Scheidemann had condemned the Belgian deportations. The political credentials of Germany's socialists were assessed with equanimity: the industrial and social demands of the reconstruction programme of the SPD, the report observed, 'are of interest owing to the similarity between them and the reconstruction programme of the British Labour Party'.[247] Admiralty Intelligence offered an equally reassuring picture of the Council of People's Commissioners in Berlin, noting that 'they are determined to have nothing to do with Bolshevism in any shape or form' but were planning for early democratic elections. The Soldiers' and Workers' Councils, similarly, were taking a 'strong line against hooliganism' and had 'set their face against anything like Bolshevism'.[248] The new German government, it was admitted, had shown 'the most marked anxiety' to obey all the armistice terms and had pleaded

[242] Harper Diary, 24 Nov. 1918, Harper Papers, HRPR 2/5. See also official support for Beatty's decision on the ensign in DCNS minute, 25 Nov. 1918, Fremantle Papers, FRE/311.
[243] Crawford Diary, 25 Nov. 1918, vol. xxxiii, Crawford Papers.
[244] Godfrey-Fausset Diary, 29 Nov. 1918, Godfrey-Fausset Papers, 1/70.
[245] *Evening Standard*, 22 Nov. 1918.
[246] *Pall Mall Gazette*, 'Beatty and the Red Flaggers', 22 Nov. 1918.
[247] Admiralty Intelligence Report, 12–14 Nov. 1918, Drax Papers, DRAX 5/4.
[248] Admiralty Intelligence Report, 19–21 Nov. 1918, Drax Papers, DRAX 5/4.

with the sailors of the High Seas Fleet and submarines to obey their Sailors' Councils in undertaking the peaceful delivery of ships and submarines to England.[249] In short, Admiralty Intelligence had little time for the image of the revolution as a 'revolution of deception' which was peddled so assiduously in the British press in these same first weeks of the revolution. Admiralty Intelligence took exactly the opposite view: 'All the information available indicates that the reports of imminent famine and transport chaos are little if at all exaggerated by the German Government and that their fear of Bolshevism and appeals to modify the terms of the Armistice are to that extent sincere.'[250]

The Royal Navy opened another 'window into Germany' in early December with the arrival of the Allied Naval Armistice Commission in the northern naval ports. Again the makers of the revolution and the representatives of the republic were snubbed, and again the intelligence collected pointed to the revolution in Germany being quite genuine and radicalized by serious food shortages. When Admiral Browning steamed HMS *Hercules* into Wilhelmshaven on 5 December 1918, he followed Beatty's example by signalling ahead that he would not negotiate with representatives of the Workers' and Soldiers' Council of Wilhelmshaven. Similarly, Browning's staff and sailors were carefully instructed in advance to have only the bare minimum of contact with the Germans and to take all meals separately.[251] At their first conference, the German and British Admirals were immediately preoccupied by the 'problem' presented by the revolution, a subject calculated to induce a degree of solidarity between the two. The German Admiral Goette supplied to Browning copious details of the difficulties under which he laboured as a result of the power of the Sailors' and Soldiers' Councils not only in Wilhelmshaven but in all the northern port cities. German officers, he explained, had no control over their men or dock workers. Spartacism in Berlin was a further danger. Browning declared that he could not concern himself with the political situation inside Germany.[252] But clearly, in excluding the Sailors' Council from his discussions, he had already shown his political colours. At Kiel on 12 December a formal request from the Workers' and Soldiers' Council to partake in the negotiations was again rejected. Goette replied on behalf of Browning, announcing that, as at Wilhelmshaven, 'the Allied Naval Commission has refused to countenance this demand'. Browning endorsed Goette's reply: 'The instructions of this commission are that we are not authorised to meet or deal with any but Naval Officers.'[253]

---

[249] Admiralty Intelligence Report, 22–5 Nov. 1918, Drax Papers, DRAX 5/4.

[250] Admiralty Intelligence Report, 26–8 Nov. 1918, Drax Papers, DRAX 5/4.

[251] Capt. Ernest Thring, 'Diary of Events connected with the Allied Naval Commission to Germany, December 1918, H.M.S. Hercules', entry for 4 Dec. 1918, E. W. C. Thring Papers.

[252] Document headed 'The following Notes on the Political Situation in Germany are based upon statements made by Rear Admiral Goette on 5th December 1918 on H.M.S. Hercules', FO 371/3224, and 'Meeting between Allied Naval Commission and German Naval Commission on board "Hercules" at Wilhelmshaven, Thursday afternoon, 5 December 1918', Thring Papers, 71/30/1.

[253] 'Report of Meeting held on board H.M.S. Hercules at Kiel, 12 Dec. 1918', Thring Papers, 71/30/1.

No one with Admiral Browning's mission could have been in any doubt about the dire food shortages in northern Germany. Henry McCall, a young officer on a motor boat accompanying the mission, recalled that there was 'tremendous privation' in Hamburg when he was there in December 1918. The rules against contacts with the Germans quickly buckled under the pressures created by the food shortage. McCall remembered throngs of Germans crowding around the dockyard gates bartering anything they had to spare with the British sailors. There was 'an enormous swarm of Germans outside and sailors with food, tobacco, exchanging their goods for marks'. Indeed the captain of McCall's motor boat was not above seeking to exploit the situation. The captain slipped back briefly to Harwich with a British destroyer retrieving mail. He bought up £30 or £40 worth of margarine and cigarettes at the Harwich naval canteen, and upon his return sold the lot to the post-master at Hamburg for three crisp £100 notes.[254]

Officers on other ships travelling to Baltic German ports to retrieve British prisoners of war in November and December had similar experiences. Leslie Hollis, an officer who received a batch of prisoners of war in a 'desperately cold' Danzig, recalled that the population of the city showed 'unmistakable signs of the effect of the blockade'. 'Most of the men and many of the women and children were shockingly emaciated.' The British sailors began to share food. Nevertheless, there were violent scenes when one train arrived with British prisoners in an appalling condition and six German soldiers were killed by the ship's company.[255] Admiral Tyrwhitt on HMS *Curlew*, who sent back detailed descriptions, also found the civil population of Danzig 'apathetic' and the women and children exhibiting a characteristic 'pastiness' as a result of the food shortages. There was 'effusive cordiality' shown by the people towards the British sailors.[256]

The British army also began to gather similar factual material on the condition of Germany in the first weeks of December from at least three sources, British prisoners of war released from Germany, the British Army of Occupation as it advanced into Belgium and Germany, and a British Military Mission that was set up in Berlin in mid-December.

One of the most complete accounts of conditions in Germany came in mid-December from Brigadier General H. C. Rees and Lieutenant A. Campbell, two prisoners of war at Bad Colberg who undertook a journey to Berlin from 12 to 15 December in order to take stock of the political and economic situation before returning to England via Holland.[257] Rees's report was emphatic: 'Germany appears to be completely beaten and disorganized; further hostilities on any

[254] Admiral Sir Henry McCall, interviewed by Peter Liddle, Oct. 1976, Peter Liddle Archive, Tape 403.
[255] General Sir Leslie Hollis, typescript memoir entitled 'Random Reminiscences', Hollis Papers, 86/47/1.
[256] Telegram from Rear-Admiral R. Tyrwhitt, H.M.S. *Curlew*, Danzig, 12 Dec. 1918, FO 371/3776.
[257] 'Report by Brigadier General H. C. Rees, D.S.O., on the Condition of Affairs in Germany between the 12th and 15th December [1918]', FO 371/3776.

appreciable scale are most improbable'. Rees debunked immediately the myth that the Germans were unaware of their defeat: 'The German people are, in my opinion, fully aware of this fact and accept it as a lesser evil than the continuance of the war.' Campbell agreed: 'They fully acknowledge that they are beaten', he wrote. In fact, Rees's diary reveals that the much criticized receptions for returning troops in Berlin were scarcely the victory parades calculated to propagate the illusion of an undefeated army as the British press alleged at the time. Rees recorded his impressions on 13 December:

During the day Campbell and I saw the Guards march into Berlin. It was a pitiful display from a military point of view. The companies were only some 90 to 100 strong, mostly composed of very young boys and men. The machine-gun limbers behind each company were drawn by the most sorry looking nags I've ever seen and the guns were often rusty. All the horses and guns bedecked with flowers, but there was no cheering and the reception was not that accorded to victorious troops.[258]

Similarly, Rees and Campbell accepted without question that the food crisis was genuine. 'The nation as a whole', Rees wrote in his formal report, 'is on the verge of starvation.' A third prisoner of war, Lieutenant G. H. Beyfus, provided a report endorsing the views of Rees and Campbell. Beyfus had also been set at liberty by a Soldiers' Council from his camp south of Berlin and remained in Germany for a month after the revolution. In his report he agreed that 'the revolution is a real and genuine movement' and that there was 'no serious danger' of Germany wishing to resume the war. The best course, advised Beyfus, would be for the Allies to offer real support to the moderate socialist government. 'I think that men like Ebert and Scheidemann—whatever may be thought of their attitude to the war—must be regarded as the main political bulwark against Bolshevism', reasoned Beyfus.[259]

Still more details emerged as the British Second Army under General Plumer advanced into Belgium and the Rhineland and finally entered Cologne at the centre of the British zone of occupation in the first week of December. As the army moved forward, intelligence officers gathered information on the revolution from Belgians and British prisoners of war who had witnessed its impact on the retiring German army. Captain George Gedye of the Intelligence Corps, for example, reported that for a period of three or four days after the signing of the armistice there was a wholesale collapse of discipline within the German army, 'saluting almost entirely ceased and in most cases officers' badges of rank were removed'.[260] But quite apart from the revolution, it was the condition of inner

[258] H. E. C. Rees Diary, 13 Dec. 1918, Rees Papers 77/179/1.

[259] 'Report as to Conditions in Germany by Lieutenant G. H. Beyfus, 3rd Duke of Wellington's Regiment, From the 10th November to the 10th December, 1918', included in 'Report by Brigadier General H. C. Rees, D.S.O., on the Condition of Affairs in Germany between the 12th and 15th December [1918]', FO 371/3776.

[260] See 'Revolutionary Tendencies in the German Army' in 'Report by Capt. G. E. R. Gedye, Intelligence Corps, on information acquired while attached to the 1st Cavalry Division and 9th Cavalry Brigade, 18–28 Nov. 1918', Gedye Papers, 8.

Germany which excited most interest. In this respect, the experiences of the ordinary British troops preserved in the sources show a remarkably consistent pattern: the German people whom they encountered and with whom they were billeted were genuinely hungry, vulnerable, and disconcertingly friendly. After crossing the frontier British troops observed from the people 'dead silence, no hostility, curiosity, a certain amount of apprehension'. The advance guard were fearful on entering Cologne, but the Germans behaved 'with dignity and self-control'.[261] The soldiers marvelled that they were accepted into billets 'without any apparent rancour'.[262] It was 'just as if we were on holiday in England', recalled one NCO.[263] The sharing of rations began instantly.[264] 'They were short of food. They were thin and white and they were delighted if we gave them anything to eat', recalled Captain J. Macmurray.[265] A former British military mounted policeman who had to deal later with Spartacist demonstrators in Cologne noted that 'the poor devils were white and starving'.[266] The British soldiers themselves were on the most meagre rations, one soldier listing the Spartan fare in his diary and his complaint that the troops were 'all half-empty'.[267] Photographs of the British troops entering German towns show children often accompanying the marching ranks.[268] In Solingen, a steel town, groups of children milled expectantly around the British horse-drawn cookers whenever troops paused at institutional billets made available to them such as schools and halls.[269] Those British soldiers who ventured out to shop for food discovered that 'everything seemed to be poverty-stricken' and they discovered 'terrible prices' and 'hardly anything in the eating line'.[270] Demobilized German soldiers were not ashamed to approach the British 'Tommies' and 'wanted to buy cheese, sugar, bread and tea'.[271] Cafes were soon placed 'out of bounds' by British military authorities in Solingen so that troops did not compete for the meagre supplies of food for sale. The reason was obvious and recorded in one soldier's diary: 'there being a great shortage of food in Germany, due to our naval blockade.'[272] Even

[261] Philip Gibbs, 'The Entry into Cologne', in *The Cologne Post-Christmas Souvenir 1919*, in Lieutenant A. Murch Papers, Peter Liddle Archive.

[262] G. R. F. Bredin, interviewed by Peter Liddle, July 1978, Peter Liddle Archive, Tape 524.

[263] William J. Hooker, interviewed by Peter Liddle, Sept. 1982, Peter Liddle Archive, Tape 733.

[264] Major-General S. W. Joslin, 'Typescript of a talk delivered January 1982', Joslin Papers, Peter Liddle Archive, H. K. Fisher, interviewed by Peter Liddle June 1988, Peter Liddle Archive, Tape 714.

[265] Captain J. Macmurray, interviewed by Peter Liddle, Sept. 1977, Peter Liddle Archive, Tape 476.

[266] Lieutenant-Colonel R. Ledingham, typescript memoir, 'War Diary, 1914–1918', Ledingham Papers, Peter Liddle Archive.

[267] J. A . Douglas Diary, 27 Dec. 1918, J. A. Douglas Papers, Imperial War Museum, 81/20/2.

[268] R. M. Kilby photo album, Kilby Papers, Peter Liddle Archive.

[269] J. A . Douglas Diary, 14 Dec. 1918, J. A. Douglas Papers, Imperial War Museum, 81/20/2.

[270] William J. Hooker, interviewed by Peter Liddle, Sept. 1982, Peter Liddle Archive, Tape 733, and J. A . Douglas Diary, 14 Dec. 1918, J. A. Douglas Papers, Imperial War Museum, 81/20/2.

[271] F. W. Davey Diary, 23 Dec. 1918, Davey Papers, Peter Liddle Archive.

[272] J. A . Douglas Diary, 25 Dec. 1918, J. A. Douglas Papers, Imperial War Museum, 81/20/2.

the commanding generals, ensconced at the Dom Hotel in the centre of Cologne, were soon writing to their colleagues in a similar vein: 'Food you cannot buy; it is all in the cellars of the food hoarders. I have not been so short of provisions during this war.'[273] In the light of these experiences, and in marked contrast to some British journalists, few soldiers in the Rhine Army appear to have been in any doubt whatsoever that the privations endured by the majority of ordinary Germans during that winter were very real.

The explosion of venereal disease in the Rhine Army testified, of course, to widespread prostitution. Among the many causes, no doubt, the vulnerability and hunger of the German people must be listed. To give but one soldier's experience, J. A. Douglas, on sentry duty on his first night in Germany at Gressenich in December 1918, was approached by a whole family, father, mother, two sisters, and a boy, all wanting food. 'From what we could gather they and all the inhabitants around were in a state of semi-starvation', Douglas jotted in his diary. The girls returned later, lifted their aprons, and vainly offered themselves for food. The girls, Douglas recorded, 'had the dark shadows under their eyes, and white pasty faces I had seen since crossing the German frontier'.[274] By the spring of 1919 the VD rate in the Rhine Army was estimated at 4,000 per week, a rate which threatened to debilitate the entire army before the year was out.[275] General Robertson conceded that the Rhine Army was 'practically non-effective due to VD'.[276] Officers on Robertson's staff recognized the cause: 'the people were starving and had lacked the necessities of life for years.'[277]

The absence of hostility from the German population is a recurring theme in the sources. Diaries and letters that survive reveal the British soldiers' amazement that they encountered no animosity, no truculence, and no want of trusting civility from German civilians and soldiers alike. 'It is difficult to treat them as they deserve to be treated', wrote one soldier, for the people were always 'very civil'.[278] There were 'no outward signs of demonstration or hate'.[279] One officer described the Germans as 'very servile and anxious to please by taking off their caps'.[280] In Cologne, the German troops in uniforms from which their shoulder straps had been torn, 'were polite and disposed to be friendly'.[281] In early

---

[273] General Godley to Sir James Allen, 31 Dec. 1918, quoting a letter from 'a general in Cologne', Allen Papers, MI/15.

[274] J. A . Douglas Diary, 6 Dec. 1918, J. A. Douglas Papers, Imperial War Museum, 81/20/2.

[275] Maj.-General L. A. Hawes, typescript memoir 'Kwab-o-Kayal—the Memories and Dreams of an Ordinary Soldier', 65, Hawes Papers, 87/41/1.

[276] Air Chief Marshal Sir John Whitworth Jones, interviewed by Peter Liddle, Apr. 1979, Peter Liddle Archive, Tape 580.

[277] Maj.-General L. A. Hawes, typescript memoir 'Kwab-o-Kayal—the Memories and Dreams of an Ordinary Soldier', 65, Hawes Papers, 87/41/1.

[278] e.g. A. C. Wilkinson to his father, 19 Dec. 1918, A. C. Wilkinson Papers, Peter Liddle Archive.

[279] Lieutenant-Colonel R. Ledingham, typescript memoir, 'War Diary, 1914–1918', Ledingham Papers, Peter Liddle Archive.

[280] Brigadier Eric Foster Hall Diary, 16 Dec. 1918, Eric Foster Hall Papers, Imperial War Museum.

[281] Philip Gibbs, 'The Entry into Cologne', in *The Cologne Post-Christmas Souvenir 1919*, in Lieutenant A. Murch Papers, Peter Liddle Archive.

December British onlookers were amazed at the actions of a Cologne crowd observing a parade near the Cathedral to welcome General Sir Charles Fergusson, the new Military Governor of Cologne: when four horses of the escorting 9th Lancers went down on the wet cobbles when rounding a corner, the Germans 'rushed forward, they picked up the soldiers, they picked up the horses, put them back on their horses and so. Never any sign of animosity.'[282] Impulsive and private acts of reconciliation took place during that December: a woman, one of two sisters who ran a family cafe in Solingen frequented by a British soldier, suddenly presented to him the army cap of her dead brother whom she explained had been killed at Passchendaele.[283] The troops as a whole were impressed with the standard of housing and public amenities in Germany, compared with France and Belgium, and the co-operative spirit of the public officials who arranged their accommodation.[284] Even beyond the Rhineland, in places where the sight of British uniforms was rare, such as Hamburg, surprised British officers discovered that the people 'were politeness and efficiency itself'.[285] A letter home from one soldier in December 1918 captured the feelings of many:

I suppose it is too soon to make up one's mind about the Germans yet but what I have seen I am pleased with. One thing they are neither sullen nor full of hate. A portion are frankly on the cadge but the majority are most obliging and anxious to make us comfortable. They are not obsequious nor fawning but have a certain dignity. Their attitude seems to be—'We have fought a good fight and we have lost. We will do what you tell us—you are the victors, we hope you won't be too hard on us'. [286]

How should this be interpreted? Many soldiers and officers at the time were simply mystified by the attitude of the Germans whom they encountered. Having habitually underestimated the progressive forces inside Germany it was mystifying to come face to face with so many people with progressive expectations and attitudes. Certainly, the German people did not act as a people who had endured a death-wound to their pride, a lost people whose beloved Kaiser had been torn from them, a truculent and defiant people whose militarism still burned in their hearts. Rather, they acted as a people with some hope, a people expecting a degree of reconciliation with the victor. The remarkable absence of animosity towards the conqueror may suggest the very deep influence of the German revolution on the temper of the nation. Presumably it was interpreted by the Germans themselves as their nation's belated but genuine answer to the political

[282] Major-General Sir Edmund Hakewill Smith, interviewed by Peter Liddle, Oct. 1976, Peter Liddle Archive, Tape 406.

[283] J. A . Douglas Diary, 16 Dec. 1918, J. A. Douglas Papers, Imperial War Museum, 81/20/2.

[284] e.g. Mr Prosser, interviewed by Peter Liddle, Feb. 1977, Peter Liddle Archive, Tape 476, or A. C. Wilkinson to his father, 23 Dec. 1918, A. C. Wilkinson Papers, Peter Liddle Archive.

[285] Admiral Sir Henry McCall, interviewed by Peter Liddle, Oct. 1976, Peter Liddle Archive, Tape 403.

[286] F. W. Davey to his parents, 24 Dec. 1918, Davey Papers, Peter Liddle Archive.

pressures coming from the West throughout 1918. The German people's hope no doubt reflected their faith in a Wilsonian settlement. The political forces exercizing power in Berlin had effectively encouraged this optimism towards the conquerors from the West. In a sense, the objective of British and Allied propaganda had been achieved: the German people were less afraid of defeat at the hands of Western liberalism than of war in the interests of the *Kaiserreich*.

However, once again the British commanders of the occupation force made no secret of their distaste for the revolution in Germany. Upon arrival in the Rhineland the British forces were used to discourage the political manifestations of the revolution. Naturally, orders were issued for British intelligence police to guard against 'Bolshevist propaganda among our troops'.[287] Plans were made even before the British troops arrived in Cologne to depoliticize the population: posters were prepared in advance informing the city that all assembling in crowds was forbidden and that all political meetings would require the permission of General Plumer.[288] Responding to requests from German military authorities and from the Mayor of Cologne, Konrad Adenauer, the British hurried an advance guard of the Second Army into Cologne on 6 December in order to forestall a rumoured Bolshevik rising. General Lawson, the commander of the advance guard, informed Adenauer that he would deal only with him and ruled out any discussions with the USPD-dominated Workers' and Soldiers' Council based at the Cologne Town Hall. Excluded from any share of power with the occupying forces, the Workers' and Soldiers' Council at Cologne dissolved itself on 20 December.[289] General Fergusson, as Military Governor with responsibility for the civilian population, then issued a proclamation demanding that all Workers' and Soldiers' Councils in districts occupied by the British 'cease their political activities in the localities and immediately leave all public buildings'.[290] The Workers' and Soldiers' Councils in and around Solingen, a USPD stronghold, were the next to resign rather than be politically neutered.[291] In the days and weeks that followed, the British military willingly lent assistance to the authorities in various towns in taking steps to crush Spartacist demonstrations and strikes.[292] British intelligence agents went to work immediately to recruit informers in order to infiltrate the local USPD and Spartacist organizations.[293] The

[287] 'War Diary—General Staff, Fourth Army—November 1918: Orders and Instructions for the Advance to the Rhine', Major-General A. A. Montgomery-Massingberd Papers, 85, Liddell Hart Centre for Military Archives.

[288] Proclamation dated 2 Dec. 1918 in Brigadier General Weston Papers, Peter Liddle Archive.

[289] David G. Williamson, *The British in Germany, 1918–1930: The Reluctant Occupiers* (New York, 1991), 18 and 45.

[290] *News of the World*, 22 Dec. 1918.

[291] Jürgen Tampke, *The Ruhr and Revolution: The Revolutionary Movement in the Rhenish Westphalian Industrial Region, 1912–1919* (Canberra, 1978), 88–9.

[292] Major-General Sir Edmund Hakewill Smith, interviewed by Peter Liddle, Oct. 1976, Peter Liddle Archive, Tape 406, Lieutenant-Colonel R. Ledingham, typescript memoir, 'War Diary, 1914–1918', Ledingham Papers, Peter Liddle Archive, and J. A . Douglas Diary, 9 Dec. 1918, J. A. Douglas Papers, Imperial War Museum, 81/20/2.

[293] Williamson, *The British in Germany*, 45.

leading British officers were divided over the degree of leniency or severity to be shown to the German population as a whole, with General Plumer veering towards severity and Fergusson towards leniency.[294] But dampening down the remnants of the revolution was not a controversial assignment; the task was clearly to the taste of the British military authorities. Certainly, some of the British brass-hats in the Rhineland discerned in German socialism merely the reflection of the same labour enemy which they despised at home. For example, General Godley, the commander of the New Zealand troops in Germany, foresaw that the only military objective that remained in Germany was the defeat of advanced socialism. He advised the New Zealand defence minister in these terms: 'I think we may safely count the war over now, though there is always the possibility that we may, as an Army of Occupation, have to put down Bolshevism in Germany.' The problem was, as Godley described it, 'the considerable development of Red-Fedism in the country', 'Red-Fedism' being an allusion to the socialist-left trade union organization which was very active in New Zealand prior to the war.[295]

Finally, reports on conditions in Germany began to flow back to the British War Office from mid-December following the opening of another 'window into Germany', this time in Berlin itself. General Richard Ewart and six other officers arrived in Berlin on 12 December to establish a British Military Mission as part of the Inter-Allied Commission on Repatriation. The mission's official purpose was to assist in the return of Allied prisoners of war, but opportunities for the gathering of intelligence were seized upon and an official diary sent back to the War Office.[296] That the revolution was real was obvious to Ewart from the beginning. On his journey to Berlin from Berne via Frankfurt, Ewart witnessed the confusion and indiscipline accompanying the spontaneous demobilization of German troops.[297] On his first day in Berlin, Ewart also witnessed the parade of returning troops. The march and reception did not strike Ewart as truculent in mood. 'The old strict march discipline has entirely disappeared', he wrote.[298] In common with so many other British officers in Germany in the first weeks after the revolution, Ewart marvelled at the lack of animosity.[299]

In his work concerning prisoners of war in Berlin, Ewart was soon in touch with other Red Cross officials, both German and Allied, with neutral diplomats,

[294] George Clive Diary, 14 Dec. 1918, Clive Papers, II, 4, Liddell Hart Centre for Military Archives.

[295] Godley to James Allen, 15 Nov. 1918, Allen Papers, M1/15. On 'Red-Fedism' see Erik Olssen, *The Red Feds: Revolutionary Industrial Unionism and the New Zealand Federation of Labour, 1908–1914* (Auckland, 1988).

[296] Ewart records sending the first official diary of his impressions back to the War Office on 15 Dec. 1918, Ewart Diary, Ewart Papers, 73/88/1.

[297] Ewart manuscript Diary, 11 Dec. 1918, and typescript document inserted entitled 'Journey to Berlin to superintend the Re-patriation of British Prisoners of War from Germany', Ewart Papers, 73/88/1.

[298] Ewart Diary, 12 Dec. 1918, Ewart Papers, 73/88/1.

[299] Ewart manuscript Diary, 11 Dec. 1918, Ewart Papers, 73/88/1.

and with the German War Ministry. From all these sources he gained further insights into the internal condition of Germany. He learned that the new revolutionary structures in Berlin did indeed oversee the workings of the old officialdom. At the German War Ministry Ewart encountered a soldier called Schlesinger, the representative of the Soldiers' and Sailors' Council, who 'insisted on signing all important papers', including Ewart's passport upon his arrival, 'much to the annoyance of the regular officers'.[300] Ewart's own antagonism to the revolution was obvious in his reports to the British War Office. The friendly relations between some Workers' and Soldiers' Councils and British prisoners disturbed Ewart. He observed that the Germans were 'giving very large number of passes' so that 'the men are leaving the camps and getting away into Berlin'.[301]

From the beginning also, Ewart was aware that food in Germany was undoubtedly in short supply and 'horribly expensive'.[302] Ewart soon learned that the deplorable condition of British prisoners of war in some German camps was not the result of calculated brutality but merely a reflection of the exhausted state of the nation.[303] At his meetings with neutral diplomats Ewart was told that the cause of the food shortages was undoubtedly the blockade.[304] All these judgements Ewart dutifully wrote into his official diary for dispatch to the War Office.

British intelligence on the revolution and the British government

Did this great range of naval and military intelligence from within Germany itself reach the government during November and December 1918? The politicians at the top, it must be said, were seldom permitted to see or hear anything but the most negative intelligence on Germany. Much of the material that was delivered to the members of the government failed to reflect the insights gained by the men on the ground in Germany especially. Instead, intelligence was sifted in London. The most important intelligence summary which circulated among all members of the War Cabinet was the 'Appreciation of Western and General Report', produced by a team of intelligence experts within Hankey's War Cabinet Secretariat. Not surprisingly, considering the editorial control exerted by George Aston and William Ormsby-Gore, these weekly reports maintained an attitude of intense scepticism towards the new German government.[305] The very first report after

---

[300] Ewart's caption with his passport in Ewart scrapbook, Ewart Papers, 73/88/1.

[301] Ewart Diary, 18 Dec. 1918, Ewart Papers, 73/88/1.

[302] Ewart manuscript Diary, 11 Dec. 1918, Ewart Papers, 73/88/1.

[303] Interview with Pedersen of the Danish Red Cross, Ewart Diary, 16 Dec. 1918, Ewart Papers, 73/88/1.

[304] Account of dinner with Baron and Baroness van Gevers, Ewart Diary, 17 Dec. 1918, Ewart Papers, 73/88/1.

[305] The 'Appreciation of Western and General Report' series was edited by Aston himself, except for the period from mid-Nov. to early Dec. 1918, when Aston undertook a mission to Egypt; see Aston Diary, 21 Nov. 1918, Aston Papers, 6/11.

the revolution put forward the sweeping claim that the majority of German socialists had 'supported the war and the militarist policy'.[306] The political embarrassment of the change of government in Berlin was stressed in the second report. 'The present German policy', Aston reported, 'seems to be to maintain constantly and vociferously that power no longer lies with the parties responsible for the war.' Never afraid to offer polemical advice, Aston suggested that the new German government had no credentials to make such a claim. According to Aston, there were 'no signs or expressions of repentance, from those now claiming to govern, for having given their whole-hearted support to the war policy for over four years—until the Associated Powers defeated the armed forces of Germany'.[307]

In assembling 'evidence' against the German government, Aston and his colleagues generally chose the sceptical judgements still coming from British consulates in the neutral countries. 'Republicanism in Germany is reported to be a sham, intended to mislead', reported Aston, on the strength of a dispatch from Walter Townley in the Netherlands. In early December, prominence was given to Harold Williams's assessment from Switzerland that 'the German spirit is unchanged and that the revolution is unreal'. The Germans, the War Cabinet was told, 'do not feel any anger against the old regime, do not admit that they are beaten, and have the old inveterate hatred of the British'.[308] Aston's reports also repeated the accusation that the German government was behind the social unrest throughout Europe. Aston assured the War Cabinet that the new German socialist government was attempting 'to stir up internal strife in enemy countries, with a view to weakening their power of imposing just conditions of peace'.[309]

The military élite did little to present material from Germany itself that might have balanced this negative portrait. One reason, no doubt, was that the highest ranking army officers were themselves receiving some private information, especially from the French-occupied districts in Germany, that cast doubt on the severity of conditions. For example, Edward Spears, the head of the British Military Mission in Paris, visited Alsace Lorraine in mid-November and wrote a long report to Henry Wilson, circulated also to Hankey, insisting that there was 'no shortage of any kind'.[310] Similarly, Haig himself made a visit to Metz and Strasburg in mid-December and came back convinced that there was no serious food problem.[311] An array of evidence gathered from inside Germany which

[306] 'Appreciation of Western and General Report, no. 94', 14 Nov. 1918, signed by Aston, CAB 24/149.

[307] 'Appreciation of Western and General Report, no. 95', 21 Nov. 1918, signed by Aston, CAB 24/149.

[308] 'Appreciation of Western and General Report, no. 97', 4 Dec. 1918, unsigned, CAB 24/149.

[309] 'Appreciation of Western and General Report, no. 98', 12 Dec. 1918, signed by Aston, CAB 24/149.

[310] Edward Spears to Henry Wilson, 29 Nov. 1918, marked with an explanation that copies had also been sent to Hankey and General Sackville-West, Spears Papers, 1/14.

[311] Haig to Esher, 14 Dec. 1918, Esher Papers, 4/10.

pointed in other directions could have been brought to the War Cabinet by Henry Wilson as CIGS, but Wilson reported little. From all the material flowing back to the War Office from the Armistice Commission at Spa, Henry Wilson chose to report to the Imperial War Cabinet that the latest intelligence from Spa showed that 'the German troops were passing on their way through to Germany in orderly and well-disciplined formation, in good condition, and not at all like a broken army'.[312] Wilson's motives in making this very selective choice of facts are not difficult to discern. At the time, the CIGS was in earnest communication with other generals assuring them of his determination to resist demands for the rapid demobilization of British forces. Thus, the latest information from Spa pointing to German truculence was exactly the type of intelligence that served Wilson's purpose.[313]

The one military figure who had an unmatched opportunity to gain insights into Germany, and to give the Prime Minister himself the details, was Admiral Wemyss. As a member of the original Armistice Commission, Wemyss travelled with Foch to Trèves (Trier) in the American zone of occupation for the negotiations with the Germans over the renewal of the armistice on 12 and 13 December 1918. Wemyss may well have been willing to consider the Germans' plight in a more generous spirit on this occasion. Evidently Lady Wemyss put him under some pressure to take seriously the political and economic situation inside Germany. In the fortnight preceding the negotiations in Trèves, Lady Wemyss organized two personal meetings between W. H. Dawson and her husband, and sent letters to Dawson full of praise for his moderation and good sense while condemning the Admiralty staff as 'devoid of idealism and imagination'.[314]

The negotiations at Trèves, however, were formal and brief, only two one-hour sessions being held before a simple instrument renewing the armistice for another month was signed. The proceedings were dominated by Foch, and the entire affair conducted in the same atmosphere of unrelieved hostility as at Compiègne.[315] Most significantly, as in other contacts with the Germans, the Allies once again advertised their disapproval of the revolution: the German delegation, it was specified, was to be composed of exactly the same members as previously, led by Erzberger, Winterfeldt, Oberndorff, and Vanselow. As Wemyss explained in his diary, 'We had refused to meet anyone else'.[316] The

---

[312] Minutes of the Imperial War Cabinet, 28 Nov. 1918, CAB 23/42.

[313] '[Henry Wilson] is anxious because the Cabinet will not take up the question of the army of the future and will make no provision for the British Army in the East. Now with the election in prospect they will do nothing but electioneering' (Rawlinson Diary, 15 Nov. 1918, Rawlinson Papers, 1/11).

[314] Lady Wemyss to Dawson, 8 Dec., 'Thursday', 12 Dec., undated, 23 and 28 Dec. 1918, Dawson Papers, WHD 401, 403–4, 407–8, 411–12. The paper may well have been the article Dawson published at this time, 'The End and the Beginning', *Contemporary Review*, 114 (Dec. 1918), which praised the revolution and the SPD, and urged the Allies to send immediate food aid to Germany in order to sustain the transition to democracy.

[315] See extracts from Erzberger's memoirs in Epstein, *Erzberger*, 292–3.

[316] Wemyss Diary, 18 Dec. 1918, Wemyss Papers, 5/7.

meaning of this gesture was plain: the Allies denied the revolution's legitimacy; only those delegates appointed by Prince Max before the outbreak of the revolution were acknowledged, and the Allies ruled out any contact with the appointees of the revolutionary Ebert-Haase government.

Outside the formal conferences, there were opportunities to gain some insight into German conditions as Captain Marriott, Wemyss's assistant, interviewed Vanselow. Wemyss gleaned three obvious facts: the Ebert-Haase government was weak and vulnerable to challenge from the Left; Germany's military forces were no longer a credible military threat to the Allies; and the food situation in Germany was critical. On the food issue, the Germans were eloquent: 'The people are tired of the war and are ill, and have no resistance left, and the sooner they get more food the sooner will there be a Government and the smaller the chance of Revolution.' Wemyss did his own tour of Trèves to examine the food situation and he appeared unable to make up his mind on the matter. The people 'did not look actually underfed, though they had not that rather bucolic and well-fed appearance that one generally connects with Germans', he wrote. Food shops, he noted, 'were certainly but sparsely furnished'. But Wemyss found it difficult to feel sympathy for the conquered people. 'I believe them all to be tarred with the same brush of brutality', he confessed in his diary.[317]

Nevertheless, Wemyss did stress in his report to Lloyd George on the Trèves conference the seriousness of the food crisis: 'A Naval officer told my secretary that he believed the sooner food was put into the country the sooner they would be able to get a more stable government.' But Wemyss did nothing to break down prejudice against the Council of People's Commissioners presided over by Ebert and Haase. As Wemyss reported, 'this council has no mandate from anybody'.[318] Wemyss's report for Lloyd George was only a brief document, and again, as in the wake of the Compiègne meeting, no private interview was sought on either side, a mark of the continuing frostiness between the two men.

With so little detailed military intelligence percolating through to the political élite, the only other major source of information on inner Germany was the Diplomatic Service and Foreign Office. During November and December 1918, intelligence on Germany gleaned from secret agents, informers, and the local press was relayed back to London by the diplomats. From the British legations in the neutral countries in particular, but also from Lord Derby in Paris, came a flow of telegrams many of which were circulated to the War Cabinet. In these reports, a number of themes stood out.

First, the diplomats portrayed the new governments in both Berlin and Munich as dangerous and devious. According to their reports, the new German socialist governments were likely to make a propaganda effort directed at social-

---

[317] Wemyss Diary, 18 Dec. 1918, Wemyss Papers, 5/7.
[318] Wemyss to Lloyd George, 15 Dec. 1918, FO 800/201. See also a summary of Wemyss's discussions with Derby, Derby to Balfour, 14 Dec. 1918, Balfour Papers, 49744.

ist opinion in Britain and France.[319] Most importantly, only a week after the revolution, Rumbold revealed in a telegram to London that the German diplomatic service in Switzerland had been ordered by the new government in Berlin to retain its staff and begin a programme of socialist propaganda throughout Western Europe.[320] The new government's denials of any such intentions were also reported, but the essential message in this intelligence was plain: the German revolution had an evangelical potential which threatened to undermine the military victory of the Allies by appealing to the international labour movement.[321]

Secondly, it is clear that the Foreign Office diplomats and staff doubted the German claims to be short of food and in danger of a Bolshevik outbreak. Although the Foreign Office legations passed on Dr Solf's pleas for some revision of the armistice terms, for food to contain the risk of Bolshevism, and for an Allied mission to investigate conditions in Germany, there was unremitting scepticism shown towards the German diplomatic effort. 'German whine' wrote Lancelot Oliphant on one report. 'No doubt the situation is bad: but this is all part of a German campaign to secure easier terms', he wrote on another.[322] Equally dismissive of all German complaints and warnings was Lord Derby in Paris.[323] The refusal to take seriously the food crisis in Germany was paralleled by an indefatigable confidence in Germany's inherent power to resist Bolshevism. Most intelligence generated in the Foreign Office in response to the revolution in November and December 1918 was united in this judgement: Germany was too educated and the German middle class too strong for a Bolshevik regime to gain power. The Bolshevik cry, therefore, was condemned from the outset as German scaremongering.[324] This became a shared conviction across the political, military, and diplomatic élites. In private letters and diaries the British leaders comforted themselves with the observation that Germany could still be dealt with sternly, because the Germans were too 'well-drilled' a people, too 'educated', too

---

[319] e.g. see especially the reports from Berne and Zurich: Rumbold to Foreign Office, 12 Nov. 1918, FO 371/3224; Rumbold to Foreign Office, 15 Nov. 1918, FO 371/3224; Rumbold to Foreign Office, 22 Nov. 1918, enclosing 'Professor Förster to the Allied Governments', dated 20 Nov. 1918, FO 371/3224; French Ministry of Foreign Affairs to Lord Derby, 6 Dec. 1918, FO 371/3226; Zurich Legation to Foreign Office, 12 Nov. 1918, FO 371/3224; and Zurich Legation to Foreign Office, 13 Nov. 1918, FO 371/3224.

[320] Rumbold to Foreign Office, 16 Nov. 1918, FO 371/3224.

[321] On the German Government's denial, see 'Memorandum' recording an interview with Count Leyden, 25 Nov. 1918, FO 371/3224, and Rumbold to Foreign Office, 28 Nov. 1918, FO 371/3224.

[322] e.g. see W. Townley to Foreign Office, 17 Nov. 1918, FO 371/3224, and minute by Oliphant; Lord Kilmarnock to Foreign Office, 23 Nov. 1918, FO 371/3224, and minute by Oliphant.

[323] See Derby to Balfour, 15 Nov. 1918, Derby Papers, 28/2/1; Derby to Foreign Office, 23 Nov. 1918, and Pichon to Balfour, 23 Nov. 1918, FO 371/3224; and Derby to Balfour, 18 Nov. 1918, Derby Papers, 28/2/1.

[324] See e.g. Rumbold to Foreign Office, 13 Nov. 1918, and covering minute by J. Y. Simpson, FO 371/3224; Zurich Legation to Foreign Office, 15 Nov. 1918, FO 371/3224; Rumbold to Foreign Office, 7 Dec. 1918, FO 371/3224; and 'Memorandum on Socialist Theory and Socialist Parties in Germany', by Mr Robieson, 24 Nov. 1918, FO 371/3224.

'solid', and with too much 'common sense' and 'natural discipline' to lapse into Bolshevism.[325]

The Political Intelligence Department of the Foreign Office was, at least initially, as distrustful of the new government and its socialist politics as the ambassadors and permanent diplomats. The revolutionary events of early November were deeply disturbing to the PID. As has been seen, in the last days of October 1918 the PID had advocated a more moderate response to Prince Max's government in order to avoid revolution. The German revolution and the formation of an all-socialist government derailed the strategy completely. To say that the German revolution was unwelcome to the PID is an understatement—it was the dreaded outcome. The German Liberalism which the PID had always hoped to bolster had apparently evaporated. The moment for Germany's redemption as a Liberal state appeared to have come and gone, displaced by the socialist menace. German history had refused to be British history. As Headlam-Morley lamented in the midst of reports of revolution in Germany, 'at this moment events progress more rapidly than thought'.[326]

The cautious response of the PID to the revolution of November, therefore, was no surprise. On the day of the armistice, the PID produced a memorandum for the War Cabinet on the German socialist parties and their leaders. The memorandum, based on interviews with an Estonian socialist leader, gave a fully rounded portrait of Germany's socialists, acknowledging the resistance of the USPD leaders in particular to militarism. But the report conveyed warnings. First, the moderate SPD leaders were presented as only temporarily in command of the situation. In the opinion of the PID, Ebert and Scheidemann were most likely to be supplanted by the Independent Socialists of the left-wing USPD in the near future. Second, while the USPD were quite properly not equated with Bolshevism, the party was accused nevertheless of being strongly internationalist in orientation and hence likely to embark on international propaganda. The PID anticipated that 'they would try and spread their ideas to England, France, and Italy with a view to bringing about radical changes in the social and political conditions of those countries'.[327] Thus the USPD, whose unblemished record of opposition to the war might otherwise have been expected to appeal to the War Cabinet, were presented as potentially subversive. Other PID reports stressed that the victory of socialism in Germany did not necessarily make the realization of British war aims easier. For example, the PID reported that opinion was divided in the SPD on the issue of Germany's need for colonies, with a section of the party advocating German colonialism as a means of realizing raw materi-

[325] e.g. Derby to Balfour, 17 Nov. 1918, Derby Papers, 28/2/1; Godley to Allen, 15 Nov. 1918, Allen Papers, MI/15; Rawlinson Diary, 9 Dec. 1918, Rawlinson Papers, 1/11.

[326] PID Memorandum, 'The Old and the New', undated but late Oct. or early Nov. 1918, HMP, HDLM, Acc. 727, Box 2.

[327] PID Memorandum, 'The Social Democratic Parties and Leaders in Germany', 11 Nov. 1918 (PID catalogue no. Germany /022), GT 6264, CAB 24/69, and FO 371/3224.

als and full employment.[328] Similarly, George Saunders also advised that the German socialists were less likely than the radical liberals to accept the argument that the new German regime should bear the guilt and pay the price of reparation as much as the old.[329] In this way the PID encouraged the Lloyd George government in its determination to shun the new socialist government in Berlin. In the judgement of the PID, the reasons for isolating Germany were plain enough. After her revolution, Germany was more untrustworthy than ever. William Tyrrell's view, for example, just a week after the revolution, was summarized in a cablegram from the PID to Arthur Murray, the Washington agent:

He [Tyrrell] says you cannot lay too much stress on the importance of dealing effectively with Bolshevism. Having freed the small nationalities of Europe from Prussianism, we must do all in our power to preserve them from Bolshevism, which is a menace as great, if not greater, to their national life; and not only to them but to all civilisation. He thinks the present German government will play on Bolshevism for all it is worth in order to get off more lightly, and thinks that Scheidemann is closely connected with the present revolutionary agitation in Holland.[330]

Headlam-Morley agreed with this assessment. In a memorandum produced by Headlam-Morley in late November he explained that the six-man revolutionary committee in Berlin had to be reluctantly acknowledged as the *de facto* government of Germany during the initial period of armistice and armistice renewal because there was no viable alternative. However, such a self-appointed government would be quite unacceptable when it came to actual peace negotiations. 'The central government, such as it is', he wrote, 'has been established purely by revolutionary action in Berlin. It has no right of any kind to speak for Germany as a whole.' Headlam-Morley even ventured the reactionary judgement that the only holders of legitimate power were the members of the old Reichstag and Bundesrat. He advised that this should be explained to Berlin in blunt terms. The Allies must say 'that they can have no dealings with Germany, and in particular cannot enter into any peace negotiations, until a government has been established which is a genuine representative of the public'.[331] Thus, the Allies' decision to deal with Germany only through the Armistice Commission until the Peace Conference could convene pleased the PID. The unfortunate socialist revolution was effectively isolated.

At first, the PID also did nothing to counter the campaign in the popular press suggesting that the revolution was in some way counterfeit. Indeed, the PID fell

---

[328] PID Memorandum, 'Memorandum on German Colonies and Popular Feeling in Germany' (PID Catalogue no. Germany /023), 15 Nov. 1918, CAB 24/70, and PID Memorandum, 'German Colonies and German Socialism' (PID Catalogue no. Germany /026), 31 Dec. 1918, GT 6609, CAB 24/73.

[329] George Saunders, minute dated 11 Nov. 1918, on Acton to Balfour, 31 Oct. 1918, FO 371/3224.

[330] Cablegram to Col. Arthur Murray, 15 Nov. 1918, from 'C. S. A.', Elibank Papers, 8807.

[331] Memorandum entitled 'The Government in Germany', Headlam-Morley to Tyrrell, 25 Nov. 1918, HMP, HDLM, Acc. 727, Box 16.

in behind the campaign. Harold Williams, the Geneva correspondent of Lloyd George's *Daily Chronicle*, was prominent among those journalists pursuing this theme and he sought to persuade his friends in the PID to be on guard against the revolution. Writing to the PID from Geneva just days after the armistice, he claimed to have information on the revolution, chiefly from the American Professor George Herron, a Christian Socialist with close connections to the Bavarian USPD. This amounted to a string of quite unsubstantiated but extremely damaging allegations about the 'spirit' of the revolution. Everything pointed to the German revolution being 'a very rotten thing'. According to Williams, 'the danger is this':

The revolution is not in any sense a real one. The German spirit is unchanged. There is not a sign of repentance. Democracy is a new mode now, and people are simply changing their dress. They are not really angry with the old regime, the whole thing is simply a dodge to save the Germans' face. They do not admit they are beaten, they hate us as much as ever, and under the new forms, so long as they last, they will pursue the old policy. I have never felt the poison of the modern German spirit so much as I feel it here and now. It affects me like the odour of Bolshevism, which, of course, is one of its by-products.

The leaders of this 'so-called revolution' were merely 'the herpes of yesterday'. Even the best of them were 'hampered by their devitalising Marxian creed'. In essence, the revolution was simply a new 'peace offensive' which, laced with socialist slogans, might prove to be 'even more dangerous' than the old. 'In any case', Williams concluded, 'it seems clear that any relaxation of the armistice is quite impossible under present conditions.' Here was an emotional and comprehensive condemnation. The revolution was both too moderate and too radical, too insincerely reformist and yet incipiently Bolshevik. Opponents of all things German could take their pick. In spite of the absence of facts in Williams's assessment, the PID decided to print it.[332] The letter was turned into an official PID memorandum for circulation to the War Cabinet in late November.

During much of December 1918, attitudes in the PID remained hostile. Antisocialist themes pervaded its advice. For example, the PID advised the government to resist the labour and socialist proposal for an international labour conference in parallel with the coming peace conference. Such a labour conference was bound to attempt to go over the heads of government representatives, according to the PID. 'It is to be argued that the British Government will oppose any proposals of this kind and that their whole influence will be thrown into maintaining the existing order in regard to these matters', preached the PID.[333]

---

[332] PID Memorandum, 'Extracts from a letter from Mr Harold Williams, *Daily Chronicle* correspondent in Geneva' (PID catalogue no. Germany /025) undated, GT 6389, CAB 24/70 and FO 371/3224.
[333] Typed memorandum on the proposal for an international Labour conference to be 'sitting side by side with the Peace Conference', undated, but, judging from the content, prepared for the Entente Conference in London, 3 Dec. 1918, HMP, HDLM, Acc. 727, Box 11, in file marked 'Preparations for the Peace Conference'.

In addition, a special preoccupation of the PID at this time was the advocacy of measures to moderate the German revolution. A wider occupation of Germany was favoured as the best option. In early December Saunders and Headlam-Morley prepared a memorandum for Tyrrell arguing that the occupation of Berlin itself was 'for political reasons extremely desirable'. It was unfortunate, argued the memorandum, that the armistice terms had not provided for whole-sale occupation. This would be good for all Germans, wrote Headlam-Morley, as it would be 'an actual demonstration before their eyes of their defeat'.[334] Saunders, in particular, looked forward to the ruthless suppression of Bolshevism by military forces loyal to the central government in Berlin. Anticipating the cre-ation of the *Freikorps*, Saunders advised that the real test for the new government was its willingness to form 'a trustworthy military force capable of acting swiftly and firmly against local insurrection'. Similarly, if the Allies were to send in food commissioners, argued Saunders, then these should be 'backed by an adequate show of military force'.[335] Again, Saunders's political preferences shaped his intelligence advice; his day books for this period are littered with expressions of horror and contempt for the influence of left-wing socialism in the new govern-ment in Berlin. For example, a speech from Ebert looking forward to the cre-ation of a great republic in Germany on American lines was condemned with the words 'Sucks up to Wilson. Dangerous spirit'. A speech from Haase expressing a preference for the consolidation of the revolution before rushing to elections was denounced as a plot to establish a 'Socialistic Republic'.[336]

Beyond the official memoranda and telegrams, the private sources of the key Foreign Office staff also reveal this same intense suspicion towards the revolu-tion. In late November, for example, Lord Hardinge wrote privately to his friend General Sir Reginald Wingate in Cairo:

> What a wonderful thing this German débâcle has been! It really has been almost too good to be true. Still, I am not very satisfied with the so-called revolution in Germany; there appears to me to be a good deal of camouflage about it. One must remember that Solf and Erzberger were two of the most prominent members of the party desiring our destruction and German domination in Europe. Our terms under these circumstances cannot be too hard, and when the Allies have made up their minds as to what those terms should be they must be forced upon the Germans without discussion. The big stick is what bullies like them understand better than anything else.

Hardinge's effusion demonstrated all the characteristics of the typical Whitehall reaction: the revolution was condemned as a charade, a sweeping and most inac-curate judgement of the wartime record of the new German leaders was employed to discredit all the changes in Berlin, and the school playground language in denunciation of the 'bullies' was steadfastly maintained. Most

---

[334] Headlam-Morley to Tyrrell, 7 Dec. 1918, HMP, HDLM, Acc. 727, Box 16.
[335] Saunders minute, dated 28 Dec. 1918, on Rumbold to Foreign Office, 7 Dec. 1918, FO 371/3224.
[336] Saunders Day Book VI (Nov. 1918–Feb. 1919), HMP, HDLM, Acc. 800/1.

importantly, this vehement denial of the legitimacy of the revolution was linked to the victors' plans for a stern peace settlement to be imposed without any genuine negotiations.[337]

In conclusion, the very close coincidence of the two key events that ended the First World War, the revolution in Germany and the armistice at Compiègne, had enormous consequences for the history of the peacemaking. When the armistice documents were constructed at the Versailles Council on 4 November, all the delegates, including the British, understood that the process being initiated was to be a conditional armistice. In agreeing to the Lansing note all the Associated Powers agreed that they were committed to an eventual peace settlement based not only on the Fourteen Points but on all Wilson's speeches of 1918. In this sense, under great pressure to obtain an armistice, the British accepted the fact that a 'dictated peace' in the pure sense of the phrase had been given up. It was to be an armistice as conventionally understood, with formations facing each other in the field, their arms silenced, while a peace settlement was negotiated. Certainly, the terms ensured the military paralysis of Germany, but the armistice and peace to follow were still to be conditional. The British did secure two reservations to the Fourteen Points, but these did not threaten the conditional nature of the armistice contract. The British were still bound to the bulk of the Wilsonian programme. Balfour acknowledged the pressures that he and Lloyd George were under in accepting these limitations when he addressed the British Empire Delegation in June 1919: 'The Prime Minister and he suddenly found themselves faced with the Fourteen Points and time was short to discuss them. There really was no question whether there ought to be an armistice or not. There had to be an armistice. Time was the essence of the matter. They had to take the Fourteen Points'.[338]

Within the space of a week, the revolution in Germany transformed the situation. German military power was not just paralysed, it melted away. The Germans were powerless to resist any of the terms. Thus, what had been envisaged as a conditional armistice on 4 November could be represented as an 'unconditional surrender' on 11 November. The new situation was full of perils, and opportunities, for the British. There were the perils that the armistice might collapse, that the German battleships might not be given up, that the British forces or the British people might succumb to revolution, and even that progressive politicians might persuade the British people that a democratic Germany deserved a moderate peace. On the other hand there were great opportunities. There was the opportunity to exploit the helplessness of the enemy, to flaunt from the hustings the victory as an unlimited victory, and—most importantly— to quietly ignore the Wilsonian restraints that had been accepted before the revolution rendered Germany powerless.

[337] Hardinge to Wingate, 28 Nov. 1918, Hardinge Papers, vol. 39.
[338] Minutes of the British Empire Delegation, 1 June 1919, CAB 29/28.

5

Electioneering and the Shunning of Socialist Germany, November–December 1918

... I must solemnly say that I think it will stand recorded that in the critical week in November, after the armistice, when the world was malleable as never before, the Prime Minister, who had more power to mould it than any other single man, definitely took the lower rather than the higher course, thereby doing irreparable damage to British prestige, setting up currents of feeling which rendered wise statesmanship infinitely difficult in the following months, and delaying, and perhaps endangering, the whole process of European recuperation.

Alfred Zimmern to Philip Kerr, 15 March 1919[1]

ONLY three days after the armistice, a new factor was introduced into British policy-making that would heighten pressures on all those associated with the 'knock-out blow' Coalition to denigrate the German revolution—the announcement of a general election. In the House of Commons on Thursday, 14 November, Bonar Law revealed the intensely controversial timetable for the long-awaited dissolution. After months of speculation, it was at last official: the old parliament was to be prorogued within a week and the people were to vote for a new parliament on 14 December. The results of counting were not to be announced before 28 December, a gesture supposedly to ensure ample opportunity for the counting of the soldiers' votes.[2] On the same day that Bonar Law made this announcement, a special conference of the British Labour Party decided to withdraw from Lloyd George's Coalition, a decision violently condemned by the Coalition press.[3] The campaign had begun. Domestic politics, therefore, was to be roughly intruded into the process of preparation for peace for at least the next six weeks.

How then did the general election of 1918 affect the British response to the German revolution? The key factor in the situation can be briefly stated: after 10 November Germany had a government that was much more politically progressive than the government of any of the nations that sat in judgement upon her,

[1] R. Brand Papers, 42.   [2] *The Times*, 15 Nov. 1918.
[3] e.g. *Daily Express*, editorials, 'A Colossal Blunder' and 'Advice to Labour Leaders', 15 and 16 Nov. 1918.

including the Lloyd George Coalition government. At this point, the details of the new German government are worth recalling. The exclusively socialist Council of People's Commissioners was the most advanced government Germany had ever seen, and its anti-militarist credentials were strong. The three left-wing socialist members included Hugo Haase, the USPD leader and defender of Karl Liebknecht in the courts during the war. His companions were Wilhelm Dittmann, a stout anti-militarist only recently released from prison, and Emil Barth, the leader of the Revolutionary Shop Stewards organization which led the strikes in Berlin in January 1918. The three SPD members, Ebert, Scheidemann, and Landsberg, were compromised in many eyes by their record of support for the war. However, their followers were correct in stressing that the SPD leaders had often condemned German annexationists and that they had vigorously advocated domestic democratization throughout the four years of war. Notwithstanding the fact that the SPD representatives had only smuggled themselves into the actual revolution at the last moment, their progressive political outlook was not in doubt.

But socialism of either brand, USPD or SPD, at the helm in Berlin created a situation big with political menace for the governing élite in Britain, as political intelligence advisers close to the top in London instantly appreciated. For example, Basil Thomson, the domestic intelligence chief, advised the War Cabinet on the eve of the German revolution that a democratized Germany would only serve to strengthen the hands of British Radicals. As Thomson explained, the 'line taken by the [British] pacifists is that a vindictive policy towards Germany will cause future wars and that as the Germans have got a more democratic government than England, we should only antagonize the German democracy by insisting on indemnities'.[4] It followed logically from this advice that, if the British government wished for a profitable peace, with a large indemnity, then the best tactic was to counter the 'pacifist' premiss by denying that any satisfactory shift to a democratic government had taken place in Germany. This was exactly the political tactic adopted by the government in the context of an election aimed to neutralize the Labour challenge at home.

Procrastination: Britain, the United States, and the question of food for revolutionary Germany

Nevertheless, in the hours immediately after the armistice, the crisis inside Germany competed with the election for Lloyd George's attention. On armistice night, Lloyd George dined with F. E. Smith, Henry Wilson, and Churchill at Downing Street. The group discussed 'principally the coming General Election', but also the reports of starvation in Germany. As Churchill recalled, the conversation turned on the 'great qualities of the German people' and the need to

---

[4] 'Fortnightly Report on Pacifism and Revolutionary Organisations in the United Kingdom and Morale in France and Italy', 4 Nov. 1918, GT 6201, CAB 24/69.

enlist them in the reconstruction of Europe. Churchill suggested that the British should immediately 'rush a dozen great ships crammed with provisions into Hamburg' to stave off Bolshevism.[5] The next day Lloyd George received the report he had so urgently requested on Armistice Day from Sir Joseph Maclay and Sir John Beale on the practicalities of sending immediate aid. Their report confirmed that it was indeed possible to provide shipments of flour and cereals 'at once'.[6]

The possibility of a rapid British response, however, receded almost immediately. A number of factors worked to dissipate interest in the project: British suspicion of German-American collusion, British resentment of American economic leadership, and British preoccupation with social stability at home. On 10 November Ebert, from his position as the new Chancellor, had directed at least three urgent requests for relaxation of the blockade, not to the victors as a whole, but to President Wilson alone.[7] These messages presented the new German government as one animated by 'the common aims and ideals of democracy' and reminded Wilson that he had promised not to make war on the German people. Food assistance was vital, pleaded Ebert's notes, if Bolshevism was to be avoided. At least one of these messages was intercepted and delayed by the British Foreign Office, a minute upon the document informing Lloyd George that 'we are of course holding it up as it has a reference to one of the armistice terms', that is, to the blockade.[8] In any case, Wilson answered the German requests in his address to Congress on 11 November, and in a formal note to Germany the next day, promising speedy assistance. In addition, he warned the Germans against Bolshevist excesses—as Ebert had urged him to do. These exchanges, in giving the appearance of continuing unilateral negotiations between Germany and the United States, antagonized the British leaders against Wilson and raised suspicions regarding the real internal state of Germany.

Hostility to the American President was still commonplace among Lloyd George's satellites. Henry Wilson, for example, recorded in his diary on 9 November that the British were intercepting all the cablegrams between House in Europe and Wilson in Washington and that they were 'amazing reading'. 'I believe Wilson to be an unscrupulous knave and hater of England and House to be a poor miserable tool', wrote General Wilson.[9] Similarly, Lord Crawford, who thought Britain scandalously unprepared to take on the essential task of relief in Europe, wrote contemptuously of 'the ostentation and vainglory of Wilson

---

[5] Henry Wilson Diary, 11 Nov. 1918, Henry Wilson Papers, DS MISC/80, and Winston Churchill, *The World Crisis: The Aftermath* (London, 1929), 21.

[6] Joseph Maclay, Shipping Controller, to Lloyd George, 12 Nov. 1918, Lloyd George Papers, F/35/2/85.

[7] Klaus Schwabe, *Woodrow Wilson, Revolutionary Germany and Peacemaking, 1918–1919* (Chapel Hill, NC, 1985), 121–2, and Arno J. Mayer, *Politics and Diplomacy of Peacemaking* (London, 1968), 97–8.

[8] Solf to Lansing, 10 Nov. 1918, Lloyd George Papers, F/47/4/5.

[9] Henry Wilson Diary, 9 Nov. 1918, Henry Wilson Papers, DS MISC/80.

posing as the universal benefactor'. Germany's pleas to Wilson, wrote Crawford, were issued 'with an insistence that arouses my suspicion'.[10] In addition, news of Wilson's decision to dispatch the head of his Food Administration, Herbert Hoover, to Europe immediately in order to take command of relief was not likely to impress British opinion.[11] During the war Hoover had antagonized many in the British governing élite and he had come to be seen as a mere stalking-horse for American economic interests.[12] Moreover, in the days following the armistice, the idea that Britain's own food resources should be mustered as a first priority for Britain herself, as an insurance against social discontent, was recommended at the highest level. For example, on 12 November Alfred Mond circulated to the War Cabinet a document entitled 'Suggestions to Prevent the Spread of Revolutionary Ideas in the United Kingdom' which cautioned against the feeding of liberated areas or enemy nations. Mond caught the mood of the moment, warning that 'a certain fever of revolutionary Bolshevist ideas' was evident in Britain; if projects for feeding 'our late enemies' and other people in far away places went ahead, while food in England was short, then he anticipated that 'a very dangerous spirit indeed may be generated here'.[13] On 13 November, Lloyd George told a meeting of trade unionists and employers at the Caxton Hall that Britain was under no obligation to feed the Germans. Their shipping would have to be surrendered first, he explained. 'But at the same time', said Lloyd George, 'when one's enemy surrenders I do not think one ought to let him starve.'[14] Finally, the French also cautioned the British against acting hastily on the matter of food. Clemenceau suggested on 14 November that any revictualling of the Central Powers must be linked to their surrender of shipping. By 19 November Lloyd George had committed himself to this position in a reply to the French premier.[15]

The plunge into the general election: the Coalition as a rampart against revolution at home and abroad

In any case, by mid-November the leaders of the British government were distracted from the whole business of peacemaking. The rush into electioneering, above all, ensured that the German food issue lost all urgency. Indeed, the pri-

---

[10] Lord Crawford Diary, vol. xxxiii, 10 and 15 Nov. 1918, Crawford Papers.

[11] Herbert Hoover, *The Memoirs of Herbert Hoover: Years of Adventure, 1874–1920* (New York, 1951), pp. 277–9.

[12] e.g. see the typical disparaging reference In Lord Crawford Diary: 'Nobody exploits & blackmails us with greater zest than Hoover. He cd. not act in a more unfriendly way towards us. Is the man straight?', vol. xxxi, 7 Dec. 1917. Other unfriendly remarks in Lord Crawford Diary, vol. xxxi, 1 Dec. 1917, and vol. xxxii, 25 July and 13 Aug. 1918, Crawford Papers.

[13] Alfred Mond, 'Suggestions to Prevent the Spread of Revolutionary Ideas in the United Kingdom', 12 Nov. 1918, GT 6270, CAB 24/69.

[14] *Daily Express*, 15 Nov. 1918.

[15] Clemenceau to Lloyd George, 14 Nov. 1918, Lloyd George Papers, F 50/3/94, and Lloyd George to Clemenceau, 19 Nov., CAB 24/70.

macy of domestic politics was a practical reality within the Prime Minister's circle not twenty-four hours after the armistice. The electoral pact sealed between Bonar Law and Lloyd George in Paris at the beginning of November was now to be redeemed. The precise details of the deals underpinning the so-called 'coupon election' have been analysed by many writers and do not require reiteration here.[16] It is important, however, to recall the highlights of armistice week, filled as it was with political deal-making. Lloyd George began on the morning of 12 November, gathering his Liberal supporters together at Downing Street to prepare them for the continuation of his Coalition and an imminent election (although no date was given).[17] In a speech lasting an hour, Lloyd George warned against reaction, vindictiveness towards Germany, and the belief that victory could be used to delay social reform. Even the 'revolutionary spirit in the air' gained praise. The Lloyd George Liberals were assured that all the great Liberal causes, including a peace of reconciliation, were safe within a Coalition where the faithful Liberal Prime Minister held ultimate authority. Herbert Fisher, who had been sweating for two days over a final draft of the Coalition manifesto for Lloyd George, 'a Coalition document which I can sign' as he put it, was much relieved.[18] It was, as Fisher reported, 'a thoroughly satisfactory speech from the Liberal point of view'.[19] The Liberal elder, Lord Buckmaster, however, was more prescient: 'The P.M.'s speech to his supporters expressed in fine language the views I hold. I do not understand how they are to be reconciled with a Coalition.'[20] On the same day, Bonar Law, Balfour, Carson, and Long addressed the Conservative Party MPs and officers at the Connaught Rooms on Kingsway and gained their endorsement for the continuation of the great experiment of Coalition under Lloyd George's leadership into the dangerous post-war period.[21] All the great Conservative causes were safe, the Conservative leaders assured their party faithful, in a Coalition within which the Conservatives would continue to be dominant.

The 'opposition' emerged too within a week of the armistice. On 13 November Lloyd George made one last effort to keep the Labour Party within the Coalition, addressing a special meeting of 'patriotic' Labour representatives at the Caxton

---

[16] e.g. see Trevor Wilson, 'The Coupon and the British General Election of 1918', *Journal of Modern History*, 36/1 (Mar. 1964), 28–42, his account in *Downfall of the Liberal Party* (London, 1966), ch. 6, the revisionist view offered in Edward David, 'The Liberal Party Divided', *Historical Journal*, 13/3 (1970), 509–33 (which reaffirms the importance of the Maurice Debate as the great divide), K. O. Morgan, *Consensus and Disunity* (Oxford, 1979), ch. 2, and the most recent analysis in John Turner, *British Politics and the Great War* (London, 1992), ch. 9.

[17] See *Westminster Gazette, The Times,* and *Daily Chronicle*, 13 Nov. 1918.

[18] H. A. L. Fisher to L. Fisher, 10 Nov. 1918, Fisher Diary, 12 Nov. 1918, Headlam-Morley Papers, Acc. 800, HDLM 3.

[19] H. A. L. Fisher Diary, 12 Nov. 1918, Headlam-Morley Papers, Acc. 800, HDLM 3.

[20] Buckmaster to Scott, 15 Nov. 1918, C. P. Scott Papers, 335/54.

[21] 'Report of Proceedings at a Meeting of the Party Consisting of Members of both Houses of Parliament and the Members of the Central Council', Connaught Rooms, Kingsway, 12 Nov. 1918, Bonar Law Papers, BL 95/3.

Hall. He promised devotion to the cause of reconstruction, and offered assurances of a moderate peace. 'Do not let us behave like small men', he said. 'Let
us have no vengeance, no trampling down of a fallen foe.' There would be 'stern
justice', he promised, but peacemaking would proceed in such a way 'that even
the enemy will feel that we were fighting for high ideals and not fighting for mere
greed or mere vengeance'.[22] The Prime Minister's moral suasion was insufficient.
The Labour Party majority was committed to its programme for a 'New Social
Order'. A special Labour Party conference on the following day, 14 November,
voted in favour of the withdrawal of Labour from the Coalition and resolved
upon Labour competing in the election in its own right. In addition, Labour
demanded representation at the coming Peace Conference, as had been promised
by Lloyd George, so it was now revealed, in December 1916.[23] This historic
decision to leave the Lloyd George Coalition testified to the mood of distrust in
the government that had slowly permeated the Labour movement ever since the
rupture between Arthur Henderson and Lloyd George over the Stockholm affair
in 1917. Only three Labour MPs, most prominently George Barnes, agreed to
stay with Lloyd George.[24]

Similarly, while the Asquithian Liberals were loath at first to present them-
selves as a group in outright opposition to the Coalition, it was plain that the
leading men closest to Asquith could not reconcile themselves to Lloyd George's
leadership. Asquith himself sought an interview with Lloyd George on 14
November, only to learn that everything was in place already for the election.
The electoral arrangements between Freddy Guest, Lloyd George's whip, and
Sir George Younger, the Conservative Party Chairman, stitched together in late
October, could not be undone.[25] Under the deal, only 150 Liberals judged as
loyal to the Lloyd George government would be given a letter of support from
the two leaders of the Coalition, the infamous 'coupon' as the Asquithians were
to dub it. Local Conservative Associations were to be induced to stand aside for
these 150 Liberals only. Lloyd George believed, not unreasonably, that he was
saving a larger number than the electorate might otherwise tolerate. But a
Conservative majority within the Coalition was virtually guaranteed. Moreover,
in the election to come, the political forces that would be targeted as 'the enemy
within' were absolutely plain. J. A. Spender, editor of the Asquithian *Westminster
Gazette*, sketched the situation satirically:

> The sum of the matter seems to be that the Tories and the Lloyd George Liberals have
> made a compact together: the one to avoid Bolshevism, the other to avoid reaction; the
> one to obtain Tariff Reform, the other to maintain Free Trade; the one to pass Home

---

[22] *Daily Express*, 15 Nov. 1918.
[23] The proceedings are in *The Times*, 15 Nov. 1918. The promise of Dec. 1916 was revealed for
the first time on the eve of the conference in *The Times*, 14 Nov. 1918.
[24] Barnes, G. H. Roberts, and G. Wardle were the three Labour representatives who eventually
defied the conference. Barnes's decision was announced even before the conference, in *The Times*, 14
Nov. 1918.
[25] Turner, *British Politics and the Great War*, 319.

Rule, the other to obstruct it, and that this is to be presented to the county as 'reconstruction', and all opposition to it branded as disloyalty and faction.[26]

In fact, this neatly captured the thrust of the oratory when the three Coalition leaders, Lloyd George, Bonar Law, and Barnes, opened their joint campaign on Saturday, 16 November, from the one platform at the Central Hall, a platform that 'bristled with conspicuous Unionist leaders, grand old Tories; "Die-Hards" even'.[27] In their speeches, the Coalition leaders presented themselves as the earnest representatives of all true patriots, those who put national interest ahead of the demands of class and faction. Those outside the Coalition, both the Labour Party, which had chosen to go, and the Asquithian Liberals, some of whom had been pushed, were all castigated alike as wreckers. On the same day, the crucial letter from the Prime Minister to Bonar Law, dated 2 November, the letter outlining the common programme upon which the Coalition was supposedly based, was released to the press. In this letter, drafted in fact by Bonar Law, the long-established gaps between the Conservative and Liberal positions were smoothed over with slippery phrases. Significant concessions towards the 'economic warriors' were given top billing; the Coalition would introduce imperial preference (without food taxes), protection for 'key industries', and protection against 'dumping'. Similarly, the Prime Minister proclaimed the right to deliver Home Rule to Ireland, qualified by a promise not to coerce Ulster, and an assurance that Home Rule would be 'postponed until the condition of Ireland makes it possible'.[28]

In this first week of political manœuvring, it is important to note, Germany was not entirely lost from view. Indeed, in several of the key speeches launching the election adventure, Coalition politicians pointed to the German revolution as a deeply disturbing development abroad which further justified the prolongation of the Coalition at home. The victory of democratic socialism in Germany was not offered a word of welcome. On the contrary, it furnished another useful argument in favour of the solidarity of all anti-socialist forces in Britain. Addressing the Conservative parliamentary meeting at the Connaught Rooms, for example, Balfour explained his conviction that the essence of the Coalition was resistance to social disruption. 'Still more do I feel it', he said, 'when I look around the international situation and see how profound is the shock which this great war has inflicted upon the whole social fabric of civilised society.' Patriots such as himself, he averred, could not believe that Britain herself could face difficulties 'comparable to those which are breaking into fragments ancient states'. But still, Balfour advised his audience, all should beware: 'if you look back upon history', he warned, 'you will always see that any great social disease which has visited the Continent has been repeated, though faintly repeated, in this island.' For this

---

[26] *Westminster Gazette*, editorial, 'Setting the Scene', 13 Nov. 1918.
[27] *Westminster Gazette*, 16 Nov. 1918.
[28] Speeches are in *The Times*, 18 Nov. 1918.

reason 'all men of sober thought' had a duty to unite within the Coalition.[29] Similarly, in his speech at the opening of the campaign at the Central Hall, Lloyd George made a dramatic reference to the disorder on the Continent. Indeed, he appeared ready to frighten his audience with the spectre of revolution in order to muster them into the fastness of the Coalition. 'At this moment the air of Europe is quivering with revolution. Two thirds of Europe has been swept by a devastating deluge and the situation is full of perilous possibilities', he declared. If selfishness and faction prevailed in Britain, he warned his supporters, then 'the institutions even of this country may follow those in the rest of Europe'.[30] When other leading Coalition politicians spoke for the first time about the German revolution, they cast doubt upon its sincerity. Lord Reading, for example, explained that Germany had given up 'not because she had changed her views, but because she knew she was absolutely beaten'. The British people must not be taken in, he warned, by the Germans' sudden anxiety 'to fall in with the views of our country'. [31]

The new socialist leaders in Germany, it is important to note, did react to these first indications that the British political leaders were reacting negatively to the revolution. For example, in an address on 13 November Scheidemann criticized Lloyd George's Guildhall speech, in which, as has been seen, he had insisted that the German people had been at one with the militarists throughout the war. 'Mr Lloyd George knows very well', Scheidemann protested, 'that large circles of the German nation, and even a large part of its old government, have never approved the principles followed by the former Chief Army Administration, and that they have repeatedly given expression to this disapproval before the whole world.' The speech was intercepted by Admiralty wireless but not reported in Britain.[32]

Thus, at the outset of the campaign, the Coalition leaders encouraged their supporters to see the revolutions in Europe simply as further evidence of German malevolence. The revolution was used to complete a portrait of the sinister forces abroad in the world against which the Coalition was the only safe redoubt.

The 'economic warriors', the demand for an indemnity, and the capitulation of British political leadership

The story of the 'khaki election' has been told most effectively by a number of historians, most prominently Robert Bunselmeyer.[33] There is no need, therefore,

---

[29] Balfour's speech, in 'Report of Proceedings at a Meeting of the Party Consisting of Members of both Houses of Parliament and the Members of the Central Council', Connaught Rooms, Kingsway, 12 Nov. 1918, Bonar Law Papers, BL 95/3.

[30] 'Coalition Party Meeting. Report of speeches delivered at the Central Hall, Westminster, Saturday 16 Nov. 1918', transcript of shorthand notes by Miss Stevenson, Bonar Law Papers, BL 95/3.

[31] Lord Reading quoted in *Evening Standard*, 19 Nov. 1918.

[32] 'Wireless Press, Admiralty, Serial no. 7124, 13 Nov. 1918', George Cave Papers, provisional number, 62497.

[33] Robert Bunselmeyer, *The Cost of the War, 1914–1919: British Economic War Aims and the Origins of the Reparations* (Hamden, Conn., 1975). See also the most recent assessment in Bruce Kent, *The*

for a full account of the election to be offered here. Rather, the special impact of the election on British attitudes to the German revolution is examined here. The crucial point to be developed is that the election led to a further distortion of outlook on the German revolution and the internal condition of Germany. A denial that a genuine revolution had taken place in Germany, and even a denial that Germany was suffering serious privation, assisted in making the case for a 'tough peace' against the German nation. The political requirements of the election, therefore, demanded that the 'counterfeit revolution' thesis be upheld.

From the moment of the armistice, the 'economic warriors' were active in propelling the issue of the indemnity to the forefront of political discussion. The furore over the Lansing Note provoked by Hughes had alerted many in these circles to the threat posed to long-standing plans for an indemnity. For example, Sir William Bull, Chairman of the London Conservatives, received a letter from a business friend on 9 November urging him to protest against 'the secret peace' made by Lloyd George with House, because it was 'monstrous that we should have to pay for a war provoked by Germany'.[34] The issue of indemnity was raised at question time in the House of Commons on 12 November by Robert Houston, the shipowner and Conservative MP. Was it true that the Allies had actually accepted the Fourteen Points? Was it true that compensation from Germany was limited to civilian damage? Or were the Allies determined 'to make Germany pay in full for the expenditure Germany and her allies have inflicted', including 'all pensions to sailors and soldiers and their dependants'? Here was an opportunity for the government to confirm that the commitments given in the Lansing Note were made in good faith by Britain. But Bonar Law walked away from this opportunity. In a written answer, he replied that it was 'not possible for me to make any statement on this subject'.[35] Later in debate Sir Joseph Walton, a colliery owner and Coalition Liberal MP, stressed the 'huge burden' of war debt. 'We are faced with this huge taxation, and yet, in looking through the terms of the armistice I do not see any mention of the indemnities', he lamented.[36] On 18 November, General Croft asked Bonar Law point-blank whether the contemplated peace terms included 'full reparation by the German Empire, including the repayment of the net cost of the war incurred by the Allies'. Again, Bonar Law declared that he 'could not make any statement at present'.[37]

Business circles lent assistance to the campaign to put the indemnity in the forefront of public discussion. A 'Joint Council' of the Federation of British Industry, the Imperial Council of Commerce, the British Empire Producers' Organization, and the Association of British Chambers of Commerce, met on 12

Spoils of War: The Politics, Economics, and Diplomacy of Reparations, 1918–1932 (Oxford, 1989), ch. 1.

[34] Thomas Blackley to William Bull, 9 Nov. 1918, Bull Papers, 4/18.
[35] *Parl. Debs.*, 5th ser., vol. 110, 2511 (12 Nov. 1918).
[36] *Parl. Debs.*, 5th ser., vol. 110, 2633–4 (12 Nov. 1918).
[37] *Evening Standard*, 18 Nov. 1918.

November to consider 'Peace Conditions'.[38] That protection and an indemnity loomed large among the priorities of these four organizations was immediately obvious. The British Empire Producers' Organization, for example, invited Hughes to speak at the Connaught Rooms on 13 November, and there he argued that it was the duty of the victors 'to impose terms of peace on defeated Germany'. The economic terms must 'render the Empire potently, absolutely free'. If Germany received the right to equal economic treatment, he warned, 'we should have won on the field of battle, but should have lost this war'.[39] The next day the Council of the London Chamber of Commerce passed a strong resolution on indemnity, declaring that terms of peace were quite unacceptable if they did not include 'the repayment by Germany to Great Britain, the Dominions and their Allies, of their costs of war'. Without such an indemnity, warned the resolution, Britain faced 'years of excessive taxation, which would cause discontent and poverty among the whole population, would cripple industry and commerce, and would infinitely postpone the requisite public expenditure on necessary schemes of social improvement and reform'. Mr J. M. Dick, who introduced the resolution, noted the 'ominous absence' of any reference to war costs in the armistice terms. Mr E. B. Bartley Dennis, a Conservative MP, agreed that it was time for 'pressure to be brought to bear upon the Government in this matter'. The resolution was sent to Lloyd George and the press.[40]

The Federation of British Industry (FBI) was especially active. At first, the 'ton for ton' policy was endorsed; on 13 November, the Executive Council of the FBI unanimously endorsed the proposal of the Liverpool Steamship Owners' Association that the merchant fleet of the enemy must be taken over and sold by the Allies. A week later, the FBI turned to the big issue: indemnity. The FBI decided to set up a 'Terms of Peace Committee' to draw up advice to the government.[41] The members of the committee included prominent 'economic warriors' such as Sir Vincent Caillard, the chair, Charles Tennyson, Sir Algernon Firth, and Sir Robert Hadfield. The committee met for the first time on 6 December and immediately proceeded to a discussion of 'Payment of Indemnities' as its first item of business. Agreement was rapidly achieved. Unless Germany was forced to meet Britain's war costs, it was decided, there would be an immense charge on capital and labour and 'the burden would be intolerable'. Caillard produced a memorandum favouring an indemnity which the committee adopted as a working draft for a major statement. A letter was dispatched to Lloyd George informing him of the FBI committee's work and urging him to refer all questions

---

[38] Association of British Chambers of Commerce, Executive Council Mins., 18 Dec. 1918, Association of British Chambers of Commerce Papers, Guildhall, 14,476, vol. 9.

[39] *The Times*, 14 Nov. 1918.

[40] London Chamber of Commerce, Mins. of the Council, 14 Nov. 1918, London Chamber of Commerce Papers, Guildhall Library, 16,459, vol. 8.

[41] Minutes of the Executive Council of the FBI, 13 Nov. 1918, FBI Papers, MSS 200/F/1/1/6, and Minutes of the Organization and Management Committee of the FBI, 20 Nov. 1918, FBI Papers, MSS 200/F/1/1/25.

'of an industrial character' to this committee. On 10 December the Terms of Peace Committee agreed that Britain must seek 'the immediate repayment of the costs of the war by the enemy governments' and should oppose any priority for devastated areas.[42] A General Meeting of the FBI on 12 December unanimously endorsed a final version of Caillard's memorandum entitled 'Peace Aims'. The memorandum urged 'the absolute necessity of transferring the burden of the war to those nations which are solely responsible for its creation'. The memorandum listed seven categories of damage for which the Allies should seek compensation, including claims for 'all expenses incurred as a direct or indirect consequence of the War'. To collect these huge payments in annual sums, the FBI favoured the establishment of an Inter-Allied Commission in Germany.[43]

During these same weeks those within the government who prided themselves on having a 'business orientation' were being pressed to seize the business opportunities made available by the armistice. German industry was, for the moment, penned up and deprived of raw materials: now was the time for British industry to step into the breach. For example, Lord Derby in Paris kept up a steady stream of letters prodding members of the government into action in support of the cause of British industry and trade in Europe. He urged Steel-Maitland, then in command of the Department of Overseas Trade, to visit Paris in order to stake out a claim for 'the future of British trade in this country'.[44] Steel-Maitland was certainly aware that his Department of Overseas Trade was to be a weapon in the great commercial competition to come. He told a meeting of the Liverpool Chamber of Commerce on 23 November that his Department was created especially to oppose Britain's 'most serious' competitor in manufacture and trade, Germany. Thus, he explained, the staff of Britain's own War Trade Intelligence Department were all to be absorbed into his new Department.[45]

Bankers also were alert to the business opportunities presented by the period of armistice. For example, in mid-December 1918, Ernest Maxse, the British Consul-General in Rotterdam, wrote to Brien Cokayne, Governor of the Bank of England, telling him of the splendid work being done by the Standard Bank of South Africa in seeking to elbow the German banks out of Rotterdam. He urged assistance to the bank 'as it is the only instance in my knowledge in which we have really succeeded in stealing a march on the Germans'.[46] The Bank of

---

[42] Minutes of FBI Terms of Peace Committee, 6 and 10 Dec. 1918, FBI Papers, MSS 200/F/1/1/180.

[43] FBI memorandum entitled 'Peace Aims', dated 12 Dec. 1918, Hewins Papers, 72; also FBI Bulletin, 19 Dec. 1918, FBI Papers, MSS 200/F/4/24/1.

[44] Derby to Steel-Maitland, 27 Nov. 1918, Derby Papers, Steel-Maitland file, 28/3. In his reply, Steel-Maitland sympathized with the cause but pleaded that he did not have the men available to promote trade in France, as his Department was 'understaffed and underhoused' (Steel-Maitland to Derby, 29 Nov. 1918).

[45] Steel-Maitland's 'Notes for a speech to the Liverpool Chamber of Commerce on 23 November 1918', Steel-Maitland Papers, GD 193–217.

[46] Ernest Maxse to Cokayne, 16 Dec. 1918, Bank of England Archives, Governor's Miscellaneous Correspondence, G. 30/5.

England itself was softly promoting the concept of the indemnity. On 11 December Montagu Norman, the Deputy Governor, wrote to Benjamin Strong, Governor of the Federal Reserve Bank in America, on the issue. Britain quite appreciated President Wilson's idealism, Norman assured Strong, but it was a great pity that Wilson was determined to pursue such policies as 'no indemnities, though the Allies are grievously impoverished.' Moreover, observed Norman, it was clear 'the only class from whom he is *certain* of support is the socialistic class'.[47] The Governor of the Bank, Sir Brien Cokayne, had the indemnity in mind too. He sent a deftly composed note to Bonar Law on 12 December, explaining that he did not presume to know what decision the government would make on indemnity; however, if it was decided to distribute Germany's liquid assets soon, then Britain, the Governor suggested, 'is entitled to the lion's share'.[48] Thus was the expectation of economic war nurtured by government ministers and high-ranking officials in the period immediately following the armistice.

By the eve of the election, associations for manufacturing and trade were all the more vehement on these issues, and it was clear that much collaboration had taken place among the economic élite. On 12 December, the London Chamber of Commerce endorsed a report from its 'Special Committee on Trade During and After the War'. The report listed 'peace terms' which included the demand for an indemnity to cover war costs in exactly the terms laid down by the FBI. The Chamber of Commerce also demanded a peace which would deliver protection against 'dumping', the imposition of new 'discriminatory taxes' against enemy shipping using British ports, reparation on a 'ton for ton' basis, and compensation for all cargoes, ships, and men lost in the struggle with Germany. It was 'a bare act of justice', pleaded the report, that no German ship should be allowed back on the high seas until Germany accepted these terms.[49] On the same day, Caillard launched the FBI's 'Peace Aims' document at a public meeting in London. It was 'insane', said Caillard, for Britain to contemplate living under 'the tremendous burden of taxation' which must flow from her own war costs. Similarly, said Caillard, it would be 'absolutely wicked that the German nation should be allowed a big start over the other nations which it had so abominably devastated and gratuitously destroyed. (Cheers)'. Ebert in Berlin did not appreciate that Germany was beaten; an indemnity would enlighten him.[50] The FBI pressed its report upon the government, and within days the Association of

---

[47] Montagu Norman to Benjamin Strong, 11 Dec. 1918, Bank of England Archives, Governor's Correspondence, G3/175.

[48] Brien Cokayne to Bonar Law, 12 Dec. 1918, Bank of England Archives, Governor's Correspondence, G3/175.

[49] 'Fourth Report of the Special Committee on Trade During and After the War, presented and accepted by Council of the London Chamber of Commerce', 12 Dec. 1918, London Chamber of Commerce Papers, Guildhall, 16,459, vol. 8.

[50] *The Times*, 13 Dec. 1918.

British Chambers of Commerce sent to the Prime Minister a similar plan for Germany to disgorge fantastic sums for a generation to come.[51]

Britain's political leaders began moving in the direction desired by the men of property soon after the armistice. On 20 November, the Imperial War Cabinet had begun a major discussion of the treatment of the defeated enemy. Initially, the Prime Minister directed attention to the subject he had been pursuing among his intimates for the last ten days: the proposed trial of the Kaiser.[52] The shorthand notes of the meeting reveal that this was one of the very few occasions when the British leaders discussed the meaning of the internal changes in Germany in any detail. The most interesting contribution came from Austen Chamberlain who made himself the spokesman of the 'all-Germans-are-Huns' position:

Is there not another danger? We have not done with the German people yet. They are in a state of flux and transition. What is going to emerge from the welter I do not know. Any of us would be rash at this moment to prophesy. When you go back to the beginning of this war, I think it is impossible to distinguish the guilt of the ex-Kaiser from the guilt of the people who welcomed and applauded and supported him throughout. If you are going to treat the ex-Kaiser as the sole root of evil, you are going to acquit the German people. I think it is too early to do that before you are satisfied that their change of mind and heart is complete and permanent. I think there is a great danger for our own people in our teaching them the ex-Kaiser alone was to blame and that the German people were as innocent as lambs . . . My first point is that the mind of the German people has not really changed by the Kaiser's inglorious and undignified exit.[53]

Lloyd George responded immediately, insisting on the justice of his proposition for a trial of the Kaiser as 'the greatest criminal of the lot' and a 'coward' into the bargain. On the matter of the ordinary German masses, Lloyd George appeared ready to defend them. He drew the contrast with the flight of the Hohenzollerns, and noted that 'the German people have stood their punishment'. Hughes joined the battle. 'I think that 85% of the German people are as bad as the ex-Kaiser ever was, and are as deserving of death', he observed, 'but I am not in favour of this 85% getting off free and sheltering under the blood of this man.' Lloyd George immediately interjected: 'They have not got off free; they have incurred 5,000,000 or 6,000,000 casualties and they have starved for four or five years, but neither the ex-Kaiser nor his household have suffered any privations or anything else.' At length the Cabinet decided to refer the matter of the Kaiser's prosecution to the Law Officers of the Crown for investigation.[54]

[51] Caillard to Bonar Law, 24 Dec. 1918, and Caillard to Lloyd George, 24 Dec. 1918, Keynes Papers, RT/1/11 and 13; Minutes of the FBI Terms of Peace Committee, 31 Dec. 1918, Item 11, in FBI Archives, MSS 200/F/1/1/180; and see Letter to the Prime Minister, dated 23 Dec. 1918, in Minute Book of the Executive Council, 18 Dec. 1918, Association of British Chambers of Commerce Papers, Guildhall, 14,476, vol. 9.
[52] 'Lloyd George wants to shoot the Kaiser. F. E. [Smith] agrees'; Henry Wilson Diary, 11 Nov. 1918, Henry Wilson Papers, DS MISC/80.
[53] Minutes of the Imperial War Cabinet, 20 Nov. 1918, shorthand notes, CAB 23/43.
[54] Ibid.

A week later, the Imperial War Cabinet returned to the issue of the treatment of Germany, this time debating the vexed issue of indemnity. Britain's international undertakings as given in the Lansing Note were simply ignored. No one suggested that under the terms of the Lansing Note, or indeed in the light of the Prime Minister's own specific disavowal of an indemnity in his Caxton Hall speech of January 1918, it would be dishonourable for Britain to pursue an indemnity covering war costs. While advertising the difficulties of collecting an indemnity, Lloyd George allowed discussion to proceed as if Britain had a free hand. As Lloyd George explained, 'there is one thing that has deterred the Allied statesmen from demanding the full indemnity and that is the fear that it can only be paid for by Germany selling goods'.

At the very outset of the discussion Hughes observed that 'a fair reading of President Wilson's proposals would show that they did not include any suggestion as to a war indemnity'.[55] The problem, therefore, was how to evade the Wilsonian programme. Nevertheless, at the start of the discussions Lloyd George seemed ready to defy Hughes on the practical rather than the moral problems raised by the indemnity. He insisted that claims for figures of £20 billion were utterly unreal for 'it would mean that for two generations we would make German workmen our slaves'. In addition, he claimed, Britain must keep in mind the difficulties of Germany paying a vast sum unless she were able to sell vast amounts of goods. Cheap goods might be dumped in Britain, and thus the pursuit of an indemnity might do Britain great harm. At this point Lloyd George himself suggested that a committee be appointed by the Imperial War Cabinet to 'work this thing out'.[56]

The manner of composition of this proposed Indemnity Committee of the Imperial War Cabinet offers some vital insights into the power of the business and tariff reform lobby in decision-making at the top. Lloyd George initially suggested that Bonar Law, as Chancellor of the Exchequer, should be chairman of the committee, but he immediately declined. It was Lloyd George himself who then proposed Hughes as a member of the committee and invited him to suggest other experts. Hughes naturally suggested someone from his 'economic warrior' circle, Hewins, the leading tariff reformer. Bonar Law put forward Sir George Foster, the Canadian Conservative Minister of Finance, a supporter of imperial preference and the Paris Resolutions. Then, no doubt to Hughes's surprise, it was Lloyd George who invited him to be the chairman. 'I don't know if I could or not. It is a very difficult problem', confessed Hughes. At this point Bonar Law appeared to encourage those in pursuit of a high indemnity. He explained that a Treasury Committee had found that Germany could pay only £2 billion; but, he explained, in the light of Britain's war debt of £8 billion, and her debts to America of £1 billion, it was his opinion that the Treasury Committee had underestimated Germany's capacity to pay. Walter Long observed that his

[55] Minutes of the Imperial War Cabinet, 26 Nov. 1918, CAB 23/42.
[56] Minutes of the Imperial War Cabinet, 26 Nov. 1918, shorthand notes, CAB 23/43.

friends in the City were of the opinion 'that we are not asking enough of Germany'. The issue of the leadership of the Indemnity Committee remained. Lloyd George suggested Foster as an alternative chairman, but also urged Long and Hughes to join the committee as members. 'I will not serve on it', replied Hughes. Lloyd George pressed Hughes for a third time, but he brazenly confessed that 'I much prefer to remain free so that I can criticise'. Lloyd George politely chided him as 'not quite playing the game'. Reading then rallied behind the original proposal that Hughes be chairman, and at last Hughes accepted the post. Other names were added quickly from business and banking circles. Lord Cunliffe, the ex-Governor of the Bank of England was put forward by Reading. Long suggested Herbert Gibbs, of the banking firm Anthony Gibbs and Sons, as a respected City authority. Sir Joseph Cook, the second Australian representative on the Imperial War Cabinet, added candidly that there was 'a certain class of people who think that Germany ought to pay for everything, and it is a person who will represent that point of view that you want on the committee'. 'They do not realize the difficulty', Lloyd George fired back.[57] Nevertheless, having surrendered control of the Indemnity Committee to Hughes, the pursuit of full war costs was to be exactly the governing assumption of all those who eventually made up the committee, namely, Foster, Long, Hewins, Cunliffe, and, of course, Hughes himself.

Lloyd George appeared to have meekly acquiesced in the creation of a committee that was bound to make extreme demands. How can his acquiescence be explained? No doubt, political realities dictated the outcome. Lloyd George surely had no desire to revisit the embarrassing matter of his agreements with Colonel House in Versailles, which Hughes, incensed over lack of Dominion consultation, refused to put behind him. Thus, never once did Lloyd George challenge the concept of indemnity from the point of view of its inadmissibility under the terms of the Lansing Note. To do so would have confirmed Hughes's accusations that Lloyd George had compromised the Empire at the Versailles Council. Then, in the composition of the Indemnity Committee, Lloyd George had no one to blame but himself for Hughes's appointment to the vital post of chairman. Perhaps he hoped to distract Hughes by loading the complexities of the indemnity issue upon him. Perhaps he hoped for the exposure of the troublesome Australian Prime Minister as incompetent in dealing with economic matters of great complexity, and assumed that the Treasury experts would prevail. This was the explanation Hewins offered in his diary.[58] More than likely, however, the appointment was a simple effort to 'compensate' Hughes for the recent embarrassments. At the time, Hughes himself and those in his circle interpreted the appointment this way. Hughes told Munro-Ferguson that, as a result of his quarrel with Lloyd George over the armistice, 'we *are getting better treatment*'.[59]

[57] Minutes of the Imperial War Cabinet, 28 Nov. 1918, CAB 23/42.
[58] Hewins Diary, 'End of October 1918 to May 13th 1919', 10, Hewins Papers.
[59] Hughes to Munro-Ferguson, 14 Dec. 1918, Novar Papers, MS 696/2748–9, italics in original.

Eggleston described the appointment of Hughes to the committee as 'a sop to Hughes' directly related to the furore of early November.[60] The vital point to note is this: it was not on the hustings in the weeks to come that a reluctant Lloyd George was to be swept off his feet by the vengeful mood of the people and seduced thoughtlessly into the rhetoric of indemnities; the first gestures of surrender to the 'economic warriors' were made in the Cabinet room at 10 Downing Street in the first week of the election campaign.

In keeping with this trend were the decisions of the Cabinet on the German food question. When Herbert Hoover arrived in London on 21 November, he was immediately locked in disputes with British officials. Sir John Beale advised him at their first meeting not to bother to raise the subject of the food blockade on Germany because the British had no desire to relax it 'until the Germans learn a few things'.[61] Certainly, in the days that followed, it became clear that the British decision-makers were in no hurry to help Germany overcome her food crisis. At the Imperial War Cabinet on 28 November there was much opposition to co-operation with the United States in schemes for immediate relief. Lloyd George invited Lord Reading, officially still the Ambassador to the United States, while visiting London, to take charge of the negotiations for Britain. He accepted the post very reluctantly and immediately announced that it was 'very important, as a matter of principle, that we should not allow the US to think that she could dictate to us in these matters'.[62] In this context, the planning of food relief for Germany was subjected to every kind of delay. During December, the whole issue of relief became bogged down in acrimonious negotiations in London between the United States and Entente officials, with each side blaming the other for the protracted delays.[63]

The popular press, 'the Huns' counterfeit revolution', and the Northcliffe factor

No doubt the decisions of the government were encouraged also by the continuing campaign in the Coalition and ultra-patriotic press representing the German revolution as a pitiful subterfuge. The responsiveness of the Coalition politicians to this theme was scarcely surprising: there was much habitual distrust of all German developments after four years of war. But the special sensitivity of the Prime Minister to the themes of the press was shaped by another vital back-

---

[60] Eggleston, 'The Peace Conference at Paris', typescript memoir, Eggleston Papers, MS 423/6/14.

[61] Hoover, *Memoirs*, 335.

[62] Minutes of the Imperial War Cabinet, 26 Nov. 1918, shorthand notes, CAB 23/43.

[63] See the most recent account of this dispute in C. Paul Vincent, *The Politics of Hunger: The Allied Blockade of Germany, 1915–1919* (Athens, Ohio, 1985), ch. 4. The case against the United States for rejecting the British proposals for a General Economic Council is given in J. A. Salter, *Allied Shipping Control: An Experiment in International Administration* (Oxford, 1921), 220–2. The case against the British is given in Hoover, *Memoirs*, ch. 33.

ground factor, the rift with Northcliffe. To understand the quarrel we must return briefly to the period just before the armistice.

As noted previously, at the beginning of October, Lloyd George's abrupt dismissal of Northcliffe's claims to advise him on the composition of the next government had led to harsh words. At the beginning of November, a fresh dispute with Lloyd George appeared to mark a final schism. The precise cause is itself debated. According to Lloyd George and others in the political élite, Northcliffe proposed that he should be made an official British delegate at the coming Peace Conference, a suggestion which the Prime Minister rejected.[64] Northcliffe and his defenders denied that such a precise request was made in November. But certainly Northcliffe had indicated his desire to be a delegate a number of times during the war, and at the very least he was promoting himself as a propaganda chief and adviser to government during the period of peacemaking and reconstruction.[65] Whatever the truth of the matter, Northcliffe believed himself to have been spurned by Lloyd George.

He responded with an astonishing exercise in self-promotion. All Northcliffe's editors received instructions to place a personal 'manifesto' entitled 'From War to Peace' in his newspapers on 4 November.[66] The article described a three-stage process for ending the war, beginning first with an armistice, then second, an invitation to the Germans to accept a list of thirteen 'principles', and third, a peace conference. Northcliffe's principles followed the territorial demands of the Fourteen Points closely, but abandoned the references to open diplomacy, freedom of the seas, free trade, and the League of Nations. In addition, there were demands upon Germany for the replacement of merchant ships, tribunals for the trying of war criminals, and her acceptance of the loss of all colonies. There was no mention of indemnities or of the Paris Resolutions.[67] Of course, the article was soon made utterly redundant by the revolution and armistice. But Northcliffe's attempt to announce foreign policy for the government at a most critical juncture was a pretension that could not be ignored. Lloyd George was intensely annoyed. The offending manifesto, although it appeared as Northcliffe's work, was in fact a late propaganda piece on British war aims prepared by Wickham Steed at Crewe House and rejected by the Prime Minister himself in early October.[68] 'From War to Peace' caused problems at *The Times* too. Dawson bridled at the 'sloppy article', as he described it, especially as it appeared in some

[64] David Lloyd George, *Memoirs of the Peace Conference* (New Haven, 1939), i. 175–7. See also Robert Sanders Diary, 8 May 1919, in John Ramsden (ed.), *Real Old Tory Politics* (London, 1984), 125.

[65] See Reginald Pound and Geoffrey Harmsworth, *Northcliffe* (London, 1959), 676 and 682–3, and also Dawson memorandum on his dismissal from editorship of *The Times*, Feb. 1919, quoted in J. E. Wrench, *Geoffrey Dawson and our Times* (London, 1955), 175.

[66] Dawson Diary, 31 Oct. 1918, Dawson Papers, 24.

[67] 'From War to Peace', *The Times*, 4 Nov. 1918.

[68] Dawson Diary, 4 Nov. 1918, Dawson Papers, 24; Wickham H. Steed, *Through Thirty Years* (London, 1924), ii. 244–50; and Wrench, *Dawson*, 176–7.

of the Northcliffe papers alongside continuing attacks on his friend Milner. Dawson must have voiced thoughts of resignation, for a friend counselled him to stay on and 'tolerate the proprietorship of *The Times*'.[69] The denouement came quickly: Northcliffe resigned peremptorily from his post of Director of Propaganda in Enemy Countries on 12 November. Two days later he told Dawson that he had 'served notice on Ll. G that he could no longer support him'.[70]

What lay at the root of this very public friction? While the quarrel appeared to be about peace diplomacy, the origins of the dispute lay in domestic policy. Northcliffe believed that Britain faced the threat of revolution itself. In his view, this danger required a persuasive flourish of social reformist trumpets at home and the pitiless pursuit of a profitable peace at Germany's expense abroad. Only such a combination could tie down the British socialist dragon. Lloyd George, however, as Northcliffe told his brother Cecil Harmsworth, was 'tied hand and foot to the Junkers of the Tory "old gang" party'.[71] Dawson received a remonstrance from Northcliffe on 1 December warning him that Lloyd George was likely to appoint 'reactionary ministers who will not allow Ll. G. to carry out such reforms as will prevent revolution'.[72] These were the constant themes of *Daily Mail* editorials.[73]

Northcliffe's resolve to punish Lloyd George led him to some unprecedented political experimentation once the election campaign was under way. To the astonishment of all sides, Northcliffe affected a sense of 'solidarity' with Labour and generously offered a column to the Labour Party in the *Daily Mail*.[74] 'Do you notice that Northcliffe has turned against Lloyd George and that the *Daily Mail* has gone Labour?', Herbert Fisher wrote to Gilbert Murray.[75] In fact, the gesture reflected only Northcliffe's personal disenchantment with Lloyd George, not a revision of his long-standing Conservative and ultra-patriotic views. For example, he wrote privately to General Croft, the National Party firebrand, assuring him that he was in hearty agreement with the extreme policies of the National Party, 'or rather the policy which my staff say you take from my newspapers!!'.[76]

The mischievous possibilities of having Northcliffe 'at large' must have haunted the Prime Minister. At the mid-point of the election campaign, he thought about mending fences. Robert Sanders found him 'anxious to know if anyone could get at Northcliffe'.[77] Cecil Harmsworth was twice summoned to

[69] J. E. Mackenzie to Dawson, 18 Nov. 1918, Dawson Papers, Mackenzie file, *The Times* Archive.

[70] Dawson Diary, 14 Nov. 1918, Dawson Papers, 24.

[71] Cecil Harmsworth Diary, 30 Nov. 1918, quoted in Pound and Harmsworth, *Northcliffe*, 676.

[72] Northcliffe to Dawson, 1 Dec. 1918, *Times* Archive, Dawson Correspondence, Northcliffe file.

[73] e.g. *Daily Mail*, editorials, 'Test Questions', 22 Nov., 'A Very Bad Bargain', 2 Dec., 'Land of Promises', 12 Dec., 'Forecast', 14 Dec. 1918.

[74] Henderson began use of the 'Labour' column, *Daily Mail*, 2 Dec. 1918.

[75] Fisher to Murray, 2 Dec. 1918, Fisher Papers, 54.

[76] Northcliffe to General Page Croft, 28 Nov. 1918, Croft Papers, 1/17.

[77] Robert Sanders Diary, 27 Nov. 1918, in *Real Old Tory Politics*, 117.

advise the Prime Minister. He found Lloyd George 'more agitated in his manner than I have seen him during the war, save on one or two very critical occasions'. A telephone call to his brother elicited the information that there was no chance of reconciliation. 'Ll. G. was gravely perturbed by N's opposition', Harmsworth commented in his diary.[78] Clearly it was in the Prime Minister's interests to be ever watchful of the leading themes of the 'patriotic' press.

The coverage of German events in the British Coalition and ultra-'patriotic' press during the election was, to say the least of it, poisonous. The political purpose of this was obvious. It was not simply to whip up hatred: the political inspiration of what had happened in Germany had to be deliberately countered. As J. A. Spender pointed out as soon as the election campaign began, the Germans were more than likely to build 'an orderly Socialist Government on a more democratic foundation than any that has been seen in the world'. For Spender, the political consequences in Britain were full of danger for the Coalition. 'The spectacle of the German working-classes gaining complete power in a rapid and orderly manner would have enormous influence in all countries, and especially in this country', wrote Spender, 'and the more so if there were any suspicion that our working classes were at the same time being excluded from any effective voice by a combination of middle-class politicians.'[79] The press campaign against the German revolution must be seen in this context. The proprietors and editors of the Coalition divined the political dangers inherent in the situation only too well. The remedy was a withering campaign against the evils, hypocrisies, and bogus achievements of the German revolution.

In this campaign, the pro-Coalition, Northcliffe, and ultra-patriotic papers co-operated. A number of themes can be identified. First, the 'new Germany', it was argued, failed every test of 'good faith'. The poor condition of the returning British prisoners of war, and the Germans' failure to hunt down and punish their own war criminals, were adduced as evidence that there had been no 'change of heart'. Second, the German socialists were accused of deliberately fomenting mutiny and industrial unrest in the victorious nations. Third, reports of starvation in Germany were treated with remorseless suspicion. Fourth, Bolshevism was depicted as a minor danger, deliberately played up by the new government, and probably engineered by it, to frighten the victors. Here, supposedly, was further evidence of the insincerity of Germany's socialists, co-operating with reactionary militarists one moment, while fomenting domestic and international Bolshevism the next. Some examples from the leading newspapers must suffice to give the flavour of the campaign.

The Northcliffe papers were in the vanguard of this anti-German interpretation. The emotional temperature was heightened with vivid front-page accounts of the suffering of released British prisoners of war in Germany. From 19

---

[78] Cecil Harmsworth Diary, 30 Nov. 1918, quoted in Pound and Harmsworth, *Northcliffe*, 676 and 680.

[79] *Westminster Gazette*, editorial, 'The Germans and the Allies', 16 Nov. 1918.

November, the *Daily Mail* and *Evening News* reported on 'THE MARCH OF DEATH', as British prisoners were released by their pitiless captors. The German government was to blame, it was alleged, for the abandonment of these prisoners 'in a barren frozen land'.[80] The Northcliffe press, however, drew a clear lesson from this. The *Evening News* opined: 'If anything were wanted to convince our people that the talk of Germany's "democratic" Government about humanity and kindness is blasphemous cant it is this ghastly story of the procession of death making its way towards our lines.'[81] Similarly, the *Mail* professed little faith in the claims that Germany was already suffering from starvation. By mid-November Tower was ridiculing reports of hunger in Germany. He insisted that there was 'plenty of food' in Cologne. Indeed, the old élite of 'Cologne guzzlers' were living it up and only biding their time before returning to take power.[82] The *Daily Mail* endorsed what it called 'the widely held Entente view that affairs in Germany are being stage managed to "bluff" the Allies into thinking that the old Germany is no more'.[83]

Such excesses were expected, no doubt, in the *Daily Mail*. The attitude of *The Times*, whose editor was often in the company of the Prime Minister, was the more telling.[84] The same suspicion and hostility towards the revolution in Germany pervaded its pages. During November, J. E. Mackenzie, the former Berlin correspondent, wrote a series of articles in his 'Through German Eyes' column casting doubt on the permanence and sincerity of the German government.[85] The Germans' alleged mistreatment of British prisoners, 'an outrageous breach of the plain dictates of humanity', was also given great prominence.[86] Denunciations of the new government in Berlin became more passionate. Mackenzie provided a major assessment of the revolution as a virtual hoax on 23 November. His suspicions centred on the speed and order of the change of government. According to Mackenzie, 'the supreme authorities quietly disappeared, and their machinery then went on running much as if nothing had happened'. It was, wrote Mackenzie, 'much the same as during any summer holiday'.[87]

Both wings of the German socialist movement were unworthy of trust, according to *The Times*; neither Ebert, who 'had little or no quarrel' with the old regime, nor Karl Liebknecht, who was described as a man 'whose imprisonment

---

[80] e.g. *Evening News*, 19 Nov. 1918. There was no doubt that real suffering was endured by British POWs, some of whom were released haphazardly in the first days of the revolution. When the subject was discussed in the Imperial War Cabinet, it was decided to warn Germany against any neglect or mistreatment of prisoners; but here even Hughes acknowledged that the root of the problem was the food shortage in Germany. See Minutes of the Imperial War Cabinet, 20 Nov. 1918, shorthand notes, CAB 23/43.

[81] *Evening News*, editorial, 'The Latest Hun Atrocity', 20 Nov. 1918.

[82] *Daily Mail*, 22 Nov. 1918.   [83] *Daily Mail*, 25 Nov. 1918.

[84] e.g. Dawson's diary records several 'long meetings', encounters and meals with the Prime Minister at this time; see Dawson Diary, 12 and 15 Nov. 1918, Dawson Papers, 24.

[85] Dawson Diary, 10 Nov. 1918, Dawson Papers, 24.

[86] *The Times*, editorial, 'Prisoners: A Last Horror', 21 Nov. 1918.

[87] *The Times*, 'The German Revolution—A Retrospect', 23 Nov. 1918.

has obviously clouded his formerly keen intelligence and probably turned his brain'.[88] Even the independent socialists' efforts to distance themselves from the foreign policy of the former regime were condemned. When Kurt Eisner's Bavarian socialist government released documents from the foreign ministry in Munich pointing to Berlin's guilt at the time of the July 1914 crisis, Dawson reacted angrily. Socialist efforts to 'shift the blame' on to the old Prussian élite, cautioned Dawson, would do nothing to shake England's convictions regarding the 'common crime' of all Germans: 'Germany sinned as a whole, she fought as a whole, she has been beaten as a whole; she will have to negotiate as a whole to the terms dictated to her. We are not going to negotiate with chaos.'[89]

Through until election day *The Times* provided a flow of reports all allegedly pointing to the lack of repentance of the German people. The new government apparently failed to abase itself to the satisfaction of *The Times*. Any attempt to rescue national dignity in the midst of the disaster of the war was presented by *The Times* as evidence of an unreconstructed nationalism at work. For example, the receptions for returning troops in German towns and cities were a target for criticism.[90] Attempts by government speakers at these receptions to take some solace from the long and successful defence of German territory were all interpreted as evidence of German truculence.[91] Most consistently of all, *The Times* charged the Germans with refusing to recognize the scale of their defeat and of believing themselves 'unbeaten'.[92] The evidence for such a claim in November–December 1918 was always scarce—*The Times* cited the flowers and cigarettes for returning troops, the flags hanging from windows, the absence of red flags in the crowds, the snippets of belligerent pavement conversation picked up by correspondents. Nevertheless, the 'unbeaten' enemy was one of the most powerful myths of the period created in the British press. It did not seem to matter that some of *The Times*'s own reports failed to accord with this myth. For example, *The Times* itself described the reception for returning troops in Cologne as a most subdued affair: 'Sometimes, but rarely, a little group of bystanders tried to raise a cheer, but it failed to evoke a response, and the troops marched in silence—the deadliest silence imaginable.'[93] Even the report in *The Times* of Ebert's controversial speech at the Brandenburg Gate on 11 December—the speech in which he told returning soldiers that 'No enemy has overcome you'— made it clear that this was not the speech of a nationalist. As *The Times* showed, Ebert spent quite as much time in praising 'the German freedom of the new

[88] *The Times*, 'German Chaos. Terrorism in Berlin', 21 Nov., and 'The Future of Germany' and 'Soviet Struggle', 27 Nov. 1918.

[89] *The Times*, editorial, 'Rifts in the German Flute', 26 Nov. 1918.

[90] *The Times*, 'Scenes in Berlin and Cologne. Indifference to Revolution', 2 Dec. 1918.

[91] *The Times*, 'Through German Eyes', 2 Dec. 1918.

[92] e.g. *The Times*, 'Kaiser-minded', 7 Dec. 1918, 'In Cologne. "Unbeaten" Germans', 9 Dec. 1918, and 'The Take Over at Coblenz. An Unrepentant People', 12 Dec. 1918.

[93] *The Times*, 'Scenes in Berlin and Cologne. Indifference to Revolution', 2 Dec. 1918.

People's State of Germany' as he did in thanking the troops for their protection of the homeland from enemy invasion.

But neither the political promise of the revolution nor the food shortages in Germany moved Dawson and his staff. *The Times* condemned the 'hubbub about the German food supply' begun by Dr Solf's appeals to the United States for assistance. Mackenzie supplied material from the German papers to prove that there was 'no question of a shortage of food in Germany'.[94] At the end of November, Dawson wrote a stern editorial critical of the 'absurd story' that the Allies might contemplate the abolition of the blockade. The very idea testified to the Germans' 'inbred arrogance'.[95]

The Northcliffe papers were by no means alone in fulminating against the new German government. Lloyd George's own *Daily Chronicle* also endorsed the view that the German revolution was insincere. The paper's special correspondent in Switzerland, Harold Williams, supplied a series of articles expressing disappointment with the revolution.[96] More extreme versions of this thesis were available in such papers as Hulton's *Illustrated Sunday Herald*. On 1 December, it began a serialization of the latest work of William le Queux, the celebrated writer of invasion-scare novels and a member of the British Empire Union. Under the title, 'The Secret History of the Kaiser's Shame', le Queux claimed to have obtained the secret confessions of a member of the Kaiser's entourage. The German socialists, alleged le Queux, were in constant touch with the Kaiser, Ebert himself making pilgrimages to Holland to receive his instructions.[97] The *Evening Standard* proclaimed that 'the very men now in power in Berlin are those who rapturously cheered all the brutalities of the late regime'.[98] For Henry Dalziel's *Pall Mall Gazette*, democracy in Germany was simply irrelevant because 'the vices of Kaiserism were simply those of the German people at large'.[99]

Significantly, Beaverbrook's *Daily Express*, after showing some initial moderation towards Germany's new socialist rulers, appeared to change its mind as soon as British Labour withdrew from the Coalition and the election campaign began in earnest.[100] Now plainly at war with British socialism, the *Express* discovered within days that the German socialists were colluding with the old authorities in

---

[94] *The Times*, 'America and Dr Solf's Appeals', 21 Nov., and 'Through German Eyes', 22 and 25 Nov. 1918.

[95] *The Times*, editorial, 'Abolish the Blockade', 28 Nov. 1918.

[96] *Daily Chronicle*, 'No Change of Heart', 21 Nov. 1918, and Daily Chronicle, 'Berlin Government Stirring Up Hatred Against Allies', 30 Nov. 1918.

[97] These entirely fictional revelations from the pen of le Queux were eventually published in an expanded version in early 1919, including further claims of German manipulation of British strikes and demobilization riots in Jan. and Feb. 1919. See William le Queux, *The Secret Shame of the Kaiser: His Dastardly Plots at Amerongen, Disclosed by Dr Franz Seeliger, Late Director of the Political Section of the German Ministry of Foreign Affairs, and attached to the entourage of the Kaiser in his exile* (London, 1919). I am grateful to Dr Michael Birch for alerting me to the existence of this work.

[98] *Evening Standard*, 'A Test of Justice', 16 Nov. 1918.

[99] *Pall Mall Gazette*, editorial, 'Pity the Poor German!', 19 Nov. 1918.

[100] On initial moderation, see e.g. the article, 'The Socialists of Germany', *Daily Express*, 11 Nov. 1918, which praised the USPD politicians in particular for their courageous opposition to the war.

a giant international conspiracy. In a leading article entitled 'IS GERMANY PLOT-TING TO TRICK THE WORLD?', the outlines of the plot were unveiled: the new government's plans to foment revolution in Europe and England; the government's toleration of Hindenburg; and the fact that much of the old bureaucracy was still in place co-operating with the new socialist government. 'Something is brewing in Germany; significant facts point to the existence of a great and mysterious plot to trap the Allies', announced the *Express*.[101]

The government, it must be stressed, did nothing to dampen down such stories—on the contrary, it endorsed them. Robert Cecil was quoted in the *Pall Mall Gazette* on 18 November as cautioning against the possibility that the German revolution was 'a huge trap'.[102] Thus, when the *Daily Express* revealed its giant conspiracy on the next day, its account ended with the assurance that suspicion of the conspiracy was common among 'leading Allied diplomats and statesmen, including Lord Robert Cecil, Assistant Secretary of State for Foreign Affairs'. It is intriguing to note, however, that when Cecil's name was linked with the hoax thesis, this was too much even for Cecil's own relations. In the privacy of family correspondence, Ruth Balfour, the Foreign Secretary's niece, confessed amazement that the Foreign Office should be seen to endorse such fanciful propositions. 'What on earth is cousin Bob [Cecil] up to giving interviews to the press to say that William II shd. be tried and that perhaps the present Government in Germany is a huge plot?', she asked. 'Funny sort of plot when they are perfectly helpless. As a private citizen his remarks would be excusable but as a member of the government what does he mean by trying to force their hand. Wonder Nunkie [Arthur Balfour] does not keep him in order . . . Never in history has there been a peace so completely the result of a military victory, nor a victory so complete.'[103]

Of all the issues canvassed in the press with respect to Germany, none generated as much heat as the issue of starvation in Germany. The opportunity for the press to offer first-hand accounts on the condition of defeated Germany was afforded by the advance of Allied and American troops into Belgium and the Rhineland under the terms of the armistice. The advance into Germany began on 1 December, and consequent press reports on inner Germany thus coincided with the last two weeks of the election campaign in Britain. In company with the advancing troops went some of the leading lights of British journalism including Philip Gibbs of the *Daily Chronicle*, Percival Phillips of the *Westminster Gazette*, Henry Nevinson of the *Nation*, Cecil Roberts of the *Daily News*, W. Beach Thomas of the *Daily Mail*, and C. E. Montague of the *Manchester Guardian*. These correspondents accompanied the first British troops across the Belgian frontier into Germany near Malmédy on 1 December, and they arrived in

[101] *Daily Express*, 19 Nov. 1918.
[102] *Pall Mall Gazette*, editorial, 'Distrust of Germany', 18 Nov. 1918.
[103] Ruth Balfour to her mother, 18 Nov. 1918, Whittingehame Correspondence, GD 433/2/362.

Cologne on 7 December.[104] In addition, a dozen foreign correspondents were soon reporting from the occupied territories and from deep inside Germany and Austria for the *Daily Mail* and *The Times*. As Steed advised Dawson, the press recognized that it was vital to send in correspondents in order to get 'reliable accounts of the state of mind of the German population'.[105] Thus, the Northcliffe correspondents normally based in the neutral countries, such as Delmer in Switzerland and Tower in Holland, received instructions to undertake journeys to Munich and Berlin. Two other correspondents, Alexander Thompson and Herbert Bailey, were assigned to accompany the American and French troops as they advanced into Germany.

The image of 'inner Germany' that emerged was confused. The inconsistent reports which appeared in the *Daily Mail* and *The Times* may serve to exemplify the point. At first their reports appeared to cater for the entrenched assumptions of the two papers. Tower reported that the populations of Berlin and Cologne were 'entirely indifferent to the revolution'.[106] Bailey found no food shortage in Metz, and Thompson met only 'unrepentant Huns' in Saarbrücken.[107] Beach Thomas's first reports stressed that there were no obvious signs of revolution or hunger. People were 'a little hysterical when food is mentioned', he observed, but food in the shops and hotels was 'excellent'.[108] Sifting through all these reports in London, the reliable Frederic Wile, who composed his 'Germany Day By Day' for the *Daily Mail*, claimed that the correspondents' reports were confirming his suspicion that the German revolution was all bluff.[109] But Delmer's and Thomas's columns soon struck a different note. After attending dramatic meetings of the Workers' and Soldiers' Councils in Munich, Delmer warned of the insidious appeal of 'Bolshevism' amidst a very genuine food crisis.[110] By the time Thomas reached Cologne he too had decided that 'the revolutionary movement is real'. That the old order was discredited he did not doubt. 'The great bulk of folk rejoice in the republican ideal. Significant signs of this are everywhere', wrote Thomas. After touring the working-class suburbs of Cologne, he declared that there was indeed a stark problem of hunger. Even a slight break in the food supply, he concluded, 'would cause starvation, so narrow is the margin'.[111] Reports in *The Times*, in contrast, remained optimistic. Report after report, from Aix-la-Chapelle, Metz, Trèves, and Cologne stressed that the people had evi-

[104] Henry Nevinson Journal, Nevinson Papers, MS Eng. Misc. c. 620. Published accounts include Henry W. Nevinson, *Last Changes, Last Chances* (London, 1928), 149–54, Philip Gibbs, *Since Then* (London, 1930), ch. 3, Philip Gibbs, *The Pageant of the Years* (London, 1946), 235–41, Cecil Roberts, *Halfway* (London, n.d.), ch. 10.
    [105] Steed to Dawson, 28 Nov. 1918, Dawson Papers, Steed File.
    [106] *Daily Mail*, 2 Dec. 1918.   [107] *Daily Mail*, 7 and 11 Dec. 1918.
    [108] *Daily Mail*, 4 and 6 Dec. 1918.
    [109] e.g. *Daily Mail*, 7 and 9 Dec., accusing the German government of doing all it could 'to keep alive the spirit of militarism'.
    [110] *Daily Mail*, 7 Dec. 1918.   [111] *Daily Mail*, 9 and 10 Dec. 1918.

dently been spared all suffering in the war and were amply supplied with all manner of 'luxurious food'.[112]

The journalists themselves were soon bitterly divided. For, in stark contrast to the Coalition newspaper journalists, those filing reports for the Asquithian and Radical press came to a very different view of the food situation very rapidly. The poor condition of children, in particular, began to sicken Nevinson and Phillips.[113] Thus, there was suspicion among the journalists at the Domhof Hotel in Cologne when the *Daily Mail* journalist G. Ward Price arrived from London on 22 December to investigate the alleged German food shortage for the Northcliffe press. Harsh words were exchanged, Nevinson being convinced that Price was 'evidently pushed by Northcliffe to represent Germany as unharmed and unrepentant'.[114] Montague was disgusted when Price, following lunch, an afternoon nap, and tea at the Domhof Hotel, declared that he must be getting on with his 'mission of hate' and retired to write his first article, based solely on his observations during his short walk from the station to the hotel that morning.[115] His article, headlined 'WELL-FED HUNS—STARVATION BLUFF', duly appeared in the *Daily Mail* on 27 December. The Allies must beware of the German 'bluff' on food. 'They have bluffed us often enough in the past', Price warned.[116] Meanwhile, Nevinson and Gibbs quarrelled with British army censors when they discovered that their own reports on malnourished babies and children at Lindenburg hospital had been erased from the Cologne press under British censorship. To add to Nevinson's disappointment, his own telegrams to London carrying the same reports 'went missing'.[117]

The khaki election and the German revolution: the campaign against Labour, the role of the press, and the Committee on Indemnity

The election campaign itself (16 November–14 December) might have been a simple affair. As A. F. Whyte jotted in his diary on Armistice Day, most electors 'will simply say that Lloyd George, having won the war, must stay in power for the Treaty of Peace'.[118] Certainly, Lloyd George started the campaign with tremendous advantages. But it was not to be a straightforward campaign towards a predictable result.

[112] See reports in *The Times*, 'Occupation of Germany', 3 Dec. 1918, 'To the Rhine' and 'Americans Beyond Trèves: Sleek Germans', 4 Dec. 1918, 'The Rhine March' and 'With the French in Germany', 6 Dec. 1918, and 'The Occupation of Cologne', 10 Dec. 1918.

[113] e.g. see Percival Phillips in *Westminster Gazette*, 10 Dec. 1918, and Philip Gibbs in *Daily Chronicle*, 14 Dec. 1918.

[114] Henry Nevinson Journal, 22 Dec. 1918, Nevinson Papers, MS Eng. Misc. c. 620.

[115] C. E. Montague, *Disenchantment* (London, 1922), 176, quoted in Nevinson, *Last Changes, Last Chances*, 151.

[116] *Daily Mail*, 27 Dec. 1918.

[117] Henry Nevinson Journal, 21 and 29 Dec. 1918, Nevinson Papers, MS Eng. Misc. c. 620.

[118] A. F. Whyte Diary, 11 Nov. 1918, Whyte Papers, MSS EUR D 761/3.

In examining the election's impact on the making of policy towards the German revolution, three aspects of the infamous campaign deserve special emphasis: the Coalition's hostility to Labour as 'soft' on Germany; the pressure exerted by the press on the leading politicians to take a strong line against Germany; and the impact of the Imperial War Cabinet's Committee on Indemnity on the campaign. The effect of the so-called 'coupon election' on foreign policy towards the German revolution can be swiftly summarized: the Coalition campaign, in its increasingly anti-Labour orientation, and especially in its promotion of a huge indemnity, further entrenched the tendency of the chief decision-makers to focus on German guilt and to belittle the German revolution. Each of these aspects of the campaign deserves explanation and illustration.

First, the election campaign must be seen, as most Coalition politicians came to see it at the time, as a manœuvre designed chiefly to keep Labour at bay. For the first time in its history, the Labour Party presented itself as the chief opponent of the existing government. In response, it was natural for the Coalition to seek to redirect attention back to the issues of war and to claim the vindications of victory. In addition, the threat of a national rail strike during the campaign itself did much to concentrate the minds of the Coalitionists on the danger of a Labour revolt. Only a government surrender on the principle of an eight-hour day for all railway workers, a concession made just a week from polling day, averted the strike.[119] It was in this atmosphere that the leading Coalition politicians chose their chief political tactic: to smear their opponents, especially their Labour opponents, as 'soft' on Germany. For example, in his first speech of the campaign, at Glasgow on 25 November, Bonar Law exulted in his membership of the victorious 'knock-out blow' Coalition. Then he proceeded, quite inaccurately, to label the whole of the Labour Party as advocates of peace by negotiation during the war.[120] Lloyd George levelled the same charges against the Labour Party in his campaign speeches. In his first provincial speech of the campaign, his 'Land Fit For Heroes' address at Wolverhampton on 23 November, Lloyd George attacked 'revolutionary elements in this country' who were taking foreign money, as in Russia, in an effort to subvert the government.[121] In his final speech of the campaign at Camberwell on 13 December, Lloyd George directly implicated Labour in this plot. The Labour Party, he warned, wanted a class government which would turn Britain into the chaotic state being endured by Russia. He accused Macdonald, Snowden, and Smillie of forming a dominating 'clique' which ran the Labour Party. 'We should have been the slaves and bondmen of Germany if we had listened to these men, and they are the real Labour Party of the present moment', declared Lloyd George. These same men, he alleged, had pulled the Labour Party out of the Coalition when the work of reconstruction was about to begin because the leaders really believed in 'Bolshevism'.[122] Running a campaign to save Britain from socialism, Lloyd George and Bonar

[119] *The Times*, 7 Dec. 1918.   [120] *The Times*, 26 Nov. 1918.
[121] *Daily Chronicle*, 23 Nov. 1918.   [122] *Daily Chronicle*, 13 Dec. 1918.

Law could scarcely afford generous estimates of the new socialist republic of Germany lying vanquished at Britain's feet.

The Coalition press pursued the same themes; the British Labour leaders and the Radicals were 'friends of Germany'. The Hulton *Daily Sketch*, for example, reminded electors that those who had sought 'conversations' with German socialists at the time of the Stockholm conference were now seeking to 'let Jerry off with a caution'.[123] *The Times* savaged Ramsay MacDonald and Philip Snowden in particular as opponents of every measure that had been required to win the war.[124] Even Lloyd George's *Daily Chronicle* descended to the most facile denunciations of Labour as pro-German. For example, a special correspondent for the *Daily Chronicle*, lurking outside the ex-Kaiser's refuge in Amerongen in Holland, reported that he happened to see 'quite by accident' newspapers on the British election with passages marked for the Kaiser's special attention by his staff. 'In several cases, passages underscored in red, were seen to refer to the British Labour Party's prospects and policy', reported the *Daily Chronicle*, apparently in all seriousness.[125]

That the election was part of a vast effort to contain a seismic movement from below—and not just to prevent an historic electoral breakthrough on the part of the Labour Party—was widely admitted in governing circles. Lord Selborne wrote anxiously to Bonar Law pleading with him that, in any reform of the second chamber, the House of Lords should be preserved for the storms ahead, because 'in five years time there will very probably be a Labour government in power'.[126] Even Liberal candidates without the Coalition 'coupon' were by no means free of nervousness at social disruption at the time of the election. Violet Markham, sister of the late Liberal MP Sir Arthur Markham, explained privately that she was standing in her brother's place as an Independent Liberal in order to act 'as a dyke against the revolution'.[127] The economic élite saw society dissolving. From the Bank of England, Cokayne wrote to Benjamin Strong that economy was the need of the hour in Britain, but the great problem facing the government was that 'wage-earners are spending infinitely more than in peacetime and living far more luxuriously'. Only 'the well-to-do classes' were showing any responsibility, he complained.[128] F. S. Oliver detected 'a general disturbed readiness to see a grievance everywhere in a working class which has

---

[123] e.g. see *Daily Sketch*, 'Our Sea', 29 Nov., and 'A Square Deal', 3 Dec., and 'The Choice', 14 Dec. 1918.

[124] e.g. see Valentine Chirol's letter to the editor, *The Times*, 29 Nov. 1918, and 'Mr Snowden On His Record', *The Times*, 7 Dec. 1918.

[125] *Daily Chronicle*, 'Kaiser's Interest in British Elections', 9 Dec. 1918.

[126] Selborne to Bonar Law, 19 Nov. 1918, and Bonar Law to Selborne, 20 Nov. 1918, Bonar Law Papers, 95/1.

[127] Violet Markham to Prothero, 11 Nov. 1918, Prothero Papers, PP1/10.

[128] Cokayne to Benjamin Strong, 19 Nov. 1918, and Strong to Cokayne, 22 Nov. 1918, Governor's Personal Files, G1/420, Bank of England Archives. Strong consoled him with the observation that the social and political unrest would probably die down, now that 'the real centre of infection is in course of being rooted out, namely Germany'.

learned to shoot'.[129] Lord Esher told Stamfordham that if the monarchy itself was to survive the imminent turmoil, then changes of style and even some frugality would be required in order to achieve 'the democratisation of the monarchy'.[130]

The fear of Labour permeated even the international councils hosted by the British government during these same weeks of electioneering. Indeed, it was clear that the whole of the Allied leadership believed itself to be locked in a struggle to deflect the influence of Labour over peacemaking as much as over domestic reconstruction. This emerged from discussions in London on 3 December when, in the middle of the election campaign, the Imperial War Cabinet was joined by the French and Italian leaders to consider the demand of Labour for an international conference to coincide with the Peace Conference. As Barnes noted, the Labour organizers' objective was 'to exercise what influence they could on the peace discussions'. The parallels with Stockholm were painfully obvious. It was decided that a denial of passports was too dangerous and might prompt serious unrest. At the same time, a Labour and socialist conference in the same city as the formal peace conference would, in Clemenceau's words, 'be sure to lead to undesirable public demonstrations'. Eventually it was decided that a Labour and socialist peace conference would be permitted, but that it must be restricted to a neutral country, that is, to a city far away from Paris, the site of the projected Peace Conference.[131]

The struggle with Labour had another crucial effect on the election: the Labour Party's election manifesto of 28 November, which ignored indemnity and argued instead for a capital levy and 'the conscription of wealth', undoubtedly encouraged the enemies of Labour to promote indemnity as part of an antisocialist package.[132] That the Germans should pay, rather than the British taxpayer, was naturally an argument of first resort against confiscatory taxation. For example, Dawson's analysis of the Labour manifesto in *The Times* on 29 November attacked the demand for 'a capital levy and heavily graduated direct taxation' as the only thoroughly objectionable feature of Labour policy. The 'conscription of wealth', announced Dawson, was 'a dangerous experiment at a moment when we need all the capital and all the enterprise at our command to restart our industries and maintain our capacity for employment'.[133]

On 29 November, the day after the release of the Labour Party manifesto, Lloyd George made a fateful election commitment. In a major speech at Newcastle, for the first time from an election platform, he used the word 'indemnities' (rather than the Wilsonian terms 'restoration' or 'reparation') and he embraced the idea of the recovery of Britain's war costs from Germany. He

---

[129] F. S. Oliver to W. E. Oliver, 26 Dec. 1918, Oliver Papers, 77.

[130] Lord Esher to Lord Stamfordham, 26 Nov. 1918, Royal Archives, RA GEO V Q 724/113.

[131] Minutes of a joint conference between the Allied leaders and the Imperial War Cabinet, 11.15 a.m., 3 Dec. 1918, CAB 23/42.

[132] The Labour Manifesto appeared in *The Times*, 29 Nov. 1918.

[133] *The Times*, editorial, 'The Labour Party's Manifesto', 29 Nov. 1918.

declared: 'There is absolutely no doubt about the principle, and that is the principle we should proceed upon (cheers)—that Germany must pay the costs of the war up to the limit of her capacity to do so. (Renewed cheers).'[134] The idea of a German indemnity had been absent altogether from his Wolverhampton address of 23 November. Now the war debt itself was to be recovered from Germany. How can this shift in policy between 23 and 29 November be explained? The only significant developments between the two dates were the creation of the Imperial War Cabinet Committee on Indemnity on 26 November and the release of the Labour manifesto on 28 November. That Labour's emphasis on the 'conscription of wealth' to cover war debt may have encouraged Lloyd George to make this decisive change seems likely.

Once Lloyd George had placed the indemnity on the government's agenda, it was common for Coalition candidates to use it in order to repel the Labour demand for taxation of wealth. To give just two examples from the constituencies, Laming Worthington-Evans, Coalition Unionist candidate for Colchester, in his first campaign speech lambasted the Labour leaders Henderson and Macdonald as advocates of a negotiated peace, and promised that the Coalition would insist on 'indemnities' coming from Germany. Later, he complained that the Labour manifesto contained 'not one word' about payments to be exacted from Germany. 'She must be made to pay to the uttermost farthing', he declared. In his election material he cited the creation of the government's Committee on Indemnity as proof of its good faith.[135] Similarly, Ernest Pretyman, Civil Lord of the Admiralty, in his election speech contrasted the Labour Party's proposal for the 'conscription of wealth' with the Coalition's determination to extract indemnities.[136] Lloyd George himself made the same contrast. In an official statement of Coalition policy released to the press on 6 December, Lloyd George reaffirmed the pursuit of an indemnity as government policy. His statement argued that 'confidence' in Britain was the key to economic progress. 'To capital I say: You shall not be plundered or penalised', declared Lloyd George. This *The Times* instantly interpreted as a timely repudiation of recent speeches by the Labour leader J. R. Clynes who had put the case for steep increases in personal taxation in order to meet the costs of war debt.[137]

The intense conflict between the Labour Party and the Coalition at the centre of the election also produced a last-minute embarrassment in the campaign, an embarrassment which encouraged the Coalition to descend into German-baiting. In early November 1918, General Ivor Maxse began circulating among his

[134] *The Times* and *Daily Chronicle*, 30 Nov. 1918.
[135] *Essex County Standard*, 30 Nov. 1918, *East Anglian Daily Times*, 4 Dec. 1918, Worthington-Evans to A. London, no date [reply to a soldier elector's enquiry]. On his own copy of the Labour candidate's manifesto, against Labour's demand for a capital levy to pay for Britain's war debt, Worthington-Evans scrawled 'Germans?'; see A. Conley, Labour candidate for Colchester, election manifesto. All in Worthington-Evans Papers, MS Eng. Hist. c. 892.
[136] *The Times*, 9 Dec. 1918.
[137] *The Times*, 6 Dec. 1918, and 'City Notes', *The Times*, 7 and 9 Dec. 1918.

brother generals a letter advocating a scheme for post-war Universal Compulsory Military Training. In the letter, Maxse suggested that the politicians would not touch the scheme at the moment, but might be persuaded to do so after the election and the discussion of the 'League of Nations nonsense'.[138] Somehow, in the last days of the campaign, a copy of this letter reached J. H. Thomas, a senior figure in the Labour Party. Without identifying Maxse as the author of the letter, Thomas read its contents at a Labour election meeting at Manchester on 10 December.[139] As Lord Crawford observed, Thomas's disclosures 'caused some excitement and people are clamouring for pledges against conscription'.[140] Indeed, the Labour Party, the Radicals, and the Asquithians all demanded that Lloyd George repudiate his generals' plans for post-war conscription.[141] Lloyd George's penultimate campaign speech at Bristol on 11 December was Lloyd George's first opportunity to reply to Labour's conscription scare. At the commencement of his speech, Lloyd George promised to end conscription in Britain, just as soon as the Peace Conference succeeded in abolishing it in Germany. Then Lloyd George turned back to the issue of indemnity. He produced the figure of £24,000 million for the first time as the total cost of the war, the sum Germany was liable to pay the Allies.[142] Next morning, Lloyd George's own newspaper, the *Daily Chronicle*, had no doubt that he had endorsed this figure in his speech: PREMIER ON GERMANY'S HUGE INDEMNITY. ALLIES TO DEMAND £24,000,000,000, announced the headline.[143] It was a dazzle of noughts—even greater than those flourished by Horatio Bottomley—and it took conscription off the front page.[144] Thus, it is important to note that the major themes of the Coalition campaign, even the notorious indemnity, emerged not simply as the product of anti-German emotionalism, but as deliberate political choices on the part of the Coalition politicians who were determined to drive back an historic challenge from the Labour Party.

Second, as is readily apparent, the role of the press in whipping up anti-German fervour was a most significant factor in the campaign. Demands in the press for the trial of war criminals, the expulsion of aliens, the boycott of German commerce, and the indemnity, all served the Coalition in that they distracted attention from Labour's programme for thoroughgoing domestic reform and the capital levy. However, it would be a mistake to imagine that the strong press campaign in favour of indemnity during the last two weeks of the campaign was

---

[138] Replies to the letter from Tim Harrington, William Robertson, Henry Wilson, and Milner, all referring to the plan for some form of universal training, and noting the likelihood of political opposition to it, are in the folder marked 'Post Bellum' in Ivor Maxse Papers, 69/53/12.

[139] *Westminster Gazette*, 11 Dec. 1918.

[140] Crawford Diary, 11 Dec. 1918, vol. xxxiii, Crawford Papers.

[141] e.g. *Westminster Gazette*, editorial, 'Conscription and Electioneering', 11 Dec. 1918. For a full description of the development of this crisis, see Lorna Jaffe, *Decision to Disarm Germany* (London, 1985), ch. 7.

[142] *The Times*, 12 Dec. 1918.   [143] *Daily Chronicle*, 12 Dec. 1918.

[144] *Westminster Gazette*, editorial, 'Electioneering and Indemnities', 12 Dec. 1918. Bottomley had demanded an indemnity of £10,000 million (*The Times*, 9 Dec. 1918).

merely a stunt conceived in the heat of the election. For some ultra-patriotic newspapers and journals, this was merely the culmination of a long-standing campaign. It was in the shadow of the approaching armistice that articles and letters pleading the case for an indemnity had begun appearing regularly in the newspapers of the 'economic warrior' interest and in some Conservative papers. The *Globe*, for instance, had asked for the proverbial 'uttermost farthing' on 25 October.[145] Hulton's *Evening Standard*, had pressed for the widest possible interpretation of the word 'restoration' as early as 6 November: 'It should mean—and we presume it does mean—every kind of damage suffered by every population, including the very real damage represented in a high income-tax.'[146] The *Pall Mall Gazette* also rejoiced over the British insistence on civilian damage in the Lansing Note, hopefully interpreting this as a dismissal of 'the monstrous and cynical doctrine of "No Indemnities" '.[147] Thus, it cannot be said that the indemnity demand was simply a last-minute hubbub produced by a few journalists to enliven the campaign.

During the first two weeks of the campaign, it is true that the Coalition leaders dodged the pet issues of the Conservative Right and the ultra-patriots, namely, the expulsion of German aliens and the indemnity. The initial Coalition manifesto, published on 22 November, was silent on the subject of indemnity.[148] At Wolverhampton the next day Lloyd George dismissed the question of aliens as one of the 'stunts' of the campaign.[149] He seemed content to pursue only one major concession to ultra-patriotic opinion, the punishment of the Kaiser and other German war criminals. Having persuaded the Imperial War Cabinet on 28 November to accept his plan for a trial of the Kaiser, Lloyd George featured this in all his remaining election addresses.[150] Bonar Law also did not touch upon the subject of indemnity in his first major address, at Glasgow on 25 November. Law told his listeners that they must trust the government to negotiate the best terms of peace at the Peace Conference, for these 'cannot be settled by public discussion'.[151] The only rumble of dissatisfaction in the press on indemnity came in response to a speech from Winston Churchill. On 26 November, Churchill told an audience that the government sympathized with the demand that the Germans pay the costs of war. 'If the Allies had not claimed this', he explained, 'it was for one reason only. It is not physically possible for them to do so. Reparation for damage will alone run into thousands of millions.'[152] Churchill's interpretation followed that of Lloyd George; indemnity was ruled out not by Britain's international engagements under the Lansing Note but simply by practical

---

[145] *Globe*, editorial, 'To the Uttermost Farthing', 25 Oct. 1918.
[146] *Evening Standard*, editorial, 'Reparation and Punishment', 6 Nov. 1918. The same point is made in *Evening Standard*, 'A Londoner's Diary', 7 Nov. 1918.
[147] *Pall Mall Gazette*, editorial, 'Germany to Pay', 6 Nov. 1918.
[148] *The Times*, 'Coalition Manifesto', 22 Nov. 1918.
[149] *The Times*, 25 Nov. 1918.
[150] Minutes of the Imperial War Cabinet, 28 Nov. 1918, CAB 23/42.
[151] *The Times*, 26 Nov. 1918.   [152] *Evening Standard*, 27 Nov. 1918.

considerations. On 27 November, the *Evening Standard* professed horror at Churchill's revelation that the government had 'decided not even to consider ways and means of making Germany pay'.[153] But there was no great outcry from the Coalition press as a whole.

The Northcliffe press was not crusading on the indemnity during the first fortnight of the election campaign; the *Daily Mail* was not pressing for war costs or even using the word 'indemnity'. Its sole criticism of the Wolverhampton speech of 23 November was in response to Lloyd George's dismissal of the aliens question as a 'side issue'.[154] The *Daily Mail* sought assurances on the exclusion of German goods, and on the 'ton for ton' compensation policy.[155] Even on 29 November, the morning of the Newcastle speech, an editorial urged electors to pin Coalition candidates down on compensation for shipping losses.[156] The Northcliffe press began to promote the indemnity with real enthusiasm only *after* Lloyd George introduced the subject in his Newcastle speech of 29 November. Certainly, the Northcliffe press, and the Coalition press in general, reacted to the novel feature of Lloyd George's speech immediately. The Coalition press was full of praise for the 'additions to his electioneering speeches' and rejoiced over the 'immense relief' and 'satisfaction' felt, supposedly throughout the country, at the Prime Minister's apparent abandonment of the lesser claim to reparation.[157] Dawson produced an editorial in *The Times* praising the Prime Minister's stand on the legal principle that Germany be forced 'to pay costs of the actions she has lost'. Dawson advised, however, that the wisest course was still for Britain to pursue as a first priority the quantifiable shipping losses she had suffered.[158]

Northcliffe's response was most significant. Immediately *after* the speech, he intervened to instruct his editors on the importance of this new departure in the election. On 30 November, he wrote to Dawson urging him to push harder for the indemnity, and warning him that Lloyd George had friends such as the financier Baron Schröder 'who like every other financier is trying to prevent Germany having to pay for the war'.[159] In his communiqué to the staff of the *Daily Mail* on 2 December, Northcliffe insisted that details on Germany's wealth be published. 'Someone who understands the subject', he instructed, 'should keep it before the public prominently each day.'[160] The effects of the instructions

[153] *Evening Standard*, editorial, 'Our Claims on Germany', 27 Nov. 1918.

[154] *Daily Mail*, editorial, 'Tests For the Prime Minister', 25 Nov. 1918.

[155] *Daily Mail*, letters to the editor under the heading 'Mr Lloyd George and the Huns', 26–8 Nov., and editorial, 'A Test For Candidates', 27 Nov. 1918.

[156] *Daily Mail*, editorial, ' "Ton for Ton": Germany Must Pay', 29 Nov. 1918. Only the *Daily Sketch* was pressing Lloyd George to embrace indemnity on the morning of 29 Nov; see *Daily Sketch* editorial, 'What the Voters Demand', 29 Nov. 1918.

[157] e.g. *News of the World*, editorial, 'Germany Must Pay the Price', 1 Dec. 1918, and *Pall Mall Gazette*, editorial, 'Retribution', 30 Nov. 1918, and editorial, 'Can Germany Pay?', 3 Dec. 1918.

[158] *The Times*, editorial, 'The Kaiser—and Ton For Ton', 30 Nov. 1918.

[159] Northcliffe to Dawson, 30 Nov. 1918, Dawson Correspondence, Northcliffe file, *The Times* Archive.

[160] Northcliffe communiqué, 2 Dec. 1918, Northcliffe Communiqués, D 303.5.

were seen immediately in the *Daily Mail*.[161] Northcliffe's motives were both personal and political. Personally, from this point on he was committed to the indemnity as an alternative to high taxation, of which he was a bitter critic.[162] By no means was he alone in this on the Right; during the election, for example, a correspondent of Leo Maxse reminded him that 'a large annual contribution from German taxes' would assist in the liquidation of debt and in the defeat of 'all this Bolshevism at the Treasury and in this government'.[163] But it is important to note that Northcliffe began to badger his editors on the issue *after* Lloyd George had made his first commitment. Northcliffe's notorious 'From War to Peace' manifesto of 4 November had not mentioned an indemnity to cover war costs, only reparation. Therefore, in introducing the idea of indemnity into the campaign, with all his prestige as Prime Minister, Lloyd George was not caving in to pressure from Northcliffe or the Coalition press. Rather, he was reaching over to the Right to borrow one of the leading points in the programme of the National Party and the 'economic warriors'.

This is not to minimize the important role played by the press in the last two weeks of campaigning. The right-wing press as a whole began to celebrate indemnity and to hound Coalition ministers on anti-German themes. Coalition ministers and candidates in turn sought to defend themselves from criticism by embracing the most extravagant rhetoric on the indemnity. Even the most infamous phrase from the campaign, Geddes's 'until the pips squeak', was extracted under pressure from the newspapers. The story behind the phrase is instructive. Speaking in Cambridge on 27 November, Geddes dwelt on the practical difficulties of obtaining an indemnity and especially the danger of encouraging German manufacturing by demanding a vast payment. Echoing the Prime Minister's reservations of the previous day (spoken in the privacy of the Imperial War Cabinet), Geddes explained that indemnities of fifty to sixty thousand million pounds, paid in goods, gold, or labour, might ruin British manufacturing and employment. Geddes complained that he 'had never yet found anyone to tell him how, without hurting ourselves, an indemnity of that kind could be received'.[164] Geddes found himself suddenly portrayed in the press as 'pro-German or weak-kneed'. The *Daily Mail*, significantly enough, did not attack him on the indemnities question. Rather, he was attacked for pointing out that the danger of forcing Germany to rebuild all Britain's ships under the ton-for-ton policy was that Britain might encourage German supremacy in ship-building.[165] He responded on 2 December with two letters to his constituency chairman pleading that his speech had been misunderstood; he was entirely in favour of

---

[161] *Daily Mail*, editorial, 'Germany Can Pay: If the Allies Make Her', 3 Dec. 1918.

[162] See Northcliffe to Harold Harmsworth, 10 Apr., 1919, and his income tax statistics, quoted in Pound and Harmsworth, *Northcliffe*, 712 and 685 respectively.

[163] Bernard Mallet to Leo Maxse, 7 Dec. 1918, Maxse Papers, vol. 475.

[164] *Cambridge Daily News*, 28 Nov. 1918.

[165] *Daily Mail*, editorial, ' "Ton for Ton": Germany Must Pay', 29 Nov. 1918.

extracting full war costs from Germany.[166] Then, speaking at the Guildhall in
Cambridge on 9 December, he answered his accusers in the press directly:

I was rather amused that I should be a pro-Boche, but it does not fit me a bit. Did you
think that the terms of the naval armistice were pro-Boche? I would like to tell you this:
I fought for three days at Versailles to get 'em stronger and I couldn't . . . And I am the
man that is weak-kneed about the Germans! (Laughter) If I am returned, Germany is
going to pay restitution, reparation and indemnity, and I have personally no doubt we
will get out of her all you can squeeze out of a lemon, and a bit more. (Prolonged
applause). [167]

The following evening, addressing the Beaconsfield Club, he refined the fateful
metaphor: 'The Germans, if this government is returned, are going to pay every
penny; they are going to be squeezed as a lemon is squeezed—until the pips
squeak.'[168]

The intimidation of Coalition ministers by the press extended even to those
chosen to serve in the Imperial War Cabinet's Indemnity Committee. Referring
to meetings of the committee, the Northcliffe *Evening News* of 6 December
alleged, quite incorrectly, that 'the only objector to making Germany pay was a
well-known Tory Junker, of the bee-keeping variety', an unmistakable reference
to Walter Long, the Colonial Secretary.[169] The accusation exemplified the determination of the Northcliffe press to root out 'reactionary' Conservatives, those
who, according to 'the Chief', might favour the Milner policy of 'soft' treatment
for Germany. On this occasion, the accusation in the *Evening News* was quite
incorrect, for Long was co-operating quite happily in the committee with the
plans of Hughes and Hewins for an indemnity. Long threatened legal action
against the *Evening News*. Admitting the error, Associated Newspapers deposited
a cheque for one hundred guineas in favour of St George's Hospital as an out-
of-court settlement. It was a small incident, but illustrated how eager the
Northcliffe press was to detect and punish any suspicion of departure from the
now 'correct' position on indemnity.[170] In his own election speeches, Long
proved how unfair Northcliffe's slurs had been, campaigning for both indemnity
and protection: he was adamant that Germany would pay 'to the last farthing',
even if it took thirty years, and would not be permitted to raise the funds by
'dumping articles on our markets'.[171]

Similarly, Lloyd George was pursued by the Northcliffe press on the indemnity immediately *after* the Newcastle speech of 29 November. While the Unionist
press congratulated the Prime Minister for the indemnities proffered at

---

[166] *Cambridge Daily News*, 3 Dec. 1918.   [167] *Cambridge Daily News*, 10 Dec. 1918.
[168] *Cambridge Daily News*, 11 Dec. 1918.
[169] *Evening News*, 'Diary of a Man About Town', 6 Dec. 1918. Notoriously, Walter Long had recommended that ex-soldiers could be given small lots of land and keep bees. See also a poem mocking Long in *Daily Mail*, 7 Dec. 1918, and Long's complaints about bullying by the press reported in
Daily Mail, 10 Dec. 1918.
[170] Long to Beevor, 8 Dec. 1918, and Beevor to Long, 19 Dec. 1918, Long Papers, WRO 947/674.
[171] *The Times*, 5 Dec. 1918.

Newcastle, the *Daily Mail* lacerated him for 'wobbling', that is, for attaching the phrase 'up to her capacity' to his indemnity demand upon Germany.[172] Steady pressure was maintained in both *The Times* and the *Daily Mail*.[173] In addition, a personal cable from Northcliffe reached Lloyd George on 6 December, urging him to strip away any qualifications from his pledge to pursue full recovery of war costs. Lloyd George appeared defiant; he cabled Northcliffe in response: 'Don't be always making mischief.'[174] Moreover, at Leeds on 7 December he said nothing about indemnity. But his defiance was short lived. In his notorious speech at Bristol on 12 December, he returned to the subject. Here he combined frank warnings about the problems and dangers inherent in an indemnity, and even a declaration that he had no wish to raise 'false hopes', with a renewed commitment to pursue the entire cost of the war. He made no pretence of shrouding the indemnity in the language of restoration or reparation. The words 'indemnity' and 'cost of the war' were used constantly. Drawing an analogy between a lost war and the settlement of costs after unsuccessful litigation, Lloyd George explained: 'The costs of the winning party must come before the costs of the litigant who has lost the suit. Therefore, whatever our indemnity is, it must come before the six or seven thousand millions which is owing to the Germans themselves in their own country'. While Lloyd George did insist that the indemnity be collected in ways that would avoid doing damage to Britain, this was no longer presented as a reason for caution on the principle of indemnity itself. 'There is absolutely no doubt about the principle', he assured his audience. Thus he capitulated completely on the question of recovering war costs. The climax of the speech included this blunt summary: 'Now let me summarise first, as far as justice is concerned. We have an absolute right to demand the whole cost of the war from Germany. The second point is that we propose to demand the whole cost of the war. (Cheers).'[175] Moving to an adjoining hall where an overflow crowd had gathered, Lloyd George then delivered a second short address, probably extempore, which added an unforgettable image to the indemnities theme: 'Those who started it [the war] must pay to the uttermost farthing, and we shall search their pockets for it. (Laughter and cheers).'[176]

Thus the press did play a critical role in drumming up support for the indemnity. But it was the Prime Minister himself who opened the door to this orchestrated effort in his speech at Newcastle on 29 November. No sustained or overwhelming campaign in the press for the full recovery of war costs *preceded* his Newcastle pledge. But, having introduced the idea, Lloyd George found that the ultra-patriots, the National Party, the Northcliffe press, his own election

[172] *Daily Mail*, editorial, 'Wobbling', 30 Nov. 1918.

[173] *Daily Mail*, editorials, 'A Straight Question to the Prime Minister', and 'A Caution to Voters', 6 and 9 Dec. 1918, and *The Times*, editorials, 'What is the Whole Bill?' and 'Making Germany Pay', 7 and 9 Dec. 1918.

[174] Pound and Harmsworth, *Northcliffe*, 682.

[175] *Morning Post*, 12 Dec. 1918.   [176] *The Times*, 12 Dec. 1918.

advisers, and several of his own Conservative ministers, provided a formidable team determined to make his promise an unequivocal one.

A third aspect of the campaign that was important in shaping the British reaction to events in Germany was the role of the Imperial War Cabinet's Indemnity Committee. As might have been expected, the Indemnity Committee became a vehicle for promoting the views of the 'economic warriors' on indemnity during the election. The 'experts' summoned to appear before the committee, and those who supplied written testimony, were naturally enough the business friends of Hewins and Long, men with tariff reform and FBI connections such as Herbert Gibbs, the banker, Charles Tennyson, Basil Peto, Hugh Chisolm, financial editor of *The Times*, and Hugo Hirst, chairman of the General Electric Company and a founder of the protectionist British Manufacturers' Association.[177] Under Hughes's chairmanship, the Indemnity Committee was not long delayed over any consideration of the legal niceties of the Lansing Note. Within three days of its first meeting, the committee resolved upon Britain's right to pursue indemnity. Hughes, eager to have some impact on the developing election campaign, immediately dispatched a cable to Lloyd George at Newcastle on 29 November informing him that the committee had 'agreed unanimously to recommend a claim for an indemnity'.[178] Walter Long also sought to bring the committee's work to bear upon the election. He wrote to Bonar Law on 28 November assuring him of the 'useful work' being done in the Indemnity Committee, and decrying the fact that some ministers were quoting such low figures for indemnity as £2,000 million pounds, a figure that was 'quite insufficient', in his view, given the 'strong feeling' in the City. He recommended that no figures be given in Coalition election material, a suggestion which Law commended as 'very good'.[179] Long was even more candid in the committee. 'We have an election coming on and this is one of the questions which is exercising the public mind more than any other.'[180] Members of the committee kept a sharp eye on the Prime Minister's speeches. When Lloyd George at Newcastle on 29 November committed himself to an indemnity from Germany 'up to the limit of her capacity to pay', Long was much perturbed: 'I am afraid the P. M. made some bad *faux pas* in Newcastle. Where are we drifting?', he wrote to Hewins.[181] The committee scarcely misconceived its essentially political role.

Indeed, the extraordinary nature of the committee's deliberations within the conference room of the Colonial Office betrayed this all too plainly. At the formal meetings, any experts who suggested moderate opinions on indemnity were

---

[177] On Hirst, see Hugo Hirst, 'Two Autobiographical Fragments', in R. P. T. Davenport-Hines, *Speculators and Patriots: Essays in Business Biography* (London, 1986), 124–33.

[178] Hughes to Long, and Hughes to Lloyd George, 29 Nov. 1918, Long Papers, WRO 947/673.

[179] Long to Bonar Law, 28 Nov. 1918, Bonar Law Papers, BL 84/3/24.

[180] Minutes of the Imperial War Cabinet Committee on Indemnity, 29 Nov. 1918, CAB 27/43, quoted in Albert Lentin, *Lloyd George, Woodrow Wilson and the Guilt of Germany* (Leicester, 1984), 21.

[181] Long to Hewins, 30 Nov. 1918, Hewins Papers, 72.

treated as tainted witnesses. Hughes explained to the Imperial War Cabinet that those experts who knew Germany best provided unsafe evidence because they 'leaned to the German side'.[182] Sir Charles Addis of the Hong Kong-Shanghai Bank was one such witness; he described in his diary how he was 'heckled for an hour' by Hughes when he appeared before the committee.[183] Addis was dumbfounded at the ignorance of Hughes, telling friends that the idea of his leading an 'expert' committee was laughable.[184] 'Neither Hughes nor Walter Long seemed to know anything about the subject', even Hewins conceded, 'and I had to suggest the materials and course of procedure for the enquiry.'[185] The careless approach to the assembly of evidence provoked much comment behind the scenes. Even the Australian camp had doubts about the proceedings. Reporting purely on the economic issues, Eggleston argued that the deleterious effects of an indemnity were exaggerated and that an indemnity could be 'safely fixed at a very large figure'.[186] But his friend Latham, on the other hand, reported that the Lansing Note was 'the point of honour', and that an indemnity was clearly ruled out by it. 'Surely the demand for a general war indemnity in effect treats the peace agreement as a "scrap of paper" ', Latham argued provocatively. He advised that it 'cannot honourably be contended that the Allies are not bound by the Fourteen Points'.[187] Such unwelcome advice was simply cast aside. Hewins's influence proved to be paramount, especially outside the committee's formal meetings. He visited Hughes at his flat and, with Robert Garran's assistance, the two produced an initial draft report; 'I dictated the conclusions', Hewins jotted in his diary.[188] The Indemnity Committee adopted the inspired guess of Lord Cunliffe that Germany could pay an indemnity of £24,000 million. Only George Foster, much perturbed over the slapdash manner of the proceedings of the committee, resisted signing the draft report, but at the last moment 'he gave way'.[189] Hughes's motives were plain: he was avenging Lloyd George's blunder, as he saw it, in saddling the Empire with the Fourteen Points. This was revealed in his private correspondence with Munro-Ferguson on 14 December:

We have put in a very hot report in favour of Germany paying the entire cost of the war . . . But of course Wilson's 14 Points are the law of the Medes and Persians and it is doubtful whether we *can even ask for an indemnity*. The Versailles Conference did a most extraordinary thing when it agreed to make terms upon Wilson's 14 Points!! Why the devil

[182] Minutes of the Imperial War Cabinet, 3 Dec. 1918, CAB 23/42.

[183] Addis Diary, 5 Dec. 1918, Sir Charles Addis Papers, 36.

[184] Addis to D. Mills, 14 Dec. 1918, Sir Charles Addis Papers, 179.

[185] Hewins Diary, 'End of October 1918 to May 13th 1919', 11, Hewins Papers.

[186] Eggleston, 'Memorandum on the Economic Effects of Indemnity', undated, Eggleston Papers, MS 423/6/342–360.

[187] Latham, 'Preliminary Notes on the Fourteen Points', dated 'London, Nov. 1918', Australian Archives, A 981/6.

[188] Garran Diary, 30 Nov. 1918, Garran Papers, Series 5, Box 3, and Hewins Diary, 'End of October 1918 to May 13th 1919', 10, Hewins Papers.

[189] Hewins Diary, 'End of October 1918 to May 13th 1919', 11, Hewins Papers.

they did it, no man knows. However, we must make the best of it—and I shall argue stoutly that we can ask for an indemnity under the Reparation clause.[190]

Whatever their private opinions, in public the Coalition leaders did not treat the Indemnity Committee with anything but respect. Indeed, Lloyd George boosted its reputation. When an Inter-Allied Conference of French, Italian, and British leaders met in London on 2 December, at the mid-point of the British election campaign, it was decided to set up an international Reparations and Indemnities Committee; the next day, the Imperial War Cabinet agreed that Hughes's committee should itself produce the names of the three British representatives for the new inter-Allied body (eventually Hughes, Cunliffe, and Lord Sumner were put forward). Lloyd George made no protest. Thus, Hughes's influence over the indemnity question was to be extended to the Peace Conference itself. Nor did Lloyd George resist Hughes's pointed suggestion that the terms of reference of the new inter-Allied body should include both reparations *and indemnity*. As he promised Hughes, he secured this change to the resolution setting up the new body on 3 December, informing the joint conference of the Imperial War Cabinet and the visiting Entente leaders that 'it was proposed to ask for *indemnity* as well as reparation'.[191]

Meanwhile, Hughes's Indemnity Committee did not have to force its extreme conclusions on the Coalition leaders as the election campaign proceeded; rather, the committee was cited approvingly and even invited to throw its weight into the election. At Newcastle on 29 November Lloyd George told his audience that the Committee on Indemnity, 'a very strong committee of experts representing every shade of opinion', had assured him that there was 'no doubt as to the justice of the demand'.[192] On 10 December, on the eve of his Bristol speech, Lloyd George pressed Hughes for a copy of the Indemnity Committee's interim report; the draft was rushed to him on the same day.[193] In the election speeches that followed, Lloyd George and Bonar Law put the committee's appointment and decisions to good political use, citing them in major speeches as evidence of the government's eagerness to hunt an indemnity.[194] Thus the cynicism behind the production of the report was matched only by the cynicism of its exploitation in the election by the Coalition leadership.

Finally, the Coalition's decision to embrace indemnity undoubtedly helped shape commonly held views of the German revolution. Throughout the election campaign as before, propaganda in favour of the indemnity was often linked with

---

[190] Hughes to Munro-Ferguson, 14 Dec. 1918, Novar Papers, MS 696/2748–9, emphasis in the original.

[191] Minutes of the Imperial War Cabinet, 10.30 a.m., 3 Dec. 1918, and Minutes of a joint conference between the Allied leaders and the Imperial War Cabinet, 11.15 a.m., 3 Dec. 1918, CAB 23/42. Italics in original.

[192] *The Times*, 30 Nov. 1918.

[193] L. F. Fitzhardinge, *William Morris Hughes*, ii. *The Little Digger* (Sydney, 1979), 380–2.

[194] For example, see Bonar Law at Bootle, *The Times*, 4 Dec. 1918, the press release summarizing government policy in *The Times*, 6 Dec. 1918, and Lloyd George at Bristol, *The Times*, 12 Dec. 1918.

an assertion of the guilt of the whole of the German people, and the belittling of the German revolution. The Prime Minister's own speeches on indemnity demonstrated the point. When promoting indemnity he insisted on the guilt of 'the German people' just as earnestly as the writers of the *Globe* or *National Review*. At the Queen's Hall, London, on 9 December he condemned highly placed Germans, but added that 'the German people, who sanctioned the war, who went into the war with a full and enthusiastic mind, who would now have been acclaiming the victory if there had been one—they must be held responsible too'.[195] 'You may depend upon it', Lloyd George told his audience at Bristol, 'that the first consideration in the minds of the Allies will be the interests of the people upon whom Germany has made war, and not the interests of the German people who have been guilty of this crime against humanity.'[196] Bonar Law, similarly, was busily denying any distinction between the German government and people in his election addresses. At Mile End on 11 December, he asserted that 'the country is responsible for its government, and for the crimes of its government, and has a right to suffer for them'. The next day at Glasgow, Bonar Law was equally firm. 'About the justice of making them pay no one had any doubt. It would be a monstrous thing', he pleaded, 'if the German nation—for a nation was responsible for the crimes that the government committed—got off as easily as a nation against whom its crimes had been committed.' The revolution was cited as another reason for caution and toughness: 'And more—there has been a revolution in Germany, everything is turned upside down', said Bonar Law, 'but nobody knows what the meaning of that is.' The new Germany might seek to avenge its defeat. Thus a punitive indemnity had the added advantage of impoverishing Germany so that 'they will have no money to pile up arms'.[197] Even Churchill, who came later than most to the support of an indemnity, assured the electors that the whole German nation was guilty: 'They were all in it and they must all suffer for it.'[198]

These assertions of the guilt of the 'German people' always earned special praise in the Coalition press. J. A. R. Marriott, the Conservative MP and a leading personality on the Unionist Business Committee, produced a definitive statement for *Nineteenth Century* declaring that the payment to the 'uttermost farthing' was founded on the belief that the German people were '*criminis participes*'. The death of the Kaiser 'shall not purge the guilt of the people'.[199] In the last week of the campaign the indemnity was defended typically in the Coalition press with articles stressing the 'emptiness' of the German revolution. 'The basis of any [German] Government will be the same, whether it flies the

[195] *The Times*, 10 Dec. 1918.　　　　[196] *The Times* and *Morning Post*, 12 Dec. 1918.

[197] Text of Bonar Law speeches, Mile End, 11 Dec., and Glasgow, 12 Dec. 1918, Bonar Law Papers, 97/1/9.

[198] *The Times*, 27 Nov. 1918. Churchill ascribed his own abandonment of the distinction between reparation and indemnity to the pressure of electioneering; see Winston Churchill, *The World Crisis: The Aftermath* (London, 1929), 42–8.

[199] J. A. R. Marriott, 'The Final Test', *Nineteenth Century*, 502 (Dec. 1918).

eagle or the red flag.'[200] Inspired by Bonar Law's speeches on German popular
guilt, the *Daily Chronicle* produced an article entitled 'Why the German people
are Responsible for the Crimes of the Kaiser'. It explained that, although
Germany had no democracy at the time of the war, this 'does not lessen the guilt
of the German nation, for the only reason they had not the power was that they
had not the moral energy to use it'.[201] The German people, it seemed, were to
blame for not having a democracy as well as for fighting the war. Thus contempt
for the new German democracy gained respectability during the election campaign because the leading Coalition politicians peddled contempt in justifying
punishment and the indemnity. In locking indemnity into Coalition policy, the
Coalition leaders also entrenched ultra-patriotic views on national guilt and the
sham revolution in Germany.

Similarly, material submitted to the Indemnity Committee assumed hostility
to the revolution. For example, Hewins commended the views of Professor
J. Shield Nicholson, professor of political economy and mercantile law at
Edinburgh University, who argued that indemnities were required to assist the
'moral recovery' of the German people, and to bring home the reality of defeat.
The revolution was at best incomplete, at worst a deliberate deception, argued
Nicholson. 'The people made what they called a revolution but they left the control of the Army in the hands of the old High Command. The Kaiser and the
princes and kinglets were all allowed to escape in first-class comfort.'[202] Other
evidence submitted to the committee presented the German socialists as a threat
to the indemnity demand. Hugo Hirst, for example, noted that he had made no
allowance for Germany's own needs for pensions in his estimates of Germany's
capacity to pay, but added that pensions were 'a measure on which the German
Socialists are very insistent'.[203]

The linking of indemnity with the assertion that the German revolution was
all bluff was evident also in Unionist election material. The election manifesto of
W. Burdett-Coutts, the Coalition Unionist candidate for Westminster and a
prominent tariff reformer, illustrates the point. Under the heading, 'A GREAT
INDEMNITY', Burdett-Coutts heaped scorn on Germany:

a nation which has suddenly, under stress of circumstances, put on the garb of democracy
and comes forward under the red flag as the German people. They profess to have thrown
over their former rulers, their Junkers, tradition and pervading war spirit . . . I do not
trust the change. All the pacifists in this country, who tried their best for a peace without

[200] *Pall Mall Gazette*, editorials, 'Chaos in Germany', and 'The Unchanging Hun', 9 and 10 Dec.
1918.
[201] *Daily Chronicle*, 'Why the German People are Responsible for the Crimes of the Kaiser', 13
Dec. 1918. For a similar explanation see *Pall Mall Gazette*, editorial, 'Mr Lloyd George's Manifesto',
6 Dec. 1918.
[202] Clippings from the *Scotsman*, 14 Dec. 1918, sent to Long by Hewins, endorsed as 'very useful' by Long and Hughes, 22 and 23 Dec. 1918, Long Papers, WRO 947/673.
[203] Hirst to Hughes, 10 Dec. 1918, and Hirst to Hewins, 12 Dec. 1918, with enclosed
'Memorandum', Hewins Papers, 72/341.

victory; all the forces of International Socialism . . . will be arrayed to make the world believe that the reformation is complete and trustworthy, that the German democracy will be safe to deal with, and that easy terms of peace should be granted to Germany. I distrust the change all the more when supported by such authorities. I have never had the slightest faith in the distinction attempted to be drawn between the German rulers and the German people.

Burdett-Coutts concluded that the only way to deal with such a recalcitrant people was to impose a great indemnity which would 'relieve the Allies of at least a part of the unbearable taxation which Germany has wantonly imposed on them'. Only an indemnity could make another war impossible, he asserted.[204]

The jingoism of the election: popular passions or political choices?

How should the campaign as a whole be interpreted? A great many historians have examined the Coalition's pledges to 'make Germany pay' and puzzled over the Prime Minister's motives in particular.[205] Lloyd George is often depicted as a man driven by an irresistible popular clamour. Indeed, only a year later this was the interpretation Lloyd George himself offered, telling an incredulous Sidney and Beatrice Webb that the 'stunt which they put up about indemnities was most unfortunate'.[206] Those close to Lloyd George tended to blame the crowds. At Paris in 1919, Kerr told Eggleston confidentially that in the course of the election Lloyd George had been simply swept off his feet whilst speech-making at Bristol, so that 'the statesman was betrayed by the orator'.[207] Historians who defend Lloyd George offer similar explanations; they have pointed out, correctly, that he did not lead the jingoist chanting, that he was by no means alone in indulging in wild rhetoric, and that the pledges he eventually gave regarding an indemnity were never unqualified.[208] It is true that he called for an indemnity up to Germany's 'capacity to pay', and that he often mentioned the difficulties of obtaining a large indemnity without endangering British trade and manufacturing. Nevertheless, his commitment to an indemnity to cover war costs as distinct from reparation was an absolutely clear election pledge.

---

[204] W. Burdett-Coutts Election Manifesto, dated 27 Nov. 1918, Hewins Papers, 72.

[205] Accounts hostile to Lloyd George, depicting him as capitulating to political and economic pressure groups during the election, include Wilson, *Downfall of the Liberal Party*, ch. 6, Bunselmeyer, *The Cost of the War*, ch. 8, Lentin, *Lloyd George, Wilson and the Guilt of Germany*, ch. 1, and Kent, *Spoils of War*, 28–40. A muted defence of Lloyd George as reluctant to pursue anti-German themes is given in Morgan, *Consensus and Disunity*, ch. 2. Lloyd George's own argument that public opinion was all in favour of indemnity, and that Mr Asquith also was in favour, is given in his *The Truth About Reparations and War Debts* (London, 1932), ch. 3, while his defence of his own election speeches is in his *Memoirs of the Peace Conference*, i, ch. 9.

[206] G. L. Dickinson to Keynes, no date (filed as 1920), Keynes Papers, EC/2/2/106.

[207] Eggleston, 'The Peace Conference at Paris', typescript memoir, Eggleston Papers, MS 423/6/14. Eggleston reported that this explanation of the Bristol speech was given to him by 'someone close to Lloyd George's entourage', probably Philip Kerr, the only member of Lloyd George's circle with whom Eggleston was intimate at Paris.

[208] e.g. Morgan, *Consensus and Disunity*, 39–40.

Did the push towards jingoism during the election campaign come from the British people? Of course, this was the view favoured in the 'patriotic' press. According to this version, the jingoism of the electorate was elemental; the politicians, supposedly sheltered from the populace in Westminster, had simply underestimated the spontaneous passion of the people and were surprised to be confronted by it on the hustings.[209] It is true that the 'public mood', such as it may have been discerned from enthusiastic audiences at political meetings, affected politicians, by their own admission. Not that all succumbed to a mood of jingoism if indeed it was dominant. The Labour Party continued to denounce indemnity as a 'stunt' to the end, and put up 'A Peace of Justice and Reconciliation' as the first of its own 'Fourteen Points' for the election.[210] Asquith defended the priority of reparation, condemned notions of economic boycott, and spoke of the need for a 'clean slate'. Only under hostile questioning late in the campaign did he declare himself in favour of Lloyd George's views on indemnity.[211] Even on the government side, Barnes bluntly disavowed indemnities because 'he did not believe they would ever get them'. It was more important, said Barnes, to seek reparation only.[212] Bonar Law also showed some restraint. While insisting on indemnity, he conceded that it was unlikely Germany could ever pay all of Britain's war debt.[213] There were some signs of moderation, therefore, from the platform orators. However, a good many of Lloyd George's political allies claimed at the time to have been pushed in a jingoist direction by the crowds. Amery, for example, recorded in his diary that he had dropped the theme of reconstruction and turned to indemnity, aliens, and the Kaiser's trial instead in order to please his audiences—but, one suspects, not reluctantly.[214] 'Like everybody else Lloyd George a month ago thought that reconstruction and domestic issues would absorb attention', wrote Lord Crawford. 'But contact with the electorate has directed the public mind to other factors—notably the punishment of the Kaiser and the question of indemnities.'[215] The Liberal Coalitionists were not so definite on the mood of the people.

---

[209] The *Spectator* was typical: 'One of the few satisfactory features of the present General Election is the way in which electoral pressure has stiffened the attitude of the Government with regard to the indemnity' (*Spectator*, editorial, 'The German Indemnity', 14 Dec. 1918). For other examples, see the views of *The Times*'s Parliamentary Correspondent, 'Two Vital Questions: Punishment and Payment', *The Times*, 30 Nov. 1918, or *Daily Sketch*, 'Man in the Street', 2 Dec. 1918.

[210] e.g. see *Daily Mail*, Labour Column, 'Election Stunts no. 1: Making the Germans Pay', 12 Dec., and 'Labour's Fourteen Points', 13 Dec. 1918. In a speech at Cardiff on 7 Dec. Henderson used the phrase 'full indemnity', but he made it clear that this was to be applied to 'restitution for devastation and wrong-doing' and that Britain's claims were limited by the armistice document which was in danger of being treated as a 'scrap of paper'; see reports of speeches by Henderson and Ramsay MacDonald, *The Times*, 9 Dec. 1918.

[211] In his early speeches he avoided the word indemnity altogether; see Asquith's speeches at Rochdale and Nottingham reported in *The Times*, 9 and 11 Dec. 1918. For his announcement of agreement with Lloyd George's views, see report of the speech at Pittenweem, *The Times*, 13 Dec. 1918.

[212] *The Times* and *Daily Mail*, 11 Dec. 1918.   [213] *Morning Post*, 12 Dec. 1918.

[214] Amery Diary, 29 Nov.–14 Dec. 1918, Amery Papers.

[215] Crawford Diary, 6 Dec. 1918, vol. xxxiii, Crawford Papers.

Herbert Fisher found one meeting 'noisy and troublesome', but at another he was well received when he chose to speak on the League of Nations. But, he wrote from Crewe, 'the people here are very violent against Germany—especially the mothers. I am afraid it will take a long time before the feeling dies down'.[216] Defeated Asquithian Liberals and Radicals also blamed 'the people', especially women voters, for being easily swayed by 'vulgar catch-words', but only as much as they blamed Lloyd George's 'demagogic declamations' and the 'patriotic' press.[217] Bryce was typical: in his view, the 'mass of the people' had been 'swept away', and the press had 'never been so successful in misrepresentation or vilification'.[218] So great is the weight of contemporary opinion that the 'public mood' must be included as a factor in any explanation.

However, neither the intangible temper of the public, nor the inflammatory work of the press, can provide a complete explanation. No doubt it suited some of the Coalition politicians to believe that they faced a more or less spontaneous wave of anti-German anger arising from the people, pushed along by the irresponsibility of Northcliffe's journalism; for, according to this explanation, the more shameful excesses of the campaign could be seen to have originated outside the Coalition. However, this has all the appearance of a rationalization after the event. The political pressures and expectations were to a large extent encouraged by the Coalition politicians, by the influential economic élites allied to the Coalition, and by the Coalition press. Northcliffe, estranged from the Coalition and giving a free column to Labour, was scarcely the evil genius of the campaign. While the Prime Minister might have given his final and most extreme public pledges on the indemnity only after having been run to earth by the Northcliffe press, other members of the 'knock-out blow' Coalition willingly employed the catch-cry of indemnity without the press barking at their heels. Even a moderate Conservative like Robert Cecil appeared to endorse the indemnity claim without qualification: he told a meeting at Letchworth late in the campaign that the only course was to determine how much Germany could pay and 'demand the whole of that'; he specifically repudiated 'any distinction between reparation, compensation or indemnity'.[219] The ultra-patriotic pressure groups behind the developing 'public mood' should also not be allowed to slip from view. The National Party, the British Commonwealth Union, and other right-wing bodies all campaigned on the indemnity, and their election material deprecated any

---

[216] H. Fisher to L. Fisher, 4, 10, and 11 Dec. 1918, Fisher Papers, 205.

[217] e.g. Asquith to Sylvia Henley, 31 Dec. 1918 and 8 Jan. 1919, Asquith Papers, MSS Eng. Lett. c. 542/5. For similar opinions, see Bryce to Asquith, 31 Dec. 1918, Asquith Papers, 33; R. McKenna to A. G. Gardiner, 29 Dec. 1918, and Gilbert Murray to A. G. Gardiner, 6 Dec. 1918, Gardiner Papers, 1/22, 1/24; Arthur Haworth to W. Runciman, 17 Dec. 1918, R. D. Holt to Runciman, 17 Dec. 1918, and J. M. Hogge to Runciman, 17 Dec. 1918, Runciman Papers, WR 169; Arthur Ponsonby to Charles Trevelyan, 30 Dec. 1918, Charles Trevelyan Papers, CPT EX 79; Courtenay Ilbert to Bryce, 15 Dec. 1918, Bryce Papers, 14; C. F. G. Masterman, 'The General Election and After', *Contemporary Review*, 115 (Feb. 1919).

[218] Bryce to A. V. Dicey, 31 Dec. 1918, Bryce Papers, 31.

[219] *The Times*, 11 Dec. 1918.

qualifications on indemnity 'as stated by some professional politicians'.[220] While the National Party stood in supposed isolation on the right, its rhetoric made an appeal to the same anti-German emotions so long fostered by the 'knock-out blow' Coalition.

Some of those caught up in the elections discerned pressure from this outflanking movement on the Right at the time. William Bridgeman, for example, wrote to his wife on 26 November observing that the sustained questioning he was encountering on the expulsion of aliens and on economic boycott pointed to some party organization. 'I think it is the National Party', he wrote. Then, two days later, he noted that 'vindictive action against Germany is the great cry—and huge indemnities'.[221] Believing himself under pressure to declare a position on indemnities, Bridgeman solicited and received a letter from Bonar Law, pledging the government's determination to extract from Germany 'as large a part of the cost of the war for which she was responsible as it is possible for her to pay'.[222] This he read to his meetings. Only later in the campaign, on 10 December, did Bridgeman believe he could discern the influence of the *Daily Mail* in his election meetings.[223] The pressures, Bridgeman believed, were manipulated by the ultra-patriots to the right of the Conservative Party as well as the press. But, like many Conservatives, he was happy to meet this pressure and give the pledge on indemnities.

The truth is that the 'pressure from below' interpretation is too kind to Lloyd George. He was not the principled Liberal leader overcome by 'the hot squalid rush of the event', ambushed by vengeful audiences, tormented by pressure groups and 'stunts'.[224] To a certain extent, he gave these forces a platform. Having voiced doubts about the indemnity, he did nothing to oppose but rather assisted in the formation of the Imperial War Cabinet's Indemnity Committee, a committee dominated by those very forces determined to roar for an indemnity. Moreover, Lloyd George had abandoned objections to a transfer of war costs in principle when he chose to deny the plain meaning of the Lansing Note during his clashes with Hughes in early November. A public commitment in favour of the indemnity, which Lloyd George must have known would be recommended by his own committee, was but a short step. Moreover, what pressures there were upon Lloyd George were quite predictable. They were the consequence of the combination of political forces and personalities which Lloyd George had himself assembled and with whom he had worked for two years. In arguing against an early election, C. P. Scott had told Lloyd George in August 1918 that the

---

[220] e.g. election manifesto of J. B. Cronin, independent naval candidate for Gillingham, in Hannon Papers, H 11/6; and Brigadier General Makins's election manifesto, dated 25 Nov. 1918, Beveridge Papers, IV/28.

[221] Bridgeman to Mrs Bridgeman, 26 and 28 Nov. 1918, Bridgeman Papers, 4629/1/1918/94 and 96.

[222] Bonar Law to Mrs Bridgeman, 28 Nov. 1918, Bridgeman Papers, 4629/1/1918/96.

[223] Bridgeman to Mrs Bridgeman, 10 Dec. 1918, Bridgeman Papers, 4629/1/1918/109.

[224] This version is given in Churchill, *The Aftermath*, 49.

Tories 'will fight on an orgy of anti-Germanism and the aliens hunt. The Liberals can hardly beat them on that ground.'[225] Lloyd George was not so untutored in the mechanics of his own Coalition to be caught unawares by the demands for a 'knock-out blow' peace.

Certainly it is a mistake to see the Coalition as surrendering before an irresistible wave of jingoism which had engulfed the electors. In fact, the languor of the electors struck many observers. Austen Chamberlain reported that only four out of forty women and only forty out of eight hundred men on his committee rolls had responded to requests for help in the election. 'The voters are apathetic', he wrote.[226] At the outset of his campaign Bridgeman told his wife that 'everyone takes it for granted that the Coalition will win and are too busy to attend or work-up meetings'.[227] 'No one seems to take any interest. I don't believe most of the people realise its an election at all', wrote Dorothy Lubbock, the daughter of Conservative MP Henry Forster, half-way through the campaign. 'I am afraid lots won't trouble to vote at all', she warned.[228] The threat of a mass abstention from the poll in the army was a danger signal too. Milner was frightened that the soldiers' vote would be scandalously low; in the last days of the campaign he pressed Haig to encourage officers to drum up voters, and urged Bishop Gwynne to request chaplains to tell the men it was 'their duty' to vote.[229] Lord Cavan in Italy warned Wilson on 5 December that probably only 10 per cent of British troops there would vote, most soldiers grumbling that 'I want to see the b—— before I vote'. According to Cavan's assessment of opinion among the troops, 'our men have no desire to remain in Germany to secure the indemnities which were being foreshadowed'.[230]

Fear of this apathy began to prey on the minds of those at Conservative Central Office; it was appreciated that such apathy in the Coalition's electorate might allow Labour to score well. Election agents from across the country reporting to Bonar Law on 3 December observed 'a distinct lack of enthusiasm about the election', 'a quietness and want of excitement in the campaign', 'little interest', and 'marked apathy'.[231] The same election agents delivered a statistical report to Bonar Law the very next day showing that, in this slow election, such interest as there was centred on 'full indemnities and reparation from Germany', 'punishment for the Kaiser and other responsible persons', and 'repatriation and

[225] C. P. Scott Diary, 8 Aug. 1918, C. P. Scott Papers, Box 134.
[226] Austen Chamberlain to Ida Chamberlain, 8 Dec. 1918, Austen Chamberlain Papers, AC 5/1/113.
[227] Bridgeman to Mrs Bridgeman, 27 Nov. 1918, Bridgeman Papers, 4629/1/1918/95.
[228] Dorothy to Rachel Forster, 28 Nov. and 5 Dec. 1918, H. W. Forster Papers.
[229] Milner to Haig, 5 Nov. [Dec.] 1918, and Milner to Gwynne, 5 Dec. 1918, Milner Adds., MS Eng. Hist. c. 696/2.
[230] Cavan to Wilson, 5 Dec. 1918, Henry Wilson Papers, HHW 28B, and Gainford Diary, 9 Dec. 1918, Gainford Papers, 44.
[231] 'Synopsis of Confidential Reports by Unionist Central Office on the Progress of the Coalition Campaigns', 3 Dec. 1918, Bonar Law Papers, 95/2.

exclusion of enemy aliens'—in short, the National Party programme.[232] Thus, it was signalled to the men at the top that anti-German election cries at the very least might help produce voters. This was the main lesson drawn by the *Daily Chronicle* the morning after Lloyd George's Bristol speech on indemnities; apathy, 'the only danger there has been since the campaign opened' was swept away by the speech, said the *Daily Chronicle*.[233] Lloyd George certainly gave indications of his own nagging concern over a low turn-out. In his speeches at the Queen's Hall and at Camberwell late in the campaign, he pleaded vigorously with voters, and especially women, above all else to make certain that they exercised their vote. The necessity to vote was also a prominent theme in the pro-Coalition press's coverage of the Prime Minister's addresses on the eve of the poll.[234] Smuts probably had in mind the warnings of the Unionist election agents regarding the measures required to drum up a higher turn-out when he gave Scott his own explanation for Lloyd George's indemnity pledge at Bristol: 'I besought him then not to commit himself, told him he was bound to win easily and that he need give no pledges. But letters came pouring in from all over the country declaring that the people were caring about nothing but punishments and indemnities and Lloyd George gave way.'[235] Advisers in the electorates were influential in this manner too. Arthur Steel-Maitland claimed later that he was 'warned of failure *by my supporters* unless I would proclaim my enthusiastic and wholehearted support to Lloyd George and policy of squeezing Germans [for] every penny'.[236] Thus, the focus on anti-German themes such as indemnity resulted, at least in part, from the simplest of political calculations: it was a device to inject life into the campaign against the opposition, a lure to bring the electors to the polling stations.

Thus Lloyd George may be seen to have bent before advice coming from within the Coalition—not before a great whirlwind of public feeling. No such whirlwind existed. The voting on the day, a day of drizzle, bore this out: 'no more signs of life than in a well tenanted cemetery', observed Hughes of the London booths on election day.[237] Crawford was of the same view: 'the percentage of votes cast must have been very small.'[238] Indeed, when the results were announced, the huge rate of abstention was the one consoling fact for the beaten Radicals and socialists. Philip Snowden exaggerated when he told Ponsonby that no more than 25 per cent of the registered electors had voted—the figure finally given was 57.2 per cent—but, even from this perspective, his claim that 'Lloyd

---

[232] 'Summary of Reports from Unionist Agents indicating the subjects in which the electors are most interested', 4 Dec. 1918, Bonar Law Papers, 95/2.

[233] *Daily Chronicle*, 'Danger of Apathy Swept Away by Premier's Speech', 13 Dec. 1918.

[234] See 'Women's Duty to Vote', the headline reporting the Queen's Hall speech, *The Times*, 10 Dec. 1918, and *Daily Chronicle*, editorial, 'Eve of the Poll', 13 Dec. 1918.

[235] C. P. Scott Political Diary, 5 July 1919, C. P. Scott Papers, Box 134.

[236] Arthur Steel-Maitland to Keynes, 4 Jan. 1920, Keynes Papers, EC/2/2/27. Italics added.

[237] Hughes to Munro-Ferguson, Novar Papers, MS 696/2747.

[238] Crawford Diary, 15 Dec. 1918, vol. xxxiv, Crawford Papers.

George has signally failed to sweep the country' had some justice to it.[239] As Sydney Buxton noted 'half the electorate stood aside'.[240] Paltry numbers at the declaration of polls compared to previous elections, wrote Arnold Rowntree, were also a measure of 'the lack of interest in the election and of its unreality'.[241] Among the services, only 641,632 soldiers voted of the 3.9 million registered service voters, (that is, about 16.5 per cent), figures which were suppressed by Lloyd George.[242] Nevertheless, the scandal of the low soldiers' vote was soon common knowledge among the political élite.[243]

At the end of the day, the Coalition produced a splendid victory. With 53 per cent of the national vote, the Coalition won a clear majority. Counting all those likely to support the Coalition in the House of Commons, the Coalition had some 554 seats out of the total of 707. Among the Coalition supporters were 332 Conservatives and 132 Liberal Coalitionists. The Asquithian Liberals won a mere 36 seats. Labour was confined to just 57 seats. But the ominous fact for the future was the steady rise in the nationwide Labour Party vote—the percentage rose from 6.4 per cent in 1910 to 20.8 per cent in 1918, although this was largely attributable to the fact that extra Labour candidates stood in 1918.[244] The long-term significance of this Lloyd George himself dramatically acknowledged two days after the close of voting, telling Hankey, only half in jest, that 'Arthur Henderson is your new Chief'.[245] In fact, despite the blossoming of the Labour vote, the Coalition had succeeded in stopping the Labour Party. In the eyes of many, this was, after all, the real point of the election; for example, Sir George Trevelyan was so caught up in this atmosphere that he told Lord Bryce that the only unfortunate thing in the election was that 'all sections of the party of order should not have united in the face of the Executive of the Labour Party'.[246]

However, the 'complete rout of Labour', as General Rawlinson described it, did not lay to rest the dread of some post-war uprising.[247] The ambiguity of the Labour result cast a shadow over the victory. Indeed, many observers now believed the danger from the working classes was greater than ever. The defeated Liberals, naturally, made much of this theme. As Buckmaster wrote, it was disastrous that in the new parliament Labour was to be 'inadequately represented

---

[239] Snowden to Ponsonby, 2 Jan. 1919, Ponsonby Papers, MS Eng. Hist. c. 667. The voter turn-out is given in Turner, *British Politics and the Great War*, 329.

[240] Sydney Buxton to Walter Runciman, 26 Jan. 1919, Walter Runciman Papers, WR 177.

[241] Rowntree to Ponsonby, 3 Jan. 1919, Ponsonby papers, MS Eng. Hist. c. 667.

[242] Turner, *British Politics and the Great War*, 331–2.

[243] See J. A. Pease to Asquith, 29 Dec. 1918, Gainford Papers, 91, where the estimate is given as 30% and C. F. G. Masterman, 'The Rise and Fall of the Coalition', *Nineteenth Century*, 508 (June 1919), where the figure is put at 25%.

[244] All figures are taken from Turner, *British Politics and the Great War*, 333, 395, 403. Turner provides a major analysis of the election results in ch. 11. He concludes that there was 'no sudden explosion of Labour strength', but rather steady growth, 435.

[245] Lloyd George, quoted in Hankey to Lady Adeline Hankey, 16 Dec. 1918, Hankey Papers, 3/23.

[246] G. O. Trevelyan to Bryce, 15 Dec. 1918, Bryce Papers, 18.

[247] Rawlinson Diary, 30 Dec. 1918, Rawlinson Papers, 1/11.

and in sullen and dissatisfied opposition'.[248] Haldane regarded it as certain that the Unionists would block reform and 'stimulate Bolshevism'.[249] Even those within the Coalition agreed on the danger from Labour. The Conservative triumph was too sweeping. As F. E. Smith told Bonar Law, the Coalition had won by 'too large a majority'; to keep the masses in line, the new ministry would require flamboyant characters such as himself who had 'a power with the democracy'.[250] Amery wrote in his diary that, unless the government produced something in the nature of bold reform, 'there will be a Labour landslide in the next few years'.[251] Crawford lamented that there was no effective 'safety valve of Parliament' for Labour, and predicted 'strikes and violence'.[252] At the Foreign Office, Knatchbull-Hugessen permitted himself the private expression of regret in his diary that thirty or forty extra Labour MPs had not been elected because 'the danger in that quarter is extra-parliamentary activity'.[253]

But the cost of stopping Labour, of buttressing the Lloyd George prime ministership, and of flattening Asquith, was a high one in terms of the moral credibility of the government. Many former supporters shuddered at the Coalition's electioneering themes. The election even endangered Lloyd George's relationship with C. P. Scott. The veteran editor was much perplexed by the election, 'a really wicked thing to have dragged across the trail of the [Peace] Conference'. Lloyd George, he feared, 'doesn't know (it is an intellectual defect) what principle means'.[254] At the mid-point of the election Scott met privately with a group of Radical MPs led by Richard Holt who came away convinced that the editor viewed Lloyd George as 'not strictly an honest man'.[255] Indeed, in a series of editorials in the *Manchester Guardian* in early December Scott let fly. He fulminated against the Coalition for the 'slump in idealism' and against Lloyd George for 'vulgarising the issue'. He accused Lloyd George of 'doing nothing to restrain the forces he has let loose'. A demand for a vast indemnity was 'precisely the way in which we should expect Germany to act were she victorious', he wrote. Most stinging of all, he professed to hear 'the very voice of the Kaiser' in Lloyd George's speeches on indemnities.[256] In his private interview with President Wilson in late December, Scott explained how disappointed he was that Lloyd George had descended 'so low' in his election addresses, and he explained this in terms of his tendency to act 'on feeling, impulse, and vision'.[257] Taking stock

[248] Lord Buckmaster, 'The General Election I', *Contemporary Review*, 114 (Dec. 1918).
[249] Haldane to Edmund Gosse, 1 Jan. 1919, Gosse Papers, vol. 9.
[250] F. E. Smith to Bonar Law, 30 Dec. 1919, Bonar Law Papers, 84/4/25.
[251] Amery Diary, 29 Dec. 1918, Amery Papers.
[252] Crawford Diary, 28 Dec. 1918, vol. xxxiv, Crawford Papers.
[253] Knatchbull-Hugessen Diary, 28 Dec. 1918, Knatchbull-Hugessen Papers, KNAT 1/3.
[254] C. P. Scott to Dr C. Weizmann, 19 Nov. 1918, C. P. Scott Papers, 335/56.
[255] Richard Holt to Runciman, 1 Dec. 1918, Runciman Papers, WR 169.
[256] *Manchester Guardian*, editorials, 'The Slump in Idealism', 3 Dec., 'The Prime Minister's Manifesto', 6 Dec., 'Vulgarising the Issue', 11 Dec., and 'Points for the Peace Conference', 12 Dec. 1918.
[257] C. P. Scott Diary, 29 Dec. 1918, Scott Papers, Box 134.

in January, Scott reflected on the extraordinary situation that Lloyd George, a Liberal, had presided over a supposedly non-party election which had resulted in 'the return of a great and solid Tory majority and the striking of such a blow that has never been struck before at the Liberal Party'.[258] Scott's voice was not alone. Even the *New Europe*, another staunch supporter of Lloyd George during the war, noted the 'supreme irony of the moment that in the hour of its triumph in Europe, Liberalism should seem to suffer overwhelming defeat in the British Isles'.[259] That Lloyd George had saddled the new Coalition with reactionary pledges and personalities became the new consensus among the progressive wing of the old 'knock-out blow' alliance. As Sir Horace Plunkett confided to Woodrow Wilson in March 1919: 'It is notorious that the recent general election resulted in a triumph for Mr Lloyd George and at the same time surrounded him with colleagues who on all questions of domestic politics (including Ireland) are what would be called elsewhere reactionary.'[260]

In the final analysis, the campaign was a triumph of domestic political priorities. The Coalition leaders had deliberately chosen to inflate the demand for a German indemnity in order to lift the Coalition's fortunes above the numerous threats they believed surrounded them—threats from the Labour Party, from the National Party, from the Northcliffe press, and from the apathy of the voters. The crucial back-flip was performed by Lloyd George: he vowed to pursue 'the full cost of the war' and endorsed the old ultra-patriotic formula of the irreducible guilt, not just of Germany, but of 'the German people'. There can be no doubt that the Coalition leaders had pandered to the most reactionary opinions on Germany and her future. Some passed across their desks in the weeks that followed. The effusive letter of one exultant military officer who wrote to Walter Long full of praise for the Coalition's stand on an indemnity from the Germans will serve to illustrate: 'I am all for it, and hope they will mortgage everything they have got until they have paid up. I would make them work for the world for 100 years, for they are *all* equally culpable, and cannot ride off now on the Kaiser's back and that of the military party.'[261] In high places too, the notion of collective guilt and the need for punishment became entrenched. Archbishop Randall Davidson, for example, rejected the proffered opinion of an American general that the vindictive British press ignored the fact that 'the German people have been poisoned and misled by men without honour'; in Davidson's opinion, 'punishment' was the need of the hour, and he condemned the 'mawkish' tendency of some Christians to 'emasculate Christianity into a sort of sentimental good nature and forget the principles of justice on which Christ laid such stress'.[262]

[258] *Manchester Guardian*, editorial, 'Politics of the New Year', 2 Jan. 1919.
[259] *New Europe*, editorial, 'La Victoire Integrale in 1919', 2 Jan. 1919.
[260] Plunkett to Wilson, 2 Mar. 1919, Plunkett Papers, WILS 8.
[261] A. Weston Tarns to Long, 5 Jan. 1919, Long Papers, Add. MSS 62424 (provisional number).
[262] General B. Brent to Davidson, 29 Nov. 1918, and Davidson to Brent, 11 Dec. 1918, Davidson Papers, vol. 366.

Britain's 'scrap of paper': the perceived breach of faith over the Lansing Note and indemnities

Perhaps the most important outcome of the election for the peacemaking to come was the sense of a degradation in Britain's moral prestige felt by advisers to the government. At Newcastle and at Bristol the Prime Minister had departed not only from the specific terms of his own Caxton Hall speech of January 1918, but, much more importantly, he had turned his back on the Lansing Note. The Asquithian Liberal press made much of this 'breach of faith' at the time, and for some weeks after the election even the *Spectator* was bothered by it.[263] Radicals regarded the fantastic sums used to dazzle the electorate as further evidence of Lloyd George's moral bankruptcy. As Richard Holt wrote, the general election was 'the most unscrupulous election, for the L. G. gang promised the electors things in the anti-German line which are wholly inconsistent with Wilson's Fourteen Points on which they got the armistice and are therefore a bargain with Germany'.[264] Most importantly, many of the progressive members of Lloyd George's 'knock-out blow' Coalition, civil servants as much as political figures, lost confidence in the moral foundation of their own nation's cause as a result. Britain had her own 'scrap of paper' scandal and it seared the consciences of many Wilsonians who had lent themselves to the 'no peace until victory' cause.

Maynard Keynes was only the first among a number of civil servants to undergo a virtual conversion experience as a result. Keynes had told his mother during the last week of October that he suspected 'a possibility of wickedness on our part and an unwillingness to subscribe to the whole of Wilson's fourteen commandments'. Then, during the Versailles discussions of early November, he was ordered to write 'a memorandum on indemnities at top speed for an airman to fly to Versailles'. The stress on reparation for damage to 'civilians' in the Lansing Note may well have been influenced by this memorandum. Keynes knew well the appalling damage of Belgium and northern France, for he toured the devastated areas on French invitation for a week from 7 November.[265] On his return, Keynes revised his document on reparation, so as to include developments under the terms of the armistice. The final 31-page document did not simply present the figures on damage, German capacity to pay, and compensation.

---

[263] For the Liberal press, see e.g. *Westminster Gazette*, editorial, 'Electioneering and Indemnities', 12 Dec. 1918. On the debate in the *Spectator* see editorial, 'German Affairs and the Indemnity', 21 Dec. 1918, and an ongoing debate in the letters column 18 Jan., 25 Jan., 1 Feb. 1919. On Strachey's struggle with his conscience see Strachey to Mrs Carruthers, 23 Dec. 1918, Strachey Papers, S/18/5/18, until a correspondent in the *Spectator* on 15 Feb. pointed out, to Strachey's evident relief, that Article XIX of the original armistice terms had outlined a catch-all reservation that 'future claims and demands of the Allies and the United States of America remain unaffected'. The idea that Article XIX was intended to displace the Lansing Note was raised by nobody in authority at the time. Keynes disposed of this excuse in his *Economic Consequences of the Peace*, 71–2.

[264] Richard Holt to W. Runciman, 17 Dec. 1918, Runciman Papers, WR 169.

[265] J. M. Keynes to F. A. Keynes, 25 Oct., 3 Nov., and 6 Nov. 1918, Keynes Papers, PP 45, J. N. and F. A. Keynes, vol. 9/18/36–38, and Keynes's passport, Keynes Papers, 1/17.

An introduction stressed that Britain could make a claim for reparation only. After carefully reviewing the pronouncements of President Wilson and the Entente during the war and the armistice documents, Keynes rejected any attempt at 'straining' the meaning of the Lansing Note. He announced that in his terms of reference he had assumed that Britain was bound to 'exclude any repayment of the general costs of the war'. Thus Keynes advised the pursuit of the figure of £2,000 million in reparation from Germany as 'a very satisfactory achievement' for Britain. To pursue the larger figure for total war costs, estimated by Keynes at £25,000 million, would be to court the repudiation of Germany's own internal war debt and political radicalism. 'If all war debts east of the Rhine have been repudiated, the proletariat of Western Europe may object to be[ing] shut out from the advantage of such a situation. Repudiation is a contagious disease', Keynes warned.[266] This was the advice rejected by the Imperial War Cabinet at the creation of the Committee on Indemnity on 26 November. The election speeches of the Coalition leaders consequently filled Keynes with consternation and anger. As the election reached its climax, Keynes had a visit from the American financial official Paul Garratt who 'spoke to me most hotly (and quite definitely) namely that we were honourably engaged not to ask for the general cost of the war, but only for reparation'.[267] The Americans may have been agog at British duplicity; Keynes was distraught. In mid-December, he exclaimed in a note to his mother, 'every voice should be lifted, however vainly, against this dishonouring Coalition'.[268]

At the Political Intelligence Department a similar awakening was in progress during the election. In the last week of the campaign Headlam-Morley received a request from Balfour that the PID investigate 'whether President Wilson has said anything for or against the view that the costs of war as distinguished from the spoils of war, are excluded by the terms of the armistice from discussion at the Peace Conference'. The request may well have been prompted by a telegram from Lord Derby dated 6 December suggesting that, in Colonel House's opinion, Wilson 'will press the distinction between indemnity on the one side and reparation on the other'. Headlam-Morley submitted a response on 10 December arguing that any loose interpretation of the Lansing Note was quite unacceptable. 'We venture to suggest', replied the PID, 'that such interpretation is clearly ruled out by the fact that in the Allies' memorandum there is no reference to loss, but only to damage, and in addition that it is put forward merely as an explanation of what is meant by restoration.' The PID pointed out tartly that 'even if lawyers were found' to support a new interpretation of the Lansing Note, the fact

---

[266] There is a copy of the original document, 'Memorandum by the Treasury on the Indemnity Payable by the Enemy Powers for Reparation and Other Claims', in Brand Papers, 18. See also *Collected Writings of John Maynard Keynes*, (1971) xvi. 313–34.

[267] Paul D. Garratt to J. M. Keynes, 12 Dec. 1918, with endorsements from Keynes dated 12 Dec. 1918, Keynes Papers, RT/1/3.

[268] J. M. Keynes to F. A. Keynes, 16 Dec.1918, Keynes Papers, PP 45, J. N. and F. A. Keynes, vol. 9/18/41.

remained that 'nothing was said to warn the Germans that the words were capable of this interpretation'. As an illustration of this, the PID adduced *The Times* editorial of 7 November which, as noted above, acknowledged that war costs had been waived under the terms of the Lansing Note.[269] In a second memorandum the PID was even more blunt:

The war has not ended with an unconditional surrender of Germany. What has happened is that the Germans have accepted an armistice which practically means unconditional *military* surrender, but they have done so on the express stipulation that the terms of peace shall be in accordance with President Wilson's statements. The result of this is that when the time comes to negotiate peace, the Allies will find their hands very strictly tied. They will not be able to add anything except what can be included in a reasonable interpretation of President Wilson's notes.

All the Allies, insisted the PID memorandum, were 'absolutely bound'. The obligation was described as 'a moral and legal one'. Moreover, 'we cannot ignore the fact that in these matters all special responsibility will, whether rightly or wrongly, appear to attach to His Majesty's Government'.[270]

What was the response of the government to such advice? A clue to the fate of the PID's uncompromising memoranda is given in a letter which Headlam-Morley wrote (but did not send) to Keynes after reading in December 1919 *The Economic Consequences of the Peace*. Headlam-Morley revealed in his letter that he had indeed protested over the twisting of the Lansing Note, and he hinted that his advice had been held up or ignored either by his immediate superiors, Tyrrell and Hardinge, or by Balfour himself. In any case, in Headlam-Morley's view, not only Lloyd George but most members of the Cabinet, and especially Balfour, were ultimately responsible for the dishonouring of the Lansing Note. He described events in this way:

As soon as the PM began to make his extended promises, I put up the matter in the strongest possible way; the result was most unsatisfactory, but surely it was the absolute duty of Mr Balfour as Foreign Secretary to insist on the most thorough examination of the question. Obviously it would not be desirable for me to put on paper any further details, but I took a good deal of trouble when I was in Paris to find out what had happened and the result left on my mind a most disquieting sense of a complete absence of serious responsibility on the part of the PM's colleagues.[271]

Headlam-Morley's fellow German experts at the PID were similarly conscience stricken during the election. Zimmern, the most convinced Wilsonian,

[269] Untitled memorandum, dated 10 Dec. 1918, Headlam-Morley Papers, file marked 'Preparation for the Peace Conference', HDLM Acc. 727, Box 11.

[270] Memorandum entitled 'Germany', undated, Headlam-Morley Papers, file marked 'Preparation for the Peace Conference', HDLM Acc. 727, Box 11. A 'Progress Report' on preparations for the Peace Conference shows a PID memorandum entitled 'Germany' as 'Draft submitted to Lord Hardinge and under revision'.

[271] Headlam-Morley to Keynes, 16 Dec. 1919 (marked 'not sent'), Headlam-Morley Papers, OS Box 1. For Keynes's stress on the Lansing Note see J. M. Keynes, *The Economic Consequences of the Peace* (Cambridge, 1971), ch. 5, esp. 91.

was particularly disappointed by the apparent intention of the Prime Minister and his Cabinet colleagues to endorse the claims for the 'full cost of the war' under the cloak of reparations. He sought out a figure of influence within the élite, Archbishop Randall Davidson. On 6 December he wrote to Davidson, describing himself as 'very distressed' at the 'absolutely infamous' proposals of Lloyd George. As Zimmern expressed it:

There is no possible room for confusion between the 'reparation' inserted in the terms on the strength of which Germany disarmed, and the 'indemnity' which it is now proposed to exact from her. If the proposal stands I do not see how we can with any decency go on with the plans for a League of Nations. We shall [have] violated an agreement made only a few weeks ago and forfeited all possibility of being trusted by the enemy or even by neutrals.[272]

The morally tormented Zimmern gained an interview at the bedside of the Archbishop, laid low at this moment by a dose of influenza. But Zimmern won no satisfaction from the fevered prelate. As the Archbishop explained in his diary, he had 'got up the case carefully' in preparation for the visit from the earnest Foreign Office expert, and he endeavoured to persuade Zimmern 'that he a little overrates the certainty that there is such a definite breach of faith'.[273] Apparently Zimmern's sense of guilt was not assuaged: he remained a resolute critic of the 'short-visioned statesmen' of the British Empire throughout the months of peacemaking to come.[274]

The shunning of socialist Germany

The British political élite's refusal to see any good in the German revolution was driven not only by the needs of the general election. There were diplomatic purposes to be served also, in particular the deflection of anticipated American pressure to moderate British peace terms. If Germany could be depicted as still dangerous and unreconstructed, then pressures for moderate treatment of the new regime in Berlin could be resisted. Indeed, as diplomacy in preparation for the peace conference proceeded during November and December, Britain acquiesced in French decisions which effectively shut out the new regime in Berlin from any participation in the coming peace negotiations. Depicting Germany in such negative colours as they did during the election, the British leaders were scarcely in a position to resist the French premiss that the socialist government of Germany was led by a bunch of desperadoes who could not be trusted to undertake any role in the coming peace conference.

The Lloyd George government's chief foreign policy concern in December 1918 was undoubtedly the 'threat' represented by Wilsonianism. In anticipation of the President's visit to Britain, scheduled for the week immediately after

[272] Zimmern to Davidson, 6 Dec. 1918, Davidson Papers, vol. 366.
[273] Davidson Diary, Sunday, 8 Dec. 1918, Davidson Papers, vol. 13.
[274] Zimmern to H. B. Higgins, 14 Dec. 1919, Higgins Papers, MS 1057, series 1, item 375.

Christmas, anti-Wilsonian sentiment was obvious throughout Whitehall. This was deliberately encouraged by Wilson's political enemies in America, some of whom sent private letters to British friends in the civil service and government, urging resistance to Wilson's 'authoritarianism' and even his 'doctrinaire socialism'.[275] More officially, British diplomats in America commended and sent on correspondence from the Republican leaders attacking Wilson and noting pointedly that the Republicans would control both Houses of Congress from March 1919.[276] Resentment at Wilson's failure to pay homage to British military achievement was very strong.[277] In addition, feeling ran high over the continuing American effort to take control over all food relief in Europe.[278] Lord Crawford noted 'dangerous tensions between us and the USA'.[279] So dispiriting did Reading find the quarrel that he pleaded at the end of December to be liberated from the whole business of food relief.[280]

Even the arrangements for Wilson's trip to Britain raised tensions. In Paris Colonel House confided to Derby that both he and the President distrusted 'the little man', and he confessed that he had no desire to accompany Wilson to London to meet with Lloyd George.[281] Reminders of the ideological gap between the British and American leaders were in the air too; House astonished Derby by announcing that the President wished to see people of all shades of opinion while he was in Britain, including the Labour Party leaders Henderson and MacDonald—these 'weird creatures', as Derby described them to Balfour.[282] For his part, House was in constant communication with the Liberal and Radical editors in England, pleading for their support for Wilson in his battle with chauvinism.[283] Indeed, praise for Wilson on the British Left excited opinion against Wilson among stalwarts of the 'knock-out blow'. F. S. Oliver, for example, railed against Wilson as 'an exceedingly vain and ignorant person' and he ridiculed the 'noisy little band of pacifists who want to make a hero of him'.[284]

Behind these irritants lay the more substantial and familiar issues inviting

[275] e.g. see Sara Norton to George Prothero, 20 Nov. 1918, George Prothero, War Letters, bundle 3, packet 3; J. Rogers to Prothero, 3 Dec. 1918, George Prothero, War Letters, bundle 1, packet 1; R. E. Prothero to Lloyd George and Bonar Law, 30 Nov. 1918, and Bonar Law to Prothero, 2 Dec. 1918, Bonar Law Papers, BL 84/3/27; Philip D. Phair to Esme Howard, 1 Dec. 1918, Howard Papers, DHW 1/24; and Rodd to Balfour, 28 Dec. 1918, Rodd Papers, 19.

[276] Colville Barclay to Lord Reading, 22 Nov. 1918, Reading Papers, EUR F 118/2.

[277] Crawford Diary, 6 Dec. 1918, vol. xxxiii, Crawford Papers.

[278] Derby to Balfour, 19 and 26 Dec. 1918, Derby Papers, 28/2/1.

[279] Crawford Diary, 8 Dec. 1918, vol. xxxiii, Crawford Papers, and Knatchbull-Hugessen Diary, 1 Dec. 1918, Knatchbull-Hugessen Papers, KNAT 1/3.

[280] For Reading's desire for resignation, see Reading to Lloyd George, 19 Dec. 1918, Reading Papers, MS EUR F 118/95, and Minutes of the Imperial War Cabinet, 31 Dec. 1918, CAB 23/42.

[281] Balfour to Derby, 16 Nov. 1918, Derby to Balfour, 18 Nov. 1918, Derby to Balfour, 11 and 20 Dec. 1918, Derby Papers, 28/2/1.

[282] Derby to Balfour, 21 Dec. 1918, Derby Papers, 28/2/1. House withdrew his request a few days later, but did insist that the President meet Lord Grey; see Derby to Balfour, 24 Dec. 1918, Derby Papers, 28/2/1.

[283] e.g. House to Gardiner, 7 Dec. 1918, Gardiner Papers, 1/17.

[284] F. S. Oliver to W. E. Oliver, 5 Dec. 1918, Oliver Papers, 65.

mutual distrust: the fate of the German colonies and the indemnity. Wilson, it was assumed, was opposed to Britain retaining all the former German colonies. Pressure from the Dominions, especially Australia, for the retention of the colonies, was intense.[285] British diplomats backed this up, submitting grave warnings that Wilson's slogan of 'self-determination' would 'set many political tongues wagging' and invite serious unrest in Britain's own colonies, especially Egypt.[286] Admirals and generals debated how to deflect Wilson's 'wildcat schemes' for a League of Nations so that there was still a place for military force in the world; the British admirals advised the absorption of the German fleet into the Royal Navy in order that a future American naval challenge might be resisted.[287] In the shadow of Wilson's visit, plans were made to meet the challenge. The Imperial War Cabinet earnestly debated various schemes to counter his anti-imperialism. At the outset Lloyd George announced, unequivocally, that it was his policy that no colonies would be returned to Germany and that the Dominions whose forces had conquered German territories would remain in possession of them. The chief stratagem proposed for Wilson was that of drawing the United States into a sharing of the spoils, an inducement dressed up in the white robe of guardianship over distressed peoples. Lloyd George explained British intentions with frankness: by 'making the offer to America we would remove any prejudice against us on the ground of "land grabbing" '. So cynical was the tone of the discussion that Montagu, summoning his resources of sarcasm, advised his colleagues that it would be 'very satisfactory if we could find some convincing argument for not annexing all the territories in the world'.[288] Montagu wrote to Balfour the same day of his distress at the 'hypocrisy' on display; it was an 'unhappy spectacle' he had just witnessed, when 'the trusted of the Empire, the custodians of the future, the translators of victory, the instruments of lasting peace' were to be found locked in a huddle and hatching schemes to defeat President Wilson, just in case 'he meant what he said'.[289]

Hostility to Wilson was equally strong when, on Christmas Eve, the Imperial War Cabinet turned to discuss the Indemnity Committee's report. At the outset Hughes boldly announced that his committee 'did not even consider whether under the terms of the Armistice they were entitled to ask for indemnity at all', because, in his opinion, there was 'no just distinction' between indemnity and reparation. Germany could safely be lumbered with a vast indemnity, he

[285] e.g. Munro–Ferguson to Milner, enclosing Australian Hansard,14 Nov. 1918, and Munro–Ferguson to Long, 14 Nov. 1918, Milner Adds., MS Eng. Hist. c. 709.
[286] On the troubles anticipated in Egypt in response to Wilsonianism, see R. Wingate to Rennell Rodd, 26 Nov. 1918, Rodd Papers, 19; George Aston Diary, 21 Nov. 1918, Aston Papers, 6/11; and Milner to Balfour, 13 Dec. 1918, Milner Adds., MS Eng. Hist. c. 696/1.
[287] e.g. H. Rawlinson to H. Wilson, 29 Dec. 1918, H. Wilson Papers, 2/88; Charles Madden to Beatty, 26 Nov. 1918, Beatty Papers, BTY 13/29/3; and Charles Madden to Jellicoe, 29 Nov. 1918, Jellicoe Papers, 49009.
[288] Minutes of the Imperial War Cabinet, 18 and 20 Dec. 1918, CAB 23/42.
[289] Montagu to Balfour, 20 Dec. 1918, Balfour Papers, 49748. Balfour wrote on Montagu's letter: 'It has all the truth of good satire but no more.'

concluded, for surely 'there was no country less likely to fall under the sway of Bolshevism'. Lloyd George was equally unashamed: endorsing the concept of indemnity, he suggested that it was wrong to argue that President Wilson had ruled out indemnities, because it 'was covered by his use of the word reparation'. Bonar Law was untroubled by his conscience, remarking that, until the recently appointed Entente Commission on Reparation and Indemnity had examined the German capacity to pay 'why should they raise the question of principles'? Not all were persuaded, however, that a vast indemnity was practical. Milner was worried about Bolshevizing Germany, Churchill about impoverishing her. Montagu raised the possibility of a large army of occupation proving to be necessary to enforce an indemnity. Borden doubted Germany could ever pay, while Foster revealed that the committee's work had been rather rushed and was 'really based on the opinions of its members'. Long countered with the observation that the Federation of British Industries and the Associated Chambers of Commerce were 'emphatic' that Germany could pay. Only Barnes and Borden found the moral courage to challenge the attempted abandonment of the distinction between reparation and indemnity itself. The British demand for indemnity was 'an afterthought', Barnes declared: until the election Britain had been aiming at compensation for Belgium and for the families of drowned British seamen only. Borden agreed, asking how Lloyd George and Balfour could possibly answer Wilson if he insisted on the plain meaning of the Fourteen Points and the Lansing Note. Helpfully, Bonar Law suggested that 'they could point to the great deal of public feeling which prevailed in this country on the subject'. At length, the Imperial War Cabinet decided to instruct its delegates on the Inter-Allied Commission on Reparation and Indemnities at the coming Peace Conference in Paris to aim at 'the greatest possible indemnity' from Germany consistent with 'the economic well-being of the British Empire and the peace of the world, and without involving an army of occupation in Germany for its collection'.[290]

Such was the immediate background to the meeting between Lloyd George and Wilson which eventually took place in London on Boxing Day. There was an 'informal interchange of views', without minutes being taken. Reporting his conversation to the Imperial War Cabinet several days later, Lloyd George put the best gloss on his exchanges with Wilson. It had emerged that 'the League of Nations was the only thing he really cared much about', reported Lloyd George. This, he explained to his colleagues, might prove to be Britain's opportunity. The setting up of the League of Nations would enable the President to return to the United States saying that he 'had achieved his purpose'. If Wilson could be accommodated on this point, reasoned Lloyd George, then he might leave Britain room to secure her own cherished objectives in other areas. The President, after all, was not immovable on some of the other more controversial matters, according to Lloyd George: on 'freedom of the seas' he was 'very vague'; on the German

---

[290] Minutes of the Imperial War Cabinet, 24 Dec. 1918, CAB 23/42.

colonies, he agreed that they 'could not be returned to Germany, and that they should be put under some power acting as a mandatory'; this was likely to advantage Britain and the Dominions, for Wilson was 'very much opposed' to the idea of America undertaking colonial responsibilities. Differences remained, however. Lloyd George explained ominously that on the issue of indemnity he had found the President 'stiffer than on any other question'.[291]

Meanwhile, away from the public glare, key advisers laboured to produce reports designed to assist the government in repelling such American pressure. For example, Amery spent Christmas evening writing a long memorandum to Balfour pleading for the Entente's right to pursue an indemnity to cover the '*total loss suffered*' and observing that it was simply 'not necessary' to discuss how far the Entente was limited by President Wilson's correspondence with Germany. The Germans, he argued, must simply learn to do without luxuries 'for a generation', and live under a 'severe limitation' of internal consumption that would amount merely to a prolongation of war conditions.[292] Balfour instructed the War Trade Intelligence Department to produce a report 'which he could use at the Peace Conference' showing that British territories in the past had maintained a relative 'open door' in trade matters in comparison with territories under the control of other imperial powers.[293] Round Table members wrote to American friends imploring their support in breaking down American prejudice against Empire, and pleading for an acceptance of the idea of new American colonies, so that the two great English-speaking powers might co-operate in a 'common task'.[294]

While the United States was looming as a threat to the kind of peace settlement being marketed from the Coalition's election platforms, the French approach to the peacemaking could not but appear more attractive. Thus, during the same weeks of electioneering, the British government accepted French plans to keep Germany in a state of total diplomatic isolation during the coming period of peacemaking. Only a week after the armistice it was common knowledge among those close to the centre of power in London that plans were afoot to impose peace terms on the Germans by means of an eventual ultimatum which would give the Germans only a week to consider a treaty agreed upon in advance by the victors.[295] The American Right was also pushing for this solution.[296] On the eve of the Inter-Allied Conference in London in early December, the French proposed officially that the Entente powers should discuss peace terms first, and then present these to Germany, 'and compel them to accept without any

[291] Minutes of the Imperial War Cabinet, 30 Dec. 1918, CAB 23/42.

[292] Amery to Balfour, 26 Dec. 1918, FO 800/215, and Amery Diary, 25 Dec. 1918.

[293] Headlam-Morley to A. Teixiera, 21 Dec. 1918, Headlam-Morley Papers, Acc 727, Box 36.

[294] Brand to Charles Altschul, 6 Dec. 1918, and Brand to Hartley Withers, 13 Dec. 1918, Brand Papers, 12.

[295] Davidson memorandum, 17 Nov. 1918, Randall Davidson Papers, 13.

[296] Colville Barclay to Balfour, 21 Nov. 1918, containing Lodge to Balfour, 21 Nov. 1918, Balfour Papers, 49748.

discussion on their part the Preliminaries of Peace and the conditions already arrived at between us'. [297] The French documents made it clear that the victors could not contemplate discussions with the current socialist German government: 'The Allies cannot indeed deal with anything but a constituent Assembly elected freely by universal, secret and direct suffrage.'[298] According to this argument, therefore, any meeting with the Germans would have to be delayed at least until after the German elections scheduled for February (later brought forward to January) 1919. Clemenceau wrote officially to Lloyd George pleading for delay, and arguing that 'it would not be a bad idea to let the German Revolution settle itself a little in order that we may know, before proceeding, whom we have to confront'.[299] Citing Clemenceau's need for a week's rest, Poincaré also implored Balfour, as 'a personal favour', not to press for an early opening of the conference.[300] The British did not resist these efforts, and accordingly the Peace Conference was not to begin until mid-January 1919.

As France gained the leading influence over preparations for the coming conference, Britain proved to be remarkably acquiescent. Absorbed in the election, the leaders of the government agreed, apparently without demur, to these fateful French recommendations. This delighted the British Right.[301] Among the government's advisory bodies, only the PID appears to have raised any doubt about the wisdom of such a course of action. Headlam-Morley prepared a memorandum declaring the French proposals for the conference as acceptable, but 'subject to one proviso; the Allies are bound by the conditions of the armistice that the terms of peace shall be in accordance with President Wilson's statements'.[302] The Prime Minister did not see it that way. Regaling the Imperial War Cabinet on 30 December with an account of his meeting with Wilson, Lloyd George lingered on the most startling of all Wilson's pronouncements: the President had suggested that 'the general Peace Conference would be a sham if definite conclusions were simply arrived at beforehand and then presented to Germany'. Wilson's preference for a negotiated settlement with Germany was, declared Lloyd George, 'a grotesque proposal'.[303]

In this way the general election undoubtedly helped push into the background the moderate option in British foreign policy towards Germany. Having so publicly committed his government to a policy of coercion of the new republic, what-

[297] 'French Proposals for the Preliminaries of Peace with Germany, communicated by the French Ambassador, 26 Nov. 1918', CAB 1/27/24.

[298] 'Note Verbale: Programme of Work and Principles suggested by the French Government for the Peace Negotiations, 28 Nov. 1918', communicated by the Italian Ambassador, 3 Dec. 1918, CAB 1/27/26.

[299] Clemenceau to Lloyd George, n.d., reproduced in Lloyd George, *Memoirs of the Peace Conference*, i. 88.

[300] Derby to Balfour, 20 Dec. 1918, Derby Papers, 28/2/1.

[301] *The Times*, 3 Dec. 1918.

[302] 'Notes on the French Proposals for the Preliminaries of Peace', undated, Headlam-Morley Papers, Acc 727, Box 11.

[303] Minutes of the Imperial War Cabinet, 30 Dec. 1918, CAB 23/42.

ever the colour of the government in Berlin, Lloyd George appeared to abandon altogether the option of consolidating democratic Germany. He acted as if victory had solved everything and the composition of the government in Berlin a matter of complete indifference to him. In so doing, he exposed how hollow had been his own argument, so often employed during the war in justification of its prolongation, that only victory could achieve a lasting peace, because only victory could be relied upon to discredit Prussian militarism and bring to power a popular government in Berlin. It seemed in late 1918 that the advent of democracy in Germany was of no importance whatsoever to the victorious 'knock-out blow' Coalition.

In conclusion, the general election of 1918 was a triumph for the right wing of the 'knock-out blow' Coalition. The triumph was registered in terms both of the personnel elected to high office and the issues given such prominence before the public. The prolongation of Conservative dominance within the administration emerged clearly enough upon the formation of Lloyd George's new government on 10 January 1919. As contemporaries observed, the new ministry was 'hardly more than a reshuffling of the old', with the genuinely progressive elements still playing second fiddle.[304] At the centre of the government, the 'War Cabinet' title and system were retained, with Lloyd George, Curzon, Bonar Law, Chamberlain, and Barnes comprising the permanent members, while ministers most concerned in particular subjects were also to attend. Curzon was appointed both to chair the Cabinet in London and to deputize for Balfour at the Foreign Office, while Lloyd George and Balfour were attending the Paris Peace Conference.[305] Almost all the great departments and institutions of state remained firmly in Conservative control: Balfour retained the Foreign Office, Chamberlain became Chancellor of the Exchequer, Milner shifted to the Colonial Office, Walter Long took control of the Admiralty, Bonar Law continued to lead the government in the House of Commons and Curzon in the House of Lords. Lloyd George held on to the handful of Liberals who had assisted him in the previous government: Churchill gained the War Office, Addison the Local Government Board, Edward Shortt the Home Office, while Montagu retained the India Office, and Herbert Fisher the Board of Education. Significantly, a single promotion for a former leading Liberal, Churchill's elevation to the War Office, brought about renewed howls of horror from the service chiefs, the Conservative leaders, and 'the usual anti-Winston ramp in the Tory press'.[306] At least one other senior Liberal did offer himself, Jack Pease, because, as he put it, 'the PM will require more *liberal* assistance in delivering his goods'.[307] But nothing came of the offer. Curzon tried to

[304] Godfrey-Fausset Diary, 12 Jan. 1919, Godfrey-Fausset Papers, 1/70.
[305] Hankey to Curzon, 10 Jan. 1919, Curzon Papers, MS EUR F 112/212.
[306] Wemyss to Beatty, 7 Jan. 1919, Beatty Papers, BTY 13/40/26, A. Weston Tarns to Long, 5 Jan. 1919, Long Papers (British Library collection), Add. MSS 62424 (provisional number), and, on the press reaction, A. M. Scott Diary, 3 Jan. 1919, A. M. Scott Papers, MS Gen. 1465.
[307] J. A. Pease to W. S. Churchill, 20 Dec. 1918, Gainford Papers, 91.

talk Lloyd George into replacing the First Commissioner of Works, Sir Alfred
Mond, whose Jewish background offended the Conservative Right, with Viscount
Harcourt, a more senior Liberal. Lloyd George, however, confessed his hatred
for Harcourt.[308] Thus, Liberal representation in the government remained limited and the bulk of the spoils of office flowed to loyal Coalition Conservatives.
Notwithstanding this triumph, Conservatives were very bitter over the actual
process of forming the government. In allocating ministerial positions, Lloyd
George negotiated in advance with very few of the leading Conservative personalities, and many ministers were astonished to read of their appointments for the
first time in the newspapers. There was anger that the Prime Minister would dare
treat his Conservative colleagues in this way—as if they were 'subordinates' to
whom he could be 'condescending', as Robert Cecil had complained in the dying
days of the previous government.[309] This was more than a flutter in the dove-
cotes; it highlighted the Conservatives' belief in their party's natural superiority
within the Coalition, a conviction amply justified by their domination of the
House of Commons.

Beyond matters of personnel, the most important consequence of the general
election was a further poisoning of public opinion against Germany, and even
against the new Germany. The Coalition's election campaign helped entrench the
fable that the German people were all guilty of making war and were dishonestly
attempting to hide behind a fake revolution. 'The Huns are the same old Huns
trying to trick us and bluff us at every turn' was the interpretation of first
resort.[310] This interpretation, widely disseminated in the course of the election
campaign, undoubtedly strengthened the hands of all those hardliners in the
Conservative Party and in Lloyd George's circle determined to push through a
severe, avenging peace unencumbered by Wilsonian ideals. It must be said that,
in the course of the campaign, Lloyd George put up scarcely any resistance to
those forces. In his speeches he endorsed the views of the Conservative Right,
on collective guilt, on colonies, and on the indemnity. In so doing, he truckled
to those most determined to disparage Germany's revolution. Thus the interpretation of a defiant and dishonest Germany took hold. As it served the immediate political and diplomatic needs of the Coalition, it was to be repeated, with
breathtaking indifference to the facts, for months to come.

Yet, it is important to note, British idealism had not evaporated completely.
As has been seen, the election was not proof of an ineluctable tide of hatred. As
C. P. Scott explained to President Wilson at a private interview in late December,
the election was simply 'an expression of pure anti-Germanism inflamed by
Lloyd George's appeals'. He assured the President that 'the better and deeper

---

[308] Curzon to Bonar Law, 28 Dec. 1918, Bonar Law Papers, 84/4/20.
[309] Robert Cecil to Walter Long, 30 Nov. 1918, Long Papers (British Library collection), Add.
MSS 62423 (provisional number); W. Bridgeman to Mrs Bridgeman, 21 Jan. 1919, Bridgeman
Papers, 4629/1/1919/16/1; Crawford Diary, 26 Jan. 1919, vol. xxxiii, Crawford Papers.
[310] W. E. Oliver to F. S. Oliver, 3 Dec. 1918, Oliver Papers, 70.

feeling of the nation was on his side and only needed to be appealed to'.[311] Nor were all Conservatives impressed by the histrionics of the 'make the Germans pay' campaign. Even the Court had blushed; Lord Stamfordham told Archbishop Davidson that he was 'disgusted' at the 'absurd vote-catching claim of a huge indemnity, apart from reparation, which can only do mischief'.[312] As has been seen, some advisers in government service, especially the German experts of the PID, were so offended that they felt released from any compulsion to support the government and would emerge in the new year eager to defy their political masters. The Radical and Liberal press continued to rail against the inhumanity and economic vandalism of the 'starvation blockade'. Prophetic counsel was not hard to find. In the December *Contemporary Review*, for example, W. H. Dawson defended the revolution in Germany as a transformation likely to be 'real and permanent'. Moderate social democratic leadership was 'a blessing', argued Dawson, for it would help carry the German masses into the new era. The victors' policy towards Germany, he advised, ought to be 'to encourage her in every endeavour which she may make to retrieve the errors of the past and rebuild her national life on sound and healthy foundations'. According to Dawson, food assistance would convince the German people that the tough armistice conditions were not dictated by vindictiveness, and this would help sustain Germany's democratic transformation; this was an achievement worth more to the victorious powers than the surrender of any number of battleships or the occupation of a hundred miles more German territory beyond the Rhine. As Dawson concluded, 'Germany has made a good end of her old political life: let us help her, according to our opportunities, to make a good beginning with the new.'[313] Clearly, beyond the 'hard men', there were other forces at work in British political life, and there was other expertise to be drawn upon, if Lloyd George's government wished to assist in making Germany safe for democracy.

[311] C. P. Scott Political Diary, 29 Dec. 1918, C. P. Scott Papers (Rylands Library), Box 134.

[312] Davidson Diary, 15 Dec. 1918, Davidson Papers, vol. 13.

[313] William Harbutt Dawson, 'The End and the Beginning', *Contemporary Review*, 114 (Dec. 1918).

6

In Fear of a Second German Revolution
December 1918–March 1919

What I feel myself is that everything has gone wrong owing to the perverted view of the general political situation [in Germany] at the highest quarters; as far as I can see they are beginning to realise some of the mistakes which have been made but I see no symptom of anything like the courage required for a radical change.

James Headlam-Morley, 10 March 1919[1]

THE popular interpretation of the German revolution as a sham may have been good politics. However, in the weeks that followed Lloyd George's victory at the polls, more and more evidence accumulated against it. Intelligence on the 'condition of Germany' increasingly stressed the genuine nature of the revolution, and the severe food shortages that were destabilizing the new German government. A demand for more reliable and complete intelligence soon arose from within the government itself, and this was inspired in part by the increasingly anxious reports of the PID. As a result, early in the new year, a series of military missions were dispatched into the interior of Germany to discover the true facts. These missions, led by British army officers, confirmed the view that the German republic faced an immense internal crisis. The officers on the ground in Germany reported that great damage was being done to the cause of moderate and progressive politics by the continuing economic blockade and by the diplomatic isolation of the new regime.

This chapter aims to show how this evidence, clearly sympathetic to the plight of Germany's government and people, was assembled. It reviews the struggle that was required to bring this material to the attention of the British government, and the political quarrel that erupted when this evidence was used in advocating a moderation of British policy towards Germany. The 'facts' did make a difference. As the chapter will show, in the face of this new intelligence, British leaders lurched from their previous conviction that the German revolution was all a charade, to a dread that Germany was probably on the edge of an irresistible

---

[1] Headlam-Morley to Zimmern, 10 Mar. 1919, Zimmern Papers, 16.

Bolshevik revolution. Even this dread, however, was insufficient to bring about any decisive moderation of British policy.

The domestic context: industrial and military unrest in Britain

The contest for the 'facts' about revolutionary Germany which absorbed British politicians and their advisers in the early months of 1919 did not, of course, take place in isolation from British domestic affairs. Indeed, to understand the debate about revolutionary Germany, it is important to appreciate that, from January to March, Britain itself was the scene of considerable industrial turmoil and military unrest. A wave of fear swept over the members of the newly elected government and the civil servants and military officials who sat with them in the offices of Whitehall, and in the gilded chambers of the Quai d'Orsay—fear of the labour movement, fear of international socialism, fear of a monstrous indiscipline that seemed to herald the break-up of the class society which the governing élite believed had been made safe by victory. Policy towards Germany, where the socialist movement was in actual occupation of government, was bound to be affected by this powerful domestic factor.

The spate of big strikes and the spread of demobilization riots have been examined at length by other historians, most notably by Chris Wrigley in his *Lloyd George and the Challenge of Labour*.[2] The essential details can be stated swiftly. On the industrial front, major disputes occurred in the coal, cotton, engineering, and shipbuilding industries, while a national strike loomed on the railways. Pressure for the reduction of the working day to eight hours was immense, and the railwaymen gained this victory on 1 February. However, disputes over the implementation of the eight-hour day produced a highly visible and inconvenient strike for Londoners, a strike on the underground railway in February. In addition, a power strike was threatened, and a string of sympathy strikes was organized in the north of England. Long-simmering trouble in the police force was also in the headlines, and strikes were with great difficulty held in check until mid-March. In the midst of the crisis, Lloyd George returned from Paris on 8 February, ostensibly for the opening of the new Parliament; he was immediately absorbed by the industrial crisis. In response, he announced in mid-February an unparalleled event, a National Industrial Conference, scheduled to begin on 27 February. Next, in an effort to ward off the most dangerous threat of all, a national coal strike, Lloyd George announced the establishment of a Royal Commission on the Coal Industry under Mr Justice Sankey to consider not only wage increases but also the possible nationalization of the mines. With these grand gestures behind him, the Prime Minister was able to return to Paris on 5 March. That these dramatic events shook the government is hardly open to

---

[2] Chris Wrigley, *Lloyd George and the Challenge of Labour: The Post-War Coalition, 1918–1922* (Hemel Hempstead, 1990). On the unrest of the new year of 1919 see ch. 5.

question. As Wrigley has written, 'The key feature of the industrial unrest of late January and early February 1919 was the conjunction of so many challenges in a very short period.'[3] For a government always ready to contemplate the use of troops against strikers, the other deeply perturbing element of the crisis was the simultaneous appearance of a mutinous spirit in the victorious armies, both in Britain and on the Continent. The process of demobilization was intensely controversial among the troops. Troubles began at Folkestone on 3 January and spread rapidly. Demonstrations by soldiers in London included one very noisy assembly outside a War Cabinet meeting in Downing Street itself on 8 January. Serious unrest spread to army camps in France and even to Germany. Churchill, the new Secretary of State for War after 10 January, produced a new plan for demobilization, ensuring that soldiers with the longest service or with war wounds gained precedence. However, Churchill's plan for an interim continuation of conscription, and his exuberant support for intervention in Russia, kept suspicion and unrest bubbling along among the troops.[4]

Two points require emphasis: first, the very real fear among the traditional governing classes that what was being seen was a fundamental shift in relations between the classes; and second, the awareness in the same circles of the similarities between the demands being made by the British and the German labour movements.

The fear gripped both Conservative and Liberal political leaders and civil servants alike. As previously noted, just such an outburst of social radicalism and lawlessness in the post-war period had long been dreaded. As private letters and diaries reveal, few were measured in their reaction. Milner and then Churchill faced the apparent dissolution of discipline in the British and Empire forces in January 1919 and both were extremely nervous. At the height of the demobilization riots in January, Milner told Lloyd George that 'drastic action' was required, and 'there is no time to be lost'.[5] Churchill told Curzon in mid-January that 'under the present pressure the Army is liquifying fast'.[6] Churchill informed Lloyd George that discipline in the army in Britain and France was steadily 'being rotted' and predicted that soon 'there will be nothing left but a demoralised and angry mob'.[7] The reaction to the labour unrest was equally extreme. Lord Crawford predicted that in the coming 'death struggle with Capital, Labour will win the day'.[8] The labour unrest 'staggers me', wrote Robert Brand in mid-January.[9] Lord Bryce believed that Britain was 'heading straight for bankruptcy

---

[3] Chris Wrigley, *Lloyd George and the Challenge of Labour: The Post-War Coalition, 1918–1922*, 112.

[4] Ibid., ch. 3.

[5] Milner to Lloyd George, 7 Jan. 1919, Milner Add. Papers, MS Eng. Hist. c. 696/2.

[6] Churchill to Curzon, 16 Jan. 1919, MS EUR F 112/209.

[7] Churchill to Lloyd George, 19 and 20 Jan. 1919, Lloyd George Papers, F/8/3/3 and 5.

[8] Lord Crawford Diary, 31 Jan. 1919, vol. xxxiv, Crawford Papers.

[9] Brand to Dr A. L. Bowley, 20 Jan. 1919, Brand Papers, 17.

or confiscation of private property', for 'we are already in the beginning of a revolution'.[10] Alfred Pease, railway director and Second Civil Lord of the Admiralty, told his brother Jack Pease that in pursuit of socialism 'the world has gone quite mad'.[11] The government's men in Paris were not free of the stress. On 4 January the train carrying the main body of Foreign Office staff to the Peace Conference via Folkestone was diverted to Dover two minutes before departure when news arrived of the rioting over demobilization.[12] Dozens of letters describing the new world of topsy-turvydom in Britain made their way to the letter box of the Hôtel Majestic. Hardinge received a typical one from Sir Arthur Davidson, a naval equerry to the king, telling him that the 'whole labour world is now completely out of hand'.[13] In Berne, Rumbold learned from Lord Drogheda that Britain was 'in a really serious state. The Labour question gets worse every day.'[14] Dozens of similar letters are scattered through the letter files of the governing élite for this period.

Because the Ebert government in Berlin was believed to be taking comfort from these events, in the governing circles it was widely assumed that the Germans were in some way responsible. 'One wonders what is really happening in Berlin now. Perhaps the Bolsheviks are telling sensational accounts about demobilization riots in London', mused Sir Courtenay Ilbert, Clerk of the House of Commons.[15] But the connection was not just idle gossip. Edward Shortt told the War Cabinet on 7 February that undoubtedly 'there were Bolsheviks in the country with German money' promoting the unrest. A number of ministers drew from this the lesson that the government must root out aliens from Britain. Auckland Geddes declared that he would invoke the death sentence against such alien agitators mixed up in strikes.[16] The German connection was taken for granted. Austen Chamberlain told his sister that the strikes 'play straight into the hands of recalcitrant Germany'.[17] Christabel Pankhurst wrote to Bonar Law to offer her suffragette services against the 'minority of Bolshevik and pro-German mischief-makers'.[18]

The obvious parallels in style and policy between the movement pursuing power in Britain and the movement exercising power in Germany buttressed this belief. Lord Derby, for example, told Henry Wilson during the demobilization troubles that the government must not consult with the soldiers' representatives for 'that looks too much like the soldiers' committees that wrecked the Russian

[10] Bryce to Dicey, 22 Jan. 1919, Bryce Papers, 4.
[11] Alfred Pease to J. A. Pease, 5 Mar. 1919, Gainford Papers, 91.
[12] Knatchbull-Hugessen Diary, 4 Jan. 1919, Knatchbull-Hugessen Papers, KNAT 1/3.
[13] Sir Arthur Davidson to Hardinge, 21 Mar. 1919, Hardinge Papers, vol. 40.
[14] Lord Drogheda to Rumbold, 21 Jan. 1919, Rumbold papers, 25.
[15] Ilbert to Bryce, 10 Jan. 1919, Bryce Papers, 14.
[16] Minutes of the War Cabinet, 7 Feb. 1919, CAB 23/9. See also Long to Lloyd George, 14 Mar. 1919, Long Papers, WRO 947/746.
[17] A. Chamberlain to Ida Chamberlain, 16 Feb. 1919, Chamberlain Papers, AC 5/1/119.
[18] Christabel Pankhurst to Bonar Law, Bonar Law Papers, 96/10/1.

and German armies'.[19] The short-lived committees of men's representatives that were often found to be at the centre of military unrest in units of the British and Dominion forces were, of course, vaguely similar to the Soldiers' Councils on which the German revolution was initially based. Lord Crawford detected a German influence in most of the social evils proliferating in post-armistice British cities: the social deterioration, the distaste for toil, and the passion for dance saloons in London were all part of 'the same temperament that has invaded Berlin'.[20] More dramatic parallels were starkly visible in the actual demands of the striking workers. The great issue of the British railwaymen's campaign was the eight-hour day—this had been granted to most German workers immediately after the revolution under the terms of the Stinnes-Legien Agreement of 15 November 1918. The great issue in the British police dispute was recognition of the union—employer recognition of unions as agents in collective bargaining had also been conceded in Germany under the same agreement.[21] The great issue in the coal dispute, the issue making headlines during the hearings of the Sankey Royal Commission during March, was socialization of the mines—in Germany, the revolutionary government had appointed a Socialization Commission under Karl Kautsky in November 1918, and in early March 1919 the new German government put forward a general socialization bill and a coal industry bill to socialize the industry.[22] George Saunders, the PID expert closest to a Conservative outlook, wrote to Headlam-Morley in March 1919 pointing out that if the Labour press got hold of the Committee Reports on coal socialization from the Weimar Assembly, then 'large sections of the British working classes may fling them at the heads of our government'.[23] In the light of these fearful parallels, the reluctance of the politicians of the Coalition government to utter a single word in praise of the advent of democracy in Germany can be well understood—the democracy was not to their taste. Their resistance to the idea that the socialist-led government in Germany required help from the victors was well-entrenched, and it would take a great inundation of facts on 'the condition of Germany' to dislodge it.

The demand for new intelligence on Germany

Allegations that the full facts on Germany were not being made available, either to the British government or to the people, appear to have been given prominence in the press for the first time in late December 1918. The *Nation* and *Manchester Guardian* protested against the inhumanity of the continuing economic blockade of Germany, and gave much valuable publicity to a new Radical

[19] Derby to Wilson, 5 Jan. 1919, Henry Wilson Papers, HHW 2/89.
[20] Lord Crawford Diary, 15 Mar. 1919, vol. xxxiv, Crawford Papers.
[21] Richard Bessel, *Germany After the First World War* (Oxford, 1993), 135 and 143.
[22] Richard Breitman, *German Socialism and Weimar Democracy* (Chapel Hill, NC, 1981), 29 and 44.
[23] Saunders to Headlam-Morley, 29 Mar.1919, HMP, HDLM, OS Box 2.

pressure group, the Fight the Famine Council, established in mid-December to mobilize public opinion against the blockade.[24] Even the *Spectator* acknowledged the reality of the suffering in Germany, publishing a letter from a British officer in Cologne describing the distress of the ordinary people and especially their children whose 'drawn, anaemic, thin, little faces and bodies' haunted the officer.[25] While *The Times* eschewed reports of imminent famine, it did concede that too little was known about the internal condition of Germany. J. E. McKenzie wrote of the 'ever thicker fog that obscures the most vital factor in all our deliberations—the true condition of Germany', and he urged the sending of Allied commissioners into the new Germany to ascertain the facts.[26]

Members of the government were evidently experiencing some difficulties with their consciences on the humanitarian issue. Finding that hearsay from private sources disagreed over Germany, several members of the Cabinet expressed dissatisfaction at the want of reliable information. 'Are their clothes made of nettles and their boots of cardboard?', asked Lord Crawford in his diary. 'We still get little news from our armies in Germany', he complained.[27] Neville Lytton, the press officer at GHQ, told Herbert Fisher that he had heard conflicting reports in Brussels, some maintaining that in Alsace there was 'plenty and abundance everywhere, fat horses, fat women', while other reports cited the death by starvation of relatives in Germany.[28] Milner received a personal appeal from a German woman whom he had known in the past imploring him to recognize the dire plight of Germany, and insisting that only immediate food assistance could stem the tide of Bolshevism and 'preserve the whole world from ruin'.[29] As Christmas approached, Smuts received several passionate letters from Emily Hobhouse urging the raising of the blockade in the interests of children, and reminding him of Prince Max's opinion 'that the Entente's treatment of the new Germany is making the League of Nations dead before it is born'.[30]

The flow of intelligence on Germany from the Diplomatic Service to the Foreign Office also began to look more ambiguous during December. Even Horace Rumbold, initially so dismissive of the revolution and of all reports of imminent starvation and Bolshevism, now endorsed his spies' opinions that the political mood in Berlin was drifting steadily to the left and that the triumph of Bolshevism in Germany was 'not impossible'.[31] One eloquent report from an unidentified British spy ('S.8'), received in London on Christmas Eve, argued

[24] *Nation*, 21 Dec. 1918, 'Expediency and the Blockade', and *Manchester Guardian*, editorial, 'The Slaughter of the Innocents', 28 Dec. 1918. On the establishment of the Fight the Famine Council, see Kate Courtney to Gilbert Murray, 15 Dec. 1918, Gilbert Murray Papers, 38.

[25] *Spectator*, 28 Dec. 1918.

[26] Letter to the editor from J. E. McKenzie, the former Berlin correspondent, *The Times*, 6 Dec. 1918.

[27] Crawford Diary, 12 and 29 Dec. 1918, vol. xxxiv, Crawford Papers.

[28] H. Fisher Diary, 19 Dec. 1918, HMP, HDLM, Box 3.

[29] Kate Cajetan to Milner, 8 Dec. 1918, Milner Papers, 355.

[30] Emily Hobhouse to Smuts, 19 and 20 Dec. 1918, Smuts Papers (microfilmed), vol. 20.

[31] Rumbold to Balfour 23 Dec. 1918, received 28 Dec. 1918, FO 371/3224.

that famine was probable in Germany by February. In the opinion of 'S.8', the revolution of November was certainly genuine. The flight of the Kaiser, Ludendorff, and Tirpitz had discredited the old militarist leadership completely, and monarchist opinion had been reduced to insignificance. 'In this sense [the] revolution is irrevocable and complete', observed 'S.8'. While the socialist leadership of the revolution was firmly in place, 'S.8' believed that liberal democratic political parties were likely to grow in strength; therefore, 'S.8' concluded, the political situation was 'entirely satisfactory'. But grave dangers lay in the economic sphere:

I feel it is impossible to over estimate [the] necessity for extreme care and [the] fullest possible understanding on our side of [the] economic situation in Germany which[,] failing economic supplies[,] is literally desperate. Continuation of [the] blockade without explanation or promises for the future creates a fatalistic spirit of helpless fear in the minds of those who should be endeavouring to prepare for [the] reorganisation of economical life. This increasing possibility of irrevocable disaster [is] only slightly less damaging to us than to the GERMANS.[32]

'S.8' also urged the 'vital necessity' of sending observers into Germany to keep the British government and public opinion accurately informed.

Such reports only added to the general sense of disillusionment now overtaking the men of the German section of the Political Intelligence Department in London. The staff, as already seen, had reacted angrily to the government's indemnity claims. The Foreign Office's lack of interest in ongoing intelligence work inside Germany also fuelled resentment within the PID. Headlam-Morley was astonished that the intelligence experts he had assembled were apparently no longer required. Almost immediately after the armistice the temporary PID staff began to enquire concerning the future of their employment with the PID.[33] Headlam-Morley kept up a flow of polite but urgent letters to Tyrrell and to Hardinge requesting that the PID be made a permanent institution, and that the staff be offered more lucrative salaries lest the expertise gathered during the war be dispersed.[34] All to no avail. Various members began to look around for more secure employment. The staff steadily diminished.[35] Those who remained complained about overwork and, most importantly, about the steady erosion of the intelligence sources used by the department.[36] For the PID was not alone in

[32] Report from 'S.8', dated 21 Dec. 1918, received in London via Stockholm, 24 Dec. 1918, FO 371/3776/51–2.

[33] e.g. A. J. Toynbee to Headlam-Morley, 21 Nov. 1918, HMP, Acc. 727, Box 36.

[34] e.g. letters from Headlam-Morley to Tyrrell, 20 Nov., 9 and 12 Dec. 1918, and to John Tilley, 22 Feb., and to Hardinge, 12 Mar. 1919, HMP, Acc. 688, OS Box 1.

[35] Among notable departures, Toynbee left in Feb. 1919, in order to take up an academic appointment. Zimmern was increasingly drawn away from German intelligence work to concentrate on Palestine, before taking up a post at the University College of Wales, Aberystwyth, in early May 1919. Bevan resigned in Apr. 1919 but kept at work on German material in a voluntary capacity at the PID on most days. On the flow of departures from the PID see Percy Koppel to Headlam-Morley, 23 Apr., 3, 10, and 21 May 1919, HMP, Acc. 688, OS Box 2.

[36] e.g. Allen Leeper to Rex Leeper, 11 Jan. 1919, Allen Leeper Papers, 2.

suffering from a winding down of activities. For example, the German experts of MI7d at the War Trade Intelligence Department were also allowed to disperse. Their publications, such as the *Daily Review of the Foreign Press* and *Enemy Press Supplements*, considered vital by the PID, were allowed to lapse. Only strenuous protests by Headlam-Morley led to their eventual revival.[37]

Not surprisingly, during December 1918 the PID staff began to reorient their opinions on Germany. Headlam-Morley, Bevan, Zimmern, and Saunders now openly challenged the reliability of the FO telegrams and military reports presented to them hitherto. On 9 December Headlam-Morley urged Tyrrell to agree to the dispatch of 'thoroughly reliable correspondents' into Germany who could 'write to us directly free from military censorship'.[38] Headlam-Morley was particularly uneasy about the lack of expertise on the crucial subject of German socialism within the British Delegation being assembled for the Paris Peace Conference. Headlam-Morley himself was appointed to join the delegation, but he pleaded more than once with his superiors to be given more staff to assist him in Paris on the key subject of German and international socialism.[39] He requested that his colleague Zimmern be allowed to accompany him to the Peace Conference, in spite of the difficulties that might be raised about his German name.[40] This request was apparently turned aside. Zimmern himself was thoroughly disillusioned. He was disturbed by the swing to the right in Britain and France and wrote to his friend Wallas concerning his fears that 'important sections of French opinion would like to break up Germany if they can, and would be quite happy to see the whole of North Germany go Bolshevik'.[41] Another friend, Herbert Croly, the progressive *New Republic* journalist, agreed with Zimmern that the 'most discouraging aspect of it [the situation] is that no responsible people in the Allied countries seem to have the slightest interest in trying to nourish the growth of a liberal and united Germany'.[42]

Events in Germany itself at the end of the year at least partially confirmed the PID's premonitions of looming disaster in Germany. On Christmas Eve, serious

[37] Headlam-Morley had pleaded for their maintenance as early as Armistice Day; see Headlam-Morley to Lt.-Col. E. Wake, 11 Nov. 1918, HMP, Acc. 727, Box 36. On the continuing struggle to preserve this service see also Headlam-Morley to William Percy, 9 Dec. 1918, ibid., and more letters to Wake 10 Feb. and 11 Apr. 1919, HMP, Acc. 688, OS Box 1.

[38] Headlam-Morley to Tyrrell, 9 Dec. 1918, HMP Acc. 727, Box 16.

[39] Memorandum entitled 'The Allied Conference and Peace Conference—Note on the Work of the PID', undated, in file endorsed 'Preparations for the Peace Conference', HMP Acc. 727, Box 11; and Headlam-Morley to Tyrrell, 14 Nov. 1918, HMP, Acc. 727, Box 16; and Headlam-Morley to Sir Henry Penson, 20 Nov. 1918, and Headlam-Morley to Alwyn Parker, 21 and 29 Nov. 1918, HMP, Acc. 727, Box 36.

[40] Headlam-Morley to Tyrrell, 28 Nov. 1918, two letters, HMP, Acc. 727, Box 16. At the last moment Headlam-Morley was informed that Captain W. Stephen Sanders, the well-known Fabian and patriotic labour personality, would accompany him as resident expert on German socialism. But, for some reason (not explained in the sources), this appointment also did not eventuate; see J. R. H. Pinckney to Headlam-Morley, 11 and 14 Dec. 1918, HMP, Acc. 727, Box 36.

[41] Zimmern to Graham Wallas, 28 Nov. 1918, Wallas Papers, 1/61.

[42] Croly to Zimmern, 6 Dec. 1918, Zimmern Papers.

fighting erupted for the first time in the centre of Berlin. The left-wing People's Naval Division, in occupation of the Royal Palace in Berlin, was attacked by some of the last units of regular soldiers available to the government, the attack being launched on Ebert's instructions and without the knowledge of the USPD. The fighting resulted in the withdrawal of USPD members from the government in protest and the formation of the Communist Party of Germany (KPD) at the end of the year. There was a general expectation of more bloodshed.[43] In the aftermath of the 'Christmas Eve massacre', even George Saunders, always the most reluctant of the PID staff to write sympathetically of Germany, was moved to complain that British intelligence was seriously underestimating the dangers confronting Germany. Considering the grave economic crisis, wrote Saunders, any repetition of the fighting of Christmas Eve would create 'all the conditions for civil war'.[44]

For Headlam-Morley, the bloodshed in Berlin was an unmistakable danger signal. On 28 December, he again urged his FO superiors to consider mounting a special effort to discover the true inner state of Germany. 'The political situation is so confused that no reliance can be placed on any opinion', wrote Headlam-Morley. 'I feel convinced', he continued, 'that we should take active steps by sending commissioners to find out the truth.'[45] So troubled was Headlam-Morley that he broke with established procedures and bypassed his superiors; he directed a personal letter to Hankey, pleading that Germany be given food and raw materials in order to restore her economic life as soon as possible. He warned that a catastrophe was near in Central Europe, a catastrophe which would render the coming Peace Conference 'abortive'. 'I should like to urge in the strongest way that this matter should be given precedence over everything else', he wrote. Hankey promised to help, but politely directed him to work through the correct channels.[46]

Dissatisfactions over the state of British intelligence apparently reached the ears of the Foreign Secretary. On 28 December, Balfour complained to the office of the Director of Military Intelligence, General Sir William Thwaites, that there was 'an absence of reliable news from Berlin'. Thwaites's office sent a consoling reply: it announced that, at that very moment, a number of British officers, including several British military attachés at British legations in the neutral countries, were preparing to embark on special missions to survey conditions inside Germany.[47] A struggle for possession of 'the facts' on Germany was about to begin.

---

[43] The incidents in Berlin may be followed in 'Joint Meeting of the Cabinet and Zentralrat in the Reich Chancellery, 28 Dec. 1918', in Charles B. Burdick and Ralph H. Lutz (eds.), *The Political Institutions of the German Revolution, 1918–1919* (New York, 1966), 119–65.

[44] George Saunders Minute, dated 27 Dec. 1918, on cover of Report from 'S. 8', FO 371/3776/49.

[45] Headlam-Morley Minute, dated 28 Dec. 1918, on Rumbold to Foreign Office, 7 Dec. 1918, FO 371/3224.

[46] Headlam-Morley to Maurice Hankey, and Hankey to Headlam-Morley, both 28 Dec. 1918, HMP, Acc. 727, Box 35. Hankey advised that it was the Foreign Secretary, Arthur Balfour, who alone could relay recommendations for special actions from the PID to the War Cabinet.

[47] Balfour to Thwaites, and DMI to Balfour, 30 Dec. 1918, FO 800/201.

Missions into Germany: the boosting of the British intelligence effort in Germany, January–February 1919

From mid-January until the beginning of March 1919, British military intelligence officers undertook a total of eight missions into Germany. The primary objective of each mission was to investigate economic conditions and food shortages, but the officers also carefully recorded material on the military and political situation inside Germany. The orders under which these missions operated revealed the scepticism still prevailing among the British brass hats. Lieutenant-General Haking, for example, issued orders instructing his officers to 'carefully study the whole question of the supply of food by the Allies to Germany and report on the extent to which food shortage is a real menace to the country, and whether assistance if sent can be made proper use of, and will reach those who are most in need of it. You will understand that it is no part of the Allied plan to feed the poorer classes so as to release more food for the wealthy classes.'[48] The British officers dispatched on these missions operated quite openly, wore military uniform, and undertook their investigations with the eager co-operation of the local municipal and health officials, normally the *Oberbürgermeister* and his assistants at the local city *Rathaus*, men whose positions of authority predated the revolution. The officers generally took up residence in the best hotel in the city and ate well in the hotel restaurants. They were often escorted in their investigations into the condition of the people by German military officers, some of whom were *Freikorps* activists. Usually, the British officers on mission spurned officials of the local Soldiers' and Workers' Councils and preferred to deal with the surviving officer corps of the old army. However, the first missions generally found some contacts thrust upon them because, early in the revolution, the local Workers' and Soldiers' Councils were sharing power with town hall officials. Again, the victorious powers' reluctance to give any sign of endorsement to the new regime was clearly signalled.

The first mission was undertaken by two officers, Lieutenant-Colonel J. H. M. Cornwall and Captain Hinchley Cooke, from the Military Section of the British Delegation in Paris set up in early January. They proceeded via Spa to Leipzig and investigated conditions in the city between 12 and 15 January. The two men then separated, and Cooke went on to Dresden and Berlin from 15 to 20 January. In their reports Cornwall and Cooke depicted a nation in the throes of a mild but quite genuine revolution, with the Workers' and Soldiers' Councils operating efficiently and moderately, keen to exercise a stabilizing influence and to hurry forward demobilization. They discovered that the German people were sick of the war and 'heartily glad at its conclusion'. Contempt of the old monarchy was commonplace. 'All present had lost all respect for the Kaiser', wrote Cornwall of his conversation with soldiers in one railway carriage. The soldiers were 'very

---

[48] 'Instructions for officers proceeding to Germany to ascertain the economic conditions as regards food supply', wrongly dated 4 Jan. 1918 (*sic*) but should be 1919, Gedye Papers, 8.

friendly' and full of expectation at newspaper reports that American bacon was on its way to Germany. Political discussion was dominated by reports of the suppression of the Spartacist unrest in Berlin in early January. There was widespread 'detestation' of Spartacism as a dangerous minority doctrine, but the report also noted that 'all hoped fervently for the triumph of the Majority Socialists' in the elections of 19 January. The military situation also intrigued the British officers. An official from the USPD-controlled Leipzig Workers' and Soldiers' Council accompanied Cooke and Cornwall to the HQ of the XIXth Army Corps, where they found a General Franke, in mufti, commanding the remnants of the corps in co-operation with the Soldiers' Council. 'It was really pathetic to see the unfortunate general who was a powerless puppet in his own headquarters', announced the report. The two officers also investigated closely the rationing system and the communal kitchens for the poor in Leipzig, and concluded that the food situation in Leipzig was 'serious and getting worse'.[49]

A further three missions were undertaken during January. One three-man team visited Munich between 22 and 26 January, and another investigated Hamburg and Hanover between 28 January and 9 February.[50] A third mission was led by a senior intelligence officer, Lieutenant-Colonel E. Dillon, also from Military Intelligence in Paris, who explored Kassel and the surrounding district in western Germany during the last ten days of January. Dillon's conclusions were typical. He reported that Germany was prostrate from a military viewpoint, and 'incapable of any further effort for the present'. The collapse of military discipline was very evident. 'During the whole of my time in unoccupied Germany I never saw a soldier salute an officer', he wrote. He was unequivocal concerning the danger of famine, reporting that 'the Germans are very short of food, especially fats'. He was more confident of the political future. There was 'no likelihood of Bolshevism breaking out in Germany, nor is there any immediate probability of a return to the old regime'. It was probable, he argued, that the Germans would quickly establish a stable government, a government 'with rather advanced tendencies, the backbone of which will be formed by the old social democratic party'.[51] All these reports stressed undernourishment, the depth of German despair over the maintenance of the blockade, and the serious danger of Bolshevism. All urged the delivery of emergency food assistance to Germany.

The urgent tone and unanimity of opinion offered in these first reports appear to have prompted a considerable beefing up of the intelligence effort inside Germany. During the first fortnight of February 1919 at least four more missions were sent into Germany. This second wave of investigators came from all cor-

---

[49] 'Report on Visit to Leipzig, 12th to 15th January 1919', by Lt.-Col. J. H. M. Cornwall and Capt. W. E. Hinchley Cooke, in Armistice Commission Report, WO 144/8.

[50] See the reports by Captains J. R. Somerville and J. E. Broad and Lieutenant D. Pease on Munich, and the report by Captains A. D. Seddon and H. M. Henwood and Lieutenant H. A. Rose on Hamburg and Hanover in 'Reports by British Officers on the Economic Conditions prevailing in Germany: December 1918–March 1919' (London, 1919).

[51] 'Extracts from report by Lt.-Col. Dillon, 31 Jan. 1919', FO 371/3776 and FO 608/129.

ners of the British intelligence network, from the Directorate of Military Intelligence at the War Office in London, from the Armistice Commission in Spa, from the Military Section of the British Delegation in Paris, and from the Second Army intelligence unit in Cologne. Because the reports submitted by these intelligence officers were to prove so controversial, it is worth briefly surveying their content.

The first mission was dispatched from the Armistice Commission at Spa and was composed of two officers, Captain E. Christie-Miller and Captain E. B. Trafford. These two men investigated the Hanover district in central Germany between 2 and 10 February. Their report was blunt: Germany faced the threat of political radicalization as a consequence of a genuine and rapidly worsening economic crisis. The two officers seemed aware that their report would not be readily believed; in a special preface to the document the two officers explained that each had been a prisoner of war in Germany during the war and had suffered mistreatment at the hands of the Germans. 'We can therefore hardly be accused of having any friendly feelings towards them', the officers pleaded. The officers argued strongly for a moderation of the blockade on behalf of the German people. 'There cannot be the slightest doubt that the Hannover district and town are extremely short of food', the report insisted. It was noted that many Germans regarded the blockade as 'a breach of faith'.[52]

A second mission was dispatched from the Directorate of Military Intelligence (DMI) in London. Captain W. Stewart Roddie led the mission, with Captain C. W. Bell and Captain E. W. D. Tennant, two German language specialists, in support. On 2 February the three officers went by train to Berlin, and took rooms at the plush Adlon Hotel. In company with members of the Berlin Charity Organization Committee, they spent the next week investigating the condition of the poor of Berlin, and taking soundings of German opinion in meetings with employers, military officers, and officials of the new government. The evidence of severe privation, and of genuine dread of Bolshevism, was quite overwhelming. Nor did the officers have doubts that anti-militarism was the dominant mood in Berlin. War Ministry personnel described 'the war party as finished'. The officers were amazed to observe a total absence of hostility towards themselves, and a widespread expectation of reconciliation with the victorious powers if only the blockade could be lifted.[53] The officers found the state of Berlin such a revelation that Roddie arranged for Tennant to fly to Paris in order to present an interim report as soon as possible to British military intelligence. The two remaining officers then extended their investigations, Roddie proceeding to Leipzig and Bell to Kassel. Roddie was so distressed by the suffering he

[52] The original report, 'Report by Captains E. B. Trafford, Scots' Guards, and E. Christie Miller, Coldstream Guards, on a visit to Hanover, 2–10 Feb. 1919', FO 608/265.

[53] 'Report on a visit to Berlin, 2nd February, 1919, to 11th February, 1919, by Captains W. S. Roddie, Claude W. Bell and E. W. D. Tennant', FO 371/3776. The story of the mission is also told in Stewart Roddie, *Peace Patrol* (London, 1932), 19–30.

encountered in Saxony that he also attached a passionate and eye-catching preface to his additional report: 'To those who have had the opportunity of studying Germany recently from the inside, the policy of continuing the starvation of that country must appear not only senseless but utterly harmful to ourselves.' Roddie's report catalogued evidence pointing to the disastrous economic state of the city of Leipzig, and the evidence of a continuing demobilization of the demoralized German Army. Roddie offered political insights also: he grasped the immense opportunity which presented itself to the victorious powers to consolidate the transition to democracy in Germany. 'Militarism is dead' was on the lips of 'people of all classes and professions'. 'The popular belief is that as soon as food comes into the country and work is resumed, the change from Monarchism to Republicism [*sic*] will prove to be one wholly for the better.'[54] Captain Bell was equally emphatic: 'All that I have seen and heard during my fortnight in Berlin and Kassel goes to convince me that the country is helpless and that its condition may become desperate at any moment. Hunger is at the bottom of a good deal of the unrest.' Bell also advised allowing supplies into the country and argued that 'it is in the Allied interests not to drive Germany *beyond* the limits of her endurance'.[55]

A third exhaustive mission into western Germany, Bavaria, and Berlin was undertaken from Berne by a lone investigator, a secret service officer, Lieutenant Thornely Gibson of the Irish Guards. Gibson was a former professional singer, fluent in German, and a man with wide experience and many contacts in pre-war Germany. (He was also married to a stepdaughter of Stanton Coit, the Ethical Church leader and Labour Party candidate, and was presumably well disposed to progressive political causes.) Leaving Berne on 2 February, Gibson travelled to Munich, Berlin, Kassel, Frankfurt, Mannheim, Heidelberg, Karlsruhe, Baden-Baden, and Offenburg. He undertook dozens of interviews with municipal authorities, politicians, including Prince Max of Baden, and members of the General Staff and the Foreign Office in Berlin. He also sought to 'check the information' by widening his sources; in civilian clothes he attended both Spartacist demonstrations and Soldiers' and Workers' Council meetings. His report focused on the problem of Bolshevism in Germany. Gibson found the threat of Bolshevism to be very real. It was founded upon the hunger of ordinary people, wrote Gibson, people who were in 'a condition of desperation the danger of which cannot possibly, I think, be exaggerated. They have waited for food from the West and so far waited in vain.' In Gibson's opinion there was evidence of 'prolonged under-nourishment'. Unless some hope was given the people, he predicted, Germany would sink into 'complete and universal anarchy'. Gibson reported graphically on the mood inside Spartacist meetings and on the

---

[54] 'Report on Visit to Leipzig, 13th to 14th February 1919, by Captain Stewart Roddie', Milner Add. Papers, MS Eng. Hist. c. 697.

[55] 'Further Reports on Visits to Germany, 13th to 15th February 1919', Milner Add. Papers, MS Eng. Hist. c. 697.

discrediting of the moderate socialist government that was taking place as a result of Allied treatment. According to Gibson, the blockade and the shunning of the new German government were furnishing useful arguments in favour of a radicalization of the revolution. Most importantly, Gibson sought to nail the contention that Bolshevism was a mere ruse of war being exploited by the government to get easier terms. He concluded that the moderate socialist-led government was 'making a genuine effort to resist the spread of Bolshevism'. If any unreconstructed elements were deliberately inciting Bolshevism to deceive the West, Gibson argued, their party was 'infinitesimally small and entirely without influence'.[56]

A deeper foray extending into eastern Germany was undertaken by a fourth mission. Major Grasset and Captain George Gedye of the Second Army's political intelligence unit left Cologne on 13 February with instructions to investigate social conditions and the military preparations of the volunteer forces in Frankfurt-on-Oder, Stettin, and Danzig. Grasset and Gedye learned at first hand of the strength of the influenza pandemic in Germany, both succumbing to the infection. Grassett lay at death's door for a week in a hotel in Frankfurt-on-Oder, and the journey was cut short there. On their return to Cologne on 1 March, Gedye drew up a document that was a mirror image of his brother officers' reports, that is, an impressive catalogue of statistics on rations and death-rates combined with an emotional plea for assistance to ameliorate the obvious privation inside Germany. The report began, as others did, with a passage imploring the delivery of immediate food aid to Germany. 'The poor people are undoubtedly suffering misery and hardship through lack of food', wrote Gedye. Outside assistance was 'urgently necessary' in order to stave off Bolshevism. On the state of 'militarism' in Germany, Gedye also confirmed the great themes of the other reports: the German army had 'ceased to exist' as a fighting formation, demobilization was occurring 'rapidly', and discipline was in tatters. As Gedye observed, 'red flags are flown over all Barracks'.[57]

The arrival of such gloomy reports at the DMI in London and the Military Section in Paris clearly shocked the officers in authority there. By the end of February a total of seventeen army officers had investigated the condition of Germany. And not only were their written reports submitted; Christie-Miller, Tennant, and Roddie presented themselves at the War Office in London upon their return from the Continent and supplemented their reports with personal interviews. These officers' arguments prompted a sudden and stunning reversal of position on the part of the chief intelligence officers in London. Even before the final reports of Gedye and Gibson had been delivered, the prevailing

---

[56] 'Conditions in Germany', by V.77, dated 28 Feb. 1919, CAB 24/76, printed as 'Bolshevism in Germany', 5 Mar. 1919, Milner Adds. MS Eng. Hist. c. 697. The quotations in this paragraph are all underlined in Milner's copy of the report.
[57] 'Report on Visit to Frankfurt on Oder', typescript undated, and Gedye Private Diary, 13 Feb.–1 Mar. 1919, Gedye Papers, 8. The journey is also described in George Gedye, *The Revolver Republic: France's Bid for the Rhine* (London, 1930), 26–33.

opinion on Germany changed dramatically. Lieutenant-Colonel Twiss wrote on 24 February to General Sir William Thwaites, now in Paris, informing him that the 'unanimous opinion of British officers who have visited Germany is that, unless the food situation is relieved at a very early date, there will be a Bolshevist outbreak in Germany'. A supporting opinion from Brigadier General Bartholomew followed, decrying the 'fashion' of saying that it was German policy to 'flourish the bogey of Bolshevism in the faces of the Entente powers'. The danger was real and 'very serious', wrote Bartholomew.[58] The Military Intelligence Branch of the Military Section under Thwaites's command in Paris needed little convincing. The officers returning from Germany had already been debriefed by Lieutenant-Colonel Cornwall in Paris and he appeared willing to endorse at least the claims concerning the disappearance of any credible military threat from Germany. On 22 February the Military Section of the British Delegation produced a report on the state of the German army which acknowledged that discipline had been 'entirely broken down by the events of the past few months'. Only German orderliness prevented 'universal confusion and riot'. The report concluded that the German army was 'no longer fit to take the field'.[59]

The new view on Germany did not long remain confined to military circles. The officers recently returned from Germany were also treated to a round of interviews with civilian intelligence officers and with government figures in London. On 22 February, Tennant and Christie-Miller obtained an interview with Lord Crawford at the Ministry of Food. They were only partially successful in shifting his opinion. 'I credit their alarming accounts of the situation, but I ask myself why under such conditions the Germans are so obstinate about handing over their mercantile marine', wrote Crawford.[60] By 28 February the same officers, plus the articulate Stewart Roddie, had been eagerly interviewed at the Foreign Office by Saunders, Bevan, and Zimmern. The PID officers reacted with enthusiasm. Saunders found Roddie's report 'so vivid and important' that he arranged for Roddie to proceed to an immediate interview with Lord Curzon.[61] The War Office itself acted swiftly to publicize the officers' revelations concerning inner Germany. The officers' reports were all printed immediately for circulation by the DMI, without significant amendment. Thus, under the imprimatur of the DMI itself, a series of eloquent indictments of the economic block-

---

[58] 'Food Conditions in Germany', dated 5 Mar. 1919, including 'Minute to D. M. I. from Lieutenant Colonel Twiss, 24 Feb. 1919', 'Letter to D. M. I. from Brigadier General Bartholomew, 28 Feb. 1919', and 'Report by reliable Agent recently returned from Berlin, middle of February, 1919', FO 608/130.

[59] 'Summary of Intelligence', dated 22 Feb. 1919, with 'Annexe: The Present State of the German Army', dated 18 Feb. 1919, from the Military Section, British Delegation, WO 106/349.

[60] Lord Crawford Diary, 22 Feb. 1919, vol. xxxiv, Crawford Papers.

[61] Zimmern to Headlam-Morley, 27 Feb. 1919, Saunders to Headlam-Morley 28 Feb. 1919, and Percy Koppel to Headlam-Morley, 28 Feb. 1919, HMP, Acc. 688, OS Box 2.

ade of Germany were circulating among British ministers and officials in London and Paris from the first week of March 1919.[62] In one sense, the officers' reports ought to have been unnecessary. During January and February, the existing 'windows into Germany', the Armistice Commission in Spa, the Berlin Military Mission, and the Naval Armistice Commission in north Germany, were all directing a wealth of material back to the War Office and Admiralty in London about deteriorating social conditions in Germany. Some quick examples must suffice to give a sense of this mass of evidence. From Spa, Haking sent a flow of reports to the War Office expressing a deepening concern over the food situation in Germany and the danger of Bolshevism. Haking advised both a wider occupation of Germany in order to crush Bolshevism, and Allied distribution of emergency food aid constantly in his reports. The *Freikorps* were doing 'good work' in crushing the Spartacists, he told the War Office. Photographs of the destruction in Berlin were entrusted to him by the German Armistice Commission on 16 January.[63] Pages of data on the measures undertaken by the government in Berlin to suppress Bolshevism were also given to Haking and these were forwarded to London with Haking's endorsement. These documents pointed out forcefully that the blockade was compounding the difficulties inside Germany and that the new political leaders in Berlin were 'not receiving any moral support in their difficult task from the Entente, which does not even refrain from morally weakening them'.[64] Haking clearly began to sympathize with this view; on 1 March, he telegraphed to Balfour his conclusion that food from Rotterdam should be sent in 'at once to strengthen [the] existing German Government or an assurance given that Germany will be supplied up to [the] next harvest by [the] Allies'.[65]

General Ewart at the British Military Mission in Berlin submitted much similar material, and his reports were included with Haking's Armistice Commission Reports. Ewart was the man on the spot during the suppression of the Spartacist uprising of early January. Personal observations of the *Freikorps* troops' use of flame-throwers against the Spartacists, and personal interviews with Count Brockdorff-Rantzau, the new German Foreign Minister, persuaded Ewart that the commitment of the Ebert government in opposing Bolshevism could scarcely be doubted. Brockdorff-Rantzau himself impressed Ewart as sincere and 'very helpful'; indeed, a fabricated French newspaper report suggesting friction

[62] The official printed versions of the reports show that they were circulated from early March. An uncorrected proof of 'Bolshevism in Germany', by Gibson, is marked as printed on 5 Mar. 1919; 'Report on a visit to Berlin, 2nd February, 1919, to 11th February, 1919, by Captains W. S. Roddie, Claude W. Bell and E. W. D. Tennant', is dated 10 Mar. 1919 by the DMI, and 'Report on a Visit to Frankfurt-on-Oder' (by Gedye), is marked as printed on 13 Mar. 1919.

[63] Armistice Commission Reports, 7, 10, 11, and 16 Jan. 1919, WO 144/7.

[64] e.g. 'Notes concerning the development and counteracting of Bolshevism', and 'German notes on Blockade', mid-Feb. 1919, Armistice Commission Reports, WO 144/10.

[65] Haking to Balfour, 1 Mar. 1919, Milner Papers, MS Eng. Hist. c. 697.

between the two men infuriated Ewart and he lodged a formal complaint.[66] Brockdorff-Rantzau 'begged' Ewart to intervene to hasten the delivery of food to Germany.[67] When in late February Dr Schairer of the German Red Cross provided evidence of 'acute distress among children at Düsseldorf', Ewart decided to release tinned milk he had in store for British prisoners of war.[68] Ewart's social contacts in Berlin at this time all testified either to the German government's good faith or to the widespread social distress they had witnessed.[69] Working with Ewart in Berlin were two representatives of the British Red Cross, Sir Martin Abrahamson and Arthur Mayne, both of whom sent additional detailed reports on the distress in Germany to London and Spa.[70] Ewart also gained insights into political opinion in Germany from a source he despised. The Soldiers' Council representative at the German War Ministry, A. Schlesinger, told Ewart that the victorious powers' refusal to release German prisoners of war, and the refusal even to allow German Red Cross officials to visit German prisoners, was helping to discredit the new government in the eyes of the German public. He angrily informed Ewart in mid-February that his own request to visit the Armistice Commission in Spa itself had been rejected on the grounds that he was the representative of the Soldiers' Council in Berlin.[71]

Naval Intelligence received a flow of material from officers on British ships of the Naval Armistice Commission. The British officers who visited Wilhelmshaven and Bremerhaven in mid-January found red flags still flying from most ships and buildings, although they learned that a less extreme Sailors' Council had just deposed a Spartacist-leaning council in Wilhelmshaven in the wake of the Spartacist uprising. In Hamburg, however, the British found a general strike in place, and conditions 'very chaotic'; only three German officers were said to be still at their posts in Hamburg.[72] The officers of the Armistice Commission continued to insist on seeing Admiral Schroeder in their negotiations and were gratified to notice the disappearance of Sailors' Council delegates by mid-February. Similarly, the suppression of Spartacism by *Freikorps* units in the German naval ports was applauded.[73] The weekly official Admiralty

---

[66] Ewart Diary, 6, 10, 12, 26 Jan. 1919 and Brockdorff-Rantzau to Ewart, 28 Jan. 1919, with annotations from Ewart in Ewart Scrapbook, Ewart Papers, 73/88/1. The French newspaper was the *L'Echo de Paris*.

[67] Ewart Diary, 3 Feb. 1919, Ewart Papers, 73/88/1.

[68] Ewart Diary, 25 Feb. 1919, Ewart Papers, 73/88/1.

[69] Ewart socialized with the Anglo-German aristocracy (Prince and Princess Blücher), the neutral diplomats (Baron van Gevers of the Netherlands, Count Moltke of Denmark, and Baroness von Essen of Sweden), and members of a visiting American economic mission; see Ewart Diary, 1–2, 4, 6, 9, 11, 14 Feb. 1919, Ewart Papers, 73/88/1.

[70] e.g. Kilmarnock to Foreign Office, 11 Jan. 1919, FO 371/3776, and Ewart Diary, 29 Jan. 1919, Ewart Papers, 73/88/1.

[71] Ewart Dairy, 17 Jan., 6, 11, and 20 Feb. 1919, Ewart Papers, 73/88/1.

[72] 'Report of Second Inspection of Surface Ships and Submarines, 9–10 Jan. 1919', by Capt. F. L. Tottenham, and Commander H. F. Leary to Commander Squadron Three Patrol Force, 19 Jan. 1919, both in Thring Papers, 71/30/1.

[73] 'Notes on General State of Affairs in Wilhelmshaven and Bremen', from Inspection Committee, HMS *Comus*, to Allied Naval Armistice Commission, 11 Feb. 1919, Thring Papers, 71/30/1.

Intelligence reports in January and February, based on the material coming from Germany, remained generally favourable to the German government, the Scheidemann Cabinet being described as dominated by 'the better, more moderate, and saner element' of the SPD. The murder of Luxemburg and Liebknecht during the suppression of the Spartacist Uprising was described as 'a happy event tending to the establishment of order'.[74] Ebert was praised as a moderate of great ability, and a man who had 'consistently condemned any war of conquest and annexation'. Character sketches of Scheidemann and Rantzau were also positive, both men being described as trenchant critics of the old order and sincere moderates. The idea in 'newspaper reports' that the new German government might be secretly conniving with Bolshevism was rejected as quite improbable.[75]

Some of the officers in the Naval Armistice Commission were clearly reluctant to discover that the German people were starving. Edward Hilton Young, the naval officer and Liberal MP, for example, was ambivalent on the food shortage. In a private letter from Hamburg in mid-February, he wrote that he had seen 'a good many double chins and paunches' among German men, and he concluded that the people were not starving. However, in the same letter he conceded that women looked 'emaciated' and that the suffering among children was 'the saddest thing'.[76] Admiralty Intelligence in London was more definite in its judgements. In January, American sources were cited as showing that the food crisis had been crucial to the collapse of the nation even in November 1918.[77] By the beginning of March, the official Admiralty Intelligence Report conceded that the evidence pointing to dire food shortages in Germany was overwhelming. Newspaper stories that the German government was deceiving the Allies over the food crisis were 'definitely false'. Chaos was quite certain, argued Admiralty Intelligence, 'unless the Allies strengthened the hands of the Moderate Socialist Party by promptly sending food and raw materials into the country'.[78]

In reality, therefore, the British army officers' reports from inside Germany during February merely confirmed the insights of a great many other observers whose official reports were piling up in the War Office and Admiralty. But these latest army officers' reports clearly carried greater weight than those emanating from Haking at Spa, from Ewart and his Red Cross assistants, or from the naval officers visiting the north German ports. These army officers were trained in intelligence, they had travelled widely and deeply into Germany, and they were unanimous in their analysis. Their missions were focused upon the food issue and planned by the DMI. Such credentials were necessary if the fog of prejudice and suspicion was to be dispersed. One of the officers, Stewart Roddie, gained

[74] Admiralty Intelligence Report, 21–3 Jan. 1919, Drax Papers, DRAX 5/5.

[75] Admiralty Intelligence Report, 11–13 and 18–20 Feb. 1919, Drax Papers, DRAX 5/5.

[76] Hilton Young to Kathleen Scott, Asquith Papers, 18. Young also applauded the work of the *Freikorps* in 'cleaning out' the north German ports.

[77] Admiralty Intelligence Report, 10–13 Jan. 1919, Drax Papers, DRAX 5/5. This includes a long interview with an American citizen who lived in Berlin from 1902 until Dec. 1918.

[78] Admiralty Intelligence Report, 28 Feb.–3 Mar. and 4–6 Mar. 1919, Drax Papers, DRAX 5/5.

some insight into the strength of this prejudice upon his return to London: at one society dinner party where he related his experiences he overheard 'a stalwart peeress' spreading the rumour that he had 'a German mistress'.[79]

It should be borne in mind that the reports of the British officers from Germany were a slap in the face to a deeply entrenched orthodoxy operating in Whitehall and Paris, an orthodoxy which the leading intelligence personalities themselves had helped to construct. Up until this time, it had been common practice among the intelligence chiefs closest to the War Cabinet to ridicule reports of famine and Bolshevism in Germany as all part of a cunning German propaganda campaign designed to secure easier terms in Paris. For example, throughout January and February, Basil Thomson of New Scotland Yard stressed in his fortnightly reports to the War Cabinet that Bolshevism in Germany was tolerated by the government in Berlin in the hope that 'the poison may spread among the Allies'. Spartacism was a threat in Germany, wrote Thomson, but he claimed to have evidence that 'the old military authorities are designedly allowing it some rope'.[80] The DMI in Paris had endorsed this view in late January, claiming to have gathered evidence proving that 'the Germans are intriguing with Bolshevism in their own country, using it both as an excuse for not fulfilling the armistice terms and for obtaining food from the Allies'. The DMI qualified this conclusion only slightly, observing that 'the evidence does not conclusively show who is the moving spirit behind the secret organisation'; nevertheless, the DMI was prepared to list the Ebert-Scheidemann government, the German Foreign Office, and the German High Command, in that order, as the most likely culprits.[81] Colonel J. H. Morgan of the Military Section told Latham in Paris that the Germans in Cologne were 'lying, appealing, fainting, dying—all sham'.[82] It is important to note also that the War Office in London continued to regard any newspaper criticism of the blockade as pernicious pro-German propaganda. Thus, citing specifically the need to guard against any campaign for the lifting of the blockade, the War Office successfully petitioned the Home Office to prolong the life of the Press Bureau, the government's chief wartime vehicle for censorship of the British press, from November 1918 until April 1919.[83] As late as 26 January, Sir Henry Wilson agreed with Admiral Wemyss in Paris that the real danger at the Peace Conference was the American determination 'to drive

[79] Roddie, *Peace Patrol*, 23.

[80] 'Fortnightly Report on Revolutionary Organisations in the United Kingdom and Morale Abroad', Report no. 31, 28 Jan. 1919, GT 6713, CAB 24/74, 'Fortnightly Report on Revolutionary Organisations in the United Kingdom and Morale Abroad', 10 Feb. 1919, GT 6816, CAB 24/74, and 'The Progress of Bolshevism in Europe—Memorandum by Mr Basil Thomson', GT 6857, CAB 24/75.

[81] Minute by the Military Section, British Delegation, 29 Jan. 1919, entitled 'Existence of a Secretly Organised Control in Germany', FO 608/129.

[82] Latham notebook, no date, Latham Papers, MS 1009/21/1410. Morgan repeated his view that the 'hunger blockade' was purely an invention of German propaganda in his memoir, J. H. Morgan, *Assize of Arms* (London, 1945), i. 183–90.

[83] Tania Rose, *Aspects of Political Censorship, 1914–1918* (Hull, 1995), 32–3.

a hole through the blockade on the plea of feeding the Boches'.[84] It was a most spectacular paradox, therefore, that the 'missions into Germany' dispatched by British Intelligence itself had now produced a series of first-hand reports unanimous in condemnation of the blockade.

The British brass hats, it must be said, were swiftly persuaded by this great wave of detail. Haig saw Milner and Henry Wilson on 19 February, and argued that the question of emergency food shipments for Germany must be settled 'without any delay' for the latest reports revealed that 'Germany was on the verge of famine'. Haig made his motives clear: 'If we don't feed her, Bolshevism will spread, this will result in the destruction of Germany and probably in our having to intervene. And further Bolshevism is likely to spread to France and England. There is therefore every reason for feeding Germany.'[85] Wilson did not resist for long. On 28 February he wrote in his diary that 'Germany *must* be fed to save her from Bolshevism'.[86]

The rallying of moderate opinion

The evidence produced by military intelligence in January–February 1919 did much to strengthen the moderate spirits among the British political and civil service élites. For moderate spirits there were. As has been seen, the excesses of the election campaign had scandalized many within the government and among its advisory agencies. They now began a campaign to mobilize opinion for a new policy: moral support and food assistance for the newly elected government in Berlin, and even the abandonment of the blockade altogether, in order to consolidate the German transition to democracy.

The agency in the best position to drive home the lessons of the new intelligence flowing from Germany, and even to press for a moderation of policy towards the German republic, was the Political Intelligence Department. As has been seen, the leading spirits within the PID were already most impatient with the 'anti-German' intelligence presented to the Foreign Office and the War Cabinet. Even before the unrest of Spartacist week, Germany's predicament appears to have softened even Headlam-Morley's considerable hostility towards the SPD. 'It is in the interests of the Allies as well as Germany to give active support to the moderate socialists', he had minuted on 3 January 1919, thus becoming surely one of the very first British advisers to recommend Allied gestures of support for the SPD-led government.[87]

When Headlam-Morley arrived in Paris in mid-January his impatience with the complacency and ignorance shown towards Germany grew swiftly. In spite of all his pleas for extra assistance, he found himself alone in Paris, apparently

---

[84] Henry Wilson Diary, 26 Jan. 1919, Henry Wilson Papers, DS Misc/80.

[85] Haig Diary, 19 Feb. 1919, Haig Papers, 136.

[86] Henry Wilson Diary, 28 Feb. 1919, Henry Wilson Papers, DS Misc/80.

[87] Headlam-Morley Minute, dated 3 Jan. 1919, on cover of Rumbold to Balfour, 23 Dec.1919, FO 371, 3224.

the sole British expert on German internal political development whom the British Empire could afford to maintain at the Peace Conference. He claimed to be deliberately starved of resources, and was soon so absorbed in advising the delegation on territorial matters that he confessed he had 'no time to study German things at all carefully'.[88] German newspapers, he discovered, were deliberately kept from him.[89] He was to complain bitterly that military intelligence had sought to monopolize all material on Germany, and that the War Office must have deliberately withheld information from the PID.[90] His accusations were almost certainly true. The PID did not see any of the intelligence flowing back to the War Office and Admiralty from Spa and north Germany. Even the press had some reports before the PID. J. H. M. Cornwall sent his first intelligence officer's report, Christie-Miller's report, to Headlam-Morley on 18 February.[91] Up until this time he was forced to rely instead on the memoranda and letters sent by his three PID colleagues in London, Saunders, Zimmern, and Bevan.[92] They in turn found themselves embarrassed by their reliance upon an irregular flow of out-of-date German newspapers, and increasingly cynical about the French and military intelligence material presented to them. Under these conditions, Zimmern explained to Headlam-Morley, he had doubts about the ultimate value of their work in the London office.[93] Thus, while Headlam-Morley hoped to rely on his colleagues in London, they were throwing up their hands in despair.

The successful suppression of the Spartacist uprising in the first two weeks of January 1919, and the clear-cut victory of the moderate Centre and Left parties in the elections of 19 January (in addition to the reassuring fact that the SPD could not govern alone), helped sway opinion in the PID in favour of the new German government. The elections, Saunders happily declared, 'have produced a vast majority for law and order'.[94] As an illustration of the spectacular movement in opinion in the London office of the PID, the views of Namier are worth citing. Horrified by the outburst of anti-Semitism in Poland at this time, and the obvious reluctance of the new Polish government to hold any genuine democratic elections comparable with those in Germany, Namier could not help passing on to Headlam-Morley the comparisons he now drew in Germany's favour:

---

[88] Headlam-Morley to Bevan, 14 Mar. 1919, HMP, Acc. 688, OS Box 2. 'We are I think not well-represented for dealing with the German problem . . . It is almost incredible that we have not been able to get any system by which we can even see a German newspaper' (Headlam-Morley to Zimmern, 3 Feb. 1919, HMP, Acc. 688, OS Box 2). 'I am afraid that since I have been here I have had no time to follow, as I should have wished, the current events in Germany' (Headlam-Morley to Lt.-Col. E. Wake, 12 Apr. 1919, HMP, Acc. 688, OS Box 1).

[89] Headlam-Morley to Bevan, 7 Feb. 1919, HMP, Acc. 688, OS Box 2.

[90] Headlam-Morley to Tyrrell, 15 July 1919, HMP, OS Box 1, and Headlam-Morley to C. K Webster, 16 Aug. 1920, Charles Webster Papers, 1/4.

[91] J. H. M. Cornwall to Headlam-Morley, 18 Feb. 1919, HMP, OS Box 1.

[92] Rex to Allen Leeper, 14 Jan. 1919, Leeper Papers, 1.

[93] Zimmern to Headlam-Morley, 22 Feb. 1919, HMP, Acc. 688, OS Box 2.

[94] Saunders to Headlam-Morley, 22 Jan. 1919, HMP, Acc. 688, OS Box 2.

The Poles are no better than the Huns, in fact much worse. They have all their vices without their virtues. At least the Germans fought like men, showed great abilities and a sense of duty, and now will probably put up one of the most decent governments in Europe. You know that I dislike them, and I think you were right in saying that no-one in this office dislikes them as thoroughly as I do. But I admit that an Ebert-Naumann Government will be an enormous asset for order and progress in Europe and that everything possible should be done to give them a fair chance.[95]

For this to be realized there was much earth to move. Throughout February 1919 the German section staff of the PID worked hard to counteract the unrelentingly hostile interpretations of the German revolution which still circulated in the Foreign Office, and among the men of power in London and Paris—much fortified, of course, by the British 'patriotic' press. On the press' portrait of the intractable Hun in socialist garb, Namier was particularly scathing. 'Much of what our and the French press describe as arrogance strikes me as simple human self-respect and dignity which one likes to see in a great nation, even if it is a conquered enemy', he wrote to Headlam-Morley in mid-February.[96]

The prejudice of the press and too many of the government's advisers, the PID experts were now agreed, prevented the British leadership from finding the wisdom and courage to lift the economic blockade of Germany. Hostile interpretations of the German revolution, from both Left and Right, they believed, had to be challenged. From the Left came the interpretation that the revolution was aborted, that the SPD had sold its soul completely to the militarists, and that the Allies should support the only true democrats and anti-militarists in Germany, the left-wing socialists of the USPD. From the Right came an equally antagonistic interpretation: the revolution in Germany was counterfeit, the moderate socialists were in league both with militarists and Bolsheviks, and Bolshevism and starvation were being paraded in front of the Allies as bogeys to scare them into a moderate peace. According to this right-wing interpretation, the Allies must retain the blockade in order to coerce the unrepentant and unreformed Germans.

The PID set out deliberately to puncture both interpretations. The left-wing critique of the revolution was promoted in Paris chiefly by Professor George Herron, the American Christian Socialist, USPD supporter, and confidant of Colonel House. Herron was in close touch with a section of the disaffected German intellectual *émigré* and pacifist group in Geneva, led by Dr Muehlon, the former Krupp director who had been converted to the anti-militarist cause during the war. Herron supplied a flow of intelligence reports to Paris transmitting and endorsing the views of the Geneva group. By February 1919, Herron

[95] Namier to Headlam-Morley, 28 Jan. 1919, HMP, Acc. 688, OS Box 2. Many further denunciations of Polish imperialism and Polish anti-Semitism were to flow from Namier's pen in the months that followed, and more praise for the German and Austrian socialists. For example, see Namier's view that Otto Bauer was 'thoroughly honest and trustworthy, one of the best men in office in Europe', in Namier to Headlam-Morley, 3 Feb. 1919, HMP, Acc. 688, OS Box 2.

[96] Namier to Headlam-Morley, 13 Feb. 1919, HMP, Acc. 688, OS Box 2.

announced that, after long interviews with his Genevan-based sources, he was now thoroughly convinced 'the present German revolution is a lie, and that the Government of Ebert and Scheidemann is a mere masquerade of the old regime'.[97] The PID Director was inclined to Herron's views, writing that they were 'worth serious consideration'. In response, the PID staff declared the Genevan intelligence the work of 'unpractical visionaries' and 'sentimentalists'. Headlam-Morley protested at the preposterous claim that nothing had changed in Germany; all attempts to measure Germany's 'change of heart' were 'unnecessary and misleading', he argued. It was 'absurd and presumptuous', he wrote, for the Allies to find fault with figures in the new government. The real cause of the faltering of the revolution in Germany, he complained, was the inexcusable delay on the part of the Allies in providing either food or a preliminary peace. 'We have got to a stage in which mere words are no good. What we want is action', he wrote.[98]

The right-wing interpretation took even more effort to dislodge because the core of it, the German-Bolshevik conspiracy theory, was a time-honoured interpretation of Russia's revolution in Entente and American propaganda. Moreover, the labour unrest in Britain in early 1919 created fertile ground for a continuing belief in a SPD–Bolshevik master plan to undermine the Allies from within. Headlam-Morley and the PID staff poured scorn on the view that the new German government was spreading Bolshevism and revolution either at home or abroad. They argued that there was ample blood in the gutters in Germany to show that the resistance of the SPD to Bolshevism in Germany was quite real. Intelligence spread by French and Polish sources, designed to show that Germany's new leaders were in league with both Lenin and Ludendorff, was denounced as a transparent fraud.[99] As Headlam-Morley concluded, the situation in Germany was 'far too serious for anyone except perhaps a few quite reckless men of the military class to play with Bolshevism'.[100]

Of course, it was not enough simply to discredit false intelligence. The PID in London had to create its own assessments of the situation in Germany. This process began well before the British army officers' reports were received. In early February, Bevan produced a lengthy two-part memorandum provocatively entitled 'The Inner Change in Germany' for circulation to the War Cabinet. Bevan debunked the idea of a counterfeit revolution quite mercilessly.[101] The evidence for a genuine transformation of German politics, for a decisive shift in

[97] Herron Memo, 'Germany's Eleventh Hour', 12 Feb. 1919, FO 608/129.

[98] See Tyrrell's and Headlam-Morley's comments on the Herron Memo, 'Germany's Eleventh Hour', 12 Feb. 1919, dated 18, 20, and 27 Feb. 1919, FO 608/126 and 129.

[99] See Bevan's comments on Horace Rumbold's Polish sources, 5 Feb. 1919, FO 608/129.

[100] Jacket endorsements on 'Military Intelligence Reports from MI1c', dated 20 Feb. 1919, FO 608/129. See also Saunders's opinion that the German socialists 'have their hands too full at home' to sponsor Bolshevism abroad, in Saunders, 'Day Book, vol. vii, 12 Feb. to 31 Mar. 1919 (Headlam-Morley Papers, Acc. 800/1).

[101] PID Memorandum, 'The Inner Change in Germany', 4 Feb. 1919, FO 608/129.

favour of democracy, and for the widespread revulsion of militarism and autocracy inside Germany was quite overwhelming, argued Bevan. Based on his continuing study of the German press since the revolution, Bevan's memorandum used editorials and features in the major German newspapers to illustrate the disgrace now attaching to the militarist cliques and the vigour of the new pro-democratic spirit. Enclosing his first memorandum when it was just hot off the press in a letter to Headlam-Morley on 5 February, Bevan explained his purpose in writing these new assessments:

You will see that my memorandum is directed against the view that the change in Germany is illusory. I am convinced that the change is real and profound, and that the people now dominant in the country have quite different ideals of political life and international action from those of the old régime. I am afraid that if we fail to realise this and to give them credit for it, if we are misled by all the silly talk about the new Germany being only the old imperialism in disguise, etc. we shall miss the opportunities of the hour.[102]

Headlam-Morley was eager to contribute to the campaign. 'I should like to get in a very short memorandum combating some of the current heresies [on Germany]', he explained to Zimmern in mid-February.[103] Headlam-Morley's memorandum appeared later the same month. He was emphatic in his positive estimation of the German revolution and its impact on the national psyche. A militarist reaction in Germany was 'unthinkable', concluded the memoranda. Nor was Headlam-Morley in any doubt concerning the social distress threatening the stability of German democracy: the food situation was 'extremely serious', and the Germans were being driven to Bolshevism through 'despair'. Indeed, Headlam-Morley scolded his superiors as responsible for a materializing disaster:

It is impossible to over-estimate the seriousness of the situation. We still have perhaps the opportunity of guiding and forcing the German nation into the way in which we want it to go. We have had an unparalleled opportunity for the legitimate extension of British influence. We seem to have been throwing it away. Partly, no doubt, we have been misled by false interpretation of the situation in Germany from French sources, but the natural and just resentment the French feel towards Germany makes them the worst possible guides in action towards Germany. The catastrophe, if it comes, will be a terrible one. Whether justly or unjustly, the world will lay the responsibility for it on the Allies in general and particularly on Great Britain.[104]

'Disagreeable reading', wrote Lord Hardinge on the cover of Headlam-Morley's memorandum.

In writing his memorandum, Headlam-Morley undoubtedly profited from a series of interviews which he had arranged with a number of the British officers returning from Germany via Paris during February. As Headlam-Morley

---

[102] Bevan to Headlam-Morley, 5 Feb. 1919, HMP, Acc. 688, OS Box 2.
[103] Headlam-Morley to Zimmern, 18 Feb. 1919, HMP, Acc. 688, OS Box 2.
[104] Headlam-Morley Memorandum 'Political Situation in Germany', 28 Feb. 1919, FO 608/129.

explained in a letter of 27 February to Rex Leeper, the PID's expert on Bolshevism, he had met several of these officers and their opinions were remarkably consistent regarding the plight of ordinary Germans. According to Headlam-Morley, 'they are unanimous that unless food is supplied there will be a collapse of social order which will take the form of Bolshevism'. He was careful to note also the most serious of their accusations: that anger against the moderate democratic and socialist government was growing among the working class, an anger drawn out by left-wing speakers who explained to the crowds that 'Our Government is no good, not even the Allies trust it; if they did they would give food'.[105]

By early March, Headlam-Morley and his colleagues in the PID were by no means alone in recommending a change of policy. Other centres of moderate opinion had appeared in the British Delegation in Paris, especially among the economic advisers. The issue of emergency food shipments to Germany increasingly polarized opinion. In December, British and French delegates to the Allied Blockade Committee had successfully thwarted Hoover's proposals for lifting the blockade in order to allow American food sales to Germany via the neutrals. Instead, a new Supreme Council of Supply and Relief, created in mid-January, accepted the need for some provisioning of Germany in principle, but only on condition that Germany agreed to surrender its entire cargo and passenger fleet.[106] British economic experts attached to the Supreme Council of Supply and Relief (and to the Supreme Economic Council which superseded it in mid-February 1919) were increasingly divided over the morality and expediency of the blockade itself. Keynes confessed later to having been opposed totally to the post-armistice blockade. Reading and Sir John Beale, however, were most reluctant to see any major dismantling of the system lest the Allies lose their power to coerce Germany.[107] In conferences, Keynes worked strenuously to smooth the way towards early relief for Germany, and he became extremely bitter over French objections to Germany paying for food from the gold reserves which France coveted as an indemnity. At the same time, even Keynes shared some cynicism that Hoover's motives included a desire to sell 'low grade pig products at high prices'. 'When Mr Hoover sleeps at night visions of pigs float across his bedclothes', he wrote.[108]

As the debates raged over food for Germany, the Supreme Council of Supply and Relief was building up its own intelligence on the food crisis in Germany. This intelligence, from American and British sources, made converts to the mod-

---

[105] Headlam-Morley to Bevan, 7 Feb. 1919, and Headlam-Morley to Rex Leeper, 27 Feb. 1919, and see a similar view in Headlam-Morley to Saunders, 26 Feb. 1919, HMP, Acc. 688, OS Box 2.

[106] See Klaus Schwabe, *Woodrow Wilson, Revolutionary Germany, and Peacemaking, 1918–1919*, (Chapel Hill, NC, 1985), 153, and C. P. Vincent, *The Politics of Hunger* (Athens, Ohio, 1985), 88.

[107] Alonzo Taylor to Keynes, 6 Nov. 1920, and Keynes to Alonzo Taylor, 27 Nov. 1920, Keynes Papers, EC/2/5/51 and 56.

[108] Keynes to Sir John Bradbury, 14 Jan. 1919, Keynes Papers, RT/1/36, and Keynes to J. N. Keynes, 14 Jan. 1919, Keynes Papers, PP 45, J. N. and F. A. Keynes, vol. 9/19/2.

erate standpoint on the peace settlement. William Beveridge, an official of the Ministry of Food, played a significant role here. Beveridge undertook a special month-long mission to investigate food conditions in Austria, Czechoslovakia, and Hungary beginning in December 1918. He discovered 'a spectacle of economic destruction which I could never have imagined'.[109] In Paris, at the end of his mission, Beveridge produced a report which he ensured was well circulated, and gained a personal interview with Lloyd George.[110] On his return to London in late January, Beveridge was appointed Permanent Secretary at the Ministry of Food; he continued to advocate rapid relief for Europe among his contacts in Paris, and he secretly encouraged the work of the Fight the Famine Council in Britain.[111] In Paris itself, Sir Robert Cecil became a focus of hope for moderate opinion. Officially an adviser to the British Delegation on League of Nations questions, Cecil was appointed the first Chairman of the Supreme Economic Council in February (following the resignation of Lord Reading from the Supreme Council of Supply and Relief on 21 January). As a former Minister for Blockade, Cecil's views carried great weight, and he favoured a rapid resolution of the food crisis. On 7 January he had written that the food situation in Germany was 'the key to the political situation'.[112] An interview in mid-January with Alonzo Taylor, the recently returned leader of an American economic mission to Austria and Germany, persuaded him of the extreme urgency of the situation.[113] By mid-February, under the influence of Keynes and Alonzo Taylor, Cecil had been converted to the necessity of making a major relaxation of the blockade, not only to allow the passage of food but also selected raw materials and exports in order to restart German industry. In a submission to the War Cabinet he declared that there was now 'an overwhelming mass of evidence' pointing to imminent disaster in Germany.[114] In a decisive move, he used his authority as Chairman of the Supreme Economic Council to release to the press a document summarizing the findings of fourteen of the British officers who had been investigating conditions in Germany. Details of the food crisis in Germany were soon filling the columns of every British newspaper. Cecil had shouldered a most difficult task, and apparently doubted his prospects. Lady Betty Balfour who visited Paris in early March found Cecil 'very gloomy' about Germany. In private, he explained to her his humanitarian motive, confessing that he had been 'specially

[109] Beveridge to Walter Runciman, 18 Jan. 1919, Runciman Papers, WR 177.

[110] Beveridge to J. R. Clynes, 25 Jan. 1919, Beveridge Papers, IV 27 pt. ii.

[111] G. H. Roberts to A. Chamberlain, 11 Feb. 1919, Beveridge Papers, IIb 18, and Lady Anna Barlow to Beveridge, 30 Jan. 1919, Beveridge Papers, IV 27 pt. i, and the series of letters from Edward Backhouse, E. M. Leaf, and H. M. Hyndman, Feb. 1919, Beveridge Papers, IV 27 pts. ii and iii.

[112] Cecil Diary, 7 Jan. 1919, Cecil Papers, 51131.

[113] Cecil Diary, 16 Jan. 1919, Cecil Papers, 51131, and Robert Cecil to Lord Reading, 17 Jan. 1919, Reading Papers, EUR F/118/10.

[114] Cecil to Balfour, 23 Feb. 1919, FO 800/215, Cecil Diary, 2 and 6 Mar. 1919, Cecil Papers, 51131, and Robert Cecil's paper, 'The Economic Situation in Europe', dated 2 Mar. 1919, CAB 29/8.

moved by the accounts of the ill-nourished and sickly children'. He declared that it was 'almost too late to help them effectively'.[115]

Support for any major retreat from blockade was still difficult to muster, even among the British delegates to the new Supreme Economic Council. This emerged clearly in the first full debate in the council on 25 February concerning the condition of Germany. The British submissions admitted the seriousness of German privation, but backed away from recommending the abandonment of the blockade altogether. Sir John Beale, the Ministry of Food delegate to the Supreme Economic Council, and previously a trenchant opponent of Hoover's plans for immediate relief, now acknowledged the desperate nature of the food crisis in Germany and the imminence of 'economic and political disaster, with consequences which may spread to Allied countries'. Beale advocated the lifting of the blockade on foodstuffs going to Germany, but no relinquishment of the blockade against other imports and exports. The economic blockade itself, he insisted, was still required 'as a lever to secure acceptance of the terms'. Peace, therefore, should be arranged as swiftly as possible, so that further concessions might follow.[116] British military intelligence agreed. The DMI produced a special 'Combined Report on Food Conditions in Germany' for the council summarizing the evidence collected by a total of fourteen of the British officers who had entered Germany during January and February. The conclusions were clear: the need for feeding Germany was 'really urgent', and the danger of 'either famine or Bolshevism' before the next harvest was extreme. Food should be permitted to slip through the blockade, but the mechanism of blockade must remain. Because 'Germany is still an enemy country which has not yet signed Peace Terms', argued the DMI, 'it would be inadvisable to remove the menace of starvation by a sudden and abundant supply of food-stocks. This menace is still a powerful lever for negotiations at an important moment.'[117] Hunger, in other words, was too valuable an ally to be dismissed from the field altogether.

The tensions among the economic advisers at this time must have been considerable. In London, Lord Crawford, still in close touch with the Ministry of Food, filled his diary with complaints about the continuing bungle over relief for Europe; Reading lacked 'the courage of a flea', Hoover was 'consumed with ambition', Beale was 'tactless and overbearing'; together they were 'the most flabby and impotent set of talkers ever assembled'.[118] In late February, Beale suddenly

---

[115] 'Memoir of a trip to Paris by Gerald and Mrs Balfour', 3 Mar. 1919, Whittingehame Papers, GD 433/2/363.

[116] 'Relief Supplies for Germany', Memorandum by Sir John Beale, dated 21 Feb. 1919, CAB 24/76, included as appendix (a) to Minutes of the Supreme Economic Council, 25 Feb. 1919, in Kenneth Bourne and D. Cameron Watt (gen. eds.): *British Documents on Foreign Affairs: Reports and Papers from the Foreign Office Confidential Print. Series I, The Paris Peace Conference of 1919*, ed. Michael Dockrill (University Publications of America, 1989), xii. 174–7.

[117] 'Combined Report on Food Conditions in Germany During the Period January 12 to February 12, 1919', dated 16 Feb. 1919, by the Military Section, British Delegation, ibid., 177–9.

[118] Crawford to Rodd, 13 Jan. 1919, Rodd Papers, 20, and Crawford Diary, 5, 9, 23, and 24 Jan., 16 Feb., and 1 Mar.1919, vol. xxxiv, Crawford Papers.

resigned; he told Kerr of his frustration that while the Reparation Commission wished to suck Germany dry, the Supreme Economic Council debated measures to assist her economic recovery; and nobody at the Peace Conference had 'a grip on the economic side of things'.[119] On the heels of Beale, Keynes now joined Cecil as a Treasury expert and delegate to the new Supreme Economic Council, with Chamberlain's full backing.[120] J. A. Salter, the Secretary of the Allied Maritime Transport Council, was also advocating the feeding of Germany for the whole year to come and a rapid abandonment of the blockade.[121] The battle lines were being drawn for a major confrontation over British policy in the light of the 'condition of Germany'.

For Cecil and his economic experts to prevail within the British Delegation, they needed allies in high positions within the government. Two advocates of a moderate peace for Germany did appear during January and February, both rather unlikely personalities to take on the roles: Lord Milner, the new Colonial Secretary, and Winston Churchill, the new Secretary of State for War. Both Milner and Churchill were shaken by the demobilization riots, and acutely conscious that British military power was melting away. Both, therefore, advocated an early peace, and both were willing to moderate Britain's claims to get it. Milner also had an optimistic view of political events inside Germany that defied the conspiracy-driven analyses of the early military intelligence on the revolution. On new year's day, Milner wrote to Lloyd George rejecting Foch's demands for a large force to be maintained against the German threat. Milner explained that in his view it was ridiculous to imagine that the German army had much fight left in it: 'German "militarism" is a thing of the past. I have never doubted that since she sued for an armistice.'[122] In this regard, Milner's letters to the Governors-General of the Dominions in the new year also give some unique insights into his own thinking on Germany; in short, they reveal that he rejected completely the view of the German revolution which the Governors-General might care to read any morning in their newspapers. For Milner, there was no fraudulent revolution in Germany, no conspiracy to affect hunger, and no persistence of an unrepentant militarism. Milner stated bluntly that a most promising German republic was in formation and needed only a swift restoration of economic life to strengthen its political reformation. He described the January election result in Germany as 'the one most favourable so far as political conditions go to stable and reasonable government in Germany'. He conceded that 'the foreign policy of the socialist and democratic parties also seems to imply a sincere repudiation of the aggressive *Weltpolitik* of the old regime'. The requirement of the moment was economic revival: 'All hopes of orderly government in

---

[119] Kerr to Lloyd George, undated but filed as late Feb. 1919, Lloyd George Papers, F/89/2/26.

[120] Chamberlain to Robert Cecil, 24 Feb. 1919, Keynes Papers, RT/1/60.

[121] J. A. Salter, 'Note summarising various discussions on relief of Germany', 8 Mar. 1919, E. M. H. Lloyd Papers, 3/3.

[122] Milner to Lloyd George, 1 Jan. 1919, Lloyd George Papers, F 39/1/1.

Germany depend on the possibility of regular industry being set going in the future'. Milner was also in no doubt that the suppression of Bolshevism by the government in Berlin was undertaken vigorously, and he praised the work of Noske. He ridiculed the idea that the Germans were deliberately inciting Bolshevism to spook the victors. Bolshevism, he wrote on 2 March, 'should not be ascribed to political motives but to the complete lack of the essentials of life'. Reports of starvation in Germany, he added, left no doubt as to the 'suffering, famine and physical degeneracy of the people'.[123]

Believing all this, it is remarkable that Milner did so little to bring about change in the government's policy, and nothing in public to enlighten popular opinion. He warned his Round Table colleagues in early March that the victorious powers were 'simply reducing Germany and Austria to Bolshevism and will find themselves without any enemy to make peace with'.[124] He told Bishop Hamilton-Baynes that the government would have to approach Germany with terms 'far more moderate than those usually contemplated' if Bolshevism was to be avoided, but cautioned him in the next breath that 'All this is deeply confidential'.[125] Thus, Milner never aligned himself in public during 1919 with the advocates of a moderate peace. Various factors may account for this. Without doubt Milner's savage lashing at the hands of the Northcliffe press, as noted above, following his suggestion in October 1918 that not all Germans were in love with militarism, made him chary of taking any public stand as a moderate again. Moreover, as Colonial Secretary he was scarcely in a good position to preach moderation; he presided already over the spoils of war and was expected by his Dominion leaders to stand firm against Wilson in the battle for possession of the new colonies. If Milner was to work for a moderate peace settlement it would be done behind the scenes.

Not so diffident was Winston Churchill. Fanatical opponent of Bolshevism as he was, Churchill believed that everything needed to be done to prevent Germany going down the same road. On 29 January he informed Lloyd George that he was having 'searching enquiries made through all the sources open to me into the conditions of German demobilization'.[126] These missions into Germany, as has been seen, produced not only evidence of the breakdown of the German military machine, but also overwhelming evidence of hunger and Spartacist agitation. At the War Office, Churchill was among the first to see the officers' reports and he took fright. He did his best to advertise the findings and to use them in his ceaseless campaigning for the maintenance of a large Army of the Rhine; armed strength, he argued, was a much better weapon than starvation to enforce peace terms. He told Henry Wilson on 20 February that the blockade

[123] Milner to 2nd Earl of Liverpool, New Zealand Governor-General, 25 Jan., 22 Feb., and 2 Mar. 1919, New Zealand Archives G 44/1.
[124] Amery Diary, 10 Mar. 1919, Amery Papers.
[125] Milner to Bishop Hamilton-Baynes, 24 Mar. 1919, Milner Papers, 46.
[126] Churchill to Lloyd George, 29 Jan. 1919, Lloyd George Papers, F/8/3/9.

should be raised as soon as Germany accepted a preliminary peace, for Britain had 'no right whatever to go on starving the great mass of German women and children'.[127] In late February, Churchill spoke publicly of the importance of preventing Germany from making common cause with the Bolshevik 'baboons'; once punished, he declared, Germany should be welcomed back into the comity of nations.[128] On 3 March he told the House of Commons that the reports he had received from intelligence officers proved conclusively that 'Germany is very near starvation'; indeed, there was 'the danger of a collapse of the entire structure of German social and national life under the pressure of hunger and malnutrition'. The only solution was a rapid conclusion of peace and early abandonment of the blockade.[129] But again, Churchill was not in a strong position to advocate a moderate peace with Germany. As noted above, he was deeply distrusted by his Conservative Cabinet colleagues. At exactly this time also, his credibility was under attack because he promoted himself as the chief advocate of armed intervention against the Bolshevik government. Lloyd George himself regarded Churchill's pugnacious approach to Russia as evidence of an unbalanced judgement: 'He is a dangerous man. He has Bolshevism on the brain', Lloyd George said to Riddell.[130] Cecil also noted that Churchill was 'mad' on intervention.[131] Churchill, no doubt, was not the first choice of moderates as an ally.

If moderate opinion was to have any chance, some support in the press in Britain was also essential. Between January and March that support in the Liberal press most certainly appeared. The issue of famine in Europe was a prominent theme, but there was also some stress on the importance of treating Germany without vindictiveness in order to consolidate the victory of German democracy. Most importantly, these themes were taken up not only in the Radical and Labour papers, the *Nation*, *Common Sense*, *Labour Leader*, and *Daily News*, but also in the *Manchester Guardian*. As a paper which had supported the Lloyd George Coalition through until military victory, this was a most significant development. In the editorial columns of the *Manchester Guardian*, C. P. Scott kept up a constant propaganda in favour of a Wilsonian peace. On the eve of the opening of the Paris Peace Conference, he demanded a relaxation of the blockade, in order to preserve 'an orderly Germany', and an abandonment of the absurd claim to a huge indemnity.[132] In early March Scott raised his voice again, condemning the blockade as 'an absurd and disastrous policy'. That Germany was starving was 'admitted on all hands', he claimed. 'Hunger is the parent of revolution', he warned. He implored Lloyd George to 'use his great influence in order to remove the obstacles, whatever they may be, to the opening of the ports and the relief of

---

[127] Churchill to Henry Wilson, 20 Feb. 1919, in Martin Gilbert (ed.), *Winston S. Churchill*, iv. *Companion Volume I: January 1917–June 1919* (London, 1977), 548.
[128] *The Times*, 24 Feb. 1919.   [129] *Parl. Debs.*, 5th ser., vol. 113, 84 (3 Mar. 1919).
[130] Riddell Diary, 11 Apr. 1919, Riddell Papers, 62983.
[131] Cecil Diary, 9 Mar. 1919, Cecil Papers, 51131.
[132] e.g. *Manchester Guardian*, editorials, 'The Conference and the Peace' and 'The Conference at Last', 10 and 13 Jan. 1919.

starving peoples'.[133] But the Liberal and Radical papers did not confine their campaign to the danger of famine and revolution. The *Nation*, in particular, was willing to acknowledge that the changes in Germany from an authoritarian monarchy to a progressive republic were praiseworthy. For example, assessing the result of the elections in January, the *Nation*, noted that the vote had been free and large, in fact, a huge increase on the turn-out in Britain in December. The militarist parties had suffered a 'reduction to impotence', and there had been a 'renaissance of German Liberalism' in the Democratic Party. The election as a whole, argued the *Nation* was 'the best answer that Germany can give to the nation's [Britain's] request for a stable government'.[134] The *Daily News* agreed that the thumping majority for the socialists and liberals in Germany had 'fulfilled alike President Wilson's demand for the democratisation of Germany and Lord Robert Cecil's call for the establishment of a "trustworthy" Government as a condition of German entry into the League of Nations'.[135] By early March, even Lloyd George's own *Daily Chronicle* agreed with the analysis of the Radical press, scolding the victorious powers for their 'blindness' in sticking with the 'disastrous' blockade and failing to recognize the 'common interest' between the Allies and 'the forces working for a German Democracy'. Ebert and Scheidemann had their weaknesses, said the *Daily Chronicle*, 'but we have to ask ourselves whether the Associated Powers have ever given them a chance'.[136] In looking to Germany's future, Hugh Spender, a Liberal supporter of Lloyd George, captured the outlook of much of the Liberal and Radical press:

A great deal will depend on the conquerors. If the spirit and substance of Mr Wilson's Fourteen Points, which Germany accepted when she signed the armistice, as a pledge against a penal and vindictive peace, are preserved by the Peace Congress, a new and better Germany, purified by her sufferings, may arise. But if the same power-peace which Germany imposed on Russia is imposed on her by the Allies, and Germany is made to pay for generations to come to the uttermost farthing for all the wrong which she has done, then there will be counter-revolution, followed perhaps by despair and anarchy in Germany, and that very system of Prussianism which we waged the war to destroy will be established in our land. Then, indeed, the Kaiser and the Junker would have their revenge.[137]

Finally, among the moderate forces, elements of the British financial community must be numbered. From January to March, some prominent men were raising doubts about the viability of the indemnity which was still being advocated so remorselessly by the 'economic warriors'. The Institute of Bankers arranged a series of progressive lectures for members in the new year on taxa-

[133] *Manchester Guardian*, editorials, 'Obstacles to Peace' and 'Starvation as a Weapon', 3 and 5 Mar. 1919.
[134] *Nation*, 'The German Republic', 25 Jan. 1919.
[135] *Daily News*, editorial, 'The German Elections', 22 Jan. 1919.
[136] *Daily Chronicle*, editorials, 'German Anarchy' and 'Germany in Chaos', 3 and 5 Mar. 1919.
[137] Hugh F. Spender, 'Downfall', *Contemporary Review*, 115 (Jan. 1919).

tion, the distribution of wealth, and the indemnity.[138] Sir Charles Addis, the banker whose moderate views had so irritated Hughes when he addressed his Indemnity Committee in December, was still actively opposing the indemnity. In February he addressed a private meeting of the Political Economy Club, with Herbert Samuel in the chair, and made plain his views.[139] On 5 March, having taken counsel from the Radical publicist Lowes Dickinson, he delivered a major address on 'The Economics of the War Indemnity' to the Institute of Bankers. On the basis of his experiences in China and a study of precedents in European history, Addis explained, he was convinced that a penal indemnity was quite impossible and economically destructive. Germany would be able to fund reparation in the territories she had occupied, but no indemnity for war costs could be anticipated. Moreover, Addis had the courage to remind the audience that in the Entente powers' own statement of their reservations to the Fourteen Points, reproduced in the Lansing Note, Britain had undertaken not to ask for an indemnity but only compensation for civilian damage. 'By what alchemy of thought civilian damage has since been transmuted into an amalgam of civil damage *and* military expenditure has not yet been explained', Addis observed.[140] He was even more frank in his private correspondence: it was a matter of honour and Britain must not 'break faith', he wrote.[141] In his address, Addis had touched a sensitive nerve, and he found himself inundated with supportive letters.[142] The argument for a moderate peace, for conscience's sake, was there to be made.

The forces of resistance: pressure for indemnity and the maintenance of the blockade

There were people for whom it seemed that the facts concerning political progress or any humanitarian crisis inside Germany were quite irrelevant. In the first months of the new year, formidable personalities on the Right in Britain, opposed to any weakening in the policy of the coercion of the German republic, were actively mobilizing opinion in receptive quarters. With the triumph of the election behind them, the ultra-patriotic Right of the Conservative Party, the 'economic warriors', the Coalition press, and the Northcliffe press, all maintained steady pressure upon the government for an unrelentingly 'tough' policy towards Germany. In particular, industry lobbies urged the government to realize the promises of the election, bring home a big indemnity, and, under the cover of protecting 'key industries', destroy Germany's capacity to compete with British industry in the post-war world. In these 'knock-out blow' circles, the

---

138 Council Minute Book, Institute of Bankers, 15 Jan., 19 Feb. 1919, Institute of Bankers Papers.
139 Charles Addis Diary, 12 Feb. 1919, Addis Papers, 37.
140 Charles Addis Diary, 1 and 5 Mar. 1919, Addis Papers, 37. The text of the address is given in *Journal of the Institute of Bankers* (Apr. 1919).
141 Addis to Dudley Mills, 6 Mar. 1919, Addis Papers, 180.
142 Charles Addis Diary, 11 Mar. 1919, Addis Papers, 37.

maintenance of the blockade, without any concessions for emergency food shipments, was the acid test of the government's commitment to a tough peace.
In the midst of industrial tumult in Britain itself, men of mercantile and industrial wealth voiced their continuing support for a stupendous war indemnity. The
FBI itself was still the centre of power for the chief 'economic warriors' determined to exert pressure upon the government. The mood was grim, but the
blockade gave promise of a brighter future. FBI literature revealed an intense
awareness that, thanks to the continuation of the blockade through the armistice
period, British industry had a golden opportunity to steal a march on Germany
in her pre-war markets.[143] It was clear from the outset that fears over the 'condition of Germany' would not be allowed to stand as an obstacle in this campaign
to keep Germany prostrate. The Federation's literature also firmly upheld the
sham revolution line. 'There is much show of "democracy" and "Bolshevism" in
Germany at present', announced the *FBI Bulletin* in January, but it was probably eyewash. The FBI called on members to 'be ready with unyielding hearts to
resist the German wail'.[144] The 'unyielding hearts' certainly dominated the FBI
Terms of Peace Committee during January 1919. After some resistance from a
lone free trader (Godfrey Isaacs), the committee pledged itself to the pursuit of
a maximum indemnity from all the defeated states.[145] R. T. Nugent, the FBI's
Director, steered a second special memorandum in the 'Peace Aims' series
through the Terms of Peace Committee at the end of the month, and it was
widely distributed among Coalition MPs. The memorandum argued that 'the
total cost of the War should be regarded as a liability of the enemy countries irre-
spective of any investigation or opinion as to the capacity of those countries to
pay the full amount'. Without a large indemnity Britain faced 'industrial stagna-
tion' under a crushing taxation. It was vital, argued Nugent, that 'no consideration whatever' should deter the British government from pursuing '*full*
payment'.[146] In addition, the FBI pressed the government for FBI representation
at the Paris Peace Conference. Caillard, together with Lloyd Graeme of the
British Commonwealth Union, interviewed Bonar Law on 25 January and gained
his agreement in principle to industry representation in Paris. Indeed, Bonar Law
invited the FBI to put forward a man to serve on the Peace Conference's
'Indemnity Committee' (as the Reparation Commission in Paris was always
described by the FBI and Bonar Law). However, much to the embarrassment of
all concerned, Lloyd George had already appointed Hughes, Sumner, and
Cunliffe as the British Empire's delegates to the Reparation Commission, and
Bonar Law was forced to apologize because it was too late to carry his offer for-

---

[143] See the report 'The Rebuilding of British Trade Abroad and Achievements of the Federation
during the Armistice Period', in *FBI Bulletin*, 13 Mar. 1919, FBI Archive, MSS 200/F/4/24/2.
[144] *FBI Bulletin*, 2 Jan. 1919, FBI Archive, MSS 200/F/4/24/2.
[145] Minutes of the FBI Terms of Peace Committee, 7, 14, 28 Jan. 1919, FBI Archive, MSS 200,
F/1/1/180.
[146] Federation of British Industries, 'Peace Aims', no. 2, 30 Jan. 1919, Worthington-Evans Papers,
MS Eng. Hist. c. 915.

ward. Caillard was disappointed not to have an FBI man on the commission but understood the mix-up, and he promised Bonar Law he would send to Paris all reports already produced by his Terms of Peace Committee on the prospects of getting 'a pretty full indemnity'.[147]

Despite this setback, the FBI and other commercial pressure groups continued to lobby the government. In February, the Terms of Peace Committee studied the difficult problem of 'the transmission of war costs' to Germany. A third 'Peace Aims' memorandum stressed that Britain could not fund both war costs and the higher living standards which workers were demanding. There was only one way out: an indemnity from Germany. Even the costs of a big Rhine Army to enforce an indemnity 'cannot be as burdensome as the taxation which must be imposed if such a course is not adopted', argued the FBI.[148] All the FBI's memoranda were circulated to the War Cabinet.[149] In early March a delegation of thirty members of the FBI visited Paris for ten days and were fêted by the leading French protectionists and enthusiasts for indemnity, Clémentel and Louis Loucheur.[150] Britain's commercial pressure groups were closely aligned with the FBI in this campaign. For example, in mid-January, a meeting in London of more than one hundred delegates from Chambers of Commerce throughout Britain pledged themselves to support the FBI's plan for retrieving war costs from the enemy.[151] The London Chamber of Commerce, similarly, resolved in February to print material in favour of an indemnity and to send this to government ministers and departments.[152]

Within the ranks of the Coalition, in the government itself, and in the British Delegation, powerful voices from the Right were calling for the maintenance of all the pressure upon Germany which Britain could muster. In London, the minister feeling much of the heat was Cecil Harmsworth, a Coalition Liberal MP, who was the new Minister of Blockade. On 20 January, after just ten days in office, Harmsworth sided with those seeking to maintain the blockade. He advised Reading in Paris that the civil servants were divided on the question. According to Harmsworth's analysis, the Treasury, the Board of Trade, the War Trade Intelligence Department, and the new Department of Overseas Trade were inclined towards relaxation of the blockade, while the Foreign Office, War

[147] Minutes of the FBI Terms of Peace Committee, 7, 14, 28 Jan. and 4 Feb. 1919, FBI Archive, MSS 200, F/1/1/180, Caillard to Nugent, 29 Jan. 1919, Caillard to H. G. Tetley, 29 Jan. 1919, Bonar Law to Caillard, 29 Jan. 1919, and Caillard to Bonar Law, 31 Jan. 1919, FBI Archive, MSS 200/F/3/01/2/2. For the appointments of Hughes, Sumner, and Cunliffe see Minutes of the British Empire Delegation, 23 Jan. 1919, CAB 29/28.

[148] Federation of British Industries, 'Peace Aims', no. 3, 18 Feb. 1919, Worthington-Evans Papers, MS Eng. Hist. c. 915.

[149] See the 'Peace Aims' memoranda, GT 6822 and GT 6854, CAB 24/74.

[150] *FBI Bulletin*, 24 Mar. 1919, FBI Archive, MSS 200/F/4/24/2.

[151] Minutes of the Association of British Chambers of Commerce, Quarterly Meeting, Connaught Rooms, 15 Jan. 1919, Item 1, Association of British Chambers of Commerce Papers, Guildhall, 14,476, vol. 9.

[152] Minutes of London Chamber of Commerce, Council Meeting, 13 Feb. 1919, London Chamber of Commerce Papers, Guildhall, 16,459, vol. 8.

Office, and Admiralty were adamant that it be maintained. Harmsworth preferred the latter advice. The blockade was 'the most effective weapon left to the Associated Powers for speedily obtaining our Peace Terms', argued Harmsworth. The hunger and unemployment caused by the blockade in Germany would serve to ensure that the Germans did not seek to 'play for time' but would rapidly agree to peace terms. Moreover, under conditions of free trade, the victorious powers would begin 'the most fierce trade competition'. Once abandoned, he warned, the blockade could never be reconstructed. The appendices to Harmsworth's report gave candid insights into pro-blockade opinion. The Admiralty described the blockade as 'the principal means we have of forcing Germany to an early peace'. General Sir William Thwaites for the General Staff urged that 'the full blockade pressure should still be maintained', while conceding that the Associated Powers might distribute emergency food 'in order to avoid the danger of complete Bolshevism'. The Foreign Office noted that during the period of blockade Britain would 'retain our enemy markets and widen our scope for export forthwith'; an end to blockade would see Britain 'lose our trade to the neutrals'.[153]

In mid-February, working closely with Lord Curzon, Harmsworth began an effort to shore up opinion on the issue in London and Paris. He first enlisted Curzon's aid, telling him that the Prime Minister did not attach 'anything like the same importance to the Blockade that we, and the Naval and Military authorities do'.[154] Then he wrote to Lloyd George, recently returned from Paris, warning him that the Board of Trade and Treasury were trying to 'destroy' the blockade. This was a great mistake, he argued, for the blockade was 'the easiest and cheapest instrument' for coercing Germany. The recent demobilization riots and the obvious weakening in British armed strength on the ground in Europe also furnished a useful argument for Harmsworth. As it was 'ever more difficult to keep the armies of the Allies in the field', he wrote, 'so is the importance of the blockade as a weapon enhanced'.[155] To Robert Cecil, at this point the newly appointed first British delegate to the Supreme Council on Supply and Relief in Paris, Harmsworth was even more blunt. He pleaded with Cecil to stand firm against the 'formidable influences working against the blockade'. He specified the dangers: Mr Hoover, 'our own trade community at home', and the Board of Trade and Treasury, all of whom were plotting to overturn the blockade. Harmsworth declared that he was more fearful of discontent at home if the Germans were given food than of the danger of Bolshevism in Germany if they were not. Harmsworth added just a hint of pressure: he announced that he was

[153] Harmsworth to Reading, 20 Jan. 1919, and 'Memorandum Respecting the Continuance of the Blockade', with Appendices: Admiralty, 'Proposals as to the Relaxation of the Blockade', 20 Jan. 1919; General Sir William Thwaites, 'Memorandum embodying the views of the General Staff respecting the continuance of the Blockade', 20 Jan. 1919; and unsigned 'Memorandum on continuance of Blockade until peace', Reading Papers, MS EUR F 118/30.

[154] Harmsworth to Curzon, 11 Feb. 1919, FO 800/250. 'I *entirely agree* and will back you to the full', wrote Curzon on this letter.

[155] Harmsworth to Lloyd George, 11 Feb. 1919, FO 800/250.

sending over William Mitchell-Thompson, a right-wing Conservative MP, to act for him on the economic councils of the conference, and he urged Cecil to accept him as an adviser on blockade matters.[156] The next day the Cabinet in London was enlisted in this campaign. Harmsworth presented his original memorandum advising the rigorous maintenance of the blockade, and the Cabinet decided that Cecil should endeavour to speak to President Wilson on the importance of maintaining the blockade.[157]

Other important figures from the Right were orchestrating political pressures and seeking to influence public opinion in favour of the maintenance of the blockade and the collection of a large indemnity. Not surprisingly the leading figures engaged in this campaign were Walter Long, Hewins, and the other familiar agitators aligned to the Tariff Commission and the Unionist Business Committee. Long worked behind the scenes to remind the Prime Minister both of his election pledges and the power of those in the Conservative Party anxiously waiting for him to redeem them. In a series of unconvincingly friendly letters sent between January and March, Long kept Lloyd George informed on 'gossip' as he put it on the Coalition back bench and in the press. In January he told Lloyd George bluntly that Northcliffe was obviously out to 'destroy' him, and added the intimidating detail that 'rumours are going about that he has got some Marconi letters of yours'. The Coalition MPs, however, would support him, Long assured Lloyd George, but there was a danger of 'severe attack' unless the British negotiators in Paris could be seen to be 'demanding of Germany every farthing they can get'.[158] On 1 February Long warned Lloyd George that reports of the government's 'climbing down' on indemnity were causing 'violent hostility'.[159] On 11 February, he sent to Lloyd George a private letter he had received from Balfour of Burleigh; the letter claimed that trustworthy (but unnamed) British sources in Cologne were now convinced that 'we are being much too soft on the Hun', and that the Germans were secretly arming for revolt 'under the guidance and inspiration of their former military chiefs'.[160] In early March, Long wrote to Lloyd George of the great resentment felt at President Wilson's attempts to supplant Britain as the leading power at the conference; he assured Lloyd George that the people would back him if he stood up to Wilson. Of course, all these letters transmitted Long's own favoured right-wing interpretations of current politics dressed up as impartial political advice. The references to the power of the back bench, however, could scarcely be ignored by Lloyd George, as he was well aware that Long had considerable influence there himself.[161]

---

[156] Harmsworth to Cecil, 11 Feb. 1919, FO 800/250.

[157] Minutes of the Cabinet, 12 Feb. 1919, CAB 23/9, and Harmsworth's memorandum, no date, CAB 1/28.

[158] Long to Lloyd George, 23 Jan. 1919, Long Papers, WRO 947/746.

[159] Long to Lloyd George, 1 Feb. 1919, Long Papers (British Library), Add. MSS 62424.

[160] Long to Lloyd George, 11 Feb. 1919, enclosing Balfour of Burleigh to Long, 10 Feb. 1919, Lloyd George Papers, F/33/2/9.

[161] Long to Lloyd George, 7 Mar. 1919, Long Papers, WRO 947/746.

The tariff reform propagandists were also busily working up opinion among the ranks of the Coalition MPs. The failure of the government to recommit itself to collecting the whole cost of the war early in the new parliament worried prominent ultra-patriots. From mid-January, prominent ultra-patriots and tariff reformers such as Walter Morrison, Walter Guinness, Leo Maxse, Gwynne, Hewins, and John Gretton debated the likelihood of Lloyd George seeking to 'wriggle out of his pledge', and plans were made at the Carlton Club to rally Coalition MPs if firm evidence of betrayal on the part of the Prime Minister emerged.[162] Meanwhile, Hewins and other prominent advocates of tariff reform did their best to keep the spotlight upon the 'economic warrior' programme and the pressure upon the government. Herbert Gibbs, former member of the War Cabinet Committee on Indemnity, addressed the City of London Conservative Association on the economics of indemnity on 20 February. Gibbs stressed both the right of Britain to seek war costs, and held out the hope that the burden of an indemnity would almost certainly depress the German export industries, thus achieving a measure of protection for British industry.[163] The Finance Subcommittee of the Unionist Business Committee, led by J. A. R. Marriott and Gretton, attended a similar special lecture from Hewins on 26 February in favour of the indemnity. A large burden of indemnities, Hewins assured the meeting, would advantage British industry for it would 'affect the whole economic position of Germany in relation to the world'. As a result of Hewins's address, the Unionist Business Committee decided to send a delegation to the Colonial Office to press for progress on imperial preference, and another delegation to the Treasury to enquire as to progress on the indemnity and protection from 'undesirable competition'.[164] Laming Worthington-Evans, the government's new Minister for Pensions, also campaigned constantly on this issue during February, widely distributing details of his own plan to collect an indemnity by placing a punitive tax on all German exports (a proposal scorned by the Treasury). Worthington-Evans's explanation of his plan was most revealing: it was essential, he argued, to restrain rather than stimulate the German export trade as part of the process of collecting an indemnity, for a stronger German industrial performance would lead to unemployment in Britain and, as a consequence, the labour movement would agitate to end payments under the indemnity. For Worthington-Evans, the pacification of British labour was an essential objective of the indemnity.[165]

---

[162] See Walter Morrison to Leo Maxse, 18 Jan. 1919, and Walter Guinness to Leo Maxse, 21 Jan. 1919, Maxse Papers, vol. 476, and Gretton to Hewins, 21 Jan. 1919, Hewins Papers, 73.

[163] Printed address, 'The Hon. Herbert Gibbs on Indemnity', dated 20 Feb. 1919, Hewins Papers, 74/40.

[164] Minutes of a meeting of the Finance Sub-Committee of the Unionist Business Committee, 26 Feb. 1919, Hewins Papers, 30.

[165] 'Proposal for Neutralising Germany's Advantage from a Depreciated Mark and for Collecting an Indemnity', 11 Feb. 1919, R. T. Nugent to Worthington-Evans, 25 Feb. 1919, E. T. Davies (Ministry of Blockade) to Worthington-Evans, 22 Feb. 1919, and Worthington-Evans to E. T. Davies, 5 Mar. 1919, Worthington-Evans to Hankey, 20 Mar. 1919, Worthington-Evans Papers, MS Eng. Hist. c. 915.

Yet another sign of the mobilization of right-wing opinion came in the formation of new pressure groups among the Coalition MPs in the first weeks of the fresh parliament. On 21 February a lunch was given for MPs by the Federation of British Industries and a new House of Commons Committee of the FBI was formed. Sir William Pearce, a prominent advocate of indemnity within the FBI Terms of Peace Committee, became the chairman of the new body.[166] A Coalition Foreign Affairs Group was formed on 27 February. The new group included such prominent ultra-patriots and tariff reformers as Sam Hoare (chair), Walter Guinness (secretary), the Duke of Northumberland, and Halford Mackinder. The priorities of the new group were clear from their first meeting when motions were passed seeking assistance for 'White' forces in Russia and even the mobilization of Russian prisoners of war in Germany to fight the Bolshevik government.[167]

Acting as the megaphone of these 'economic warriors' in Paris, as ever, was the Australian Prime Minister, Billy Hughes.[168] During the Paris Peace Conference, the tense relationship between Hughes and Lloyd George deteriorated even further, and it became obvious to many observers that Lloyd George was in fear of the Australian Prime Minister and his connections. Lloyd George had already made important concessions to Hughes. As seen above, Lloyd George had steered Hughes into a position of great influence as head of the War Cabinet's Indemnity Committee during the general election campaign. In late December, Lloyd George had eventually accepted Hughes's argument that there should be a system of dual representation for the Dominions at the Paris Peace Conference, that is, representation in their own right plus representation as British Empire delegates on various commissions. Lloyd George loyally pressed for this awkward formula in Paris and it was confirmed.[169] As noted above, Lloyd George also personally invited Hughes to become a British Empire representative on the Peace Conference's Reparation Commission (which Hughes always pointedly described as the Indemnity Commission).[170] None of these appointments or concessions pacified Hughes. If they were intended to buy his loyalty to Lloyd George, they failed altogether. Hughes's loyalties lay elsewhere, with the 'economic warriors' and irrepressible Germanophobes on the British Right, from Maxse to Northcliffe, who flattered him with admiring letters and interviews beseeching him to stand firm for the right-wing agenda—outright

[166] 'Minutes of the First Meeting of the Committee of Members of Parliament connected with the Federation of British Industries', 5 Mar. 1919, FBI Archive, MSS 200 F/1/1/50.

[167] Hoare to Churchill, 27 Feb. 1919, and Churchill to Lloyd George, 2 Mar. 1919, Lloyd George Papers, F/8/3/24.

[168] For full details on Hughes's performance at Paris see L. F. Fitzhardinge, *William Morris Hughes*, ii. *The Little Digger* (Sydney, 1979), ch. 16, W. J. Hudson, *Billy Hughes in Paris* (Melbourne, 1978), and Peter Spartalis, *The Diplomatic Battles of Billy Hughes* (Sydney, 1983).

[169] For a full discussion of the establishment of separate Dominion representation see L. F. Fitzhardinge, 'Hughes, Borden and Dominion Representation at the Paris Peace Conference', *Canadian Historical Review*, 49/2 (June 1968), 160–69.

[170] Hughes to Munro-Ferguson, 17 Jan. 1919, Novar Papers, 696/2757.

annexation of the German colonies, protection from a German economic revival, a long period of blockade, and a big indemnity.[171] Once installed at the Hôtel Majestic, Hughes was constantly supping with right-wing personalities and a great many journalists. As Eggleston, Hughes's press officer, noted in late January, 'Billie is up in arms and is rallying round him every reactionary politician and pressman in Europe'.[172] The ultra-patriots continued to cultivate Hughes. Gwynne of the *Morning Post*, always a reliable ally, visited Hughes soon after his arrival in Paris and set up contact between Hughes and his various journalists.[173] Hughes's cosy relationship with the Northcliffe press in particular was revealed spectacularly in late January. Hughes planted an article in the Paris edition of the *Daily Mail* attacking Wilson, and accusing Lloyd George of selling out the Dominions' interests in the former German colonies by agreeing to the Wilsonian formula of mandates. The incident astonished many in the American, the British, and Australian delegations, and Hughes's reputation for probity sagged. Eggleston went immediately to Lionel Curtis to discover the British reaction to the 'abominable column', and was told that Hughes was 'doing us a terrible amount of harm'.[174] Kerr was soon made aware, doubtless via Curtis, that the 'mischievous article' had been read and corrected in proof by Hughes himself.[175] However, it was not only in Paris that Hughes had been seeking to manipulate public opinion. On receiving only lukewarm support from the Australian Cabinet for his outspoken views, Hughes sent a series of inflammatory cables back to Australia announcing that he had been 'abandoned' by Lloyd George and asking the Australian government to place 'strong statements' in the press and 'arrange immediate demonstrations [of] public support'.[176] In the final outcome, the top Allied negotiators evolved a compromise on the German colonies through the invention of the system of A, B, and C class 'mandates', the purpose clearly being to create something under the C class quite close to the 'direct control' desired by Hughes.[177]

More importantly, this first major dispute between Hughes and Lloyd George in Paris advertised certain realities of the situation in any ongoing rivalry between

---

[171] e.g. Maxse to Hughes, 13 Jan. 1919, Hughes Papers, MS 1538/24/12.

[172] Eggleston Diary, 29 Jan. 1919, Eggleston Papers, MS 423/6/81. The diaries of Robert Garran and Eggleston show that Hughes socialized with an array of journalists in Jan. and Feb. 1919, including Sydney London and Dr E. J. Dillon of the *Daily Telegraph*, George Sims of the United Press, Wickham Steed of *The Times*, and the reactionary 'Pertinax' of *L'Echo de Paris*; see Garran Diary, 14, 15, 16 Jan. 1919, Garran Papers, Series 5, Box 3, and Eggleston Diary, 31 Jan., 18 and 19 Feb. 1919, Eggleston Papers, MS 423/6/58, 86–7, and Dillon to Hughes, n.d., Hughes Papers, 1538/24/512.

[173] H. A. Gwynne to Hughes, 15 and 18 Jan. 1919, and 18 June 1919, Hughes Papers, MS 1538/24/14, 15, and 421.

[174] Eggleston Diary, 30 Jan. 1919, Eggleston Papers, MS 423/6/82–3.

[175] Kerr to Milner, 31 Jan. 1919, Milner Add. Papers, MS Eng. Hist. c. 700.

[176] See the exchanges of cables between Hughes and Watt, the Deputy Prime Minister, 20–31 Jan. 1919, in Australian Archives, CP 290/3. The plan for demonstrations was not followed up, according to Watt, because the influenza epidemic made public meetings in Australia too dangerous.

[177] Fitzhardinge, *The Little Digger*, 391.

moderates and extremists in the British Delegation. Both men had been bruised in this encounter. But the incident underlined Hughes's capacity to mobilize Lloyd George's most formidable enemy in the press, Lord Northcliffe, on the side of the extremists. Certainly, the fall-out from the *Daily Mail* article continued to poison relations between Lloyd George and Hughes. In early February, Amery attempted to act as an intermediary and pleaded with Hughes to go to Lloyd George and 'have it out with him, as a colleague, between four walls'.[178] To no avail. Apparently, mutual distrust, if not fear, now governed the relationship. Lloyd George told Amery that Hughes was 'quite impossible' and 'a regular little cad'.[179] For some days Hughes was seen by his staff to be deliberately avoiding the precincts of the Hôtel Majestic where he might encounter Lloyd George.[180] Those closest to Hughes understood the forces with whom he was allied. In fact, the Round Table men on the Australian Delegation, Eggleston and Latham, were more and more disillusioned by the role of their Prime Minister. 'Hughes is in his element', wrote Eggleston, 'He is the leader of the most extreme chauvinist groups singing songs of hate against the Germans all day long.'[181]

The right-wing press in Britain as a whole, of course, was still the most powerful factor at work in the contest for 'public opinion'. Throughout January and February, the Coalition press, and the Northcliffe press, maintained a steady flow of articles calculated to buttress the policy of extreme claims against Germany. According to the pages of the popular press, the German revolution was still a fraud, the German people were still guilty, and—until late February—reports of hunger in Germany were still wildly exaggerated.

The tone of the Northcliffe papers changed little from the period of the election campaign. On domestic issues, Lloyd George's government was still constantly criticized as too 'Tory'. Meanwhile, coverage of German events remained exceptionally hostile. In the *Daily Mail*, articles provided by Sefton Delmer from Berlin, Charles Tower from Weimar, and Ward Price from Paris, made up a tedious gruel of negative reports hostile to every side of politics in Germany. According to the *Daily Mail*, Spartacism was nothing but a plot to 'dissipate resources' in Germany so that the Allies would be denied their indemnity.[182] Thus the murders of Luxemburg and Liebknecht were applauded because the dangerous Spartacist leaders, it was claimed, had spread a propaganda of 'pure destruction'.[183] At the same time, the moderate ministers of the new government,

---

[178] Amery to Hughes, 2 Feb. 1919, Hughes Papers, MS 1538/24/32.

[179] Amery Diary, 2 Feb. 1919, Amery Papers; and see Kerr's suggestion to Eggleston a fortnight later that Lloyd George liked Hughes but was still 'frightfully angry' about the *Daily Mail* article, Eggleston Diary, 19 Feb. 1919, Eggleston Papers, MS 423/6/58.

[180] Latham Diary, 3 Feb. 1919, Latham Papers, MS 1009/21/1409, and Eggleston, 'Paris Peace Conference', typescript memoir, Eggleston Papers, MS 423/6/29.

[181] Eggleston Diary, 14 Feb. 1919, Eggleston Papers, MS 423/6/58.

[182] *Daily Mail*, 'Berlin Bolsheviks', 9 Jan. 1919.

[183] *Daily Mail*, editorial, 'The End of the Tigers', 18 Jan. 1919.

socialist and bourgeois alike, were denounced as simply the 'old Huns'.[184] The return of the Kaiser, courtesy of a plot organized by the still powerful High Command, was constantly predicted to be just around the corner.[185] Not until late February did the *Daily Mail* acknowledge that there was any real danger of Bolshevism in Germany as a result of the food shortage.[186] Throughout these same weeks, Britain's right to claim a large indemnity was constantly reasserted, and the Prime Minister was served with none too subtle reminders that he was 'pledged to demand from Germany the full cost of the war'. 'No evasion of that pledge will be tolerated by this country', declared the *Daily Mail*.[187]

The predicability of themes in the Northcliffe newspapers in January and February belied major changes taking place behind the scenes, changes full of menace for Lloyd George. The most important was Northcliffe's dismissal of Geoffrey Dawson as editor of *The Times* in early February. The rupture had been in sight for some months. Its causes were obvious. Dawson, the loyal Conservative and Round Table man, bitterly resented Northcliffe's campaign against Milner for alleged 'Lansdowneism' which had begun in October 1918. Northcliffe's feud with Lloyd George lay at the root of the trouble too. Dawson disagreed with Northcliffe's campaign against Lloyd George, interpreting it as a vindictive reaction to Lloyd George's principled decision to defy Northcliffe on government and peace conference appointments in November 1918. Dawson had also been openly critical of Northcliffe's articles in the *Daily Mail* since the election, with their 'Hang the Kaiser' refrain and constant 'sneers at the Tory Party'. He refused to make *The Times* conform to this pattern.[188] Northcliffe warned his editor on 25 January that he must 'endeavour to see eye to eye' with him, or relinquish his position.[189] By early February, Dawson confessed that he found Northcliffe's interference at *The Times* 'quite intolerable'.[190] He resigned. Northcliffe selected as his replacement Wickham Steed, the foreign editor of *The Times* who was at that time covering the Peace Conference. The change was announced on 25 February. From Lloyd George's point of view, Steed's appointment could only mean an increase in hostile reporting in the pages of the Northcliffe press. It was soon common knowledge that Dawson had quit because he refused to pursue 'Northcliffe's personal vendetta against Lloyd George'.[191]

---

[184] See, e.g. the denunciation of Rantzau, *Daily Mail*, 17 Feb. 1919, and the comparison between Ebert and the Kaiser, *Daily Mail*, 26 Feb. 1919.

[185] *Daily Mail*, 'Kaiser Plot in Berlin', 27 Feb. 1919.

[186] *Daily Mail*, 'Germany and Bolshevism', 24 Feb. 1919.

[187] *Daily Mail*, editorial, 'Reparation Means Indemnities', 22 Feb. 1919.

[188] For a full account, see Dawson's memorandum on his resignation from *The Times*, typescript, dated Mar. 1919, Dawson Papers, 68. Much of this is reproduced in J. E. Wrench, *Geoffrey Dawson and Our Times* (London, 1955), 175–87.

[189] Northcliffe to Dawson, 25 Jan. 1919, marked as received on 29 Jan. 1919, Dawson Papers, Northcliffe file, *The Times* Archive.

[190] Dawson to Kitty Perfect, 11 Feb. 1919, Dawson Papers, 57.

[191] Milner to Jim, 26 July 1919, Milner Add. Papers, MS Eng. Hist. c. 690, and J. St Loe Strachey, 5 Mar. 1919, Dawson Papers, 68.

The new editor, presumably, had no such qualms. Many observers believed also that the change would strengthen still further the anti-German prejudice in the columns of the leading British daily. Even the diplomats regarded Steed as an extremist.[192] Thus there was consternation at the PID in London. Bevan wrote to Headlam-Morley to tell him of the bad news, predicting that, with Steed at the helm, *The Times* would be 'given over more completely than before to the French view of things'.[193] Steed himself could have been under no illusions concerning what was required of him in this direction. On his first official day in the editor's chair, Northcliffe pressed the issue of the indemnity upon him, remarking that everyone he met was 'grumbling' that 'the question of Germany paying is not dealt with'.[194]

Soon after came another resignation from among the Northcliffe journalists, a departure not well publicized, but in fact all the more revealing of the determination of the Northcliffe press to manipulate news from Germany. In the middle of March, F. Sefton Delmer, the Northcliffe journalist in Berlin, resigned in great anger. He had been reporting for the *Daily Mail* in Germany since the onset of the revolution and his articles, as has been seen, appeared to be in accord with the requirements of the Northcliffe papers—that is, generally hostile to the revolution and the new German government. After his resignation Delmer wrote a passionate letter to George Saunders at the PID, complaining that the copy he had sent from Germany was constantly interfered with at the paper. As Saunders recorded, the substance of Delmer's complaint was that the *Daily Mail* 'will only print the bad and refuses to print the good about the place [Germany]'. After four months in Germany, Delmer had finally come to a position anathema to the *Daily Mail*. 'In many ways Germany today is sounder than England from all I can make out', he confided to Saunders.[195]

The Northcliffe press, of course, was not alone in jeering at the new German government. The Coalition press was equally antagonistic. The ultra-patriotic Right, the *Morning Post*, the *Globe*, and the *National Review*, maintained their familiar themes. The demand for evidence of 'repentance' and a 'change of heart' was ubiquitous. Thus the more promising events in Germany—the stunning success of the pro-democratic parties in the election of January 1919, and the formation of the socialist-led coalition government under Scheidemann in February—all passed off without impressing the right-wing press in Britain. The mood can be neatly summarized in Maxse's editorial in the *National Review* for February:

In a word, we have not to deal with a new and innocent Germany under new and innocent men, but with the old and guilty Germany under men only one degree less guilty

[192] Rodd to Curzon, 2 Mar. 1919, Rodd Papers, 20.
[193] Bevan to Headlam-Morley, 25 Feb. 1919, Headlam-Morley Papers, HDLM OS Box 2.
[194] Northcliffe to Steed, 25 Feb. 1919, Steed Papers, Northcliffe file, *The Times* Archive.
[195] Delmer to Saunders, 18 Mar. 1919, notes preserved in Saunders's Day Book VII (12 Feb.–31 Mar. 1919), Headlam-Morley Papers, HDLM Acc. 800/1. Delmer's return to London, but not his resignation from the paper, is reported in *Daily Mail*, 17 Mar. 1919.

than the Kaiser and his Ministers, who upheld Frightfulness in all its forms with no less zest than the 'militarists' who executed the Kaiser's orders in Belgium, France and elsewhere.[196]

Naturally, the same newspapers and journals were the last to acknowledge that there was danger of Bolshevism in Germany or real hunger. Indeed, the ultrapatriotic Right simply refused to acknowledge that Germany was in need, and refused to quake at the danger of Bolshevism overrunning the defeated land. Leo Maxse maintained this flinty outlook even when confronted with first-hand evidence. For example, over lunch with Lord Denbigh in late February, Maxse listened to a report on conditions in Germany from Colonel Pollock, an assistant to General Ewart, just back from Berlin. Pollock argued that he was 'all for feeding the Germans to prevent Bolshevism spreading'; Maxse was unconvinced and announced that he was 'all for letting the Germans turn Bolshevik and cut each other's throats—the more the better because the fewer Germans will be left'.[197]

The tilt towards moderation: the Brussels Agreement and the Fontainebleau Memorandum of March 1919

The turning-point in this campaign came in the first week of March. The new British intelligence which had now been amassed on Germany was potentially a powerful new factor. But first, the intelligence reports had to be placed in the hands of the key men, read, and believed. This was not always easy, as Thornely Gibson discovered on his arrival in Paris on 1 March. He was invited to lunch with Arthur Balfour the next day, Sunday, 2 March, but found the Foreign Secretary absent having been 'carried off' to play lawn tennis with Tyrrell, Vansittart, and Ian Malcolm, Balfour's secretary; thus, by chance, it was Lady Betty Balfour, waiting patiently for lunch with Gibson, who received an emotional account of the privation he had witnessed in Germany. She carefully recorded his conviction that, if the food shortage in Germany was permitted to worsen, the victorious powers would 'destroy all possibility of stable government in Germany'. The very different convictions still prevailing among the Foreign Office élite emerged when the tennis players returned. Balfour asked Gibson 'what chance he thought there was of a military revival in Germany, as there were still people here who seemed to think their depression was a bluff'. Gibson must have wondered if he lived in the same world as these other men: he replied that 'he could not believe this—that from a military point of view they were done'.[198]

Almost immediately, further dramatic events in Germany itself had an important effect in shaking loose such convictions concerning German 'bluff'. On 3 March a general strike was called in Berlin by the Workers' Council in protest at the deployment of *Freikorps* troops against left-wing demonstrations in differ-

[196] *National Review*, 432 (Feb. 1919).
[197] Sir Arthur Davidson to Hardinge, 25 Feb. 1919, Hardinge Papers, vol. 40.
[198] Lady Betty Balfour to family, 2 Mar. 1919, Whittingehame Papers, GD 433/2/270.

ent cities during February. The government had moved to declare the socialization of the coal and potash industries, but this move to the Left failed to distract the strike movement. As the strike spread through central Germany, the nation seemed suddenly on the threshold of a 'second revolution'. There was a renewal of savage street-fighting in Berlin between Noske's *Freikorps* and Spartacist forces which continued until 12 March. The fighting appears to have turned many heads in Paris. A certain sense of panic was discernible in the British Delegation in Paris. 'The news from Berlin far from reassuring', wrote Knatchbull-Hugessen in his diary on 3 March.[199] 'I am convinced the necessity for feeding Germany is fully justified', wrote General Thwaites on 4 March.[200] 'The news from Germany is gloomy, from whatever source it comes. Bolshevism appears to be making almost rapid headway, even among that disciplined people', wrote Ian Malcolm to Long on 5 March. It was now crucial to 'feed the brutes', he added.[201] 'Everyone here regards the Bolshevism in Germany as very real', wrote Edward Spears to Churchill on 6 March.[202] Even Wickham Steed seemed momentarily convinced, writing to Northcliffe of 'alarming reports' from Germany which had persuaded him that food assistance was vital to dampen Bolshevism; he noted there was now an 'acute' fear in Paris that the German government would fall.[203] Memories of the German difficulties with the Russian Bolsheviks at the Brest-Litovsk negotiations had begun to stalk military imaginations. Haking advised from Spa that the victorious powers must keep a stable government in Berlin if they wished to conclude a peace treaty and garner 'at least some indemnity for their losses'. He warned that, if the Bolsheviks in Berlin succeeded in turning out the permanent officials, 'chaos will supervene, and it will become just as impossible to make peace with Germany as Germany found it impossible to make peace with Russia'.[204]

Gibson, the resident expert in Paris on German Bolshevism, suddenly found himself surrounded by more sympathetic listeners. Headlam-Morley proved to be an important ally in advertising his views. Gibson was, in fact, not a complete stranger to the PID staff, having been a student in Zimmern's classes at Oxford before the war. Zimmern vouched for his credibility.[205] Headlam-Morley arranged a personal interview with the young officer and received an advance copy of his vivid report on 5 March. Headlam-Morley wrote immediately to Philip Kerr, warning him that a first-class report was arriving on his desk the

[199] Knatchbull-Hugessen Diary, 3 Mar. 1919, Knatchbull-Hugessen Papers, 1/3.

[200] Thwaites's minute on Pichon to Balfour, 3 Mar. 1919, FO 608/129.

[201] Ian Malcolm to Walter Long, 5 Mar. 1919, Long Papers, WRO 947/751.

[202] Spears to Churchill, 6 Mar. 1919, Spears Papers (Liddell Hart Centre), 1/21.

[203] Wickham Steed to Northcliffe, 5 Mar. 1919, Steed Papers, Daily Memorandum to Northcliffe Box.

[204] 'Extract from Report D. 102', from R. Haking, undated but filed as late Feb., FO 371/3776/313, and Armistice Commission Report, 1 Mar. 1919, WO 144/11.

[205] Zimmern vouched for his reliability; Zimmern to Headlam-Morley, 17 Mar. 1919, HMP, Acc. 688, OS Box 2.

next morning and urging him to bring it to Lloyd George's attention promptly. Food for Germany was absolutely essential, pleaded Headlam-Morley: 'to this everything else is subordinated.'[206] Unbeknown to Headlam-Morley, Sir Henry Wilson also sent copies of the report to Lloyd George, with a letter announcing that he had 'full confidence in Lieutenant Thornely Gibson's judgement'.[207] When Lloyd George returned to Paris on 5 March, after a month in London negotiating his way through the sudden outbreak of industrial unrest, multiple copies of the Gibson report awaited him, together with Gibson's own covering letter arguing that it was 'essential that the present government receive definite support from the Entente'.[208] Within two days Riddell recorded that Gibson's report had made 'much impression in Government circles, and particularly on the PM'.[209]

Meanwhile in Berlin itself, the German government was using the few face-to-face contacts available to it to put its case. On 6 March Brockdorff-Rantzau asked to see General Ewart. In semi-darkness (the general strike having cut the electricity supply), Brockdorff-Rantzau told Ewart of his 'very deep anxiety' over the future. He noted that in recent speeches Lloyd George had expressed concern over the spread of Bolshevism in Germany. In a tone that deeply impressed Ewart, the German Foreign Minister explained that 'if the German people do not receive a definite assurance *within the next two or three weeks* that food is coming to them, the position of himself and other ministers would become untenable, and the government would have to go out. This would mean that Spartacists would come into power and Bolshevism would spread like lightning.'[210] Ewart dutifully relayed this information to Spa, and Haking endorsed his conclusion: the Germans were not bluffing. 'The German Government will collapse unless it is strengthened by assurance of food within the next fortnight', wrote Haking from Spa on 8 March.[211]

Fresh reports, all in this same desperate tone, now crowded in upon Lloyd George and his entourage. A Ministry of Food report from the occupied zones of Germany, based upon conversations with General Herbert Plumer (Commander of the British Army of the Rhine) and his staff at Cologne, warned that even in the Rhineland there was 'considerable suffering' and that without emergency food imports 'famine in a very few weeks' was certain. The report announced that food assistance was vital for military as much as for humanitarian reasons, because 'the task of policing and repressing a starving population' was dissolving the military discipline of those British and American troops in the Rhineland who might yet be called upon to move forward into Germany to

[206] Headlam-Morley to Kerr, 5 Mar. 1919, HMP, Acc. 688, OS Box 2.
[207] H. Wilson to Lloyd George, 5 Mar. 1919, Lloyd George Papers, F/47/8/6, and Wilson Diary, 5 and 6 Mar. 1919, Wilson Papers, DS Misc/80.
[208] Thornely Gibson, 'Bolshevism in Germany', 28 Feb. 1919, Lloyd George Papers, F/47/8/6.
[209] Riddell Diary, 7 Mar. 1919, Riddell Papers, 62983.
[210] Ewart Diary, 6 Mar. 1919, Ewart Papers, 73/88/1.
[211] Haking to Thwaites, 8 Mar. 1919, FO 608/130.

enforce the terms of peace.[212] General Plumer himself had written to Haig stating exactly these anxieties on 6 March—with the important reservation that he did not want the blockade in its entirety abandoned, only the ban on food imports.[213] On 6 March Lloyd George met with Balfour, Wilson, Austen Chamberlain, Hankey, and Cecil to discuss the feeding of Germany. Cecil was much gratified by the discussion: Lloyd George, he wrote in his diary, was now 'recognising to the full the necessity of keeping Germany from revolution'.[214] A series of crucial discussions took place on 7 March. General Plumer saw Lloyd George in Hoover's presence and pressed his views upon him. Hoover took the opportunity to catalogue the history of British and French obstruction to the relief of Germany.[215] In discussions with the French Prime Minister on that same day, however, Clemenceau outlined his continuing opposition to feeding Germany, and protested that the Bolshevik scare was 'purely a German story, circulated with a view to intimidating the Allies'. It was vital, Clemenceau said, to maintain 'the demeanour of a conqueror towards Germany'.[216] By chance, a weapon for Lloyd George to use in a showdown with the French materialized on the same day. Frank Tiarks, a director of the Bank of England recently returned from Cologne, dined with Lloyd George in the evening and showed him a cable concerning the food crisis from yet another general in Cologne, but a general whose name Lloyd George did not recognize. Lloyd George asked Tiarks to obtain a similar cable from the more well-known General Plumer and he promised to make use of it the next day. Tiarks was 'very excited', describing Lloyd George as 'magnificent'.[217]

A major breakthrough came the following day, 8 March. During a tense session of the Supreme War Council on the food crisis in Germany, the British and Americans pushed for a renewal of negotiations with the Germans and an acceptance of the German proposal, namely, a guarantee of the provisioning of Germany until September in return for the surrender of the German merchant fleet. The French stood firm for the provisioning of Germany only a month at a time, after the surrender of the fleet, and without the Germans touching their gold reserves. In his speech, Lloyd George begged the council to break this impasse. Using hunger as a weapon in Germany was 'like stirring an influenza

---

[212] E. F. Wise (Principal Assistant Secretary of the Ministry of Food), 'Note on Food Supplies for the Left Bank of the Rhine', enclosed with George H. Roberts to W. S. Churchill, 3 Mar. 1919, Lloyd George Papers, F 8/3/26. (The printed report is dated 6 Mar.; see Milner Add. Papers, MS Eng. Hist. c. 697.) Churchill breakfasted with Lloyd George on 8 Mar. and probably reinforced his support for the Wise report which he had received from G. H. Roberts on 3 Mar.; see A. J. P. Taylor (ed.), *Lloyd George: A Diary by Frances Stevenson* (London, 1971), 170.

[213] Plumer to Haig, 6 Mar. 1919, Haig to Churchill, 11 Mar. 1919, B. B. Cubitt to Churchill, 5 Apr. 1919, FO 608/279, and Haig Diary, 11 Mar. 1919, Haig Papers, no. 136.

[214] Cecil Diary, 6 Mar. 1919, Cecil Papers, 51131.

[215] Herbert Hoover, *The Memoirs of Herbert Hoover* (New York, 1951), 341, and Riddell Diary, 7 Mar. 1919, Riddell Papers, 62983.

[216] 'Notes on an interview between Clemenceau, House and Lloyd George', 7 Mar. 1919, FO 800/215.

[217] Riddell Diary, 7 and 8 Mar. 1919, Riddell Papers, 62983.

puddle next door', he said. He referred directly to the new British intelligence officers' reports, and to Plumer's opinions, that Bolshevism was very near in Germany. He warned the council: 'As long as order was maintained in Germany, a breakwater would exist between the countries of the Allies and the waters of revolution beyond, but once that breakwater was swept away, though he could not speak for France, he trembled for his own country.' While making a second speech, late in the session, Lloyd George received a cable at his seat: a cable from Plumer. This cable, of course, had been arranged with Tiarks the evening before. Summoning all his resources of drama and passion, Lloyd George read the cable to the council, beseeching the victorious powers to promise food deliveries as soon as possible as the only means of preventing disorder in the occupied zone, for British troops were refusing to repress the starving people. With this cable as up-to-the-minute proof of the seriousness of the situation, Lloyd George angrily depicted the obdurate French delegates as the Bolsheviks' best friends in Germany. The performance undoubtedly helped break the deadlock. With the French isolated, it was accepted, after a short adjournment, that negotiations with the Germans should be resumed. French objections to payment in gold were overridden. The council clung to its demand for ships, but it was clear that long-term provisioning was to be offered to Germany in return. The final resolutions specified that new negotiations with the Germans were to be conducted by a British admiral.[218] The talks were set down to begin in Brussels on 13 March.[219]

But even this breakthrough did not scatter the hard men of the British Delegation. In particular, the British representatives on the Reparation Commission, Hughes and Cunliffe, were roused by these events, and worked to undermine fear of the German food crisis. Hughes's assistant noted that Walter Guinness came to see Hughes on 9 March, and he overheard Hughes say that 'starvation would do anything. That is how you will exact any terms from Germany'.[220] Cunliffe went on the same day to complain to Ian Malcolm over the procuring of Plumer's cable. Tiarks, he explained, was really 'Tiarchs', a 'son of a German, married to a German'. According to Cunliffe, Tiarks himself admitted that he had suggested the terms of Plumer's cable; the theatrical intervention at the Supreme War Council on the previous day, therefore, was a mere stunt. Cunliffe had personally dressed down Tiarks for his 'improper' interference in foreign policy.[221] Balfour was evidently told of the story immediately, and he passed on the information to Kerr the next day. Balfour wrote that he disliked

---

[218] 'Minutes of the Third Meeting of the Seventeenth Session, Supreme War Council, held in M. Pichon's room at the Quai d'Orsay, Paris, on Saturday, March 8, 1919, at 3 p.m.', in *British Documents in Foreign Affairs: The Paris Peace Conference of 1919*, ed. Dockrill, ii. 325–41.

[219] Kerr had suggested to Lloyd George that Brussels was a better venue for talks with the Germans, because the French were so 'unreasonable' and 'tricky' in their dealings with the Germans that they no longer trusted the honesty of Allied dealings (Kerr to Lloyd George, 3 Mar. 1919, Kerr Papers, GD 40/17/1240).

[220] Eggleston Diary, 9 Mar. 1919, Eggleston Papers, MS 423/6/58.

[221] Ian Malcolm to Balfour, 9 Mar. 1919, FO 800/215.

the suggestion that Plumer had acted on the advice of a 'semi-Hun friend'. The Germans were still not sincere, he added, for it was his belief that they were deliberately leaving Cologne short, thus 'distributing their food in the manner most likely to influence [the] Allies on their behalf'.[222] Hughes also contributed to this ongoing propaganda battle. He appears to have realized that, if a harsh peace was to be imposed, it was vital for the Right to discredit Germany's claim to be an emaciated democracy. To this end, Hughes resorted to his own private sources of intelligence in an effort to refute the reports of the British officers. On 10 March, Hughes circulated to the War Cabinet and British Delegation the views of one Corporal A. F. Ross, a former Australian prisoner of war in Germany for two years, which Ross happened to send in a personal note to Hughes during the previous week. Ross gave a first-hand account of his experiences in revolutionary Germany since his release from a prisoner of war camp in November 1918. Ross insisted that the 'alleged revolution' in Germany was a fraud, that he had seen masses of food stores in the possession of the German army, and that the demobilization of the German army was 'a gigantic fake'. According to Ross, the people of Germany would willingly welcome back the Kaiser, and even the soldiers' council delegates were not really republicans. Ross concluded that 'German authority remains more or less where it was prior to the armistice'. The Germans, alleged Ross, were secretly preparing 'a final effort for victory'.[223] Hughes circulated this memorandum as an official British Empire Delegation paper. However, comments on the file-jacket were scathing. Colonel Cornwall of the Military Section commented that these were the views of one inexperienced soldier which counted for little against the great number of reports testifying to the revolutionary mood in Germany. Headlam-Morley was more devastating: 'If what has happened in Germany is not a revolution, our whole political terminology will have to be changed', he wrote on the document.[224]

For the moment, Lloyd George seemed determined to force through the moderate proposals for the feeding of Germany. Riddell was prevailed upon to approach the press and prepare public opinion for a concession to the Germans on food. Of course, winning over the Coalition press, and if possible even the Northcliffe press, to a recognition of the reality of the hunger in Germany was vital if a more moderate policy on Britain's part was to be sustained—and, of course, in order to minimize the political danger to Lloyd George from the Conservative back bench. On 9 March extracts from Gibson's report were released to the British press by Lord Riddell. The impact was profound. Even the *Daily Mail* declared that food deliveries to Germany were clearly necessary in order to make a good peace.[225] However, some of the Prime Minister's sternest

[222] Balfour to Kerr, 10 Mar. 1919, FO 800/215.
[223] Corporal A. F. Ross to Hughes, 4 Mar. 1919, circulated as 'The Situation in Germany', Australian Archives A 981/43 and FO 608/130.
[224] Headlam-Morley minute on W. M. Hughes', paper, 'The Situation in Germany (4 March 1919)', FO 608/130.
[225] 'Feeding the Huns', editorial, *Daily Mail*, 13 Mar. 1919.

critics among the press corps reserved a modicum of scepticism. Steed wrote to Northcliffe a typically ambivalent explanation of the Gibson report, acknowledging that 'the danger of starvation and of wild revolution is certainly great', while noting also that it was 'very hard to assess the exact degree in which the reactionary element in Germany are toying with the Bolshevist danger in the hope of scaring us'.[226]

Meanwhile, Lloyd George used General Haking at the Armistice Commission in Spa to alert the Germans, secretly, to expect genuine negotiations at Brussels at this time. On Lloyd George's instructions, on 10 March Wilson dispatched a note to Haking asking him to convey to the Germans 'by nods and nudges' that the Allied proposals in Brussels this time would be '*real* honest bona fide proposals and that if they agree to our shipping terms we will see to it that they are fed'. Haking wired back the same day to say that he had given the required intimations to General Hammerstein in a private meeting, without the knowledge of the American or French Armistice Commissioners. Indeed he had gone further. Haking asked if the Germans would find useful a public assurance from the Allies that, once the ships were handed over, Germany would be supplied with food up to the next harvest. The Germans confirmed that this would be most welcome. But the reference to a public assurance apparently scared off Lloyd George. The 'little civilian', wrote Wilson, wanted Haking to reply with renewed promises of British good faith, but to 'shut down' the arrangements he had mooted for a public promise. Haking saw the Germans privately once again on the afternoon of 12 March. He requested their confidentiality at Brussels respecting these private exchanges, and fobbed them off on the public assurance with a story of his communications in that respect not having been answered. He reported to Wilson that the Prime Minister's experiment in secret diplomacy had been 'a good one', and that it would probably assist in breaking the deadlock at Brussels.[227]

Admiral Wemyss, who was to preside over the negotiations at Brussels on 13–14 March, was apprised of all this over breakfast with the Prime Minister in Paris on the morning of 12 March.[228] Wemyss was similarly determined that his negotiations at Brussels should be successful, and for a mixture of motives. Lady Wemyss was still sharing afternoon teas with W. H. Dawson and was enthusiastically recommending to her husband Dawson's policy of generous assistance to Germany in order to prevent all Europe being 'engulfed in the ever rising tide of Bolshevism'.[229] Admiral Wemyss was also deeply perturbed over his continuing feud with Beatty, and Beatty's alleged machinations to displace him as First

[226] Steed to Northcliffe, 9 Mar. 1919, Steed Papers, Daily Memorandums to Northcliffe Box.

[227] Henry Wilson to Haking, 10 Mar., Haking to Wilson, 11 Mar., Wilson to Haking, 12 Mar., and Haking to Wilson, 12 Mar. 1919, Henry Wilson Papers, HHW 2/90. The correspondence is marked with a note that all items were copied for Wemyss's information.

[228] Wemyss Diary, 12 Mar. 1919, WMYS 12/5.

[229] Lady Wemyss to Dawson, 10 Feb and 6 Mar. 1919, W. H. Dawson Papers, WHD 417 and 425.

Sea Lord which Wemyss was openly challenging.[230] Success in Brussels, Wemyss believed, would add to his credibility in the Prime Minister's eyes. As Wemyss explained to his wife from Paris, 'if I get this matter through I shall be in a stronger position than ever' regarding 'my personal business'.[231]

Not surprisingly, considering all these preparations, and the Germans' dire need for food, the two days of negotiations with the Germans in Brussels on 13 and 14 March went very smoothly. The heart of the agreement was simple: the German negotiators agreed to the surrender of their entire merchant fleet (and they were promised that the future disposal of the ships was not prejudiced), while the Allies agreed to supply Germany with 270,000 tons of food in March and 370,000 thereafter until September. Germany was to be permitted to export a very few products in order to assist her raise the funds to purchase food. The blockade itself, on all other prohibited imports and exports, would remain in place until 12 July. Under the terms of the agreement, the first German ships to be surrendered sailed for British ports on 21 March, and the Germans made the first payment for food on 22 March. Three days later the first American ship began unloading a cargo of flour in Hamburg. Food at last was beginning to flow. However, it should not be imagined that the food crisis inside Germany ended in March. In fact, serious food shortages inside Germany persisted for many months. Difficulties over the financing of food purchases kept deliveries to Germany well behind schedule. Not until the end of May did German ships loaded with American foodstuffs begin to arrive in German harbours.[232]

With the successful conclusion of the Brussels Agreement, a dent in the policy of the blockade had been made—a psychological dent too in the policy of coercing Germany to accept whatever terms were to be devised in Paris over the next months. For the moderates in the British Delegation and the government, however, the Brussels Agreement was only a first step towards a bold new policy. The next step was to win the Prime Minister to a moderate outlook in the construction of the peace as a whole. For a fortnight in late March this too seemed possible, for the Prime Minister appeared suddenly more than willing to revise his whole approach.

At this point, it is important to note the evolving views of those advisers closest of all to Lloyd George, Philip Kerr and Maurice Hankey. In Kerr's case, a strong streak of scepticism, and an evangelical desire to 'punish' the German nation, were still discernible in his advice to the Prime Minister. In mid-February, a month after the elections had returned a clearly pro-democratic majority in Germany, Kerr told Lloyd George that 'Germany is still in my judgement fundamentally unrepentant and requires very firm and uncompromising

---

[230] Wemyss to Beatty, 28 Feb. 1919, Wemyss to Long, 10 Mar. 1919, Wemyss Papers, WMYS 11, and Long to Beatty, 19 Mar. 1919, Beatty Papers, BTY 13/28/5.

[231] Wemyss to Lady Wemyss, 12 Mar. 1919, Wemyss Papers, WMYS 7/11/14.

[232] For details of the Brussels Agreement and the actual deliveries made, see Harold Temperley (ed.), *A History of the Peace Conference of Paris* (London, 1920), i. 313–19.

handling'.[233] Soon after, he advised Lloyd George that Germany's troubles were only just beginning, and no improvement could be expected 'until she is able to bring to the top a more honest and capable set of men than she managed to produce at the Weimar Assembly'. Kerr could scarcely have been looking forward to a more *left*-wing government. In early March, Kerr was still in two minds about concessions to Germany. 'I doubt if we know enough of the internal [situation in Germany] as yet', he wrote, 'to warrant us in supposing that we shall not want to modify our terms, especially in the economic sphere, after we have heard what the Germans have got to say.'[234] This particular document was prepared for Lloyd George just prior to his return to the conference in early March, that is, after most of the officers' reports (but not Gibson's) were already circulating. Hankey's position was very similar. In a note to Jones written on 5 March, he conceded that the evidence gathered in Paris showed that 'there really is an appalling state of affairs in Germany'. But Hankey was still not prepared to drop all his suspicions of German deviousness: 'My impression is that the Germans may have deliberately allowed the Spartacists a good deal of rope in order to frighten us into the idea that we cannot get an indemnity.'[235] Thus neither the Prime Minister's personal secretary nor his Cabinet secretary, were of the stamp to be easily won over to a moderate position.

The reluctance of his two chief advisers underlines as all the more remarkable the sudden strengthening of moderate opinion in the Prime Minister's entourage after the breakthrough of the Brussels Agreement. The mood appears to have shifted decisively. On 19 March, Hankey, inspired by a long session with Henry Wilson, sent Lloyd George a memorandum expressing deep disquiet over the direction of the peace conference. Hankey complained that Germany was being loaded with exactions that would place her 'in an utterly impossible position'. Terms that could only be described as 'humiliating' were being prepared for Germany, terms that would hasten her 'disintegration'. The crucial need was to maintain Germany as 'a barrier against Bolshevism'. He recommended three principles. First, 'the enormity of their crimes must be brought home to the German people' by the imposition of 'drastic penalties' at the outset, but penalties which could be liquidated quickly. Second, the Germans should be assured assistance in their battle with the internal Bolshevik enemy. And third, the Germans should be given 'self-respect' by promising them membership of the League of Nations and a share in the trial of war criminals. It was vital, advised Hankey, throughout the treaty 'to avoid the appearance of Vindictiveness'. The underlying theme in Hankey's advice was the need to combat Bolshevism.[236] Gone was the suggestion that the unrest in Germany might be a sham.

[233] Kerr to Lloyd George, undated but 18 or 19 Feb. 1919, Kerr Papers, GD 40/17/1223.
[234] Kerr to Lloyd George, 3 Mar. 1919, Kerr Papers GD 40/17/1240.
[235] Hankey to Jones, 5 Mar. 1919, Jones Diary for 1919, Thomas Jones Papers.
[236] Hankey to Lloyd George, 19 Mar. 1919, Lloyd George Papers, F/23/4/39.

Other moderate voices also were now heard. Herbert Fisher, an eminent historian of Europe as well as Education Secretary, wrote to Lloyd George to object strenuously to the plans for the cession of Danzig to Poland.[237] Lloyd George, always a great believer in mopping up details in conversations with experts, was also widening his contacts at the conference. Symbolic was his decision to invite Oswald Garrison Villard, the American pacifist and leading Radical journalist, to breakfast on 22 March. (President Wilson had turned aside the chance to meet Villard.) Villard had just returned to Paris after a month's sojourn in Germany where he had interviewed dozens of revolutionary socialists and moderate government ministers in both Munich and Weimar. According to Frances Stevenson, Villard gave Lloyd George extraordinary details of the 'terrible' privation in Germany, and explained that the German people were 'looking to the Allies for salvation'. There was no question that the Kaiser and the old regime were blamed for the war, said Villard, and the people would 'hear nothing against the Allies'.[238] Lloyd George listened attentively, but when Villard announced that the Germans would not accept a harsh treaty, Lloyd George responded 'in that case we will slap the blockade on again'.[239]

This may well have been sheer bravado on Lloyd George's part. For certainly, inspired by Hankey's memorandum, the Prime Minister was veering away from such harsh solutions. Indeed, he was about to embark upon a major experiment: a gentle tilt in British policy towards a peace of moderation. A weekend away had been planned for the Prime Minister and his intimates at Fontainebleau. The idea was Lloyd George's; he had told Riddell that he was profoundly dissatisfied with the peace process so far and wanted 'to put in the hardest 48 hours thinking I have ever done' in order to put things right.[240] After breakfast with Villard on the morning of Saturday, 22 March, Lloyd George drove to Fontainebleau for an intensive review of Britain's stance at the peace conference. He took with him Henry Wilson, Kerr, Hankey, and Montagu, a team of advisers in which liberalism was scarcely the dominant ingredient.[241] The Saturday was spent listening to specially prepared lectures: Wilson spoke on the peace terms from the German perspective; Hankey spoke on the war aims of the British Empire; Montagu spoke on the peace terms from the point of view of a 'Man from Mars'; Wilson spoke again on French perspectives; and Kerr kept notes. As this book's chief focus is upon the precise issue of the German revolution as a factor in shaping British

[237] Fisher to Lloyd George, 17 Mar. 1919, in typed version of Fisher Diary, HMP, HDLM Acc. 800.

[238] Taylor, *Lloyd George: A Diary*, 23 Mar. 1919, referring to events on 22 Mar. 1919, 175.

[239] Quoted in Michael Wrezsin, *Oswald Garrison Villard: Pacifist at War* (Bloomington, Ind., 1965), 117.

[240] Riddell Diary, 21 Mar. 1919, Riddell Papers, 62983.

[241] In his memoirs, Lloyd George incorrectly listed Smuts among those attending the conference and left out Montagu; see David Lloyd George, *Memoirs of the Peace Conference* (New Haven), i. 266. Smuts was definitely not present as he was in England until Sunday, 23 Mar. Montagu's papers include a document attesting to his contributions at Fontainebleau on Saturday, 22 Mar.; see 'Memorandum', by E. S. Montagu, 4 Apr. 1919, Montagu Papers, Box 5, AS1/12/18.

policy, these complex lectures delivered on the Saturday need not be examined here. It was on the Sunday that the issue of Germany and her revolution received attention. Lloyd George dictated a memorandum giving his general observations. His 'preface' document announced:

The whole of Europe is filled with the spirit of revolution . . . I am told on all hands that workmen have lost their taste for toil . . . Her [Russia's] ideas may yet triumph in Germany. There are many indications that Sparticism [*sic*] has not been completely over-thrown, and a stern peace may make the life of any government impossible and drive Germany into Bolshevism. This is the immediate danger. The present government is weak; it has no prestige; and its authority is challenged. I do not believe it will dare to sign an over-stern peace treaty. If it does, I am told it will be swept away within 24 hours . . . A Spartacist Germany in alliance with Bolshevist Russia is the immediate peril which confronts us. [242]

This preliminary version of what was to become the famous 'Fontainebleau Memorandum' makes it clear that one factor above all was driving the British leadership to consider adopting a more moderate approach: fear of Bolshevism in Germany. The negative motive held sway. It is clear also from the records of the meetings on that weekend that Lloyd George was pursued, even to the quiet of his forest retreat at Fontainebleau, by the irreconcilable men devoted to indemnity. Hankey's records show that, before addressing his advisers for a second time on the Sunday, Lloyd George was closeted away in a 'long conference' with two of the British delegates from the Reparation Commission, Lords Cunliffe and Sumner. [243] When Lloyd George emerged from this conference, it became clear that, for all his determination to project a new moderation, the programme of the 'economic warriors' was still on the agenda. A list of 'British Empire Interests' drawn up by Hankey and Kerr, based on Lloyd George's second speech, made this clear:

The British Empire must get as large an indemnity out of Germany as possible in order to lighten the burden it has to carry, which is a heavy handicap in commercial competi-tion with the United States and other nations. It is also necessary because otherwise Germany will be in a more favourable position for commercial competition than Great Britain as her debt will be less. [244]

[242] 'Prime Minister's "Preface" Version', dated 23 Mar. 1919, listed as Appendix 2, in 'Final Treaty of Peace—Diary Showing its Development', by Sir Maurice Hankey, CAB 1/28.

[243] 'Final Treaty of Peace—Diary Showing its Development', by Sir Maurice Hankey, CAB 1/28.

[244] 'British Empire Interests', dated 23 Mar. 1919, attached to a typed draft of the 'Fontainebleau Memorandum', endorsed by Henry Wilson with the words 'Drawn up by L. G. on the morning of 23 March (Sunday) and as reflections on lectures given last night', and dated by Henry Wilson 23 Mar. 1919, Henry Wilson Papers, HHW/2/90. Hankey's record of the Fontainebleau meetings explains that, after Sumner and Cunliffe had seen Lloyd George, he delivered a speech on 'his prin-ciples and general outline of peace terms'. From this address, Kerr and Hankey prepared 'a prelim-inary rough draft of Peace Terms based on the Prime Minister's observations'. This document is attached as Appendix 3 in Hankey's file and is entitled 'British Empire Interests'; see 'Final Treaty of Peace—Diary Showing its Development', by Sir Maurice Hankey, CAB 1/28.

Even at Fontainebleau, therefore, moderation had to give some ground to the expectations of the 'economic warriors.

The final version of the Fontainebleau Memorandum, sent privately to Clemenceau and President Wilson on 26 March, put the case for offering to Germany 'a peace which, while just, will be preferable for all sensible men to the alternative to Bolshevism'. Above all, it signalled Lloyd George's flirtation with the idea of peace terms which, by implication, would *not* require coercion in order to obtain either German signature or compliance. While not going so far as to argue for a change in procedure, that is, genuine negotiations with the Germans, Lloyd George declared that the treaty must be 'a settlement which a responsible German Government can sign in the belief that it can fulfil the obligations it incurs'. Freedom from coercion was implied. In addition, deep in the text was a sign that Lloyd George was prepared to throw over a key item in the 'economic warrior' programme, the future strangulation of German trade. Lloyd George advised that he was prepared to put 'in the forefront of the peace' with Germany, the principle that 'once she accepts our terms, especially reparation, we will open to her the raw materials and markets of the world on equal terms with ourselves, and will do everything possible to enable the German people to get upon their legs again'.[245] While the vague commitment to 'reparation' remained, Lloyd George was here propounding free trade sentiments which, if known, would have instantly driven the tariff reformers of the Conservative Party into conspiratorial huddles.

In conclusion, the 'struggle for the facts' on Germany in January and February had produced a remarkable change among the British peacemakers. The struggle to gain a new reliable intelligence on Germany, free from the presumption of conspiracy on Germany's part, had been very successful. Perhaps unexpectedly in many quarters, it had been the trained intelligence officers of the British army, many with experience in the trenches or in prisoners of war camps, whose reports from Germany had demolished—in many but not all minds—the myth of coun-terfeit revolution and sham hunger in Germany. Having been sent deep into Germany, without exception they had found the evidence of great privation quite overwhelming, and they had reported that the starvation of the country was undermining the successful advent of German democracy.

The change in mood which this new intelligence induced among the leading British policy-makers, however, should not be exaggerated. Certainly, the 'con-dition of Germany' was now taken seriously at the highest levels. But it was the danger of Bolshevism and the prospect of losing a peace treaty altogether that captured the imaginations of the men at the top. How resilient a commitment to a moderate peace had been created was an open question. Fear, not democratic idealism, was the dominant emotion. There was no appreciation of the argument that moderation was required in order to bolster the credit of the existing

---

[245] 'Some considerations for the Peace Conference before they finally draft their terms', in 'Final Treaty of Peace—Diary Showing its Development', by Sir Maurice Hankey, CAB 1/28.

socialist-led government in Berlin. The idea that the new regime required unmistakable expressions of support, in order to consolidate the new spirit and the new democratic institutions in Germany, was being put by the men of the PID in particular, but Lloyd George and his chief advisers made no moves in this direction. The policy of coercing Germany to accept a peace treaty, a treaty to be made entirely without German participation, was still in place, and the military power to make it happen, though weaker than it had been in the autumn of 1918, was still deployed. No words of support for the Scheidemann government in Germany had accompanied the conclusion of the Brussels Agreement. Nothing in the Fontainebleau Memorandum showed that Lloyd George regarded any of the developments in Germany since the armistice as praiseworthy. The Scheidemann government was simply pilloried as a 'weak' government, a government with 'no prestige'.

It is a mistake to imagine that, in all of this, Lloyd George and his ministers had simply overlooked the achievements of the period of revolution in Germany. From the point of view of the British government, many of the 'achievements' were simply embarrassments. The government in Weimar was dominated by socialists, trade unionists, Catholics, and liberals; the constitution presented to the Weimar Assembly was of the most advanced and democratic character; the government promised sweeping social reforms and had already conceded the eight-hour day; the government had announced its preference for a capital levy and a steeply graduated income-related tax to pay for the war; the government had already announced the socialization of the coal industry as the first of a series of measures towards nationalization; the government promised that factory councils would be enshrined in the constitution. Lloyd George's government did not fail to express support for Weimar in spite of its achievements, but, rather, because of them. The revolutionary foundations of the new state, and its constant teetering on the brink of another revolution, ensured that Lloyd George and his ministers refused to give any clear message of support for the new democratic and social German republic.

The more far-sighted moderates of the British Delegation, however, still hoped that the precedent set at Brussels might be repeated. Under the influence of Wilsonian idealism, they prophesied, Lloyd George might yet grasp the opportunity to make a peace of reconciliation face to face with the representatives of Weimar, a peace that would boost the electoral stocks of the creators of the new Germany, the socialists and democrats. At least the camp of discernible 'moderates', of a kind, was enlarging around Lloyd George; it now included leading Conservatives, such as Cecil and Milner, surviving Liberals such as Churchill, Montagu, and Fisher, key advisers to the government such as Keynes and Headlam-Morley, and the men of the PID. One more key figure was to declare himself immediately after Fontainebleau. In a long and emotional letter delivered to Lloyd George a couple of days after his return from Fontainebleau, General Smuts threw the weight of his prestige into the struggle for a peace reflecting 'political magnanimity'; and yet even Smuts's idealism had its limits, for he openly proclaimed that his chief objective was to treat Germany 'in a different spirit' so that the victors might 'have the effect of turning her into a bulwark against the oncoming Bolshevism of Eastern Europe'.[246] The men constantly in the vehicles ferrying Lloyd George about in Paris, Hankey, Wilson, and Kerr, were scarcely yet determined 'moderates': each was shifting ground, each retained an elemental scepticism concerning Germany, but all three were genuinely disturbed over the deterioration of social and political conditions inside Germany. Were the men closest to the Prime Minister willing to press upon him the case for the abandonment of the policy of coercion of Germany altogether? Would a policy of moderation towards Germany be adopted, for the positive objective of bolstering German democracy, even if the immediate danger of Bolshevism receded? The events of January to March had shown that Britain's leaders would consider moderation only if fear of Bolshevism could be brought home to them. Undoubtedly, it had been this aspect of the new intelligence on the 'condition of Germany' which had led to Lloyd George's decision to make a breakthrough over food and to his experiment of the Fontainebleau Memorandum. Over the next three months, as Bolshevism in Germany *was* progressively defeated, the struggle to influence the conscience of the government would intensify. The objective of the moderates in the British Delegation was now a grand one: to persuade the British leaders to embrace moderation, not to save themselves from the hordes of masterless men, but in order to make German democracy strong.

[246] Smuts to Lloyd George, 26 Mar. 1919, Lloyd George Papers, F/45/9/29.

7

Towards Peace by Coercion
March–June 1919

One of the worst features of the Peace terms is the treatment accorded German democracy. Again and again our statesmen have declared that their quarrel was not with the German people but with their rulers. Again and again they have repeated that some evidence was required of a change in a more democratic direction. That change has now come in a far more emphatic form than the statesmen, when they made these declarations, ever contemplated. Yet it had made no difference . . . The terms could hardly have been more severe if they had been imposed upon a Germany which retained the Kaiser on his throne and submitted tamely to a government of the old type. It seems, indeed, as if the Allied and Associated Governments regarded the coming of socialism to power in Germany as a greater danger than Prussian militarism . . .

UDC Pamphlet, *The Betrayal of the Peoples*, May 1919[1]

THE Brussels Agreement and the Fontainebleau Memorandum of March 1919 were moderate breakthroughs which were bound to lead to major political disputes over the direction of the peace settlement still taking shape. Between March and the signing of the Versailles Treaty on 28 June 1919, the British government and its delegation in Paris was wracked by an increasingly bitter debate between the proponents of coercion and the proponents of moderation towards Germany. In the final analysis, the debate was won by the 'hard men'. While Lloyd George did succeed in modifying several territorial aspects of the draft treaty in June, he did not challenge the essential policy underpinning the peace, namely, the coercion of Germany in order to gain its acceptance of peace terms, without negotiation. Nor did he retreat from the crucial demand for an indemnity, a commitment that eventually tied him firmly into the camp of the chauvinist blowhards. Britain did nothing, in the end, to save the makers of Weimar from the humiliation of Versailles—in spite of the best economic, political, and military intelligence advice, generated by British advisers, that such a course might fatally damage the electoral prospects of the democratic forces inside Germany.

---

[1] UDC Pamphlet, no. 37*a*, *The Betrayal of the Peoples*, May 1919, UDC Archives, DDC 5/340.

It is not the intention of this chapter to review in detail the British contribution to the making of the Versailles Treaty in its entirety; there are a number of excellent studies that already provide such a review.[2] Rather, this chapter examines the ongoing struggle within the British government, and among its advisers, over the most fundamental question, the wisdom or folly of the government's supporting the basic policy of coercion, the policy symbolized by Britain's enforcement of the continuing economic blockade. The chapter focuses in particular on the effect of two forces in determining the British commitment to coercion: first, domestic pressures on the Prime Minister from the 'economic warriors' of the British Right; and second, the slowly receding threat of a second revolution inside Germany which liberated the government from the fear of pushing Germany over the edge. In the final analysis, Lloyd George proved to be more afraid of the power of his right-wing domestic critics than of the Bolshevik threat in Germany. He insisted upon the coercion of Germany in order to satisfy his Conservative constituency. Those British advisers still clinging on to hopes that their leaders might do something for the future of German democracy were left disappointed and embittered.

The attempt of the British moderates to abolish the economic blockade of Germany, March–April 1919

During late March and April 1919, British moderates attempted to build on the precedent of the Brussels Agreement and secure the complete abolition of the blockade. Using new evidence on the still steadily deteriorating 'condition of Germany', evidence gathered once again by military intelligence officers and economic missions inside Germany during late March and April, the moderates within the government and the delegation attempted to steer Britain into partnership with the United States behind the policy of a revival of German economic life as soon as possible.

The group seeking moderation towards Germany contained diverse elements working towards a variety of objectives. In the case of the PID, as we have seen, the overriding motive was to assist in the transition to democracy in Germany. The economic advisers serving Robert Cecil in Paris wanted to assist in the recuperation of European economic life, for humanitarian motives above all. Those moderates in the inner circle of power around Lloyd George, were driven by a determination to avoid Bolshevism. Following the accession to power of the Hungarian Communist, Bela Kun, in Budapest on 22 March, the anti-Bolshevik motive was bound to be uppermost in the minds of several key British figures. Saving Germany was Churchill's special interest, and he moved immediately after the conclusion of the Brussels Agreement to drum up a more sympathetic

---

[2] e.g. Erik Goldstein, *Winning the Peace* (Oxford, 1991), M. L. Dockrill and J. D. Goold, *Peace without Promise* (London, 1991), and Howard Elcock, *Portrait of a Decision: The Council of Four and the Treaty of Versailles* (London, 1972).

press and public opinion on the issue. He sought and obtained Lloyd George's permission to compile all the British army officers' reports received so far on the inner condition of Germany into a single printed report for distribution to the press and to all MPs. At the end of March, Churchill sent copies to leading members of the government, with a letter carefully noting that he had Lloyd George's express approval, and declaring that the distribution of the document was vital if parliament was to gain a 'proper understanding' of the situation inside Germany.[3] Quite plainly Churchill wished to feed Germany and settle peace quickly in order to enlist German aid in a wider war against Bolshevism in eastern Europe.[4] When Henry Wilson spoke of moderation towards Germany, he too thought along the same lines. Full of scorn for all talk of the League of Nations as a device for quashing Bolshevism, Henry Wilson told Churchill that instead he would like to see 'a combination of England, France and Germany in an Alliance against Russia and Japan'.[5] Smuts, similarly, kept the anti-Bolshevik theme prominent in his advocacy of a new moderation. Just after Bela Kun's take-over in Hungary, Smuts told Curzon that 'the whole European order seems to be dissolving' and he warned that 'the complete fiasco of the Conference' might soon have to be faced.[6]

During late March and April, the flow of intelligence from Germany, now recognized by all as a key weapon in the struggle over policy, increased in volume and became ever more desperate in tone. The DMI sent a number of further missions into Germany. The leading theme of the reports submitted by these missions was the same: the concession of emergency food made at Brussels was too little, and probably too late. Once again the army officers sent into Germany appear to have been shocked by what they saw, and they assembled highly emotional reports. The first reports to come in after the Brussels Agreement were a series submitted by Major Bertie, Captain Brandt, and Lieutenant Harding. These three officers were sent to Berlin originally, their purpose being to examine a supposed cache of evidence on Bolshevik agitation in Germany found by the German police upon the arrest of the Russian emissary, Karl Radek. The Radek documents were so few that they were quickly copied ('a one man job', as Bertie described it) and the officers then concentrated on an investigation of conditions in Berlin, and east to Stettin, Danzig, Königsberg, Memel and Courland. The officers' reports described 'fearful conditions'. 'The Mayor of Stettin who has 8 children looked a mere skeleton. I was afterwards told that his hatred for England for carrying on the blockade after the armistice knew no bounds', wrote Bertie. The vehement opinions of dozens of employers and ordinary citizens against the blockade were reported, with much content betraying the officers'

---

[3] Churchill to Lloyd George, 14 Mar. 1919, Lloyd George Papers, F/8/3/32, and Churchill to Curzon, 28 Mar. 1919, Curzon Papers, MS EUR F 112/209.

[4] For a detailed analysis of Churchill's motives see Donald Graeme Boadle, *Winston Churchill and the German Question in British Foreign Policy, 1918–1922* (The Hague, 1973), esp. ch. 2.

[5] Henry Wilson to Churchill, 18 Mar. 1919, Henry Wilson Papers, HHW 18.

[6] Smuts to Curzon, 26 Mar. 1919, Curzon Papers, MS EUR F 112/214.

own sympathy for this viewpoint. For example, summarizing attitudes towards the British, the Bertie report noted, with the emphasis of capital letters in the original: 'BUT WHAT ABSOLUTELY BEATS THEM IS THE CONTINUANCE OF THE BLOCK-ADE, BECAUSE THEY CANNOT REALIZE THAT THERE ARE STILL PEOPLE IN ENGLAND WHO HAVE NOT YET GRASPED THE FACT THAT GERMANY HAS BEEN BEATEN IN THE WAR AND SO BADLY BEATEN THAT SHE MAY REQUIRE HELP TO DEFEND HERSELF AGAINST INTERNAL AND EXTERNAL ENEMIES.' Bertie also reported on the condition of the German army, describing it as 'far more serious than we imagine'. In the east, wrote Bertie, Germany was wholly reliant on volunteer corps. This mobilization against Poland did not impress Bertie as a reversion to militarism. Social democracy was no mask, he reported. In interviews with socialist ministers in Berlin, Bertie was assured that there was 'not a man living in Germany today who did not consider the pre-war foreign policy of Germany as hopelessly wrong'.[7]

Another major report came from the still more tumultuous regions of southern Germany. Captain James Broad, Lieutenant G. H. Beyfus, and Lieutenant Wareing were sent to Bavaria on 31 March, and between them the three officers explored Würzburg, Nuremberg, and Munich. Beyfus sent an interim report from Berlin on 9 April. The officers had been in northern Bavaria when the Councils' Republic, the most serious left-wing threat to the moderate Berlin government yet to appear in Germany, was proclaimed in Munich on 6 April.[8] Thus the British officers happened to be in that part of Germany where a bloody conflict for power between the moderate and radical wings of German socialism was about to explode. Beyfus described the political battle between the moderate Johannes Hoffmann government, which promised food from the West, and the Workers' Council government in Munich, which promised food from Russia and Hungary. The Bavarian people as a whole were 'in the depths of despair', wrote Beyfus, because for five months since the great promises of food from the West contained in the armistice itself the food situation had not improved. 'The Germans have read so much and heard so much of the promised food supplies that they no longer believe in them', wrote Beyfus. Prompt arrival of supplies might avert tragedy, but Beyfus agreed with the many Bavarians who told him that it was 'too late' for the Allies to save the situation.[9] The final report submitted by Broad and Beyfus included details of the still more serious armed confrontation which arose following the proclamation of a 'Second Councils' Republic' in Munich under Max Levien and Eugen Leviné in mid-April. In explaining these events, Beyfus and Broad wrote vividly of the 'nervous depression and moral collapse' of the ordinary people after years of 'undernourishment'.

[7] 'Report of Major Bertie, Captain Brandt and Lieutenant Harding, 17 March to 12 April 1919', dated 12 Apr. 1919, WO 144/15.
[8] On developments in Bavaria, see F. L. Carsten, *Revolution in Central Europe, 1918–1919* (London, 1972), 218–23.
[9] 'Interim Report on Conditions in Bavaria (March 31st to April 8, 1919)', by Lieutenant Gilbert H. Beyfus, dated 9 Apr. 1919, Armistice Commission Report, WO 144/15.

The fearful shortage of food, they proclaimed, was undoubtedly 'the root of all the industrial and political unrest prevailing'. Beyfus and Broad also took issue with the Entente press for suggesting that Bolshevism was 'inspired from high quarters'. They had found no evidence of this: 'we are convinced that the Bolshevist movement in Bavaria is a genuine one and no stage play designed to terrorise the Peace Conference into granting easier terms.' Beyfus and Broad recommended 'the promptest action on the part of the Entente' so that food supplies would be on hand the moment Munich was retaken by *Freikorps* forces.[10]

Perhaps the most impressive of all the reports from within Germany was produced in mid-April by a team of technical and commercial experts sent in by the DMI. The team comprised a professor of chemistry, Henry L. Smith, and four businessmen, S. N. Jenkinson, F. T. Johnston, Wallace Ellison, and Frederic Wise, later a Conservative MP. The original purpose behind the sending of this team of experts is probably revealed in a jacket comment by Headlam-Morley; he noted that he had heard the criticism that the British officers' reports were valueless, unless supported by 'technical experts'.[11] In fact, the businessmen submitted a lengthy report which must rank as the most humane to appear on the German problem. Based on extensive interviews and visits to factories, the technical experts argued vehemently for sweeping changes in the policies of the victorious powers: food and raw materials should be sent into Germany 'to defeat Bolshevism', the blockade should be raised, a preliminary peace should be signed 'at once', and the Allies should announce that they 'support the present Ebert-Scheidemann Government as long as [they] are satisfied that it is non-military'. The businessmen had clearly been astonished at the privations they were forced to observe. 'Starvation is an ugly word', wrote Wise from Berlin, 'but when the ordinary cab-driver asks for bread instead of his fare one realises that there is something very wrong in a city.' Wise estimated deaths from malnutrition in Berlin among the old, very young, and invalids at 800 per day. Jenkinson and Johnston, who toured factories in Bavaria, were scathing about Allied expectations of an indemnity:

. . . there is nothing here except angry, despairing, hungry men, tubercular children and living skeletons called women. We came here as commercial men to see the conditions as to what sum Germany could pay, with the feeling that we would make her pay and pay well. We feel convinced that the Allies, unless they give help quickly, will get no indemnity, but in its place they will get Bolshevism.

The tone of the report was nothing if not emphatic. 'The fate of European civilization is hingeing on a quick and wise decision on these problems', declared the concluding sentence of the report.[12]

---

[10] 'Report by James E. Broad and G. H. Beyfus', dated 23 Apr. 1919, FO 371/3777.

[11] Headlam-Morley Minute on jacket of 'Conditions in Germany', 15 Apr. 1919, FO 608/130.

[12] 'Conditions in Germany', 15 Apr. 1919, WO 144/15, and Milner Add. Papers, MS Eng. Hist. c. 697.

These reports added to the mountain of information on German privation which, one might have imagined, was now undeniable. But even more important, intelligence reports from Berlin also predicted the long-term political consequences of the Allies' apparent refusal to grant any declaration of support, any real chance of economic recovery, or any forum for negotiations to the new German government during the months of armistice. A flow of individual reports from Berlin confirmed the political lessons being drawn. Certainly the Allies were blamed. 'There is *real* want. Feeling is that we are now murdering women and children unnecessarily', wrote Major Knyvett to the DMI on 20 March.[13] But the moderate government in Berlin was also being blamed. For example, in late March Stewart Roddie circulated a letter from Dr Reinhold Schairer of the German Red Cross, which gave graphic descriptions of the bloody fighting in Berlin; Schairer explained that the Berlin government's use of such extreme measures of repression against Spartacism would bring it enormous discredit unless moderate peace terms emanating from Paris eventually vindicated its tactics. Spartacism was winning adherents, wrote Schairer, because the German people 'cannot see *one* glimmer of hope'.[14] On 4 April Keynes sent to Kerr a similar statement from Dr Melchior, a German banker and economic negotiator with whom Keynes had dealt in Brussels. Melchior argued that Germany faced two crises, the food supply crisis, plus a crisis of 'disillusionment' among the working class. The armistice had given hope of 'a Peace of justice and reconciliation', wrote Melchior; but the people did not expect that the armistice would last so long, and now there was a growing conviction that the terms of peace 'will not fulfil the conditions on which arms were laid down'. The Berlin government, attacked from Left and Right, was likely to fall, and then the Allies would face, in Melchior's words, 'men like those whom we met at Brest-Litovsk'.[15] An interview with a leading German USPD politician, Herr Strobel, was also circulated by the DMI, Strobel making a passionate plea for Allied support for the existing government lest it be overwhelmed by Bolshevism or by the reactionary militarism of a slowly reviving German Right.[16] Dr Winthrop Bell, a Foreign Office adviser sent into Germany at the request of Robert Borden, the Canadian Prime Minister, sent in a report showing economic conditions in Berlin becoming 'steadily graver', while the emergency food supplies from the West were having only a small effect.[17] A British Foreign Office agent, von Wiegand, sent a report of an hour's interview with Ebert. He argued that Ebert was 'no great statesman', but conceded that he was obviously sincere in his opposition to communism and

[13] Major Knyvett to DMI, 20 Mar. 1919, FO 608/130.

[14] Reinhold Schairer to Stewart Roddie, 23 Mar. 1919, FO 371/3776.

[15] Keynes to Kerr, 4 Apr. 1919, enclosing 'Statement by Dr. Melchior on the General Situation in Germany', dated 3 Apr. 1919, Kerr Papers, GD 40/1771.

[16] 'Political Tendencies in Germany since the Revolution, by Herr Strobel of the Independent Socialist Party', Milner Add. Papers MS Eng. Hist. c. 697.

[17] Winthrop Bell to Robert Borden, from Berlin, 17 Apr. 1919, FO 800/216, and Borden to Lloyd George, 21 Apr. 1919, Lloyd George Papers, F/5/3/39.

would only support the socialization of 'monopolies'. Ebert stressed that his government would only sign a peace based on the Fourteen Points, and implored emergency food deliveries for this 'would prove a great stabiliser for the present government'. The people of Berlin, von Wiegand confirmed, were in a state of 'desperation, despair, indignation, [and] humbled pride'.[18]

The recently promoted Captain Thornely Gibson, whose reports had made such an impact in early March, also began to focus on the disastrous political consequences of the long armistice when he undertook a second mission into Germany beginning in late March. On 4 April he sent a handwritten report to Kerr, accompanied by a private note. Gibson warned Kerr that 'Spartacus is a marvel of energy and organisation'. The 'desperate' people of Berlin, he wrote 'still do not believe that food is coming—or if it is coming that it will ever reach them'. Gibson pleaded with Kerr to show his report to Lloyd George as soon as possible: 'I feel strongly that he is the only man who could and would deal with the situation.' His new reports stressed that the poorer classes of Berlin were 'literally starving' and that 'the danger of Germany embracing Bolshevism is both real and imminent'. He argued that the Ebert-Scheidemann government was losing its hold on the German working class because its promises of food and a quick peace had not materialized. The Bolshevik ideals, wrote Gibson, had 'gripped the imagination of a diseased and starving people'.[19] Gibson sent a second and even more gloomy report from Berlin on 17 April. This time Gibson argued that the collapse of the Scheidemann government was probably a foregone conclusion. According to Gibson the best that the Western powers could do was to seek influence over the USPD-controlled government that was bound to follow Scheidemann's by rushing in food to stabilize the situation. The advantage of this was two-fold: the proletariat would be satisfied with a more leftist government, and such an all-socialist government was much more likely to sign the peace than the socialist-bourgeois ministry of Scheidemann. However, if the Allies did not wish a USPD government, they would have to prepare for the occupation of the country as a whole to prevent anarchy and civil war.[20]

It is important to note also that Gibson's views were not based simply upon his impressions of life in the capital. Gibson was more than an observer; he was a go-between in secret British contacts with Brockdorff-Rantzau, the German Foreign Minister. During his April mission to Germany, Gibson visited Brockdorff-Rantzau on two occasions, once on 10 April at Weimar and again in Berlin on 13 April. On the first occasion he passed on a special communiqué from Cecil, summarizing the food shipments scheduled for Germany under the Brussels Agreement, and asking the German government to publicize the details

---

[18] Wiseman to Balfour, 21 Mar. 1919, FO 800/215.

[19] Gibson to Kerr, 4 Apr. 1919, enclosing report, Kerr Papers, GD 40/17/71. The report was later printed as 'Bolshevism in Germany', dated 10 Apr. 1919, War Cabinet Paper GT 7092, Milner Add. Papers, MS Eng. Hist. c. 697.

[20] Gibson to Kerr, 17 Apr. 1919, enclosing report entitled 'Conditions in Germany', Kerr Papers, GD 40/17/71 and FO 608/130.

of this assistance together with the Allies' threat that such food shipments were dependent on the maintenance of 'order'. Quite explicitly, therefore, Britain gave the German government assurances that its forceful suppression of Spartacism would lead to favourable treatment from the Allies. In response, Brockdorff-Rantzau pointed out that the shipments scheduled under the Brussels Agreement were insufficient to consolidate the existing government. Something more decisive was required to restart the German economy. Moreover, the British did not seem to understand the realities in Germany, he insisted. Citing the *Daily Mail*, Brockdorff-Rantzau protested that the British press was still peddling the ludicrous claim that the German government was inciting Bolshevism in a cynical manœuvre to scare the Allies into offering easier terms. Brockdorff-Rantzau insisted that resistance to Bolshevism was fundamental to the government's position, and had been a condition of his joining the Cabinet. He reminded Gibson that he had demonstrated his own good faith in making Radek available for British interrogation.[21] On his return to Paris on 23 April, Gibson gained immediate access to Lloyd George, joining him and Cecil for breakfast. Cecil recorded the burden of the discussion: 'Gibson urged strongly, as he had done privately to me, that we ought to make some suspension of the blockade before the Germans are asked to sign; that at present the great weapon of the Spartacists is the threat that the Entente mean to crush Germany utterly, and that therefore there is no reason for avoiding Bolshevism.'[22]

For the moderates among the British delegates in Paris, these intelligence reports were a flow of first-class ammunition for use in their campaign. The lesson of all these reports was absolutely plain: the breakthrough at Brussels was hopelessly inadequate as a means of rescuing the situation in Germany; another major concession was required, even before the peace terms were ready for presentation to Germany—a further relaxation or even a total abolition of the economic blockade. This implied, of course, that the peace terms, not yet presented to Germany, would have to be genuinely negotiated; for the victors would no longer have their fingers on the throat of the German nation. Hence the proposal to raise the blockade was bound to excite much opposition.

Nevertheless, the economic advisers working with Cecil were determined to demolish the blockade. Once again Cecil took a leading role both in Paris and London in attempting to swing opinion around to a more moderate position. Cecil was personally 'oppressed', his word, by the evidence of witnesses concerning the hunger on the Continent.[23] On 4 April he wrote to Lloyd George informing him that the economic situation was 'more and more alarming' and that the only chance to retrieve the situation was 'the immediate conclusion of

---

[21] The interviews between Gibson and Brockdorff-Rantzau, based on material in the German Foreign Ministry, are summarized in Arno J. Mayer, *Politics and Diplomacy of Peacemaking* (London, 1968), 756–8.

[22] Cecil Diary, 23 Apr. 1919, Cecil Papers, 51131, and Riddell Diary, 23 Apr. 1919, Riddell Papers, 62983.

[23] Cecil Diary, 3 Apr. 1919, Cecil Papers, 51131.

Peace with the subsequent removal of all artificial restrictions such as the blockade'.[24] Cecil was now heavily reliant on his two advisers Brand and Keynes. Both were pushing for a retreat from indemnities and blockade on Britain's side, as part of a package which would include American assistance to Europe and reductions in the Entente's debts to the United States.[25] On 5 April Cecil circulated a paper written by Brand urging exactly this formula: reparation needed to be mild if German economic life was to recover, while American assistance would have to be generous, not an easy objective considering 'the ignorance of Congress and the public'.[26] Cecil was all the more ardent when he learned the latest on conditions in eastern Europe from Smuts who returned from a special mission to Budapest via Vienna on 9 April. From Smuts Cecil heard of children fighting over buns in the streets of Vienna. One of the businessmen just back from Bavaria gave Cecil similar accounts of women and children 'all in the last stages of exhaustion' in the hospitals of Munich.[27] Keynes also heard a first-hand account from Smuts of his mission; with his encouragement Keynes began work on a large-scale version of Brand's plan to be entitled 'Scheme for the Rehabilitation of European Credit and for Financing Relief and Reconstruction'.[28] However, on 12 April Bernard Baruch, an American economic adviser, gave Cecil an early indication of the probable American reaction to such proposals. He wrote to Cecil arguing that complex government financial arrangements were all very well, but the first thing to be done was to raise the blockade. Everyone was aware, wrote Baruch, 'since the signing of the armistice, of the increasingly difficult economic situation in Europe. The Allied Governments have it in their power to correct this situation by removing restrictions that are hampering trade, but all have refused to do it'. Trade was 'smothered' by restrictions. The blacklist should have been abolished and the freedom of mail and cables restored five months ago, advised Baruch. He invited Cecil, in effect, to prove his good faith; it was the task of moderates to 'bend our energies to convincing our governments to do these things now'.[29]

But first the War Cabinet in London had to be persuaded. Among the leading figures of the government there was some sympathy for Cecil's position, as has been seen, but almost nobody from the front bench of the government was willing to take a public position. The silence of Milner was notable. Milner was thoroughly roused by the British press coverage of events in Germany, but he still would not venture out from the safety of privately circulated letters. For exam-

[24] Cecil to Lloyd George, 4 Apr. 1919, Cecil Papers, 51076.
[25] Brand to Altschul, 8 Apr. 1919, Brand Papers, 18, and Brand to Keynes, 9 Apr. 1919, Keynes Papers, RT/1/79.
[26] 'Notes submitted by Lord Robert Cecil on the general economic position (as circulated to the British Delegation)', 5 Apr. 1919, Brand Papers, 18.
[27] Cecil Diary, 10 Apr. 1919, Cecil Papers, 51131.
[28] Keynes to F. A. Keynes, 12 and 17 Apr. 1919, Keynes Papers, PP 45 F. A. and J. N. Keynes, vol. 9/19/13–14, and 'Scheme for the Rehabilitation of European Credit and for Financing Relief and Reconstruction', Apr. 1919, Brand Papers, 19.
[29] Baruch to Cecil, 12 Apr. 1919, Brand Papers, 18.

ple, he wrote in April to Kerr complaining of the tragic mistake of the 'lumping together by the press and public of all Germans in one indiscriminating category of abuse'. But Milner shied away from directly recommending a moderation in policy towards Germany: instead, he wrote that the division of Germany was probably inevitable, and even suggested that western Germany might require some encouragement, as he put it, 'to detach itself from the possibly Bolshevised, in any case chaotic, remainder'.[30] In any case, as new Colonial Secretary, Milner was distancing himself from the German problem. In mid–April he agreed to lead a Commission to Egypt to enquire into the severe nationalist unrest which had engulfed the Protectorate during March. Crawford captured the reaction of many to the news: 'He is tired and I fancy wants to quit the Government and get one of those cushy and agreeable jobs . . . On all sides one sees people trying to evacuate their posts, leaving the others the thankless task of cleaning up the war mess.'[31] Milner, one of the most well-informed moderates on the German problem, was in effect turning his back on the problem which had landed him in such hot water in the press, British policy towards the new Germany.

In London, Cecil found only one ally from within the government willing to face the chauvinists on the issue in public: Churchill. The Secretary of State for War had been doing his best to advertise all the latest intelligence from Germany and also the determination of his military chiefs, as he claimed, to raise the blockade.[32] Churchill carried his argument to the Prime Minister himself. To alert Lloyd George to the latest material, he sent a telegram to him on 7 April drawing his attention to the recent reports from Germany coming via Spa. 'I feel it my duty', he declared 'to tell you that all my military advisers without exception are all agreed that [the] interior situation in Germany is fast approaching catastrophe through want of food, raw materials and settled conditions'. Lloyd George returned a telegram assuring Churchill that he was 'fully alive' to the situation, and asking, perhaps impatiently, if Churchill had 'any suggestions as to anything more that can be done to improve [the] position.'[33] Churchill was also using public speeches to send signals to the Germans on the issue. On 11 April he told a lunch meeting of the Aldwych Club that 'a way of atonement is open to Germany. By combating Bolshevism, by being the bulwark against it, Germany may take the first step towards ultimate reunion with the civilised world.'[34] Both food and a milder peace, Churchill indicated, awaited Germany once she had dealt firmly with her own Bolsheviks. Next, on 14 April he told his colleagues in informal discussion at the War Cabinet that 'the War Office were

---

[30] Milner to Kerr, 24 Apr. 1919, Kerr Papers, GD 40/17/1176.

[31] Crawford Diary, 28 Apr. 1919, vol. xxxiv, Crawford Papers. The mission itself did not depart for Egypt until later in the year.

[32] *Parl. Debs.*, 5th ser., vol 114, 1199 (2 Apr. 1919), and Churchill to J. A. Spender, 8 Apr. 1919, Spender Papers, Add. MSS 46388.

[33] Churchill to Lloyd George, 7 Apr. 1919, and Lloyd George to Churchill, 8 Apr. 1919, Lloyd George Papers, F/8/3/37 and 38.

[34] *The Times*, 12 Apr. 1919.

strongly in favour of raising the blockade' and he quoted the opinions of Haking.[35] Alerted to Churchill's machinations, Cecil Harmsworth, the Minister for Blockade, immediately confronted Churchill, assuring him that the blockade was maintained 'exclusively on military grounds' (and not just to please the protectionists, he implied); the Americans, he warned, 'would jump at the proposal to raise the blockade', but only because of their plans for gaining commercial supremacy in Europe.[36] Harmsworth then rallied his men. Curzon, another opponent of any softening towards Germany, was informed of the exchange with Churchill, but he replied that feeling in the War Cabinet was swinging against the blockade.[37] Cecil's resolve on the issue was clear. He told Fisher that England 'doesn't realise a bit the serious economic situation on the Continent, that Germany is starving, and that every effort must be made to save her'.[38]

On 17 April, a decisive confrontation took place. Cecil took on Harmsworth at a War Cabinet meeting called to consider the 'relaxation' of the blockade. Harmsworth pleaded for the maintenance of the 'machinery' of the blockade as a weapon of war. Much to his relief, Henry Wilson supported him, insisting that, because Britain was 'still at war with Germany', the blockade could not be abandoned altogether; it was, he insisted, the victors' most powerful weapon to impose terms.[39] Cecil got the best of the debate and a resolution was passed 'in favour of the general principle of relaxation of trade restrictions' and empowering Cecil to proceed in that manner at the Supreme Economic Council 'subject to the approval of the Prime Minister'.[40] The first round went to Cecil.

Cecil's next hurdle was the Supreme Economic Council itself. At a meeting of the council on the afternoon of 23 April, Cecil introduced from the chair a series of handwritten resolutions designed to demolish the blockade. The resolutions proclaimed that in view of the 'exceedingly critical economic conditions of Europe' it was 'of urgent importance to re-establish as soon as possible normal commercial conditions in European countries', and especially Germany. Cecil proposed that all remaining regulations governing the trade of the Scandinavian countries, Holland, and Switzerland, especially the controls on the re-export of goods to Germany, and all restrictions on Germany's imports and exports (excepting gold, silver, securities, and war material), should be suspended. Each of the Allied and Associated Governments would be free to decide how much trade with Germany they wished to undertake. The relaxations were declared to be 'temporary' in character, and it was noted that they would be withdrawn 'if the German Government takes up a hostile attitude', or if it were replaced by a

---

[35] Thomas Jones Diary, 14 Apr. 1919, Thomas Jones Papers.

[36] Harmsworth to Churchill, 15 Apr. 1919, FO 800/250.

[37] Harmsworth to Curzon, 16 Apr. 1919, and Curzon to Harmsworth, 16 Apr. 1919, FO 800/250.

[38] H. Fisher to L. Fisher, 14 Apr. 1919, Fisher Papers, 206.

[39] Harmsworth was cheered by Wilson's stand, writing to Curzon that 'Winston must have been under a misapprehension as to the opinion of his military advisers' (Harmsworth to Curzon, 18 Apr. 1919, FO 800/250).

[40] Minutes of the War Cabinet, 17 Apr. 1919, CAB 23/10.

government which could not guarantee 'order and stability'—code, of course, for the threat to reimpose the blockade on a pro-Bolshevik government. The French delegates announced that they were 'forbidden' even to discuss relaxation of the blockade until *after* the signing of a preliminary peace. The United States and Italian delegates supported Cecil's resolutions and, as the recommendation of the three powers, the resolutions went forward to the Council of Four.[41]

The passage of these resolutions, at Cecil's urging, was without doubt a critical moment in the history of the British response to revolutionary Germany. In defiance of the wishes of the 'economic warriors', Britain was seeking to join with the United States in an effort to restore normal trade in Europe as soon as possible. The timing of this most significant gesture towards the government in Berlin was crucial. The Supreme Economic Council was suggesting that the blockade should be raised on the very eve of the victorious powers' first meeting with the German peace delegation in Paris. For, on 21 April, the Germans had replied to the Allies' invitation to send delegates to receive the treaty at Versailles, and the arrival of a large peace delegation was expected on 25 April. Moreover, when the resolution went through the Supreme Economic Council, the situation in Bavaria was still unresolved; not until 1 May did the *Freikorps* troops overwhelm the forces of the Councils' Republic and retake Munich. The raising of the blockade, therefore, before peace terms were accepted by the Germans, and before the communist threat in Bavaria was known to have been liquidated, would undoubtedly have been interpreted in Germany as a most significant move to bolster the Scheidemann government. What was proposed was tantamount to the Allies declaring to the world that they were leaving their most lethal weapon outside the peace conference room. It would have been an unmistakable signal that actual negotiations were contemplated at Versailles. The whole tone of the proceedings, and the entire process of negotiating terms with the Germans, might well have been different if the blockade had been raised before the presentation of the treaty to the Germans on 7 May.

However, it was not to be. On 2 May Lloyd George replied to Cecil on behalf of the Council of Four. He explained, with an almost sheepish economy of words, that 'some of us thought, on political grounds, that the present moment was not propitious and that it would be better to hold our hands, at any rate for a few days'.[42] The letter of rejection was read to the Supreme Economic Council on 5 May.[43] Thus the best efforts of the British moderates to overturn the policy of coercion, the policy which had underpinned the whole peace process up until this time, had come to nought.

[41] Minutes of the Supreme Economic Council, 23 Apr. 1919, in Kenneth Bourne and D. Cameron Watt (gen. eds.), *British Documents on Foreign Affairs: Reports and Papers from the Foreign Office Confidential Print. Series I, The Paris Peace Conference of 1919*, ed. Michael Dockrill (University Publications of America, 1989), xii. 323–9; and Cecil Diary, 23 Apr. 1919, Cecil Papers, 51131.

[42] Lloyd George to Cecil, 2 May 1919, Lloyd George Papers, F/6/6/39.

[43] Minutes of the Supreme Economic Council, 5 May 1919, in *Reports and Papers from the Foreign Office Confidential Print. Series I, The Paris Peace Conference of 1919*, ed. Dockrill, xii. 323–9.

Lloyd George and domestic pressure against a moderate peace

Why did Lloyd George make this choice? Part of the answer lies in the pressure put upon him in Paris at the end of April. On the precise issue of the raising of the blockade Lloyd George came under significant pressure from within the British delegation to stick to the weapon of economic warfare. Sir William Mitchell-Thompson, Harmsworth's appointee to the Supreme Economic Council, fought doggedly for his Minister of Blockade and against Cecil and the moderate majority of advisers around him. It is noteworthy that, in common with many of the leading advocates of indemnity in the House of Commons, men such as Claude Lowther and Gilbert Parker, Mitchell-Thompson was a front-rank figure in the Anti-Socialist Union.[44] In understanding his motives, therefore, it can be assumed that he had no sympathy whatsoever for the socialist-led government in Germany, and that he had a heightened awareness of the importance of obtaining a big indemnity in order to smother the advance of socialism at home, this being the characteristic position of British politicians on the ultra-patriotic Right.

Mitchell-Thompson and Cecil crossed swords first in early April. Mitchell-Thompson pressed Cecil to make preparations, not for the relaxation of the blockade, but for its tightening, especially with respect to food, in case the Germans refused to sign the preliminary peace; Cecil put him off and directed that the whole matter be 'postponed'.[45] A great quarrel naturally erupted when Cecil openly declared himself in favour of the raising of the blockade. On 23 April, the day Cecil achieved his breakthrough on the Supreme Economic Council, Mitchell-Thompson wrote immediately to Lloyd George recording his dissent from the Council's recommendation to raise the blockade. Such a move would only strengthen the Germans and delay their signature to any peace document, he argued. The sting was in the tail of Mitchell-Thomson's letter: raising the blockade, he wrote, would have a 'catastrophic' effect on 'British public opinion'—a calculated threat, of course, from a man representing forces whom the Prime Minister knew only too well had formidable powers to mould such 'public opinion', both in the press and in the House of Commons.[46] Mitchell-Thompson wrote a letter of protest to Cecil along the same lines. The blockade had 'enfeebled Germany, which is precisely what it was designed to do', he argued. 'Our object was and is, not to do what is best for Germany, but to do what is best for ourselves, by bending the German will to our own so they will sign our peace terms.' What Mitchell-Thompson dreaded was that the demoli-

---

[44] See the Appendix to K. D. Brown, 'The Anti-Socialist Union', in K. D. Brown (ed.), *Essays in Anti-Labour History* (London, 1973), 260.

[45] 'Note by Sir William Mitchell-Thompson, 8 Apr. 1918', with endorsement from Henry Wilson, FO 608/265.

[46] Mitchell-Thompson to Lloyd George, 23 Apr. 1919, Lloyd George Papers, F/45/4/1.

tion of the blockade would take away the Allies' power to dictate the complete programme of Victory. To raise the blockade, 'on the eve of the arrival of the German delegates', would convince the Germans that the Allies 'are losing cohesion', he warned.[47] That same evening Mitchell-Thompson was on the phone to Harmsworth in London complaining of the developments in Paris.[48] A letter that followed gives some indication of the reaction within the camp of the 'economic warriors'. Mitchell-Thompson described his 'wild and whirling day' at the Supreme Economic Council, battling against Cecil, Keynes, and Llewellyn Smith on the issue of blockade. He had been beaten, he explained, by a secret cabal at a lunchtime adjournment between Cecil, Keynes, and Llewellyn Smith. 'You will now have to bring what guns you can to bear', he advised Harmsworth. 'I think the House of Commons will surely rise in revolt at the idea of taking off the blockade before the signature of peace', he predicted darkly.[49]

Harmsworth swung into action. From Wemyss he obtained an instant opinion, over the telephone, that the Admiralty regarded the blockade as vital and that, with the German delegates' arrival at Versailles imminent, the concession Cecil planned should not be contemplated.[50] Walter Long came also to his assistance. Long's secretary, E. K. Packe, obligingly sent to Balfour, and he in turn to Lloyd George, his impressions of a recent journey through the occupied Rhineland to Spa. According to Packe factory chimneys in Belgium were clear, while every factory chimney in the Rhineland was smoking 'day and night', even on Sundays, and 'every man working like a beaver'. By this remarkable chimney test, Packe detected the looming danger of German commercial supremacy on the Continent, and argued that it was the Allies' duty to ensure that their own industries were geared up and could 'compete against the German trade' before unleashing the monster.[51] On 26 April, Mitchell-Thompson, no doubt encouraged by London, again took up his pen to send protests to the Prime Minister and to Cecil, but this time with the addition of his own intelligence on the condition of Germany. Against the dozens of detailed reports submitted by the officers of military intelligence, Mitchell-Thompson pitted a Foreign Office telegram recording the opinions of one secret agent 'Max', a source used by Walter Townley, British Ambassador in the Netherlands. According to 'Max', the German government's suggestion that they would refuse to sign a harsh peace was all 'bluff', for, under blockade conditions, the Germans were 'well aware that they can be starved into submission'. Mitchell-Thompson argued that the import of this was clear: the Germans were bluffing in every sense, even with regard to the seriousness of privation inside Germany. He sought to discredit the intelligence of Thornely Gibson in particular: 'Captain Gibson's views are entitled to

[47] Mitchell-Thompson to Cecil, 23 Apr. 1919, Lloyd George Papers, F/45/4/1.
[48] 'Secretary's Notes, 23 Apr. 1919', FO 800/250.
[49] Mitchell-Thompson to Harmsworth, 23 Apr. 1919, FO 800/250.
[50] H. W. Kennard to Harmsworth, 23 Apr. 1919, FO 800/250.
[51] E. K. Packe to Eric Drummond, 26 Apr. 1919, Lloyd George Papers, F/3/4/22.

respect, but there is a considerable body of opinion on the other side.' Furthermore, Mitchell-Thompson reminded the Prime Minister that the opposition of Henry Wilson and Admiral Hope to any abandonment of the blockade was on the record, and he noted that a further memorandum from Hope would soon be submitted.[52]

That opinion within the leadership circle was slipping back towards coercion was clear from the outcome of a War Cabinet meeting in London on 29 April. Churchill sought to build on Cecil's coup at the Supreme Economic Council by presenting a paper to the War Cabinet in favour of the 'relaxation' of the blockade, a paper purporting to be a summary of the views of 'the General Staff'. The paper put the case for the raising of the blockade in order to bolster the present government in Germany. However, Henry Wilson's opposition to Cecil's plans for raising the blockade, expressed to the War Cabinet on 17 April, was well remembered. This time the forces of opposition were better prepared. Bonar Law refused to discuss the paper, arguing that the resolution already given to Cecil by the War Cabinet on 17 April ought to have closed the matter. Curzon announced that he was firmly opposed to any further relaxation of the blockade for it would be impossible to reimpose it. Long, as First Lord of the Admiralty, supported Curzon's position. Eventually it was decided to come to 'no decision' in view of the fact that the German delegates had arrived in Paris and would be meeting the Allies to receive the terms of peace in the coming week. The old argument about avoiding any sign of 'weakness' won the day.[53]

Clearly, in opposing the moderation of Robert Cecil in Paris, Mitchell-Thompson was not speaking just for himself. A 'considerable body of opinion', as he had put it, on the Right of the British delegation had indeed been alarmed by the signs of a moderate consensus forming among those close to the Prime Minister. During April, among the Foreign Office staff and among the brass hats in particular, it became clear that the thesis of sham hunger and sham Bolshevism in Germany was down but not out. Sceptical remarks returned to the file-jackets of the Foreign Office documents. Significantly, new doubts were expressed about the quality of the intelligence reports coming from Germany. Eyre Crowe, one of the Foreign Office's most experienced Germany-watchers, commented on Captain Harding's report on 1 April that he found such reports a puzzle: one moment the officers suggested food was the 'panacea' for Germany, while the next they suggested military occupation by the Allies—'I remain sceptical', he minuted on his copy.[54] When Gibson's report of 4 April arrived Crowe reacted with irritation, demanding to know who Gibson was and declaring that he was 'quite at a loss to know what to do with a paper like this'.[55] On 17 April

[52] Mitchell-Thompson to Cecil, 26 Apr. 1919, copy in Lloyd George Papers, F/45/4/2.

[53] Minutes of the War Cabinet, 29 Apr. 1919, CAB 23/10.

[54] Crowe Minute, 1 Apr. 1919, on jacket of 'Harding to DMI, 30 Mar. 1919', FO 608/130.

[55] Crowe Minute, undated, on jacket of 'Report of situation in Germany by Capt. Thornely Gibson', FO 608/130.

Crowe spent two pages of a Foreign Office file-jacket lashing the 'sweeping generalisations' of the five business experts' report on internal conditions in Germany.[56] Tempers were evidently running short among the Foreign Office élite: Headlam-Morley minuted on Gibson's next report that he was fed up with the 'purely negative attitude' so many people adopted towards the internal problems of Germany—the comment clearly being directed at his superiors.[57] Cecil's staff also received remonstrances from the sceptics. Philip Waterlow, for example, was told by T. H. Urwick, a staff member of the Inter-Allied Economic Committee for the Rhine Territories, that Germans in the occupied territories were showing 'no signs whatever of malnutrition'. The 'Hun' had a plan to win the peace, Urwick wrote, 'to pretend that he is dying and on the verge of disruption'. Urwick accepted the conspiracy thesis. 'I am beginning to think it is all organised; his revolution, his uprisings, his riots, his army that silently disappears.'[58]

Most importantly, Gibson's evidence, and his access to the Prime Minister, came under attack from the brass hats. General Thwaites was displeased to discover Gibson at breakfast with Cecil and the Prime Minister on 23 April, the very day Cecil piloted his resolutions through the Supreme Economic Council. 'I rather object to these personal reports to the Prime Minister but as I was there myself I was able to control the discussion on this occasion', Thwaites assured Henry Wilson.[59] Then came a damaging blow to Gibson's credibility. On 1 May, General Haking, widely regarded as the senior officer with his finger closest to the German pulse (after almost six months of day to day negotiations on the Armistice Commission), and an opponent of the blockade, sent a memorandum attacking Gibson's report of 17 April. According to Haking the Gibson paper was too pessimistic; it contained opinions that were 'extraordinary'. Bolshevism was not imminent in Germany; and neither a USPD government nor an Allied occupation of Germany was required to eliminate the threat. General Hammerstein had assured Haking that very morning, he wrote, that 'the German Government is stronger now than it has ever been'.[60] The timing of Haking's memorandum was most significant: 1 May was the day of the liquidation of the Councils' republic in Munich. While Haking did not resile from his own personal support for the raising of the blockade as a requirement for the final destruction of Bolshevism in Germany, he had done the moderate cause a grave disservice; he had damaged the reputation of Thornely Gibson as a reliable observer, the key intelligence officer with privileged access to the Prime Minister. It was on the

[56] Crowe Minute, 17 Apr. 1919, on jacket of 'Conditions in Germany', by Henry Smith *et al.*, FO 608/130.

[57] Headlam-Morley Minute, 21 Apr. 1919, on jacket of 'Conditions in Germany', by Thornely Gibson, 17 Apr. 1919, FO 608/130.

[58] T. H. Urwick to P. Waterlow, FO 608/281.

[59] Thwaites to Henry Wilson, 23 Apr. 1918, Henry Wilson Papers, HHW 45.

[60] The memorandum was printed as Haking, 'Notes on a Paper by Captain Thornely Gibson, dated Berlin, 17 April, 1919', 1 May 1919, FO 371/3777.

very next day, 2 May, that Lloyd George wrote to Cecil to shut down the proposal to lift the blockade.

However, it was not only the pressure on Lloyd George in Paris on the issue of the blockade at the end of April 1919 that accounts for his desertion of the moderate programme with which he had flirted at Fontainebleau. Political pressures at home were considerable too. In fact, his decision to stick with the policy of coercion came after more than a month of sustained hostility from the Northcliffe newspapers and from the Conservative Party back bench over rumours of the Prime Minister's switch to the side of the moderate peacemakers.

From about the middle of March, with memories of the general strike and bloodshed in Berlin fading, the Northcliffe press pumped out a stream of articles advising against any consideration being shown to the Germans in the coming peace terms. The newspapers offered the special Northcliffe mixture of populist chauvinism: anti-German and anti-Bolshevik articles appeared side by side with articles almost left-wing in tone—for example, articles sympathetic to the miners' case at the Sankey Royal Commission and articles taking swipes at the 'old Tories' in the Lloyd George government. The *Daily Mail* in particular launched frequent editorial salvoes against the Prime Minister because of his 'weakness' at the Peace Conference. Readers received almost daily harangues on the timidity of Lloyd George and Wilson, the consequent delay in the peace settlement, the refusal of the leaders to send military forces against the Russian Bolsheviks, the reluctance of the leaders to pressure Germany to surrender Danzig to the Poles, and the alleged concern of Wilson and Lloyd George for a treaty that would leave no grievances in Germany.[61] For the *Daily Mail*, the place of the German revolution in all of this was clear: it had never taken place. Democracy was a mask obscuring Junkerdom. To drive this point home to readers every day, beginning on 7 April, the *Daily Mail* inserted in pride of place at the head of every leader column a quotation encapsulating this necessary myth. Entitled 'The Warning', the quotation read: 'They will cheat you yet those Junkers! Having won half the world by bloody murder, they are going to win the other with tears in their eyes crying for mercy.'[62] The quotation remained in place every day until the peace was concluded.

From his new position as editor of *The Times*, Wickham Steed appeared to be Northcliffe's loyal lieutenant in this campaign to ensure a 'stern' peace. He promised Northcliffe that he would keep up the pressure on Lloyd George and 'keep the bayonet in the ribs of them all'.[63] Steed lacked no small sense of his own importance. He wrote to G. S. Freeman, his deputy editor, that 'I am convinced that if the paper is to wield all the influence it ought to have it will need

[61] e.g. *Daily Mail* editorials, 'The Parting of the Ways', 20 Mar., 'Ten Weeks of Talk', 24 Mar., 'Conference Talks, Bolsheviks Act', 25 Mar., 'Real Weakness of Bolshevism', 27 Mar., 'Trying to Tickle the Tiger', 7 Apr., and 'The Danzig Wobble', 8 Apr. 1919.

[62] *Daily Mail*, 7 Apr. 1919. The source was given as 'Carl Rosemeier, a German in Switzerland, to the Allies'. Rosemeier was a German exile, and the quotation was, of course, originally directed at the wartime German government, not the Scheidemann government.

[63] Steed to Northcliffe, 30 Mar. 1919, Steed Papers, Daily Memorandums to Northcliffe Box.

to lay down the law rather than to follow the guidance of any sort of constituted authority'.[64] Part of the process of 'laying down the law' was to attack the intelligence on Germany which clearly provided support for the moderate approach to peacemaking. To this end, the Northcliffe press attempted, once again, to discredit reports of famine in Germany. By 17 March *The Times* was cautioning against placing any faith in the casual observations of soldiers or in the Germans' own representations concerning famine. The letters page featured testimonials from men in occupied Germany, one a bishop, who had failed to detect any famine in Germany.[65] Those serving the government were quick to notice the new line in *The Times*. Edwyn Bevan at the PID was moved to protest, sending a letter to the editor complaining of his 'thoroughly dishonest' leaders on the German hunger; it was rejected for publication. As Bevan complained to Headlam-Morley, it was difficult for the government to rely on public opinion to support a wise policy in Germany 'if public opinion is constantly misled'.[66] It should be stressed that this campaign against the reality of privation in Germany was undertaken in the Northcliffe press in spite of the fact that first-hand accounts of the food crisis were dispatched to Northcliffe himself by his journalists in Paris. For example, on 12 March Valentine Williams sent to Northcliffe his account of a conversation with two of the British officers just returned from Berlin. Williams declared that 'their evidence is conclusive of the famished conditions of the Germans' who were 'half out of their minds with shock, worry and privation'.[67] That Lloyd George felt the pressure of the Northcliffe press was obvious. He complained to Riddell on 28 March that Wickham Steed had 'a personal animus against him because he [had] snubbed him'. Lloyd George openly confessed that 'these attacks in the press are most harmful'. The next day Riddell found Lloyd George 'still very angry about press criticism'.[68]

News of the Prime Minister's Fontainebleau Memorandum, first reported in general terms in the British press on 1 April, alarmed those at the centre of this press campaign. Steed told Northcliffe that Lloyd George was drifting to the Left, pulling at Wilson to follow 'on to a pro-German and pro-Bolshevik basis', and 'filling him up with the *Manchester Guardian*'.[69] The central obsession at the heart of the campaign against Lloyd George became clear. It was the indemnity that still shone brightest for Northcliffe among the spoils of war, and it was the indemnity—under the polite euphemism of 'reparation'—that was being decided in Paris in March and April. Northcliffe's bitterness over high taxation still

[64] Steed to Freeman, 13 Apr. 1919, Steed Papers, Freeman file.

[65] *The Times*, letter to the editor from Bishop Frodsham (chaplain to the Australian Imperial Force), 17 Mar. 1919.

[66] Bevan to Headlam-Morley, 17 Mar. 1919, HMP, HDLM OS Box 2.

[67] Valentine Williams to Northcliffe, 12 Mar. 1919, Northcliffe Papers, 62210A.

[68] Riddell Diary, 28 Mar. 1919, Riddell Papers, 62983. This was a reference to the quarrel with Steed in Oct. 1918 when Lloyd George had rejected Steed's submission on propaganda for the transition from war to peace, the article later printed under Northcliffe's signature.

[69] Steed to Northcliffe, 1 Apr.1919, Steed Papers, Daily Memorandums to Northcliffe Box.

fortified his determination to achieve a spectacular indemnity. In early March, Chamberlain had suggested that he might have to consider higher progressive taxes in his coming budget. This immediately provoked sharp attacks against him in the Northcliffe press.[70] Behind the scenes Northcliffe was especially fervent. In a note to Steed on 8 March, Northcliffe denounced the idea of higher taxes on profits as 'a mad proposition' and predicted that 'every ambitious young man will leave the country'; he warned Steed that Chamberlain was 'a fool', and 'quite capable of this madness'. Northcliffe announced that he was asking Freeman to 'see what active opposition to this insane idea can be commenced'.[71] The Northcliffe press was soon crusading on the issue of the indemnity from Germany as the alternative to confiscatory taxation at home. On 3 April the *Daily Mail* warned that, without an indemnity, British business and British workers would be 'under bondage for a century or more'. 'If we are to have a "levy of capital", let us begin with a levy of German capital', the paper suggested.[72] On 10 April the *Daily Mail* pinned down the Prime Minister on the issue. The Prime Minister was pledged to demand the whole cost of the war from Germany as a matter of right, argued the *Daily Mail*, helpfully reproducing large slabs of Lloyd George's election speech at Bristol on 12 December just to ram home the point. In making the case for the indemnity, it did not escape the *Daily Mail* that both the revolution in Germany and the claim to imminent famine needed to be discredited. The same editorial asserted that 'As Germany so often during the war "shammed dead" so now she is shamming poverty and Bolshevism'.[73]

Similar articles suddenly appeared elsewhere in the 'patriotic' press, all showing the same concern for discrediting the revolution in order to justify the indemnity. In the *Nineteenth Century*, for example, readers were assured that just as the revolution was a 'conjuring trick' to secure easier terms, so too the 'Jewish socialists' were being permitted to create chaos in Germany in order to deceive the Allies before the imminent return of the Kaiser. Harold Wyatt, the Navy Leaguer and recent National Party candidate, supplied even more alarmist copy. Lloyd George's pledges were all 'election gas'. Failure to get the indemnity would make 'financial disaster' inevitable, 'and revolution is likely to follow in its trail'. To secure the indemnity, the people had to realize that what was happening in Germany was all 'revolutionary camouflage'. 'The real truth is that the military party have never been shattered and have never relinquished command of the situation.' According to Wyatt, it was the unreconstructed German militarists who had organized, in a giant conspiracy, the recent strikes and riots in France, Britain, India, and Egypt.[74] Thus, to serve the needs of the indemnity demand, the counterfeit revolution thesis, no matter how fanciful, was revived.

[70] *Daily Mail*, editorial, 'A Warning to Mr Lloyd George', 15 Mar. 1919.
[71] Northcliffe to Steed, 8 Mar. 1919, Steed Papers, Northcliffe file.
[72] *Daily Mail*, editorial, 'Indemnities. How Much Shall We Get?', 3 Apr. 1919.
[73] *Daily Mail*, editorial, 'The Whole Cost: The Premier's Election Pledges', 10 Apr. 1919.
[74] Gertrude Kingston, 'Plus ça change, plus c'est la même chose!', and Harold F. Wyatt, 'Growth, or Dissolution?—Peace, or War?' *Nineteenth Century*, 606 (Apr. 1919).

Lloyd George did not hide his discomfort at the Northcliffe campaign from those closest to him in Paris. 'They call me a pro-German. That is a libel. I have a good mind to bring an action. I shall certainly say in public what I think about Northcliffe', he told Riddell on 5 April.[75] By no means, however, was the renewed hue and cry over the indemnity a mere propaganda stunt in newspapers and journals to embarrass the Prime Minister. Northcliffe and others were lending the support of their newspapers and journals to a broad movement being stirred up in the House of Commons by 'economic warriors' on the Conservative back bench. This movement had been long prepared. Leading members of the Unionist Business Committee and the Tariff Commission were in constant touch concerning the indemnity. Hewins noted in his diary that he was 'invariably' lunching at the Carlton Club, where he was 'very active on the indemnity question'. 'I have done my best daily on this question', he wrote.[76] Crawford also believed that Hewins was the focus of lobbying on the indemnity.[77] During March, Bonar Law came under sustained questioning in the House on the indemnity and gave evasive replies. In response, on 22 March Colonel Claude Lowther, a Conservative MP and former chairman of the Anti-Socialist Union, sent to Bonar Law a scheme of his own for extracting payments from Germany over the next fifty years. Lowther argued that it was the duty of the government to resist the 'whining German people' and 'International Jew financiers' who were desperately seeking 'to prove German's débâcle and inability to pay'. The government must present 'the bill in full'.[78] Bonar Law simply sent on the memorandum to Lloyd George, and to the three British members of the Reparations Commission, Hughes, Cunliffe, and Sumner.[79]

The strain on Bonar Law increased when the Right in the House of Commons got wind of the new attitude being adopted by Lloyd George in the aftermath of his Fontainebleau meetings. In an effort to combat the right-wing press, as Riddell had suggested, the Prime Minister himself gave an interview to Sisley Huddleston of the *Westminster Gazette* summarizing the new moderate course he intended to pursue.[80] On 1 April the existence of the Fontainebleau Memorandum, but not its contents, was reported in the *Daily Mail*.[81] The next day, Colonel Lowther launched a three-hour adjournment debate in the Commons on the problem of indemnities and the apparent intention of the government to treat its election pledges as disposable. Lowther insisted that Germany could pay the war costs of the victors, given time, International Commissioners who should act

---

[75] Riddell Diary, 5 Apr. 1919, Riddell Papers, 62983.

[76] Hewins Diary, summary entry for Oct.1918–13 May 1919, Hewins Papers.

[77] Crawford Diary, 7 Apr. 1919, vol. xxxiv, Crawford Papers.

[78] Lowther to Bonar Law, 22 Mar. 1919, and see Keynes's scathing commentary upon it in Keynes to Gower, 29 Mar. 1919, Bonar Law Papers, 97/1/9 and 16.

[79] Bonar Law to Lowther, 24 Mar. 1919, Bonar Law Papers, 101/3/34.

[80] Riddell Diary, 29 and 30 Mar. 1919, Riddell Papers, 62983, and Mayer, *Politics and Diplomacy of Peacemaking*, 627.

[81] *Daily Mail*, 'A Sane and Just Peace', 1 Apr. 1919.

like receivers for a bankrupt firm, and an Army of Occupation. Those who
pleaded Germany's present suffering were the same 'anti-English Englishmen'
who opposed the war, led by financiers whose real names were 'often biblical'.
Lowther also read a great slab from Lloyd George's speech at Bristol to remind
all of the pledges of the government. Lowther explained that he had only contempt for the argument that Germany might refuse to sign a treaty which
included payment for war costs: 'I take it that this is a peace by dictation, and
not a peace by negotiation', he declared. Other speakers from the Right, including Kennedy Jones, a former editor of Northcliffe's *Evening News*, and Page Croft
of the National Party, eagerly supported Lowther. Some drew the same lesson as
the press with regard to the condition of Germany: if stories of German starvation and Bolshevism were preventing the exaction of an indemnity, then these
stories must be German lies aimed at 'camouflaging the issue to get the Allies to
let her down lightly'. In reply, Bonar Law rather unconvincingly insisted that he
and the Prime Minister had only ever promised to collect from Germany what
she could pay, and not the whole cost of the war.[82] There was much bitterness
on the issue. In the smoking-room afterwards, Lowther told MacCallum Scott
that Bonar Law was '. . . a bounder . . . a pip . . . a small man. He has no insight,
no imagination, no big view'.[83] On 3 April Bonar Law confessed to Lloyd George
that he was having 'a bad time about indemnities' in the House of Commons. He
was perfectly frank about the political affiliation of the discontented: 'I do not
think I convinced anyone and probably nine out of ten of the Unionist members
at least were very disgusted.'[84]

The consequences were not long in emerging. At the House of Commons,
MacCallum Scott noticed Jones 'gathering around him a crowd of toughs who
are invading parlours hitherto sacred'.[85] Within a week of the adjournment
debate, Jones and Lowther formed a small committee, including Percy Hurd (the
Secretary of the Unionist Business Committee) and Edward Goulding (a prominent member of the FBI) to organize for a telegram and petition to be sent to
the Prime Minister on indemnities.[86] The telegram, eventually boasting the signatures of more than 300 MPs, was sent on 8 April and called upon Lloyd
George to stand by his election pledges and present 'the complete financial claim
of the Empire' to Germany.[87] The telegram was a signal of grave danger for
Lloyd George. He reacted bitterly, describing Kennedy Jones as 'a dirty dog'.
Bonar Law, who had flown to Paris to consult with Lloyd George, declared it to
be a matter of 'grave importance'. He implored Lloyd George to return to
England for a few days.[88] In the first instance, a telegram in reply was drawn up

[82] *Parl. Debs.*, 5th ser., vol. 114, 1304 ff. (2 Apr. 1919).
[83] MacCallum Scott Diary, 2 Apr. 1919, MacCallum Scott Papers, MS Gen. 1465.
[84] Bonar Law to Lloyd George, 3 Apr. 1919, Bonar Law Papers, 101/3/40.
[85] MacCallum Scott Diary, 8 Apr. 1919, MacCallum Scott Papers, MS Gen. 1465.
[86] *The Times*, 9 Apr. 1919.
[87] Lowther, 'Germany's Debt', *Daily Mail*, 10 Apr. 1919.
[88] Riddell Diary, 29 and 30 Mar. 1919, Riddell Papers, 62983,

assuring Kennedy Jones that the government intended 'to stand faithfully by all the pledges we gave to the constituencies in respect of the peace terms and of the social programme'. The reference to 'the social programme' was then deleted from the telegram before its dispatch, Bonar Law telling Lloyd George that the words would be 'unnecessarily provocative in the state of his party's mind at that moment'—a telling admission of the Conservative Party's continuing reluctance to acknowledge the expectations of social reformers within the Coalition.[89]

Lloyd George must have been in no doubt that his right-wing critics in Paris and London were now working in harmony against him. For, while the House of Commons erupted during the first ten days of April, the great battle over reparations was reaching a climax in Paris. As usual, resistance to moderation in Paris was led by the Australian Prime Minister, Billy Hughes. The long negotiations over reparations need not be detailed here, but the connections used by Hughes in an effort to maintain pressure on Lloyd George do deserve emphasis. The diary of Robert Garran, Hughes's most supportive aide during his sojourn in Paris, contains details of the press coverage of the conference and of Hughes's various meetings with pressmen. On 1 April Garran noted that 'For three days the *Daily Mail* has been beating its joss and giving some shrewd blows to Lloyd George and Wilson'. On the same day Hughes dined with Leo Maxse who was 'very bitter against L. G. and [his] excessive deference to Wilson'. The Northcliffe journalist G. Ward Price was a guest at a special dinner in mid-April, and Colonel J. H. Morgan, the member of the DMI most sceptical of the German hunger, was also in contact with the Australian camp.[90] An emissary from the 'economic warriors' in London, Christabel Pankhurst, visited the Australian Prime Minister's headquarters during early April, and was ferried to and fro between Hughes, Cunliffe, and Sumner.[91]

The final debate over reparations among the British delegates is also noteworthy as it illustrates the difficulties facing both moderates and 'hard men' as they tried to weigh two different factors: the danger to the Lloyd George Coalition coming from the right-wing press and the 'economic warriors' if the peace were seen to be too moderate, on the one hand, and the danger of driving Germany to revolution if the peace were too harsh, on the other. Hughes faced his showdown with Lloyd George on 11 April, with the newspapers still filled with news of the Conservative back-benchers' telegram. Hughes was summoned to Lloyd George's flat for an early breakfast meeting, with Lloyd George, Bonar Law, the three other Dominion Prime Ministers, and Cunliffe and Sumner. Lloyd George introduced the compromise which he had evolved after long discussions with Wilson, Clemenceau, and Smuts, over the preceding fortnight. About £10,000 million was the most Germany could pay. Under the formula to

---

[89] David Lloyd George, *Memoirs of the Peace Conference* (New Haven, 1939), i. 375.

[90] Garran Diary, 1 and 17 Apr. and 1 May 1919, Garran Papers, Series 5, Box 3, and Latham to Ella Latham, 2 June 1919, Latham Papers, MS 1009/21/1450.

[91] Sumner to Hughes, 7 Apr. 1919, Hughes Papers, MS 1538/24/88.

be adopted, Germany would accept responsibility for all loss and damage arising from the war—so that Lloyd George could go through the motions of presenting 'the whole bill'—and then, under the cover of reparations, the British Empire would claim a share in order to fund her pensions. This transparent attempt to get war costs by the back door was agreed to by the Americans, as Lloyd George explained, only after 'considerable difficulty'. (In fact, Smuts had been inveigled into defending the idea in a controversial memorandum sent to Wilson in late March.)[92] Bonar Law estimated that the British Empire would get £2,200 million. Lloyd George added the sweetener that the German colonies were worth probably £5,500 million.

Hughes, and only Hughes, refused to accept the compromise. Unless war costs were specifically claimed, he threatened, the politicians would have to reckon with 'a most formidable public opinion'—he might have spelled Northcliffe's name. After two hours of debate, Lloyd George announced that he must go to the Supreme Council and demanded the support of the Dominion Prime Ministers. Still Hughes held out. The discussion continued in Lloyd George's absence. There were surprisingly candid admissions. Sumner pleaded with Hughes to appreciate the sleight of hand achieved by Lloyd George: although war costs were not listed as a recoverable claim for the British Empire, pensions were, and 'this was a very wide interpretation of reparations'. Cunliffe acknowledged that he had estimated the German capacity to pay at a much larger figure in December 1918, but, he admitted, 'at the time this had really been little more than a shot in the dark as he had been pressed to arrive at it between a Saturday and a Monday'. Bonar Law's fear of the House of Commons was visible in all his contributions to the debate. He declared that if the Dominion Prime Ministers refused to support Lloyd George's compromise 'if he were in the Prime Minister's place, he would not be prepared to face the House of Commons'. Speaking for himself, he explained, if he were to tell the House of Commons that Britain had abandoned a claim to the principal costs of the war then 'the position would be hopeless'. But the compromise offered a face saver. It was, explained Bonar Law, tantamount to saying 'we think you ought to pay the whole costs and you must recognise this; recognising, however, that you cannot pay the whole you must pay on the categories that have been proposed'. Under this formula, said Bonar Law, 'he would not be afraid to face the House'. Hughes reminded all that 'the real trouble originated with the acceptance of the Fourteen Points', a reference back to the original sin of Lloyd George, as he saw it, in agreeing to the Lansing Note. It was Botha who introduced the German revolution into the debate. He supported Lloyd George's compromise, arguing

---

[92] On Smuts's controversial memorandum of 31 Mar. 1919 in favour of pensions being included within the meaning of the British proviso to the Fourteen Points, see the 'Memorandum' in W. K. Hancock and Jean van der Poel (eds.), *Selections from the Smuts Papers, iv. November 1918–August 1919* (Cambridge, 1966), 96–8, and Robert Skidelsky, *John Maynard Keynes: Hopes Betrayed, 1883–1920* (New York, 1986), 396.

that 'another reason for closing with the present agreement was that Germany must not be allowed to become Bolshevist. If Germany should join Russia, the situation would be very serious.' Here was a reminder of the great external factor hanging over the proceedings in Paris, in the forefront of Botha's mind no doubt following discussions with his Defence Minister Smuts, just back from Hungary. Hughes, secure in his belief that the German revolution was all humbug, as already seen, remained immovable. Private talks with Hankey following the meeting produced no solution. Indeed, Hughes sent a letter to Lloyd George later that same day refusing his agreement to the bargain that had been struck on reparations, and even complaining that he should be pressured to assent. As Hughes put it in cables to Australia, 'I was asked to swallow every word I had said about the inclusion of costs of war'. It was obvious to Lloyd George and Hankey that Hughes was signalling his intention to grandstand against the compromise on reparations, courtesy of his contacts in the Northcliffe press.[93]

Lloyd George himself, savaged daily by the Northcliffe papers, pursued by telegrams from his angry back bench in London, threatened by Hughes in Paris—yet surrounded by intelligence on the threat of a second revolution in Germany—appears to have vacillated constantly on the central issue of the coercion of Germany. On the matter of the indemnity, he presented two faces. Riddell recalled him saying 'one day' that 'If they want a man who will compel German women to give their jewels up, they had better get someone else to make the peace. Let us deal on broad lines. Don't let us be small and petty. Don't let us do things that will make for bitterness in the future.' And yet, on 9 April, in the aftermath of the famous telegram from London, Riddell found his tone on indemnities 'very changed'. 'Today he said the Germans would have to pay the uttermost farthing. He pushed aside economic difficulties and said that if the Germans decline to fulfil their obligations we can compel them by an economic blockade involving starvation and stoppage of trade.'[94]

Only a week later, however, he appeared to have set his course on resistance to the hard men. Having faced down Hughes in Paris, Lloyd George announced that he was returning to London to answer his accusers on the back bench in a major speech to the House of Commons. He appeared before the House to give a report on progress at the Peace Conference on 16 April. The parting of the ways, perhaps, had been reached. However, it is vital to note that Lloyd George did not use the opportunity to argue the merits of a peace of moderation for Germany as he had done before his audience of intimates at Fontainebleau. In his speech, he did attack the idea of a full-scale military intervention in Russia, denouncing it as 'the greatest act of stupidity that any Government could

[93] Hankey to Hughes, 9 Apr. 1919, Hughes to Lloyd George, 11 Apr. 1919, and Hankey to Hughes, 11 Apr. 1919, Hughes Papers, MS 1538/24/89, 92, and 95; Minutes of the British Empire Delegation, no. 19A, 11 Apr. 1919, CAB 29/28; Hughes to Watt, Cable no. 343, 13 Apr. 1919, Australian Archives, CP 290/3.
[94] Riddell Diary, 9 Apr. 1919, Riddell Papers, 62983.

possibly commit'—a stance which mollified the Labour Party. He also declared support for the League of Nations. But there was little else in the speech that reflected moderation. Lloyd George defended the decision not to publish the peace terms before presenting them to the enemy. He defended the speeches that he had made during the election campaign, going so far as to assert that practically all shades of opinion and 'every political leader' had been in favour of indemnities at the time of the election. Then, turning to his tormentors in the press, he launched a wickedly entertaining attack on Northcliffe as the very travesty of the 'reliable source' who, he suggested, had taken it upon himself to tip off the back-bench MPs concerning the Prime Minister's alleged treachery in Paris. Without actually naming Northcliffe, but naming 'Broadstairs' as his abode, he reviewed the recent record of the 'reliable source'. He recalled Northcliffe's 'War to Peace' manifesto of November 1918, noting that it had 'not a word about indemnities, not a word about the cost of the War', but rather, only a commitment to reparation. He recalled the Northcliffe newspapers' free columns for the Labour Party during the election campaign, and warned that, had things gone the way of the press baron, Ramsay MacDonald and Philip Snowden might well have been Britain's representatives at the Peace Conference. Tapping his forehead, Lloyd George announced that he would rather rely on a grasshopper than on such a 'reliable source'.[95]

The speech was generally regarded as a triumph. Certainly it had been carefully prepared; Lloyd George had rehearsed it in front of his trusted advisers on the destroyer returning him to England.[96] Without doubt it was superbly crafted to shore up Lloyd George's leadership of the Coalition. As Chamberlain wrote, 'there was but one verdict throughout the House as to his success'.[97] The secret of its success was obvious. Lloyd George had chosen to attack one of the most widely despised advocates of a harsh peace towards Germany—Northcliffe—but Lloyd George did not dare attack the idea itself of a harsh peace towards Germany. Instead, he personalized the issue. In focusing upon Northcliffe, he focused upon a man distrusted in the Conservative Party as dangerously unreliable, a man with a vaulting ambition and a penchant for populism, and a carping critic of the 'old Tories' still in command of the Conservative Party. He was the only press baron who had dared to offer the Labour Party gestures of support during the election, the miners gestures of support in the face of a coal strike, and the soldiers gestures of support during the demobilization riots, all of which had scandalized both Liberals and Conservatives.[98] On the key issue of

[95] *Parl. Debs.*, 5th ser., vol. 114, 2936 ff. (16 Apr. 1919); Crawford Diary, 17 Apr. 1919, vol. xxxiv, Crawford Papers, 34.

[96] Alice Blanche Balfour Diary, 17 Apr. 1919, Whittingehame Papers, GD 433/2/11.

[97] Chamberlain to Ida Chamberlain, 18 Apr. 1919, Chamberlain Papers, AC 5/1/125.

[98] For examples of criticism of the Northcliffe press for encouraging unrest during the demobilization period see Crawford Diary, 14 Jan. 1919, vol. xxxiv, Crawford Papers, F. S. Oliver to Austen Chamberlain, 16 Mar. 1919, Chamberlain Papers, AC 14/6/107, and J. A. Pease to Elsie Pease, 29 Jan. 1919, Gainford Papers, 525.

peace with Germany, however, Lloyd George did not attack Northcliffe as promoting an impossibly harsh programme. Quite the reverse. In his speech he presented Northcliffe as an unprincipled opportunist on indemnity, and he, Lloyd George, as the original proponent of the concept, and the only reliable man to see it through. The reaction among Conservatives was all that Lloyd George could have hoped for—that is, if defending his hold on office was the vital objective. 'This afternoon the Carlton [Club] was full of men rejoicing in the savage punishment inflicted on Northcliffe by the Prime Minister. No castigation could have been better deserved', wrote Crawford. 'The man is a bully and deserves no sympathy.'[99] Those 'old Tories' who had suffered so much criticism in the Northcliffe press were delighted too. Chamberlain believed that Lloyd George had now broken spectacularly with Northcliffe. 'Lloyd George did his part admirably . . . I never liked him better', wrote Chamberlain.[100] 'It was wonderfully well done', wrote Bonar Law to Carson.[101] 'Lloyd George seems to have wiped the floor with Northcliffe', wrote Derby to Curzon.[102] Throughout the Tory establishment the speech was regarded as a triumph—as an attack on Northcliffe, not as an attack on Germanophobia and indemnity hunting.

Had Lloyd George chosen to present and defend the position he had taken at Fontainebleau, or had he chosen to argue for the suspension of the blockade, the speech would have been far more controversial. Lloyd George may well have chosen to prepare public opinion for the major shift in British policy on the blockade, to which Cecil, as has been seen, was now committed. However, Lloyd George did not for a moment suggest that the raising of the blockade was a possibility. He spoke of the dangers of Bolshevism, and to illustrate the seriousness of hunger on the Continent he related Smuts's story of children fighting for bread distributed by British soldiers in the streets of Vienna. At this point Commander Kenworthy, the new Labour member for Central Hull, interjected 'The blockade?', but Lloyd George ignored it. Not once in the remainder of his speech did he refer to the economic blockade. It was left to Robert Cecil to indicate some movement in that direction, a difficult task, for he would not have the permission of the War Cabinet to pursue relaxation until the next day. He was forced to declare at the outset of his speech that he was speaking as Chairman of the Supreme Economic Council: 'I am not speaking in any sense as a member of the Government.' He then made an eloquent plea for the removal of the blockade as soon as possible, on humanitarian grounds, and gave evidence from Bavaria and Austria of the terrible suffering of the ordinary people. 'It is essential to get rid of the blockade completely, and at the earliest possible moment', he declared. 'The whole fabric of our civilisation is in danger.' But Cecil did not definitely put the case for the removal of the blockade against Germany *before* the terms

[99] Crawford Diary, 16 and 17 Apr. 1919, vol. xxxiv, Crawford Papers.
[100] Austen Chamberlain to Ida Chamberlain, 18 Apr. 1919, Chamberlain Papers, AC 5/1/125.
[101] Bonar Law to Carson, 17 Apr. 1919, Bonar Law Papers, 101/3/47.
[102] Derby to Curzon, 17 Apr. 1919, Derby papers, 28/2/2.

were presented, in order that a signature to peace terms could be negotiated
rather than coerced from the defeated enemy.[103]

Considering all the events of April, therefore, the decision of Lloyd George in
early May to shut down Cecil's proposal for the raising of the blockade must be
seen primarily as the end result of domestic pressure. In mid-April Lloyd George
had decided to stand and fight against one prominent Germanophobe, but not
against Germanophobia. Accused of abandoning plans for a great indemnity, he
had rounded on his accusers, but had not thrown over the indemnity. On the eve
of the presentation of the treaty to the Germans, he dared not risk alienating the
majority of the House of Commons. Thus Cecil was to be disappointed, and the
policy of coercion cemented in place for the coming process of peacemaking with
Germany.

Without doubt there was a second factor of significance also in Lloyd George's
decision not to take up the struggle for a moderate process in the negotiation of
peace: the receding threat of a second revolution in Germany. During the last
week of April news arrived in Paris of the successful progress of the *Freikorps* in
its military campaign against the revolutionaries in Bavaria. By 1 May, the city
of Munich was in the hands of General von Epp's *Freikorps*. The government in
Berlin had now survived the uprising of the Spartacists in Berlin in January, the
general strike and street-fighting in Berlin in March, numerous smaller engagements in the smaller cities of northern Germany, and finally the crisis of the
Councils' Republic in Bavaria. When Lloyd George rejected the Supreme
Economic Council's advice for the lifting of the blockade, therefore, he could do
so secure in the knowledge that the most significant 'Bolshevik' eruption in
Germany had just been brutally extinguished.

There is no doubt that such considerations were placed before Lloyd George
at this time. For example, on 2 May Borden sent to him a copy of the 'Daily
Review of the Foreign Press' containing an interview with Karl Kautsky; Borden
urged Lloyd George to note especially the view of Kautsky that Bolshevism
would never be able to triumph in Germany for reasons of history and economy.[104] Lloyd George was apparently still ready to believe that things inside
Germany were not so bad. This was clear to General Ewart when he visited Paris
on 6 May, the day before the terms were to be handed to the Germans. He
received a last-minute invitation to lunch with the Prime Minister, and there gave
a report on conditions in Berlin, including details of his interviews with
Brockdorff-Rantzau. Whether Germany would or would not sign a peace treaty
interested Lloyd George above all, and Ewart informed him that Brockdorff-
Rantzau was unlikely to recommend signing an unduly harsh treaty. At that
Lloyd George turned to the subject of food. Ewart's diary records the conversation: 'He asked me if the reports he had heard about there being plenty of food
in Germany were true, and I explained to him that it was only the rich who got

---

[103] *Parl. Debs.*, 5th ser., vol. 114, 2961 ff. (16 Apr. 1919).
[104] Borden to Lloyd George, 2 May 1919, Lloyd George Papers, F/5/3/50.

it by swindling over the food cards.' Later that day, Ewart discovered Cecil much more concerned about food, but he too admitted to having received 'conflicting reports'. Ewart even encountered a readiness to use food as a weapon on Cecil's own staff. E. F. Wise of the Ministry of Food interviewed Ewart in the evening and appeared ready to slow down the food assistance. 'I told him what I had done in the matter of food relief for the Germans', wrote Ewart in his diary, 'and that I proposed seeing Agnew [of the Red Cross] about the disposal of the surplus food parcels in Rotterdam. He advised doing nothing about selling more food-stuffs to the Germans for the next two or three weeks, when the position as regards the Germans might be clearer.'[105]

Not only was the economic blockade still locked in position, but Britain had acquiesced further in arrangements laid down by France for the actual process of peacemaking. The Germans had been invited to send delegates to Versailles in mid-April. Brockdorff-Rantzau responded at first that Germany would send only messengers unless it was the intention of the victorious powers to negotiate.[106] The Allies replied that messengers were unacceptable and that the Germans must send fully accredited representatives with power to sign a peace. To this the Germans agreed on 21 April, 'supposing that, after the remittance of the project of the preliminaries, it is intended to negotiate on their contents'.[107] When the Germans accepted the invitation to set out to Versailles, therefore, the possibility of a negotiated settlement hung in the balance. On 26 April, however, Hankey had agreed to French arrangements whereby the Germans would be strictly confined to their hotels at Versailles until summoned forth to receive the terms. All communication with the Allied delegations, including telephone calls, was to be conducted through Colonel Henry, the French officer in charge of managing the Germans at Versailles.[108] On 27 April, Clemenceau told Steed proudly that 'he had succeeded in eliminating all verbal discussion with the Germans'.[109] With these arrangements in place, and with Lloyd George's decision to overrule Cecil and hold the economic blockade in place too, the last chance for a negotiated peace at Versailles was quietly snuffed out.

The Trianon Palace ceremony and the reassertion of an unrepentant Germany

The German Peace Delegation, led by Brockdorff-Rantzau, arrived in Versailles by train on 29 April. The Germans were housed in a number of adjoining hotels in Versailles, surrounded by barbed wire and gawking tourists.[110] In choosing

---

[105] Ewart Diary, 6 May 1919, Ewart Papers, 73/88/1.

[106] On German Foreign Office representations at Spa, see Haking to Thwaites, 19 Apr. 1919, Henry Wilson Papers, HHW 45.

[107] General Nudant to Foch, 21 Apr. 1919, Henry Wilson Papers, HHW 45.

[108] Hankey, 'Draft Instructions for the German Delegation at Versailles', 26 Apr. 1919, WCP 658, copy in Australian Archives, A 981/1/41 part 1.

[109] Steed to Northcliffe, 27 Apr. 1919, Steed Papers, Memorandums to Northcliffe Box.

[110] Jessie Whitehead to her mother, 26 May 1919, Whitehead Papers, Peter Liddle Archive.

persons for the delegation, the new German government had agreed in March that 'the guiding principle is that of including personalities who might facilitate the renewal of international contacts of all sorts—men of world renown who are qualified to represent the Reich and whose presence might prevent degrading treatment'. Walter Simons told the Cabinet that it was vital to separate the old Germany from the new in the minds of the victors. There were six major German delegates, giving a fair representation of the balance of power in the new republic: Brockdorff-Rantzau, the aristocrat and diplomat who had declared for the republic, Otto Landsberg of the SPD, the former People's Deputy from the revolutionary government, now the Minister of Justice, Robert Leinert of the SPD, former Chairman of the National Congress of Soldiers' and Workers' Councils and now President of the Prussian National Assembly, Josef Giesberts of the Centre Party, founder of the Christian Trade Union movement and Minister for Posts, Karl Melchior, the banker, and Professor Walter Schücking of the German Peace Society.[111] The Associated Powers could scarcely complain about its composition. It was a delegation led by a reformed member of the old ruling class—the type of man whom the victors, by means of countless gestures of hostility to the revolution, had signalled was their preference in dealing with Germany—and supported by men of the Centre and Left of German politics. None the less, the German preparations were all in vain. No contact and no verbal discussion were permitted. The political forces whose influences were now so dominant in Paris and London were determined to ignore the new Germany and pin the sins of the old upon it.

The ceremony organized for the actual handing over of the peace terms was to be most controversial and deserves some analysis. The occasion was planned for the afternoon of 7 May, the fourth anniversary of the sinking of the *Lusitania*, and took place at the Trianon Palace in Versailles, the headquarters of the Supreme War Council and 'a fashionable hotel in the summer for naughty Parisians'.[112] Much stage-management attended the ceremony. On arrival the German delegates faced a walk down a long corridor to a large salon past dozens of military officers. Here Latham, the Australian, had suggested that all the officers remove their caps in order to avoid the necessity of saluting. His description of the delegates captures that typical desire among the victors to see the Germans as both defeated and defiant. 'They looked beaten men . . . thrashed—but with nastiness left beneath', wrote Latham. 'Brockdorff-Rantzau looks a gentleman—some of the others [do not] possess any distinction and the appearance of some of them is almost repulsive. They are typically Boche.'[113] Brockdorff-Rantzau led his delegation into the salon, the pre-war dining-room of the hotel,

---

[111] Minutes of the German Cabinet, 18 and 22 Mar. and 25 Apr. 1919, Charles B. Burdick and Ralph H. Lutz (eds.), *Political Institutions of the German Revolution, 1918–1919* (New York, 1966), 264, 277, and 281.

[112] 7th Earl Stanhope to 6th Countess Stanhope, 9 Jan. 1918, Stanhope Papers, U 1590 C. 578/18.

[113] Latham to Ella Latham, 8 May 1919, Latham Papers, MS 1009/21/1443 (*a*).

where more than 200 invited guests had fallen into absolute silence. The German delegates were seated at one end of a square of tables facing the leaders of the Allied and Associated Powers at the other. Clemenceau stood up and gave a short speech. He explained that the Germans would have fifteen days to respond to the treaty in writing—there would be no discussion. The treaty, printed in French and English only, was handed to Brockdorff-Rantzau.

The German Foreign Minister, while remaining seated, then gave a speech in response. This speech was to excite outrage in the press, and much anger too among Allied delegates. The content, written by Walter Simons and Kurt Hahn, was indeed strong, but not defiant. It contained a frank admission of German defeat and German defencelessness. But it noted also that the Germans had one protection left which the victors had themselves supplied, namely, their commitments to the Fourteen Points as conveyed to the Germans in the Lansing Note. The former German government, he conceded, had contributed to the disaster of war, but Brockdorff-Rantzau protested at the idea that Germany alone was guilty of causing the war. The policy of competitive imperialism was to blame, he asserted, and he asked for a neutral commission to determine the issue of the causes of the war. The German people, he noted, sincerely believed they were engaged in a war of defence. He proclaimed Germany's willingness to contribute to the reparation of the devastated areas. Most importantly, he upbraided the Allies for causing the deaths of hundreds of thousands of civilians in Germany as a result of the blockade during the six months since the armistice.

As this was the only face-to-face encounter permitted between the victors and the vanquished, the dynamics of the meeting are worthy of some attention. Brockdorff-Rantzau's decision to remain seated caused offence as it was represented as a calculated insult. Two explanations soon circulated; one, that he was too nervous and ill to stand, and the other, that he wished to give the character of a round-table negotiation even to this first encounter between victor and vanquished.[114] The second of these explanations is certainly consistent with the policy he had pursued over the preceding weeks. Possibly it was Billy Hughes who first roused resentment at Brockdorff-Rantzau's decision to remain seated and portrayed this as an insult. He scribbled a note to Lloyd George during the ceremony: 'Why does Clemenceau allow Rantzau to address him seated? He stood up and so did we all.'[115] The delivery of the speech caused adverse comment too. Clemenceau's speech was read through as a whole and then translated into English and German. Brockdorff-Rantzau's speech, however, was translated sentence by sentence, by two German translators, working from the one copy of the speech passed back and forth.[116] A number of persons present noted that the

[114] *Observer*, 11 May 1919, and Klaus Schwabe, *Woodrow Wilson, Revolutionary Germany, and Peacemaking, 1918–1919* (Chapel Hill, NC, 1985), 331.
[115] Note on torn piece of paper headed 'To the Prime Minister', Hughes Papers, MS 1538/24/510.
[116] Lord Hankey, *The Supreme Control at the Paris Peace Conference, 1919* (London, 1963), 153–4.

German speakers and English speakers gained different impressions of the speech. This may well have been due to the translation. One German-speaking English secretary, for example, found the speech in German 'unrepentant certainly, but not without a certain impressiveness', while English speakers found the German translator used language of 'insolence and studied offensiveness'.[117] One journalist noted that the speech was translated into 'raucous Middle West American by a German from St. Louis'.[118] Latham reported that the translator had 'a most objectionable American accent—the real offensive sort'.[119] President Wilson also told Derby that the translator had made the impression worse by seeming to 'spit out venom in every word'.[120]

Whether it was the delivery, the translation, or the content itself that was offensive, the reaction of the leading British and Dominion delegates to the speech was almost universally hostile. Bonar Law professed to find in Brockdorff-Rantzau's speech 'the old unteachable Prussian Spirit' and he told Henry Wilson that it made him 'tingle with rage'.[121] Lloyd George returned from the ceremony 'exhausted with emotion'. He told Frances Stevenson that he wanted to get up and hit Brockdorff-Rantzau, and explained the story of Billy Hughes's note of protest. He confessed that, for the first time, he 'felt the same hatred for them that the French feel'.[122] In the evening, while the band of the Royal Artillery played to a huge crush of people at the Hôtel Majestic, Headlam-Morley had a word with Lloyd George. He found him 'full of indignation. He said they were insolent beyond description, not so much merely in what they said, but in the manner in which they said it; he said that he had never been so angry with the Germans throughout the war and that the Colonials were in such a state of indignation that they would like to have gone for the Germans at once.'[123] Next day, Lloyd George was still complaining to Riddell about 'those insolent Germans'. 'Their conduct', he said, 'showed that the old German is still there. Your Brockdorff-Rantzau is still there.'[124] In his diary on the night of 7 May Hankey wrote that Brockdorff-Rantzau was 'a sinister looking rascal, a typical Junker. His speech was a strange mixture of cringing and insolence.' In a letter to his wife the next day Hankey's views were even more extreme: Brockdorff-Rantzau was 'an incarnation of the whole Junker system. I can imagine no more typical exponent.'[125] Kerr explained in a letter written a week later that 'by the time

[117] Jessie Whitehead to her mother, 26 May 1919, Whitehead Papers, Peter Liddle Archive.
[118] Sidney Dark, *Mainly About Other People* (London, 1925), 205.
[119] Latham to Ella Latham, 8 May 1919, Latham Papers, MS 1009/21/1443 (a).
[120] Derby to Curzon, 9 May 1919, Derby Papers, 28/2/2.
[121] H. Fisher to L. Fisher, 13 May 1919, Fisher Papers, 206; Henry Wilson Diary, 8 May 1919, Henry Wilson Papers, DS MISC/80.
[122] Frances Stevenson Diary, 7 May 1919, in A. J. P. Taylor (ed.), *Lloyd George: A Dairy by Frances Stevenson* (London, 1971), 183.
[123] Headlam-Morley to Percy Koppel, 8 May 1919, HMP, HDLM OS Box 2.
[124] Riddell Diary, 8 May 1919, Riddell Papers, 62983.
[125] Hankey Diary, 7 May 1919, Hankey Papers HNKY 1/5, and Hankey to Adeline, 8 May 1919, Hankey Papers, 3/25.

Brockdorff-Rantzau had finished speaking, most people were almost anxious to recommence the war'.[126] Hughes, not surprisingly, was probably the most intemperate of all in his reaction. In a letter to the Australian Governor-General, Munro-Ferguson, Hughes explained that Brockdorff-Rantzau had sat down because he was 'not only a Junker but a pig'. 'He looks what he is: a typical Prussian Junker: arrogant: intolerant: unrepentant: the War has taught him nothing.' He had posed as the representative of Social Democracy, explained Hughes.[127] The Brockdorff-Rantzau speech, therefore, appeared to give almost all the chief British delegates a licence to retreat back to the right-wing newspapers' familiar interpretations of Germany since the armistice: the old Germany was still unchanged; democracy was a mere mask. Even those who were not present at the Trianon Palace drew this same easy conclusion. Henry Wilson, for example, having heard Bonar Law's account, jotted in his diary: 'What fools to think that Boches can be other than our Boches.'[128] In London, Crawford wrote that the speech was classic German 'cadishness' and proof that 'even in defeat their psychology remains as blind as ever'.[129]

The explanation for this outpouring of emotion in letters and diaries is not difficult to determine. It is noteworthy that virtually nobody took up the points of fact raised in Brockdorff-Rantzau's speech but rather almost everybody resorted immediately to chauvinist name-calling. Quite apart from the controversies arising from Brockdorff-Rantzau's decision to sit, or the translator's alleged hostility, it was the substance of the speech that pricked consciences. The speech had touched on two points which were especially sensitive for the British: the Lansing Note and the blockade. Apart from the few with troubled consciences, such as Keynes, Headlam-Morley, and his colleagues in the PID, most people in the British Delegation had put the inconvenient matter of the Lansing Note out of mind. The reality of the blockade and the resulting hardship throughout central Europe was even more challenging to the notion of British moral rectitude, as Cecil's agonies of conscience in his diary reveal so very clearly. For the German Foreign Minister to raise both questions, in the only public forum to be permitted them in the peacemaking process, was more than many of the leading British delegates could bear.

But some in the British Delegation did see through this smokescreen of outrage. Within a few days, Headlam-Morley was hearing different accounts of the meeting with the Germans at the Trianon Palace. He told Tyrrell that, while the Prime Minister was extremely indignant at the German behaviour, 'I hear from another person who was present that he thought they were very dignified'.[130] Explanations for the notorious 'insolence' of Brockdorff-Rantzau in sitting down

[126] Kerr to his mother, 13 May 1919, Kerr Papers, GD40/17/466/25.
[127] Hughes to Munro-Ferguson, 17 May 1919, Novar Papers, MS 696/2805-6.
[128] Henry Wilson Diary, 8 May 1919, Henry Wilson Papers, DS MISC/80.
[129] Crawford Diary, 9 May 1919, vol. xxxv, Crawford Papers.
[130] Headlam-Morley to Tyrrell, 11 May 1919, HMP, HDLM, OS BOX 1.

during his speech to the Trianon session also reached the PID through none other than Captain Thornely Gibson, now a Liaison Officer responsible for managing the German Delegation. Gibson reported to Saunders that the Germans in conversation had revealed the real reason for Brockdorff-Rantzau's sitting down; the Germans had thoroughly researched the precedents beforehand and found that 'people stood or sat when addressing international conferences just as they liked'. Thus the decision not to stand as Clemenceau had done, Saunders concluded, was 'probably pure stupidity and not deliberate rudeness'.[131] But these, of course, were exceptional responses.

The reaction of the leading British delegates gave to the British journalists present all the encouragement they needed to resume beating the 'unrepentant Germany' drum. The Conservative, Coalition Liberal, and Northcliffe press united in a spectacular bout of German-baiting. The Huns 'strutted'—'haughty', 'arrogant', 'insolent', 'truculent', and 'impudent'—through page after page of the British dailies. For a week at least, the word 'unrepentant' became the most overworked adjective in the journalists' armoury. Valentine Williams of the *Daily Mail* collected all the outraged comments of the Allied delegates as they left the Trianon Palace and listed them all in his paper's coverage. Pity was wasted on the Germans, readers of the *Daily Mail* were assured, for they were 'malefactors who arrogantly shout abuse to their judges from the dock'.[132] *The Times* was no less strident: 'Those who expected the Germans to come to Versailles in a mood of penitence for the wrongs inflicted must by now be woefully disappointed.'[133] Sidney Dark of the *Daily Express* heard 'the voice of Potsdam' in Brockdorff-Rantzau's speech—and even the red beard of the socialist Landsberg struck him as 'truculent'. 'The Hun has displayed the braggart insolence and incorrigible insolence of his character', declared the *Daily Express*.[134] Percival Landon of Lloyd George's own *Daily Chronicle* found the speech 'arrogant and aggressive'.[135] The *Observer*'s Paris correspondent found Brockdorff-Rantzau to be 'the very symbol of feudal Prussia', and he warned that 'whatever happens, the beaten Prussians will look for revenge'.[136] Down market at the *Daily Sketch*, the headlines reported 'COUNT RANTZAU'S INSOLENT REPLY TO THE ALLIES'.[137] Almost without exception, the pro-Coalition press presented the Germans' appearance at the Trianon Palace as a vital moment, when the shallowness of the changes in 'unrepentant' Germany, and the need for continuing coercion, had been exposed.[138]

---

[131] Saunders to Headlam-Morley, 12 May 1919, HMP, HDLM, OS BOX 2.

[132] See e.g *Daily Mail*, editorial, 'Impudent and Unrepentant', 9 May 1919.

[133] *The Times*, 8 May 1919.

[134] *Daily Express*, 'Voice of Potsdam at Versailles', 9 May 1919, and ' "Terms" from the Hun!', 12 May 1919, and Dark, *Mainly About Other People*, 205.

[135] *Daily Chronicle*, 8 May 1919.　　　　　　　　　[136] *Observer*, 11 May 1919.

[137] *Daily Sketch*, 8 May 1919.

[138] The exception was the *Observer*, where the leader columns of J. L. Garvin took on a moderate tone, in conformity with the argument pursued in his new book, *The Economic Foundations of the Peace* (London, 1919). See his leader columns 'First Steps to the Real Settlement' and 'How to Mend It' arguing against the draft treaty, *Observer*, 18 and 25 May 1919.

Towards peace by coercion

With the defeat of the Councils' republic in Bavaria in the first days of May, the proponents of a second revolution in Germany appeared to have been decisively crushed. Reports from Germany continued to stress the suffering of ordinary Germans, but the burden of the reports was that the danger of Bolshevism had passed. The *Freikorps* had the situation 'well in hand'.[139] Major-General Neill Malcolm, who replaced Ewart as head of the British Military Mission in Berlin in early May, reported constantly from Berlin that the politicians of the existing government were incensed by the draft treaty, but also that the danger of a Bolshevik uprising was much diminished.[140] Indeed, it was the long-anticipated revival of the nationalist Right in Germany that concerned Malcolm and other military intelligence officers; although this, of course, was never likely to dissuade the victors from imposing peace terms.[141] Thus, from the Trianon session of 7 May to the signing of the Versailles Treaty on 28 June, the German revolution as a factor in British policy-making, the main focus of this study, rapidly declined in importance. Therefore, the evolution of British policy during the remaining seven weeks before the peace was signed may be swiftly summarized here.

The cause of moderation within the British Delegation was not quite defeated. In fact, the presentation of the draft treaty itself was the spark for an eleventh-hour revival. Because the document had been assembled in great haste over the first week of May, many of the British delegates read the peace treaty through for the first time only *after* its presentation to the Germans. The German counter-proposals submitted on 29 May excited much sympathy, even admiration. Under these pressures, a number of consciences snapped. Barnes, Smuts, Cecil, and Churchill, in particular, worked hard in the cause of revision of the treaty, and all pleaded with Lloyd George to support negotiation rather than the resort to armed force and blockade in order to coerce Germany into acceptance of the existing treaty.[142] However, Lloyd George knew well that none of these advocates of moderation stood on very strong ground within the Coalition or in the House of Commons: Barnes was seen as the token Labour representative cast

---

[139] e.g. see 'Preliminary Report by Major Knyvett, Major Bertie, and Captain Bell on visits to Hannover, Hamburg and Berlin between 28th April and 19th May, 1919', which stated that 'The Government believed they had the bolshevist danger well in hand' (FO 371/3777). See also Lt.-Col. Thelwall to Major-General N. Malcolm, 13 May 1919, FO 371/3777.

[140] See the series of weekly reports entitled 'Report by Major-General Neill Malcolm, Chief of the British Military Mission in Berlin on the Situation in Germany', in FO 371/3777.

[141] See e.g. Malcolm's reports of interviews with Gustav Noske, Minister of Defence, General Hoffmann, and the right-wing military contact man Count Rechberg, 30 May, 6, 11, 13, 17 June 1919, in Malcolm Diary, Neill Malcolm Papers; General Charles Fergusson to DMI, 7 June 1919, FO 608/131; and 'Memorandum on the Political Situation in Germany', dated Berlin, 7 June 1919, Kerr Papers, GD 40/17/71.

[142] See Barnes to Lloyd George, 16 and 18 May 1919, Lloyd George Papers, F/4/3/15 and 16; Smuts to Lloyd George, 5 and 14 May 1919, Smuts Papers, vol. 101; Cecil to Lloyd George, 14 May 1919, Lloyd George Papers, F/6/6/45, and Cecil to Lloyd George, 27 May 1919, Cecil Papers, 51076; Churchill to Lloyd George, 20 May 1919, Lloyd George Papers, F/8/3/55.

adrift by his own party; Smuts was known to have been as keen as anyone to retain all German colonies and it was he who had persuaded Wilson to accept the inflated British claim to compensation under the cover of 'reparation'; Churchill was disliked by the Conservative majority in the government and was regarded as anything but a moderate on the issue of Russian intervention; Cecil was seen by his critics as a notorious Tory Free Trader and a Christian sentimentalist. None of these was likely to be of much assistance to Lloyd George if it came to defying the Conservative back-benchers.

Nevertheless, in the face of these representations, Lloyd George called a meeting of the British Empire Delegation to discuss the German counter-proposals on 30 May. After three long discussions within the British Empire Delegation over the weekend of 30 May–1 June, a clear majority advised revision. Smuts, Barnes, Churchill, Milner, Montagu, and Cecil all argued with great emotion for a peace treaty reconcilable with the Fourteen Points. Significantly, Balfour, one of the few who resisted, resorted to the argument of lack of repentance on Germany's part to justify his position: 'it had apparently been assumed that Germany was repentant, that her soul had undergone a conversion, that she was now absolutely a different nation from the Germany which in the past had built up armaments and had caused the war. But why', he asked, 'should there be faith in Germany altering her course?' At length, it was agreed that four changes should be recommended in the treaty: revisions to the territorial settlement with Poland, including the greater use of plebiscites in doubtful areas; a statement favouring early admission of Germany to the League of Nations; earlier termination of the occupation of the Rhineland; and a modification of the reparation clauses so that Germany could be faced with a fixed sum. What was missing from the list, it should be noted, was any demand for the commencement of verbal negotiation with the Germans. Still, the list included significant changes, and, in order to persuade the Council of Four to revise the draft treaty, the delegation even armed the Prime Minister with 'the full weight of the entire British Empire'; if it came to the point of forcing the hand of Wilson and Clemenceau, the Prime Minister was empowered to refuse British military assistance for a march into Germany and naval assistance for the reimposition of the full blockade. Tough as this sounded, it was agreed that these were guidelines and that in negotiation Lloyd George 'should be allowed a certain latitude'.[143] To accomplish this task, however, Lloyd George required the support of President Wilson. He did not get it. The personal relations between the two men were now at a low ebb. It was too late in the day, according to Wilson, for Lloyd George and he to form a common front of liberalism against Clemenceau. He refused to undo the treaty to please, as he saw it, such an unreliable opportunist as Lloyd George. At the last moment, the British were united, as Wilson put it, 'in their funk'.[144]

[143] Minutes of the British Empire Delegation, 30 May and two meetings 1 June, CAB 28/28.
[144] Albert Lentin, *Lloyd George, Woodrow Wilson, and the Guilt of Germany* (Leicester, 1984), 99–100; Elcock, *Portrait of a Decision*, 273–85.

Moreover, Lloyd George's pressure for moderation on territorial matters had no parallel in any determined effort on his part to moderate the British position on reparations. In particular, he abandoned the advice which the British Empire Delegation had given him to pursue a fixed sum for Germany in the reparations chapter of the treaty, a concession to Germany which Wilson would have supported.[145] The explanation for this is clear. The same pressures upon Lloyd George which had caused him such difficulties in April were reapplied in June. As soon as rumours of the latest effort at moderation reached the ears of Cunliffe and Sumner, both submitted memoranda to Lloyd George insisting that there be no retreat on indemnity.[146] The way Lloyd George's mind was working could be seen in a response to another letter from Barnes, a letter denouncing the dishonesty in Britain's pursuit of war costs, which Lloyd George sent off on 2 June: 'I made it quite clear both in the Cabinet and on the platform at the date of the General Election what I conceived to be the policy of the Government on the subject of the compensation to be levied on Germany. That was the time for you to object.'[147] The election pledges were back in the news soon after. Rumours of the renewed push in the direction of moderation had reached Fleet Street. On 6 June, both *The Times* and *Daily Mail* shouted warnings from their editorial columns about 'wobbling' and 'pusillanimity' on the Prime Minister's part regarding the hunt for the indemnity.[148] Soon after, Walter Long also sent a memorandum to Lloyd George announcing ominously that, judging from 'a good many conversations recently with very well-informed people', Long believed that support for the indemnity was still strong and Britain's case watertight. Long attempted, in particular, to argue that the Lansing Note was not an obstacle because pensions and 'the enormous weight of taxation' arising from the war were 'surely' covered by the British insistence on compensation for damage to the 'civilian population'. The German people deserved to pay in taxes for the war, wrote Long, 'since whatever the post-war apologists for Germany may say, it was the German nation as a whole which was responsible for the war'.[149] For Lloyd George, knowing Long's association with Hewins and the Unionist War Committee and Business Committee, such a letter could only be regarded as something between a stern warning and blackmail. Thus the last ill-timed British effort to moderate the peace foundered on the same rocks as had the Fontainebleau Memorandum—the realities of politics within the 'knock-out blow' Coalition.

---

[145] Schwabe, *Woodrow Wilson, Revolutionary Germany, and Peacemaking*, 370–1.

[146] Cunliffe to Kerr, 1 June 1919, Kerr Papers, GD/40/17/62; Sumner to Lloyd George, 3 and 5 June 1919, Lloyd George Papers, F/46/2/4 and 10.

[147] Barnes to Lloyd George, 2 June 1919, and Lloyd George to Barnes, 2 June 1919, Lloyd George Papers, F/4/3/17 and 18.

[148] *The Times*, editorial, 'An Amazing Rumour', 6 June 1919, and *Daily Mail*, 'No Wobbling!', editorial, 6 May 1919.

[149] Long to Lloyd George, 11 June 1919, Long Papers, WRO 947/746.

In effect, therefore, by mid-June, the moderates within the British Delegation had made their protests in vain. The victors were united behind the only remaining policy towards Germany on which they could all agree: coercion. The German counter-proposals were rejected on 16 June. The Germans were given five days to sign the treaty, with its schedule of minor amendments, or face the full reimposition of blockade and the resumption of the war on land. Philip Kerr undertook to write a covering letter to accompany the documents announcing the decision of the Allied and Associated Powers to Germany. This letter was important in that it was to be released to the world's press and used as a final summary of the position of the victors on the peace terms. It covered the usual ground: the Germans had caused the war, and they had waged it with unparalleled brutality. Punishment was required, for the sake of the world. Stern Justice. The letter also included a memorable paragraph referring directly to the judgement made by the victors upon the German revolution:

It is said that the German Revolution ought to make a difference and that the German People are not responsible for the policy of the rulers whom they have thrown from power. The Allied and Associated Powers recognise and welcome the change. It represents a great hope for peace, and for a new European order in the future. But it cannot affect the settlement of the war itself. The German Revolution was stayed until the German armies had been defeated in the field and all hope of profiting by a war of conquest had vanished. Throughout the war, as before the war, the German people and their representatives supported the war, voted the war credits, subscribed to the war loans, obeyed every order, however savage, of their government. They shared the responsibility for the policy of their government, for at any moment, had they willed it, they could have reversed it. Had that policy succeeded they would have acclaimed it with the same enthusiasm with which they welcomed the outbreak of the war. They cannot now pretend, having changed their rulers after the war was lost, that it is justice that they should escape the consequences of their deeds.

Later in the document, in justification for Germany's exclusion from the League of Nations, Kerr noted again that 'The German revolution was postponed to the last moments of the war, and there is as yet no guarantee that it represents a permanent change'.[150]

Here was a crowning piece of unction from a leading British 'moral warrior' to finish the war. The victors had made a definitive finding against the sincerity of the German revolution. The revolution was too late; it was a pretence; it was not yet sufficiently consolidated. Through the words of the British Prime Minister's secretary, the absurd doctrine of collective guilt was enshrined in a central document of the peace: the doctrine that whole peoples are responsible for the actions of their governments, even authoritarian governments, even in

---

[150] 'Letter to the President of the German Delegation covering the Reply of the Allied and Associated Powers' (16 June 1919), 6, Headlam-Morley Papers, Acc 727, Box 13, now reproduced in *British Documents on Foreign Affairs: Reports and Papers from the Foreign Office Confidential Print, Part II, From the First to the Second World War. Series I, The Paris Peace Conference of 1919*, ed. Dockrill, vii. 377.

times of war, and even when those governments deployed power with all the instruments of censorship, the state of siege decrees, and all manner of emergency legislation at their command. To remove such a government by popular revolution was, apparently, no defence, no contrition, and no atonement. The idea that the German revolution was not authentic, that it was a last-minute conversion to democracy, that it was not sufficiently thorough, was given official approval. The idea that the revolution had done nothing to lessen the perceived guilt of a whole people or the perceived need for their punishment in Allied eyes—an idea fundamental to the German Right in their campaigns to discredit the revolution in Weimar Germany—was built in to the moral justification of the treaty. In short, Kerr's letter argued, as the German Right was to argue with such devastating effect, that the revolution was pointless 'funk'. Considering the British authorship of the document, it is only fair to point out that the inconsistencies and cynicism in the argument were quite breathtaking. The German revolution was declared to be 'welcome'—when, in fact, not a word or gesture of welcome or approval of the revolution had ever been made by any minister of the Lloyd George Coalition since 9 November 1918. The German revolution was said to have arrived too late to be convincing—when, in fact, from the moment of the outbreak of the revolution, the British government and British military forces had given countless indications to the Germans that the revolution and its institutions were anathema and that the sooner the more thorough revolutionaries within Germany were liquidated the better. The revolution and its democratic institutions were declared to be insufficiently consolidated—when, in truth, the British had rejected all advice to bolster the democratic regime with open declarations of support and had resisted for months the one change desperately needed to consolidate the new regime, the raising of the blockade.

Nevertheless, when Kerr's letter appeared in print it soothed many a troubled conscience among the British élite. Apparently, it recaptured a sense of certainty that the British were still standing on high moral ground. Archbishop Randall Davidson, for example, who had confided to the Prime Minister that he was much troubled by the vindictive spirit pervading the Peace Conference during the early months of 1919, declared at a dinner attended by Herbert Fisher and various other political notables in mid-June that he considered Kerr's letter 'the finest document of the war'. Fisher wrote to his wife: 'The reply to Germany was written by Philip Kerr, and how good it was.'[151] The Prime Minister himself was impressed too. The indictment against the whole German people, which Kerr had included in the famous 'covering letter', was repeated and emphatically endorsed by Lloyd George in a major speech to the House of Commons in July 1919 when the Treaty of Versailles was debated. Lloyd George explained his own position in these words:

---

[151] Randall Davidson to Lloyd George, 24 May 1919, Davidson Papers, vol. 366; Herbert Fisher to L. Fisher, 18 June 1919, Fisher Papers, 206, and Fisher Diary, 17 June 1919, HMP, Acc. 800 HDLM 3.

But it is said, 'Are you not punishing Germany for the crime of her rulers?' Well, I am sorry to have to answer this, but I must. If Germany had been committed to this war against the will of her people, I say at once that we ought to have taken that into account in the terms of peace. But was that so? [Hon. Members: 'No, no!'] The nation approved, the nation applauded; the nation had been taught to approve and to applaud. From the Baltic to the Bodensee the nation was united and enthusiastic behind this enterprise.[152]

In such remarkable passages as these, the complexities of Germany's political development before and during the war, and the baffling moral issues of responsibility, were reduced to the simplicities of the *Daily Mail*. The German people were to blame. And yet even the government's own documents made the absurdity of this claim clear. For example, in the official report of the Department of Propaganda in Enemy Countries produced in February 1919, it was proudly explained that the whole purpose of the department had been to enlighten the German people because 'The truth was being concealed from them by their own leaders'. This propaganda, the report claimed, had reached a climax in the final weeks of the war, when it had helped promote the revolution 'which put an end to the war'.[153] By June 1919, the German people were both misled and guilty. Their revolution made no difference, and their enthusiastic support for the war became the justification for their punishment.

The moderate men within the British Delegation who had fought against this outcome knew that the revolution had made a great deal of difference. There were many ashamed of the terms of peace; there were many ashamed of the fact that the conditional armistice had been forgotten when the revolution broke out and rendered Germany militarily helpless; and there were many ashamed of the indemnity that had been guiltily smuggled into the treaty under the cover of reparations. Some of the best and brightest of the advisers to the British Delegation—Headlam-Morley, Zimmern, Bevan, Keynes, Brand, Alan Leeper, Lionel Curtis, Eggleston, Temperley—all acknowledged that the British government's disregarding of the plain meaning of the Lansing Note was a 'breach of faith'.[154] Here was a sense of moral betrayal that would sap faith in all aspects of the Treaty of Versailles in the years to come.

The men of the PID, in particular, had slowly come to a view of the German revolution totally at odds with that insisted upon by Kerr and Lloyd George in their justifications of the Treaty of Versailles. Zimmern, Bevan, and Headlam-

---

[152] *Parl. Debs.*, 5th ser., vol. 117, 1221 (3 July 1919).
[153] 'Report on the Work of the Department of Propaganda in Enemy Countries', n.d. but filed as Feb. 1919, CAB 24/75.
[154] e.g. Headlam-Morley to Keynes, 16 Dec. 1919, HMP, HDLM, OS Box 1; Zimmern to Wallas, 20 May 1919, Wallas Papers, 1/62; Zimmern to Toynbee, 10 Aug. 1919, Toynbee Papers, (temporary) 86; Alan Leeper to Seton Watson, 17 Apr. 1919, Seton-Watson Papers, 'filing cabinet correspondence', Leeper file; Lionel Curtis to Keynes, 28 Dec. 1919 and 5 Jan. 1920, Keynes Papers, EC/2/1/137 and EC/2/2/41; Brand to Keynes, 27 Dec. 1919, Keynes Papers, EC/2/1/109; Keynes to Temperley, 14 Nov. 1920, Keynes Papers, CO/19; Eggleston, typescript memoir 'The Peace Conference at Paris', Eggleston Papers, MS 423/6/15.

Morley had overcome, to a certain extent, their own middle-class prejudices and their deep distrust of German socialism. A month after the signing of the Versailles Treaty, Headlam-Morley was emphatic in his criticisms. Looking back he gave this prophetic judgement on the German revolution, the enfeeblement of Weimar democracy, and the tragic failure of Allied policy:

Had we taken the opportunity when it was open to us, directly after the armistice, we could I think have done with Germany what we liked; now we have allowed time for the bad elements to come to the top again. The revolution in Germany was, as far as I can make out, as thorough, complete and sincere, as any revolution of which there is any record. But we have allowed the effect to wear itself out during a futile period of waiting, and we have only ourselves to blame if the effect is beginning to disappear.[155]

In conclusion, the real British response to the German revolution can be seen to have evolved full circle between the outbreak of revolution and the signing of the Versailles Treaty. At the outset, the Lloyd George government professed to believe that the German revolution was bogus. How much the various ministers and candidates really believed in this counterfeit revolution thesis is not clear; it suited domestic political requirements at least to affect belief in it. Then, thrown off balance by a great deal of evidence pointing to imminent famine and the growth of Bolshevism in Germany, the British had decided it was no sham at all, but a deadly peril, and ministers agonized over how much food to rush in to the defeated nation in order to avoid catastrophe. Having avoided it, many simply resumed the old interpretation, again for political purposes—there had not really been a deep-seated revolution at all, Germany was still unrepentant, and the nation might throw off the garb of democracy at any moment. Brockdorff-Rantzau became a useful symbol for reviving the old interpretation that there was no 'new Germany', and Kerr revived it to justify the coercion of the Weimar Republic. In a sense, the *Freikorps* forces had done their murderous work too swiftly. The fear of a second revolution had been extinguished. In British eyes, the danger of pushing Germany over the brink was no longer credible. Thus was the policy of coercion saved.

After the Bolshevik peril in Germany had dissipated, only two possible factors remained that might have prompted a successful and sustained effort on the part of the British to moderate the peace process, conscience and democratic idealism. Conscience reminded a few troubled souls that a Wilsonian contract was supposed to underpin the whole peace process, as promised in the Lansing Note. Conscience reminded some others that the German government had been encouraged to extirpate its Bolshevik enemies, and stood in danger of political discredit if it had nothing to show its people for the brutality. Democratic idealism prompted a very few advisers to recommend that Britain should do what was best for German democracy—if not for Germany's sake, then for the safety of Europe. Neither conscience nor democratic idealism existed in sufficient supply

---

[155] Headlam-Morley to Dr R. P. Scott, 29 Aug. 1919, HMP, HDLM Acc. 688, OS Box 1.

among the British leaders for these views to prevail. Lloyd George himself had tested the limits of moderation in the weeks that followed Fontainebleau and had been scorched. He would not risk his political life again for moderation in the making of peace. After all, a peace dictated to the enemy had always been part of the rhetoric of his 'knock-out blow' Coalition.

Conclusion

When Germany overthrew her military autocracy it was undoubtedly in the
hope and belief that, as a democratic state in line with other democratic states
of Europe, she might escape from her past and be regarded as having in some
degree at least atoned for its errors. So she was told, and so we ourselves at
one time honestly believed. Who does not remember the declarations that to
a democratic Germany much might be conceded which to a Germany still
militarist, still autocratic, could not be allowed. So Germany parted with her
militarism, parted with her autocracy, only then to discover that she was still
regarded in the same light as before. Such discoveries breed disillusionment
and are apt to be followed by reaction. If the worst has happened to her in
her democratic state, might she not perhaps have fared as well or better had
she not thrown her traditions and her Emperor overboard?

C. P. Scott, Manchester Guardian, 10 May 1919[1]

THE German revolution was a most unwelcome international and domestic complication for the Lloyd George Coalition at the end of the First World War. The
government was fiercely hostile both to the revolution and to the democratic
Weimar Republic that followed in its wake. It is the essential argument of this book
that British antipathy towards republican Germany in 1918–19 was politically
driven: it was shaped by a long-standing abhorrence of German and international
socialism. British animosity towards the new politics in Germany was maintained
and exploited during the eight-month period of peacemaking chiefly for reasons of
domestic political calculation. The policy that triumphed was a policy of ignoring
and even denying the transition to democracy in Germany; that policy had its roots
in the determination of the increasingly anxious governing élites in Britain to wring
every possible advantage from victory in order that bold new movements seeking
unprecedented social changes in post-war Britain might be smothered. For a great
many reasons, no doubt, the revolutionary period in Germany did not culminate
in the creation of a robust democracy; British policy, it must be said, made it all
the more difficult for the Germans to achieve the democratic outcome which an
overwhelming majority of the people clearly wished.

At this point, a brief summary of the argument of this book may be outlined
here, chapter by chapter, to show how these themes outlined above have emerged
within the narrative:

---

[1] *Manchester Guardian*, editorial, 'The German Protests', 10 May 1919.

1. Lloyd George's 'knock-out blow' Coalition of 1916–18 was an improvised government tilting towards reactionary politics at the war's end. It was beholden to powerful interest groups which looked forward to a profitable victory against Germany, especially in the economic sense. The 'knock-out blow' government was an amalgam of Conservatives, 'economic warriors', and imperial idealists, and as such it was bound to be instinctively hostile towards any progressive revolution in Germany, but especially a socialist-led revolution.

2. The British governments of 1914–18, while willing to exploit the democratic theme as a propaganda weapon to divide the German enemy, especially during 1918, never had a genuine commitment to the democratization of Germany as a war aim. The Lloyd George Coalition in particular was most suspicious of the idea of German democratization. The majority of the men around Lloyd George regarded belief in the inner regeneration of Germany as a Liberal and Radical delusion fostered by those opposed to the ideology of the 'fight to the finish' and a 'dictated peace'. The Russian Revolution, the American entry into the war, and Labour Party pressure prompted a propaganda asserting democratic purposes, but the men of the 'knock-out blow' Coalition never accepted this ideology with any conviction.

3. The German armistice proposal of early October 1918 was, at first, vehemently opposed by Britain as a Wilsonian threat to the 'knock-out blow'. However, the idea of an armistice was eventually accepted by Britain in late October for a mixture of military, diplomatic, but chiefly domestic motives. Wilsonian influence over the armistice terms had been effectively blocked. Lloyd George discerned the domestic political advantages to be obtained from a snap election following a very tough armistice. In the light of Britain's waning military power, the British government also perceived the advantages of claiming a victory in 1918, when British rather than American arms appeared to be crucial in delivering victory. Thus, eager to obtain an armistice, Lloyd George accepted a conditional formula for armistice at Versailles on 4 November 1918. As originally envisaged, the armistice would deliver a sweeping military victory, but it would still be conditional in that Britain accepted that the peace to follow would have to be based on Wilsonian principles.

4. The German revolution of early November 1918, as a socialist-led uprising, disappointed and frightened the chief British political and military leaders, and encouraged them to shun the new government. It imperilled the anticipated smooth passage towards military and diplomatic triumph. However, coming on the eve of the armistice, the revolution also encouraged the British government to exploit the moment of German weakness as a providential opportunity. As the revolution demolished the German capacity to resist, Britain sought to strengthen the armistice terms still further. In the days that followed, the reality of the revolution was realized, and British politicians were tempted to deny the Wilsonian restraints over peacemaking which had been acknowledged in the pre-

armistice correspondence with Germany, and to misrepresent the armistice as an unconditional surrender on Germany's part.

5. Lloyd George and his Conservative partners exploited the general election of December 1918 essentially as a manœuvre to pre-empt and contain the much feared outbreak of socialist politics in post-war Britain. To that end they promoted the familiar politics of war, smearing their opponents as apologists for the enemy and inflaming anti-German hatreds. The strategy for the election, in essence the deliberate choice of Lloyd George but made worse by a spectacular newspaper campaign, was to dazzle the apathetic electorate with the vision of a stupendous indemnity. The indemnity demand was endorsed in order to deflect the Labour Party's demands for high taxation, and to appease the 'economic warriors' of the Right who had gained so much influence in the business lobby. In choosing this strategy for the election, Lloyd George and his partners promoted the preposterous doctrine of the collective guilt of the German people, and, as a logical corollary, they encouraged the popular press in its interpretation of the German revolution as an elaborate attempt to gull the Allies.

6. With the general election behind it, the British government sought in January and February 1919 to discover the truth of what was happening inside Germany. Expeditions into Germany by officers of Military Intelligence followed. The bulk of the military and political intelligence that was submitted argued that the revolution in Germany was not phoney at all but quite alarmingly genuine. The army officers insisted that food shortages were disastrous, and that the political situation in Germany was extremely serious. German democracy itself was in danger, they argued, because the new government failed to secure economic revival, food aid, or negotiations on a quick peace. The Spartacist uprising of January, and the still more serious street-fighting which accompanied the general strike in Berlin in early March, finally persuaded the Prime Minister and his advisers that the crisis in Germany was real. However, despite the constant efforts of a far-sighted minority in the government and the intelligence services to secure some dramatic moderation of British policy, in order to buttress democracy in Germany, little was achieved. The gesture of emergency food shipments to Germany under the Brussels agreement of March 1919 was regarded as too little to make a difference. The best chance for a more imaginative response came at the end of March when Lloyd George produced his Fontainebleau Memorandum arguing for a moderate peace for Germany, in order to prevent it collapsing into Bolshevism.

7. The new spirit of the Fontainebleau Memorandum, however, was short lived. Events in April were to show that fear of a Bolshevik Germany was not sufficient to produce any bold new British response to the troubles inside Germany, certainly not a repudiation of the process already adopted in Paris for the dictation of peace terms. Robert Cecil launched a bold initiative in Paris in late April, when he secured the support the Supreme Economic Council for the raising of the

economic blockade altogether. By this time, however, Lloyd George had been subjected to a major domestic political scare; the Right of the Conservative Party, the Northcliffe press, and the 'economic warriors' raised a great hubbub against any retreat from the indemnity demand. In response, Lloyd George delivered a major address to the Commons in which he attacked the good faith of his tormentors in the press but promised to honour his election pledges. Moreover, at the end of April, the last great left-wing rebellion in Germany, the Bavarian Councils' republic, was crushed. As a result, Lloyd George decided to stick with the policy of coercion. The peace was dictated to Germany. In justifying the Treaty of Versailles, Lloyd George and his companions again professed contempt for the German revolution, and cynically encouraged the fiction that the new German government was both unrepentant and unreformed.

In essence, the British reaction to the German revolution was driven by the considerations of domestic politics. Again and again Lloyd George demonstrated his judgement that any softening in the approach to Germany was politically inexpedient in the light of the powerful anti-German constituency which his own government had inflamed and with whom he shared political power. Against these considerations, the facts on the appalling internal condition of Germany, and the best political advice concerning security for Europe in the future, could scarcely make headway. Thus the British government reacted with unremitting hostility to the revolution and to the foundation of the Weimar Republic under a progressive socialist-led government. The chance of combining in Paris with the representatives of the United States from the very beginning of the Peace Conference, and of making a progressive response to the unfolding of events in Germany, was allowed to slip past. British policy—in standing firm for indemnity and blockade—contributed decisively to the debilitation of Weimar democracy.

Other explanations for this tragic outcome, of course, can readily be found in the vast storehouse of scholarship on the lost peace. There are at least four other common explanations and each deserves some necessarily brief consideration here.

First, in some accounts it almost appears as if the planet was to blame. That is, it is asserted that geographic and demographic factors gave to Germany such inherent strength for the future, such abundant resources, and so fecund a population, that no defeat could destroy these God-given endowments. Thus, it is argued, no military reversal was likely to be permanent, and thus, by extension, no treatment of the 'new Germany' could really be too harsh. However tough the peace, all the permanent advantages still lay with Germany. According to this explanation, therefore, those chauvinists of the Entente who sought a still more draconian treaty were only too correct; the sentimentalists who wrung their hands at the 'starvation blockade' were paving the way for more German aggression. The most rigorous blockade, and the Versailles Treaty, were too mild if anything, for even these burdens could not guarantee the security of the states surrounding Germany. Only German illusion, parochialism, political sensitivity, and chauvinism, it is said, prevented the Germans themselves from seeing that they were being treated comparatively leniently in 1918–19.[2] This geo-economic argument is correct in its premiss but surely wrong in its conclusion. If the geographic and demographic strengths enjoyed by Germany were immutable, then surely it was all the more vital to assist her transition to democratic institutions under social democratic leadership. Surely the folly of neglecting the political path in the peace settlement, the consolidation of German democracy from within, is revealed all the more clearly.

Second, it is suggested that the vengeful people of the victorious nations were to blame. In the literature there are countless references to 'public opinion' demanding harsh treatment of the defeated nations. It was easy for political leaders to blame their own peoples. Both Wilson and Lloyd George blamed the elections of November and December 1918 respectively for placing them under the pressure of chauvinist opinion. The difference, of course, was that Wilson had campaigned against chauvinism while Lloyd George had played up to it. In the case of Britain, it simply was not true that her peacemakers cowered before a monstrous and irresistible wave of popular support for harsh treatment of the new Germany. It is said that, in the aftermath of a war, hatred and vindictiveness is a normal human reaction, and that ordinary people naturally wish to hit out at their defeated opponents and heap miseries upon them. The ordinary people of Britain, as represented by the soldiers who occupied the Rhineland in 1918–19, overwhelmingly showed exactly the opposite spirit, as shown here in the many references to the letters, diaries, and interviews in the valuable Peter Liddle Personal Experience Archive. The ordinary people appeared to believe that the war was a bloody disaster, for both sides, and that it ought to be buried in a spirit of reconciliation. As Philip Gibbs argued, 'Long before peace was signed at Versailles it had been signed on the Rhine. Stronger than the hate of war was human nature.'[3] As has been seen, the themes pursued by the Coalition in the khaki election secured it victory, but a victory on the basis of a turn-out of just over half the electorate. By-elections in the next six months saw big swings against Coalition candidates. The Asquithian Liberal, Radical, and Labour press, all urged a peace of reconciliation and consolidation for German democracy. Thus there was no overwhelming opinion for the starvation of Germany and the spurning of the new government. The forces in Britain preaching a peace worthy of the 'knock-out blow' were not irresistible. Lloyd George judged them to be irresistible—in the press, in the House, and on the side of politics which he had chosen to lead. He judged them to be irresistible, unless he was to endanger his personal hold on office.

---

[2] e.g. this argument is alluded to in Gerhard Weinberg, 'The Defeat of Germany in 1918 and the European Balance of Power', *Central European History*, 2 (Sept. 1969), 248–60.

[3] Philip Gibbs, *Now It Can Be Told* (London, 1920), 507.

Third, it is said that the emotion of the politicians was to blame. According to this version, the treatment of Germany was an act of vengeful passion on the part of all the Allied leaders. The most recent history of the war published in Britain, Martin Gilbert's massive *First World War*, explains the ideas of Kerr's 'covering letter' of June 1919 in this way: 'For the Allies, the wounds of war were too close, and the victory too close, to allow any other response.'[4] There is an element of truth within this. Without doubt the personal bereavements endured by many people in the British ruling circle did have an effect on attitudes to the defeated enemy. Indeed, stationed as they were in Paris in the first six months of 1919, many of those responsible for guiding British policy had the unhappy privilege of being able to make the first visits of anyone in England to the war graves of sons, brothers, friends, and relations. These journeys through battlefield cemeteries, amidst the appalling destruction of northern France and Belgium, could scarcely have left any person untouched by intense emotions. Some of those close to Lloyd George in Paris in 1919 made such pilgrimages to grave sites. Frances Stevenson visited the grave of her brother Paul in April.[5] In letters to his mother during the Peace Conference, Kerr made a number of references to the grave of his younger brother David, and he persisted in calling the Germans 'Huns' in his private letters.[6] Among the leading British figures, Bonar Law, Hankey, Tyrrell, Hardinge, Long, Derby, and Selborne, all endured family bereavements.

But powerful as this factor may have been in some cases, it cannot on its own account for the development of British policy towards the defeated enemy over the period October 1918 to June 1919. It must be remembered that the Coalition government which made the peace was made up of the same individuals who had championed conscription, and had even sent boys of only 18 and a half years of age into the line.[7] It was the same government that had turned out Asquith in December 1916 for fear of a negotiated peace after more than two years of war, and then immediately set aside the German offer of a negotiated peace. It was the same government that resisted every Russian request for a reconsideration of war aims to smooth the way towards negotiations. This was the same government that had endured hundreds of thousands of casualties rather than contemplate anything short of military victory and a dictated peace. It is impossible to credit that such men made mistakes in Paris because they were overwhelmed by emotion over so much human suffering. Their papers give no such impression. The peace treaty was created over many months and the decision to coerce Germany into acceptance was made eight months beyond the armistice. Thus British pol-

---

[4] Martin Gilbert, *First World War* (London, 1994), 515.

[5] Frances Stevenson Diary, 15 Apr. 1919, in A. J. P. Taylor (ed.), *Lloyd George: A Diary by Frances Stevenson* (London, 1971), 180.

[6] Kerr to his mother, 29 Apr., 7 and 25 June 1919, Kerr Papers, GD 40/17/466/24, 27, 28. Later Kerr paid a thousand francs for land in which David was buried; see Kerr to his mother, 8 Sept. 1919, Kerr Papers, GD 40/17/466/34.

[7] Keith Grieves, *The Politics of Manpower, 1914–18* (Manchester, 1988), 185.

icy towards defeated Germany was not constructed by men in the heat of the moment, with tears in their eyes.

Fourth, it is said that the Germans themselves were ultimately responsible for the fragility of their own republic. As this is undoubtedly the most popular explanation of 'what went wrong' in 1918–19 to be found in the historical literature, it demands some treatment in greater depth. While this book is primarily about British policy and British pressures upon Germany during the revolutionary period, it does not seek to obscure the fact that the Germans made their own mistakes. The blunders of the moderate German socialists are all well known and are reproduced in all the standard accounts of the revolution: such mistakes as the secret Ebert–Groener pact in which Ebert appeared to make himself beholden to the High Command, or the SPD leaders' decision to use troops on Christmas Eve 1918 in an effort to evict the People's Naval Division from the Royal Palace in Berlin. The moderate German socialists most certainly may be charged with having made serious miscalculations. Their fear of Bolshevism was certainly as exaggerated as the Spartacists' faith in a second revolution that would propel Germany forward to full socialism. The fateful decision of SPD leaders like Gustav Noske to deploy the brutal *Freikorps* forces against the German Spartacists in January 1919, and their redeployment time and again in the months that followed, was to create a hatred beyond all powers of forgiveness on the German Left.[8]

Yet even here the pressure of the victors cannot be overlooked. The Allied and Associated Powers, with a stranglehold on German economic life through the blockade and troops in possession of the Rhineland, were poised to intervene if they so chose. Their antagonism to the revolution in Berlin was well known. As early as mid-December 1918, Konstantin Fehrenbach, the president of the defunct Reichstag, attempted to recall that body on the grounds that 'the Entente Powers are unwilling to negotiate with the present German Government, but that they recognise the competence of the Reichstag and Federal Council to create a legitimate Government'.[9] The possibility of armed intervention by the Allies in Berlin against the socialist-led government was always present. The minutes of the Council of People's Commissioners and of the Scheidemann Cabinet in Berlin during this period show that, on many occasions, demands for moderation and order were based on the premiss that such caution on the part of the new government was demanded in view of the hostile attitude of the Allies.[10] At one

---

[8] Richard Breitman, *German Socialism and Weimar Democracy* (Chapel Hill, NC, 1981), ch. 2.

[9] Admiralty Intelligence Report, 17–19 Dec. 1918, Drax Papers, 5/4.

[10] See Charles B. Burdick and Ralph H. Lutz (eds.), *The Political Institutions of the German Revolution, 1918–1919* (New York, 1966): for example, the Council of People's Commissioners' decision to reject the return of the Soviet Ambassador to Berlin, because the Entente was judged to be ready to 'intervene with all its might to forestall the rise of Bolshevism' (18 Nov. 1918, 70); Cohen's demand for order in Berlin in order to prevent 'a British general as Commandant in Berlin' (7 Dec. 1918, 86); General Groener's speech against the Hamburg Points in order to appease the Americans (20 Dec. 1918, 103); Winnig's report that 'the English have demanded that we protect the country [the Ukraine] from the Bolsheviks', and Scheidemann's speech on keeping on good terms

point even Hugo Haase, the leader of the USPD, advised his impatient left-wing friends in the Berlin executive of the Workers' and Soldiers' Councils, who were advocating a closer relationship with Russia, that they 'should be made to realise the decisive impact of foreign affairs in this matter'.[11]

Indeed, the British constantly signalled their desire for a moderate revolutionary outcome in Germany. As has been seen, they dispersed the Workers' and Soldiers' Councils wherever they encountered them in the areas of occupation, and they gave every indication of preferring to deal with the respectable officials of the old regime rather than with the socialist politicians or with the revolutionary sailors and soldiers who had overturned 'Prussian militarism'. One poignant example may serve to underline this. In March 1919 local town council elections were forbidden by the occupying armies in the Rhineland. The General Staff (Intelligence) of the British Second Army in Cologne recorded a candid explanation for this in their weekly 'Political Notes':

The Allies have forbidden the local town council elections, because relations with the German local authorities as at present constituted are satisfactory and they refuse to have the situation upset by a change of officials. Owing to the alteration of the franchise from the so-called 'Three Class System' to universal suffrage, the elections, if allowed, would probably result in a complete change of officials.[12]

In other words, having ejected the Soldiers' and Workers' Councils from the town halls, the victorious armies had no intention of presiding over democratic elections that would see socialists and liberals march back in through the front doors. And this at the end of a war supposedly to make the world safe for democracy. Even the Prussian three-class suffrage was preferable to the victors.

Thus, in many ways, the winding down of the revolution sprang from the moderates' belief that only by shutting down radical experiments would Germany be granted food and a just peace. A limited revolution was positively demanded by the victors. Indeed, during the worst excesses of the revolution, the bloody street-fighting between the *Freikorps* and the socialist Left in Berlin and Munich, the victorious powers may be said to have applauded the grisly work of the *Freikorps* organized by right-wing officers of the old army. It was surely absurd for those who barracked for the triumph of the *Freikorps* from inside and outside the borders of Germany then to denounce the government in Berlin for having made concessions to 'militarism'. The truth is that many of the compromises made within Germany in 1918–19 were made in order to appease the victorious powers.

---

with the Entente powers 'in order to get food supplies from them' (26 Dec. 1918, 115); Landsberg's speech justifying the attempted ejection of the mutinous People's Naval Division from the Royal Palace, because in the light of such challenges to the government's authority 'hostile armies are given every incentive to march in' (28 Dec. 1918, 139).

[11] Haase's speech in 'Cabinet Meeting of November 18' [1918], ibid. 74.
[12] 'Political Notes' by General Staff (Intelligence), Second Army, 5 Mar. 1919, Gedye Papers, 8.

Significantly, some of those who lived through these events in Germany at the centre of power were in little doubt concerning the relative importance of German political errors and Allied pressures as factors in the hobbling of Weimar democracy at its birth. For example, Arnold Brecht, the civil servant who worked at the Chancellery with Prince Max, Ebert, Scheidemann, and Bauer in 1918–19 (and later a prominent opponent of Nazism) argued in his memoirs that even the horrific acts of the *Freikorps*, committed under the direction of the new government, need not have doomed the republic:

> It was not actually necessary that the connection between German democracy and the remnants of the old army should lead to the collapse of democracy. If Germany had been given a peace treaty which was less challenging to all national concepts of honour; if the honest democratic governments of Ebert, Scheidemann, Fehrenbach, Wirth, Marx, Stresemann, Hermann Müller, etc., had received support comparable to that offered the Adenauer government after the Second World War—then it would by no means have been impossible to keep control over the military. That all this was to be denied the German governments, Ebert and Noske could not know during the first months after the revolution.[13]

Certainly the German revolution was a limited revolution, but adjectives stronger than this invite readers to ignore the very real gains that were made in establishing a new parliamentary republic, under democratic socialist leadership. While there were many marks of compromise, the reality of the revolution remained. A new republic was set up. Weimar democracy was launched. The government of Ebert, Scheidemann, and Erzberger, whatever charges of compromise may be laid at its door, was progressive, in its social, economic, and foreign policy. There was surely a chance for a 'new Germany'.

But the historical consensus is against this. There are very few sympathetic accounts of the revolution and most are content to condemn the revolution as both unfinished and insincere.[14] The inference is that there was no real basis for a genuine shift to a democratic future in 1918–19. In those accounts which do acknowledge the burden of the peace process, it is often the Germans themselves who bear the brunt of the blame for the intensity of their disappointment. As Gordon Craig writes in his magisterial *Germany 1866–1945*, German faith in a Wilsonian spirit guiding the peacemaking was founded upon 'an extraordinary feat of wishful thinking'.[15] Sally Marks complains that the German people expected a just peace from the Allies 'without reason'.[16] Similarly, A. J. Nicholls

---

[13] Arnold Brecht, *The Political Education of Arnold Brecht: An Autobiography, 1884–1970* (Princeton, 1970), 144–5.

[14] e.g. in Breitman, *German Socialism and Weimar Democracy*, the revolution appears as 'The Limited Revolution'; in Mary Fulbrook, *The Fontana History of Germany, 1918–1990: The Divided Nation* (London, 1990), it is 'The Incomplete Revolution'; in Gordon Craig, *Germany 1866–1945* (Oxford, 1986), the revolution is billed as 'The Aborted Revolution'; in Harold James, *A German Identity, 1770–1990* (London, 1990), it is 'Improvised Democracy'.

[15] Craig, *Germany 1866–1945*, 424.

[16] Sally Marks, *The Illusion of Peace: International Relations in Europe, 1918–1933* (London, 1976), 16.

blames the government of Philip Scheidemann for not preparing the German people for the blunt reality of total defeat and suggests that Germany's conversion to democracy was something of a sham. 'The Army, the Foreign Office, and the Government all thought that the "democratic" card was the one to play', writes Nicholls.[17] In the most recent general account published in Britain, John Lowe's *The Great Powers, Imperialism and the German Problem, 1865–1925*, one finds a stern judgement: German disillusionment over the peacemaking process was a product of those destructive German 'self-delusions' that ought to have been punctured by a wider occupation of German soil by Allied forces in 1918–19.[18]

This focus on German errors distracts attention, of course, from the disastrous consequences of Allied and British policy. The refusal of the Western powers to consider measures to consolidate the new democracy in Germany at its foundation was undoubtedly a spectacular blunder. The political consequences were readily apparent in Germany by the summer of 1919. The perceived humiliations of the peace process constituted a devastating blow to the political credibility of the founders of the new republic. After all, the progressive politicians in Germany had promised that democratic reforms in Germany would enable a peace of conciliation. The fledgling democracy was discredited as näive and powerless. The word democracy itself came to symbolize humiliation. The progressive German politicians who had secured the long-awaited peace of November—those who might have gone down in German history as the 'November heroes' given a happier outcome—were easily transformed by right-wing extremists into the 'November criminals', the traitors of the 'stab in the back' legend.

The major new study of *Germany after the First World War* by Richard Bessel is instructive on these points. Bessel shows that the widespread revulsion against war experienced by so many in Germany in the immediate aftermath of the armistice and revolution was deep-seated and 'not a mere passing phenomenon'. He speculates that a passionately anti-militarist work like Remarque's *All Quiet on the Western Front* would not have provoked much reaction at all in Germany had it been published in 1918–19, given the widespread disillusionment at that time with the 'swindle' of the war. Bessel estimates that it was only in the mid- to late 1920s that 'the more conservative and militarist set of values made a comeback and shaped public discussion of the War'. The revulsion against war, therefore, was only slowly checked by the almost universal revulsion against the manner and terms of the Versailles diktat of 1919 and the years of economic difficulty that were believed to spring from the unjust treatment of the new republic. Progressive politics in Germany clearly received a decisive set-back. The unsatisfactory process of peacemaking, therefore, must be considered a crit-

---

[17] A. J. Nicholls, *Weimar and the Rise of Hitler* (London, 1977), 53–4.

[18] John Lowe, *The Great Powers, Imperialism and the German Problem, 1865–1925* (London, 1994), 246–7.

ical factor in the destabilization of Weimar politics and society. 'After the First World War', as Bessel concludes, 'Germany never really made the transition from a "war society" (*Kriegsgesellschaft*) to a "peace society" (*Friedensgesellschaft*). Instead, it remained a post-war society'.[19]

As a direct result of the events associated with the armistice and the peace, the forces of the German Right enjoyed the unexpected prospect of political rehabilitation. Allied treatment of the new republic, so the men of the Right could claim, had justified their stand during the war. They had warned that the democratic promises of Wilson and Lloyd George were a snare. They had preached militarism, reliance on force, steadfast resistance to the invader at any cost, and harsh discipline against the democratic reformers at home. The slogans of liberalism and democracy had been shown to be hollow. The grand internationalist themes of British and American propaganda during 1918, so important in undermining faith in Kaiserism inside Germany, could credibly be attacked as cruel deceptions.[20]

Thus the enormity of what was squandered in Germany in 1918–19 still deserves reiteration. From the point of view of the victors the initial political outcome of the war could scarcely have been more promising. The Kaiser was deposed and his ignominious flight to Holland cost the nationalist and conservative Right much prestige. At first, the traditional élites and the officer class were thoroughly discredited and dejected. The advocates of militarism, unrestricted submarine warfare, economic security through annexationism, and food from the East through the Brest-Litovsk Treaty, had all been proved wrong. 'The War had bankrupted the old regime in every sense: militarily, politically, financially, and morally', as Bessel expresses it.[21] In November 1918, the political gains were bound to be scooped up by those who could credibly claim either to have opposed the war at the outset, or to have offered only cautious support for a just war, a war of defence, while pressing all the while for democratic reforms against the ruling oligarchy. The major parties of opposition to the *Kaiserreich*, the Social Democrats and some of their liberal and Catholic allies, could make such claims, with varying degrees of sincerity. The potential for a successful transition to democracy under the leadership of these political forces was clearly present in 1918–19. Indeed it may be seen as a natural development. The essential centre-left alliance, the Weimar Coalition as it was to become, was poised to take Germany forward into a peaceful future. The alliance was no hasty, deathbed improvisation: its formation had been discernible in Germany since the elections of 1912. The centre-left alliance had produced the Peace Resolution in 1917. Nor was democracy a foreign ideology. Democratization had been an objective of the

[19] Richard Bessel, *Germany after the First World War* (Oxford, 1993), 283. On the revulsion against war see also 260 and 265–6.

[20] e.g. see the historic lessons drawn by Gustav Stresemann in a speech in Dortmund, 21 Feb. 1923, in Eric Sutton (ed.), *Gustav Stresemann: His Diaries, Letters and Papers* (New York, 1935), i. 42.

[21] Bessel, *Germany After the First World War*, 48.

socialists from the foundation of the party in 1863. Some 34.8 per cent of the German electorate had voted SPD in 1912, in spite of the Prussian power élite's habitual and frantic attempts to demonize the socialists.[22] In post-war Germany, the prestige of such large and long-established parties as the SPD and Catholic Centre Party, once wedded to the republic, promised to provide a large majority in Germany in favour of democracy. Moreover, while the revolution of November 1918 was led by the socialists, a development which frightened the victorious powers, it soon became clear that this did not imperil a democratic outcome; both wings of German socialism rejected the option of socialism through dictatorship, that is, the option of Bolshevism. The socialist government of November–December 1918 saw itself as provisional only and, in part to please the Allies, moved towards national elections for a Constituent Assembly as swiftly as possible. In the elections of January 1919, the Weimar Coalition parties secured a large majority. Together the SPD, Centre Party, and German Democratic Party garnered 76.1 per cent of the popular vote. The socialists, with 37.9 per cent, were the most successful party but had just failed to gain an outright majority—again, a perfect outcome from the point of view of the victors. The German nationalists and conservatives could attract only a pitiful 10.3 per cent of the popular vote.[23] Germany, by any measure, had turned the corner. But all this political promise was frittered away. The next Reichstag election, in June 1920, less than a year after the signing of the Treaty of Versailles, saw the majority enjoyed by the pro-democratic parties wiped out; the Weimar Coalition of the SPD, Centre Party, and German Democrats registered only 43.6 per cent of the vote.[24] The thumping majority achieved for democracy, republicanism, and peace in January 1919 had been destroyed.

Perhaps the cruellest irony in all of this, from Britain's point of view, was to be glimpsed in the later debate over appeasement in the 1930s. From amongst the leading figures of the 'knock-out blow' Coalition of the First World War were to come some of the leading advocates of appeasement on the Right in the 1930s, most notably Kerr and Geoffrey Dawson. From the great newspaper empires that had supported the vision of the 'knock-out blow' came proprietors and journalists sympathetic to Nazism, such as Rothermere and Ward Price.[25] These men, resistant to any gesture of political support to the German republic in 1918–19, were ready to advocate an accommodation with the Nazis in the 1930s. 'Appeasement', from a position of dominance, that would have strengthened the hands of the founders of the Weimar Republic, was refused; but 'appeasement', from a position of weakness, designed to buy time and deflect the threat of Nazism on to others, was granted to the Nazi destroyers of that same republic.

---

[22] H. W. Koch, *A Constitutional History of Germany in the Nineteenth and Twentieth Centuries* (London, 1984), table 4, 385.
[23] Ibid., table 5(a), 386.   [24] Ibid.
[25] See e.g. Martin Gilbert and Richard Gott, *The Appeasers* (London, 1963), and Richard Griffiths, *Fellow Travellers of the Right* (London, 1980).

Finally, as the moral superiority of Britain and the Empire was asserted so strongly at the time, and is still heard in so many histories, the gap between wartime rhetoric and ultimate performance is worth stressing. On many occasions during the war British and Empire statesmen had insisted on the principle of seeing the war through until total victory in order that German tyranny could be completely destroyed. It was the hard but the only prudent path, they said. Lloyd George himself had declared that the only peace that could last would be a peace delivered by victory, for only with the total defeat of the reactionary clique around the Kaiser could Germany be regenerated and the German people invited to participate in the making of the peace. Only on such democratic foundations, as he so often insisted, could an 'enduring peace' be built. For this reason, he claimed, he had made the agonizing decisions to turn aside the possibility of a negotiated peace with undefeated 'Prussianism', a 'patched-up peace' as he always characterized it.[26] In the event, at the end of 1918, with complete victory in Britain's grasp, and three-quarters of a million men of the British Empire killed in delivering it, the British governing élite discarded its own rhetoric and approached the peacemaking with scarcely a thought for the future safety of German democracy. All the nations with empty bellies made terrible mistakes in 1918–19—but so too did those with full bellies. It is a matter of personal judgement to decide which were the more culpable.

[26] See e.g. Lloyd George's speech in response to the Lansdowne letter, *Parl. Debs.*, 5th ser., vol. xxvii, 2221–4 (20 Dec. 1917).

SELECT BIBLIOGRAPHY

A. GOVERNMENT PAPERS

Public Record Office, Kew
Foreign Office Papers
  FO 371 General Correspondence: Political
  FO 608 Paris Peace Conference of 1919–20: Correspondence
  FO 800 Private Collections
Cabinet Papers
  CAB 23 Minutes of the War Cabinet and Imperial War Cabinet
  CAB 24 Cabinet Papers
  CAB 28 IC Series
  CAB 29 Minutes of the British Empire Delegation
  CAB 63 Hankey's 'Magnum Opus' Files
War Office Papers
  WO 106 Directorate of Military Operations and Intelligence: Papers
  WO 144 British Armistice Commission
Admiralty Papers
  ADM 116 Geddes Papers

Australian Archives, Canberra, Australia
  A 981 War: Peace Conference Files
  CP 290 Watt-Hughes Cables
  CP 351 Peace Conference Files
  CP 360 Watt-Hughes Cables

New Zealand National Archives, Wellington, New Zealand
G Series (G 40–7)

B. PRIVATE PAPERS

Bank of England, London
  Governor's and Secretary's Letterbooks for 1918–19

Bodleian Library Oxford
  Christopher Addison, Herbert Henry Asquith, Robert H. Brand, James Bryce, Lionel
  Curtis, Geoffrey Dawson, Maurice de Bunsen, R. D. Denman, Willoughby Dickinson,
  R. C. K. Ensor, H. A. L. Fisher, H. A. Gwynne, J. L. and L. B. Hammond, Lewis

Harcourt, Alfred Milner, Gilbert Murray, H. W. Nevinson, William Palmer (Second Earl of Selborne), Arthur Ponsonby, James Rennell Rodd, Evelyn Sharp, John Simon, Arnold J. Toynbee, Laming Worthington-Evans, Alfred Zimmern

Borthwick Institute of Historical Research, University of York

Lord Halifax

Bowood Estate, Calne, Wiltshire

E. G. Petty-Fitzmaurice (Baron Fitzmaurice), H. C. K. Petty-Fitzmaurice (5th Marquess of Lansdowne)

British Library, British Museum, London

Arthur Balfour, John Burns, George Cave, Robert Cecil (Cecil of Chelwood), John Jellicoe, Walter Long, Lord Northcliffe, Ralph Paget, George Riddell, C. P. Scott, George Bernard Shaw, J. A. Spender, Harold Whitmore Williams

British Library of Political and Economic Science, London

Colville Barclay, William Beveridge, Robert Dell, A. G. Gardiner, George Lansbury, E. M. H. Lloyd, Andrew Macfadyean, Violet Markham, Graham Wallas, Charles Webster

Brotherton Collection, Leeds University Library, Leeds

Edmund Gosse, Glenesk-Bathurst Papers

Brynmor Jones Library, University of Hull

Mark Sykes, the Union of Democratic Control Archive

Cambridge University Library, Cambridge

Lord Crewe, Lord Hardinge, Jan Smuts (microfilm), Edgar Abraham, Samuel Hoare (Lord Templewood)

Centre for Kentish Studies, Maidstone

7th Earl of Stanhope

Chartered Institute of Bankers, London

Institute of Bankers Papers

Churchill Archives Centre, Churchill College, Cambridge

W. B. Adam, Tufton Percy Hamilton Beamish, Colin R. Buist, William Bull, Henry Page Croft, Cunninghame Graham of Gartmore, A. G. Denniston, Admiral Drax, Admiral Dreyer, Bryan Godfrey-Fausset, Reginald Hall, Geoffrey Harper, James Headlam-Morley (including the Herbert Fisher diary within it), H. Knatchbull-Hugessen, Allen and Rex Leeper, Reginald McKenna, Viscount Norwich, Herbert Packer, Eric Phipps, Arthur Pridham, Bertram Ramsay, John de Robeck, Henry Rawlinson, George Saunders, Edward Spears, James Somerville, Algernon Willis, and Wester Wemyss

City of Liverpool, Brown, Picton, and Hornby Libraries, Liverpool
17th Earl of Derby

Cumbria Record Office, Carlisle
Esme Howard

Eaton Square, London
Leopold Amery (diaries only)

Glasgow University Library, Glasgow
Alexander MacCallum Scott

Guildhall Library, London
Papers of the Association of British Chambers of Commerce, Federation of Commonwealth Chambers of Commerce, London Chamber of Commerce

Hartley Library of the University of Southampton
Wilfrid William Ashley

House of Lords Record Office
Lord Beaverbrook, Andrew Bonar Law, David Lloyd George, Patrick Hannon, Herbert Samuel, J. St Loe Strachey

Imperial War Museum, London
Lord Burnham, George Cockerill, C. R. Cockcroft, John Cowans, J. A. Douglas, Richard Ewart, John French, George Gedye, J. E. B. Gray, H. A. Gwynne, E. Foster Hall, H. N. Harding, L. A. Hawes, Sir Leslie Hollis, Ivor Maxse, Hubert C. Rees, Christopher Thomson (Lord Thomson of Cardington), E. W. C. Thring, N. E. Tyndale-Biscoe, R. L. Venables, Henry Wilson

India Office Library of the British Library, London
Lord Curzon, Lord Reading, A. F. Whyte

John Rylands University Library of Manchester
C. P. Scott, *Manchester Guardian* Archive

King's College Library, Cambridge
J. M. Keynes, J. T. Sheppard

Lambeth Palace Library, Lambeth, London
Archbishop Randall Davidson

Lepe House, Exbury
Henry Forster

Liddell Hart Centre for Military Archives, King's College, London

George Aston, Sidney Clive, Alexander Godley, F. Lister, Frederick Maurice, H. Montgomery-Massingberd, William Robertson, Edward Spears

Modern Records Centre, University of Warwick, Coventry

Federation of British Industry Archive

National Library of Australia, Canberra

Joseph Cook, Frederick Eggleston, Andrew Fisher, Robert Garran, Henry Gullett, William Morris Hughes, John Latham, Keith Murdoch, Ronald Munro-Ferguson (Viscount Novar), George Pearce, E. L. Piesse, H. B. Higgins, John Baird (Viscount Stonehaven)

National Library of Scotland, Edinburgh

David Lindsay (27th Earl of Crawford and 10th Earl of Balcarres), Douglas Haig, R. B. Haldane, F. S. Oliver, Arthur C. Murray (Viscount Elibank)

National Library of Wales, Aberystwyth

Thomas Jones

National Maritime Museum, London

David Beatty, Walter Cowan, Sydney Fremantle, John Donald Kelly, Charles Madden

New Zealand National Archives, Wellington, New Zealand

James Allen

Norfolk Record Office, Norwich

H. W. Massingham

Northampton Shire Record Office, Northampton

Brien Cokayne

Nuffield College, Oxford

J. A. Pease, Alfred Emmott

Peter Liddle's Personal Experience Archive, Leeds University Library

G. R. F. Bredin, Lord Willoughby de Broke, F. W. Davey, H. K. Fisher, W. J. Hooker, George Hope, H. Innes, John Whitworth Jones, S. W. Joslin, R. J. Leadingham, Henry McCall, J. MacMurray, A. Murch, Michael S. Pease, Mr Prosser, Edmund Hakewill Smith, J. M. D. Stancomb, Charles H. Stringer, W. G. Tatham, Brig. Gen. Weston, Miss J. Whitehead, A. C. Wilkinson, J. C. H. Willett

Plunkett Foundation, Long Handborough

Horace Plunkett

Rhodes House Library, Oxford
Charles Roden Buxton

Richmond Borough Library
Douglas Sladen

Robinson Library, University of Newcastle upon Tyne
Charles Trevelyan, Walter Runciman

Royal Historical Society, University College, London
George Prothero

Royal Archives, Windsor Castle, Berkshire
King George V Papers

School of Oriental and African Studies, University of London
Charles Addis

School of Slavonic and East European Studies, University of London
R. W. Seton-Watson

Scottish Record Office, Edinburgh
Philip Kerr (Lord Lothian), Arthur Steel Maitland, Whittingehame Correspondence (of the Arthur Balfour Papers)

Shropshire Records and Research Centre, Shrewsbury
William Clive Bridgeman

Sissinghurst Castle, Kent
Harold Nicolson

St Anthony's College, Oxford
Neill Malcolm

'The Times' Archive, London
Valentine Chirol, Geoffrey Dawson, G. S. Freeman, J. E. McKenzie, Lord Northcliffe, Wickham Steed

Trinity College Library, Cambridge
Edwin Montagu, F. W. Pethick-Lawrence

University of Birmingham, Edgbaston, Birmingham
Austen Chamberlain, William Harbutt Dawson

University of Sheffield, Sheffield
W. A. S. Hewins

University of Sussex, Brighton
Leonard and Virginia Woolf, Rudyard Kipling

West Sussex Record Office, Chichester
Leo Maxse

Wiltshire County Record Office, Trowbridge
Walter Long

C. OFFICIAL PAPERS

Hansard, Great Britain, Parliamentary Debates, Official Report, Fifth Series.

D. COLLECTIONS OF DOCUMENTS

BOURNE, KENNETH, and WATT, D. CAMERON (gen. eds.), *British Documents on Foreign Affairs: Reports and Papers from the Foreign Office Confidential Print, Part II, From the First to the Second World War. Series H, The First World War*, ed. by David Stevenson (12 vols., University Publications of America, 1989).
BOURNE, KENNETH, and WATT, D. CAMERON (gen. eds.), *British Documents on Foreign Affairs: Reports and Papers from the Foreign Office Confidential Print, Part II, From the First to the Second World War. Series I, The Paris Peace Conference of 1919*, ed. by Michael Dockrill (15 vols., University Publications of America, 1989).
SCOTT, JAMES BROWN (ed.), *Official Statements of War Aims and Peace Proposals, December 1916 to November 1918* (Washington, 1921).

E. NEWSPAPERS AND JOURNALS

Common Sense
Contemporary Review
Daily Chronicle
Daily Express
Daily Mail
Daily News
Daily Sketch
English Review
Evening News
Evening Standard
Fortnightly Review
Globe
Nation
National Review

New Europe
News of the World
Nineteenth Century and After
Observer
Pall Mall Gazette
Reynold's Newspaper
Spectator
Star
The Times
Westminster Gazette

F. PUBLISHED PERSONAL PAPERS

ADDISON, CHRISTOPHER, *Four and a Half Years* (2 vols., London, 1934).

BARNES, J., AND NICHOLSON, D. (eds.), *The Leo Amery Diaries* , i. *1896–1929* (London, 1980).

BELL, ANNE OLIVIER (ed.), *The Diary of Virginia Woolf*, i. *1915–1919* (London, 1979).

BLAKE, ROBERT (ed.), *The Private Papers of Douglas Haig, 1914–18* (London, 1952).

BOYCE, GEORGE, (ed.), *The Crisis of British Unionism: The Domestic Political Papers of the Second Earl of Selbourne* (London, 1987).

BURTON, HENDRICK J. (ed.), *The Life and Letters of Walter H. Page* (London, 1930).

CALLWELL, C. E. (ed.), *Field Marshal Sir Henry Wilson: His Life and Diaries* (2 vols., London, 1927).

GILBERT, MARTIN (ed.), *Winston S. Churchill, iv, companion volume i. January 1917—June 1919* (London, 1977).

GWYNN, STEPHEN (ed.), *The Letters and Friendships of Sir Cecil Spring Rice, A Record* (2 vols., London, 1929).

HANCOCK, W. K., and VAN DER POEL, JEAN (eds.), *Selections From the Smuts Papers*, iv. November 1918–August 1919 (Cambridge, 1966).

HEADLAM-MORLEY, JAMES, *A Memoir of the Paris Peace Conference 1919* ed. Agnes Headlam-Morley, Russell Bryant, and Anna Cienciala (London, 1972).

HEPBURN, JAMES (ed.), *The Letters of Arnold Bennett* (3 vols., Oxford, 1966).

JEFFERY, KEITH (ed.), *The Military Correspondence of Field Marshal Sir Henry Wilson, 1918–1922* (London, 1985).

JONES, THOMAS, *Whitehall Diary*, i. *1916–1925*, ed. Keith Middlemass (London, 1966).

KENNET, LADY KATHLEEN (Lady Scott), *Self Portrait of an Artist* (London, 1949).

MCEWEN, JOHN M. (ed.), *The Riddell Diaries, 1908–1923 : A Selection* (London, 1986).

MEINERTZHAGEN, Colonel R., *Army Diary, 1899–1926* (London, 1960).

MORGAN, KENNETH O. (ed.), *Lloyd George Family Letters: 1885–1936* (Cardiff, 1973).

RAMSDEN, JOHN (ed.), *Real Old Tory Politics: The Political Diaries of Sir Robert Sanders, Baron Bayford, 1910–1935* (London, 1984).

RIDDELL, Lord, *Lord Riddell's Intimate Diary of the Peace Conference and After* (London, 1933).

—— *War Diary, 1914–1918* (London, 1933).

TAYLOR, A. J. P. (ed.), *Lloyd George: A Diary by Frances Stevenson* (London, 1971).

VINCENT, JOHN (ed.), *The Crawford Papers: The Journal of David Lindsay, Twenty-Seventh Earl of Crawford and Tenth Earl of Balcarres, 1892–1940* (Manchester, 1984).

WILSON, KEITH (ed.), *George Saunders on Germany 1919–1920: Correspondence and Memoranda* (Leeds, 1987).
—— *The Rasp of War: The Letters of H. A. Gwynne to the Countess Bathurst 1914–1918* (London, 1988).
WILSON, TREVOR. (ed.), *The Political Diaries of C. P. Scott, 1911–1928* (London, 1970).

G. MEMOIRS

ADDISON, CHRISTOPHER, *Politics From Within, 1911–1918* (2 vols., London, 1924).
AMERY, L. S., *My Political Life* (3 vols., London, 1953–5).
OXFORD and ASQUITH, Earl of, *Memories and Reflections, 1852–1927* (2 vols., London, 1928).
ASTON, Sir GEORGE, *Secret Service* (London, 1930).
BARNES, G. N., *From Workshop to War Cabinet* (London, 1924).
BEAVERBROOK, Lord, *Politicians and the War, 1914–1918* (London, 1928).
—— *Men and Power, 1917–1918* (London, 1956).
BONSAL, STEPHEN, *Unfinished Business* (London, 1944).
BRAILSFORD, HENRY N., *Across the Blockade: A Record of Travels in Enemy Europe* (London, 1919).
BROWNRIGG, Sir DOUGLAS, *Indiscretions of the Naval Censor* (London, 1920).
BUTLER, Sir HAROLD, *Confident Morning* (London, 1950).
CECIL of CHELWOOD, Lord ROBERT CECIL, *A Great Experiment: An Autobiography* (London, 1941).
—— *All the Way* (London, 1949).
CHAMBERLAIN, AUSTEN, *Down the Years* (London, 1935).
CHIROL, VALENTINE, *Fifty Years in a Changing World* (London, 1927).
CHURCHILL, WINSTON, *The World Crisis: The Aftermath* (London, 1929).
CLYNES, J. R., *Memoirs* (2 vols., London, 1937).
COCKERILL, Sir GEORGE, *What Fools We Were* (London, 1944).
COOPER, DUFF, *Old Men Forget* (London, 1953).
DARK, SIDNEY, *Mainly About Other People* (London, 1925).
DAVIES, JOSEPH, *The Prime Minister's Secretariat* (London, 1951).
ESHER, LORD, *Journals and Letters* (4 vols., London, 1934–8).
FISHER, H. A. L., *An Unfinished Autobiography* (London, 1940).
FOCH, FERDINAND, *Memoirs of Marshal Foch* (London, 1931).
GARRAN, ROBERT, *Prosper the Commonwealth* (Sydney, 1958).
GIBBS, PHILIP, *The Pageant of the Years: An Autobiography* (London, 1946).
GLEICHEN, Major General Lord EDWARD, *A Guardsman's Memories* (London, 1932).
GREENWALL, HARRY J., *I Hate Tomorrow* (London, 1940).
HANKEY, Lord, *The Supreme Command, 1914–1918* (2 vols., London, 1961).
—— *The Supreme Control at the Paris Peace Conference, 1919* (London, 1963).
HARDINGE of PENSHURST, Lord, *The Old Diplomacy* (London, 1947).
HENDERSON, NEVILLE, *Water Under the Bridges* (London, 1945).
HEWINS, W. A. S., *The Apologia of an Imperialist: Forty Years of Empire Policy* (London, 1929).
HIRST, FRANCIS, *In the Golden Days* (London, 1947).

HOOVER, HERBERT, *The Memoirs of Herbert Hoover: Years of Adventure, 1874–1920* (New York, 1951).
HOWARD, ESME, *Theatre of Life: Life Seen From the Stalls* (2 vols., London, 1936).
HUGHES, WILLIAM M., *Crusts and Crusades* (Sydney, 1947).
JONES, KENNEDY, *Fleet Street and Downing Street* (London, 1920).
JONES, Sir RODERICK, *A Life in Reuters* (London, 1951).
JONES, THOMAS, *Lloyd George* (London, 1951).
KENWORTHY, J. M., *Soldiers, Statesmen and Others: An Autobiography* (London, 1933).
KEYNES, JOHN MAYNARD, *Two Memoirs* (London, 1949).
KNATCHBULL-HUGESSEN, Sir Hughie, *Diplomat in Peace and War* (London, 1948).
LLOYD GEORGE, DAVID, *The Truth About Reparations and War Debt* (London, 1932).
—— *War Memoirs* (2 vols., London, 1938).
—— *Memoirs of the Peace Conference* (2 vols., New Haven, 1939).
LONG, Lord, *Memories* (London, 1923).
MACFADYEAN, A., *Recollected in Tranquillity* (London, 1964).
MACREADY, General Sir NEVIL, *Annals of an Active Life* (London, 1924).
MALCOLM, IAN, *Lord Balfour: A Memory* (London, 1930).
MONTAGUE, C. E., *Disenchantment* (London, 1922).
MORGAN, Brigadier General J. H., *Assize of Arms: Being the Story of the Disarmament of Germany and Her Rearmament, 1919–1939* (2 vols., London, 1945).
NEVINSON, H. W., *Changes and Chances* (London, 1923).
—— *More Changes and Chances* (London, 1925).
ORPEN, Sir WILLIAM, *An Onlooker in France* (London, 1921).
PARMOOR, Lord, *A Retrospect* (London, 1936).
PERCY, EUSTACE, *Some Memories* (London, 1958).
PETHWICK-LAWRENCE, F. W., *Fate Has Been Kind* (London, 1943).
PRICE, M. PHILIPS, *My Three Revolutions* (London, 1969).
REPINGTON, C., *The First World War 1914–1918: Personal Reminiscences* (2 vols., London, 1920).
RODD, Sir RENNELL, *Social and Diplomatic Memories, 1902–1919* (London, 1925).
SALTER, Lord, *Memoirs of a Public Servant* (London, 1961).
SIMON, Sir JOHN, *Retrospect* (London, 1952).
SPENDER, J. A., *Life, Journalism and Politics* (2 vols., London, 1928).
SNOWDEN, PHILIP, *An Autobiography* (2 vols., London, 1934).
STEED, WICKHAM H., *Through Thirty Years* (2 vols., London, 1924).
STUART, Sir CAMPBELL, *The Secrets of Crewe House* (London, 1920).
THOMSON, Basil, *Queer People* (London, 1922).
—— *The Scene Changes* (New York, 1937).
TOYNBEE, ARNOLD, *Acquaintances* (Oxford, 1967).
—— *Experiences* (Oxford, 1969).
TREVELYAN, CHARLES, *From Liberalism to Labour* (London, 1921).
—— *Fifty Tumultuous Years* (London, 1955).
WEDGWOOD, JOSIAH, *Memoirs of a Fighting Life* (London, 1940).
WELLS, H. G., *An Experiment in Autobiography* (2 vols.; London, 1934).
WILLERT, Sir ARTHUR, *The Road to Safety: A Study in Anglo-American Relations* (London, 1953).

Wood, Edward F. L., First Earl of Halifax, *Fullness of Days* (London, 1957).
Woodward, E. L., *Short Journey* (London, 1942).

H. BIOGRAPHIES

Ayerst, David, *Garvin of the Observer* (London, 1985).
Blake, R., *The Unknown Prime Minister: The Life and Times of Andrew Bonar Law, 1858–1923* (London, 1955).
Butler, J. R. M., *Lord Lothian (Philip Kerr), 1882–1940* (London, 1960).
Churchill, Randolph S., *Lord Derby: King of Lancashire* (London, 1959).
Cline, Catherine, E. D. *Morel, 1873–1924: The Strategies of Protest* (Belfast, 1980).
Collier, Basil, *Brasshat: A Biography of Field Marshal Sir Henry Wilson* (London, 1961).
Davenport-Hines, R. P. T., *Dudley Docker: The Life and Times of a Trade Warrior* (Cambridge, 1984).
Dugdale, Blanche, *Arthur James Balfour* (2 vols., London, 1936).
Dutton, David, *Austen Chamberlain, Gentleman in Politics* (Bolton, 1985).
—— *Simon: A Political Biography of Sir John Simon* (London, 1992).
Epstein, Klaus, *Matthias Erzberger and the Dilemma of German Democracy* (New York, 1971).
Eyck, F., *G.P. Gooch: A Study in History and Politics* (London, 1982).
Fisher, H. A. L., *James Bryce* (2 vols., London, 1927).
Fitzhardinge, L. F., *William Morris Hughes* (2 vols., Sydney, 1964–79).
Fraser, Peter, *Lord Esher: A Political Biography* (London, 1973).
Gilbert, Martin, *Sir Horace Rumbold: Portrait of a Diplomat, 1869–1941* (London, 1973).
—— *Winston S. Churchill*, iv. *1917–1922* (London, 1975).
Gollin, A. M., *Proconsul in Politics: A Study of Lord Milner in Opposition and in Power* (London, 1964).
Grieves, Keith, *Sir Eric Geddes: Business and Government in War and Peace* (Manchester, 1989).
Grigg, John, *Lloyd George: From Peace to War, 1912–1916* (London, 1985).
Hammond, J. L., *C. P. Scott of the Manchester Guardian* (London, 1934).
Harrod, R. F., *The Life of John Maynard Keynes* (London, 1963).
Havighurst, Alfred F., *Radical Journalist: H. W. Massingham, 1860–1924* (Cambridge, 1974).
Hudson, W. J., *Billy Hughes in Paris: The Birth of Australian Diplomacy* (Melbourne, 1978).
Hutcheson, John A., *Leopold Maxse and the National Review, 1893–1914* (New York and London, 1989).
Hyde, H. Montgomery, *Lord Reading* (New York, 1967).
Ingham, Kenneth, *Jan Christian Smuts: The Conscience of a South African* (London, 1986).
Jackson, Stanley, *The Sassoons: Portrait of a Dynasty* (London, 1968).
James, Sir William, *The Eyes of the Navy: A Biographical Story of Admiral Sir Reginald Hall* (London, 1955).
Jenkins, Roy, *Asquith* (London, 1964).
Jones, Raymond A., *Arthur Ponsonby* (London, 1989).
Judd, Denis, *Lord Reading: Rufus Isaacs, First Marquess of Reading, Lord Chief Justice and Viceroy of India, 1860–1935* (London, 1982).

Koss, STEPHEN, *Fleet Street Radical: A. G. Gardiner and the 'Daily News'* (London, 1973).

LEVENTHAL, F. M., *The Last Dissenter: H. N. Brailsford and His World* (Oxford, 1985).

—— *Arthur Henderson* (Manchester, 1989).

MACKAY, RUDDOCK F., *Balfour: Intellectual Statesman* (Oxford, 1985).

MACKENZIE, NORMAN, and MACKENZIE, JEANNE, *The Time Traveller: The Life of H. G. Wells* (London, 1973).

McKENNA, STEPHEN, *Reginald McKenna* (London, 1948).

McKERCHER, B. J. C., *Esme Howard: A Diplomatic Biography* (Cambridge, 1989).

McNEILL, WILLIAM H., *Arnold J. Toynbee: A Life* (Oxford, 1989).

MARLOWE, JOHN, *Milner: Apostle of Empire* (London, 1960).

MASTERMAN, LUCY, C. F. G. *Masterman: A Biography* (London, 1939).

MORRIS, A. J. A., *C. P. Trevelyan, 1870–1958: Portrait of a Radical* (London, 1979).

MOSLEY, LEONARD, *Curzon: The End of an Epoch* (London, 1960).

NEWTON, Lord, *Lord Lansdowne* (London, 1929).

NICOLSON, HAROLD, *Curzon: The Last Phase, 1919–1925: A Study in Post-War Diplomacy* (London, 1934).

O'BRIEN, T. H., *Milner* (London, 1979).

PETRIE, CHARLES, *Walter Long and His Times* (London, 1936).

POUND, REGINALD, and HARMSWORTH, GEOFFREY, *Northcliffe* (London, 1959).

ROSE, KENNETH, *Curzon: A Most Superior Person* (London, 1985).

ROSKILL, STEPHEN, *Hankey: Man of Secrets* (2 vols., London, 1970–2).

—— *Admiral of the Fleet, Earl Beatty: The Last Naval Hero: An Intimate Biography* (New York, 1981).

SKIDELSKY, ROBERT, *John Maynard Keynes, Hopes Betrayed 1883–1920* (London, 1983).

SPARTALIS, PETER, *The Diplomatic Battles of Billy Hughes* (Sydney, 1983).

WEST, FRANCIS, *Gilbert Murray: A Life* (London, 1984).

WRENCH, J. E., *Geoffrey Dawson and Our Times* (London, 1955).

WRESZIN, MICHAEL, *Oswald Garrison Villard: Pacifist at War* (Bloomington, Ind., 1965).

WRIGLEY, CHRIS, *Arthur Henderson* (Cardiff, 1990).

ZEBEL, S. H., *Balfour: A Political Biography* (Cambridge, 1973).

I. SECONDARY STUDIES

ADAMS, R. J. Q. (ed.), *The Great War, 1914–18: Essays on the Military, Political and Social History of the First World War* (London, 1990).

ANDREW, CHRISTOPHER, *Secret Service: The Making of the British Intelligence Community* (London, 1985).

AYERST, DAVID, *Guardian: Biography of a Newspaper* (London, 1971).

BARNETT, CORRELLI, *The Collapse of British Power* (London, 1972).

—— *The Audit of War: The Illusion and Reality of Britain as a Great Nation* (London, 1986).

BEESLY, P., *Room 40: British Naval Intelligence, 1914–1918* (London, 1982).

BIRNBAUM, KARL E., *Peace Moves and U-Boat Warfare: A Study of Imperial Germany's Policy toward the United States, April 18, 1916–January 9, 1917* (Hamden, Conn., 1970).

BOADLE, DONALD G., *Winston Churchill and the German Question in British Foreign Policy, 1918–1922* (The Hague, 1973).

BOND, BRIAN (ed.), *The First World War and British Military History* (Oxford, 1991).

BOURNE, J. M., *Britain and the Great War, 1914–1918* (London, 1989).

BOYCE, GEORGE, CURRAN, JAMES, and WINGATE, P. (eds.), *Newspaper History from the Seventeenth Century to the Present Day* (London, 1978).

BREITMAN, RICHARD, *German Socialism and Weimar Democracy* (Chapel Hill, NC, 1981).

BUNSELMEYER, ROBERT E., *The Cost of the War, 1914–1919: British Economic War Aims and the Origins of Reparations* (Hamden, Conn., 1975).

BURK, KATHLEEN (ed.), *War and the State* (London, 1982).

CARSTEN, FRITZ, *Revolution in Central Europe, 1918–1919* (Los Angeles, 1972).

—— *War Against War: British and German Radical Movements in the First World War* (London, 1982).

COMFORT, RICHARD A., *Revolutionary Hamburg: Labor Politics in the Early Weimar Republic* (Stanford, Calif., 1966).

COWLING, MAURICE, *The Impact of Labour, 1920–1924: The Beginning of Modern British Politics* (Cambridge, 1971).

CROSBY, GERDA R., *Disarmament and Peace in British Politics, 1914–1919* (Cambridge, Mass., 1957).

DAVENPORT-HINES, R. P., *Speculators and Patriots: Essays in Business Biography* (London, 1986).

DOCKRILL, M. L., and GOOLD, J. D., *Peace Without Promise: Britain and the Peace Conferences, 1919–1923* (London, 1981).

FISCHER, FRITZ, *Germany's Aims in the First World War* (London, 1967).

FLOTO, INGA, *Colonel House in Paris: A Study of American Policy at the Paris Peace Conference 1919* (Aarhus, 1973).

FOSTER, LEONIE, *High Hopes: The Men and Motives of the Australian Round Table* (Melbourne, 1986).

FOWLER, W. B., *British-American Relations, 1917–18: The Role of Sir William Wiseman* (Princeton, 1969).

GATZKE, HANS, *Germany's Drive to the West: A Study of Germany's Western War Aims during the First World War* (Baltimore, 1966).

GOLDSTEIN, ERIK, *Winning the Peace: British Diplomatic Strategy, Peace Planning, and the Paris Peace Conference, 1916–1920* (Oxford, 1991).

GRIEVES, KEITH, *The Politics of Manpower, 1914–18* (Manchester, 1988).

GUINN, PAUL, *British Strategy and Politics, 1914–18* (Oxford, 1965).

HARTLEY, STEPHEN, *The Irish Question as a Problem in British Foreign Policy, 1914–18* (London, 1987).

HAZLEHURST, CAMERON, *Politicians at War, July 1914 to May 1915: A Prologue to the Triumph of Lloyd George* (London, 1971).

HINSLEY, F. H. (ed.), *British Foreign Policy under Sir Edward Grey* (Cambridge, 1977).

JAFFE, LORNA, *The Decision to Disarm Germany: British Policy towards Postwar German Disarmament, 1914–1919* (London, 1985).

JOHNSON, PAUL BARTON, *Land Fit for Heroes: The Planning of British Reconstruction, 1916–1919* (Chicago, 1968).

KENDLE, J. B., *The Round Table Movement and Imperial Union* (Toronto, 1975).

KENT, BRUCE, *The Spoils of War: The Politics, Economics and Diplomacy of Reparations, 1918–1932* (Oxford, 1989).

KITCHEN, MARTIN, *The Silent Dictatorship: The Politics of the German High Command under Hindenburg and Ludendorff, 1916–1918* (London, 1976).

KOCH, H. W., *A Constitutional History of Germany in the Nineteenth and Twentieth Centuries* (London, 1984).

KOSS, STEPHEN, *The Rise and Fall of the Political Press in Britain* (2 vols.; London, 1984).

LENTIN, ALBERT, *Lloyd George, Woodrow Wilson and the Guilt of Germany: An Essay in the Pre-History of Appeasement* (Leicester, 1984).

LOUIS, WILLIAM R., *Great Britain and Germany's Lost Colonies, 1914–1919* (Oxford, 1967).

LOWE, C. J. and DOCKRILL, M. L. *The Mirage of Power, ii. British Foreign Policy 1914–1922* (London, 1972).

MARTIN, LAURENCE W., *Peace Without Victory: Woodrow Wilson and the British Liberals* (New Haven, 1958).

MAYER, ARNO J., *Political Origins of the New Diplomacy, 1917–1918* (New Haven, 1959).

—— *Politics and Diplomacy of Peacemaking: Containment and Counter-revolution at Versailles, 1918–1919* (London, 1968).

MESSINGER, GARY S., *British Propaganda and the State in the First World War* (Manchester, 1992).

MITCHELL, A., *Revolution in Bavaria, 1918–1919: The Eisner Regime and the Soviet Republic* (Princeton, 1965).

MORGAN, DAVID, *The Socialist Left and the German Revolution: A History of the German Independent Social Democratic Party, 1917–1922* (Ithaca, NY, 1975).

MORGAN, KENNETH O., *Consensus and Disunity: The Lloyd George Coalition Government, 1918–1922* (Oxford, 1979).

NIMOCKS, WALTER, *Milner's Young Men: The 'Kindergarten' in Edwardian Imperial Affairs* (London, 1970).

OCCLESHAW, MICHAEL, *Armour Against Fate: British Military Intelligence in the First World War* (London, 1989).

OFFER, AVNER, *The First World War: An Agrarian Interpretation* (Oxford, 1989).

ORDE, ANNE, *British Policy and European Reconstruction after the First World War* (Cambridge, 1990).

PORTER, BERNARD, *Plots and Paranoia: A History of Political Espionage in Britain, 1790–1988* (London, 1992).

RETALLACK, JAMES N., *Notables of the Right: The Conservative Party and Political Mobilization in Germany, 1876–1918* (London, 1988).

ROBBINS, KEITH, *The Abolition of War: The 'Peace Movement' in Britain, 1914–1919* (Cardiff, 1966).

ROTHWELL, V. H., *British War Aims and Peace Diplomacy, 1914–1918* (Oxford, 1971).

RYDER, A. J., *The German Revolution of 1918: A Study of German Socialism in War and Revolt* (Cambridge, 1967).

SANDERS, MICHAEL, and TAYLOR, PHILIP M., *British Propaganda during the First World War, 1914–18* (London, 1982).

SCALLY, ROBERT J., *The Origins of the Lloyd George Coalition* (Princeton, 1976).

SCHWABE, KLAUS, *Woodrow Wilson, Revolutionary Germany, and Peacemaking, 1918–1919: Missionary Diplomacy and the Realities of Power* (Chapel Hill, NC, 1985).

SETON-WATSON, HUGH, and SETON-WATSON, CHRISTOPHER, *The Making of a New Europe: R. W. Seton-Watson and the Last Years of Austria-Hungary* (London, 1981).

SHARP, ALAN, *The Versailles Settlement: Peacemaking in Paris, 1919* (London, 1991).

STEVENSON, DAVID, *The First World War and International Politics* (Oxford, 1988).

SWARTZ, MARVIN, *The Union of Democratic Control in British Politics during the First World War* (Oxford, 1971).

TAMPKE, JÜRGEN, *The Ruhr and Revolution: The Revolutionary Movement in the Rhenish Westphalian Industrial Region, 1912–1919* (Canberra, 1978).

TERRAINE, JOHN, *To Win A War—1918 The Year of Victory* (London, 1978).

THIRLWELL, A. P. (ed.), *Keynes as a Policy Adviser* (London, 1982).

TILLMAN, SETH P., *Anglo-American Relations at the Paris Peace Conference of 1919* (Princeton, 1961).

TRASK, DAVID F., *The AEF and Coalition Warmaking, 1917–1918* (Lawrence, 1993).

TURNER, JOHN, *Lloyd George's Secretariat* (Cambridge, 1980).

—— (ed.), *Businessmen and Politics* (London, 1984).

—— (ed.), *Britain and the First World War* (London, 1988).

—— *British Politics and the Great War: Coalition and Conflict, 1915–1918* (London, 1992).

VINCENT, C. PAUL, *The Politics of Hunger: The Allied Blockade of Germany, 1915–1919* (Athens, Ohio, 1985).

WAITES, BERNARD, *A Class Society at War: England 1914–1918* (Leamington Spa, 1987)

WALDMAN, ERIC, *The Spartacist Uprising of 1919* (Milwaukee, 1958).

WALLACE, STUART, *War and the Image of Germany: British Academics 1914–1918* (Edinburgh, 1988).

WALLACH, JEHUDA L., *Uneasy Coalition: The Entente Experience in World War I* (Westport, Conn., 1993).

WALWORTH, ARTHUR, *America's Moment 1918: American Diplomacy at the End of World War One* (New York, 1977).

WILLIAMS, JOYCE G., *Colonel House and Sir Edward Grey: A Study in Anglo-American Diplomacy* (Lanham, Md., 1984).

WILSON, KEITH, *A Study of the History and Politics of the Morning Post, 1905–1926* (Lewiston, NY, 1990).

WILSON, TREVOR, *The Downfall of the Liberal Party 1914–1935* (London, 1966).

—— *The Myriad Faces of War: Britain and the Great War, 1914–1918* (London, 1986).

WOODWARD, DAVID, *Lloyd George and the Generals* (East Brunswick, NJ, 1983).

—— *Trial by Friendship: Anglo-American Relations, 1917–1918* (Lexington, Mass., 1993).

WRIGLEY, CHRIS, *Warfare, Diplomacy, and Politics: Essays in Honour of A. J. P. Taylor* (London, 1986).

—— *Lloyd George and the Challenge of Labour: The Post-War Coalition, 1918–1922* (Hemel Hempstead, 1990).

J. ARTICLES

ABRAMS, P., 'The Failure of Social Reform, 1918–1920', *Past and Present*, 24 (1963), 43–64.

ADAMS, R. J. Q., 'Asquith's Choice: The May Coalition and the Coming of Conscription, 1915–1916', *Journal of British Studies*, 25 (July 1986), 243–63.

ADAMS, W., 'Lloyd George and the Labour Movement', *Past and Present*, 1 (1952–3), 55–64.

BAILEY, STEPHEN, 'The Berlin Strike of January 1918', *Central European History*, 13/2 (1980), 158–74.

BEAVERBROOK, BARON, and TAYLOR, A. J. P., 'Two War Leaders: Lloyd George and Churchill', *History Today*, 23/8 (1973), 546–53.

BERNSTEIN, GEORGE L., 'Yorkshire Liberalism during the First World War', *Historical Journal*, 32 (Mar. 1989), 107–29.

BLOUET, BRIAN W., 'The Political Career of Sir Halford Mackinder', *Political Geography Quarterly*, 6/4 (1987), 355–67.

BOSWELL, JONATHAN S., and JOHNS, BRUCE R., 'Patriots or Profiteers? British Businessmen and the First World War', *Journal of European Economic History*, 11 (1982), 423–45.

BOYCE, DAVID G., 'British Opinion, Ireland and the War, 1916–1918', *Historical Journal*, 17/2 (1974), 575–93.

BROOKS, DAVID, 'Lloyd George, For and Against', *Historical Journal*, 24/1 (1981), 223–30.

CAPIE, FORREST, 'The Pressure for Tariff Protection in Britain, 1917–1931', *Journal of European Economic History* 9/2 (1980), 431–47.

CLINE, CATHERINE ANN, 'British Historians and the Treaty of Versailles', *Albion*, 20/1 (1988), 45–58.

CLOSE, DAVID, 'Conservatives and Coalition After the First World War', *Journal of Modern History*, 45/2 (1973), 240–60.

——— 'The Collapse of Resistance to Democracy: Conservatives, Adult Suffrage, and Second Chamber Reform, 1911–1928', *Historical Journal*, 20/4 (1977), 893–918.

COATS, A. W., 'Political Economy and the Tariff Reform Campaign', *Journal of Law and Economics*, 11 (1968), 181–229.

COETZEE, F., and COETZEE, M. R., 'Rethinking the Radical Right in Germany and Britain Before 1914', *Journal of Contemporary History*, 21 (1986), 515–37.

DAVID, Edward, 'The Liberal Party Divided, 1916–1918', *Historical Journal*, 13/3 (1970), 509–33.

DOCKRILL, M.L., and STEINER, Z., 'The Foreign Office at the Paris Peace Conference in 1919', *International History Review*, 2/1 (1980), 56–86.

DOUGLAS, ROY, 'The Background to the "Coupon" Election Arrangements', *English Historical Review*, 339 (1971), 318–36.

——— 'The National Democratic Party and the British Workers' League', *Historical Journal*, 15 (1972), 533–52.

——— 'A Classification of the Members of Parliament Elected in 1918', *Bulletin of the Institute of Historical Research*, 47/115 (1974), 74–94.

ENGLANDER, DAVID, 'Military Intelligence and the Defence of the Realm: The Surveillance of Soldiers and Civilians During the First World War', *Bulletin of the Society for the Study of Labour History*, 52/1 (1987), 24–32.

FAIR, J. D., 'Politicians, Historians and the War: A Reassessment of the Political Crisis of December, 1916', *Journal of Modern History*, 49/3, (1977), Abstract iii.

FEST, W. B., 'British War Aims and German Peace Feelers during the First World War (December 1916–November 1918)', *Historical Journal*, 15/2 (1972), 285–308.

FITZHARDINGE, L. F., 'W. M. Hughes and the Treaty of Versailles', *Journal of Commonwealth Political Studies*, 5 (July 1967), 130–42.

——— 'Hughes, Borden and Dominion Representation at the Paris Peace Conference', *Canadian Historical Review*, 49/2 (June 1968), 160–9.

FRASER, PETER, 'British Policy and the Crisis of Liberalism in May 1915', *Journal of Modern History*, 54/1 (1982), 1–26.

FRENCH, DAVID, 'The Meaning of Attrition, 1914–1916', *English Historical Review*, 103 (Apr. 1988), 385–405.

FRY, MICHAEL G., 'Political Change in Britain, August 1914–December 1916: Lloyd

George Replaces Asquith: The Issues Underlying the Drama', *Historical Journal*, 31 (Sept. 1988), 609–27.

GALBRAITH, JOHN S., 'British War Aims in World War 1: A Commentary on "Statesmanship" ', *Journal of Imperial and Commonwealth History*, 13/1 (1984), 25–45.

GILBERT, BENTLEY B., 'Lloyd George and the Historians', *Albion*, 11/1 (1979), 74–86.

GOLDSTEIN, ERIK D., 'New Diplomacy and the New Europe at the Paris Peace Conference of 1919: The A. W. A. Leeper Papers', *East European Quarterly*, 21/4 (1987), 393–400.

—— 'The Foreign Office and Political Intelligence 1918–1920', *Review of International Studies*, 14/4 (1988), 275–88.

—— 'Historians Outside the Academy: G. W. Prothero and the Foreign Office Historical Section, 1917–1920', *Historical Research*, 63 (June 1990), 195–211.

GOLLIN, ALFRED, 'Freedom or Control in the First World War: The Great Crisis of May 1915', *Historical Reflections*, 2/2 (1975), 135–55.

GRIFFIN, ROBERT A., 'A Communicative Study of the Dissenting Views of John Maynard Keynes and Thorsten Veblen on the Treaty of Versailles', *Revue d'economie politique*, 95/2 (1985), 174–98.

GRIGG, JOHN, 'Nobility and War: The Unselfish Commitment?', *Encounter*, 74 (Mar. 1990), 21–7.

HART, MICHAEL, 'The Liberals, The War, and the Franchise', *English Histories Review*, 97/385 (1982), 820–32.

HOPKIN, D., 'Domestic Censorship in the First World War', *Journal of Contemporary History*, 5/4 (1970), 151–69.

KENNEDY, PAUL M., 'Idealists and Realists: British Views of Germany, 1864–1939', *Transactions of the Royal Historical Society*, 25 (1975), 137–56.

—— 'The Tradition of Appeasement in British Foreign Policy, 1865–1939', *British Journal of International Studies*, 2/3 (1976), 195–215.

KOSS, STEPHEN E., 'The Destruction of Britain's Last Liberal Government', *Journal of Modern History*, 40/2 (June 1968), 257–77.

KURTZ, HAROLD, 'The Lansdowne Letter', *History Today*, 18 (1968), 84–92.

LOCKWOOD, P.A., 'Milner's Entry into the War Cabinet, December 1916', *Historical Journal*, 7/1 (1964), 120–34.

LOWE, RODNEY, 'The Failure of Consensus in Britain: The National Industrial Conference, 1919–1921', *Historical Journal*, 21 (1978), 647–75.

LOWRY, BULLITT, 'Pershing and the Armistice', *Journal of American History*, 55, (1968–9), 281–329.

MCDERMOTT, JOHN, 'Total War and the Merchant State: Aspects of British Economic Warfare against Germany, 1914–1916', *Canadian Journal of History*, 21 (Apr. 1986), 61–76.

—— ' "A Needless Sacrifice": British Businessmen and Business as Usual in the First World War', *Albion*, 21 (1989), 263–82.

MCEWEN, J. M., 'The Coupon Election of 1918 and Unionist Members of Parliament', *Journal of Modern History*, 34 (1962), 294–306.

—— 'The Liberal Party and the Irish Question during the First World War', *Journal of British Studies*, 12/1 (1972), 109–31.

—— 'The Press and the Fall of Asquith', *Historical Journal*, 21/4 (1978), 863–83.

—— 'The Struggle for Mastery in Britain: Lloyd George Versus Asquith', *Journal of British Studies*, 18 (1978), 131–56.

McEwen, J. M., 'Lloyd George's Liberal Supporters in December 1916: A Note', *Bulletin of the Institute of Historical Research*, 53/128 (1980), 265–72.

—— 'Northcliffe and Lloyd George at War, 1914–1918', *Historical Journal*, 24/3 (1981), 651–72.

—— 'The National Press during the First World War: Ownership and Circulation', *Journal of Contemporary History*, 17 (1982), 459–86.

—— 'Lloyd George's Acquisition of the *Daily Chronicle* in 1918', *Journal of British Studies*, 22/1 (1983), 127–44.

McGill, Barry, 'Asquith's Predicament, 1914–1918', *Journal of Modern History*, 39 (1967), 283–303.

—— 'Lloyd George's Timing of the 1918 Election', *Journal of British Studies*, 14/1 (1974), 109–24.

McIvor, Arthur, ' "A Crusade for Capitalism": The Economic League, 1919–1939', *Journal of Contemporary History*, 23/4 (1988), 631–65.

Marks, Sally, 'Behind the Scenes at the Paris Peace Conference of 1919', *Journal of British Studies*, 9/2 (1970), 154–80.

—— 'The Misery of Victory: France's Struggle for the Versailles Treaty', *Historical Papers* (1986), 117–33.

Marrison, A. J., 'Businessmen, Industries and Tariff Reform in Great Britain, 1903–1930', *Business History*, 25/2 (1983), 148–78.

Martin, Ged, 'Asquith, The Maurice Debate and the Historians', *Australian Journal of Politics and History*, 31/3 (1985), 435–44.

Morgan, Kenneth O., 'Lloyd George's Premiership: A Study in "Prime Ministerial Government"', *Historical Journal*, 13/1 (1970), 130–57.

Murphy, Richard, 'Walter Long, the Unionist Ministers, and the Formation of Lloyd George's Government in December 1916', *Historical Journal*, 29/3 (1986), 735–45.

Naylor, J., 'The Establishment of the War Cabinet Secretariat', *Historical Journal*, 14 (1971), 783–803.

Nottingham, Christopher J., 'Recasting Bourgeois Britain? The British State in the Years which Followed the First World War', *International Review of Social History*, 31/3 (1986), 227–47.

O'Boyle, Lenore, 'The German Independent Socialists During the First World War', *American Historical Review*, 56/4 (July 1951), 824–83.

Occleshaw, M. E., 'The "Stab in the Back"—Myth or Reality?', *Journal of the Royal United Services Institute for Defence Studies*, 130/3 (1985), 49–54.

Panayi, Panikos, 'Anti-German Riots in London During the First World War', *German History*, 7 (1989), 184–203.

—— 'The British Empire Union in the First World War', *Immigrants and Minorities*, 8 (Mar. 1989), 113–28.

Pugh, Martin D., 'Asquith, Bonar Law and the First Coalition', *Historical Journal*, 17/4 (1974), 813–36.

Renshaw, P., 'Anti-Labour Politics in Britain, 1918–1927', *Journal of Contemporary History*, 12 (1977), 693–705.

Ridley, Jane, 'The Unionist Social Reform Committee 1911–14: Wets Before the Deluge', *Historical Journal*, 30 (1987), 391–413.

Roskill, Stephen W., 'Lord Hankey—the Creation of the Machinery of Government', *Journal of the Royal United Services Institute for Defence Studies*, 120/3 (1975), 10–18.

RUBINSTEIN, W. D., 'Henry Page Croft and the National Party, 1917–1922', *Journal of Contemporary History*, 9/1 (1974), 129–48.

SANDERS, M. L, 'Wellington House and British Propaganda During the First World War', *Historical Journal*, 18/1 (1975), 119–46.

SHARP, A. J., 'The Foreign Office in Eclipse, 1919–22', *History*, 61 (1976), 198–218.

SKOP, ARTHUR L., 'The British Labour Party and the German Revolution, November, 1918–January, 1919', *European Studies Review*, 5/3 (1975), 277–97.

SNELLING, R. C., 'Peacemaking 1919: Australia, New Zealand and the British Empire Delegation at Versailles', *Journal of Imperial and Commonwealth History*, 4/1 (1975), 15–28.

SPEAR, SHELDON, 'E. D. Morel's UDC International', *Peace and Change*, 7/1–2 (1981), 97–108.

STEINER, ZARA, and DOCKRILL, M. L., 'The Foreign Office Reforms, 1919–1921', *Historical Journal*, 17/1 (1974), 131–56.

STERLING, KERNEK, 'The British Government's Reactions to President Wilson's "Peace" Note of December 1916', *Historical Journal*, 13/4 (1970), 721–66.

STEVENSON, DAVID, 'The Failure of Peace By Negotiation in 1917', *Historical Journal*, 34/2 (1991), 65–86.

STUBBS, J. O., 'Lord Milner and Patriotic Labour, 1914–1918', *English Historical Review*, 87 (1972), 717–54.

—— 'The Unionists and Ireland, 1914–18, *Historical Journal*, 33/4 (1990), 867–93.

SYKES, ALAN, 'The Radical Right and the Crisis of Conservatism Before the First World War', *Historical Journal*, 26/3 (1983), 661–76.

TANNER, DUNCAN, 'The Parliamentary Electoral System, The "Fourth Reform Act" and the Rise of Labour in England and Wales', *Bulletin of the Institute of Historical Research*, 56/134 (1983), 205–19.

TAYLOR, PHILIP M., 'The Foreign Office and British Propaganda during the First World War', *Historical Journal*, 23/3 (1980), 875–98.

TRACHTENBERG, MARC, ' "A New Economic Order": Etienne Clémentel and French Economic Diplomacy during the First World War', *French Historical Studies*, 10/2 (1977), 315–41.

—— 'Reparation at the Paris Peace Conference', *Journal of Modern History*, 51 (Mar. 1979), 24–85.

—— 'Versailles After Sixty Years', *Journal of Contemporary History*, 17/3 (1982), 487–506.

TURNER, JOHN, 'The Formation of Lloyd George's "Garden Suburb": "Fabian–like Milnerite Penetration"?', *Historical Journal*, 20/1 (1977), 165–84.

—— 'The British Commonwealth Union and the General Election of 1918', *English Historical Review*, 93 (July 1978), 528–59.

WARD, STEPHEN R., 'Intelligence Surveillance of British Ex-servicemen, 1918–1920', Historical Journal, 16/1 (1973), 179–88.

WARMAN, ROBERTA, 'The Erosion of Foreign Office Influence in the Making of Foreign, Policy 1916–1918, *Historical Journal*, 15 (1972), 113–59.

WEINROTH, H., 'Peace By Negotiation and the British Anti-War Movement, 1914–1918', *Canadian Journal of History*, 10/3 (1975), 369–92.

WILSON, TREVOR, 'The Coupon and the British General Election of 1918', *Journal of Modern History*, 36/1 (Mar. 1964), 28–42.

WINTER, J. M., 'Arthur Henderson, the Russian Revolution and the Reconstruction of the Labour Party', *Historical Journal*, 15/4 (1972), 753–73.

WOODWARD, DAVID, 'David Lloyd George, A Negotiated Peace With Germany and the Kühlmann Peace Kite of September 1917', *Canadian Journal of History*, 6/1 (1971), 75–93.

—— 'The Origins and Intent of David Lloyd George's January 5 War Aim Speech', *The Historian*, 34 (Nov. 1971), 22–39.

—— 'Britain in a Continental War: The Civil–Military Debate over the Strategical Direction of the Great War of 1914–1918', *Albion*, 12/1 (1980), 37–65.

YEARWOOD, PETER, ' "On the Right and Safe Lines": The Lloyd George Government and the Origins of the League of Nations, 1916–1918', *Historical Journal*, 32 (Mar. 1989), 131–55.

INDEX